# The English Reference Qur'an Translation:
# The First Translation of the Qur'an from the Original Arabic into Modern English with References to the Tawrah, Zabur, and Injil

by
The Reference Qur'an Council

version 5.17 © November, 2022
original version © February, 2014

If you have any suggestions for improving the wording of this translation, or if you would like to write an endorsement for this translation, please email us at: referencequran@gmail.com

Also for sale at referencequran.com

The Kindle edition and the Arabic-English version, which also includes the original Arabic Qur'an, are also available on the same site and on Amazon.

# Contents

## TABLE OF CONTENTS

Introduction - to be read ................................................................................................ iv
Preface .............................................................................................................................. iv
The reasons for this translation ........................................................................................ v
Identifying Arabic pronouns ........................................................................................... vii
Organization of the Qur'an ............................................................................................. vii
Verse numbering ............................................................................................................ viii
Capitalization ................................................................................................................. viii
Rhyme ............................................................................................................................ viii
Challenges of translating the Arabic original of the Qur'an ........................................... ix
The Appendices ............................................................................................................... ix
Chapter ............................................................................................................................. 2
Chapter 2: Al-Baqarah ...................................................................................................... 3
Chapter 3: Aal Imran ...................................................................................................... 42
Chapter 4: Al-Nisa' ........................................................................................................ 70
Chapter 5: Al-Ma'idah .................................................................................................... 93
Chapter 6 Al-Anaam ..................................................................................................... 112
Chapter 7 Al-Aaraf ....................................................................................................... 129
Chapter 8 Al-Anfal ....................................................................................................... 149
Chapter 9: Al-Tawbah ................................................................................................... 157
Chapter 10 Yunus ......................................................................................................... 172
Chapter 11 Hud ............................................................................................................. 182
Chapter 12 Yusuf .......................................................................................................... 195
Chapter 13 Al-Raad ...................................................................................................... 206
Chapter 14 Ibrahim ....................................................................................................... 213
Chapter 15 Al-Hijr ........................................................................................................ 221
Chapter 16 Al-Nahl ....................................................................................................... 227
Chapter 17 Al-Isra ........................................................................................................ 238
Chapter 18 Al-Kahf ...................................................................................................... 249
Chapter 19: Mariam ...................................................................................................... 258
Chapter 20: Taha .......................................................................................................... 267
Chapter 21 Al-Anbiya' ................................................................................................. 278
Chapter 22 Al-Hajj ....................................................................................................... 286
Chapter 23 Al-Muminun .............................................................................................. 297
Chapter 24 Al-Noor ...................................................................................................... 304
Chapter 25 Al-Furqan ................................................................................................... 312
Chapter 26 Al-Shuara ................................................................................................... 318
Chapter 27 Al-Naml ..................................................................................................... 328
Chapter 28 Al-Qasas ..................................................................................................... 336
Chapter 29 Al-Ankabut ................................................................................................ 345
Chapter 30 Al-Roum ..................................................................................................... 352
Chapter 31 Luqman ...................................................................................................... 358
Chapter 32 Al-Sajdah ................................................................................................... 363
Chapter 33 Al-Ahzab .................................................................................................... 366

| | |
|---|---|
| Chapter 34 Saba | 375 |
| Chapter 35 Fatir | 382 |
| Chapter 36 Ya Sin | 388 |
| Chapter 37: Al-Saffat | 393 |
| Chapter 38: Sad | 400 |
| Chapter 39 Al-Zumar | 406 |
| Chapter 40 Al-Ghafir | 414 |
| Chapter 41 Fussilat | 423 |
| Chapter 42 Al-Shura | 430 |
| Chapter 43 Al-Zukhruf | 437 |
| Chapter 44 Al-Dukhan | 445 |
| Chapter 45 Al-Jathiyah | 449 |
| Chapter 46 Al-Ahqaf | 453 |
| Chapter 47 Muhammad | 458 |
| Chapter 48: Al-Fath | 462 |
| Chapter 49 Al-Hujurat | 467 |
| Chapter 50 Qaf | 470 |
| Chapter 51 Al-Dhariyat | 474 |
| Chapter 52 Al-Tur | 478 |
| Chapter 53 Al-Najm | 481 |
| Chapter 54 Al-Qamar | 484 |
| Chapter 55 Al-Rahman | 487 |
| Chapter 56 Al-Waqiah | 491 |
| Chapter 57 Al-Hadid | 495 |
| Chapter 58 Al-Mujadilah | 500 |
| Chapter 59 Al-Hashr | 504 |
| Chapter 60 Al-Mumtahanah | 508 |
| Chapter 61 Al-Saff | 511 |
| Chapter 62 Al-Jumuah | 513 |
| Chapter 63 Al-Munafiqun | 515 |
| Chapter 64 Al-Taghabun | 517 |
| Chapter 65 Al-Talaq | 520 |
| Chapter 66: Al-Tahrim | 523 |
| Chapter 67 Al-Mulk | 525 |
| Chapter 68 Al-Qalam | 528 |
| Chapter 69 Al-Haqqah | 530 |
| Chapter 70 Al-Marij | 532 |
| Chapter 71 Nuh | 534 |
| Chapter 72 Al-Jinn | 536 |
| Chapter 73 Al-Muzzammil | 539 |
| Chapter 74 Al-Muddathir | 541 |
| Chapter 75 Al-Qiyamah | 544 |
| Chapter 76 Al-Insan | 546 |
| Chapter 77 Al-Mursalat | 548 |
| Chapter 78 Al-Naba' | 550 |
| Chapter 79 Al-Naziat | 552 |
| Chapter 80 Abasa | 554 |
| Chapter 81 Al-Takwir | 556 |
| Chapter 82 Al-Infitaar | 558 |
| Chapter 83 Al-Mutaffifun | 559 |

Chapter 84 Al-Inshiqaq .................................................................................... 561
Chapter 85 Al-Buruj ....................................................................................... 563
Chapter 86 Al-Tariq ....................................................................................... 565
Chapter 87 Al-Aala ........................................................................................ 566
Chapter 88 Al-Ghashiyah ............................................................................... 567
Chapter 89 Al-Fajr ......................................................................................... 569
Chapter 90 Al-Balad ...................................................................................... 571
Chapter 91 Al-Shams ..................................................................................... 572
Chapter 92 Al-Layl ........................................................................................ 573
Chapter 93 Al-Duha ....................................................................................... 574
Chapter 94 Al-Inshirah ................................................................................... 575
Chapter 95 Al-Tin .......................................................................................... 576
Chapter 96 Al-Alaq ........................................................................................ 577
Chapter 97 Al-Qadr ....................................................................................... 578
Chapter 98 Al-Bayyinah ................................................................................. 579
Chapter 99 Al-Zalzalah .................................................................................. 580
Chapter 100 Al-Adiyat ................................................................................... 581
Chapter 101 Al-Qariah ................................................................................... 582
Chapter 102 Al-Takathur ................................................................................ 582
Chapter 103 Al-Asr ........................................................................................ 583
Chapter 104 Al-Humazah ............................................................................... 583
Chapter 105 Al-Fil ......................................................................................... 585
Chapter 106 Al-Quraysh ................................................................................ 585
Chapter 107 Al-Maoun ................................................................................... 586
Chapter 108 Al-Kawthar ................................................................................ 586
Chapter 109 Al-Kafiruun ................................................................................ 587
Chapter 110 Al-Nasr ...................................................................................... 587
Chapter 111 Al-Lahab .................................................................................... 588
Chapter 112 Al-Ikhlas .................................................................................... 588
Chapter 113 Al-Falaq ..................................................................................... 589
Chapter 114 Al-Nas ........................................................................................ 589
Appendix 1: Examples of differences in various translations of the Qur'an ............ 590
Appendix 2: Glossary: ................................................................................... 594

INTRODUCTION
# Introduction - to be read

## Preface

The translation committee, a partnership of sincere Muslim and Christian Arabic scholars, has made this translation with two purposes in mind. First, it aims to be a modern English translation of the Qur'an that keeps as true as possible to what the original Arabic text actually says rather than how the text is commonly understood to mean.

Second, this translation aims to show parallel passages and similarities between the Qur'an and the Bible for those who may not have read both books and thus it could be called a comparative translation. This is accomplished through a generous use of footnotes, which show parallel passages and similarities between the Qur'an and the Bible, which is known in the Qur'an as the Tawrah (Old Testament), Zabur (Psalms) and Injil (New Testament).

The use of cross-references is an attempt by the Reference Qur'an Committee to help readers find common truth and similarities between the Qur'an and the Bible where they seem to exist. It should not be interpreted as an attempt to affirm or deny the inspiration of the Qur'an or the Bible or to promote any specific doctrine.

This focus on the common ground between the Qur'an and the other books is not a new idea. In the 15th century, Sheikh, Imam, Erudite Scholar and Chief Abu al-Hasan Ibrahim bin Umar bin Hasan al-Biqa'i al-Shafi'i wrote a treatise called <u>The Just Verdict on the Permissibility of Quoting from the Ancient Scriptures</u> /Kitab al-Aqwal al-Qawimah fi hukm al-naql min al-kutub al-qadimah/, in which he successfully defended at al-Azhar University in Cairo his use of the former books in his commentary on the Qur'an.

More recently, Dr. Frances Wakefield published a book called <u>Islamic, Christian, and Jewish References to Elucidate the First Nine Chapters of the Qur'an</u> in 1926 (1343 AH) in Cairo. In it, she gives both internal cross-references from the Qur'an but also

INTRODUCTION

references from the Old Testament /al-Tawrah/ and New Testament /al-Injil/ for the first nine surahs of the Qur'an.

## The reasons for this translation

At last count, there were more than 80 translations of the Qur'an into English. Why another translation of the Qur'an? There are several reasons.

Readability: This translation seeks to use readable, modern English, so that modern readers are not stymied by archaic words. The word Qur'an means "reading" or "recitation", and the translation committee intends that this translation be readable.

Grammar: This translation seeks to clearly express the meaning of the Arabic of the Qur'an in modern English, using modern English word order, grammar, sentence structure, and phraseology. focusing on communicating in modern English *what the Arabic text itself says*. It is not a word-by-word translation that follows Arabic parts of speech, phraseology, word order, grammar and sentence structure.

Vocabulary: This translation seeks to use modern English vocabulary, using Arabic only when necessary to convey the meaning. It does not attempt to teach Arabic.

Clarity: This translation attempts to present in modern English the meaning of the Arabic text *as clearly as the original text does in Arabic*. It aims to let the text explain itself, and *does not attempt to be specific when the Arabic text of the Qur'an is not specific*. When the text can be translated several different ways, the footnotes will give alternate translations. Where the original Arabic is vague or does not specify a pronoun reference, this translation attempts to translate the same degree of vagueness.

Pronouns: Arabic pronouns are more specific than English pronouns. There are five Arabic pronouns that correspond to the English "you" and three that correspond to the English 'they." This translation clearly notes whether the word is singular. dual, or plural, and whether it is masculine or feminine. See note below. Where relevant, it also distinguishes between pronouns used of thinking beings versus those relating to things.

v

# INTRODUCTION

Style: This translation focuses on conveying *what the text of* the original Arabic text says in modern English prose. It does not attempt to reproduce the rhymed prose style of the Qur'an in Arabic.

Chronology: This translation uses the traditional order of chapters and does not attempt to put the Qur'an into chronological order.

Commentary: This translation aims to give a clear translation of what the Arabic text of the Qur'an *says*, without focusing on what historians, commentators, theologians, and traditions may *think* the text means. Nor does this translation focus on the background /asbab al-nuzul/ of the verses of the Qur'an. This translation does not insert commentary into the text.

Cross-references: This translation includes footnotes with cross-references between the Qur'an and the Bible (see notes in glossary on Tawrah, Zabur, and Injil) for those who want to compare verses or investigate a certain subject in more depth. The Reference Qur'an Council, a partnership of Muslim and Christian scholars seeking to build bridges between the two communities, believes that bringing to light *what the original Qur'an actually says* clearly reveals the common truths that exist in the books. Many verses from the Qur'an are consistent with this kind of comparison (29:46, 10:91,94, 16:43-44, 21:7, 2:62, 5:69, 3:113, 4:64, 2:4, 2:136, 4:136, 26:196, 20:133, etc.).

Arabic words: Some English translations of the Qur'an use the Arabic version of the names transliterated into English (like Ibrahim) while others use the English versions (like Abraham). This version of the Reference Qur'an uses the Arabic versions of the names. We plan to make another version of the Reference Qur'an that uses English names for those who prefer them.

The reasons this version uses the Arabic version of the names are as follows:
1) Many English-speaking Muslims around the world are not familiar with the English names.
2) Many English-speaking Muslims are more comfortable with the Arabic versions of the names.
3) Since the Qur'an's original language is Arabic, we felt that using transliterations of names directly from the Arabic was more

appropriate for our first edition than using English names, which are transliterated from other languages.

There are also some other Arabic words that are used in this translation. In some cases, the reason is that there are no English translations that accurately express these words.

## Identifying Arabic pronouns

Arabic has five different words that correspond to the English word "you" and three words for "they." In order to reduce the number of footnotes, these will be abbreviated as follows: /anta/ (you masculine singular) will be you[MS]; /anti/ (you feminine singular) will be you[FS]; /antumaa/ (you dual) will be you[D]; /antum/ (you masculine plural) will be you[MP]; /antunna/ (you feminine plural) will be you[FP], /humaa/ (they dual) will be they[D], /hum/ (they masculine) will be they[MP] and /hunna/ (they feminine) will be they[FP].

## Organization of the Qur'an

The Qur'an is divided into 114 chapters (surahs), arranged roughly in order of decreasing length. These chapters are numbered as well as named. Thus Chapter 2 is also known as the Al-Baqarah chapter. Since these chapter titles are names, they have not been translated, but rather transliterated and the translation given in a footnote. The names of the chapters are often taken from a key verse in the chapter.

The Qur'an is also divided into 30 sections /juz'/ of roughly equal length, which can thus be read one section a day and the Qur'an completely read in a month. Each section is subdivided into two halves /hizb/, which are traditionally also numbered, so that half can be read in the morning, for example, and half in the evening. Finally, markers are placed ¼, ½, and ¾ of the way through each subsection, so the Qur'an is divided into 240 parts. In this translation, the sections are numbered, the halves of the sections are marked A and B, and the quarters of these halves are marked 1 (at the beginning), 2 (after the first quarter), 3 (after half), and 4 (after three-quarters). Thus **23B2** refers to section /juz'/ **23**, second half, or /hizb/ **46**, after the first quarter of the /hizb/.

INTRODUCTION

## Verse numbering

We have used the standard numbering in Arabic. Other English translations may differ by up to several verses if they do not follow the Arabic numbering. As is done in the Arabic Qur'an, we have placed the verse numbers *after* the verses to give greater honor to the verses than their numbers.

## Capitalization

The Arabic language has no capitalization, so does not specify between "he" referring to a person and "He" referring to Allah, for example. We have therefore not capitalized pronouns, since this would be making specific in the translation what the text of the Qur'an does not. In the few instances where an Arabic pronoun makes clear what cannot be communicated in English, this has been footnoted. This translation uses standard English capitalization rules, whereby proper names are capitalized, but not pronouns that refer to them. The words Allah and Lord, as well as people's names, are capitalized, but when the word /ilah/ (god) is used, it is not capitalized. Titles and adjectives are not capitalized. See Allah and god in glossary for more information.

## Rhyme

The style of Arabic in which the Qur'an is written is rhymed prose. We have not attempted to reproduce the rhyme of the Arabic Qur'an in English. There are a number of different rhyme schemes the Qur'an uses, the most common of which is words ending in /eem/, /een/, /oom/, or /oon/. In most chapters of the Qur'an, there is at least one change in the rhyme scheme. Some commentators think that the change in rhyme is due to chapters containing several different revelations, which occurred at different times and were revealed in different rhyme schemes. Others think that the changes in rhyme scheme are intentional, in order to emphasize a verse or section. We have marked changes in rhyme scheme by inserting a line with *** between verses. There is some disagreement about exactly what word endings are allowed in the different rhyme schemes. In order for the English reader to be able to notice all the potential rhyme scheme changes, we have assumed the strictest definitions.

INTRODUCTION
# Challenges of translating the Arabic original of the Qur'an

Some of the challenges in translating the Qur'an from the original Arabic are the following:
1. The Qur'an has no punctuation, as was typical of classical Arabic in that era.
2. Most verses contain what would be several sentences in English in them.
3. Furthermore, verse boundaries do not always signify the end of a sentence. A verse usually ends when a word occurs which fits the rhyme scheme of the chapter.
4. Because the end of a sentence is not marked, whether a phrase belongs with the phrase before it or after it is a decision the translator must make, and even in Arabic, commentators and translators do not always agree.
5. Since there are no quotation marks in the original Arabic, the translator must decide how far the quotation extends, and different translations interpret this differently.
6. Because the ends of the verses generally rhyme, often a word from the middle of a sentence that rhymes is placed at the end of the sentence, even though grammatically it fits better elsewhere This can cause ambiguity in meaning.
7. Often words are used in the Arabic original of the Qur'an that are either unusual, or that seem to have a different meaning from their usual meaning, and thus the meaning is not clear. In such cases, it is left to the translator to try to discern what the closest equivalent is in the target language.

# The Appendices

Appendix 1 contains three examples of such verses, and how 18 translations render those verses.

Appendix 2 is the glossary, with additional information about a number of words and phrases.

This glossary is intended to give background information on key terms, usually with references. As an example, here is the glossary entry for Allah:

# INTRODUCTION

Allah: (God) is the transliteration in English of the word in Arabic for the Almighty, All-knowing Creator of the universe, the only God, He who is worthy of all praise, worship and honor, Allah most gracious and merciful.

/Allah/ is the equivalent of "God" as understood properly in the previous books. It is used 2697 times in the Qur'an. <u>All</u> Arabic-speaking Muslims, Arabic-speaking Christians, and Arabic-speaking Jews use the word /Allah/ for God, and it is used in Arabic versions of <u>all</u> the books, Qur'an, Law, Psalms, and Gospel. It is the linguistic equivalent to /elohim/ in Hebrew, which is the word used in the Law for God 7007 times. Jesus used /elo(h)i/ to talk to Allah in the Injil (Mark 15:34).

Many consider Allah not just a title denoting God, but the *name* of God in Arabic, similar to /yahweh/ in the Law. This has grammatical validity, since neither of those names have a feminine or plural, nor can they be used with a pronoun (e.g. *my* God). However, there is no widespread agreement on this subject.

The Qur'an strongly affirms that Allah (God) is the same God worshiped by true Christians, Jews, and Muslims. See 10:90, 29:46, 73:9 among many other verses listed under "god" in this glossary.

# The English Reference Qur'an: The First Translation of the Qur'an from the Original Arabic into Modern English with references to the Tawrah, Zabur, and Injil

# Chapter 1: Al-Fatihah[2]

1:1 In the name of Allah, the most gracious and merciful.[3] (1)[4] Praise be to Allah, the Lord of the universe, (2) the most gracious and merciful, (3) ruler[5] of the day of judgment. (4) You are the one we worship[6]; you are he whose help we seek. (5) Guide us to the straight path,[7] (6) the path of those whom you have blessed, with whom you are not angry,[8] who have not gone astray.[9] (7)

---

[1] The Arabic word is /surah/ (or sura) and some translations keep the Arabic word /surah/ instead of translating it. It is not used for chapters of other books beside the Qur'an.
[2] In keeping with the translation principle of transliterating names, we have left names of chapters in Arabic. This name means "opening."
[3] Zabur, Psalms 103:8, 145:8. See glossary for more details for this phrase here and in verse 3.
[4] Verse numbers in the Qur'an always follow the verse, not precede it.
[5] Or master or owner or sovereign.
[6] The Arabic word includes the idea of serving as well.
[7] See glossary for more details, and notes on 3:51, 6:153, 19:36, 36:61, and 43:61,64 on what the straight path is.
[8] The text does not say that it is Allah who is angry with them, but it is implied. This verse does not specify with whom Allah is angry, but other verses in the Qur'an make it clear: disbelievers (2:90 among others), murderers of believers (4:93), those who turn away from faith (16:106), and hypocrites and idolaters (48:6). People with the qualities above from any religion incur Allah's anger.
[9] The Arabic can also be understood as "nor [the path of] those with whom you are angry, nor [the path of] those who go astray." This verse does not specify those who have gone astray, but other verses make it clear: those who leave their faith (3:90), idol worshipers (6:74), idolaters (4:116), those who disbelieve in Allah, his angels, his books, his messengers, and the last day (4:136), the unjust (19:38), and those who have not received revelation (26:97). People with the qualities above from any religion have gone astray.

# Chapter 2: Al-Baqarah[10]

In the name of Allah, the most gracious and merciful.[11] ALM.[12] (1) There is no doubt about that book.[13] It is guidance to the reverent, (2) who believe in the unseen, perform prayers, and donate some of our[14] provision to them. (3) They believe in what we revealed to you<sup>MS</sup>[15] and what we revealed before you<sup>MS</sup>[16] and they are certain of the hereafter.[17] (4) They are guided by their Lord and are successful. (5) Disbelievers will not believe, whether you<sup>MS</sup> warn them or not. (6) Allah has sealed their hearts and their hearing, and covered their sight.[18] They will have great torment.[19] (7) Some people say, "We believe in Allah and in the last day," but they are not [really] believers. (8) They try to fool Allah and the believers, but they only fool themselves, and do not even realize it. (9) They have sick hearts,[20] and Allah made them sicker. They will have painful torment for their lies. (10) When they were told, "Do not cause destruction[21] on the earth," they said, "But we are reformers!"[22] (11) They are truly corrupt and do not realize it. (12)

---

[10] heifer or cow

[11] Zabur, Psalms 103:8, 145:8. See glossary for more details.

[12] Here and at the beginning of many chapters there are unvowelled letters of unknown meaning. Numerous theories have been proposed, but there is no agreement on the subject.

[13] i.e. the previous book. Most commentators assume the meaning is the Qur'an. However, the text says, "That book," not "This book." If the meaning were the Qur'an, it would be "this book." In addition, the Qur'an was not yet in book form, like the previous book.

[14] "We" is used throughout the Qur'an when Allah speaks. This is most probably the "royal we" as used by a king (or queen) when referring to himself. It does not imply that Allah is not one.

[15] The Qur'an

[16] The previous books

[17] The Qur'an refers to people who are certain of the hereafter here and in 27:3 and 31:4. All three passages seem to have a reference to the previous books. Injil, John 5:24

[18] Injil, Romans 11:8, 2 Corinthians 3:14, 4:3,4, Tawrah, Isaiah 6:10

[19] For "torment" here and in verses 10, 85 (twice), 90, 96, 104, 114, 126, 162, 165 (twice), 166, 174, 175, 178, 201, and 284, see Tawrah, Isaiah 50:11, Injil, Matthew 18:34, 25:41,46, Luke 16:23-28, Revelation 20:15.

[20] Tawrah, Jeremiah 8:18, 17:9-10

[21] or corruption

[22] or peacemakers

## Chapter 2

When they were told, "Believe like other people have believed," they said, "Shall we believe like fools?" They are the [real] fools, but they do not know it. (13) If they meet believers, they say, "We have believed." But when they are alone with their devils,[23] they tell them, "We are with you[MP]. We were only mocking." (14) Allah will mock them, and will increase their tyranny as they stray. (15) They have exchanged guidance for error, and their trading was unprofitable. They were not guided. (16) They are like those who light a fire, and when it shines around them, Allah takes away their light and leaves them in darkness, where they cannot see. (17) Deaf, dumb, and blind, they will not return.[24] (18) Or [they are] like a cloud in the sky with darkness, thunder, and lightning. They put their fingers in their ears because of the lightning bolts, afraid of death. Allah surrounds the disbelievers. (19)

\*\*\*

The lightning almost blinds them. Whenever it shines, they walk by its light.
When it is dark, they stand still. If Allah had willed, he would have taken away their hearing and their sight. Allah can do anything.[25] (20)

\*\*\*

People, worship your[MP] Lord who created you[MP] and those before you[MP], that you[MP] may be reverent. (21) He made the earth as a bed for you[MP] and the sky as a building. He sent rain[26] from the sky, and through it, brought forth fruits as provision for you[MP]. So do not knowingly make[MP] rivals for Allah.[27] (22) If you[MP] are in doubt concerning our revelation to our servant, bring a chapter like it, and call your[MP] witnesses besides Allah, if you[MP] are telling the truth. (23) If you[MP] do not do that, and you[MP] never will do it, beware[MP] of hellfire which burns people and rocks; it was prepared for disbelievers. (24) Give[MS] good news to the believers who do righteous deeds[28]: they will have heavenly gardens[29] with flowing

---

[23] Arabic /shayatin/ here and in verse 102 (twice). See glossary for more details.
[24] Injil, Revelation 3:17
[25] Tawrah, Job 42:2, Isaiah 14:27, Daniel 4:35, Injil, Matthew 19:26, Mark 10:27, Luke 1:37
[26] Tawrah, Deuteronomy 28:12, Job 5:10, Joel 2:23, Zabur, Psalms 68:9, Injil, Matthew 5:45
[27] Injil, 1 John 5:21
[28] Injil, 1 Corinthians 3:8, James 2:14-17, Revelation 19:8

rivers[30] underneath. Every time they get fruit as provision from it, they say, "This is what we were provided with beforehand." They were given similar to it. There they will have purified kinds[31] and live there forever. (25) 1A2 Allah is not ashamed to tell a proverb about a mosquito or something bigger. Believers know that it is truth from their Lord, but disbelievers say, "What did Allah mean by this?" It is a proverb that leads many astray and guides many. It only leads the unbelievers[32] astray. (26) Those who break Allah's covenant after it is confirmed, sever what Allah commanded to be joined, and cause destruction on the earth are lost. (27) How can you[MP] disbelieve in Allah when you[MP] were dead and he made you[MP] alive? Later, he will make you[MP] die, then make you[MP] alive, and then you[MP] will be returned to him. (28) He created everything on the earth for you[MP], and then sat[33] down in heaven,[34] and he made them[35] into seven heavens. He knows everything. (29) When your[MS] Lord told the angels, "I will make a regent[36] on earth," they said, "Will you[MS] put someone there who will cause destruction on it and shed blood, while we glorify, praise, and sanctify you[MS]?" He said, "I know things you[MP] do not know." (30) He taught

---

[29] Arabic /jannah/ here and in verses 35 and 214. See glossary for more details.

[30] Injil, Revelation 22:1-2, Tawrah, Ezekiel 47:12

[31] Other translations translate "spouses,' but the adjective "purified" refers to inanimate objects, not people. This word /azwaaj/ has two main meanings, "kinds" or "spouses." It is used often in the context of gardens with the meaning "kinds" [often of fruit] - see 20:53,131, 22:5, 26:7, 36:36, 38:58, 43:12, and 50:7. From the context in this verse, it is probable that the meaning is also "kinds" [of fruit or other plants].

[32] Or transgressors or immoral. See Injil, Matthew 13:10-17.

[33] Allah does not have a physical body, but like the Injil and Tawrah, the Qur'an uses anthropomorphisms to talk about Allah. Sitting here has the idea of reigning.

[34] Or the sky. The same word in Arabic means both. Injil, Revelation 4:2-3.

[35] The word them is used for thinking beings, so the reference here might be to those who inhabit heaven.

[36] The word in Arabic is /khalifah/, sometimes translated vicegerent. It is used for caliph and comes from the root "to be behind or after. " Only Adam (here) and Dawud (38:26) are named as regents in the Qur'an. In 7:69,74 and 27:62 people are called regents on the earth. In this meaning, see also Tawrah, Genesis 1:26-28.

## Chapter 2

Adam[37] all the names[38] and then showed them[MP][39] to the angels. He said, "If you[MP] are telling the truth, tell[MP] me the names of these." (31) They said, "May you[MS] be glorified! We know nothing except what you[MS] have taught us. You[MS] are all-knowing[40] and wise."[41] (32) He said, "Adam, tell[MS] them[MP] their[MP] names." When he told them[MP] their names, he said, "Did I not tell you[MP] that I know the unseen things of the heavens and the earth, and I know what you[MP] show and what you[MP] hide?" (33) When we told the angels, "Bow[MP] down[42] to Adam," they all bowed down, except for Iblis,[43] who refused and was proud. He was a disbeliever.[44] (34) We said, "Adam, live with your[MS] wife in the heavenly garden and eat[D] of it freely wherever you[D] want, but do not approach[D] this tree, or you[D] will be wicked." (35) Satan caused them[D] to stumble from it, and he expelled them[D] from where they[D] were. We said, "Go[MP] down,[45] enemies to one another, and on earth you[MP] will have a temporary place of stability and livelihood." (36) Adam received words from his Lord, who accepted his repentance. He is the merciful[46]

---

[37] See glossary for more details on Adam here and in verses 33, 34, 35, and 37.

[38] Possibly the animals. See Tawrah, Genesis 2:19-20. Ahmad Hulusi and other commentators believe that the names are the 99 beautiful names of God.

[39] The words here and in verse 33 for "them," "their," and "these" are masculine plural for thinking creatures. Traditionally this has been explained as the animals, but animals uses a different word for "they." Possibly thinking creatures were included, such as Eve. See Tawrah, Genesis 2:19-21.

[40] For "all-knowing" here and in verses 115, 127, 137, 158, 181, 224, 227, 231, 244, 247, 256, 261, and 268, see Tawrah, Job 37:16, Isaiah 40:14, Zabur, Psalms 33:13-15, Injil, 1 John 3:20.

[41] For "wise" here and in verses 209, 220, 228, 240, and 260, see Tawrah, Job 9:4, Proverbs 2:6, Jeremiah 9:23-24, Injil, 1 Corinthians 1:21-25, Romans 16:27.

[42] Zabur, Psalms 97:7, Injil, Hebrews 1:6

[43] The devil. See glossary for more details.

[44] This does not mean that Satan did not know of Allah's existence, but that he refused to obey Allah. See glossary for more details.

[45] Here and in verse 38, the use of the plural and not the dual implies that Adam, Eve, and Satan were all cast down. See Tawrah, Genesis 3:23-24.

[46] Here and in verses 54, 128, 143, 160, 173, 182, 192, 199, 218, and 226, see glossary for more details on "merciful."

acceptor of repentance.[47] (37) We said, "All of you[MP] go down from it.[48] When my guidance comes to you[MP], those who follow my guidance will neither fear nor grieve." (38) Disbelievers who reject our signs[49] will go to hellfire, where they will be eternally. (39) People of Israel, remember the blessings[50] I gave you[MP]. Fulfill[MP] my covenant, and I will fulfill your[MP] [part of the] covenant. Be[MP] terrified of me. (40) Believe[MP] in my revelation,[51] which confirms what you[MP] have.[52] Do not be[MP] the first disbeliever[53] in it, and do not sell[MP] my verses for a small price, but fear[MP] me. (41) And do not cover[MP] truth with vanity or knowingly hide[MP] the truth. (42) Perform[MP] prayers, pay[MP] the poor-tax,[54] and kneel[MP] together.[55] (43) 1A3 Do you[MP] command others to be righteous and forget[MP] yourselves, though you read[MP] the book? Do you[MP] not comprehend? (44) Seek[MP] help in endurance[56] and performing prayers. It[57] is a major issue,[58] except to the humble (45) who think[MP] they will meet their Lord. They will certainly return to him.[59] (46) People of Israel, remember[MP] the blessings I gave you[MP]. I preferred[60] you[MP] above all mankind.[61] (47) Fear[MP] a

---

[47] For "repentance," here and in verses 54 and 160, see glossary. Tawrah, Jeremiah 18:8, Joel 2:13, Jonah 3:9-4:2

[48] probably the garden (verse 35).

[49] Arabic /ayat/. See glossary for more details.

[50] Or grace, but here and in verse 47, as in "common grace": rain, food, relationships, etc.

[51] the Qur'an

[52] The Book that the Jews had in the days of Muhammad is here confirmed by the Qur'an as accurate. The Qur'an confirms the previous books many times (2:41,89,91,97,101, 3:3,81, 4:47, 5:48, 6:92, 35:31, 46:12,30)

[53] This word is singular in the Arabic.

[54] This word /zakah/ refers to obligatory giving. Voluntary giving is expressed by another word Sadaqaat. See glossary for more details.

[55] Or, with the (other) kneelers (in prayer)

[56] For "endure" and "endurance" here and in verses 61, 153 (twice), 155, 175, 249, and 250, see glossary for more details.

[57] The duty, or prayer.

[58] Or "great."

[59] Injil, Romans 14:12

[60] 2:122, Injil, Romans 3:1,9. Tawrah, Deuteronomy 7:7. Allah preferred them, but this does not mean they are better. Allah sent them prophets and revelation, but they often disobeyed (2:61,93, 4:155).

[61] Or "above everything in the universe" here and in verse 122.

day when no soul will benefit another, nor will its intercession[62] be accepted,[63] nor will a ransom be taken from it. They will not be saved. (48) When[64] we rescued you[MP] from the family of Pharaoh, he treated you[MP] with evil torment, slaughtering your[MP] sons and keeping your[MP] women alive. That was a great trial from your[MP] Lord. (49) When we divided the sea for you[MP], we rescued you[MP], and drowned Pharaoh's family as you watched.[65] (50) When we made an appointment with Musa[66] for forty nights, you[MP] chose the calf after that, and were[MP] wicked. (51) Afterwards, we pardoned you[MP] so that you[MP] may give thanks. (52) We gave Musa the book and the criterion,[67] so that you[MP] may be guided. (53) Then Musa told his people, "My people, you[MP] have wronged yourselves[MP] by taking[MP] the calf, so repent[MP] to your[MP] creator and kill[MP] yourselves.[68] That would be better for you[MP] with your[MP] creator." Then he accepted their repentance. He is the merciful acceptor of repentance. (54) Then you[MP] said, "Musa, we will not believe in you[MS] until we see Allah plainly." Then lightning overtook you[MP] as you[MP] watched. (55) Then we resurrected you[MP] after your[MP] death, so that you[MP] might give thanks. (56) Then we overshadowed you[MP] with the cloud and sent you[MP] down manna and quail.[69] "Eat[MP] of the good things we have provided you[MP]."

---

[62] the word "intercession" is feminine and the verb "be accepted" is masculine. There may be a different meaning here.

[63] For "intercession" here and in verse 123, the Qur'an speaks of only one intercessor (see note at 2:255). Tawrah, Exodus 32:33, 2 Chronicles 6:23, Ezekiel 18:1-32, Injil, Galatians 6:7-8.

[64] Or "since," here and in verses 50-51. There is no previous word "when" that is addressed to these people, so this verse may be a continuation of a conversation, and not the beginning. This verse and those following may also be a general admonition based on Allah's previous works and signs.

[65] Tawrah, Exodus 14:26-31, 15:4, Isaiah 43:17

[66] Moses here and in verses 53, 54, 55, 60, 61, 67, 87, 92, 108, 136, and 248. See glossary for more details.

[67] The Arabic word /furqan/ refers to a book given to Musa, and it may refer to the Ten Commandments. It comes from the root to differ or distinguish, as commandments do.

[68] Or "each other." See Tawrah, Exodus 32:27-29, Injil, Matthew 18:6, 26:64

[69] Tawrah, Exodus 16:1-35.

## Chapter 2

They did not wrong us, but they wronged themselves.[70] (57) So we said, "Enter[MP] this village[71] and eat freely from it wherever you[MP] want." Enter[MP] the door bowing down, and say[MP], "Relief!"[72] We will forgive your[MP] faults and increase the generous. (58) The wicked substituted one saying they had been told for another, so we sent a plague from heaven down on the wicked for their unbelief.[73] (59) 1A4 When Musa asked for a drink for his people, we said, "Strike the rock with your[MS] staff," and twelve springs broke forth from it.[74] All the people knew their[MP] drinking place. Eat[MP] and drink[MP] from Allah's provision, and do[MP] not trouble and cause[MF] destruction on the earth. (60) When you[MP] said, "Musa, we will not endure one food. Pray to your[MS] Lord for us. Let him bring forth for us legumes, cucumbers, garlic, lentils, and onions that the earth brings forth."[75] He said, "Will you[MP] trade what is good for what is less? Go[MP] down to Egypt.[76] You[MP] can have your[MP] request." Abasement and misery struck them. They have brought Allah's anger upon themselves, because they disbelieve in Allah's signs[77] and wrongfully murder the prophets.[78] This was because

---

[70] The injustice/wickedness, disbelief/ungratefulness, evil, unrighteousness/sin, or lostness of mankind is mentioned in a number of verses in the Qur'an as well as in the previous books. Injustice or wickedness: 2:57, 3:117,135, 4:64,97, 7:160,177, 9:70, 10:44, 11:101, 14:34,45, 16:33,61,118, 29:40, 30:9, 33:72, 34:19, 35:32, 43:76, 65:1, Tawrah, Genesis 6:5, Job 25:4, Injil, Acts 3:26, disbelief or ungratefulness: 14:34, 17:67, 22:66, 42:48, 43:15, 80:17, Injil, Hebrews 3:19, Evil: 12:53, Tawrah, Jeremiah 17:9, Injil, Matthew 15:19, Mark 7:21, unrighteousness or sin: 91:8, Tawrah, 1 Kings 8:46, Ecclesiastes 7:20, Injil, Romans 3:9-19, 5:12, Lostness: 103:2, Tawrah, Jeremiah 50:6, Injil, Luke 19:10, Romans 3:23, 6 23

[71] Or "community" if this means the people of Israel in the wilderness. Tawrah, Exodus 16:4-5

[72] Or humiliation or abasement or alleviation

[73] Or immorality or transgression

[74] Tawrah, Exodus 17:1-6

[75] Tawrah, Numbers 11:1-7

[76] Tawrah, Numbers 14:3,22,23

[77] Arabic /ayat/, here and in verse 231. See glossary for more details.

[78] For Jews murdering the prophets here and in verses 87 and 91, see also 3:21,112,181,183, 4:155, 5:70, Tawrah, Nehemiah 9:26, Injil, Matthew 23:37, Luke 11:47-49, Acts 7:52, 1 Thessalonians 2:15. The word "murder" does not imply that they thwarted Allah's will or that the Jewish people as a whole murdered them. Particularly in the case of Isa, it was

## Chapter 2

they disobeyed and attacked.[79] (61) Truly believers, the Jews,[80] the Christians,[81] and Sabeans[82] who believe in Allah and in the last day and who do righteous deeds[83] have their reward from their Lord, and will not fear or grieve.[84] (62) When we made a covenant with you[MP] and raised the mountain over you[MP], "Take what we give you[MP] firmly and remember[MP] what is in it, so that you[MP] may be reverent." (63) Then you[MP] turned away afterwards. If not for the grace and mercy of Allah toward you[MP], you[MP] would have been lost. (64) You[MP] know those of you[MP] who transgressed the sabbath,[85] so we told them, "Be despicable monkeys."[86] (65) We made them[87] a warning for what was in front of them[88] and behind them,[89] and an admonition for the reverent. (66) [Remember] when Musa told his people, "Allah commands you[MP] to sacrifice a

---

the Jewish religious leadership who were responsible. See Injil, Matthew 26:47ff.

[79] or violated or transgressed

[80] Or those who repented and turned back to the truth. This refers to the Jews, especially when they repented after worshiping the golden calf idol (2:54, 92, 7:138, 148-150, Tawrah, Exodus 32).

[81] For /nasara/ (Christian) here and in verses 111, 113 (twice), 120, 135, and 140, see glossary for more details.

[82] Sabeans are only mentioned three times in the Qur'an (here, 22:17, and in 5:69). They may be followers of John the Baptizer, as some by that name still exist in Iraq today, or a tribe of Christians in northern Arabia who were known for praying 7 times a day, or this may refer to the Mandeans. Whoever they are, they seem to be monotheists.

[83] Here and in verse 82, see Injil, 1 Corinthians 3:8, James 2:14-17, Revelation 19:8

[84] This verse promises all monotheists, Sabeans, Muslims, Christians and Jews, eternal comfort if they believe in Allah and the last day and do good deeds. There is no requirement for anyone to convert to another religion.

[85] Tawrah, Exodus 20:8-11, 31:13; Isaiah 56:6,7, 58:13,14, 66:22,23; Ezekiel 20:20, Injil, Matthew 12:8, 24:20; Mark 2:27; Luke 23:56

[86] This is probably figurative, since the noun monkeys has an adjective used for thinking beings, rather than the normal adjective for non-thinking beings. for a similar usage, see 5:60 and 7:166, in addition to Injil, Matthew 7:6, where some people are compared to pigs.

[87] The monkeys. Non-thinking plural three times in this verse.

[88] Or, "between their hands."

[89] Some translations put "The people of that day, and those after them." This is probably incorrect, since the pronoun "them" (the monkeys) refers to non-humans.

heifer."[90] They said, "Are you[MS] kidding us?" He said, "Allah forbid that I would be ignorant." (67) They said, "Pray to your[MS] Lord for us that he would clarify for us what she is." He said, "He says that it is a heifer, neither old nor virgin, but middle-aged, so do as you[MP] are told. (68) They said, "Pray to your[MS] Lord for us to clarify to us what color she is." He said, "He says it is a yellow heifer, bright yellow-colored, pleasing to look at." (69) They said, "Pray to your[MS] Lord for us, to clarify for us which one she is. The heifers look alike to us. If Allah wills, we will be guided." (70) He said, "He says it is a cow never yoked[91] to plow the ground, nor to water the furrows, whole and without blemish." They said, "Now you[MS] have brought the truth," so they sacrificed it, but they almost did not. (71) When you[MP] killed a person and fought about it, Allah brought to light what you[MP] hid.[92] (72) So we said, "Make[MP] a comparison with him[93] with a part of it[F].[94] Thus Allah gives life to the dead and shows you[MP] his signs, so that you[MP] would comprehend."[95] (73) Then your[MP] hearts were hardened after that. They were as hard as stone or harder,[96] for some stones have had rivers break forth from them;[97] some give water when split; and

---

[90] For details about the heifer here and in verses 68 and 71, see Tawrah, Numbers 19:2.
[91] For "never yoked" and "nor to water the furrows," see Tawrah, Deuteronomy 21:3.
[92] This may be a reference to Isa being killed. Musa also killed a man (28:15) and hid his body, Tawrah, Exodus 2:11-14, but "you hid" in the Arabic in this verse is plural, so "you" cannot refer to Musa. According to several Muslim commentators, it refers to those who killed Isa. See the footnotes on the following verse.
[93] Injil, Hebrews 9:13-14. The word here translated "make a comparison" can also be translated several other ways, including "strike" or "travel". See following footnotes.
[94] In other words, there are similarities between the slaughter of the cow and the murder of the person referred to.
[95] One commentary that says this verse refers to Isa and his death and resurrection is: The Holy Quran, by Zahurul Hoque, Holy Quran Publishing Project (2000), notes 72-73 (p 19). In The Message of the Quran, by Muhammad Asad, Dar Andalus (1980), note 57 (p 23), the commentary mentions the figurative sense of the verb /daraba/ including one meaning of giving an illustration. See 39:27.
[96] This hardness of the Jews accurately describes their state after Jesus' death. 3:55, 5:117, Injil, Matthew 27:62 - 28:15
[97] Tawrah, Exodus 17:6, Numbers 20:10-11

## Chapter 2

others fall down in the fear of Allah.[98] Allah is aware of your[MP] deeds. (74) 1B1 Do you[MP] expect that they will be true to you[MP] when some of them heard Allah's message and then knowingly distorted it after they comprehended it?[99] (75) When they meet believers, they say, "We believe," and when they are alone among themselves, they say, "Do you[MP] tell them what Allah explained to you[MP] so they dispute with you[MP] about it with your[MP] Lord?" Do they not comprehend? (76) Do they not know that Allah knows what they conceal and what they announce?[100] (77) Some of them are unlettered,[101] knowing only a little of the book. They only guess. (78) Woe to those who write the book with their hands and then say, "This is from Allah," to sell it for a paltry sum.[102] Woe to them for what they wrote and woe to them for their gain. (79) They said, "Hellfire will not touch us except for a few days." Have you[MP] made a covenant with Allah that he will not break? Or do you[MP] say what you[MP] do not know about Allah? (80) Rather, those who do bad deeds, and are caught in their faults, will be in hellfire eternally.[103] (81) Those who believe and do righteous deeds will go to heaven eternally. (82) So we made a covenant with the people of Israel: You[MP] will worship Allah alone,[104] do good to parents, relatives, orphans[105] and the poor. Tell[MP] people what is good, perform prayers and pay the poor-tax. Then all except a few of you[MP] turned away in aversion. (83) So we made a covenant with you[MP]. You[MP] do not shed your[MP] own blood, and you[MP] do not expel yourselves from your[MP] own houses. Then you[MP] concurred, and you[MP] are witnesses. (84) Then you[MP] kill yourselves[MP] and

---

[98] Injil, Luke 19:40

[99] There are two types of "distortion:" altering the text and altering the meaning. From the words "heard" and "comprehended," it is clear that altering the meaning is intended. See 3:78, 4:46, 5:13,41 for the other verses that deal with this subject. Injil, 2 Peter 3:16

[100] See also 11:5, 14:38, 16:19,23, 27:25,74, 28:69, 36:76, 60:1, 64:4.

[101] Or Gentiles. In modern Arabic, this word can mean illiterate, but the Qur'an's meaning here is that they do not know the Book (in this case the Tawrah, Zabur, and Injil).

[102] Trying to make money from Allah's word is warned against.

[103] Those who imagine that they will escape from hellfire after a period of time are deceived.

[104] This verse is what they do, not a command to do them.

[105] Tawrah, Job 29:12, Zabur, Psalms 82:3, Injil, James 1:27

expel a group of yourselves<sup>MP</sup> from their homes. You<sup>MP</sup> assist[106] them in guilt and hostility. If they had come to you<sup>MP</sup> as prisoners, you<sup>MP</sup> would have ransomed them, while expelling them is forbidden for you<sup>MP</sup>. Do you<sup>MP</sup> believe in part of the book, and disbelieve in the rest? The reward for those among you<sup>MP</sup> who do that is shame in this world, and on the day of resurrection,[107] they will be sent back to the severest torment. Allah is aware of your<sup>MP</sup> deeds. (85) The torment of those who trade this life for the hereafter will not be lightened, and they will not be saved. (86) We gave Musa the book and made messengers follow him. We brought Isa[108] son of Mariam[109] miracles,[110] and aided him with the Holy Spirit.[111] Whenever a messenger comes to you<sup>MP</sup> with a message you do not like, are you<sup>MP</sup> proud, calling<sup>MP</sup> some of them liars, and murdering<sup>MP</sup> some of them? (87) They said, "Our hearts are hardened." Allah has damned them for their disbelief.[112] How little they<sup>MP</sup> believe! (88) And when a book came to them<sup>MP</sup> from Allah confirming[113] what they have,[114] they used to ask for Allah's help against the disbelievers. When what they knew came to them, they disbelieved in it. Allah has damned disbelievers. (89) What

---

[106] The vowelling of this word is non-standard. If the consonants are assumed correct and the voweling is adjusted, the meaning is as translated. If another "t" were added, the meaning would be similar.

[107] For "day of resurrection" here and in verses 113,174, and 212, see Tawrah, Daniel 12:,2 Injil, Acts 24 15, 1 Corinthians 15:52-54, Revelation 20:11-15

[108] Jesus, here and in verses 136 and 253. See glossary for more details.

[109] Mary, mother of Jesus, here and in verse 253. See glossary for more details.

[110] The Qur'an lists some of his miracles in 3:49,52, 5:110,112, 19:19,20,24,30-33. Most of the miracles Isa does, with the stories behind them, are mentioned in the Injil, especially Matthew 8-11, 14-15,17,21, Mark 1-9,11, Luke 2,4-9,22, John 2,4-6,9,11.

[111] Injil, Matthew 3:16-4:10, Luke 4:1, 14, 18, 10:21. Isa is the only one in the Qur'an who was aided by the Holy Spirit. See also 2:253, 5:110. His anointing as Messiah is connected with his being aided with the Holy Spirit in all three verses of the Qur'an as well as Tawrah, Isaiah 61:1, Injil, Matthew 3:16, Romans 1:4, Hebrews 9:14.

[112] For here and verse 89, see Tawrah, 2 Kings 17:14-18.

[113] The Qur'an confirms the previous books many times (2:41,89,91,97,101, 3:3,81, 4:47, 5:48, 6:92, 35:31, 46:12,30). This passage contains four such confirmations.

[114] Here and in verses 91 and 97, the Qur'an confirms the truth of the book that existed in the days of Muhammad (s).

## Chapter 2

they sell their souls for is dreadful: insolently disbelieving in what Allah has revealed, that Allah reveals his grace to those he wills of his servants. They have gotten more and more anger. Disbelievers will have shameful torment. (90) If they are told, "Believe in what Allah has revealed," they say, "We believe in what was revealed to us."[115] They disbelieve in what is beyond that, though it is truth confirming what they have. Say[MS], "Then why did you[MP] murder Allah's prophets beforehand, if you[MP] are believers?" (91) **1B2** Musa came to you[MP] with miracles, but you[MP] chose the calf.[116] You[MP] are wicked. (92) So we made a covenant with you[MP] and raised the mountain[117] above you[MP], "Grasp what we bring you[MP] firmly and listen." They said, "We listened and disobeyed." Then they were made to drink the calf in their hearts because of their disbelief.[118] Say[MS], "What your[MP] faith commands you[MP] to do is dreadful, if you[MP] are believers." (93) Say[MS], "If you[MP] are certain of the abode of the hereafter free and clear, to the exclusion of other people, then wish for death, if you[MP] are telling the truth." (94) They will not wish for it at all because of what their hands have done. Allah knows the wicked. (95) They are the people you[MS] will find most desirous of staying alive than a polytheist. One of them wants to live a thousand years, but he will not avoid torment by living long. Allah sees what they do. (96) Say[MS], "Who is Jibril's[119] enemy?" He revealed it to your[MS] heart by Allah's permission, confirming what is in his possession,[120] guidance and good news to believers. (97) Who is an enemy of Allah, his angels, his messengers, Jibril and Mikal[121]? Allah is the enemy of disbelievers. (98) We have revealed miraclous signs to you[MS]. Only the unbelievers[122] disbelieve them. (99) Whenever they make a covenant, some of them violate it. Most of them do not believe. (100) And when a messenger from Allah comes to them confirming what they have, some recipients of the book toss Allah's book behind their backs as if they did not know (101) and

---

[115] The former books
[116] See Tawrah, Exodus 32:1-6
[117] Mount Sinai
[118] See Tawrah, Exodus 32:20
[119] The archangel Gabriel, here and in verse 98
[120] Or, "between his hands" or "in front of him."
[121] the archangel Michael
[122] Or transgressors or immoral.

follow what the devils recited about the kingdom of Sulayman.[123] Sulayman did not disbelieve like the devils, who taught people magic; what was revealed to Harut and Marut, the two angels in Babylon. They[D] did not teach anyone before telling him, "We are a temptation, so do not disbelieve." So they[MP] learn from them[D] how to separate a man and his wife,[124] but they[MP] cannot harm anyone with this except with Allah's permission.[125] They[P] also learn what harms them and does not benefit them. They[MP] knew that whoever buys it has no share in the hereafter. What they[MP] sell their souls for is dreadful, if they only knew. (102) If they had believed and been reverent, Allah would have rewarded them well, if they had known. (103) Believers, do not say[MP], "Look at us,"[126] but say, "Consider us," and listen. Disbelievers will have painful torment. (104) Disbelieving people of the book[127] and idolaters do not want anything good to come down to you[MP] from your[MP] Lord. Allah assigns his mercy to whom he wills.[128] Allah has great grace. (105)

**1B3**

\*\*\*

We will replace a sign[129] that we cancel[130] or cause to be forgotten with another one like it or better.[131] Do you[MS] not know that Allah can do anything?[132] (106) Do you[MS] not know that the kingdom of the heavens and the earth is Allah's? You[MP] have no helper or savior[133] besides Allah. (107) Or do you[MP] want to ask your[MP] messenger as Musa was asked previously? Whoever exchanges

---

[123] Solomon twice in this verse. See glossary for more details.
[124] This is a major sign of the devil's involvement.
[125] Tawrah, Job 1:12, 2:6
[126] Some commentators believe that this word was deliberately mispronounced to be an insult.
[127] Not all people of the book are believers and not all are disbelievers. See 2:253.
[128] Tawrah, Exodus 33:19, Injil, Romans 9:15,18
[129] or verse
[130] or abrogate
[131] Injil, 1 Corinthians 13:10, 2 Corinthians 3:3,7,11,13,14, Ephesians 2:15, Hebrews 7:19,22, 8:6, 9:23, 11:16, Matthew 5:17-20
[132] Tawrah, Job 42:2, Isaiah 14:27, Daniel 4:35, Injil, Matthew 19:26, Mark 10:27, Luke 1:37
[133] Tawrah, Hosea 13:4, Zabur, Psalms 106:21, Injil, Luke 1:47, Titus 1:3

## Chapter 2

faith for disbelief has gone astray from the straight path.[134] (108) Many of the people of the book wish they could turn you[MP] back into disbelievers after you[MP] had faith, because they themselves are jealous after truth became clear to them. So pardon[MP] and forgive[MP] until Allah gives his command. Allah can do anything.[135] (109) Perform[MP] the prayers and give[MP] the poor-tax. The good you[MP] present to yourselves[136] you[MP] will find with Allah. Allah sees your[MP] deeds. (110)

\*\*\*

They said, "Only Jews and Christians will enter heaven." That is their wish.
Say[MS], "Present your[MP] proof if you[MP] are telling the truth." (111) Rather those who submit their faces to Allah and are charitable have their reward from their Lord, and will neither fear nor grieve. (112) The Jews said, "Christians are without foundation," and the Christians said, "The Jews are without foundation," while they read the book. The ignorant speak similarly. Allah will judge between them on the day of resurrection concerning their differences.[137] (113) Who is as wicked as one who forbids Allah's name being mentioned in his places of worship and tries to destroy them? They should not enter them without fear. They will have shame in this world and great torment in the hereafter. (114) The East and the West are Allah's, and his face is wherever you[MP] turn. Allah is everywhere[138] and knows everything.[139] (115) They said, "Allah has taken a boy."[140] May he be glorified (above that)! Everything in heaven and earth is his, and all are subservient to him, (116) the creator of the heavens and the earth.[141] If he decrees something, he just says to it, "Be," and it is.[142] (117) The ignorant

---

[134] See glossary for more details, and notes on 3:51, 6:153, 6:153, 19:36, 36:61, and 43:61,64 on what the straight path is.
[135] Tawrah, Job 42:2, Isaiah 14:27, Daniel 4:35, Injil, Matthew 19:26, Mark 10:27, Luke 1:37
[136] Or each other
[137] Injil, Acts 17:30
[138] Zabur, Psalms 139:7-12
[139] Tawrah, Job 37:16, Isaiah 40:14, Zabur, Psalms 33:13-15, Injil, 1 John 3:20
[140] Or son. The word refers only to a physical son. All the books reject the idea that Allah took a boy to be his son.
[141] Tawrah, Genesis 1:1, Isaiah 42:5, 45:18
[142] Tawrah, Genesis 1:3-28

## Chapter 2

said, "If only Allah would speak to us or give us a sign."[143] Those before them spoke similarly. Their hearts are similar. We have made signs clear to people who are certain. (118) We truly[144] sent you[MS] as a bearer of good news and a warner. You[MS] are not responsible for those headed to hell. (119)

\*\*\*

The Jews and Christians will not be pleased with you[MS] until you[MS] follow their spiritual path.[145] Say, "Allah's guidance is guidance." If you[MS] follow their desires after you[MS] have received knowledge, there will be no one to protect or save you[MS] from Allah. (120)

\*\*\*

Those to whom we gave the book[146] read it as it deserves to be read,[147] and believe in it. Whoever disbelieves in it is lost. (121) People of Israel, remember the blessings I gave you[MP], how I preferred you[MP] above all mankind. (122) Beware of a day when no soul will receive anything from another. No ransom will be accepted from it,[148] nor will intercession benefit it; they will not be saved. (123) **1B4** When Allah tested Ibrahim[149] with words, he fulfilled them.[150] He said, "I will make you[MS] a leader of men." He said, "And my descendants?"[151] He said, "My covenant does not extend to the wicked." (124)

\*\*\*

We made the sanctuary a reward and safety for people, and they made the place where Ibrahim stood[152] a place of prayer. We made a covenant with Ibrahim and Ismail:[153] purify my house for those who walk around it, the devout and those who kneel bowing down. (125)

\*\*\*

---

[143] Injil, Matthew 12:38, 16:1, John 4:48, 1 Corinthians 1:22

[144] The phrase can also mean, We sent you with truth

[145] Arabic /millah/. See glossary.

[146] In this context, the Tawrah; see next verse.

[147] Or, "truly"or "truthfully."

[148] Zabur, Psalms 49:7

[149] Abraham here and in verses 125 (twice), 126, 127, 130, 132, 133, 135, 136, 140, 258 (three times), and 260. See glossary for more details.

[150] The words here may be symbolic, since the word "them" is used for thinking beings.

[151] Or "seed." See Tawrah, Genesis 15:2.

[152] See Tawrah, Genesis 22:2, 5, 9, 14, 2 Chronicles 3:1

[153] Ishmael here and in verses 127, 133, 136, 140, and 162. See glossary for more details.

## Chapter 2

When Ibrahim said, "Lord, make this a safe city[154]. Provide fruit for its inhabitants who believe in Allah and the last day." He said, "I will let the disbelievers have pleasure for a short time, then I will force them into the torment of hellfire, a dreadful destiny." (126)

\*\*\*

Ibrahim and Ismail set up the foundations[155] of the sanctuary: "Our Lord, accept [it] from us. You[MS] hear all and know all. (127) Our Lord, make us submitted[156] to you[MS], and make some of our descendants a nation submitted to you[MS]. Show us our rituals, and accept our repentance. You[MS] are the merciful acceptor of repentance.[157] (128) Our Lord, send[MS] them a messenger from among them who recites your[MS] signs to them, teaches them the book and wisdom, and purifies them. You[MS] are strong and wise."[158] (129) Whoever dislikes the spiritual path[159] of Ibrahim is foolish. We have chosen him[160] in this world, and in the hereafter; he is righteous. (130) When his Lord told him, "Submit," he said, "I have submitted to the Lord of the universe." (131) Ibrahim commanded[161] his sons[162] and Yaqub[163] about it,[164] "Sons, Allah has chosen your[MP] religion, so do not die unless you are submitted[MP]." (132) Or were you[MP] witnesses when Yaqub was on his deathbed,[165] when he asked his sons, "What will you[MP] worship

---

[154] Tawrah, Genesis 18, Injil, Hebrews 11:10

[155] Injil, Hebrews 11:10

[156] Injil, James 4:7. For "submit" and "submitted" here (twice) and in verses 131 (twice), 132, 133, and 136, some translators do not translate this. See glossary for more details.

[157] For "repentance," see glossary. See Tawrah, Jeremiah 18:8, Joel 2:13, Jonah 3:9-4:2

[158] Tawrah, Job 9:4, Proverbs 2:6, Jeremiah 9:23-24, Injil, 1 Corinthians 1:21-25, Romans 16:27

[159] Arabic /millah/ here and in verse 135. See glossary.

[160] i.e. Ibrahim

[161] Tawrah, Genesis 18:19

[162] The Arabic is plural (not dual referring to Ishaq and Ishmael), so assumedly the sons of Keturah, his third wife (Tawrah, Genesis 25:1-4), are also included.

[163] Jacob, here and in verses 133, 136, and 140. See glossary for more details.

[164] The word "it" here is feminine and it is not clear what the antecedent is. It could be "sect" from verse 130.

[165] Compare Tawrah, Genesis 49, Injil, Hebrews 11:21

## Chapter 2

after I die?" They said, "We will worship your[MS] god[166] and the god of your[MS] fathers[167] Ibrahim, Ismail, and Ishaq,[168] one god, and we have submitted to him." (133) That nation has passed away. They have what they deserve, and you[MP] have what you[MP] deserve. You[MP] will not be questioned about what they did. (134) They said, "Be Jews or Christians and you[MP] will be guided." Say[MS], "Rather the spiritual path of Ibrahim, a monotheist.[169] He was not a polytheist." (135) Say[MP], "We believe in Allah and what was revealed to us and what was revealed[170] to Ibrahim, Ismail, Ishaq, Yaqub, and the tribes, what was given to Musa and Isa, and what was given to the prophets[171] from their Lord. We do not distinguish between any of them,[172] and we are submitted to him." (136) If they believe similarly to your[MP] belief, they are guided, but if they turn away, they are in disagreement. Allah will suffice you[MS] regarding them, and he hears all and knows all. (137) Allah's dye;[173] who is better than Allah at dyeing?[174] We are his worshipers. (138) Say[MS], "Do you[MP] argue with us about Allah, when he is our Lord as well as your[MP] Lord? We have our works and you[MP] have your[MP] works, and we are sincere toward him. (139) Or do you[MP] say that Ibrahim, Ismail, Ishaq, Yaqub, and the tribes

---

[166] Arabic /ilah/ here three times and in verses 163 (three times) and 255. See glossary for more details.

[167] Father is used non-literally here, since Abraham was his grandfather and Ishmael his uncle.

[168] Isaac, here and in verses 136 and 140. See glossary for more details.

[169] The root of this word is "to incline" and there are other opinions about its meaning.

[170] Most of what all the prophets were given came from Allah orally, and it was later written down. The exception is Musa (Tawrah, Exodus 34:28, Deuteronomy 4:13, 10:4), when Allah himself wrote them on stone tablets.

[171] The text does not give the names of these prophets, but if the order of the people given revelation in this verse is chronological, then the "prophets" would be the ones who were given the rest of the Injil after Isa was raised to Allah.

[172] See 17:55, 2:253, where Allah prefers some prophets and messengers over others. This verse talks about distinguishing.

[173] The word also means color, baptism (which originally meant dyeing), or religion. "Dye" is in the accusative case, so the opening phrase either has an implied verb or is a continuation of another idea.

[174] See Injil, Acts 1:5, Ephesians 4:5. Some see here a reference to baptism.

Chapter 2

were Jews or Christians?" Say^(MS), "Who knows more: you^(MP) or Allah? Who is more wicked than he who conceals testimony within himself from Allah? Allah is aware of your^(MP) deeds." (140) That nation has passed away. It has received what it deserves, and you^(MP) will receive what you^(MP) deserve. You^(MP) are not accountable for their deeds. (141) 2A1 Foolish people will say, "What turned them away from their former prayer direction?" Say^(MS), "East and West belong to Allah. He guides whom he wills to a straight path."[175] (142) We have made you^(MP) a middle[176] nation, so you^(MP) can witness against people, and the messenger a witness against you^(MP). We made your^(MS) former prayer direction[177] only so that we could know who would follow the messenger and who would turn around on his heels. It was overwhelming, except for those Allah guided. Allah would not lose their faith. Allah is compassionate and merciful to people. (143) We may see the turning of your^(MS) face in the sky.[178] Thus we will certainly turn a prayer direction for you^(MS) that will please you^(MS). So turn^(MS) your^(MS) face toward the sacred place of worship,[179] and wherever you^(MP) are, turn your^(MP) faces toward it. Those who were given the book know that it is truth from their Lord. Allah is aware of what they do. (144) If you^(MS) brought every sign to those who were given the book, they would not follow your^(MS) prayer direction, and you^(MS) do not follow their prayer direction, and some of them do not follow each others' prayer direction. If you^(MS) follow their desires after knowledge has come to you^(MS), you^(MS) will be wicked. (145) Those to whom we gave the book know it as they know their children,[180] but a group of them knowingly hide the truth. (146) Truth is from your^(MS) Lord, so do not doubt. (147)
\*\*\*

---

[175] See glossary for more details, and notes on 3:51, 6:153, 19:36, 36:61, and 43:61,64 on what the straight path is.

[176] or moderate. "Moderate" is masculine and "nation" is feminine, so the meaning is probably not "moderate nation."

[177] For prayer direction, here and in verse 145, Tawrah, 2 Chronicles, 6:21,26,32,34,38, Daniel 6:10

[178] Or the heavens

[179] For "sacred place of worship here and in verses 149 and 150, see Injil, John 4:20-24, Hebrews 8:1-2, 9:24, 10:19-22.

[180] Or sons

## Chapter 2

Everyone has a direction he turns toward, so compete in goodness. Wherever you<sup>MP</sup> are, Allah will bring you<sup>MP</sup> all. Allah can do anything.[181] (148)

\*\*\*

Wherever you<sup>MS</sup> go out, turn your<sup>MS</sup> face toward the sacred place of worship. It is truth from your<sup>MS</sup> Lord. Allah is aware of your<sup>MP</sup> deeds. (149) Wherever you<sup>MS</sup> go out, turn<sup>MS</sup> your<sup>MS</sup> face toward the sacred place of worship. Wherever you<sup>MP</sup> are, turn<sup>MP</sup> your<sup>MP</sup> faces toward it, lest people have an excuse against you<sup>MP</sup>, except for the wicked among them.[182] Do not fear them, but fear me,[183] and I will complete my blessings to you<sup>MP</sup>, so that you<sup>MP</sup> may be guided. (150) We sent you<sup>MP</sup> a messenger from among you<sup>MP</sup> reading our signs to you<sup>MP</sup>, purifying you<sup>MP</sup>, teaching you<sup>MP</sup> the book and wisdom, and teaching you<sup>MP</sup> what you<sup>MP</sup> did not know. (151) So remember<sup>MP</sup> me and I will remember you<sup>MP</sup>. Thank me and do not disbelieve<sup>MP</sup> in me.[184] (152) Believers, get help from endurance and performing prayers. Allah helps those who endure. (153) Do not say<sup>MP</sup> that those killed in Allah's path are dead,[185] but alive, though you<sup>MP</sup> do not realize it. (154) We will certainly send you<sup>MP</sup> trials of fear, hunger, lack of money and of people and fruit, so give<sup>MS</sup> good news to those who endure, (155) who say when disaster strikes them, "We are Allah's and will return to him."[186] (156) They have their Lord's blessings[187] and mercy, and they are guided. (157) **2A2** Safa and Marwa[188] are Allah's ceremonies. It is not wrong for anyone who does a hajj[189] or visits the sanctuary to walk around them. Allah is grateful and all-knowing[190] of those who voluntarily do good. (158) Allah and the cursers curse those who

---

[181] Tawrah, Job 42:2, Isaiah 14:27, Daniel 4:35, Injil, Matthew 19:26, Mark 10:27, Luke 1:37

[182] this phrase may be part of the previous sentence.

[183] See the Injil, Matthew 10:28

[184] Or be ungrateful

[185] Injil, Matthew 9:24, John 11:11

[186] Tawrah, Ecclesiastes 12:7, Zabur, Psalms 31:5, Injil, Luke 23:46, Acts 7:59, Romans 14:12

[187] Literally prayers

[188] Two hills near the Kaaba, which had been part of pagan worship ceremonies before Islam. See footnote of Yusuf Ali on this verse.

[189] Pilgrimage here and in verses 189, 196 (three times), and 197 (three times). See glossary for more details.

[190] Tawrah, Job 37:16, Isaiah 40:14, Zabur, Psalms 33:13-15, Injil, 1 John 3:20

## Chapter 2

hide miracles and the guidance we have revealed after clarifying it in the book to people, (159) except for those who repent and make amends publicly. I will accept their repentance. I am the merciful acceptor of repentance. (160) Allah, angels and all men have cursed disbelievers who died in their disbelief. (161) They will be there[191] forever and their torment will not be lightened, nor will they be given more time.[192] (162) Your[MP] god is one god. He is one god, the most gracious and merciful.[193] (163) The creation of the heavens and the earth,[194] the difference of night and day,[195] the ship that sails the sea to benefit men, the rain[196] Allah sends down to give life to the dead ground and to send every living creature into it, sending off the winds, and the clouds kept between the sky and the earth are all signs to people who comprehend. (164)

\*\*\*

Some people take rivals to Allah, and they love them as much as they love Allah.[197] Believers love Allah more. If the wicked only knew when they see the torment that all power is Allah's and that Allah is severe in torment! (165) The leaders will disown the followers. They will see torment and were at their wits end. (166) The followers said, "If we had another chance, we would disown them just as they disowned us. Thus Allah will show them how sorrowful their works are to them. They will not leave hellfire. (167)

\*\*\*

People, eat what is permitted and delicious on earth. Do not follow Satan's steps; he is a clear enemy to you[MP]. (168) He commands you[MP] to do evil and promiscuity,[198] and to say things about Allah you[MP] do not know. (169) If they are told, "Follow[MP] what Allah has revealed," they say, "Rather we will follow what we found our fathers doing."[199] Even if their fathers did not comprehend

---

[191] i.e. under Allah's curse
[192] or looked at
[193] Zabur, Psalms 103:8, 145:8. See glossary for more details.
[194] Tawrah, Genesis 1:1, Isaiah 42:5, 45:18
[195] Tawrah, Genesis 1:3-5, 14-18
[196] Tawrah, Deuteronomy 28:12, Job 5:10, Joel 2:23, Zabur, Psalms 68:9, Injil, Matthew 5:45
[197] Or as Allah loves (them)
[198] Or lewdness, adultery or abomination
[199] Tawrah, Jeremiah 11:10, Injil, Acts 7:51, Galatians 1:14, Colossians 2:20-22

## Chapter 2

anything, and were not guided? (170) Disbelievers are like a man who screams to what hears nothing except for a prayer and a call. They are deaf,[200] dumb,[201] and blind;[202] they do not comprehend. (171) Believers, eat the good things we provided you[MP] and thank Allah, if you[MP] worship him. (172) He has forbidden you[MP] dead animals, pork, and meat offered to other gods.[203] If someone is forced unwillingly and unintentionally, he is not guilty. Allah is forgiving[204] and merciful. (173) Those who hide part of the book Allah has revealed and sell it for a small price[205] will feed their bellies nothing except hellfire, and Allah will not speak to them on the day of resurrection, nor purify them. They will have painful torment. (174)

\*\*\*

Those who exchange guidance for straying and forgiveness for torment are patiently seeking hellfire. (175)

\*\*\*

That is because Allah revealed the book in truth, and those who differed about the book are deeply divided. (176) 2A3

\*\*\*

Righteousness is not a matter of turning your[MP] faces eastward or westward. Rather, righteousness is believing in Allah, the last day, the angels, the book and the prophets,[206] giving money in his love to relatives,[207] orphans,[208] the poor,[209] travelers,[210] and beggars,

---

[200] Tawrah, Isaiah 6:10, 42:18, Jeremiah 6:10, Ezekiel 3:7, Injil, Acts 7:51

[201] Tawrah, Isaiah 56:10

[202] Tawrah, Isaiah 6:10, 42:18, 56:10, Injil, Matthew 15:14, Revelation 3:17

[203] Injil, Acts 15:29, 10:14, 1 Corinthians 8:13, Tawrah, Leviticus 11:7,39, Isaiah 65:4, 66:17, Daniel 1:8

[204] Here and in verses 182, 192, 199, 218, 225, 226, and 235, see Zabur, Psalms 103:3, 130:4, Tawrah, Isaiah 43:25, Exodus 34:7, Injil, Acts 26:18.

[205] Making a profit from Allah's word will be punished.

[206] Tawrah, 1 Samuel 9:9, 1 Kings 13:4, 19:10, 2 Chronicles 20:20, Nehemiah 9:26, Jeremiah 25:4, 28:8-9, 44:4, Daniel 9:6, Hosea 6:5, Zabur, Psalms 105:15, Injil, Matthew 5:12,17, 16:14, 23:29-37, Luke 13:34, 16:31, 24:25.27, Acts 3 21.24, 26:22, Romans 1:2, 1 Corinthians 14:32, Ephesians 4:11, Hebrews 1:1, James 5:10, Revelation 22:6

[207] Tawrah, Exodus 20:12, Injil, Matthew 15:4, 19:19, Ephesians 6:2

[208] Tawrah, Job 29:12, Deuteronomy 24:19, Zabur, Psalms 82:3, Injil, James 1:27

## Chapter 2

freeing slaves,[211] performing prayers, paying the poor-tax,[212] keeping their promises,[213] and enduring misery and adversity.[214] In misery, such people are honest and reverent. (177) Believers, punishment is prescribed in the case of those murdered:[215] a free person for a free person, a slave for a slave, a female for a female. If a brother pardons anything, it should be followed by kindness and good deeds to him, and will be lightening[216] and mercy from your[MP] Lord. Whoever is hostile after that will have painful torment. (178) Through punishment, you[MP] will have life, so that you[MP] thinkers may be reverent.[217] (179) If any of you[MP] is close to death, and leaves possessions, he is to will them kindly to his parents and relatives, as an obligation for the reverent. (180) Those who change it[218] after hearing it are guilty. Allah hears all and knows all. (181) He who fears that a person making a will is going to deviate or be guilty and reconciles them[219] is not guilty. Allah is forgiving and merciful. (182) Believers, Allah commanded fasting for you[MP] just as he commanded it[220] for those who were before you[MP] so that you[MP] would be reverent: (183) for a number of

---

[209] Tawrah, Exodus 23:11, Leviticus 19:10, Proverbs 14:31, 19:17, 28:27, Isaiah 58:7, Zabur, Psalms 82:3, Injil, Mark 10:21, Luke 6:20, 19:8, 1 Corinthians 13:3, Galatians 2:10

[210] Tawrah, Genesis 18:1-8, Exodus 12:49, 22:21, Leviticus 19:10,33-34, Deuteronomy 10:19, 26:12, Injil, Romans 12:13, Hebrew 13:2, 1 Peter 4:9

[211] Tawrah, Exodus 21:2-7, Leviticus 25:39-41, Jeremiah 34:8-11, Injil, Philemon 16

[212] Tawrah, Deuteronomy 14:28-29, 26:12, Injil, Matthew 19:21, Mark 12:42-43, Luke 19:8, Acts 11:29, Romans 15:26, 2 Corinthians 8:14-15, 9:12

[213] Tawrah, Leviticus 19:12, Proverbs 25:14, Zabur, Psalms 50:14, Injil, Matthew 5:33-37

[214] See "endure" in glossary

[215] Tawrah, Genesis 4:10-16, 9:6, Exodus 21:12-32, Leviticus 24:17, Numbers 35:16-34, Injil, Matthew 26:52

[216] of punishment

[217] Tawrah, Deuteronomy 22:21

[218] The reference is not clear. Possibly the obligation is intended. "Will" is feminine and the word "it" is masculine.

[219] It is not clear from the verse who is intended by "them" but may refer to the heirs.

[220] Tawrah, Leviticus 16:29-31, 23:29, 2 Chronicles 20:3, Esther 4:16, Isaiah 58:3-10, Joel 1:14, 2:12,15, Injil, Matthew 6:16-18, Mark 2:20, Luke 2:37

days.²²¹ If someone is sick or traveling, a few other days. For those who can bear it, a ransom by feeding a poor person. If someone voluntarily does good, it is better for him. Fasting is better for you^MP, if you only^MP knew. (184) The month of Ramadan is when the Qur'an²²² was revealed as guidance to men and miracles of guidance and the criterion.²²³ Whoever witnesses the month²²⁴ should fast it. Whoever is sick or traveling, several other days. Allah wants it to be easy for you^MP, not hard, so you^MP can complete the period, praise Allah for his guidance to you^MP, and give thanks. (185) If my worshipers ask you^MS about me, I am near, answering the call of him who prays when he prays to me.²²⁵ They should answer me and believe in me in order to be guided. (186) Sex with your^MP wives is permitted on the night of a fast. They are clothing to you^MP and you^MP to them.²²⁶ Allah knows that you betrayed yourselves, so he relented toward you²²⁷ and pardoned you. So now, have sex with them and desire what Allah has ordained for you^MP. Eat^MP and drink^MP until you^MP can distinguish a white thread from a black one in the dawn, then complete^MP the fast until nightfall. Do not have sex with them while you^MP are secluded in the places of worship.²²⁸ These are Allah's boundaries which should not be approached. This is how Allah shows people his signs so that they would be reverent. (187) Do not waste your^MP money on worthless things or bribe^MP rulers with it to wrongly and knowingly take people's money. (188) 2A4 They ask you^MS about new moons. Say^MS, They are times²²⁹ for people and for hajj. It is not right to approach houses from the back. Rather righteousness

---

²²¹ The feminine plural is used here and in the following phrase, rather than the normal plural here and in verse 203. There may be a different meaning to this phrase.
²²² Or recitation. See glossary for more details.
²²³ The criterion in this verse refers to the Qur'an; in 2:53 and 21:48, it refers to the Tawrah.
²²⁴ The reference is probably to the new moon, which signifies the beginning of the month of fasting. It could also mean whoever is present.
²²⁵ Zabur, Psalms 34:4-5, 50:15, 120:1, Injil, Matthew 7:7, Tawrah, Jeremiah 33:3, 23:23
²²⁶ Injil, 1 Corinthians 7:1-5
²²⁷ Or accepted your repentance. For "repentance," see glossary. Tawrah, Jeremiah 18:8, Joel 2:13, Jonah 3:9-4:2
²²⁸ Injil, 1 Corinthians 7:4-5
²²⁹ Tawrah, Genesis 1:14, Exodus 34:23-24, Numbers 10:10, Isaiah 66:23, Zabur, Psalms 81:3, 104:19, Injil, Colossians 2:16

is being reverent and approaching houses from their doors.[230] Fear[MP] Allah, so that you[MP] may succeed. (189) Fight[MP] in the path of Allah against those who fight you[MP], but do not be[MP] aggressors. Allah does not love aggressors.[231] (190) And kill[MP] them wherever you discover them,[232] and expel[MP] them from wherever they expelled you[MP].[233] Sedition is worse than murder. Do not fight[MP] them at the sacred place of worship[234] unless they fight you[MP] in it. If they fight you[MP], kill them. That is the reward of disbelievers. (191) If they stop, Allah is forgiving and merciful. (192) Fight them until there is no more sedition and religion is Allah's. If they stop, there should be no aggression except toward the wicked. (193) The sacred month: for the sacred month and punishment for forbidden things, whoever attacks you[MP], attack them as you[MP] were attacked. Fear[MP] Allah and know[MP] that Allah is with the reverent. (194) Donate your[MP] money in the path of Allah, and do not spread destruction, but do good. Allah loves those who do good. (195)

\*\*\*

Do your[MP] hajjes and minor pilgrimages[235] for Allah. If you[MP] are prevented,[236] then send what gifts are easily obtained, and do not shave your[MP] heads[237] until the gift arrives. If one of you[MP] is sick or has a head injury, then he can be ransomed[238] by fasting or alms or

---

[230] Injil, John 10:1-2
[231] Zabur, Psalms 5:4-5, 11:5, Tawrah, Proverbs 6:16-19.
[232] The Qur'an has four verses that command killing others (2:191, 4:89,91, and 9:5), but none of these apply today. Similarly, the Tawrah has many verses that refer to killing others (Exodus 23:23-24,28-30, 32:27, Numbers 21:35, 31:2,7-8,17, Deuteronomy 7:2,16, 9:3-4, Joshua 6:17-21, 8:2, Judges 21:11, 1 Samuel 15:3, 27:9,11, 2 Chronicles 15:13) and none of them apply today either.
[233] This verse is in the context of self-defense "against those who fight against you," "wherever they expelled you," "unless they fight you," and "if they fight you," and "if they stop." It cannot be used as a justification for aggression.
[234] For "sacred place of worship" here and in verses 196 and 217, see Injil, John 4:20-24, Hebrews 8:1-2, 9:24, 10:19-22
[235] Arabic /umra/ twice in this verse. See glossary for more details.
[236] Tawrah, Deuteronomy 14:24-26
[237] Probably in fulfillment of a vow of purification. See Tawrah, Leviticus 14:8, Numbers 6:9,8:7, Injil, Acts 18:18, 21:24.
[238] Tawrah, Exodus 13:13-15, 21:30, 34:20, Numbers 18:15-17

a sacrifice. If you<sup>MP</sup> are safe, whoever breaks<sup>MS239</sup> his purification between the minor pilgrimage until the hajj should offer what gifts he can easily give, or if he cannot, he should fast three days during the hajj, and then seven when you<sup>MP</sup> return. Those are ten days in all. That is for those whose families are not present at the sacred place of worship. Fear<sup>MP</sup> Allah and know<sup>MP</sup> that Allah is severe in punishment.[240] (196) The hajj is in known[241] months, and for him who does the hajj upon them<sup>FP</sup>,[242] there should not be any impurity, unbelief,[243] or argument on the hajj. Allah knows the good deeds you<sup>MP</sup> do, so make<sup>MP</sup> provision. Reverence is the best provision, so you thinkers must be fear me. (197)

\*\*\*

Seeking grace from your<sup>MP</sup> Lord is not wrong. If you<sup>MP</sup> are overflowing[244] from Arafat,[245] remember Allah at sacred Mashaar;[246] remember him just as he guided you<sup>MP</sup> even if before that, you<sup>MP</sup> went astray. (198) Then overflow<sup>MP</sup> from the place people overflowed. Ask Allah's forgiveness. He is forgiving and merciful. (199)

\*\*\*

When you<sup>MP</sup> have done your<sup>MP</sup> sacrifices,[247] remember Allah at least as much as
you<sup>MP</sup> remember your fathers. Some people say, "Our Lord, give to us in this world."[248] They have no share in the hereafter. (200) Others say, "Our Lord, give us goodness in this world and goodness in the hereafter. Protect us from hellfire's torment."

---

[239] The Arabic pronoun changes here, then changes back later in the verse.
[240] Here and in verse 211, see Injil, Matthew 8:12, 13:42,50, 22:13, 24:51, 25:30, Mark 9:48, Luke 13 28, 19:27
[241] The adjective is for thinking beings, where the normal word would be for inanimate objects (like months). There may be a different meaning.
[242] This could refer to the months as well.
[243] Or immorality or transgression
[244] The meaning may be overflowing with blessings or flowing down like water, here and in the next verse.
[245] i.e. Mount Arafat. Or, "come down from Arafat like a flood" here and in verse 199 twice.
[246] Mount Arafat and the Mashaar Mosque are connected with pilgrimage rituals.
[247] Or religious rituals
[248] Injil, Matthew 6:24

Chapter 2

(201) Those have the portion they deserve. Allah is swift in reckoning.[249] (202) 2B1
\*\*\*

Remember Allah on certain days.[250] Whoever is in a hurry in two days is not guilty, and whoever is reverent and is late will not be guilty.[251] Fear Allah and know that you[MP] will be gathered[252] to him. (203)
\*\*\*

What one person says about this life will please you[MS]. He calls Allah as witness to what is in his heart, yet he is the fiercest in conflict. (204) If he turns away, he tried to cause destruction on the earth and devastate fields and descendants. Allah does not love destruction.[253] (205) If he is told, "Fear Allah,"[254] his pride leads him to sin.[255] He is headed to hell, a dreadful destination. (206) Some people give themselves up,[256] desiring Allah's pleasure. Allah is compassionate[257] toward his servants. (207)
\*\*\*

All you believers, enter in peace, and do not follow the steps of Satan; he is a clear enemy to you[MP]. (208) If you[MP] go astray after receiving miracles, know[MP] that Allah is powerful and wise. (209)
\*\*\*

Do they wait only for Allah and the angels to come to them in a shadow of clouds[258] though the matter has been predestined? Matters are referred back to Allah. (210)
\*\*\*

Ask the people of Israel how many miraculous signs we brought them. Allah is severe in punishment to those who exchange Allah's blessings after receiving them. (211) This life has been

---

[249] Tawrah, Isaiah 19:1, Malachi 3:5, Zabur, Psalms 147:15, Injil, 2 Peter 2:1, Revelation 22:12
[250] Tawrah, Exodus 13:3, 20:8, Deuteronomy 5:15, 16:3
[251] Injil, Romans 14:5-6
[252] Tawrah, Joel 3:11-14, Zephaniah 3:8, Injil, Matthew 25:31-32, John 15:6, Revelation 16:16
[253] Zabur, Psalms 5:4-5, 11:5, Tawrah, Proverbs 6:16-19
[254] Tawrah, Deuteronomy 10:12, Isaiah 29:13, Injil, 1 Peter 2:17, Revelation 14:7
[255] Or pride seizes him in his sin (Arberry). Tawrah, Proverbs 16:18, Injil, 1 Peter 5:5
[256] Injil, Romans 6:6, 1 Corinthians 9:27, 15:31, Galatians 5:24
[257] Injil, James 5:11
[258] Tawrah, Daniel 7:9-10, 13-14, Ezekiel 1:4-28

## Chapter 2

made attractive to disbelievers, and they scoff at the believers. The godfearers will be over them on the day of resurrection.[259]
\*\*\*

Allah provides bountifully for all he wills. (212)
\*\*\*

Mankind was all one nation, and Allah sent prophets bearing good news and warnings, and he sent the book[260] with them in truth, to judge between men in the matters in which they differ. The only ones who differed about it were those who received it after miracles came to them, acting insolently.[261] Allah guides believers regarding the truth they differ about with his permission. Allah guides those he wills to a straight path.[262] (213)
\*\*\*

Or do you[MP] think you[MP] will enter the heavenly garden when the example of those who passed away before you[MP] has come to you? They were afflicted with misery, adversity, and were shaken,[263] so the messenger and the believers with him said, "When will Allah's salvation come?" Allah's salvation is close.[264] (214)
\*\*\*

They ask you[MS] what they should donate. Say[MS], The possessions you[MP] donate should be for parents, relatives, orphans, the poor, and the traveler.[265] Allah knows the good deeds you[MP] do. (215) Fighting is ordained for you[MP],[266] though it is repulsive to you[MP]. You[MP] may hate something that is good for you[MP], or love[MP] something that is evil for you[MP]. Allah knows but you[MP] do not. (216) They ask you[MS] about fighting during the sacred month. Say[MS], Fighting during it is a serious sin, but blockage from the path of Allah, disbelief in it[267] and in the sacred place of worship, and expelling its residents is a more serious sin to Allah. Sedition is a more serious sin than murder, and they continue to fight you[MP]

---

[259] 3:55, Injil, John 5:28-29.

[260] The purpose of the book the prophets brought previously (the Tawrah, Zabur, and Injil) was to judge between men. See 5:47

[261] Or, out of covetousness

[262] See glossary for more details, and notes on 3:51, 6:153, 19:36, 36:61, and 43:61,64 on what the straight path is.

[263] or "and earthquake"

[264] See Injil, 2 Corinthians 6:2

[265] See footnotes on 2:177.

[266] In modern terms, this would be like a draft.

[267] or him (Allah)

## Chapter 2

to try to[268] turn you[MP] back from your[MP] religion if they can. The works of those of you[MP] who turn back from your[MP] religion and die in a state of disbelief are void in this world and the hereafter. They are headed for hellfire, where they will remain forever. (217) Those who believe and emigrate and struggle in Allah's path hope for Allah's mercy.[269] Allah is forgiving and merciful. (218) **2B2** They ask you[MS] about wine[270] and gambling.[271] Say[MS], "There is serious sin in them[D],[272] and benefit for people.[273] Their[D] sin is greater than their[D] benefit." They ask you[MS] what they should donate. Say[MS], "Pardon."[274] Thus Allah makes signs clear to you[MP] so that you may consider (219) this world and the hereafter. They ask you[MS] about orphans. Say[MS], Helping them is good.[275] If you mix things with them, [they are] your[MP] brothers. Allah knows the difference between a corrupt person and someone who does good. If Allah willed, he would have harassed[276] you[MP]. Allah is strong and wise. (220) Do not marry idolaters[FP] until they[FP] believe. A believing[FS] slave[277] is better than a polytheist[FS] even if she pleases you[MP]. Do[MP] not give idolaters[MP] in marriage until they[MP] believe.[278] A believing slave is better than a polytheist[MS], even if he pleases you[MP]. They call for hellfire and Allah calls for the heavenly garden and forgiveness by his permission. He makes his signs clear to people, so that they may remember. (221) They ask you[MS]

---

[268] Or, until they

"Mercy" has a different spelling here and in 6 other places. See glossary.
[269]

[270] Tawrah, Leviticus 10:8-10; Injil, Revelation 1:6, Tawrah, Judges 13:4; 1Samuel 1:15; Proverbs 20:1; 23:20,21,31; 31:4,5; Jeremiah 35:1-10; Injil, Matthew 27:34, Luke 1:13-15; 21:34; 1 Corinthians 6:10; 10:31; Ephesians 5:18

[271] Tawrah, Proverbs 13:11, Injil, 2 Thessalonians 3:10-11, 1 Timothy 6:9-10, (Revelation 1:6)

[272] Tawrah, Proverbs 23:20-21,29-35

[273] Injil, 1 Timothy 5:23, Mark 15:23, Tawrah, Proverbs 31:6,

[274] The meaning could be surplus. For this meaning, see Injil, 2 Corinthians 8:13. For the meaning of pardon, see Injil, Ephesians 4:32, Colossians 3:13, 1 Peter 4:8. Forgiving others is one of the greatest things we can do.

[275] Tawrah, Job 29:12, Zabur, Psalms 82:3, Injil, James 1:27

[276] or destroyed

[277] another possible reading is "a blameworthy slavegirl"

[278] Tawrah, Genesis 24:3, Deuteronomy 7:3-4, Ezra 9:2,12, Nehemiah 13:25, Injil, 2 Corinthians 6:14

## Chapter 2

about menstruation. Say[MS], It is harm, so isolate women during their menstruation, and do not approach[MP] them[FP] until they[FP] are clean.[279] When they[FP] are clean, have[MP] sex with them[FP] from where Allah has commmanded you[MP]. Allah loves the repentant and the purifiers. (222) Your[MP] wives are a field for you[MP],[280] so go[MP] into your[MP] fields however you[MP] want, and send[MP] it[281] beforehand for yourselves[MP]. Fear[MP] Allah and know[MP] that you[MP] will meet him. Give[MS] good news to the believers. (223) Do not make[MP] Allah the object of[282] your[MP] oaths[283] to be[MP] pious, be[MP] reverent, and do[MP] good to people. Allah hears all and knows all. (224) Allah does not blame you[MP] for foolishness in your[MP] oaths, but as your[MP] hearts deserve.[284] Allah is forgiving and gentle.[285] (225) To those[MP] who swear abstinence from their wives, there is a waiting period of four months. If they[MP] return, Allah is forgiving and merciful. (226) If they[MP] insist on divorce,[286] Allah hears all and knows all. (227) Divorced women shall wait by themselves three menstruations, and they[FP] are not allowed to hide what Allah has created in their wombs if they believe in Allah and the last day. Their husbands[287] have more right to bring them back in this if they[MP] want to be reconciled. In fairness, they[FP] have as many rights as responsibilities. Men are higher in rank than they.[288] Allah is strong and wise. (228) Divorce can be done twice, then retaining kindly or dismissing generously. You[MP] may not take anything you[MP] have given them[FP] back unless they[D] fear they[D] will not observe Allah's limits. If you[MP] fear they[D] will not observe Allah's limits, it is not wrong for them[D] in her ransom of herself. These are Allah's limits, so do[MP] not exceed them. Anyone who exceeds them is wicked. (229) If he divorces her, she is no longer allowed to him

---

[279] Tawrah, Leviticus 15:19-24
[280] Tawrah, Genesis 1:28, Exodus 21:10, Zabur, Injil, 1 Corinthians 7:3-5
[281] There is no object in Arabic The meaning may be present yourselves to each other or send on good deeds.
[282] or an impediment to
[283] Tawrah, Leviticus 19:12, Proverbs 25:14, Zabur, Psalms 50:14, Injil, Matthew 5:33-37
[284] For Allah judging our hearts, see Injil, Matthew 5:21-48, Hebrews 4:13
[285] For "gentle" here and in verses 235 and 263, see Zabur, Psalms 45:4, 145:17, Injil, Matthew 11:29, Galatians 5:22.
[286] Tawrah, Deuteronomy 24:3, Injil, Matthew 10:4-5
[287] Or masters
[288] Tawrah, Genesis 3:16, Injil, 1 Corinthians 11:3, Titus 2:14

until she marries another husband. Then if that husband divorces her, it is not wrong for them[D] to return[289] if they[D] think that they[D] can observe Allah's limits. These are Allah's limits, which he makes clear to people who know. (230) If you[MP] divorce wives and their[FP] time is complete, either take[MP] them[FP] back kindly or send[MP] them[FP] away kindly. Do[MP] not take them[FP] back to harm them[FP], and thus be[MP] aggressors. Anyone who does that wrongs himself. Do[MP] not mock Allah's signs but remember Allah's blessings to you[MP] and what he revealed to you[MP] from the book and wisdom by which he preaches to you[MP]. Fear[MP] Allah, and know[MP] that Allah knows everything. (231) If you[MP] divorce wives and their[FP] time is complete, do[MP] not interfere with their[FP] marrying their husbands, if they[MP] agree kindly among themselves. That is an admonition for those of you[MP] who believe in Allah and the last day. That is holier and purer to you[MP]. Allah knows and you[MP] do not. (232) **2B3**

\*\*\*

Mothers should nurse their[FP] children[290] for two complete years if anyone[MP] wants to complete the nursing. Their[FP] provision and clothing in kindness are his[291] responsibility. No soul is burdened with more than it can bear. A mother shall not be harmed by her son, nor a newborn's father by his son. An heir has similar duties.[292] It is not wrong if they[D] willingly want to separate[293] after consultation. It is not wrong if you[MP] want to have another woman nurse your[MP] children, if you[MP] surrender what you[MP] gave kindly. Fear[MP] Allah and know[MP] that Allah sees your[MP] deeds. (233) Wives of those of you[MP] who die should wait four months and ten.[294] When they[FP] complete their[FP] time, you[MP] are not to be blamed for what they[FP] do with themselves[FP] kindly. Allah is aware of your[MP] deeds. (234)

\*\*\*

It is not wrong for you[MP] to make offers of marriage to women publicly or to keep[MP] it between yourselves[MP]. Allah knows that you[MP] will mention[295] them[FP], but do not pledge[MP] yourselves to them[FP] in secret unless you[MP] speak a kind saying, and do not

---

[289] Tawrah, Deuteronomy 24:3-4

[290] Or sons

[291] i.e. the mother's food and clothing is the baby's father's responsibility

[292] Probably implied here is "if the father dies."

[293] or wean (the baby)

[294] Probably, ten days. Fourteen months would have been said differently.

[295] or remember

make[MP] a marriage contract until the time the contract[296] is valid. Know[MP] that Allah knows what is within your[MP] souls, and beware[MP] of him. Know[MP] that Allah is forgiving and gentle. (235) There is nothing wrong with divorcing your[MP] wives before you[MP] have touched[297] them[FP] or paid them[FP] their bride price. Let[MP] them[FP] enjoy[298] as much as possible. He who is in financial straits must give provision kindly according to his means. This is an obligation for those who do good. (236)

\*\*\*

If you[MP] divorce them[FP] before you[MP] touch them[FP] but after you[MP] have given them[FP] their bride-price, then let[MP] them[FP] have half of it, unless they[FP] forego it or unless the one[299] making the marriage contract foregoes it. If you[MP] forego it, it is closer to reverence. Do not forget[MP] grace[300] between you[MP]. Allah sees your[MP] deeds. (237)

\*\*\*

Take care[MP] to perform the prayers[301] as well as the intermediate prayer, and stand[MP] devoutly before Allah. (238) If you[MP] fear, then while walking or riding. When you[MP] are safe, remember[MP] Allah's name as he taught you[MP] before you[MP] knew. (239) Those of you[MP] who die and leave[MP] wives should have a will, so their[MP] wives can enjoy life for a year without being driven out. If they[FP] leave, this is a kindness they do on their own and you[MP] are not to be blamed. Allah is strong and wise. (240) Divorcees[FP] should be provided for kindly. This is an obligation on the reverent. (241) Allah thus makes his signs clear to you[MP], so that you[MP] may comprehend. (242) 2B4 Did you[MS] not see how the thousands who left their homes avoided[302] death? Allah told them, "Die[MP]." Then he made them alive. Allah is gracious to people, but most people do not give thanks. (243) Fight[MP] in Allah's path and know that Allah hears all and knows all. (244) Who can loan Allah a good loan? Allah will repay him many-fold.[303] Allah withholds and he gives

---

[296] Literally, Book
[297] i.e. sexually, here and in verse 237. Injil, 1 Corinthians 7:1
[298] probably implied is, "pay them"
[299] the wife's representative
[300] or graciousness or generosity
[301] Zabur, Psalms 119:62,164, Tawrah, Isaiah 43:25
[302] There are several other possible meanings - for fear of death, fearing death, wary of death
[303] see Tawrah, Proverbs 19:17

## Chapter 2

forth. You[MP] will return to him.[304] (245) Did you[MS] not see how the leaders of the children of Israel after Musa told one of their prophets,[305] "Raise[MS] up a king for us[306] and we will fight in Allah's path." He said, "If fighting is your[MP] destiny, might you not fight?" They said, "How can we not fight in Allah's path, since we and our children[307] have been forced out of our homes?" When fighting was their destiny, all but a few turned away.[308] Allah knows the wicked. (246) Their prophet told them,[309] "Allah has raised up Talut[310] as your[MP] king." They said, "How can he be our king? We are more deserving of being king than he. He does not have a lot of money." He[311] said, "Allah has chosen him over you[MP], and has given him stature in knowledge and body.[312] Allah gives his kingdom to whoever he wills."[313] Allah is omnipresent[314] and all-knowing. (247) Their prophet told them, "The sign of his kingdom is that the ark,[315] in which is the presence[316] of your Lord, will come to you[MP],[317] as well as the relic of what the family of Musa and Harun[318] left,[319] carried by angels. That is a sign for you[MP] if you[MP] believe." (248) When Talut divided the troops,[320] he said, "Allah will try you[MF] at a river. Whoever drinks from it is not with me, and whoever does not taste it is with me, except for those

---

[304] Injil, Romans 14:12
[305] Samuel. See Tawrah, 1 Samuel 8:5ff
[306] Tawrah, 1 Samuel 8:5,19,20, see Deuteronomy 17:14-20
[307] Or sons
[308] Tawrah, 1 Samuel 15:9
[309] Tawrah, 1 Samuel 10:21-24
[310] King Saul, here and in verse 249. See glossary.
[311] The prophet Samuel
[312] Tawrah, 1 Samuel 10:23-24
[313] Tawrah, Daniel 2:37
[314] Zabur, Psalms 139:7-12
[315] i.e. the ark of the covenant
[316] This word /sakeenah/ can mean either /shekinah/ (an Arabized word from Hebrew, meaning Allah's presence) or tranquility. Since true tranquility comes from Allah's presence, the two meanings are not contradictory. It is used also in 9:26,40, 48:4,18,26. Here it clearly refers to Allah's presence. Tawrah, Numbers 7:89
[317] Tawrah, 1 Samuel 6-7
[318] Aaron. See glossary for more details.
[319] Injil, Hebrews 9:4 specifies what this is: Harun's rod, a pot of manna, and tablets of the covenant
[320] Tawrah, 1 Samuel 13:2

who scoop out a handful. All but a few drank from it.[321] When he and the believers crossed it together, they said, "We have no strength against Jalut[322] and his troops today." Those who thought they were about to meet Allah said, "How many small groups have defeated large groups with Allah's permission?[323] Allah is with those who endure." (249) When they showed themselves to Jalut and his troops, they said, "Our Lord, pour out endurance upon us and make our feet firm and save us from disbelieving people." (250) So they defeated them by Allah's permission, and Dawud[324] killed Jalut[325] and Allah gave him the kingdom[326] and wisdom and taught him what he willed. If Allah had not pushed people into each other, the earth would have been destroyed, but Allah shows grace to people.[327] (251) These are Allah's signs which we recite to you[MS] in truth. You[MS] are a messenger. (252) 3⚹1
\*\*\*

We preferred some of those[328] messengers over others. Allah spoke to some, and he raised some in degree:[329] We gave Isa son of Mariam miracles,[330] and aided him with the Holy Spirit.[331] If Allah had willed, those after him would not have fought after miracles had come to them, but they differed. Some of them

---

[321] see Tawrah, Judges 7, where the leader is Gideon. Sometimes the books combine two stories to make a point.
[322] Goliath, here and in verses 250 and 251. See glossary for more details.
[323] compare Tawrah, 1 Samuel 17, especially verse 37
[324] David. See glossary for more details.
[325] Tawrah, 1 Samuel 17:49-51
[326] Tawrah, 2 Samuel 2:9-11, 5:6-12
[327] or the worlds.
[328] The word for "these" is the usual word for non-thinking creatures, so the messengers included here may include other things Allah sends.
[329] Of honor or rank. From the context, it seems that Isa was raised in degree.
[330] The Qur'an lists some of his miracles in 3:49,52, 5:110,112, 19:19,20,24,30-33. Most of the miracles Isa does that are mentioned in the Injil, with the stories behind them, are in the Injil, Matthew 8-11, 14-15,17,21, Mark 1-9,11, Luke 2,4-9,22, John 2,4-6,9,11.
[331] Injil, Matthew 3:16-4:10, Luke 4:1, 14, 18, 10:21. See note at 2:87. His anointing as Messiah is connected with his being aided with the Holy Spirit in all three verses of the Qur'an as well as Tawrah, Isaiah 61:1, Injil, Matthew 3:16, Romans 1:4, Hebrews 9:14.

## Chapter 2

believed, and others disbelieved. If Allah had willed, they would not have fought.[332] But Allah does whatever he wants. (253)
\*\*\*

Believers, donate[MP] some of what we have provided you[MP] with before a day comes when there is neither buying,[333] friends,[334] nor intercession.[335] Disbelievers are wicked. (254) Allah is the only god, living and eternal.[336] He neither slumbers nor sleeps.[337] Everything in the heavens and the earth is his. Who is the one[MS] who intercedes[338] with him except by his permission? He[339] knows what is in their hands and what is behind them.[340] They know none of his knowledge except what he wills. His chair[341] covers the heavens and the earth, and protecting them[D] does not tire him. He is most high and great. (255) There is no compulsion in religion.[342] The difference between guidance and error has been made clear. Whoever disbelieves in false gods[343] and believes in Allah has grasped the firm, unbreakable handle. Allah hears all and knows all. (256) Allah protects believers and brings them out of darkness into light.[344] False gods are the protectors of disbelievers, and they bring them out of light into darkness.[345] They will be in hellfire eternally. (257) Have you[MS] not seen him who disputed with

---

[332] It seems that the Qur'an here connects those who disbelieved with those who fought.
[333] Injil, Revelation 13:17
[334] Injil, Luke 16:20-31
[335] Injil, Revelation 22:11
[336] Or the self-subsisting, or the resurrector.
[337] Zabur, Psalms 121:4
[338] Some translations say "No one can intercede" but this verse actually has a question: "Who is the one who intercedes," and the three words "one", "who" and "intercedes" are all masculine singular. 10:3, 20:109, 34:23, and 43:86 all mention conditions for an intercessor. It seems the Qur'an alludes to one intercessor, who has Allah's permission. Injil, 1 John 2:1, 1 Timothy 2:5
[339] This could refer to the intercessor or to Allah.
[340] or their future and their past
[341] or throne
[342] Injil, John 5:40, 12:32, 2 Corinthians 5:20, Tawrah, Ezekiel 18:32, Isaiah 55:1-3
[343] Arabic /Al-Taghut/ here and in verse 257. See glossary for more details.
[344] Tawrah, 2 Samuel 22:29, Isaiah 58:10, Zabur, Psalms 18:28, 112:4, Injil, Matthew 4:16, John 8:12, 12:46, Ephesians 5:8, 1 Peter 2:9
[345] Tawrah, Job 12:25, Injil, Matthew 6:23

Chapter 2

Ibrahim about his Lord, since Allah had given him kingship? Ibrahim said, "My Lord gives life and causes death."[346] He said, "I give life and death." Ibrahim said, "Allah brings the sun from the east. So bring[MS] it from the west." The disbeliever was confounded. Allah does not guide wicked people. (258)

\*\*\*

Or him who passed by a village ruined to its foundations. He said, "How can Allah make these alive after their death?" Allah made him die for a hundred years, then resurrected him. He said, "How long have you[MS] stayed?" He said, "A day or part of a day." He said, "You[MS] stayed for a hundred years. Look at your[MS] food and your[MS] drink. It has not grown moldy. Look at your[MS] donkey.[347] We will make you[MS] a sign for people. Look how we raise the bones, then cover them with flesh.[348] When he saw it, he said, "I know that Allah can do anything."[349] (259)

\*\*\*

Ibrahim said, "My Lord, show me how you[MS] give life to the dead." He said,
"Do you not believe?" He said, "Yes I do, but assure my heart."[350] He said, "Take four birds and turn them toward you. Then put a piece of each on a mountain and call them.[351] They will come quickly to you. Know that Allah is strong and wise. (260) Those who donate their money in Allah's path are like a seed that sprouts seven heads,[352] in each of which are a hundred grains.[353] Allah multiplies to whom he wills.[354] Allah is omnipresent[355] and all-

---

[346] Tawrah, 1 Samuel 2:6, Deuteronomy 32:39

[347] Some research into the usage of Aramaic words in the time of the Qur'an suggests that the meaning is "Look at your nature and your state. It has not altered. Look at your perfection." In either case, this is a miracle.

[348] Tawrah, Ezekiel 37

[349] Tawrah, Job 42:2, Isaiah 14:27, Daniel 4:35, Injil, Matthew 19:26, Mark 10:27, Luke 1:37

[350] Injil, Mark 9:24

[351] The word "they" and "them" that refers to the birds here is the one used for thinking beings, so possibly the meaning is that Allah makes them obey his will as thinking creatures can (and should).

[352] Tawrah, Genesis 41:6

[353] Injil, Matthew 13:8,23

[354] Tawrah, Proverbs 19:17

[355] Zabur, Psalms 139:7-12

Chapter 2

knowing.³⁵⁶ (261) Those who spend their money in Allah's path and then do not follow up what they spend with reproach or harm will have a reward from their Lord.³⁵⁷ They will neither fear nor grieve. (262) 3A2 A kind word and forgiveness are better than alsmgiving followed by harm. Allah is self-sufficient and gentle. (263) Believers, do not ruin your alms with reproach and harm like one who does not believe in Allah or the last day and donates his money so people will see him.³⁵⁸ He is like a rock with soil on it which was rained upon heavily and became hard and dry. They can do nothing with what they deserve.³⁵⁹ Allah does not guide disbelieving people.³⁶⁰ (264) Those who spend their money seeking Allah's pleasure to establish themselves are like a garden on a hill which was rained heavily upon, then it produced twice as much. If it had not been rained upon heavily, then dew.³⁶¹ Allah sees your^MP deeds. (265) Does any of you^MP want to have a garden³⁶² with palms and grapes, with flowing rivers³⁶³ underneath, having every kind of fruit, but be suffering from old age, with weak³⁶⁴ descendants, and then a fiery whirlwind strikes it and it burns up?³⁶⁵ Thus Allah shows you^MP signs so that you^MP may consider. (266)
\*\*\*

Believers, donate^MP some of the good things you^MP have earned, and of what we

have brought forth to you from the ground.³⁶⁶ Do not donate the evil part of it that you would not take except by closing your^MP

---

³⁵⁶ For "all-knowing" here and in verse 268, see Tawrah, Job 37:16, Isaiah 40:14, Zabur, Psalms 33:13-15, Injil, 1 John 3:20
³⁵⁷ Tawrah, Proverbs 3:9-10, Ecclesiastes 11:1, Isaiah 32:20
³⁵⁸ Injil, Matthew 6:1ff
³⁵⁹ Or earn
³⁶⁰ Injil, 2 Thessalonians 2:11, Tawrah, 2 Samuel 22:27, 1 Kings 22:20-23, Ezekiel 14:9
³⁶¹ or light rain (would be all it gets).
³⁶² Tawrah, Genesis 2:9,10, Isaiah 65:21, Exekiel 47:12, Injil, Revelation 22:1-2
³⁶³ Injil, Revelation 22:1-2, Tawrah, Ezekiel 47:12
³⁶⁴ Here and in 9:91, this word has a different spelling than in 14:21 and 40:47. Some say the reason is that this one refers to those who are weak in this world.
³⁶⁵ compare Tawrah, Job 1
³⁶⁶ Tawrah, Exodus 23:19, Deuteronomy 18:4, Proverbs 3:9

[eyes] to it.³⁶⁷ Know that Allah is self-sufficient and praiseworthy. (267)

\*\*\*

Satan promises you^MP poverty and commands you^MP to be promiscuous.³⁶⁸ Allah promises you^MP his forgiveness and grace. Allah is omnipresent³⁶⁹ and all-knowing. (268)

\*\*\*

He gives wisdom to those he wills, and whoever is given wisdom is given much good.³⁷⁰ But only thinkers remember. (269)

\*\*\*

Allah knows your^MP donations or gifts as vows. The wicked have no one to save them. (270)

\*\*\*

If you^MP give alms visibly, how excellent they are. If you hide them and give them to the poor, it is better for you,³⁷¹ and it covers³⁷² your bad deeds. Allah is aware of your^MP deeds. (271) 3A3

\*\*\*

You^MS are not responsible to guide them. Allah guides whom he wills. What property³⁷³ you^MP donate is for yourselves, when³⁷⁴ you^MP donate only to please³⁷⁵ Allah. Your donations will be paid back to you^MP, and you will not be wronged.³⁷⁶ (272) To³⁷⁷ the poor who are restricted in the path of Allah since they are not able to travel in the land. The ignorant man considers them rich because of restraint. You^MS will know them by their appearance. They do not ask people repeatedly. Allah knows your^MP donations. (273) Those who donate their money at night and day in secret and in public will receive a reward from their Lord. They will not fear or grieve. (274) Those who profit by usury will stand only as one whom Satan kicks by possessing him. That is because they say, "Selling is like usury," yet Allah allowed selling and forbade

---

³⁶⁷ Tawrah, Proverbs 11:24, Malachi, 1:8
³⁶⁸ Or lewd, adulterous or abominable
³⁶⁹ Zabur, Psalms 139:7-12
³⁷⁰ compare Tawrah, Ecclesiastes 7:11
³⁷¹ Here and in verse 274, see Injil, Matthew 6:1-4.
³⁷² or expiates. Injil, 1 Peter 4:8.
³⁷³ or good
³⁷⁴ some translations have "and"
³⁷⁵ or seek the face of
³⁷⁶ see Tawrah, Proverbs 19:17
³⁷⁷ There is no verb here. The probable meaning is "Give to"

## Chapter 2

usury.[378] If an admonition comes[379] to someone from his Lord, and he stops, he has what was previous and his matter is with Allah. Those who repeat will be in hellfire eternally. (275) Allah annihilates[380] usury and makes alms increase. Allah does not love any guilty disbeliever.[381] (276) Those who believe, do righteous deeds,[382] perform their prayers, and give the poor-tax[383] have their reward from their Lord and will not fear or grieve. (277) Believers, fear Allah[384] and leave the usury that remains if you[MP] are believers. (278) If you[MP] do not do that, then permit a war from Allah and his messenger. If you[MP] repent, you[MP] may have your[MP] capital. You[MP] will not wrong and you[MP] will not be wronged. (279) If someone is in dire straits, then he may have a delay until he prospers. Giving alms is better for you[MP] if you[MP] only knew. (280) Beware of a day when you[MP] are returned to Allah and every soul will be paid back for what it has gained,[385] and they will not be wronged. (281) Believers, if you[MP] take on a debt to each other for a specific period, write it out. Let a legal clerk write it between you[MP]. The clerk should not refuse to write as Allah has taught him. The debtor should dictate and fear Allah, his Lord. Nothing should be omitted from it. If the debtor is foolish,[386] weak, or unable to dictate by himself, let his guardian dictate fairly, and have it witnessed by two men, or if there are not two, by one man and two women you[MP] approve of as witnesses.[387] If one[FS] of them[D] goes astray, the other[FS] will remind her. Witnesses should not refuse when they are called upon. Do not disdain[MP] to write it, whether a small or large one, for its period. That is more just with Allah, straighter for testimony, and closer to your[MP] avoiding doubt, except when it is a current business you[MP] manage among

---

[378] Tawrah, Exodus 22:24, Leviticus 25:35-37, Deuteronomy 23:20-21, Zabur, Psalms 15:5

[379] The verb "comes" is for a masculine noun, whereas "admonition" is feminine. There may be an implied subject in addition to admonition.

[380] This may mean "annihilates the gain from."

[381] Zabur, Psalms 5:4-5, 11:5, Tawrah, Proverbs 6:16-19

[382] Injil, 1 Corinthians 3:8, James 2:14-17, Revelation 19:8

[383] this is different from voluntary almsgiving, and is a fixed percentage required yearly.

[384] For "fear Allah" here and in verses 282 and 283, see Tawrah, Deuteronomy 10:12, Isaiah 29:13, Injil, 1 Peter 2:17, Revelation 14:7.

[385] Tawrah, Jeremiah 32:19, Injil, Revelation 11:18, 22:12

[386] or ignorant

[387] Tawrah, Deuteronomy 17:6, 19:15

## Chapter 2

yourselves[MP]. Not writing that is not wrong. Call witnesses if you[MP] sell it to each other and do not let a a clerk or a witness be bothered. If you[MP] do, it is unbelief[388] for you. Fear[MP] Allah and Allah will teach you[MP]. Allah knows everything. (282)
\*\*\*

3A4 If you[MP] are on a trip and do not find a clerk, let it be pledges received. If you[MP] entrust things to each other, the one to whom it was entrusted should take him his pledge.[389] He should fear Allah, his Lord. Do[MP] not hide the testimony. Whoever hides it has a guilty heart. Allah knows your[MP] deeds. (283)
\*\*\*

Everything in the heavens and the earth is Allah's. Allah will reckon with you[MP] if you[MP] show what is in your[MP] hearts or if you[MP] hide it. He forgives whom he wills and torments those he wills.[390] Allah can do anything.[391] (284) The messenger believes in what was revealed to him by his Lord, and so do the believers; they all believe in Allah and his angels and his books and his messengers. We do not distinguish between any of his messengers.[392] They said, "We have heard and obeyed. Our Lord, [we seek] your[MS] forgiveness. You[MS] are [our] destiny." (285)
\*\*\*

Allah does not burden a soul with more than it can bear.[393] It has [the good] it has earned, and [the evil] it has earned. Our Lord, do not blame us if we forget or are at fault. Our Lord, do not make us bear a burden like those before us. Our Lord, do not make us bear more than we have energy for. Pardon[MS] us, forgive[MS] us, and have[MS] mercy on us. You[MS] are our master, so save[MS] us from unbelieving[394] people. (286)[395]

---

[388] Or immorality or transgression.
[389] Tawrah, Deuteronomy 24:10-17
[390] Tawrah, Exodus 33:19, Injil, Romans 9:15,18
[391] Tawrah, Job 42:2, Isaiah 14:27, Daniel 4:35, Injil, Matthew 19:26, Mark 10:27, Luke 1:37
[392] This verse is balanced by verse 2:253, which mentions that Allah has preferred some messengers over others and specifically mentions Isa, and 17:55, which mentions Dawud.
[393] Injil, 1 Corinthians 10:13
[394] Or transgressing or immoral
[395] The verses in this chapter that rhyme are put together in paragraphs, separated by \*\*\*.

# Chapter 3: Aal Imran[396]

In the name of Allah, the most gracious and merciful.[397] ALM.[398] (1) Allah is the only god[399] –living and eternal.[400] (2)
\*\*\*

He revealed the book to you[MS] in truth, confirming[401] what is in his possession,[402] and he revealed the Tawrah[403] and the Injil[404] (3)
\*\*\*

beforehand as guidance to people, and he revealed the criterion.[405] Disbelievers
in Allah's signs[406] will have severe torment.[407] Allah is strong[408] and avenging.[409] (4) Nothing on earth or in heaven is hidden from Allah.[410] (5)

---

[396] This name means "the family of Imran"

[397] Zabur, Psalms 103:8, 145:8. See glossary for more details.

[398] Here and at the beginning of many chapters there are unvowelled letters of unknown meaning. Numerous theories have been proposed, but there is no agreement on the subject.

[399] Arabic /ilah/ here and in verses 6, 18 (twice), 62, 64 (twice), 80 and 151. See glossary for more details.

[400] Or self-sustaining or resurrector.

[401] The Qur'an confirms the previous books many times (2:41,89,91,97,101, 3:3,81, 4:47, 5:48, 6:92, 35:31, 46:12,30)

[402] Or, "between his hands" or "in front of him." Allah does not have a physical body, but like the Injil and Tawrah, the Qur'an uses anthropomorphisms to talk about Allah. Hands here refers to what Allah owns or possesses.

[403] The Law, here and in verses 48, 50, 65, and 93 (twice). See glossary for more details.

[404] The Gospel, here and in verses 48 and 65. See glossary for more details.

[405] This word is only mentioned in seven verses (2:53,185, 3:4, 8:29,41, 21:48, 25:1) and not all of these verses refer to a book. It is not clear in this verse to whom it was revealed but in 2:53 it is said to be revealed to Musa and in 21:48 to Musa and Harun. 25:1 says merely "his slave." Most probably it refers to the ten commandments given to Musa on the mountain.

[406] Arabic /ayat/ here and in verses 7, 11, 13, 19, 21, 41 (twice), 49 (twice), 50, 58, 70, 97, 98, 101, 103, 108, 112, 113, 118, 164, 190, and 199. See glossary for more details.

## Chapter 3

\*\*\*

He forms you[MP] in the womb[411] as he wills.[412] He is the only god, strong[413] and wise.[414] (6)

\*\*\*

He revealed the book to you[MS]. Some of its verses are firm;[415] they are the mother of the book.[416] Others are similar to them.[417] Those with perversity in their hearts follow the similar ones, desiring strife[418] and their explanations. No one knows their explanations except Allah. Those who are firm in knowledge say,[419] "We have believed in it. Everything is from our Lord. Only thinkers will remember this. (7) Our Lord, do not let our hearts go astray after you[MS] have guided us. Give[MS] us mercy from yourself. You[MS] are the giver.[420] (8) Our Lord, you[MS] gather[421] people for a day that is

---

[407] For "torment" here and in verses 16, 21, 56, 77, 88, 91, 105, 106, 128, 129, 176, 177, 178, 181, 188 (twice), and 191, see Tawrah, Isaiah 50:11, Injil, Matthew 18:34, 25:41,46, Luke 16:23-28, Revelation 20:15.

[408] Here and in verses 6, 18, and 62, see Tawrah, Job 9:4, Zabur, Psalms 24:8, Injil, Ephesians 6:10, Revelation 18:8

[409] Tawrah, Deuteronomy 32:35, Ezekiel 25:17, Injil, Romans 12:19, Hebrews 10:30

[410] Tawrah, Jeremiah 23:24, Injil, Hebrews 4:12, Mark 4:22

[411] Zabur, Psalms 139:13-16

[412] For Allah doing whatever he wills here and in verses 13, 37, 40, 73, 74 and 129, see Tawrah, Exodus 33:19, Injil, Romans 9:15,18.

[413] For "strong" here and in verses 18,62, and 126, see Tawrah, Job 9:4, Zabur, Psalms 24:8, Injil, Ephesians 6:10, Revelation 18:8.

[414] For "wise" here and in verses 18, 62, and 126, see Tawrah, Job 9:4, Proverbs 2:6, Jeremiah 9:23-24, Injil, 1 Corinthians 1:21-25, Romans 16:27.

[415] The adjectives "firm" and similar" are for thinking beings. The reason is unknown.

[416] Or "origin of the book" or "master book." See 13:39, 43:4, Injil, Revelation 15:1-5.

[417] The meaning of these two phrases may be "universally applicable" and "applicable to a specific time and place." Another possibility is "exact/clear" and metaphorical.

[418] Injil, 2 Timothy 4:3-4

[419] Or possibly, "except Allah and those who are firm in knowledge. They say,"

[420] Injil, Matthew 7:11, James 1 5

[421] Here and in verses 12 and 25, see Tawrah, Joel 3:11-14, Zephaniah 3:8, Injil, Matthew 25:32, John 15:6, Revelation 16:16

certain." Allah does not break his promise.[422] (9) Neither the possessions nor the children[423] of the disbelievers will help them at all with Allah.[424] They are fuel for hellfire. (10) As in the case of Pharaoh's family and those before them, they have denied our signs,[425] so Allah caught them in their sins. Allah is severe in punishment.[426] (11) Say[MS] to the disbelievers, "You[MP] will be defeated and gathered into hell – a dreadful home. (12) You[MP] had[427] a sign: two groups met, one group fighting in Allah's path, and the other disbelievers who saw them with their own eyes twice as many as they were."[428] Allah supports with his salvation whomever he wills. That is a lesson for those who have eyes to see.[429] (13) People were deceived by the love of things[430] they covet: women, children, vast hoards of gold and silver, branded horses, cattle, and tilled land. These are matters of this world. Allah has the best place to return. (14) **3B1** Say[MS], "Shall I tell you[MP] of better things than that? The reverent will have heavenly gardens[431] with their Lord, with flowing rivers[432] underneath. They will live there forever, with purified kinds[433] and Allah's pleasure." Allah sees his servants (15) who say, "Our Lord, we

---

[422] Tawrah, Numbers 23:19, Injil, Titus 1:2, Hebrews 6:18
[423] Or sons, here and in verses 14, 61, and 116.
[424] Zabur, Psalms 49:7-9
[425] Tawrah, Exodus 4:17, 7:3,11-13,22, 8:3,14,15,28, 9:7,12,34,35, 10:20,27, 11:9,10, 14:4,8
[426] Tawrah, Ezekiel 25:17, Injil, Matthew 8:12, 13:42,50, 22:13, 24:51, 25:30, Mark 9:48, Luke 13:28, 19:27.
[427] The subject "sign" is feminine and the verb "had" is masculine. The reason is unknown.
[428] Tawrah, Judges 7:12,19-22, 2 Kings 7:5-7, 2 Chronicles 14:9
[429] Tawrah, Isaiah 6:9, Injil, Luke 8:10
[430] Injil, 1 Timothy 6:10, 1 John 2:15-16, James 4:4
[431] Arabic /jannah/ here and in verses 133, 136, 142, 185, 195, and 198. See glossary for more details. Tawrah, Genesis 2:9,10, Isaiah 65:21, Exekiel 47:12, Injil, Revelation 22:1-2
[432] For "flowing rivers" here and in verses 136, 195, and 198, see Injil, Revelation 22:1-2, Tawrah, Ezekiel 47:12.
[433] This word is used often in the context of gardens. 20:53,131, 22:5, 26:7, 36:36, 38:58, 43:12, and 50:7 show that the meaning is probably kinds [of fruit or other plants]. The adjective "purified" refers to inanimate objects, not people. Other translations use "mates," but this fits neither the context of gardens nor the inanimate adjectives.

## Chapter 3

have believed, so forgive us our sins[434] and protect us from the torment of hellfire." (16) They are enduring,[435] honest, humble, generous, and ask forgiveness before dawn.[436] (17)

\*\*\*

Allah, the angels, and the scholars witness that he is the only god, standing on justice.[437] He is the only god, strong and wise. (18)

\*\*\*

Religion to Allah means submission,[438] and those who received the book differed only after receiving knowledge, because of jealousy. Allah will be swift in reckoning[439] with those who disbelieve in his signs. (19) If they dispute with you[MS], say[MS], "My followers and I have submitted our faces to Allah." Say[MS] to those who were given the book and the Gentiles,[440] "Have you[MP] submitted?" If they submit, they have been guided. If they turn away, your[MS] responsibility is only to convey the message. Allah sees his servants. (20)

\*\*\*

Tell[441] those who disbelieve in Allah's signs, who wrongfully murder prophets,[442] and murder those who command justice that they will have painful torment. (21) Their works have failed both in this world and in the hereafter, and they will have no savior.[443] (22) Did you[MS] not see those who were given a portion of the book being called to Allah's book to judge between them? Then a group

---

[434] Injil, Luke 11:4

[435] See "endure" in glossary

[436] Zabur, Psalms 5:3, 55:17, 88:13, 90:14, 92:2

[437] Tawrah, Isaiah 30:18

[438] Injil, James 4:7. For "submission," "submit," and "submitted" here three times and in verses 52, 64, 67, 80, 83, 84, 85, and 102, some translators do not translate this. See glossary for more details.

[439] Tawrah, Isaiah 19:1, Malachi 3:5, Zabur, Psalms 147:15, Injil, 2 Peter 2:1, Revelation 22:12

[440] The word can also mean illiterate or unlettered here and in verse 75.

[441] Literally give good news. This may be sarcastic.

[442] For Jews murdering the prophets, here and in verses 112, 181, and 183, see also 2:61,87,91, 4:155, 5:70, Tawrah, Nehemiah 9:26, Injil, Matthew 23:37, Luke 11:47-49, Acts 7:52, 1 Thessalonians 2:15. The word "murder" does not imply that they thwarted Allah's will or that the Jewish people as a whole murdered them. Particularly in the case of Isa, it was the Jewish religious leadership who were responsible. See Injil, Matthew 26:47ff.

[443] Tawrah, Isaiah 43:11, Hosea 13:4, Injil, Hebrews 10:26

## Chapter 3

of them turn away, (23) since they said, "Hellfire will only touch us for a few[444] days."[445] The lies they fabricated beguiled them in their religion. (24) What if we gather them for a day which is certain, when every soul is repaid as it deserves? They will not be wronged. (25)

\*\*\*

Say[MS], "Allah, Owner of the kingdom, you[MS] give the kingdom to whom you[MS]
will; you[MS] take the kingdom from whom you[MS] will;[446] you[MS] exalt whom you[MS] will, and you[MS] abase whom you[MS] will.[447] Goodness is in your[MS] hand. You can do anything.[448] (26)

\*\*\*

You[MS] make night flow into[449] day, and day flow into night; you[MS] bring out the living from the dead, the dead from the living, and you[MS] provide bountifully for those you[MS] will without reckoning." (27)

\*\*\*

Believers should not take disbelievers as helpers instead of[450] believers.[451] Whoever does that is not at all from Allah, except if you[MP] are very careful of them. Allah warns you[MP] of himself. Allah is [man's] destiny. (28) Say[MS], "Allah knows what is in your[MP] hearts,[452] whether you[MP] hide or reveal it. He knows what is in the heavens and the earth. Allah can do anything. (29)

\*\*\*

On that day, everyone[453] will be presented with the good he has done. As for the evil he has done, he will wish that there were a

---

[444] There could be a different meaning here as the noun is masculine and the adjective feminine

[445] These people apparently believed in "purgatory," which the Qur'an here clearly denies, just as the Tawrah, Zabur and Injil do. See Injil, Luke 16:25,26, Hebrews 9:27

[446] Tawrah, Daniel 4:17

[447] Tawrah, 1 Samuel 2:6,7

[448] Here and in verses 29, 165, and 189, see Tawrah, Job 42:2, Isaiah 14:27, Daniel 4:35, Injil, Matthew 19:26, Mark 10:27, Luke 1:37.

[449] Or penetrate

[450] Or besides

[451] Injil, 1 Corinthians 15:33

[452] Here and in verses 35, 73, 119, 121, 129, 154, 156, and 167, see Tawrah, 1 Samuel 16:7, 1 Chronicles 28:9, Zabur, Psalms 44:21, Injil, Luke 16:15, Romans 8:27, Acts 15:8, 1 John 3:20.

[453] Literally, every soul

great distance between himself and it.[454] Allah warns you[MP] of himself. Allah is compassionate[455] with [his] servants."[456] (30)
***

Say[MS], "If you[MP] love Allah, follow[MP] me. Allah will surely love you[MP] and forgive your[MP] sins. Allah is forgiving[457] and merciful."[458] (31) Say[MS], "Obey[MP] Allah and the messenger. If they turn away, Allah does not love disbelievers."[459] (32) **3B2** Allah chose Adam,[460] Nuh,[461] Ibrahim's[462] family, and Imran's family over all mankind,[463] (33) some as offspring of others. Allah hears all and knows all.[464] (34) Imran's[465] wife said, "Lord, I have vowed to you[MS] what is in my belly to be wholly freed to you[MS]; accept[MS] it from me. You[MS] hear all and know all." (35) When she gave birth to her, she said, "Lord, I have given birth to a female." Allah well knows what she bore. A male is not like a female. "I

---

[454] Zabur, Psalms 103:12

[455] Injil, James 5:11

[456] For "servant" here and in verses 79 and 182, see glossary for more details.

[457] Here and in verses 89, 129, and 155, see Zabur, Psalms 103:3, 130:4, Tawrah, Isaiah 43:25, Exodus 34:7, Injil, Acts 26:18.

[458] Here and in verses 89, 129, and 155, see glossary for more details on "merciful."

[459] Zabur, Psalms 5:4-5, 11:5, Tawrah, Proverbs 6:16-19

[460] See glossary for more details on Adam here and in verse 59.

[461] Noah. See glossary for more details.

[462] Abraham here and in verses 65, 67, 68 (twice), 84, 95, and 97. See glossary for more details.

[463] or, above the universe

[464] Tawrah, Job 37:16, Isaiah 40:14, Zabur, Psalms 33:13-15, Injil, 1 John 3:20

[465] Mary (Mariam in Arabic) is in this passage and in 66:12 presented as the daughter of Imran. In the Tawrah, Miriam (also Mariam in Arabic), Musa, and Harun are presented as the children of Amram (see Tawrah, Exodus 6:20, Numbers 26:59). It is not known whether the same person is intended. Mary's father is not specifically named in the Injil, though Joseph (see Injil, Matthew 1:16) and Heli (Injil, Luke 3:23) have been suggested. However, Mary is called a relative of Elizabeth (Injil, Luke 1:36) and Elizabeth was descended from Harun, son of Amram (Injil, Luke 1:5). The reason the Qur'an calls her the daughter of Imran may be to designate her priestly line (descent from Harun).

Chapter 3

have named her Mariam.[466] I seek refuge in you[MS] from damned[467] Satan for her and her seed.[468]" (36)[469]

\*\*\*

And her Lord accepted her favorably[470] and caused her to grow[471] well and entrusted Zakariyya[472] to take care of[473] her. As often as Zakariyya visited her in the inner sanctuary, he found she had provision. He said, "Mariam, how did you[FS] get this?" She said, "It is from Allah. Allah provides bountifully for whomever he wills." (37) There Zakariyya prayed to his Lord. He said, "Lord, give me a good seed from you[MS]. You[MS] hear prayer." (38)

\*\*\*

The angels called to him as he stood praying in the inner sanctuary,[474] "Allah
gives you[MS] good news of Yahya,[475] confirming[476] a word from Allah,[477] a master, chaste,[478] and a righteous prophet."[479] (39)

---

[466] Mary, mother of Jesus, here and in verses 37, 42, 43, 44, and 45 (twice). See glossary for more details.

[467] Literally, stoned

[468] Tawrah, Genesis 3:15 speaks of one to be seed of a woman who will have victory over Satan. Isa was resurrected from death to life (19:33, 5:117) and gave life to the dead (3:49), so he was victorious over Satan, whose work it is to cause living people to die (see 28:15).

[469] This begins a section that refers to a number of ways Isa is unique. He is the only one who: is a "seed" of a woman (this verse), is a word from Allah (39,45), is highly exalted in this world and the hereafter (45), is named as brought near to Allah (45), speaks as an infant in the cradle (46), creates (49), heals (49), gives life to the dead (49), tells hidden things (49), confirms a book (50), permits formerly forbidden things (50), commands obedience in the context of the straight path (50), senses disbelief in people (52), and who was raised up to be with Allah, so he is with Allah now (55). For more information about this subject, see notes at 4:158, 5:46,110, 19:19, 43:59.

[470] Injil, Luke 1:28,45,49,50

[471] Literally, sprout

[472] Zechariah, father of John, here (twice) and in verse 38. See glossary for more details.

[473] Or guaranteed or provided for

[474] Injil, Luke 1:11, Hebrews 9:7, Tawrah, Exodus 30:10, Leviticus 16:34

[475] John the Baptist. See glossary for more details. Yahya is the only person in the Qur'an who confirms a person (Isa, a word from Allah, here and in verse 45).

[476] Injil, John 1:23, 29-36, in which Yahya confirms that Isa is the Lamb of God, the sacrifice.

Chapter 3

\*\*\*
He said, "Lord, How can I have a boy when old age has overtaken me and my wife is barren?"[480] He said, "Thus Allah does whatever he wills." (40) He said, "Lord, give me a sign."[481] He said, "Your[MS] sign will be that you[MS] will not speak to people[482] for three days except by symbols. Remember your[MS] Lord frequently, and glorify [him] in the evening and the morning." (41)
\*\*\*
The angels said, "Mariam, Allah has chosen you[FS],[483] purified you[FS],[484] and chosen you[FS] above all women in the universe.[485] (42) Mariam, be[FS] devout to your Lord, and bow[FS] down and kneel[FS] with those who kneel." (43) This is hidden knowledge that we reveal to you[MS]. You[MS] were not with them when they cast lots[486] for which of them would take care of Mariam, or when they quarreled. (44) When the angels said, "Mariam, Allah gives you[FS] good news of a word[487] from him, whose name will be the Messiah,[488] Isa[489] son of

---

[477] See verse 45 for his identity. See also note at verse 36, 4:171, and Injil, John 1:1-3,14, Revelation 19:13

[478] Yahya is the only one in the Qur'an called a master and chaste.

[479] Injil, Luke 1:76

[480] Injil, Luke 1:18

[481] Injil, Luke 1:18

[482] Injil, Luke 1:20

[483] Injil, Luke 1:28,42

[484] Injil, Luke 1:30

[485] Injil, Luke 1:42. Ways in which Mariam was chosen above all women include: she is the only one ever to be a virgin and bear a son (verse 47, 19:20, Tawrah, Isaiah 7:14), Allah himself breathed into her (21:91) or her womb (66:12) of his own spirit for Isa to be conceived (see Luke 1:35), and she was prophesied about in the Tawrah, Genesis 3:15 and Isaiah 7:14, and the Injil, Luke 1:31. Allah knew that she would need inner strength to suffer the shame of being an unmarried mother and to endure people's misunderstandings (19:27-28, Injil, Matthew 1:18-19) . Despite this honor, she is neither to be worshipped as a goddess (5:116, Injil, Mark 12:29), nor is she a mediator (2:255, Injil, 1 Timothy 2:5).

[486] Or "pens"

[487] See verse 39, 4:171, note at verse 36, and Injil, John 1:1-3,14, Revelation 19:13

[488] Or Christ. Arabic /Al-Masih/. See glossary for more details.

[489] Jesus, here and in verses 52, 55, 59, and 84. See glossary for more details.

Chapter 3

Mariam, highly exalted[490] in this world and the hereafter,[491] and brought near[492] [to Allah]. (45) He will speak to people in the cradle[493] and when mature, and he is righteous." (46) She said, "Lord, how can I have a boy when no man has ever touched[494] me?" He said, "Allah can create[495] what he wills. When he decrees a matter, he only says to it: "Be," and then it is."[496] (47)

\*\*\*

And he[497] will teach[498] him[499] the book,[500] wisdom,[501] the Tawrah,[502] and the Injil (48)

---

[490] Or illustrious or distinguished or highly-regarded; this word is only used twice in the Qur'an, about Musa in 33:69 and here about Isa. In the plural, this word is used for leading citizens of a city or country. See note at verse 36. Injil, Philippians 2:9

[491] Al-Baidawi has suggested that "exalted in this world" means through his prophethood and "in the hereafter" means through his intercession. See note at 2:255, Injil, 1 Timothy 2:5.

[492] Others who are brought near to Allah are the angels (4:172) and the inhabitants of the heavenly garden. (56:11,88, 83:21,28) See note at verse 36.

[493] For what he says, see 19:30-33. See note at verse 36.

[494] i.e. sexually. See Injil, Luke 1:34, 1 Corinthians 7:1.

[495] This word is used of creating something from nothing. In Isa's case, 19:15-36, 21:91, and 66:12 tell how Allah caused Isa to be conceived within Mariam: by breathing his spirit into her. This, then, is a general statement of what Allah can do. He could have created Isa from nothing, but he chose to breathe his spirit into her. By comparing this verse (Allah <u>creates</u> what he wills) with verse 40 (Allah <u>does</u> what he wills) , we see the difference between the conception of Yahya, whom Allah allowed to be conceived from Zakariya's sperm and his wife's egg, and the conception of Isa, who was conceived when Allah created something (out of nothing) that combined with Mariam's egg.

[496] Allah did this kind of creating in the beginning. See Tawrah, Genesis 1:3-28.

[497] Allah

[498] Tawrah, Isaiah 50:4

[499] Isa

[500] The book in 2:53,87, 6:153, 11:110, 17:2, 23:49, 25:35, 28:43, 32:23, 41:45 is stated to be what Allah revealed to Musa. This would be the Pentateuch, the first five parts of the Old Testament.

[501] The wisdom probably refers to what the Jews called ketubim or writings, which include the Zabur, Psalms, and Tawrah, Proverbs, Job, Ecclesiates, and Song of Solomon. The Arabic word "hikmah" means both proverb and wisdom. Injil, 1 Corinthians 15:24-28

## Chapter 3

\*\*\*

[and Isa was][503] a messenger to the people of Israel, "I have brought you[MP] a sign from your Lord: I create[504] a bird[505] for you[MP] from clay and breathe into it and it will be a [living][506] bird[507] by Allah's permission.[508] I heal[509] the man born blind[510] and the leper[511] and give life[512] to the dead by Allah's permission. I tell you[MP] what you[MP] eat[513] and what you[MP] store in your[MP] houses.[514] That is truly a sign for you[MP], if you[MP] believe.[515] (49) And [I am] a

---

[502] This three-part division of the Old Testament/Tanakh (book, wisdom and law) parallels the Jewish division of it: law of Musa, prophets, and Psalms (Injil, Luke 24:44). See glossary.

[503] Or as. The Arabic sentence here changes from talking about what Allah will do in verse 48 to what Isa will be in verse 49. In verse 50 also there are words that are not stated.

[504] Injil, John 1:3,10, Colossians 1:16, Hebrews 1:3. See note at verse 36

[505] This sign is not mentioned in the Injil, but many of Isa's signs were not mentioned in the Injil. See Injil, John 21:25. Similarly, many of Isa's miracles in the Injil are not mentioned in the Qur'an. See 10:94 for what to do in case of doubt.

[506] Or real.

[507] Most translations take this to mean a literal bird, but Muhammad Asad translates this "destiny."

[508] No one can do anything without Allah's permission. See Tawrah, Job 1:12, 2:6. Isa specifically said he could do nothing on his own authority. Injil, John 5:30.

[509] Injil, Matthew 4:23-24, 8"7-13,16, 9:35, 12:10-15,22, 14:14, 15:28,30, 17:18, 19:2, 21:14, Mark 1:34, 3:2-5,10, 5:25-34, 6:5,13, Luke 4:40, 5:17, Luke 6:17-19, 7:3-10, 8:2, 36, 43-48, 9:11,42, 13:11-14, 14:3-4, 17:12-15, John 4:47-53, 5:6-9, 9:1-9. See note at verse 36.

[510] Injil, John 9:1-25

[511] Injil, Matthew 8:2-4

[512] See Injil, Matthew 9:25, Luke 7:14-15, John 11:43-44. See note at verse 36.

[513] Injil, Luke 6:8, John 2:25. See note at verse 36.

[514] The Qur'an lists some other miracles of Isa in 3:52, 5:110,112, 19:19,20,24,30-33. In the Injil, most of the stories of the miracles that Isa does are mentioned in Matthew 8-12, 14-15, 17, 20, Mark 1-10, Luke 1, 4-9, 11, 14, 17-18, 22, John 2, 4-6, 9, 11.

[515] These particular signs were significant in that three of them (healing a man born blind, healing a Jewish leper, and giving life to a person who had been dead more than three days) were believed by the Jews to be signs that only the Messiah could do. The fourth sign was casting out a dumb demon, which is mentioned in Injil, Matthew 9:32-33 and Luke 11:14.

## Chapter 3

confirmer[516] of the Tawrah that is in my possession,[517] and [I came] to permit[518] for you[MP] some of what was forbidden to you[MP], and I have brought you[MP] a sign from your[MP] Lord, so fear[MP] Allah and obey[MP] me.[519] (50) Allah is my Lord and your Lord,[520] so worship[MP] him. This is the straight path."[521] (51) **3B3** When Isa sensed[522] their disbelief,[523] he said, "Who are my helpers toward Allah?" The disciples[524] said, "We are Allah's helpers.[525] We have

---

[516] The Tawrah that existed in his days, which he possessed, was confirmed. See note at verse 36.

[517] Or, "between my hands" or "in front of me." Injil, Matthew 5:17-19

[518] Injil, Mark 7:19 (which refers to ceremonial cleanliness, not value as food), Acts 10:15, 15:29. See note at verse 36.

[519] Injil, Matthew 7:21-27. Several prophets tell the people specifically, "obey me." (Nuh 26:108,110, 71:3, Hud 26:126,131, Salih 26:144,150, Lut 26:163, Shuaib 26:179, Harun 20:90, and Isa 3:50, 43:63) Several verses also command people to obey "the messenger" (3:32,132, 4:59, 5:92, 8:1,19,46, 24:54,56, 47:33, 58:13, 64:12), most of which probably refer to Muhammad (s). See note at verse 36.

[520] Injil, John 20:17, Mark 12:29-30, 1 Corinthians 3:23, 11:3, 15:28

521 The straight path is mentioned often in the Qur'an (1:7 and 37:118 as "the straight path", 7:16 as "your straight path," 6:126 as "your Lord's straight path," 6:153 as "my straight path," and 2:108,142,213, 3:51,101, 4:68,175, 5:12,16,60,77, 6:39,87,161, 10:25, 11:56, 15:41, 16:76, 121, 19:36,43, 20:135, 22:54, 23:73, 24:46, 28:22, 36:4,61, 38:22, 42:52, 43:43,61,64, 46:30, 48:2,20, 60:1, 67:22 as "a straight path.") However, only 3:51, 6:153, 19:36, 43:61,64, and 36:61 say what the straight path is. This passage is one of the most complete in its explanation, and we can conclude that the straight path includes (from verses 45-51) 1) believing Isa is a word from Allah, Christ, the son of Mary, and exalted in this age and the hereafter, 2) that he has been brought close to Allah, 3) that he was taught the book, wisdom, the Tawrah and the Injil, 4) that he is a messenger to the people of Israel, 5) that he brought a sign, 6) that he created a bird, healed the blind and the leper, gave life to the dead, and proclaimed what people ate and stored by Allah's permission, 7) that he confirmed the Tawrah, 8) that he allowed forbidden things, 9) fearing Allah, 10) obeying Isa, 11) believing in the one God who is Isa's and our Lord, and 12) worshipping Allah. See notes on the other four passages.

[522] Injil, John 6:64, 1 Corinthians 4:5. See note at verse 36.

[523] The Qur'an lists some of his miracles in 3:49, 5:110,112, 19:19-20,24,30-33. Most of the miracles Isa does that are mentioned in the Injil, with the stories behind them, are in the Injil, Matthew 8-11, 14-15,17,21, Mark 1-9,11, Luke 2,4-9,22, John 2,4-6,9,11.

[524] Or hawariyun. The reference is to the twelve disciples that Isa sent out as apostles. The Arabic word is of uncertain meaning. Some have

## Chapter 3

believed in Allah, so testify that we have submitted. (52) Our Lord, we believe in your[MS] revelation and follow the messenger[526] so record[MS] us as witnesses." (53) And they[527] were crafty[528] and Allah was crafty, and Allah was the craftiest:[529] (54) Allah said, "Isa, I[530] will make you[MS] die[531] and raise you[MS] up[532] to me,[533] and

---

suggested that it refers to their arguing, and others to their wearing white robes, or working in bleaching clothes.

[525] The word /ansaar/ here is from the same root as the word used for Christian /nasaaraa/. This is one theory of the origin of the word.

[526] In this conversation, which took place over 500 years before Muhammad (s) was born, the apostles call Isa "the messenger". In 48:29, Muhammad (s) is also called "the messenger," and in 73:16, Musa is called "the messenger."

[527] Reference here is to the Jews (verse 49).

[528] Or sly. Some translations use "plot" or "plan" but the Arabic word /makara/ is stronger than that. In the context of Isa's death, this probably refers to the Jews wanting him to be crucified and thus fall under the curse of the Old Testament (Tawrah, Deuteronomy 21:23, which says that all who are hanged on a tree are cursed by Allah) rather than stoning him, which would have made him a martyr. Their purpose may have been to discredit Isa and his being the Messiah with the argument that the Messiah could not be cursed.

[529] Or best of the crafty. Injil, 1 Corinthians 1:19, 3:19-20. This does not imply a defect in Allah's character but rather shows that Allah will overcome all who plot against him.

[530] 4:157 makes it clear that the Jews did not kill Isa. If they did not, then who did? Here the Qur'an makes it clear that Allah did it. Other verses that talk about Allah's sovereignty over death include 8:17.

[531] This word in Arabic /tawaffa/ means "to cause to die." Some translators ignore the clear statement of the Qur'an that Isa died, and instead translate common beliefs. The clearest commentary on the Qur'an is the Qur'an itself, not what others say about it. This verb, in its various forms, occurs 25 times in the Qur'an. Twice (here and 5:117) it refers to Isa, and everywhere else (2:234,240, 3:193, 4:15,97, 6:60,61, 7:37,126, 8:50, 10:46,104, 12:101, 13:40, 16:28,32,70, 22:5, 32:11, 39:42, 40:67,77, 47:27), it is in the context of death. Even today, it is used euphemistically to mean "to pass away," and the word "obituaries" is from the same root. For other verses which state or imply Isa's death, see 5:117, 19:33, 19:31, 2:87, etc.

[532] This word refers to Isa's ascension, not his resurrection. Injil, Acts 1:2,9-11,22, 1 Timothy 3:16. For his resurrection from the dead, see note on 19:33.

## Chapter 3

purify you[MS] from the disbelievers,[534] and make your[MS] followers higher than the disbelievers[535] until[536] the day of resurrection.[537] Then you[MP] will return to me and I will judge between you[MP] in matters about which you[MP] differ.[538] (55) But I will torment the disbelievers severely in this world[539] and the hereafter, and they will have no savior."[540] (56) But he will pay the believers who do righteous deeds their wages.[541] Allah does not love the wicked.[542] (57) What we recite to you[MS] are verses and the wise reminder.[543] (58) With Allah, Isa is like Adam, who[MS] was created[MS] from soil; then he told him, "Be[MS]!" and he was.[544] (59) Truth is from your[MS]

---

[533] Since he was raised up to be with Allah, he is with Allah now. See note at verse 36 and Injil, Acts 2:33, 5:31, 7:55-56, Romans 8:34, Colossians 3:1, Hebrews 10:12, 12:2, 1 Peter 3:22.

[534] In 19:19, the Qur'an states that Isa is pure and sinless, and the Qur'an never says that Isa committed a sin or asked Allah for forgiveness. This purification may be a reference to Isa's dying to purify the disbelievers from the guilt, shame, and uncleanness of their sins if they repent and follow him. If they do, they would be made "higher than the disbelievers" based on the next phrase in this verse.

[535] The position of Isa's followers above the unbelievers is an ethical position, as the Qur'an describes in 5:82.

[536] The order the Qur'an gives is first Isa's death, then his ascension, then his being purified of the disbelievers, then his followers being raised above the disbelievers, and finally the day of resurrection. Clearly, then, his death would have occurred before his followers were raised above the disbelievers, which in turn happened before the day of resurrection. This contradicts those who say that Isa has not died yet. See also 5:117, 19:33, Injil, 1 Peter 3:18.

[537] For "day of resurrection" here and in verses 77, 161, 180, 185, and 194, see Tawrah, Daniel 12:,2 Injil, Acts 24:15, 1 Corinthians 15:52-54, Revelation 20:11-15

[538] Injil, 1 Corinthians 15:24-28

[539] Injil, Revelation 9:5-6, Tawrah, 1 Samuel 16:14, Jeremiah 26:13

[540] For the believers, it is implied that there will be a savior. But it is not stated whether the savior is Allah or Isa. If it is Allah, see 2:106, Tawrah, Isaiah 43:11, Hosea 13:4, Zabur, Psalms 65:5, Injil, Titus 1:3, Hebrews 10:26. If it is Isa, see Injil, Luke 2:11, Acts 5:31, 13:23, Philippians 3:20.

[541] Tawrah, Isaiah 61:8, Injil, Matthew 5:12, 6:1, 10:41-42, 16:27, Luke 6:23,35, 1 Corinthians 3:8, James 2:14-17, Revelation 11:18, 19:8, 22:12

[542] Zabur, Psalms 5:4-5, 11:5, Tawrah, Proverbs 6:16-19

[543] Arabic /dhikr/. See glossary for more details.

[544] The phrase "who was created from soil" is in the singular, not the dual, and refers only to Adam. The account of Isa's conception through Allah's spirit and birth through the virgin Mary is told in 19:16ff, 66:12,

## Chapter 3

Lord, so do[MS] not doubt. (60) If someone protests about it against you[MS] after knowledge has come to you[MS], say[MS], "Come[MP] let's call our children and yours[MP] and our wives and yours[MP] and ourselves and yourselves[MP], then let us praise Allah and call down his curse on the liars." (61) This is the true story and Allah is the only god. Allah is strong and wise. (62) If they turn away, Allah knows about the corrupters. (63) People of the book, come to a common word between us and you[MP] that we will not worship any other gods besides Allah, and we will not make anything else a god,[545] nor will we take each other as gods[546] in addition to Allah. If they turn away, say[MP], "Testify that we have submitted." (64) People of the book, why do you[MP] protest about Ibrahim, since the Tawrah and Injil were not revealed until after him? Do you[MP] not comprehend? (65) You[MP] dispute about what you[MP] know. Why do you[MP] dispute about what you[MP] do not know? Allah knows, and you[MP] do not. (66) Ibrahim was neither a Jew nor a Christian, but he was a monotheist who submitted, and not a polytheist. (67) Ibrahim's followers and this prophet and the believers have the most right to Ibrahim.[547] Allah protects the believers. (68) Some people of the book want to mislead you[MP]; they mislead only themselves and they do not realize it. (69) People of the book, why do you[MP] disbelieve in Allah's signs that you[MP] witness? (70) People of the book, why do you[MP] clothe the truth with worthlessness,[548] and knowingly hide[MP] the truth? (71) Some people of the book said, "Believe in what was revealed to the believers at daybreak, and disbelieve at sunset," so they can return.

---

and 21:91, whereas Adam's creation is told in 32:9, 7:12, 18:37, 22:5, 30:20, 35:11, and 40:67. Adam was created first, from soil, and then Allah breathed of his spirit into him, whereas Allah breathed his spirit into Isa's mother Mariam, and then Isa was conceived in her womb and later born. Thus the likeness of Adam to Isa is not in the method of their birth. See Injil, Romans 5:12-21, 1 Corinthians 15:21-22,45-47 for an explanation of how they were alike.

[545] Tawrah, Deuteronomy 6:4-5, Injil, Matthew 23:9, Romans 3:29, 1 Timothy 1:17

[546] Tawrah, Deuteronomy 5:7, 6:14, 28:14, Injil, Mark 12:29, Acts 5:29, 1 Timothy 2:5

[547] Injil, John 8:32-47.

[548] Allah's words are pure and true, but many people add their explanations, doctrinal statements, creeds, traditions, catechisms, etc. to Allah's words. In comparison to Allah's words, these things are all worthless.

## Chapter 3

(72) Only trust those who follow your[MP] religion.[549] Say[MS], "Guidance is Allah's guidance,[550] that someone be given like what you[MP] have been given; or they[MP] dispute with you[MP] before your[MP] Lord." Say[MS], "Grace is in Allah's hand, and he gives it to those he wills. Allah is all-encompassing[551] and all-knowing. (73) He gives special mercy to those he wills, and Allah has great grace." (74) 3B4 Some of the people of the book you[MS] can entrust with a huge sum, and they will return it to you[MS]. If you[MS] give others of them a dinar, they will not return it to you[MS] unless you remain standing over them. That is because they say, "We have no dealing with the Gentiles." They knowingly say lies about Allah. (75) Rather, Allah loves whoever keeps his oath[552] and is reverent.[553] (76) Those who sell Allah's covenant and their oaths for a small price have no portion in the hereafter, and Allah will not speak to them or look at them on the day of resurrection, nor purify them. They will have painful torment. (77) Some of them twist[554] the book with their tongues,[555] so that you[MP] would think that it is from the book, when it is not from the book. They say, "It is from Allah," when it is not from Allah, and they knowingly tell lies about Allah. (78) A person[556] would not have been given the book, rulership, and prophecy[557] by Allah and then have told the people, "Worship[MP] me instead of Allah."[558] Rather, "Be reverent teachers in your teaching the book and your studying."[559] (79) He does not

---

[549] Religion here means "submission" (to Allah).
[550] This is similar in meaning to the saying in English, "All truth is God's truth."
[551] Zabur, Psalms 139:7-12
[552] Tawrah, Leviticus 19:12, Proverbs 25:14, Zabur, Psalms 50:14, Injil, Matthew 5:33-37
[553] Zabur, Psalms 4:3, Injil, 2 Peter 2:9
[554] or twist
[555] There are two types of "distortion:" altering the text and altering the meaning. From the words "with their tongues," "say," and "tell lies," it is clear that altering the meaning is intended. See 2:75, 4:46, 5:13,41 for the other verses that deal with this subject. Injil, 2 Peter 3:16
[556] This probably refers to Isa.
[557] or prophethood
[558] Anyone who says he should be worshipped instead of Allah is wrong. Injil, Matthew 4:10, Luke 4:8, John 4:21, Acts 24:14, Tawrah, Exodus 34:14.
[559] Injil, Matthew 5:17-20, 2 Timothy 2:15, Acts 17:11.

## Chapter 3

command you to take angels and prophets as gods.[560] Would he command you to disbelieve after you have submitted? (80) Allah made a covenant with the prophets, "The books and wisdom I gave you[MP]." Then a messenger came to you[MP] confirming[561] what you[MP] have." You[MP] would certainly believe in him[562] and aid him. He said, "Have you[MP] admitted it and made it binding on you[MP]?" They said, "We admit it." He said, "Then testify[MP] and I will testify with you[MP]." (81) Those who turn away after that are unbelievers.[563] (82) Do they seek a religion other than Allah's? All in heaven and earth submit to him willingly or unwillingly.[564] They will return to him.[565] (83) Say[MS], "We believe in Allah and what he revealed to us and to Ibrahim, Ismail,[566] Ishaq,[567] Yaqub,[568] the tribes,[569] and in what was given to Musa,[570] Isa, and the prophets from their Lord.[571] We do not distinguish between any of them, and we have submitted[572] to him." (84) Religion other than submission will not be accepted of him who seeks it, and in the hereafter, he will be lost. (85) How can Allah guide people who disbelieve after having believed and witnessed that the messenger is true, and after having seen miracles? Allah does not guide wicked people. (86) Their reward is the curse of Allah, angels, and all men upon them. (87) There they will be forever,

---

[560] Or lords, Injil, Matthew 23:29, Revelation 22:8-9

[561] The Qur'an confirms the previous books many times (2:41,89,91,97,101, 3:3,81, 4:47, 5:48, 6:92, 35:31, 46:12,30)

[562] or it

[563] Or transgressors or immoral, here and in verse 110. Injil, Matthew 7:14, 22:14, 24:12, Luke 13:23-24.

[564] Injil, 1 Corinthians 15:24-25.

[565] Injil, Romans 14:12

[566] Ishmael. See glossary for more details.

[567] Isaac. See glossary for more details.

[568] Jacob. See glossary for more details.

[569] i.e. the twelve tribes of Israel

[570] Moses. See glossary for more details.

[571] Most of what all the prophets were given came from Allah orally, and it was later written down. The exception is Musa (Tawrah, Exodus 34:28, Deuteronomy 4:13, 10:4), when Allah himself wrote them on stone tablets. The prophets listed here are all in chronological order, so the prophets listed after Isa may refer to those who were given the rest of the Injil (see Injil, 1 Peter 1:20-21, 2 Timothy 3:16).

[572] Injil, James 4:7. For "submitted" and "submission" here in verse 85, some translators do not translate this. See glossary for more details.

## Chapter 3

and their torment will not be lightened, nor will they be given more time.[573] (88) The exception is for those who later repent and do good. Allah is forgiving and merciful. (89) The repentance of believers who disbelieve, and then increase in their disbelief will not be accepted.[574] They have gone astray. (90) The earth full of gold will not be accepted as a ransom for any disbeliever who died in disbelief.[575] They will have painful torment, and no savior.[576] (91) You[MP] will not obtain righteousness until you[MP] donate what you[MP] love.[577] And Allah well knows your[MP] gifts. (92) 4A1 All food was lawful for the children of Israel[578] except what Israel forbade to himself before the Tawrah was revealed. Bring the Tawrah[579] and read[MP] it if you[MP] are telling the truth. (93) Those who later invent lies about Allah are wicked. (94) Say[MS], "Allah is true, so follow[MP] him, in the spiritual path[580] of Ibrahim the monotheist. He was not a polytheist." (95) The first sanctuary designated for men, for the one in Bakka,[581] [was] blessed and a guidance to mankind.[582] (96) It has miraculous signs, the place Ibrahim stood. Whoever entered it was safe. People who are able to do so are obligated to Allah to make a hajj to the sanctuary. As for the disbelievers – Allah needs nothing from anyone. (97) Say[MS], "People of the book, why do you[MP] disbelieve in Allah's signs? Allah is witness to your[MP] deeds." (98) Say[MS], "People of the book, why do you[MP] block believers from Allah's path?[583] You want it to be crooked.[584] You[MP] are witnesses and Allah is aware of your[MP] deeds." (99) Believers, if you[MP] obey one group of those who were given the book,[585] they will turn you[MP] back to disbelief after your[MP]

---

[573] or regarded or be looked at
[574] Injil, Hebrews 10:26-27, Tawrah, Ezekiel 18:1-20.
[575] Zabur, Psalms 49:7-9, Injil, Matthew 16:26, Luke 12:16-31, 16:19-31, James 5:1-6
[576] Tawrah, Isaiah 43:11, Hosea 13:4, Injil, Hebrews 10:26
[577] Injil, Matthew 19:21-24
[578] Tawrah, Leviticus 11
[579] This verse shows that the Tawrah was in the possession of the Jews of those days. The Qur'an here appeals to its authority.
[580] Arabic /millah/. See glossary.
[581] said to be the ancient name for Mecca. Another possibility is Baka (Zabur, Psalms 84:6)
[582] or, to the worlds
[583] Injil, Matthew 23:13, Luke 11:52
[584] Injil, Acts 13:10
[585] the reference is to the former Book

## Chapter 3

faith.[586] (100) How can you[MP] disbelieve when Allah's signs are recited to you[MP], and his messenger is among you[MP]. Whoever clings to[587] Allah has been guided to a straight path.[588] (101) Believers, fear[MP] Allah as he deserves to be feared, and do not die unless you have submitted. (102) Cling to Allah's rope,[589] all of you[MP], and do[MP] not split up. Remember[MP] Allah's blessings to you[MP]: when you[MP] were enemies, he united your[MP] hearts and you[MP] became brothers by his blessings.[590] You[MP] were at the edge of a pit of hellfire and he rescued you[MP] from it.[591] Thus Allah makes his signs clear to you[MP], so that you[MP] may be guided. (103) May there be a nation among you[MP] that pray for good, promote virtue[592] and prevent vice.[593] They are successful. (104) Do not be like those who scattered and differed after having seen miracles. They will have great torment (105) on a day when some are honored and others are shamed.[594] As for those who are ashamed, "Have you[MP] disbelieved after believing? Taste torment for your[MP] disbelief." (106) As for those who were honored, they will live eternally[595] in Allah's mercy. (107) Those are Allah's verses which we truly recite to you[MS]. Allah does not desire injustice for mankind. (108)
\*\*\*

Everything in the heavens and the earth is Allah's, and matters return to him. (109)
\*\*\*

You[MP] were the best nation presented to mankind, promoting virtue, preventing vice, and believing in Allah. If the people of the book had believed it would have been better for them. Some of

---

[586] i.e. show discernment, as being given a book is not important, but rather following it. See note at 5:82.
[587] or takes refuge in
[588] See glossary for more details, and notes on 3:51, 6:153, 19:36, 36:61, and 43:64 on what the straight path is.
[589] Tawrah, Proverbs 4:13, Injil, 1 Thessalonians 5:21, Titus 1:9, Hebrews 10:23, Revelation 2:25
[590] Injil, Romans 5:8-11, Ephesians 2:14-18
[591] Tawrah, Daniel 3:26, Amos 4:11, Zechariah 3:2, Injil, Jude 23
[592] or kindness
[593] Here and in verses 110 and 114, or command what is right/kind and forbid what is wrong.
[594] Literally, faces were whitened and faces were blackened
[595] Injil, Matthew 25:46, Mark 10:30, John 5:39, 12:25, Romans 2:7, 5:21

## Chapter 3

them are believers but most are unbelievers. (110) An insult[596] is all the harm they will do to you[MP]. If they fight you[MP], they will flee and not be saved. (111) They are vile wherever they are, except for a rope from Allah and a rope from people,[597] and they remain under Allah's anger.[598] Humiliation was stamped upon them because they disbelieve in Allah's signs and wrongfully murder the prophets in disobedience and hostility. (112) 4A2 They are not alike. Some of the people of the book are an upright nation, reading Allah's verses[599] all night[600] as they bow down. (113) They believe in Allah and the last day, promote virtue, prevent vice, and compete in good deeds. They are righteous. (114) The good they do will not be forgotten.[601] Allah knows those who fear him. (115) The money and the children of the disbelievers will be of no benefit to them with Allah. They are going to hellfire, where they will be eternally. (116) What they spend their money on in this life is like a freezing wind that blew on a field belonging to people who wronged themselves, and it destroyed it. Allah did not wrong them, but they wronged themselves.[602] (117) Believers, do not be close friends[603] to others not among you[MP] who continually

---

[596] The Arabic is more vague and could include harm or injury. Context implies minor harm.

[597] Tawrah, Joshua 2:15, Jeremiah 38:11-12, Injil, Acts 9:25, 2 Corinthians 11:33

[598] Injil, John 3:36

[599] Or signs

[600] Zabur, Psalms 42:8, 63:6, 119:55,148,164

[601] This word is actually the passive of disbelieved, but the underlying root means ungratefulness.

[602] For here and verse 135, the injustice/wickedness, disbelief/ungratefulness, evil, unrighteousness/sin, or lostness of mankind is mentioned in a number of verses in the Qur'an as well as in the previous books. Injustice or wickedness: 2:57, 3:117,135, 4:64,97, 7:160,177, 9:70, 10:44, 11:101, 14:34,45, 16:33,61,118, 29:40, 30:9, 33:72, 34:19, 35:32, 43:76, 65:1, Tawrah, Genesis 6:5, Job 25:4, Injil, Acts 3:26, disbelief or ungratefulness: 14:34, 17:67, 22:66, 42:48, 43:15, 80:17, Injil, Hebrews 3:19, Evil: 12:53, Tawrah, Jeremiah 17:9, Injil, Matthew 15:19, Mark 7:21, unrighteousness or sin: 91:8, Tawrah, 1 Kings 8:46, Ecclesiastes 7:20, Injil, Romans 3:9-19, 5:12, lostness: 103:2, Tawrah, Jeremiah 50:6, Injil, Luke 19:10, Romans 3:23, 6:23

[603] This word actually means an inner vest, but metaphorically, a close friend.

## Chapter 3

impede you<sup>MP604</sup> and want evil for you. Hatred is apparent from their mouths, and their hearts hide even worse. We have made signs clear to you<sup>MP</sup>, if you<sup>MP</sup> could only comprehend. (118)
\*\*\*

You<sup>MP</sup> love them, but they do not love you<sup>MP</sup>.<sup>605</sup> You<sup>MP</sup> believe in all the book, and when they meet you<sup>MP</sup>, they say, "We believe." When they depart, they bite their fingertips against you<sup>MP</sup> in rage. Say<sup>MS</sup>, "Die<sup>MP</sup> in your rage. Allah knows what is in [your] hearts." (119)
\*\*\*

If something good happens to you<sup>MP</sup>, they are displeased, and if something bad, they rejoice.<sup>606</sup> If you<sup>MP</sup> endure<sup>607</sup> and are<sup>MP</sup> reverent, their plots will not harm you<sup>MP</sup> at all. Allah is informed of what they do. (120)
\*\*\*

When you<sup>MS</sup> came in the morning from your<sup>MS</sup> family, you<sup>MS</sup> provide the believers chairs for the battle. Allah hears all and knows all. (121) When two of your<sup>MP</sup> sects were concerned about failing, Allah is their protector. Let the believers trust Allah. (122) Allah saved you<sup>MP</sup> at Badr when you<sup>MP</sup> were humiliated, so fear<sup>MP</sup> Allah that you<sup>MP</sup> may give thanks. (123) If you<sup>MS</sup> tell the believers, "Will it not be enough that your<sup>MP</sup> Lord supplies you<sup>MP</sup> with three thousand angels<sup>608</sup> he sends down?" (124) Yes it will! If you<sup>MP</sup> endure, are<sup>MP</sup> reverent, and they come to you<sup>MP</sup> immediately, your<sup>MP</sup> Lord will provide five thousand angels who are coerced. (125) Allah makes it all good news for you<sup>MP</sup> so that your<sup>MP</sup> hearts would be calm<sup>609</sup> in him. Victory<sup>610</sup> is only from Allah the strong and wise, (126) so that he may cut off one side of the disbelievers or crush them so that they turn back disappointed. (127) You<sup>MS</sup> have nothing to do with the matter. Either he will accept their repentance or torment them. They are wicked. (128) Everything in

---

<sup>604</sup> Injil, 1 Cor 15:33
<sup>605</sup> Zabur, Psalms 109:5
<sup>606</sup> Zabur, Psalms 35:15,26, 40:15
<sup>607</sup> See "endure" in glossary here and in verses 125, 142, 146, 186, and 200.
<sup>608</sup> For "thousands of angels" here and in the next verse, see Tawrah, Daniel 7:10, Zabur, Psalms 68:17, Injil, Matthew 26:53, Revelation 5:11
<sup>609</sup> Zabur, Psalms 107:29, Injil, John 14:27, 16:33, Philippians 4:7
<sup>610</sup> Tawrah, Isaiah 25:8, Injil, 1 Corinthians 15:57, 1 John 5:4

## Chapter 3

the heavens and the earth is Allah's.[611] He forgives whom he wills and torments whom he wills. Allah is forgiving and merciful. (129) Believers, do not get many-fold gains from usury,[612] but fear Allah[613] so that you[MP] may succeed; (130) fear hellfire,[614] which was prepared for the disbelievers; (131) obey Allah and his messenger, that you[MP] may receive mercy. (132) 4A3 Run toward forgiveness from your[MP] Lord and toward a heavenly garden as wide as the heavens and the earth, prepared for the reverent, (133) who give in good times and in bad, who suppress their rage, and who pardon other people. Allah loves those who do good[615] (134) and those who, when they commit promiscuity[616] or wrong themselves, remember[617] Allah and ask forgiveness for their sins.[618] Who forgives sins except Allah?[619] They do not knowingly persist in what they did. (135) Their reward is forgiveness from their Lord and heavenly gardens with flowing rivers underneath. They will live in them eternally.[620] What a wonderful reward for their deeds! (136) Traditions passed away before you[MP], so walk[MP] through the earth and look[MP] at the end of those who deny. (137) This is a clear statement to people, guidance, and an admonition to the reverent. (138) Do not be[MP] weak[621] or grieve;[622] since if you[MP] are believers, you[MP] are the highest.[623] (139) If you[MP] are wounded,[624] people have wounded similarly. We deal out those days with mankind, so Allah can know the believers and make

---

[611] Here and in verses 180 and 189, see Tawrah, Isaiah 45:12, Zabur, Psalms 24:1, 89:11, Injil, Hebrews 1:10.
[612] Tawrah, Exodus 22:24, Leviticus 25:35-37, Deuteronomy 23:20-21, Zabur, Psalms 15:5
[613] For "fear Allah" here and in verse 200, see Tawrah, Deuteronomy 10:12, Isaiah 29:13, Injil, 1 Peter 2:17, Revelation 14:7.
[614] Injil, Matthew 10:28, Luke 12:5, Hebrews 10:31, James 4:12
[615] Zabur, Psalms 45:7, Injil, 2 Corinthians 9:7, Hebrews 1:9
[616] Or lewdness, adultery or abomination
[617] Or, "mention."
[618] Tawrah, 1 Kings 8:35-36, Zabur, Psalms 79:9, Injil, Matthew 6:12, Luke 11:4
[619] Zabur, Psalms 86:5, 103:3, Injil, Mark 2:7, Luke 5:21
[620] Injil, Matthew 25:46, Mark 10:30, John 5:39, 12:25, Romans 2:7, 5:21
[621] Tawrah, 2 Chronicles 15:7, Joshua 1:6-9
[622] Tawrah, Genesis 45:5, Nehemiah 8:11
[623] See 3:55, Tawrah, Deuteronomy 28:13.
[624] The word is used for ulcers today.

## Chapter 3

some witnesses (Allah does not love the wicked)[625] (140) so Allah can test the believers[626] and annihilate[627] the disbelievers. (141) Or do you[MP] suppose that you[MP] will enter the heavenly garden while Allah does not show[628] those among you[MP] who struggled and he knows those who endure? (142) You[MP] desired death before you[MP] met it. You[MP] have seen it as you[MP] look. (143) Muhammad[629] is only[630] a messenger. The messengers passed away before him. So if he dies or is killed, will you[MP] turn on your[MP] heels? Whoever turns on his heels will not hurt Allah at all. Allah will reward those who give thanks.[631] (144) No soul can die without Allah's permission;[632] as a postponed book. We will give rewards in this world to those who want them, and rewards in the hereafter to those who want them. We will reward those who give thanks. (145) How many prophets fought along with myriads of reverent ones and they were not feeble, weak, or abased by what they suffered in Allah's path? Allah loves those who endure.[633] (146) Their statement was only that they said, " Lord, forgive us our sins[634] and our wastefulness in our matter and make our feet firm and save us from a disbelieving people." (147) So Allah gave them rewards in this world and good rewards in the hereafter.[635] Allah loves those who do good.[636] (148) Believers, if you[MP] obey the disbelievers, they will send you[MP] back on your[MP] heels and you[MP]

---

[625] Zabur, Psalms 5:4-5, 11:5, Tawrah, Proverbs 6:16-19

[626] Tawrah, Proverbs 17:3, Jeremiah 9:7, 11:20 Zabur, Psalms 11:5, 17:3, 139:23, Injil, 1 Thessalonians 2:4

[627] Tawrah, Genesis 6:17, 13:10,Deuteronomy 2:21,Zabur, Psalms 9:5, 145:20, Injil, Matthew 10:28

[628] Or know, based on the vowels in the text.

[629] Muhammad (s) is mentioned by name here and in three other verses (33:40, 47:2, and 48:29). In addition, he is often referred to, but he is never to be worshiped; he pointed people to Allah. There is no basis in the Qur'an to call Muslims Mohammedans.

[630] The word "only" should be taken in context of the rest of the Qur'an, where he is called, among other things, a prophet (5:81), a warner and bearer of good news (11:2), a shining lamp (33:46), etc. The Qur'an also uses the word "only" about the Messiah. See note at 5:75.

[631] Tawrah, Ecclesiastes 5:19, Injil, Matthew 5:12, Luke 6:23

[632] Tawrah, Job 1:12, 2:6

[633] Injil, James 1:12, 5:11, Matthew 10:22, 24:13

[634] Injil, Luke 11:4

[635] Injil, Mark 10:30, Luke 18:30, 2 Peter 1:10-11

[636] Zabur, Psalms 45:7, Injil, 2 Corinthians 9:7, Hebrews 1:9

will turn away and be lost. (149) But Allah is your<sup>MP</sup> Lord and he is the best savior.⁶³⁷ (150) We will cast terror into the hearts of the disbelievers because of the gods they worshiped besides Allah, since Allah gave them no authority. Their dwelling is hellfire.⁶³⁸ The wicked have a dreadful dwelling. (151) Allah fulfills his promise to you<sup>MP</sup> when you<sup>MP</sup> destroy them by his permission until you<sup>MP</sup> failed and disputed about the issue and disobeyed after he showed you<sup>MP</sup> what you<sup>MP</sup> love. Some of you<sup>MP</sup> want this world and others want the hereafter. Then he sent you<sup>MP</sup> away from them to afflict you<sup>MP</sup>, and he pardoned you<sup>MP</sup>. Allah is gracious toward the believers. (152) 4A4 You<sup>MP</sup> were going up and not turning back to anyone, as the messenger was calling you<sup>MP</sup> from behind, and he⁶³⁹ afflicted you<sup>MP</sup> with sorrow upon sorrow so you<sup>MP</sup> would not grieve over what you<sup>MP</sup> missed or what happened to you<sup>MP</sup>. Allah is aware of your<sup>MP</sup> deeds. (153)

\*\*\*

Then after the affliction, he made security descend on you<sup>MP</sup> and drowsiness covered some of you<sup>MP</sup>.⁶⁴⁰ Others were worried about themselves, and thinking wrongly and ignorantly about Allah. They said, "What do we have to do with the matter?"⁶⁴¹ Say<sup>MS</sup>, "The whole matter is Allah's." They hide within themselves what they do not reveal to you<sup>MS</sup>. They say, "If we had something to do with the matter, we would not have been killed here." Say<sup>MS</sup>, "Even if you<sup>MP</sup> were in your<sup>MP</sup> houses, those destined to be killed would have shown up on their [death] beds, so that Allah could test what is in your<sup>MP</sup> souls⁶⁴² and purify your hearts. Allah knows what is in the heart." (154)

\*\*\*

Satan made those of you<sup>MP</sup> who turned back on the day the two groups met stumble by part of what they gained. Allah has pardoned them. Allah is forgiving and gentle.⁶⁴³ (155)

\*\*\*

---

⁶³⁷ Tawrah, Isaiah 43:3, 45:21, Hosea 13:4 Zabur, Psalms 106:21, Injil, Luke 1:47, 1 Timothy 2:3, 4:10
⁶³⁸ Tawrah, Deuteronomy 32:22, Matthew 5:22, 18:9, Mark 9:43-47, Revelation 20:15
⁶³⁹ i.e. Allah
⁶⁴⁰ Injil, Matthew 25:5, Mark 13:35,36, 1 Thessalonians 5:6-7
⁶⁴¹ Or command
⁶⁴² or chests or breasts
⁶⁴³ Zabur, Psalms 45:4, 145:17, Injil, Matthew 11:29, Galatians 5:22

## Chapter 3

Believers, do not be like those who disbelieved and told their brothers when they struck out on a journey or were raiders, "If they has been with us, they would not have died or been killed," so that Allah make their hearts regret. Allah gives life and causes death.[644] Allah sees your[MP] deeds. (156)

\*\*\*

If you[MP] die or are killed in Allah's path,[645] there is forgiveness and mercy from Allah better than their booty. (157) If you[MP] die or are killed, you[MP] are gathered to Allah.[646] (158) By Allah's mercy, you[MS] were gentle[647] toward them. If you[MS] had been rude[648] and hard-hearted, they would have dispersed from you[MS]. Pardon[MS] them, ask[MS] forgiveness for them,[649] and consult[MS] them about the matter. If you[MS] are determined, trust[MS] Allah. Allah loves those who trust him.[650] (159) If Allah saves you[MP], none can defeat you[MP].[651] If he deserts[652] you[MP], then who can save you[MP]? Let the believers trust Allah. (160) No prophet should embezzle, and whoever did so will bring what he embezzled on the day of resurrection. Then each will be paid as he deserves, and will not be wronged. (161)

\*\*\*

Is someone who follows Allah's pleasure like one who receives Allah's wrath? His dwelling is hell, a dreadful destiny. (162)

\*\*\*

The others are in differing levels with Allah. Allah sees[653] what they do. (163)

\*\*\*

---

[644] Tawrah, 1 Samuel 2:6, Deuteronomy 32:39
[645] Zabur, Psalms 44:22, Injil, Luke 21:16-17, Romans 14:8, Philippians 1:21, Revelation 6:9
[646] Tawrah, Genesis 25:8,17, 35:29, 49:33, Ecclesiastes 12:7, Injil, Matthew 25:32, John 15:6
[647] or flexible, pliant, lenient or yielding
[648] or coarse. See Injil, Titus 3:2
[649] Tawrah, Exodus 32:32, Daniel 9:5,19, Injil, Luke 6:28, 23:34, Acts 7:60
[650] Tawrah, Proverbs 3:5-6, Jeremiah 17:7, Zabur, Psalms 34:8, 84:12, Injil, John 14:23
[651] Zabur, Psalms 118:6, Injil, Acts 18:10, Romans 8:31,38-39
[652] Tawrah, Numbers 32:15, Ezekiel 29:5, 32:4, Zabur, Psalms 78:60, Injil, Romans 1:24,26,28
[653] Tawrah, 2 Chronicles 16:9, Proverbs 5:21, 15:3, Injil, 1 Peter 3:12

Allah was gracious to the believers by sending them a messenger[654] from among themselves, who recited his verses[655] to them, purified[656] them, and taught them the book and wisdom,[657] though previously, they were clearly astray. (164)

\*\*\*

And when you[MP] are stricken with an affliction while having caused double the amount of affliction, you[MP] say, "How can this be?" Say[MS], "You[MP] brought this on yourselves[MP]. Allah can do anything." (165)

\*\*\*

Allah gave permission for what happened to you[MP] on the day when the two groups met so that he would know the believers (166) and know the hypocrites. It was told them, "Come fight in Allah's path or else, defend."[658] They said, "If we knew of a battle,[659] we would have followed you[MP]." They were closer to disbelief on that day than they were to faith. They say with their mouths what is not in their hearts. Allah knows what they hide. (167) Those who told their brothers and sat by, "If they had obeyed us, they would not have been killed." Say[MS], "Avert death from yourselves, if you[MP] are telling the truth."(168) Never consider[MS] that those who are killed in Allah's path are dead. They are alive and provided for with their Lord, (169) rejoicing at the grace Allah gave them, cheerful for those who have not yet joined them, that no fear should be on them, nor should they grieve. (170)

4B1 They are cheerful for the blessings and grace from Allah, and that Allah does not lose the wages of the believers (171) who responded to Allah and his messenger after they were wounded. Those of them who do good and are reverent have a great reward. (172) Those who were told by others, "People have gathered to you[MP] so fear them," but whose faith increased as a result, said, "Allah is enough for us, and he is a wonderful steward." (173) So they turned back by Allah's blessings and grace. No evil has

---

[654] Tawrah, 2 Chronicles 36:15, Malachi 3:1, Injil, Matthew 11:10, 23:34, Luke 11:49
[655] Or signs. Arabic /ayat/
[656] Tawrah, Malachi 3:3, Zabur, Psalms 19:8, 119:9,140, Injil, Acts 15:8,9,1 Peter 2:2, Titus 2:14, Hebrews 1:3
[657] 3:48, Tawrah, Exodus 31:3, Zabur, Psalms 51:6, Injil, Mark 6:2, 1 Corinthians 2:13
[658] Or pay
[659] Or how to fight

touched them and they followed Allah's pleasure. Allah has great grace. (174) Truly Satan frightens his helpers, so do not fear them but fear me if you[MP] are believers.[660] (175) Do not let those who race to disbelief grieve you[MS]. They will not harm Allah at all. Allah does not want to[661] give them a good portion in the hereafter. They will have great torment. (176) Those who have sold their faith for disbelief will not harm Allah at all. They will have painful torment. (177) Disbelievers must never think that when we give them more time, it is better for them. We give them more time so they will increase their guilt. They will have shameful torment. (178) Allah would not leave the believers in your[MP] state until he distinguishes between evil and good. Allah would not have informed you[MP] of the unseen, but Allah chooses the messengers he wills. So believe in Allah and his messengers. If you[MP] believe and are[MP] reverent, you[MP] will have a great reward. (179)

\*\*\*

Those who are miserly with the grace Allah has given to them must not think that it is good for them. It is evil for them. Their miserliness will be hung around their necks on the day of resurrection. The inheritance of the heavens and the earth is Allah's.[662] Allah is aware of your[MP] deeds. (180)

\*\*\*

Allah has heard those who said, "Allah is poor, and we are rich." We will write down their saying and their wrongful murder of the prophets. We will tell them, "Taste the fire's torment." (181)

\*\*\*

That is for their deeds. Allah does not wrong his servants[663] (182)

\*\*\*

who said, "Allah has covenanted with us not to believe in a messenger until he brings us an offering that fire will burn up."[664] Say[MS], "Messengers before me have come to you[MP] with miracles and with the same thing you[MP] said, so why did you[MP] murder them if you[MP] are telling the truth?" (183)

---

[660] Injil, Matthew 10:28
[661] Or wants to not
[662] Injil, Matthew 25:34, 1 Corinthians 6:9,10
[663] This verse is one of only five verses where the plural form /abid/ is used. All five use the same phrase. This word can also be translated "slaves." The other verses are 8:51, 22:10, 41:46, and 50:29.
[664] Tawrah, 1 Kings 18:22-38, Injil, Luke 9:54

\*\*\*

And if they reject[665] you[MS], the messengers who came before you[MS], bringing miracles, books,[666] and the enlightening book,[667] were also rejected. (184) Every soul will taste death,[668] and you[MP] will be paid your[MP] wages on the day of resurrection. He who is moved away from hellfire and enters the heavenly garden has won. The life of this world is merely an illusion. (185) **4B2** You[MP] will certainly be tested regarding your[MP] money and your[MP] souls and will certainly hear great harm from those previously given the book and from the idolaters. If you[MP] endure and are[MP] reverent, that is a determined matter. (186)

\*\*\*

Allah made a covenant with those who were given the book: show[MP] it clearly to people and not hide[MP] it, but they ignored it behind their backs and sold it for a small price. How dreadful is what they sell it for. (187) Do not think that those who rejoice over what they were given and who love to be praised for what they did not do will escape from torment. They will have painful torment. (188)

\*\*\*

The kingdom of the heavens and the earth is Allah's. Allah can do anything. (189)

\*\*\*

The creation of the heavens and the earth[669] and the difference of night and day are signs to thinkers.[670] (190) They mention[671] Allah while standing and sitting and lying on their sides, and consider the creation of the heavens and the earth. Our Lord, you[MS] have not created this in vain.[672] May you[MS] be glorified! So protect[MS] us from the torment of hellfire. (191) Our Lord, you shamed the one you[MS] caused to enter hellfire. There is no help for the wicked. (192) Our Lord, we have heard one calling us to faith, "Believe in

---

[665] Or call a liar or deny
[666] Or psalms.
[667] See 22:8, 31:20, 35:25. Here and 35:25 refer to the previous books. Zabur, Psalms 119:130, 105, 19:8
[668] Injil, Hebrews 9:27
[669] Here and in verse 191, see Tawrah, Genesis 1:1, Isaiah 42:5, 45:18.
[670] Or having minds or hearts
[671] Or remember, possibly in prayer.
[672] Tawrah, Genesis 1:1, Isaiah 42:5, 45:18

your<sup>MP</sup> Lord." So we believed. Our Lord, forgive us our sins,[673] expiate our bad deeds[674] and let us die with the righteous. (193) Our Lord, bring us what you<sup>MS</sup> promised us through your<sup>MS</sup> messengers and do<sup>MS</sup> not shame us on the day of resurrection. You<sup>MS</sup> do not break your<sup>MS</sup> promises.[675] (194) So their Lord answered them, "I do not lose the work of any of you<sup>MP</sup> workers,[676] whether male or female, some of you or others. I will expiate the bad deeds of those who emigrated and were expelled from their homes and were harmed for my sake, who fought and were killed, and make them enter heavenly gardens with flowing rivers underneath as a reward from Allah. Allah has great rewards. (195) Do not let the fickleness[677] of the disbelievers in the city beguile you<sup>MS</sup>. (196) They have a short time of enjoyment, and then their dwelling is hell, a dreadful resting place. (197) But those who fear their Lord will have heavenly gardens with flowing rivers underneath, lodging there forever in dwellings from Allah. What Allah has for the righteous is good. (198) Some of the people of the book believe in Allah and what was revealed to you<sup>MP</sup> and what was revealed to them, fearing Allah. They do not sell Allah's verses for a small price. They have a reward from their Lord, and Allah is quick in reckoning. (199)

\*\*\*

Believers, endure and strive with each other in endurance and be connected with each other. Fear Allah, so that you<sup>MP</sup> may prosper. (200)[678]

---

[673] Injil, Luke 11:4
[674] For "expiate" here and in verse 195, see Tawrah, Isaiah 27:9, Injil, Romans 3:25, Hebrews 2:17, 1 John 2:2, 4:10
[675] Tawrah, Numbers 23:19, Injil, Hebrews 6:18
[676] Injil, 2 Timothy 1:12, Romans 2:6-16.
[677] Or movement
[678] The verses in this chapter that rhyme are put together in paragraphs, separated by \*\*\*.

Chapter 4

# Chapter 4: Al-Nisa'[679]

**4B3** In the name of Allah, the most gracious and merciful.[680] People, fear your[MP] Lord who created you[MP] from one soul, then from that created its spouse[681] and from them[D] brought forth many men and women. Fear Allah,[682] by whom you[MP] ask each other, as well as those who bore you.[683] Allah watches over you[MP]. (1) Give the orphans their money and do not trade bad for good, nor take[684] their money as your[MP] money.[685] That is a great travesty. (2)
\*\*\*

If you[MP] fear that you[MP] will not be just toward the orphans, marry the women you[MP] think best, a pair or three or four. But if you[MP] fear you[MP] will not be just to them,[686] then just one, or the slave girls you[MP] own. This is better to avoid oppression.[687] (3)
\*\*\*

Give women their[FP] bride-price as a gift. If they[FP] freely give you[MP] back any of it, take[MP] it as a blessing and health to you[MP]. (4) Do not give[MP] fools[MP] the money Allah gave you[MP] for your[MP] livelihood. Rather, provide[MP] for them[MP] with it, clothe[MP] them[MP], and speak[MP] kindly to them. (5) Test[MP] the orphans until they[MP] reach marriage. If you[MP] sense they are mature, pay[MP] them their[MP] money. Do not spend[MP] it wastefully or hastily before they grow up. The rich should refrain from doing anything wrong. The poor should spend it kindly.[688] If you[MP] pay them their money, do[MP] it in front of witnesses. Allah is a suffecient reckoner. (6) Both men and women have shares in what their parents and relatives leave behind,

---

[679] women
[680] Zabur, Psalms 103:8, 145:8. See glossary for more details.
[681] Tawrah, Genesis 2:7,21,22
[682] For "fear Allah" here and in verses 9 and 131, see Tawrah, Deuteronomy 10:12, Isaiah 29:13, Injil, 1 Peter 2:17, Revelation 14:7.
[683] Or "the wombs" See Injil, Luke 11:27
[684] Literally, eat, here and in verses 4 and 10 (twice).
[685] For orphans here and in verses 3, 6, 8, and 10, see Tawrah, Job 29:12, Zabur, Psalms 82:3, Injil, James 1:27
[686] In verse 129, the Qur'an says that being just is impossible with multiple wives.
[687] The word can also mean having a large family or deviating (for the right path).
[688] The meaning her may be, let the rich be trustees without taking payment, and let the poor take the fees from the orphan's money.

## Chapter 4

whether little or much. It is a mandatory share. (7) If the distribution is attended by relatives, orphans, and the needy, provide for them with it, and speak[MP] kindly to them. (8) Let those who have weak[689] descendants for whom they fear beware. Let them fear Allah and speak appropriately. (9) Those who wickedly take orphans' money shall take fire into their bellies and be roasted in a burning fire. (10) This is what Allah commands concerning your[MP] children:[690] Each son shall inherit[691] as much as two daughters. If there are more than two women, they shall have two-thirds of what he left. If there is only one, then she inherits half. His parents shall each get one-sixth if he has a son. If he does not have a son and his parents inherit from him, his mother shall get a third. But if he has brothers, his mother shall get a sixth after deducting bequests and debts. You[MP] do not know whether your[MP] parents or your[MP] children will be closer and more beneficial to you[MP]. This is Allah's ordinance. Allah is all-knowing[692] and wise.[693] (11) **4B4**

\*\*\*

You[MP] are entitled to half of what your[MP] wives leave if they[FP] do not have a son. If they[FP] have a son, you[MP] inherit a quarter of what they[FP] left behind after deducting bequests and debts. They[FP] get a quarter of what you[MP] leave behind if they[FP] do not have a son. If you[MP] have a son, they[FP] get an eighth of what you[MP] left behind after deducting bequests and debts. If a man or a woman inherits from a distant relative,[694] and there is a brother or sister, they[D] will each get a sixth. If there are more than that, they[MP] shall share a third, after deducting bequests and debts, without harming [anyone];[695] it is Allah's commandment. Allah is all-knowing and

---

[689] Mentally incompetent.

[690] Or sons, here twice and in verses 75, 98, and 127.

[691] Throughout this chapter, for inheritance laws, see Tawrah, Leviticus 27:8-11

[692] For "all-knowing" here and in verses 12, 17, 24, 26, 35,63, 70, 92, 104, 111, 147, 148, and 170, see Tawrah, Job 37:16, Isaiah 40:14, Zabur, Psalms 33:13-15, Injil, 1 John 3:20.

[693] For "wise" here and in verses 17, 24, 26, 56, 92, 104, 111, 130, 158, 165, and 170, see Tawrah, Job 9:4, Proverbs 2:6, Jeremiah 9:23-24, Injil, 1 Corinthians 1:21-25, Romans 16:27.

[694] Here and in verse 176, possibly, people with no children whose parents have died.

[695] "Not harmful" is accusative masculine, and does not modify either debt (genitive masculine) or bequest (genitive feminine).

## Chapter 4

gentle.⁶⁹⁶ (12) These are Allah's limits. Allah will cause him who obeys Allah and his messenger to enter heavenly gardens⁶⁹⁷ with flowing rivers⁶⁹⁸ underneath where they will remain forever. That is the great victory.⁶⁹⁹ (13) If anyone disobeys Allah and his messenger and transgresses his limits, Allah will make him enter hellfire forever, and he will have shameful torment.⁷⁰⁰ (14)

\*\*\*

As for your^MP women⁷⁰¹ who commit promiscuity,⁷⁰² bring four of you^MP as witnesses against them^FP. If they witness [against them], keep them^FP in their houses until they^FP die⁷⁰³ or Allah provides a way [out] for them^FP. (15) As for the two^MD⁷⁰⁴ who commit it,⁷⁰⁵ harm^MP them^D, and if they^D repent and make^D amends, turn away^MP from them^D. Allah will accept repentance and is merciful.⁷⁰⁶ (16) Allah is obliged to accept the repentance of those who unknowingly do evil and then repent soon.⁷⁰⁷ Allah will accept their repentance. Allah is all-knowing and wise. (17) Repentance is not for those who do bad deeds, and saying when approaching death,⁷⁰⁸ "Now I repent." Nor is it for those who die in their disbelief. We have prepared painful torment for them. (18) Believers, it is not lawful for you^MP to inherit women⁷⁰⁹ against

---

⁶⁹⁶ Zabur, Psalms 45:4, 145:17, Injil, Matthew 11:29, Galatians 5:22

⁶⁹⁷ Arabic /jannah/ here and in verses 57 and 122. See glossary for more details.

⁶⁹⁸ Here and in verses 57 and 122, see Injil, Revelation 22:1-2, Tawrah, Ezekiel 47:12.

⁶⁹⁹ Tawrah, Isaiah 25:8, Injil, 1 Corinthians 15:57, 1 John 5:4

⁷⁰⁰ For "torment" here and in verses 18, 25, 37, 56, 93, 102, 138, 147, 151, 161, and 173, see Tawrah, Isaiah 50:11, Injil, Matthew 18:34, 25:41,46, Luke 16:23-28, Revelation 20:15.

⁷⁰¹ or wives

⁷⁰² Or lewdness, adultery or abomination, here and in verses 19, 22, and 25.

⁷⁰³ See Tawrah, 2 Samuel 13:1-20.

⁷⁰⁴ The Arabic dual is used also for one man and one woman, so this could be the meaning as well.

⁷⁰⁵ I.e. promiscuity, as in the previous verse. In this case, the meaning is probably homosexuality.

⁷⁰⁶ Here and in verses 23, 25, 29, 64, 96, 99, 100, 106, 110, 129, and 152, see glossary for more details on "merciful."

⁷⁰⁷ Tawrah, Numbers 15:28-30

⁷⁰⁸ Injil, Hebrews 12:17

⁷⁰⁹ Either widows as property or inheriting from women.

## Chapter 4

their will. Do<sup>MP</sup> not make it difficult[710] for them<sup>FP</sup> so you<sup>MP</sup> can cheat them<sup>FP</sup> out of part of what you<sup>MP</sup> gave them<sup>FP</sup>, except if they<sup>FP</sup> commit promiscuity openly. Live<sup>MP</sup> with them<sup>FP</sup> kindly. If you<sup>MP</sup> hate them<sup>FP</sup>, you might hate something that Allah will make very good. (19) If you<sup>MP</sup> want to trade one wife for another, though you<sup>MP</sup> have given the first a huge bride price, do not take <sup>MP</sup>any of it back. Would you<sup>MP</sup> take it back scandalously and with clear guilt? (20) How could you<sup>MP</sup> take it back when you<sup>MP</sup> have been intimate[711] with each other and they<sup>FP</sup> have made a solemn covenant with you<sup>MP</sup>? (21) From now on, do not marry<sup>MP</sup> women your fathers have married. It is promiscuity, hateful, and a bad path. (22) It is forbidden for you<sup>MP</sup> [to marry[712]] your<sup>MP</sup> mothers,[713] daughters, sisters,[714] paternal and maternal aunts,[715] daughters of your brothers or sisters, wet nurses who nursed you and girls they have nursed, mothers-in-law,[716] step-daughters in your care if you<sup>MP</sup> have consumated marriage with their mothers (if you<sup>MP</sup> have not consumated the marriage, they are allowed), and daughters-in-law if they are married to your<sup>MP</sup> biological sons.[717] Do not marry sisters[718] from now on - Allah is forgiving[719] and merciful - (23) 5A1 nor married women,[720] except if they are your<sup>MP</sup> slaves. That is Allah's command to you. Besides that, you<sup>MP</sup> are permitted to use your<sup>MP</sup> money to get married<sup>MP</sup> rather than having<sup>MP</sup> sex with a prostitute.[721] Give the wives their<sup>FP</sup> wages[722] for what you<sup>MP</sup> have enjoyed with them<sup>FP</sup>. This is a regulation. Anything that you<sup>MP</sup> agree upon after the regulation is allowed. Allah is all-knowing and wise. (24)

---

[710] Either by mistreating them so they renounce their bride-price or by making it hard for them to re-marry.
[711] i.e. had sex. Literally, come into each other
[712] Or have sex with
[713] Tawrah, Leviticus 18:7
[714] Tawrah, Leviticus 18:9,11
[715] Tawrah, Leviticus 18:12, 13
[716] Tawrah, Leviticus 18:17
[717] Tawrah, Leviticus 18:15
[718] Tawrah, Leviticus 18:18
[719] For "forgiving" here and in verses 25, 43, 96, 100, 106, 110, 129, and 152, see Zabur, Psalms 103:3, 130:4, Tawrah, Isaiah 43:25, Exodus 34:7, Injil, Acts 26:18.
[720] Leviticus 18:20
[721] the word includes fornication
[722] Here and in verse 25, the meaning may be "bride price."

## Chapter 4

\*\*\*

Those of you<sup>MP</sup> who are not able to marry believing<sup>FP</sup> wives [should marry] believing<sup>FP</sup> slave girls you<sup>MP</sup> own. Allah knows your<sup>MP</sup> faith, one and the other, so marry them<sup>FP</sup> with the permission of their<sup>FP</sup> families and give them<sup>FP</sup> their<sup>FP</sup> wages kindly, as wives, and not as prostitutes or mistresses. When they<sup>FP</sup> are married, if they<sup>FP</sup> commit promiscuity, they<sup>FP</sup> will get half the torment of married [free] women. This is for those of you<sup>MP</sup> who fear hardship.[723] But enduring is better for you<sup>MP</sup>.[724] Allah is forgiving and merciful. (25) Allah wants to show you<sup>MP</sup> and guide you<sup>MP</sup> by the traditions of those before you<sup>MP</sup>,[725] and to accept your<sup>MP</sup> repentance. Allah is all-knowing and wise. (26)

\*\*\*

Allah wants to accept your<sup>MP</sup> repentance, but those who want to follow their passions veer far from the path. (27) Allah wants to lighten matters for you<sup>MP</sup>, and man was created weak. (28) Believers, do not waste your<sup>MP</sup> money, except if it is voluntary business, and do not kill yourselves.[726] Allah is merciful to you<sup>MP</sup>. (29) We will roast in hellfire whoever does such things in enmity and wickedness. That is easy for Allah. (30) If you<sup>MP</sup> avoid the serious sins you<sup>MP</sup> have been warned not to do, we will expiate your<sup>MP</sup> bad deeds[727] from you<sup>MP</sup> and give you<sup>MP</sup> a generous entry.[728] (31) Do not covet what Allah has given one over another.[729] Men and women both have a portion of what they have earned. Ask Allah by his grace. Allah knows everything. (32) For everything left behind by parents and relatives we have appointed heirs.[730] As for you who have sworn a contract, give them their portion. Allah is witness of everything. (33) Men are guardians[731] of women, with what Allah has preferred some of them over others with, and as they donated their money. Righteous women are devout and

---

[723] i.e. in controlling your passions. See Injil, 1 Corinthians 7:9
[724] 1 Corinthians 7:6
[725] Here the reference is to the former books, especially Tawrah, Leviticus 18 and Injil, 1 Corinthians 7.
[726] Or, "each other." The reference also might be to suicide.
[727] Tawrah, Isaiah 27:9, Injil, Romans 3:25, Hebrews 2:17, 1 John 2:2, 4:10
[728] Injil, 2 Peter 1:11
[729] Or preferred. Tawrah, Exodus 20:17
[730] Or possibly executors
[731] or directors

## Chapter 4

protect what is unseen as Allah protects it. Admonish those<sup>FP</sup> you<sup>MP</sup> fear will cheat,<sup>732</sup> then desert<sup>MP</sup> them on their<sup>FP</sup> beds, and then leave<sup>MP</sup> them<sup>FP</sup>.<sup>733</sup> If they<sup>FP</sup> obey you<sup>MP</sup>, do not wish for a way against them<sup>FP</sup>. Allah is most high and great. (34) If you<sup>MP</sup> fear a split between them<sup>D</sup>, send an arbiter from his family and an arbiter from her family. If they<sup>D</sup> want to reconcile, Allah will make them<sup>D</sup> agree. Allah is all-knowing and aware. (35) **5A2** Worship<sup>MP</sup> Allah and do not worship<sup>MP</sup> any other god<sup>734</sup> beside him. Do good to your parents,<sup>735</sup> your relatives, orphans,<sup>736</sup> the needy, neighboring relatives, neighbors who are strangers, close friends, travelers, and your<sup>MP</sup> slaves.<sup>737</sup> Allah does not love the proud and boastful,<sup>738</sup> (36) those who are miserly, and who command others to be miserly, who hide what Allah has given them out of his grace. We have prepared shameful torment for disbelievers (37) and those who donate their money to be seen by people<sup>739</sup> and do not believe in Allah or the last day. Satan is a bad partner to have. (38) What harm is it to them if they believe in Allah and the last day and donate out of what Allah has provided them? Allah knows about them. (39) Allah does not cheat by so much as a speck. If it is a good deed, he himself multiplies it and gives a great reward. (40) What if we brought a witness from every nation, and we brought you<sup>MS</sup> against them as a witness? (41) On that day, disbelievers who disobeyed the messenger will wish that the earth would flatten them.<sup>740</sup> They do not conceal a saying from Allah. (42) Believers, do not go near prayers when you<sup>MP</sup> are drunk,<sup>741</sup> until you<sup>MP</sup> know what you<sup>MP</sup> are saying, nor when ritually unclean until

---

[732] See 4:128, where the same word is used of men.
[733] Most translations translate the word /daraba/ as "beat." Other meanings according to context, including "propound/tell" 59:21, 36:78, 39:27 (a parable), and "travel" 2:273, 4:101, 20:77, 38:44 (the English phrase "hit the road" is an example of a parallel meaning). "Cover" is a probable meaning in 18:11. The Message translation renders this, "separate from them," and the Reformist translation does similarly.
[734] Arabic /ilah/ here and in verses 87 and 171. See glossary for more details.
[735] Tawrah, Exodus 20:12
[736] Tawrah, Job 29:12, Zabur, Psalms 82:3, Injil, James 1:27
[737] Tawrah, Deuteronomy 26:12-13.
[738] Zabur, Psalms 5:4-5, 11:5, Tawrah, Proverbs 6:16-19
[739] Injil, Matthew 6:1-4
[740] Injil, Revelation 6:16
[741] Tawrah, Ezekiel 44:21

## Chapter 4

you have washed, unless you are traveling. If you<sup>MP</sup> are sick or traveling or have gone to the bathroom[742] or have had sex with women and do not find water, wash with pure sand and wipe your faces and hands. Allah is pardoning and forgiving. (43)

\*\*\*

Have you<sup>MS</sup> not seen that those who were given a portion of the book buy error? They want you<sup>MP</sup> to go astray from the path. (44)

\*\*\*

Allah knows your<sup>MP</sup> enemies well, and Allah is a sufficient protector. He is a sufficient savior. (45) Some Jews[743] distort the sense of words out of their context[744] and say: "We heard and disobeyed; hear<sup>MS</sup> without being heard and pay attention to us."[745] They twist with their tongues and slander religion. If they had said: "We heard and obeyed; hear<sup>MS</sup> and look at[746] us," it would have been better and more upright for them. Allah has damned them for their disbelief, for few of them believe. (46) You<sup>MP</sup> who received the book, believe<sup>MP</sup> in what we have revealed, confirming[747] what you<sup>MP</sup> have, before we obliterate faces and turn them backwards, or damn them[748] as we damned the people of the sabbath,[749] and Allah's command is done. (47) Allah does not

---

[742] i.e. have defecated

[743] Or those who repented and turned back to the truth. The meaning is the Jews, probably when they repented after worshiping the golden calf idol (2:54, 92, 7:138, 148-150, Tawrah, Exodus 32).

[744] There are two types of "distortion:" altering the text and altering the meaning. From the words "heard" and "take out of their context," it is clear that altering the meaning is intended. In this context especially, the following verse says that the Qur'an confirms the book that the people of the book had received, so altering the text is not intended. See 2:75, 3:78, 5:13,41 for the other verses that deal with this subject. Injil, 2 Peter 3:16.

[745] There is a word play that these Jews were making here. The Arabic word /ra'ina/ means "pay attention to us," "care for us," or "our shepherd." The Hebrew word /ra'ina/ with a similar pronunciation meant "our evil one."

[746] Or have patience with

[747] The Qur'an confirms the previous books many times (2:41,89,91,97,101, 3:3,81, 4:47, 5:48, 6:92, 35:31, 46:12,30). Here it specifically states that what they had in the days of the Qur'an was confirmed as correct by the Qur'an.

[748] refers to people, not the faces.

[749] Tawrah, Exodus 20:8-11, 31:13; Isaiah 56:6,7, 58:13,14, 66:22,23; Ezekiel 20:20, Injil, Mathew 12:8-10, 24:20; Mark 2:27; Luke 4:16, 23:56, Acts 17:1-2, 18:4

forgive those who believe in other gods, but he forgives those he wills for sins less serious than that. He who believes in other gods has invented serious guilt. (48) Do you[MS] not see those who purify themselves? Allah purifies those he wills,[750] and they will not be wronged at all. (49) See[MS] how they invent lies about Allah? That is clearly a sin. (50) Have you[MS] not seen those who were given a portion of the book believing in idols and false gods?[751] They say of disbelievers, "They are more rightly guided than the believers." (51) Those are the ones Allah has damned, and you[MS] will find no savior for those Allah damns.[752] (52) Or do they share the kingdom? They do not give people anything. (53) Or do they envy people because of Allah's gifts to them by his grace? We gave the family of Ibrahim[753] the book and wisdom and we gave them a great kingdom.[754] (54) Some of them believe in it, and others block it.[755] Hell is a sufficient burning fire for them. (55) We will roast those who disbelieve in our signs[756] in hellfire. As soon as their skins mature, we will exchange them with other skins so that they taste torment. Allah is strong and wise. (56) We will make those who believe and do righteous deeds[757] enter heavenly gardens with flowing rivers underneath. They will be in it forever and ever. In them they will have purified kinds[758] and we will bring them into the deep shade. (57) **5A3** Allah commands you[MP]

---

[750] Tawrah, Malachi 3:3, Zabur, Psalms 19:8, 119:9,140, Injil, Acts 15:8,9,1 Peter 2:2, Titus 2:14, Hebrews 1:3
[751] Arabic /Al-Taghut/ here and in verses 60 and 76. See glossary for more details.
[752] Tawrah, Isaiah 43:11, Hosea 13:4, Injil, Hebrews 10:26
[753] Abraham here and twice in verse 125. See glossary for more details. His "family" would include all the prophets who received or wrote down books.
[754] See for example Tawrah, 1 Kings 2:12. He who received the 'great kingdom" (Sulayman) was also he who wrote Proverbs in the Tawrah, probably called "wisdom" in the Qur'an (here and in 3:48, et al.)
[755] Here and in verses 160 and 167, see Injil, Matthew 23:13, Luke 11:52.
[756] Arabic /ayat/ here and in verses 140 and 155. See glossary for more details.
[757] Injil, 1 Corinthians 3:8, James 2:14-17, Revelation 19:8
[758] This word is used often in the context of gardens. 20:53,131, 22:5, 26:7, 36:36, 38:58, 43:12, and 50:7 show that the meaning is probably kinds [of fruit or other plants]. Other translations have "spouses" which would be possible in different contexts, but the adjective "purified" is used for inanimate objects, not people.

## Chapter 4

to restore pledges to their owners,[759] and if you[MP] judge between people, to judge justly. Allah admonishes you[MP] well. Allah hears all and sees all.[760] (58) Believers, obey Allah and obey the messenger and your[MP] rulers.[761] If you[MP] dispute about anything, take[MP] it to Allah and the messenger, if you[MP] believe in Allah and the last day. That is better, and a better explanation. (59) Have you[MS] not seen those who claim they believe in what was revealed to you[MS] and what was revealed before you[MS]? They want to be ruled by false gods and they were commanded to disbelieve in them. Satan wants to lead them far astray. (60) When they are told: "Come to what Allah revealed and to the messenger," you[MS] see the hypocrites blocking them from you[MS]. (61) What if they have a disaster because of what they did, and they come to you[MS] swearing by Allah, "We wanted only goodness and success." (62) Allah knows what is in their hearts, so turn aside[MS] from them and admonish them, and say[MS] an eloquent saying to them about themselves. (63) Every messenger we sent was to be obeyed by Allah's permission. If they had come to you[MS] when they had wronged themselves[762] and asked Allah's forgiveness, and the messenger had asked for their forgiveness,[763] they would have found that Allah accepts repentance[764] and is merciful. (64) No, by your[MS] Lord, they will not believe until they ask for your[MS] judgment regarding their controversy. Then they will find no wrong in your[MS] judgment, and they will surrender. (65) If we had written for them, "Kill yourselves,"[765] or "Leave[MP] your[MP] homes,"

---

[759] Tawrah, Exodus 22:26
[760] Injil, Matthew 6:4,15,18
[761] Injil, Romans 13:1-5
[762] For here and verse 97, the injustice/wickedness, disbelief/ungratefulness, evil, unrighteousness/sin, or lostness of mankind is mentioned in a number of verses in the Qur'an as well as in the previous books. Injustice or wickedness: 2:57, 3:117,135, 4:64,97, 7:160,177, 9:70, 10:44, 11:101, 14:34,45, 16:33,61,118, 29:40, 30:9, 33:72, 34:19, 35:32, 43:76, 65:1, Tawrah, Genesis 6:5, Job 25:4, Injil, Acts 3:26, disbelief or ungratefulness: 14:34, 17:67, 22:66, 42:48, 43:15, 80:17, Injil, Hebrews 3:19, Evil: 12:53, Tawrah, Jeremiah 17:9, Injil, Matthew 15:19, Mark 7:21, unrighteousness or sin: 91:8, Tawrah, 1 Kings 8:46, Ecclesiastes 7:20, Injil, Romans 3:9-19, 5:12, lostness: 103:2, Tawrah, Jeremiah 50:6, Injil, Luke 19:10, Romans 3:23, 6:23
[763] Tawrah, Job 42:7-9.
[764] For "repentance," see glossary.
[765] Or each other

## Chapter 4

only a few of them would have done it. If they had done what they were admonished to do, it would have been better and firmer for them. (66) Thus we would have given them a great reward from us (67) and guided them on a straight path.[766] (68) Those who obey Allah and his messenger are with those whom Allah has blessed – the prophets, the righteous, martyrs, and the good. Those are good companions.[767] (69) That is Allah's grace. Allah is totally[768] all-knowing. (70) Believers, be careful and go out in groups or all together. (71) One of you[MP] will certainly delay, so if a catastrophe happens to you[MP], he will say, "Allah has blessed me, because I was not a witness[769] with them." (72) If you[MP] receive Allah's grace, he will say, as if there is no love between you[MP] and him, "I wish I had been with them, so I could [also] be greatly victorious." (73) 5A4 So let those who sell the hereafter for this life fight in Allah's path. We will greatly reward those who fight in Allah's path, whether they are killed or victorious. (74) Why do you[MP] not fight in Allah's path, since the weak men and women and children say, "Our Lord, get us out of this village whose people are wicked and give us a helper from yourself[MS]. Give us a savior from yourself[MS]. (75) The believers fight in Allah's path, and the disbelievers fight in the path of false gods. So fight Satan's helpers. Satan's trap is weak. (76) Have you[MS] not seen those who were told, "Keep your[MP] hands back, perform the prayers, and pay the poor-tax." When they were appointed to fight, a group of them feared men at least as much as they feared Allah,[770] and said, "Our Lord, why did you[MS] appoint us to fight? Could you[MS] not postpone it until a bit later?" Say[MS], "The pleasures of the world are few, and the hereafter is better for those who are reverent. You[MP] will not be wronged at all. (77), Death will reach you[MP] wherever you[MP] are, even in a high tower." If goodness happens to them, they say, "This is from Allah," and if something bad happens to them, they say, "This is from you[MS]." Say[MS], "Everything is from Allah." What is wrong with those people? They barely understand a saying. (78)

---

[766] See glossary for more details, and notes on 3:51, 6:153, 19:36, 36:61, and 43:64 on what the straight path is.

[767] See Injil, 1 Corinthians 15:33

[768] Or sufficiently

[769] In modern Arabic, this word has come to mean "martyr" in a religious or political sense, but the original meaning was "witness." See 4:159, 5:117.

[770] Injil, John 12:42-43, Tawrah, Proverbs 29:25

# Chapter 4

The goodness that happens to you<sup>MS</sup> is from Allah, and the bad that happens to you<sup>MS</sup> is from yourself<sup>MS</sup>.[771] We sent you<sup>MS</sup> as a messenger to people, and Allah is a sufficent witness. (79) Whoever obeys the messenger obeys Allah, and we have not sent you<sup>MS</sup> to watch over those who turn away. (80) They say, "We will obey." And if they go forth from you<sup>MS</sup>, a group of them plots against your<sup>MS</sup> saying. Allah records what they plot, so turn away from them and trust Allah. Allah is a sufficent attorney.[772] (81) Do they not reflect on the Qur'an?[773] If it were not from Allah, they would have found many differences. (82) If a matter of safety or fear comes to them, they broadcast it. If they had sent it back to the messenger or those responsible among them, those who discover the truth among them would have known it. If not for Allah's grace and mercy to you<sup>MP</sup>, most of you<sup>MP</sup> would have followed Satan. (83) Fight<sup>MS</sup> in Allah's path. Do not compel<sup>MS</sup> anyone but yourself<sup>MS</sup>. Urge<sup>MS</sup> the believers. Allah may stop the vengeance of the disbelievers. Allah is more vengeful and punishing.[774] (84) He who intercedes well for it will have a portion of it, and he who intercedes badly it will have a share of it. Allah will nourish everything. (85) If you<sup>MP</sup> are greeted, greet<sup>MP</sup> them back with a better greeting, or return<sup>MP</sup> the same one. Allah reckons everything. (86) Allah is the only god. He will certainly gather you<sup>MP</sup> at the day of resurrection.[775] There is no doubt about it. Whose sayings are truer than Allah's? (87) **5B1** Why are you<sup>MP</sup> divided into two groups regarding the hypocrites? Allah has overturned them by what they gained. Do you<sup>MP</sup> want to guide those Allah has misled? You<sup>MS</sup> will not find a way with those Allah misleads.[776] (88) They wished you<sup>MP</sup> disbelieved as they do, so

---

[771] The belief that all prophets and messengers are sinless is not supported by the Qur'an. For instances of prophets or messengers asking forgiveness or committing sins, see 7:23, 20:121 (Adam), 11:47, 71:28 (Nuh), 26:82, 14:41 (Ibrahim), 28:15-16 (Musa), 7:151, 20:93 (Musa and Harun), 38:24 (Dawud), 38:32,35 (Sulayman), 21:87, 37:142 (Yunus), 48:2, 47:19, 40:55, 4:79, 106, 9:43, 13:30, 80:1-2, 110:3, 94:2, 23:118, 66:1, 33:37, 8:67, and 9:117 (Muhammad (s).

[772] Or "sufficiently trustworthy."

[773] Or recitation. See glossary for more details.

[774] Injil, Hebrews 12:29, Romans 12:19

[775] Here and in verses 140 and 172, see Tawrah, Joel 3:11-14, Zephaniah 3:8, Injil, Matthew 25:32, John 15:6, Revelation 16:16.

[776] Here and in verse 143, see Injil, 2 Thessalonians 2:11, 2 Samuel 22:27, Tawrah, 1 Kings 22:20-23, Ezekiel 14:9.

you^MP would be alike. Do not take^MP any of them as helpers until they emigrate in Allah's path. If they turn away, take^MP them and kill^MP them wherever you^MP find them.[777] Do not take them as helpers or saviors, (89) except for those who get to people with whom you^MP have a covenant, or if they come to you^MP and their hearts are besieged from their fighting you^MP or fighting their people. If Allah had willed, he would have put them in authority over you and they would have fought you. Allah has not permitted you to fight in any way those who isolate themselves from you^MP, do not fight you^MP and offer you^MP peace. (90) You will find others who want themselves and their people to be safe from you^MP. Whenever they return to strife they are overthrown by it. If they do not isolate themselves from you^MP, offer^MP you^MP peace, and restrain^MP their hands, then take them and kill them wherever you^MP discover them. We have given you^MP clear authority over them.[778] (91) A believer should not kill another believer, except by accident. Whoever kills a believer by accident must free a believing slave as a fine surrendered to the family, unless they forego it. If the believer was from people that are enemies of yours^MP, then the penalty is freeing a believing slave. If he was from people you^MP have a treaty with, then pay a fine to his family and freeing a believing slave. Whoever cannot do this must fast two consecutive months as repentance given by Allah. Allah is all-knowing and wise. (92) He who kills a believer intentionally will be punished in hell forever. Allah is angry with him and has damned him and prepared great torment for him. (93) Believers, if you^MP march in Allah's path, use^MP discernment and do not say^M' to him who gives greetings of peace to you^MP, "You^MS are not a believer." You^MP want the world's goods,[779] but Allah has much plunder. Thus you^MP were beforehand, but Allah blessed you^MP. Discern^MP that Allah is aware of your^M' deeds. (94) Believers who sit idle, except for the handicapped, are not equal to those who

---

[777] The Qur'an has four verses that command killing others (2:191, 4:89, 91, and 9:5), but none of these apply today. Similarly, the Tawrah has many verses that refer to killing others (Exodus 23:23-24,28-30, 32:27, Numbers 21:35, 31:2,7-8,17, Deuteronomy 7:2,16, 9:3-4, Joshua 6:17-21, 8:2, Judges 21:11, 1 Samuel 15:3, 27:9,11, 2 Chronicles 15:13) and none of them apply today either.
[778] Notice in this passage also that the believers are forbidden to initiate attacks, but are allowed to defend themselves. Tawrah, Esther 8:11.
[779] Injil, 1 Timothy 6:10

## Chapter 4

struggle in Allah's path with their money and themselves. Allah ranks those who struggle with their money and themselves a grade above the idlers. Allah has promised good to each of them, but Allah prefers the strugglers over the idlers by a great reward: (95) rank with him, forgiveness, and mercy. Allah is forgiving and merciful. (96) Those the angels cause to die wronged themselves. They said, "What were you like?" They said, "We were weak on the earth." They said, "Was the earth not wide enough so you$^{MP}$ could emigrate in it? Their home will be hell, an awful destiny. (97) The exception is the weak[780] men, the women, and children who cannot plan and be guided on the way. (98) Allah may pardon them. Allah is pardoning and merciful. (99) **5B2** He who emigrates in Allah's path will find much refuge and room on the earth. He who leaves his house, emigrates to Allah and his messenger, and then dies will have his reward from Allah. Allah is forgiving and merciful. (100) If you$^{MP}$ march in the land, it is not wrong to shorten prayers if you$^{MP}$ fear that disbelievers will attack you$^{MP}$. Disbelievers are a clear enemy to you$^{MP}$. (101) If you$^{MS}$ are among them and perform$^{MS}$ prayers for them, let a group of them stand with you$^{MS}$, and let them take their weapons. When they bow down, let them be behind you$^{MP}$, and let another group that has not prayed come and pray with you$^{MS}$. Let them be careful and take their weapons. Disbelievers want you$^{MP}$ to be unaware of their weapons and their equipment so they can turn against you$^{MP}$ at once. It is not wrong for you$^{MP}$ to take off your weapons if you are harmed by rain or sickness, but beware. Allah has prepared shameful torment for disbelievers. (102) When you$^{MP}$ finish performing the prayer, remember$^{MP}$ Allah, when standing, sitting, and on your$^{MP}$ sides. If you$^{MP}$ feel secure, perform$^{MP}$ the prayers. Performing prayers is an obligation to believers at specific times. (103) Do not be$^{MP}$ slack in pursuing the people if you$^{MP}$ are in pain. They are in pain like you$^{MP}$ are, and you$^{MP}$ hope from Allah and they do not. Allah is all-knowing and wise. (104) We revealed the book to you$^{MS}$ in truth so that you$^{MS}$ can judge between people based on what Allah has shown you$^{MS}$. Do not be$^{MS}$ an advocate of traitors, (105) and ask$^{MS}$ forgiveness[781] from Allah. Allah is

---

[780] Or incompetent
[781] The belief that all prophets and messengers are sinless is not supported by the Qur'an. For instances of prophets or messengers asking forgiveness or committing sins, see 7:23, 20:121 (Adam), 11:47, 71:28 (Nuh), 26:82, 14:41 (Ibrahim), 28:15-16 (Musa), 7:151, 20:93 (Musa and

## Chapter 4

forgiving and merciful. (106) Do not argue about those who betray themselves. Allah does not love guilty traitors.[782] (107) They hide from people but they cannot hide from Allah. He is with them when they plot sayings that are not pleasing. Allah knows what they do. (108) You[MP] argued with them about this life. Who will argue with Allah about them on the day of resurrection,[783] or who will be responsible for them? (109) Whoever does evil or wrongs himself, and then asks Allah's forgiveness will find Allah forgiving and merciful. (110) If anyone becomes guilty, it is against his own soul, and Allah is all-knowing and wise. (111) Whoever is at fault or guilty and then blames an innocent person has committed slander and is clearly guilty. (112) If not for Allah's grace and mercy to you[MS], a group of them would have tried to mislead you[MS]. They mislead only themselves, and they do not harm you[MS] at all. Allah revealed the book and wisdom to you[MS] and taught you[MS] what you[MS] did not know. Allah's grace to you[MS] was great. (113) 5B3 There is no good in their private counsels except for those who promote alms or kindness or reconciliation. We will greatly reward those who do that in order to please Allah. (114) We will make the one who contends with the messenger after guidance has come to him, who does not follow the believers' path, get what he has turned to. We will roast him in hell, an evil destiny. (115) Allah does not forgive those who worship other gods, but he forgives less serious sins for those he wills. He who worships gods other than Allah has gone far astray. (116) They only pray to goddesses besides Allah. They only pray to a devil[784] they follow. (117) Allah has damned him, and he[785] said, "I will take some of your[MS] worshipers as a required portion, (118) mislead them, make them desire, and command them, so they cut the ears of cattle. I will command them and they will change Allah's creation." Whoever takes Satan as a helper apart from Allah is clearly lost. (119) He promises them and makes

---

Harun), 38:24 (Dawud), 38:32,35 (Sulayman), 21:87, 37:142 (Yunus), 48:2, 47:19, 40:55, 4:79, 106, 9:43, 13:30, 80:1-2, 110:3, 94:2, 23:118, 66:1, 33:37, 8:67, and 9:117 (Muhammad (s)).

[782] Zabur, Psalms 5:4-5, 11:5, Tawrah, Proverbs 6:16-19

[783] For "day of resurrection" here and in verses 87,141, and 159, see Tawrah, Daniel 12:2 Injil, Acts 24:15, 1 Corinthians 15:52-54, Revelation 20:11-15

[784] Arabic /shaytan/. See glossary for more details.

[785] the devil

them desire. Satan promises only temptations for them. (120) Their dwelling place is hell, and they will find no escape from it. (121) We will make those who believe and do righteous deeds[786] enter heavenly gardens with flowing rivers underneath, where they will remain forever and ever. This is Allah's true promise. Who is more trustworthy than Allah in what he says? (122) It is neither by your[MP] wish nor by the wish of the people of the book; those who do evil will be repaid according to it, and will not find any helper or savior besides Allah. (123) Male and female believers who do righteous deeds will enter heaven, and will not be wronged at all. (124) Who is better in religion than one who submits[787] his face to Allah and is generous[788] and follows the monotheistic spiritual path[789] of Ibrahim? Allah took Ibrahim as a friend.[790] (125) Everything in the heavens and the earth is Allah's.[791] Allah knows everything. (126) They ask you[MS] for a religious decision about women. Say[MS], "Allah will give you[MP] the decision about them[FP], in addition to what is recited to you[MP] in the book about orphan[792] women whom you[MP] want to marry, to whom[FP] you[MP] do not give what was written for them, and weak[793] children: be[MP] just with orphans.[794] Allah knows the good you[MP] do. (127) If a woman fears her husband will cheat on[795] her or turn away from her, it is not wrong for them[D] to reconcile[D] between themselves. Reconciliation is better. Souls are covetous, but if you[MP] do good and are[MP] reverent, Allah is aware of your[MP] deeds. (128) You[MP] will never be able to treat [multiple] wives justly, even if you[MP] are careful, so do not turn[MP] aside from her completely, leaving her hanging. If you[MP] reconcile and are[MP] reverent, Allah is forgiving and merciful. (129) If they[D] split up,[796] Allah will enrich each one from his bounty.

---

[786] Here and in verse 124, see Injil, 1 Corinthians 3:8, James 2:14-17, Revelation 19:8.

[787] Injil, James 4:7. For "submit," some translators do not translate this. See glossary for more details.

[788] Or does good deeds. Injil, James 1:26-27

[789] Arabic /millah/. See glossary.

[790] Tawrah, Isaiah 41:8

[791] Here and in verses 131 (twice), 132, 170, and 171, see Tawrah, Isaiah 45:12, Zabur, Psalms 24:1, 89:11, Injil, Hebrews 1:10

[792] or orphans of

[793] or incompetent.

[794] Tawrah, Job 29:12, Zabur, Psalms 82:3, Injil, James 1:27

[795] Or mistreat

[796] The reference is probably to divorce.

Allah is omnipresent[797] and wise. (130) Everything in heaven and earth is Allah's. We commanded you[MP] and those who were given the book before you[MP], to fear Allah. If you[MP] disbelieve, everything in heaven and earth is Allah's. Allah is self-sufficient and praiseworthy." (131) Everything in the heavens and the earth is Allah's, and Allah is a sufficent trustee. (132) If he wills, he will make all you[MP] people go away, and bring others.[798] Allah can do that. (133) If anyone wants the rewards of this world, Allah has the rewards of this world and the hereafter. Allah hears all and sees all.[799] (134) 5B4 Believers, be just and fair witnesses to Allah, even if against yourselves[MP], your[MP] parents, or relatives. Whether rich or poor, Allah is better than they[D], so do not follow your[MP] desires. When you[MP] twist or turn away from justice, Allah is aware of it. (135) Believers, believe in Allah, his messenger, the book he revealed to his messenger, and the book he revealed beforehand. Whoever disbelieves in Allah, his angels, his books,[800] his messengers, and the last day has gone far astray. (136) Allah will not forgive or guide those who believe, then disbelieve, then believe, then disbelieve, then become more disbelieving. (137) Announce[801] to the hypocrites that they will have painful torment. (138) Do those who take disbelievers as helpers instead of believers seek power from them? All power is Allah's. (139) He has revealed to you[MP] in the book[802] that, if you[MP] hear his signs being disbelieved and mocked, do not sit with them until they begin talking about something else.[803] Otherwise you[MP] are like them.[804] Allah will gather all the hypocrites and disbelievers together in hell.[805] (140) If you[MP] have Allah's victory, those who watch you[MP] will say, "Were we not with you[MP]?" If [the battle] goes well for the disbelievers, they will say, "Did we not overcome you[MP] and prevent you[MP] from the believers?" Allah will

---

[797] Or bounteous. Zabur, Psalms 139:7-12. The words "omnipresent" and "bounty" in this verse are from the same root, meaning wide.
[798] Injil, Matthew 21:43
[799] Injil, Matthew 6:4
[800] Here and in 2:285, believers are told to believe not only in the Qur'an but also in the former books.
[801] This word is used for giving good news, and is used here sarcastically.
[802] The book referenced here is the Zabur. See Zabur, Psalms 1:1.
[803] Zabur, Psalms 1:1
[804] Injil, 1 Corinthians 15:33
[805] Injil, Revelation 21:8

## Chapter 4

judge between you[MP] on the day of resurrection, and will give the disbelievers no path against the believers. (141) The hypocrites try to deceive Allah, and he deceives them.[806] If they stand up for prayers, they do so lazily, just to be seen by men,[807] and they remember Allah infrequently, (142) wavering between that,[808] not toward one group nor toward another. If Allah misleads anyone, he will find no way [out]. (143) Believers, do not take disbelievers as helpers instead of believers. Do you[MP] want to give Allah clear authority against you[MP]? (144) The hypocrites are the lowest of the low in hellfire. You[MS] will find no savior[809] for them. (145) The exceptions are those who repent, make amends, deeply trust in Allah, and are sincere in their religion to Allah. They will be with the believers, and Allah will give believers a great reward. (146) What does Allah do with your[MP] torment if you[MP] give thanks and believe?[810] Allah is grateful and knows all. (147) 6A1 Allah does not love[811] publicizing evil sayings except by those who were cheated. Allah hears all and knows all. (148) Whether you[MP] show good or hide it, or pardon evil, Allah is pardoning and powerful. (149) Those who disbelieve in Allah and his messengers and want to distinguish between Allah and his messengers and say, "We believe in some and disbelieve in others," and want to take the middle path (150) are truly disbelievers. We have prepared shameful torment for disbelievers. (151) We will give rewards to those who believe in Allah and his messengers and do not distinguish between any of them.[812] Allah is forgiving and merciful. (152) The people of the book[813] ask you[MS] to make a book come down from heaven. They asked more than that from

---

[806] Injil 2 Thessalonians 2:11, Tawrah, 2 Samuel 22:27, 1 Kings 22:20-23, Ezekiel 14:9
[807] Injil, Matthew 6:5-8
[808] Injil, James 1:7-8
[809] Tawrah, Isaiah 43:11, Hosea 13:4, Injil, Hebrews 10:26
[810] Tawrah, Ezekiel 18:23, 33:11
[811] Zabur, Psalms 5:4-5, 11:5, Tawrah, Proverbs 6:16-19
[812] This verse and verse 150 are balanced by other verses that tell how some messengers are better than others. For instance, 2:253 says Allah preferred some messengers over others, and specifically mentions Isa, and 17:55 says Allah preferred some prophets and mentions Dawud.
[813] Although "people of the book" includes Jews, Christians, and Muslims in general, verses 153-157 are specifically about the Jews. Note the references here to Musa, the calf, Mount Sinai, the covenant, the sabbath, killing the prophets, and accusing Mariam.

## Chapter 4

Musa.[814] They said, "Show us Allah publicly," and they were struck by lightning for their wickedness. Then they took the calf[815] after miracles had come to them, and we pardoned that and we gave Musa clear authority. (153) We raised the Mount[816] over them by their covenant, and we told them, "Enter the door bowing down." We told them, "Do not break the sabbath,"[817] and we made a strong covenant with them. (154) Because[818] they broke their covenant and disbelieved in Allah's signs and wrongfully[819] murdered the prophets[820] and said, "Our hearts are hardened," (Allah has stamped disbelief on their hearts, for only a few believe),[821] (155) and because they disbelieved in Allah and accused Mariam[822] of a great scandal,[823] (156) and because of their saying, "We killed the Messiah,[824] Isa[825] son of Mariam, Allah's messenger,"[826] though they did not kill him[827] nor crucify him,[828]

---

[814] Moses, twice in this verse and in vese 164. See glossary for more details.

[815] Tawrah, Exodus 32:1-35.

[816] Mount Sinai, Tawrah, Exodus 19:1-25.

[817] Tawrah, Exodus 20:8-11, 31:13; Isaiah 56:6,7, 58:13,14, 66:22,23; Ezekiel 20:20, Injil, Mathew 12:8, 24:20; Mark 2:27; Luke 23:56

[818] The result of the word "because" here and in verses 156, 157, and 160 is in verse 160.

[819] or wickedly

[820] For Jews murdering the prophets, see also 2:61,87,91, 3:21,112,181,183, 5:70, Tawrah, Nehemiah 9:26, Injil, Matthew 23:37, Luke 11:47-49, Acts 7:52, 1 Thessalonians 2:15. The word "murder" does not imply that they thwarted Allah's will or that the Jewish people as a whole murdered them. Particularly in the case of Isa, it was the Jewish religious leadership who were responsible. See Injil, Matthew 26:47ff.

[821] or, they only believe a little

[822] Mary, mother of Jesus, here and in verses 157 and 171 (twice). See glossary for more details.

[823] of committing fornication (see 19:27-28). The Jews did not know that Isa was conceived by a breath of Allah's spirit (21:91, 66:12)

[824] Or Christ. Arabic /Al-Masih/ here and in verses 171 and 172. See glossary for more details.

[825] Jesus here and in verse 171. See glossary for more details.

[826] The ones specifically called Allah's messenger in the Qur'an are Muhammad (s) 48:29, 7:158, 33:21,40,53, etc., Musa 61:5, Thamud's messenger 91:13, and Isa 4:157,171, 61:6.

[827] Several explanations have been proposed for this statement in light of 2:154. The first is that Isa's body died, but the spiritual nature of Isa did

## Chapter 4

but it was made to seem so to them.[829] Truly those who differed about him are in doubt about him. They have no knowledge about him, but only follow what they guess. They did not kill him certainly.[830] (157) But Allah raised him up[831] to himself.[832] Allah is strong and wise. (158) Every one of the people of the book will certainly believe in him[833] before his[834] death, and he will be a

---

not die. (See also Injil, Matthew 27:46) The second is that although the cross was the punishment of criminals, Isa was not a criminal. Allah did not allow Isa to be left on the cross, where the birds would eat his body, but his body was taken down and buried (See Injil, Matthew 27:59). The third is that the *Jews* did not murder Isa (see following footnote also) because Isa submitted to Allah's will and lay down his life voluntarily for people. (See Injil, John 10:15,17,18)

[828] There is no contradiction between this verse and 19:33, which talks specifically about Isa's death, because this verse only says that the Jews did not kill him. It does not say that the Romans did not kill him. Thus there is no contradiction within the Qur'an itself, or between the Qur'an and the previous books, which affirm that the Romans killed him. See the Injil, Matthew 20:19, 27:26-35. For those who claim that Isa has not died yet, 5:117 is clear, where Isa speaks of his death in the past tense, and is clearly alive, for dead people do not speak at all (see note at 5:117). Furthermore, it is recorded in the Qur'an, so this happened before the Qur'an was written. In addition, 3:55 affirms this, for Allah tells Isa that he will make him die, and then that his followers will be above the disbelievers <u>until</u> the day of resurrection, not after it.

[829] This phrase does <u>not</u> say someone was made to look like him /shubbiha bihi/ or /tashaabaha alayhim (2:70) but /shubbiha lahum/ (it seemed so to them). The Jews indeed thought that they had ended Christ's message and influence by killing him, but when Allah resurrected him from death to life and then raised him to himself, Allah got the great victory (verse 158). See 3:55

[830] The text does not use /abadan/ which would mean "at all." See note at 8:17.

[831] This word refers to Isa's ascension, not his resurrection.

[832] Here begins a section that refers to some of Isa's uniquenesses. Isa is the only prophet or messenger in the Qur'an: whom Allah raised up to himself (158), who is a witness on the day of judgment (159), who is Allah's word, which was in existence before it was cast into his mother (171), who is a spirit from Allah (171). For more information about this subject, see notes at 3:36, 5:46,110, 19:19, 43:59.

[833] Isa

[834] Most commentators say "his death" means Isa's death. The singular pronouns in verses 157-159 all refer to Isa, except one, which refers to Allah.

## Chapter 4

witness over them on the day of resurrection.[835] (159) Because of the wickedness of the Jews,[836] we forbade good things from them that had been permitted. Because they often blocked others from the path to Allah,[837] (160) and because the disbelievers among them took usury,[838] which was forbidden to them, and took people's money falsely, we have prepared painful torment for them. (161) But those of them who are firm in knowledge and the believers believe in what was revealed to you[MS] and what was revealed before you[MS]. We will give a great reward to those who perform the prayers, pay the poor-tax, and believe in Allah and the last day. (162) 6A2 We inspired you[MS] just as we inspired Nuh[839] and the prophets after him.[840] We inspired[841] Ibrahim,[842] Ismail,[843] Ishaq,[844] Yaqub,[845] the tribes,[846] Isa,[847] Ayyub,[848] Yunus,[849] Harun,[850] and Sulayman.[851] We gave Dawud[852] the Zabur.[853] (163)

---

[835] See note at verse 158.

[836] Or those who repented and turned back to the truth. This refers to the Jews, probably when they repented after worshiping the golden calf idol (2:54, 92, 7:138, 148-150, Tawrah, Exodus 32).

[837] Here and verse 167, see Injil, Matthew 23:13, Luke 11:52.

[838] Tawrah, Exodus 22:24, Leviticus 25:35-37, Deuteronomy 23:20-21, Zabur, Psalms 15:5

[839] Noah. See glossary for more details.

[840] The "prophets after Nuh" include all the prophets except Adam, Idris and Salih.

[841] Most of what the prophets were all given came from Allah orally, and it was later written down. The exception is Musa (Tawrah, Exodus 34:28, Deuteronomy 4:13, 10:4), when Allah himself wrote them on stone tablets.

[842] Tawrah, Genesis 11:26-25:9

[843] Ishmael. See glossary for more details. Tawrah, Genesis 16:11-25:16

[844] Isaac. See glossary for more details. Tawrah, Genesis 17:19-35:28

[845] Jacob. See glossary for more details. Tawrah, Genesis 25:27-49:33

[846] i.e. the twelve tribes of Israel

[847] Jesus. See glossary for more details. Injil, Matthew, Mark, Luke, John, and Revelation.

[848] Job, the prophet known for patience. See glossary for more details. Tawrah, Job 1-42

[849] Jonah. See glossary for more details. Tawrah, Jonah 1-4

[850] Aaron. See glossary for more details. Tawrah, Exodus 4:14 – Numbers 33:39

[851] Solomon. See glossary for more details. Tawrah, 1 Kings 1-11, 2 Chronicles 1-9, Proverbs 1-31, Ecclesiastes 1-12, Song of Solomon 1-8, Zabur, Psalms 72, 127

# Chapter 4

We have told you<sup>MS</sup> the story of messengers beforehand. We have not told you<sup>MS</sup> the stories of other messengers. Allah spoke to Musa directly.[854] (164) [They were] messengers, bearers of good news, and warners, so that people would have no excuse[855] before Allah after the messengers. Allah is strong and wise. (165) But Allah witnesses to what he revealed to you<sup>MS</sup>. He revealed it with his knowledge. The angels witness. Allah is a sufficent witness. (166) Disbelievers who block others from Allah's path have gone far astray. (167) Allah will not forgive or guide wicked disbelievers on the path, (168) except for the path to hell, where they will be forever and ever. This is easy for Allah. (169) People, the messenger has come to you<sup>MP</sup> with truth from your<sup>MP</sup> Lord, so believe<sup>MP</sup>. It is better for you<sup>MP</sup>. If you<sup>MP</sup> disbelieve, everything in the heavens and the earth is Allah's. Allah is all-knowing and wise. (170) People of the book, do not exaggerate in your<sup>MP</sup> religion, and only say the truth about Allah.[856] Truly[857] the Messiah, Isa son of Mariam, is Allah's messenger and his word[858] which he sent down on[859] Mariam, and a spirit[860] from him. So believe in Allah and his messengers and do not say<sup>MP</sup>, "Three."[861] Stop<sup>MP</sup> it. It is better for you<sup>MP</sup>. Allah is one god. May he be glorified above having a

---

[852] David. See glossary for more details.

[853] Psalms. See glossary for more details.

[854] Tawrah, Numbers 12:8

[855] Injil, Romans 2:1ff, 3:19

[856] If all the people of the book stuck to the truth revealed in the books and did not add men's writings to them, it would be better for them.

[857] Most translations use "merely" or "only." The Arabic word is used for emphasis, and it generally has a positive meaning in the Qur'an. Indeed, the same word, used later in this same verse, if translated with a negative, would come out, "Allah is merely one god." In any case, what it says about Isa is quite positive, and gives him titles given to no one else in the Qur'an: Messiah, son of a woman, Allah's word sent down on Mariam, and a spirit from Allah.

[858] 3:39,45, Injil, John 1:1-14, Revelation 19:13. See note at verse 158.

[859] Or cast down or spoke to. Allah's word, which existed before Isa's conception, was sent down to Mariam, and the name given to the child was Isa.

[860] Isa is also called a spirit in Injil, 1 Corinthians 15:45. See note at verse 158.

[861] All the former books agree with the Qur'an that there is one God, and there is not a single verse in any of them that uses the number three in relationship to God.

boy!⁸⁶² Everything in the heavens and the earth is his. Allah is a sufficient trustee. (171) The Messiah will not disdain to be a servant⁸⁶³ of Allah, nor will the angels who have been brought near.⁸⁶⁴ Allah will gather everyone who proudly disdains his service. (172) But he will reward those who believe and do righteous deeds⁸⁶⁵ and he will give them more grace.⁸⁶⁶ He will painfully torment those who proudly disdain him. They will find no helper or savior apart from him. (173) People, a proof has come to you^MP from your^MP Lord. We have revealed clear light⁸⁶⁷ to you^MP. (174) Allah will cause those who believe and take refuge in him to enter his mercy and grace, and he will guide them to him on a straight path.⁸⁶⁸ (175)

\*\*\*

---

⁸⁶² The idea that Allah had sexual relations with a woman and fathered a son by her is not supported at all in any of the books.
⁸⁶³ See glossary. Injil, Philippians 2:6-8
⁸⁶⁴ Injil, Hebrews 1:14. This word /muqarrabun/ here refers to angels. Elsewhere in the Qur'an it refers only to the inhabitants of the heavenly garden (56:11) and Isa (3:45).
⁸⁶⁵ Injil, 1 Corinthians 3:8, James 2:14-17, Revelation 19:8
⁸⁶⁶ Injil, James 4:6
⁸⁶⁷ Tawrah, Isaiah 9:2, Injil, Matthew 4:16, John 1:4-12
⁸⁶⁸ See glossary for more details, and notes on 3:51, 6:153, 19:36, 36:61, and 43:64 on what the straight path is.

They ask you<sup>MS</sup> for a religious ruling. Say<sup>MS</sup>: Allah will give you<sup>MP</sup> a religious ruling about distant relatives. If a man dies with no child,[869] but he has a sister, she shall inherit half of what he left behind. He is her heir if she does not have a child. If there are two sisters, they shall inherit two-thirds of what he left behind between them. If there are several brothers and sisters, each male shall inherit as much as two females. Allah makes clear to you<sup>MP</sup> lest[870] you<sup>MP</sup> go astray. Allah knows everything. (176)[871]

---

[869] or son, twice in this verse
[870] literally, so that
[871] The verses in this chapter that rhyme are put together in paragraphs, separated by ***.

Chapter 5
# Chapter 5: Al-Ma'idah[872]

**6A3** In the name of Allah, the most gracious and merciful.[873] Believers, fulfill your[MP] contracts. Beasts of the herds are allowed for you[MP], except as is recited to you[MP]. Hunting is not allowed while you[MP] are consecrated. Allah judges[874] as he wants. (1)
\*\*\*

Believers, do not allow the violation of Allah's ordinances, the sacred month, offerings, garlanded ones, or those who seek grace and pleasure from their Lord in the sacred sanctuary. When you[MP] are no longer consecrated, then you[MP] may hunt. Do not let the hatred of people who barred you[MP] from the sacred sanctuary make you[MP] do wrong by aggression. Cooperate[MP] in righteousness and reverence. Do not cooperate[MP] in guilt and enmity. Fear[MP] Allah. Allah is severe in punishment.[875] (2)
\*\*\*

These are forbidden to you[MP]: dead animals, blood, pork, animals not offered to Allah, strangled, clubbed to death, fallen to their death, gored, or eaten by wild beasts, except if you slaughter it, and those sacrificed to idols [876] If you[MP] divine using headless arrows, that is unbelief.[877] Today, the disbelievers will be disappointed by your[MP] religion, so do not fear them, but fear[MP] me. Today I
have completed your[MP] religion for you[MP], and finished giving you[MP] my blessings and am pleased with submission[878] as your[MP] religion.

---

[872] The (dinner) table
[873] Zabur, Psalms 103:8, 145:8. See glossary for more details.
[874] Or decides
[875] Here and in verse 98, see Tawrah, Ezekiel 25:17, Injil, Matthew 8:12, 13:42,50, 22:13, 24:51, 25:30, Mark 9:48, Luke 13:28, 19:27.
[876] Injil, Acts 15:29. See Tawrah, Leviticus 11:7,39, Isaiah 65:4, 66:17, Daniel 1:8, Injil, 1 Corinthians 8:13, Acts 10:15, Mark 7:19.
[877] Or immorality or transgression, here and in verses 25, 26,.47, 49, 59, 67, 81, and 108.
[878] Injil, James 4:7. For "submission," and ' submitted" here and in verses 44 and 111, some translators do not translate this. See glossary for more details.

## Chapter 5

Allah is forgiving[879] and merciful[880] to him who is compelled by hunger, not desiring to be guilty. (3)

\*\*\*

They ask you[MS] what is allowed for them. Say[MS], "You[MP] may have good things, and what you[MP] have taught predators to hunt. You[MP] teach them[881] as Allah has taught you[MP]. Eat[MP] of what they[FP] catch for you, mention[MP] Allah's name over it, and fear[MP] God. Allah is swift in reckoning."[882] (4)

\*\*\*

Today, good things are allowed. In addition, the food of those who were given the book[883] is allowed for you[MP], and your[MP] food is allowed for them. Allowed are chaste,[884] believing women, and the chaste women of those given the book before you[MP] if you[MP] give them[FP] their bride price,[885] are chaste[MP], do not fornicate[MP], and do not take[MP] mistresses. The works of a disbeliever in the faith will be futile, and in the hereafter, he will be be lost. (5) Believers, when you[MP] stand for prayers, wash[MP] your[MP] faces and your[MP] hands up to the elbows, and wipe your[MP] heads and wash your[MP] feet up to the ankles.[886] If you[MP] are unclean, purify yourselves[MP]. If you[MP] are sick or on a journey, or one of you[MP] has come from the toilet,[887] or if you[MP] have had sex with women, and you[MP] do not find water, then wash with pure sand,[888] and wipe your faces and hands with it. Allah does not want to make it difficult for you[MP], but Allah

---

[879] Here and in verses 34, 39, 74, 98, and 101, for "forgiving," see Zabur, Psalms 103:3, 130:4, Tawrah, Isaiah 43:25, Exodus 34:7, Injil, Acts 26:18. See glossary for more details.

[880] Here and in verses 34, 39, 74, and 98, on "merciful," see glossary for more details.

[881] The word for "them" here and "they" in the following sentence is for thinking beings. The intention may be that with man's training, animals almost think.

[882] Tawrah, Isaiah 19:1, Malachi 3:5, Zabur, Psalms 147:15, Injil, 2 Peter 2:1, Revelation 22:12

[883] Tawrah, Leviticus 11:2-3, 9,22, Injil, Mark 7:19, Acts 15:29.

[884] the word chaste in this verse can also refer to (chaste) married women

[885] or wages

[886] the word also means heels

[887] i.e. defecated

[888] or good soil; sand makes more sense in context here and in geographical context

## Chapter 5

wants to purify[889] you[MP] and complete his blessings on you[MP] so that you[MP] may give thanks. (6)

\*\*\*

Remember Allah's blessings to you[MP] and his covenant which he made with you[MP] when you[MP] said, "We hear and obey." Fear Allah![890] Allah knows what is in the heart.[891] (7)

\*\*\*

Believers, be upright before Allah, just witnesses, and do not let your hatred of people make you[MP] do wrong by being unjust. Be[MP] just. It is nearer to reverence. Fear[MP] Allah. Allah is aware of your[MP] deeds. (8) Allah has promised believers who do righteous deeds[892] forgiveness and a great reward. (9) Those who disbelieve and reject our signs[893] are going to the blazing fire. (10) Believers, remember[MP] Allah's blessings to you[MP], when people plotted to stretch out their hands toward you[MP] and he kept their hands from you[MP]. Fear[MP] Allah. Let the believers trust[MP] in Allah. (11) 6A4

\*\*\*

Allah made a covenant with the people of Israel and we sent twelve leaders from them.[894] Allah said, "I am with you[MP]. If you[MP] perform the prayers, pay the poor-tax, believe in my messengers, assist them, and give a good loan to Allah, I will expiate your[MP] bad deeds[895] and make you[MP] enter heavenly gardens[896] with

---

[889] Tawrah, Malachi 3:3, Zabur, Psalms 19:8, 119:9,140, Injil, Acts 15:8,9,1 Peter 2:2, Titus 2:14, Hebrews 1:3

[890] For "fear Allah" here and in verses 28, 35, 88, 96, 100, and 112, see Tawrah, Deuteronomy 10:12, Isaiah 29:13, Injil, 1 Peter 2:17, Revelation 14:7.

[891] Here and in verses 54, 76, 99, and 109, see Tawrah, 1 Samuel 16:7, 1 Chronicles 28:9, Zabur, Psalms 44:21, Injil, Luke 16:15, Romans 8:27, Acts 15:8, 1 John 3:20.

[892] Injil, 1 Corinthians 3:8, James 2:14-17, Revelation 19:8

[893] Arabic /ayat/ here and in verse 86 and 114. See glossary for more details.

[894] Tawrah, Numbers 1:5-15

[895] Here and in verses 65 and 89, for "expiate," see Tawrah, Isaiah 27:9, Injil, Romans 3:25, Hebrews 2:17, 1 John 2:2, 4:10

[896] Arabic /jannah/ here and in verses 65, 72, 85, and 119. See glossary for more details.

## Chapter 5

flowing rivers[897] underneath. He among you[MP] who disbelieves after that has gone astray from the straight path."[898] (12)
\*\*\*
Because they broke their covenant, we damned them and hardened their hearts. They distort the sense of words from their context,[899] and have forgotten some of what they were reminded of. You[MS] will constantly discover new treacheries from most of them. Pardon[MS] and forgive[MS] them, for Allah loves the generous.[900] (13) We made a covenant with those who said, "We are Christians."[901] Then they forgot some of what they were reminded of, so we brought about enmity and hatred among them until the day of resurrection.[902] Allah will proclaim to them what they did. (14) People of the book, our messenger has come to you[MP] to clarify to you[MP] much that you[MP] were hiding from the book, and to pardon you[MP] much. Light and a clear book came to you[MP] from Allah. (15) With it, Allah guides whoever follows his pleasure on paths of peace and brings them out from darkness to light[903] by his permission. He guides them to a straight path. (16)
\*\*\*
Those who said that Allah is the Messiah,[904] son of Mariam[905] have truly covered [the truth].[906] Say[MS], "Who can do anything

---

[897] Here and in verses 85 and 119, see Injil, Revelation 22:1-2, Tawrah, Ezekiel 47:12.

[898] Here and in verse 16, see glossary for more details, and notes on 3:51, 6:153, 19:36, 36:61, and 43:64 on what the straight path is.

[899] There are two types of "distortion:" altering the text and altering the meaning. From the words "twist words from their context" and "forgotten," it is clear that altering the meaning is intended. See 2:75, 3:78, 4:46, 5:41 for the other verses that deal with this subject. Injil, 2 Peter 3:16

[900] Injil, 2 Corinthians 9:7

[901] For /nasara/ (Christian) here and in verses 18, 51, 69, and 82, see glossary for more details.

[902] For "day of resurrection" here and in verses 36 and 64, see Tawrah, Daniel 12:2 Injil, Acts 24:15, 1 Corinthians 15:52-54, Revelation 20:11-15

[903] Injil, Colossians 1:13, John 1:5-9

[904] Or Christ. Arabic Al-Masih, here twice and in verses 72 (twice) and 75. See glossary for more details.

[905] Mary, mother of Jesus, here twice and in verses 46, 72, 75, 78, 110, 112, 114, and 116. See glossary for more details.

## Chapter 5

against Allah, if he wanted to destroy the Messiah, son of Mariam, his mother, and everyone on the earth? The kingdom of the heavens, the earth, and what is between them[D] is Allah's. He creates whatever he wills. Allah can do anything."[907] (17) The Jews and the Christians said, "We are Allah's children[908] and his beloved ones."[909] Say[MS], "Why will[910] he torment[911] you[MP] for your[MP] sins? Rather you[MP] are humans created by Allah.[912] He forgives whom he wills and torments whom he wills.[913] Allah has the kingdom of the heavens, the earth and what is between them. He is [man's] destiny." (18) People of the book, our messenger has come clarifying to you[MP] after a period of not having messengers [lest] you[MP] say, "No bearer of good news or warner has come to us." One who bears good news and warns has come to you[MP]. Allah can do anything.[914] (19)
\*\*\*

When Musa[915] told his people, "My people, remember[MP] Allah's blessings to you[MP], since he sent prophets to you[MP] and gave you[MP] kings[916] and gave you[MP] what no one in the universe had ever been given before.[917] (20) My people, enter[MP] the holy land which Allah

---

[906] Or disbelieved. If someone said this, he would be saying that when the Messiah was on earth, there was no god in heaven, or when the Messiah prayed, there was no one to pray to. Obviously Allah was in heaven when the Messiah was on earth. None of the books say that there was no Allah in heaven when the Messiah was on earth.

[907] Tawrah, Job 42:2, Isaiah 14:27, Daniel 4:35, Injil, Matthew 19:26, Mark 10:27, Luke 1:37

[908] or sons

[909] Being loved by Allah does not mean a person is no longer human. See the rest of the verse. All the books affirm Allah's love for people. See "love" in glossary.

[910] Or does

[911] For "torment" here twice and in verses 33, 36 (twice), 37, 40, 41, 73, 80, 94, 115, and 118, see Tawrah, Isaiah 50:11, Injil, Matthew 18:34, 25:41,46, Luke 16:23-28, Revelation 20:15.

[912] this phrase could be part of the preceding sentence.

[913] Here and in verses 40, 54, and 64, see Tawrah, Exodus 33:19, Injil, Romans 9:15,18.

[914] Here and in verse 40, see Tawrah, Job 42:2, Isaiah 14:27, Daniel 4:35, Injil, Matthew 19:26, Mark 10:27, Luke 1:37.

[915] Moses here and in verses 22 and 24. See glossary for more details.

[916] Tawrah, 1 Samuel 8:6

[917] Tawrah, Deuteronomy 4:33

## Chapter 5

has decreed for you<sup>MP</sup>,[918] and do not turn<sup>MP</sup> back, or you<sup>MP</sup> will be overturned and lost.[919] (21) They said, "Musa, there are strong people in it, and we will not enter it[920] until they leave it. If they leave it, we will enter." (22) Two men[921] whom<sup>D</sup> Allah blessed among those who feared said, "Enter<sup>MP</sup> the gate against them. When you<sup>MP</sup> enter it, you<sup>MP</sup> will be victorious. Trust<sup>MP</sup> in Allah, if you<sup>MP</sup> are believers." (23) They[922] said, "Musa, we will never enter it as long as they are in it. You<sup>MS</sup> and your<sup>MS</sup> Lord go and fight. We will sit here." (24) He said, "My Lord, I cannot control anyone except myself and my brother. Make a distinction between us and unbelieving people." (25) He said, "So it is forbidden for them for forty years.[923] They will wander on the earth.[924] Do not be sad for unbelieving people." (26) **6B1** Read<sup>MS</sup> to them[925] the story of the two sons of Adam[926] truly. They<sup>D</sup> offered offerings, and it was accepted from one of them<sup>D</sup> and not from the other,[927] who said, "I will surely murder you<sup>MS</sup>."[928] He answered, "Allah truly[929] accepts from the godfearers.[930] (27) Even if you<sup>MS</sup> stretch forth your<sup>MS</sup> hand to murder me, I will not stretch forth my hand toward you<sup>MS</sup> to murder you<sup>MS</sup>. I fear Allah, the Lord of the universe. (28) I want you<sup>MS</sup> to bring my guilt[931] and your<sup>MS</sup> guilt and be destined for hellfire. That is the punishment of the wicked." (29) Yet his soul prompted him to murder his brother, so he murdered him[932] and was lost.[933] (30) So Allah sent a raven, searching in the ground[934],

---

[918] Tawrah, Deuteronomy 27:3
[919] Tawrah, Deuteronomy 1:23-35
[920] Tawrah, Numbers 13:28-33, Deutereonmy 1:28
[921] Joshua and Caleb. See Tawrah, Numbers 13:30, 14:6-9.
[922] This refers to the other ten scouts from the 12 tribes of the people of Israel. Tawrah, Numbers 14:3
[923] Tawrah, Numbers 14:29-35
[924] Tawrah, Numbers 32:13
[925] Or "recite to them." See note at 7:157.
[926] See glossary for more details on Adam. The story of his oldest two sons is in Tawrah, Genesis 4.
[927] Tawrah, Genesis 4:4-5. The one it was accepted from was Habil (Abel) and the other was Qabil (Cain).
[928] Tawrah, Genesis 4:8
[929] or only
[930] Tawrah, Genesis 4:4
[931] Or, the guilt of your killing me
[932] Tawrah, Genesis 4:8
[933] Tawrah, Genesis 4:11

## Chapter 5

to show him how to conceal the shame[935] of his brother. He said, "Woe is me. Am I unable to be like this raven, and conceal the shame of my brother?" And he became remorseful. (31) Therefore, we decreed for the people of Israel: If anyone murders a soul, except in vengeance for another soul or destruction on earth, it is as if he murdered all of mankind. Whoever gives life to a soul[936] is as if he gave life to all mankind.[937] Our messengers came[938] to them with miracles, and then after that, many of them were wasteful in the land. (32) The penalty of those who make war against Allah and his messenger and try to cause destruction on the earth is to be slaughtered, crucified, have their hands and feet on opposite sides amputated, or be banished from the land. Thus they will have shame on the earth and great torment in the hereafter, (33) except those who repent before you[MP] conquer them. Know[MP] that Allah is forgiving and merciful. (34) Believers, fear Allah, seek the way to him, and fight in his path, that you[MP] may prosper. (35) Truly if the disbelievers had everything on earth twice over as a ransom for them from the torment of the day of resurrection, it would not be accepted from them.[939] They will have painful torment. (36) They will want to leave hellfire, but they will not leave it. They will have permanent torment. (37) As for the male and female thief, cut off their hands as the punishment they[D] deserve, as an exemplary punishment from Allah. Allah is strong and wise.[940] (38) Allah will accept the repentance of a wicked person who repents and makes amends. Allah is forgiving and merciful. (39) Do you[MS] not know that the kingdom of the heavens and the earth is Allah's?[941] He torments whom he wills and forgives whom he wills. Allah can do anything. (40) **6B2** Messenger, do not be sad[MS] about those who hasten to disbelief, whether among those who said with their

---

[934] i.e. by digging or scratching

[935] or body

[936] This actually happened. See 3:49, Injil, John 11:43-44

[937] Injil, 1 Corinthians 15:22

[938] The verb for inanimate objects is used here. The meaning might be that the focus is on the message, not the messengers.

[939] Zabur, Psalms 49:7,8

[940] Here and in verse 118, for "wise," see Tawrah, Job 9:4, Proverbs 2:6, Jeremiah 9:23-24, Injil, 1 Corinthians 1:21-25, Romans 16:27.

[941] Here and in verse 120, see Tawrah, Isaiah 45:12, Zabur, Psalms 24:1, 89:11, Injil, Hebrews 1:10.

## Chapter 5

mouths, "We have believed," when their hearts have not believed, or among the Jews,[942] who listen to lies, hearken to other people who have not come to you[MS], and distort the sense of words out of their context.[943] They say, "If you[MP] have been given this, take it, and if you[MP] have not been given it, beware." If Allah wants to tempt someone, you[MS] will not be able to do anything for him against Allah. Those whose hearts Allah does not want to purify will have shame in this world and great torment in the hereafter. (41) They hearken to lies and take illicit gain, so if they come to you[MS], judge among them or turn away from them. If you[MS] turn away from them, they will not harm you[MS] at all. If you[MS] judge, judge among them justly, Allah loves those who act justly. (42) And how can they make you[MS] their judge, when they have the Tawrah,[944] which contains Allah's judgment?[945] Then they turn away after that![946] They are not believers.[947] (43) We revealed the Tawrah, in which is guidance and light.[948] The prophets who submitted, the rabbis, and the priests judge the Jews according to the portion of Allah's book with which they have been entrusted.[949] They were witnesses of it. So do not fear[MP] people, but fear me,[950] and do not sell my verses for a small price. Whoever

---

[942] Here and in verse 69, or "those who repented and turned back to the truth." This refers to the Jews, probably when they repented after worshiping the golden calf idol (2:54, 92, 7:138, 148-150, Tawrah, Exodus 32).

[943] There are two types of "distortion:" altering the text and altering the meaning. From the words "listen" and "twist out of their context," it is clear that altering the meaning is intended. See 2:75, 3:78, 4:46, 5:13 for the other verses that deal with this subject. Injil, 2 Peter 3:16

[944] The Law, here and in verses 44, 46 twice), 66, 68, and 110. See glossary for more details.

[945] Note that the verse says that the Tawrah has Allah's judgment, not that it once had it and no longer does. There is no need for a messenger to give an opinion on matters in which Allah's word (the Tawrah/Law here) has given a ruling.

[946] Injil, John 5:39-40

[947] Injil, John 5:42

[948] Note that the verse says the Tawrah has guidance and light, not that it once had and no longer does. Zabur, Psalms 119:130

[949] Injil, Romans 3:2

[950] Tawrah, Proverbs 29:25

## Chapter 5

does not judge by what Allah has revealed[951] are disbelievers. (44) And we wrote for them in it[FS],[952] 'A life for a life, an eye for an eye,[953] a nose for a nose, an ear for an ear, a tooth for a tooth, and punishment for wounds, so if someone forgoes it,[954] it will be expiation for him. Those who do not judge by what Allah has revealed are wicked. (45) We made Isa[955] son of Mariam follow in their footsteps, confirming[956] the Tawrah in his possession,[957] and we gave him the Injil,[958] in which is guidance and light, confirming the Tawrah in his possession, as guidance and an admonition to the reverent.[959] (46) So let the people of the Injil judge by what Allah has revealed in it. Whoever does not judge by what Allah has revealed are unbelievers. (47) And we revealed the book to you[MS] with truth, confirming[960] what he had of the book before it and protecting[961] it, so judge among them according to what Allah has revealed,[962] and do not follow their desires concerning[963] the truth that has come to you[MS]. We made a law and a program for each one of you[MP]. If Allah had willed, he would

---

[951] Here and in verse 47, those who use man's sayings instead of Allah's revelations are called disbelievers and unbelievers. The Qur'an thus affirms the correctness of the Tawrah and Injil.

[952] i.e. the Tawrah

[953] See Tawrah, Exodus 21:23-27, Leviticus 24:19-21, Deuteronomy 19:21, Injil, Matthew 5:38

[954] i.e. the penalty that is due from the transgressor to him

[955] Jesus here and in verses 78, 110, 112, 114, and 116. See glossary for more details.

[956] or certifying. This word is used today for certified copies. Isa is the only person in the Qur'an who certifies a book. See notes on 3:36, 4:158, 5:110, 19:19, and 43:59 for other uniquenesses of Isa.

[957] Here and in verses 46 and 48, or, "between his hands," or "in front of him." This shows that the Tawrah in Isa's day was correct.

[958] Here and in verses 47, 66, 68 and 110, Gospel. See glossary for more details.

[959] Note that the Injil is not only guidance to the Christians, but to all who are reverent or god-fearing.

[960] The Qur'an confirms the previous books many times (2:41,89,91,97,101, 3:3,81, 4:47, 5:48, 6:92, 35:31, 46:12,30). This shows that the Injil in the days of the Qur'an was correct.

[961] Or being a guardian over it. The Qur'an therefore has a role to guard the previous books.

[962] The messenger here is told to judge by what Allah has revealed, which in this context means the Tawrah, Injil and Qur'an.

[963] Or "over against"

have made you^MP one nation, but he wanted to test you^MP regarding what he gave you^MP. So compete in goodness. You^MP will all return toward Allah, and he will proclaim to you^MP your^MP differences. (48) Judge^MS between them based on what Allah has revealed and do not follow^MS their desires. Beware^MS of them, lest they entice you^MS away from some of what Allah has revealed to you^MS. If they turn away, know^MS that Allah wants to afflict them for some of their sins. Many people are unbelievers. (49) Do they want their judgment based on ignorance? Who is better than Allah in judging people who are certain? (50) **6B3** Believers, do not take Jews and Christians as protectors.[964] They protect each other. Those of you^MP who take them as protectors become part of them. Allah does not guide wicked people. (51) You^MS see those with sick hearts[965] hastening to say to them, "We fear that a calamity[966] will afflict us." Allah may bring victory or a commandment from him, so they will regret what they hid in their souls. (52) The believers say, "Are those the ones who swore by Allah with binding oaths that they are with you^MP?" Their works will be in vain, and they will be lost. (53) Believers, if you turn back from your religion, Allah will bring people whom he loves and who love him,[967] who are humble toward believers and strong against disbelievers, who struggle in Allah's path and do not fear anyone's blame. That is Allah's grace, which he gives to those he wills. Allah is omnipresent[968] and all-knowing. (54) Allah, his messenger, and the believers who perform prayers and pay the poor-tax, kneeling down are your^MP protectors. (55) As for those who turn to[969] Allah and his messenger and the believers, Allah's party are the victors. (56) Believers, do not take as protectors those who make fun of your^MP religion and mock it, whether of those given the book before you^MP or disbelievers. Fear^MP Allah if you^MP are believers. (57) If you^MP

---

[964] There is no contradiction between this verse and verse 82, which says that the closest in love to the believers are those who say they are Christians, and study Allah's commands in their book. There is a large difference between those who are Christians in name only, because of their ancestors, and those who follow their book. The former are not to be friends of the believers, but the latter are honored by the Qur'an.

[965] Tawrah, Jeremiah 8:18, 17:9-10

[966] Or a circle

[967] Injil, Matthew 21:43

[968] Zabur, Psalms 139:7-12

[969] or take as protector

## Chapter 5

call to prayer, they make fun of it and mock it. That is because they are people who do not comprehend. (58) Say[MS], people of the book, will you[MP] take revenge on us because we believe in Allah, what was revealed to us, and what was revealed beforehand,[970] whereas most of you[MP] are unbelievers?[971] (59)

\*\*\*

Say[MS], "Shall I proclaim to you[MP] the most evil reward from Allah? Allah has damned them, is angry with them, and made them monkeys and pigs.[972] They worshiped false gods.[973] They are in an evil place and have gone astray from the right path." (60)

\*\*\*

When they come to you[MP], they say, "We believe," whereas they have entered in disbelief and left with it. Allah knows what they were hiding. (61) You[MS] see many of them competing in guilt, enmity, and unjust gain. What they did was dreadful. (62) Would that the rabbis and priests would forbid them from guilty sayings and unjust gain. What they did was dreadful. (63) The Jews said, "Allah's hand is chained," but their hands are the ones that are chained, and they are damned because of their saying. His hands are stretched out, donating as he wills. What was revealed to you[MS] from your[MS] Lord will increase many of them in tyranny and disbelief. We cast enmity and hatred among them until the day of resurrection. Every time they kindle a fire for war, Allah extinguishes it. They try to cause destruction on the earth. Allah does not love destroyers.[974] (64) If the people of the book had believed and been reverent, we would have expiated their bad deeds and caused them to enter into heavenly gardens of delight. (65) If they had kept the Tawrah and Injil and what we revealed to them from their Lord, they would have eaten from above them and beneath their feet. Some of them are a nation of good intentions,

---

[970] It is ironic that the Muslims are to believe in what was revealed beforehand, while many of the people of the book do not believe it.

[971] The Qur'an carefully distinguishes between the believers and the unbelievers of the people of the book.

[972] In 2:65 and 7:166, people are compared to pigs as well, but the adjective used there is for thinking beings. The meaning may be that they have not been changed into actual monkeys and pigs, but their character qualities are like monkeys and pigs. See Injil, Matthew 7:6 for a similar usage, where some people are compared to pigs.

[973] Arabic /Al-Taghut/. See glossary for more details.

[974] Zabur, Psalms 5:4-5, 11:5, Tawrah, Proverbs 6:16-19

## Chapter 5

and many of them do evil. (66) **6B4** Messenger, deliver what was revealed to you<sup>MS</sup> from your Lord. If you<sup>MS</sup> do not do that, you<sup>MS</sup> have not delivered his message. Allah will protect you<sup>MS</sup> from the people. Allah does not guide unbelieving people. (67) People of the book, you<sup>MP</sup> have no foundation unless you<sup>MP</sup> uphold the Tawrah and Injil and what was revealed to you<sup>MP</sup> by your<sup>MP</sup> Lord. What was revealed to you<sup>MS</sup> will certainly increase many of them in transgression and disbelief. Do not sorrow<sup>MS</sup> over disbelieving people. (68) Truly believers, Jews, Sabeans, and Christians – whoever believes in Allah and in the last day and does righteous deeds shall have no fear, nor will they grieve. (69) We have made a covenant with the people of Israel and sent them messengers. Whenever a messenger brought them something they did not like, some of them they called liars, and some of them they murder.[975] (70) They thought there would be no temptation, and were blind and deaf.[976] Then Allah accepted their repentance, and many of them were blind and deaf. Allah sees what they do. (71)

\*\*\*

Those who said that Allah is the Messiah, son of Mariam have truly covered [the truth].[977] The Messiah said, "People of Israel, worship Allah, my Lord and yours<sup>MP</sup>."[978] If someone adds gods to Allah, Allah will forbid him from the heavenly garden; his abode will be hellfire. The wicked will have no helpers. (72)

\*\*\*

Those who say that Allah is the third of three[979] have truly disbelieved. There is no other god[980] besides one god, and if they

---

[975] For Jews murdering the prophets, see also 2:61,87,91, 3:21,112,181,183, 4:155, Tawrah, Nehemiah 9:26, Injil, Matthew 23:37, Luke 11:47-49, Acts 7:52, 1 Thessalonians 2:15. The word "murder" does not imply that they thwarted Allah's will or that the Jewish people as a whole murdered them. Particularly in the case of Isa, it was the Jewish religious leadership who were responsible. See Injil, Matthew 26:47ff.

[976] Tawrah, Isaiah 6:9, Injil, Mathew 13:14-15, John 9:41

[977] Or disbelieved. If someone said this, he would be saying that when Christ was on earth, there was no god in heaven, or when Christ prayed, there was no one to pray to. Obviously Allah was in heaven when Christ was on earth.

[978] See Injil, John 20:17, Mark 12:29, 1 Corinthians 15:24-28

[979] No verses in the former books use the word "three" for Allah. See glossary under "god."

[980] Arabic /ilah/ twice in this verse. See glossary for more details.

do not stop what they are saying, he will touch the disbelievers among them with painful torment. (73) Will they not repent toward Allah and ask his forgiveness? Allah is forgiving and merciful. (74) The Messiah, son of Mariam is only[981] a messenger. The messengers before him died.[982] His mother was righteous. They both ate food.[983] See how we make signs plain to them? Then see how they lie! (75) Say[MS], "Do you[MP] worship what cannot harm you[MP] or help you[MP] instead of Allah?"[984] Allah hears all and knows all. (76)

\*\*\*

Say[MS], "People of the book, do not exaggerate in your[MP] religion beyond the

truth, and do not follow the desires of people who went astray beforehand, and led many astray. They went astray from the straight path."[985] (77)

\*\*\*

The disbelievers of the people of Israel were cursed by the tongue of Dawud[986] and Isa son of Mariam for their disobedience and transgressions.[987] (78) They would not desist from doing what is forbidden. They did it, and what they did was dreadful.[988] (79) You[MS] see many of them taking disbelievers as protectors. What they did to themselves was dreadful. Allah is furious with them, and they will be tormented forever. (80) If they had believed in

---

[981] The word "only" should be taken in context of the rest of the Qur'an, where he is called, among other things, "his word, and a spirit from him" (4:171), "highly exalted in this world and the hereafter, and brought near to Allah" (3:45), "sinless" (19:19), a witness on the day of resurrection (4:159), the only one who confirmed a book (3:50), the statement of truth (19:34), etc. The Qur'an also uses the word "only" about Muhammad (ص). See note at 3:144.

[982] Some see the implication here that Christ also died, as 19:33, 3:55, and 5:117 say explicitly. See 3:144, where it is stated that the messengers before Muhammad (ص) died.

[983] Injil, Luke 24:43

[984] Zabur, Psalms 115:4-7, Tawrah, Isaiah 44:20

[985] See glossary for more details, and notes on 3:51, 6:153, 19:36, 36:61, and 43:64 on what the straight path is.

[986] David. See glossary for more details.

[987] Zabur, Psalms 12:2,3, Injil, Matthew 23

[988] There are hundreds of verses in the Tawrah that mention the people of Israel doing things Allah forbids. See as one example, Tawrah, Leviticus 19:4, 2 Kings 17:12

Allah, the prophet, and what was revealed to him, they would not have taken them as protectors, but many of them are unbelievers. (81) 7A1 You[MS] will surely find those strongest in enmity toward the believers to be the Jews and the idolaters. You[MS] will surely find those closest in love to the believers to be those who say, "We are Christians." This is because some of them are pastors and monks, and they are not proud.[989] (82) When they hear what was revealed to the messenger, you[MS] see their eyes overflow with tears because of the truth they knew. They say, "Our Lord, we believe. Record us as witnesses. (83) Why should we not believe in Allah and the truth that has come to us, and desire that our Lord make us enter along with righteous people." (84) Allah rewarded them for their sayings with heavenly gardens with flowing rivers underneath, where they will be forever. That is the reward of the generous.[990] (85) Those who disbelieve and reject our signs are destined for the blazing fire. (86) Believers, do not forbid[MP] the good things Allah has allowed for you[MP].[991] Do not transgress[MP]. Allah does not love transgressors.[992] (87) Eat[MP] the allowed and delicious [food] Allah provides you[MP], and fear Allah, in whom you[MP] believe. (88) Allah does not punish you[MP] for vain words in your[MP] oaths, but he does punish you[MP] for oaths that you[MP] take solemnly. The expiation for such is either feeding ten poor people as you[MP] would normally feed your own families, clothing them, or freeing a slave. Whoever cannot afford that should fast for three days. That is expiation for your[MP] oaths if you swear. Fulfill your[MP] oaths. Thus Allah makes his signs clear to you[MP], so that you[MP] may give thanks. (89) Believers, truly wine, gambling, idols, and witchcraft are abominable works of Satan, so avoid[MP] them, so that you[MP] may prosper. (90) Satan wants to cast enmity and hatred among you through wine and gambling, and to block you[MP] from remembering Allah and performing prayers. Will you[MP] stop? (91) Obey[MP] Allah, obey[MP] the messenger, and beware[MP]. If you[MP] turn away, know that our messenger must convey the message clearly. (92) Believers who do righteous deeds[993] are not to be blamed for what they have eaten if they are reverent, believe, and do righteous

---

[989] It is important to show discernment, as not all people of the book are alike. See 5:51, 3:55.
[990] Or doers of good deeds, here and in verse 93.
[991] Injil, Colossians 2:21-22
[992] Zabur, Psalms 5:4-5, 11:5, Tawrah, Proverbs 6:16-19
[993] Injil, 1 Corinthians 3:8, James 2:14-17, Revelation 19:8

## Chapter 5

deeds, then are reverent and believe, then are reverent and generous. Allah loves the generous. (93) Believers, Allah will test you^MP with wild animals that you^MP hunt with your^MP hands and your^MP spears. Thus Allah will know who fears him in secret. Whoever transgresses after that will have painful torment. (94)
\*\*\*

Believers, do not kill wild animals while you^MP are consecrated. The punishment for someone among you^MP who intentionally kills them is that he shall offer at the Kaaba livestock equivalent to what he killed, as judged by two just men among you^MP, or as expiation, he shall feed the poor, or fasting as a ransom for that, so that he might taste the negative consequences of the matter. Allah has pardoned what is past, but Allah will take revenge on those who repeat it. Allah is strong[994] and avenging.[995] (95)
\*\*\*

Fishing and eating what you^MP catch is allowed for your^MP provision and that of the group of travelers, but hunting is forbidden as long as you^MP are consecrated. Fear Allah to whom you^MP will be gathered.[996] (96) 7A2 Allah has established the Kaaba, the sacred sanctuary a means of support for people, along with the sacred month, the offerings, and the garlands so that you^MP will know that Allah knows everything in the heavens and the earth. Allah knows everything. (97) Know^MP that Allah is severe in punishment and Allah is forgiving and merciful. (98) The messenger is only responsible to convey the message. Allah knows what you^MP show and what you^MP hide. (99) Say^MS, "The evil and the good are not the same, even if a multitude of evil[997] pleases you^MS. You^MP thinkers, fear Allah so that you may^MP prosper. (100) Believers, do not ask about things which would be evil to you^MP if made apparent.[998] If you ask about them when the Qur'an[999] is revealed, they will be made apparent to you^MP. Allah pardons them. Allah is forgiving

---

[994] Tawrah, Job 9:4, Zabur, Psalms 24:8, Injil, Ephesians 6:10, Revelation 18:8

[995] Tawrah, Deuteronomy 32:35, Ezekiel 25:17, Injil, Romans 12:19, Hebrews 10:30

[996] Here and in verse 109, see Tawrah, Joel 3:11-14, Zephaniah 3:8, Injil, Matthew 25:32, John 15:6, Revelation 16:16

[997] The word multitude is feminine and the verb is masculine, so there may be a different meaning.

[998] Or, do not ask about things if they appear harmful to you.

[999] Or recitation. See glossary for more details.

and gentle.¹⁰⁰⁰ (101) People before you^MP asked about them, and then became disbelievers because of them. (102) Allah has not allowed idolatrous practices related to camels, whether Bahira, Saiba, Wasila, or Hami, but the disbelievers promote lies about Allah. Most of them have no comprehension. (103) When they are told, "Come to what Allah has revealed and to the messenger," they say, "What we found our fathers doing¹⁰⁰¹ is enough for us." What if their fathers know nothing, and are not guided? (104) Believers, you^MP are responsible for yourselves^MP.¹⁰⁰² Those who go astray will not harm you^MP if you^MP are guided. All of you^MP will return to Allah, and he will proclaim to you^MP your^MP deeds. (105) Believers, if one of you^MP approaches death, when making a will let there be two just witnesses from among you^MP, or two others from outside your^MP group in case you^MP are travelling when death assails you^MP. After performing prayers, hold^MP them^D and if you^MP doubt them, have them^D swear by Allah, "We will not sell it, even to a relative, and we will not hide Allah's testimony, or we will be guilty." (106) If it turns out they^D are deservedly guilty, let two others who have a claim against them^D take their^D places and swear by Allah, "Our testimony is more true than theirs^D, and we have not transgressed, or we would be wicked. (107) That way, it is more likely that they^MP will give true testimony or fear that [other] oaths would contradict their^MP oaths. Fear^MP Allah and listen. Allah does not guide unbelieving people. (108) 7A3

\*\*\*

On the day Allah gathers the messengers, he says, "How were you^MP answered?" They said, "We do not know. You^MS know what is unseen." (109)

\*\*\*

When Allah said, "Isa son of Mariam, remember my blessings to you^MS and your^MS mother:¹⁰⁰³ I aided you^MS with the Holy Spirit¹⁰⁰⁴

---

¹⁰⁰⁰ Zabur, Psalms 45:4, 145:17, Injil, Matthew 11:29, Galatians 5:22

¹⁰⁰¹ Tawrah, Jeremiah 11:10, Injil, Acts 7:51, Galatians 1:14, Colossians 2:20-22

¹⁰⁰² Or your souls

¹⁰⁰³ This is the beginning of a section that refers to a number of ways in which Isa is unique among the prophets and messengers in the Qur'an. Isa is the only one who is aided by the Holy Spirit, who speaks as an infant in the cradle, who creates, who heals a man born blind and a leper, who brings forth the dead (all in this verse, 110), and who speaks after his death, which implies he is alive after his death (117). For more

## Chapter 5

so you[MS] spoke to the people in the cradle[1005] and as an adult; I taught you[MS] the book,[1006] wisdom,[1007] the Tawrah and the Injil; you create a clay bird by my permission, then you[MS] breathe into it and it becomes a bird by my permission; you[MS] heal the one born blind[1008] and the leper[1009] by my permission; you[MS] bring forth the dead[1010] by my permission; I kept the people of Israel from you[MS] when you[MS] brought them miracles."[1011] But the disbelievers among them[1012] said: This is just magic;[1013] (110) I inspired the disciples,[1014] "Believe in me and in my messenger." They said, "We believe. Witness that we have submitted." (111) When the disciples said, "Isa son of Mariam, can your[MS] Lord make a table descend upon us[1015] from heaven?"[1016] He said, "Fear Allah, if

---

information about this subject, see notes at 3:36, 4:158, 5:46, 19:19, 43:59.

[1004] Injil, Matthew 3:16-4:10, Luke 4:1, 14, 18, 10:21. See note at 2:87. His anointing as Messiah is connected with his being aided with the Holy Spirit in all three verses of the Qur'an as well as Tawrah, Isaiah 61:1, Injil, Matthew 3:16, Romans 1:4, Hebrews 9:14.

[1005] For what he says, see 19:30-33.

[1006] Tawrah, Isaiah 50:4,5

[1007] The reference here may be to the book of Proverbs, or more broadly, the Writings, /ketubim/ which include the Zabur and several other books of the Tawrah.

[1008] Injil, John 9:1-41.

[1009] Injil, Matthew 8:1-4, 11:5, Luke 17:11-19

[1010] Injil, Matthew 11:5, Luke 7:12-17, 8:40-56, John 5:21, 11:1-53.

[1011] Injil, John 7:30, 8:20. The Qur'an lists some other miracles of Isa in 3:49,52, 5: 112, 19:19,20,24,30-33. In the Injil, most of the stories of the miracles that Isa does are mentioned in Matthew 8-12, 14-15, 17, 20, Mark 1-11, Luke 1-2, 4-9, 11, 14, 17-18, 22, John 2, 4-6, 9, 11.

[1012] The Qur'an is very just and does not condemn all the people of Israel because of the unbelief of the majority. Indeed, the hawariyun, who believed, were of the people of Israel.

[1013] Injil, Matthew 9:32-35

[1014] Or hawariyun here and in verse 112. The reference is to the twelve disciples that Isa sent out as apostles. The Arabic word is of uncertain meaning. Some have suggested that it refers to their arguing, and others to their wearing white robes, or workers in bleaching clothes.

[1015] This probably refers either to the events described in the Injil, Matthew 14:14-21, Mark 6:34-44, Luke 9:11-17, John 6:5-14, or to those in the Injil, Matthew 15:32-38, Mark 8:1-9. See Zabur, Psalms 78:19-20.

[1016] The Qur'an lists other of his miracles in 3:49,52, 5:110, 19:19,20,24,30-33. Most of the miracles Isa does that are mentioned in

## Chapter 5

you<sup>MP</sup> are believers." (112) They said, "We wish to eat from it, and our hearts be calm. We know that you<sup>MS</sup> have told us the truth, and testify to that. (113) Isa son of Mariam said, "Allah, our Lord, send down a table from heaven,[1017] to be a feast for us, from the first of us to the last, and a sign from you<sup>MS</sup> and provide for us. You<sup>MS</sup> are the best provider. (114) Allah said, "I am sending it down on you<sup>MP</sup>. I will torment any of you<sup>MP</sup> who still disbelieve more than anyone in the universe." (115)

\*\*\*

Allah said, "Isa son of Mariam, did you<sup>MS</sup> tell the people: Take me and my mother as two gods in addition to Allah?"[1018] He said, "May you<sup>MS</sup> be glorified (above that)! I could not say what I have no right to say. If I had said that, you<sup>MS</sup> would have known. You<sup>MS</sup> know what is in my soul, and I do not know what is in your<sup>MS</sup> soul.[1019] You<sup>MS</sup> know what is unseen. (116)

\*\*\*

I told them only what you<sup>MS</sup> commanded me: Worship Allah, my Lord and your<sup>MP</sup> Lord.[1020] I was a witness over them while I remained among them, and when[1021] you<sup>MS</sup> made me die,[1022] you<sup>MS</sup> yourself watched over them.[1023] You<sup>MS</sup> are witness over everything. (117)

---

the Injil, with the stories behind them, are in the Injil, Matthew 8-11, 14-15,17,21, Mark 1-9,11, Luke 2,4-9,22, John 2,4-6,9,11.

[1017] Injil, Matthew 14:19, 15:36

[1018] Nowhere in any of the books is Allah ever referred to as three. See glossary for more details.

[1019] Injil, Matthew 24:36, 1 Corinthians 2:11

[1020] See Injil, Mark 12:29, John 20:17

[1021] Isa speaks of his death in the past tense. Since he speaks, he is alive, and since this conversation is recorded in the Qur'an, it happened before the Qur'an was recorded. See first note at verse 110.

[1022] This word in Arabic /tawaffa/ means "to cause to die." Some translators ignore the clear statement of the Qur'an that Isa died and instead translate common beliefs. The clearest commentary on the Qur'an is the Qur'an itself, not what others say about it. This verb, in its various forms, occurs 25 times in the Qur'an. Twice (here and 3:55) refer to Isa, and everywhere else (2:234,240, 3:193, 4:15,97, 6:60,61, 7:37,126, 8:50, 10:46,104, 12:101, 13:40, 16:28,32,70, 22:5, 32:11, 39:42, 40:67,77, 47:27), it is in the context of death. Even today, it is used euphemistically to mean "to pass away," and the word "obituaries" is from the same root.

[1023] Even though a messenger dies, Allah does not desert the believers.

\*\*\*

If you<sup>MS</sup> torment them, they are your<sup>MS</sup> servants,[1024] and if you<sup>MS</sup> forgive them, you<sup>MS</sup> are strong and wise." (118) Allah said, "This is a day when the truthfulness of the truthful benefits them. They will have heavenly gardens with flowing rivers underneath, where they will be forever. Allah is pleased with them, and they with Allah. That is the great triumph." (119)

\*\*\*

The kingdom of the heavens and the earth and everything in them is Allah's, and he can do anything. (120)[1025]

---

[1024] See glossary.
[1025] The verses in this chapter that rhyme are put together in paragraphs, separated by \*\*\*.

# Chapter 6 Al-Anaam[1026]

In the name of Allah, the most gracious and merciful.[1027] Praise be to Allah, who created the heavens and the earth[1028] and made the darkness and the light,[1029] yet the disbelievers make others equal to their Lord.[1030] (1) He created you[MP] from clay,[1031] then predestined a period of time.[1032] The period is set with him. Yet you[MP] doubt. (2) He is Allah in the heavens and the earth. He knows your[MP] secrets and what is obvious.[1033] He knows your[MP] gains. (3) They turn aside from every sign[1034] of their Lord that comes to them. (4) They rejected the truth when it came to them. News of what they made fun of will come to them. (5) Have they not seen how many generations[1035] we have destroyed before them? We made them firmer than you[MP] in the earth. We sent abundant rain[1036] on them from the sky, and made rivers flow underneath them.[1037] Then we destroyed them because of their sins, and raised up another generation in their place. (6) If we had revealed a book written on paper to you[MS] and they had touched it with their hands, the disbelievers would have said, "This is nothing but clear magic." (7) They said, "If only an angel had descended on him." If we had sent down an angel, the matter would have been decided. Then they would not have been given more time. (8) If we had made him an angel, we would have then made him a man, and we would have further obscured what was already obscure to them. (9)

---

[1026] Cattle
[1027] Zabur, Psalms 103:8, 145:8. See glossary for more details.
[1028] Here and in verses 14, 73, 79, and 103, see Tawrah, Genesis 1:1, Isaiah 42:5, 45:18.
[1029] Tawrah, Genesis 1:3-5
[1030] Tawrah, Isaiah 46:5
[1031] Tawrah, Genesis 2:7
[1032] Zabur, Psalms 139:16
[1033] Zabur, Psalms 139:1-6
[1034] Arabic /ayat/ here and in verses 21, 27, 33, 35, 37 (twice), 39, 49, 93, 124, 130, 150, 157 (twice) and 158 (twice). See glossary for more details.
[1035] or centuries
[1036] Tawrah, Deuteronomy 28:12, Job 5:10, Joel 2:23, Zabur, Psalms 68:9, Injil, Matthew 5:45
[1037] This is probably a reference to Noah's flood, with rain from the sky and fountains of the deep producing the flood. See Tawrah, Genesis 7:11

Chapter 6

Messengers before you<sup>MS</sup> were mocked,[1038] and those who ridiculed them were surrounded by what they had made fun of. (10) Say<sup>MS</sup>, "Walk<sup>MP</sup> through the land and see the punishment of rejecters." (11) Say,<sup>MS</sup> "Who owns everything in the heavens and the earth?" Say<sup>MS</sup>, "It is Allah's, He has decreed mercy for himself,[1039] to gather[1040] you<sup>MP</sup> on the day of resurrection[1041] about which there is no doubt. Those who lose their souls do not believe. (12) 7A4 Everything that lives in the night and the day is his. He hears all and knows all."[1042] (13) Say<sup>MS</sup>, "Shall I take a protector other than Allah, the creator of the heavens and the earth? He feeds[1043] and is not fed."[1044] Say<sup>MS</sup>, "I was commanded to be the first one to submit:[1045] Do not be<sup>MS</sup> a polytheist." (14) Say<sup>MS</sup>, "I fear the torment[1046] of a great day if I disobey my Lord."[1047] (15) He from whom it is averted on that day has been shown mercy. That is the clear victory.[1048] (16)

If Allah touches you<sup>MS</sup> with harm, he is the only one who removes it. If he touches you<sup>MS</sup> with good, he can do anything.[1049] (17) He is victorious over his servants.[1050] He is wise[1051] and aware. (18)

---

[1038] Tawrah, 2 Chronicles 30:10, 36:16, Zabur, Psalms 35:16, Injil, Matthew 20:19, 27:29,31,41, Mark 15:20,31, Luke 18;32, 22:63, 23:11,36

[1039] literally, he has written mercy on himself

[1040] Here and in verses 22, 51, and 72, see Tawrah, Joel 3:11-14, Zephaniah 3:8, Injil, Matthew 25:32, John 15:6, Revelation 16:16.

[1041] Tawrah, Daniel 12:2 Injil, Acts 24:15, 1 Corinthians 15:52-54, Revelation 20:11-15

[1042] Here and in verses 80, 83, 96, 115, 128, and 139, see Tawrah, Job 37:16, Isaiah 40:14, Zabur, Psalms 33:13-15, Injil, 1 John 3:20.

[1043] Zabur, Psalms 145:16

[1044] Zabur, Psalms 50:13

[1045] Injil, James 4:7. For "submit" here and in verses 71, 125, and 163, some translators do not translate this. See glossary for more details.

[1046] For "torment" here and in verses 30, 40, 49, 70, 93, 124, and 157, see Tawrah, Isaiah 50:11, Injil, Matthew 18:34, 25:41,46, Luke 16:23-28, Revelation 20:15.

[1047] Injil, Hebrews 3:19

[1048] Tawrah, Isaiah 25:8, Injil, 1 Corinthians 15:57, 1 John 5:4

[1049] Tawrah, Job 42:2, Isaiah 14:27, Daniel 4:35, Injil, Matthew 19:26, Mark 10:27, Luke 1:37

[1050] See glossary for "servant" here and in verse 88.

## Chapter 6

Say<sup>MS</sup>, "What is the greatest testimony?" Say<sup>MS</sup>, "Allah is witness between me and you<sup>MP</sup>, and this recitation[1052] has been inspired to me so I can warn you<sup>MP</sup> and those it reaches with it. Do you<sup>MP</sup> testify that there are other gods in addition to Allah?" Say<sup>MS</sup>, "I do not." Say<sup>MS</sup>, "He is one god,[1053] and I am innocent of the other gods you believe in." (19) Those whom we gave the book know it[1054] as they know their children.[1055] Those who lose their souls do not believe. (20) Who is more wicked than him who invents a lie about Allah or rejects his signs? The wicked do not prosper. (21) On the day when we gather them all, we will say to the idolaters, "Where are those other supposed gods?" (22) Their temptation will only be that they will say, "[We swear] by Allah our Lord, we were not idolaters." (23) Look<sup>MS</sup> how they lied against themselves, and how what they invented went astray[1056] from them. (24) Some of them listen to you<sup>MS</sup> and we put veils over their hearts[1057] lest they understand, and deafness in their ears. Even if they see every sign,[1058] they will not believe. Even if they come to you<sup>MS</sup> arguing with you<sup>MS</sup>, disbelievers will say, "This is nothing but old fables." (25) They forbid it and go away from it. They destroy only themselves, though they do not realize it. (26) If you<sup>MS</sup> could see them when they are made to stand over hellfire! They will say, "We wish that we were returned. We would not reject our Lord's signs, but would believe." (27) What they had hid was made

---

[1051] For "wise" here and in verses 73, 83, 128, and 139, see Tawrah, Job 9:4, Proverbs 2:6, Jeremiah 9:23-24, Injil, 1 Corinthians 1:21-25, Romans 16:27.

[1052] Or Qur'an or qur'an. See glossary for more details.

[1053] Arabic /ilah/ here twice and in verses 46, 74, 102, and 106. See glossary for more details.

[1054] The "it" is unclear. It could refer to the Book they were given, or to the oneness of Allah. Not all of the people of the Book know their book, and the Qur'an often calls some of them disbelievers, e.g. 5:78, 59:2. The Qur'an also advises those in doubt to consult with those who actually read their book 10:94, which means some do not. However, the oneness of Allah is a clear theme in all the former books and is more probably the reference here. See for example Tawrah, Deuteronomy 6:4, Injil, Mark 12:29, 1 Timothy 2:5. See also the glossary under "god."

[1055] Or" sons" here and in verses 137, 140, and 151.

[1056] Or away

[1057] Injil, 2 Corinthians 3:14

[1058] Tawrah, Isaiah 6:9, 10, Injil, Acts 28:27

## Chapter 6

obvious to them. If they had been returned, they would have gone back[1059] to what they were forbidden. They are liars. (28) They said, "Our earthly lives are everything. We will not be resurrected." (29) If you[MS] could see them when they are made to stand before their Lord! He said, "Is this not the truth?" They said, "Yes [it is. We swear] by our Lord, yes." He said, "Taste torment because of what you[MP] disbelieved in." (30) Those who disbelieve that they will meet Allah are lost. Even when the hour[1060] comes upon them, they will say, "Alas to us because of what we neglected." They will carry their burdens on their backs. Are their burdens not evil? (31) This life is only playing and amusement. The hereafter is better for the reverent. Do you[MP] not comprehend? (32) We know that what they said saddens you[MS]. They do not reject you[MS], but the wicked deny Allah's signs. (33) Messengers before you[MS] were rejected, and they endured[1061] the rejection and harm they suffered, until our salvation came. There is no substituter of Allah's words. [1062] News of the messengers has come to you[MS]. (34) If their turning away is a big issue to you[MS], if you[MS] can, seek[MS] out a tunnel in the earth or a ladder in the sky and bring them a sign. If Allah had willed, he would have gathered them in guidance. Do not be[MS] ignorant. (35) 7B1 Those who hear will respond and Allah will resurrect the dead,[1063] and they will be returned to him. (36) They said, "If only a sign had been revealed[1064] to him from his Lord!" Say[MS], "Allah can reveal a sign," but most of them do not know. (37) We neglected nothing in the book regarding living creatures on the earth or birds that fly with their wings, which were nations[1065] like you.[MP] They[1066] will be gathered to their Lord. (38) Those who reject our signs are deaf

---

[1059] Injil, 2 Peter 2:22
[1060] Injil, Revelation 14:7
[1061] See "endure" in glossary
[1062] For being impossible to change or corrupt Allah's words, see also 18:27, 6:115, 10:64.
[1063] Injil, John 5:25
[1064] The subject ("sign" - feminine) and verb ("had been revealed" - masculine) do not agree, so the meaning might be different.
[1065] For the concept of nations of animals, see Tawrah, Proverbs 30:26
[1066] The word they and the verb "will be gathered" are for thinking beings, so the beasts and birds may be figurative, referring to nations of people.

and dumb in the darkness. Allah leads whoever he wills[1067] astray and puts whoever he wills on a straight path.[1068] (39) Say[MS], "What do you[MP] think? When Allah's torment or the hour[1069] comes to you[MP], will you[MP] pray to gods other than Allah, if you[MP] are telling the truth?" (40) He is the one you[MP] will pray to, and he removes what you[MP] pray to if he wills. You[MP] will forget your[MP] other gods. (41) We sent to nations before you[MS] and afflicted them with misfortune and adversity,[1070] so that they might be humbled. (42) If they had only supplicated when our misfortune came to them! But their hearts were hardened and Satan made their deeds seem fair to them.[1071] (43) When they forgot what they were reminded of, we opened up doors of everything for them, so that they rejoiced at what they were brought. Then we took them suddenly, and they despaired.[1072] (44) The ends of the wicked people were cut off. Praise be to Allah, the Lord of the Universe. (45) Say[MS], "What do you[MP] think, if Allah takes your[MP] hearing and sight and seals your[MP] hearts, what god besides Allah can give it[1073] [back] to you[MP]? Look how we explain the signs, and then they turn aside. (46) What do you[MS] think,[1074] if Allah's torment[1075] comes upon you[MP] suddenly or obviously? Are any besides wicked people destroyed? (47) We send messengers only as bearers of good news and warners. Whoever believes and does good will not fear or grieve. (48) Torment will touch those who reject our signs for their unbelief.[1076] (49) Say[MS], "I do not tell you[MP]: I own Allah's storehouses. Nor do I know the unseen. I do not tell you[MP]: I am an angel. I follow only what is inspired to me." Say[MS], "Are the blind and the sighted equal? Do you[MP] not consider this?" (50) Use[MS] it to

---

[1067] Injil, 2 Thessalonians 2:11, Tawrah, 2 Samuel 22:27, 1 Kings 22:20-23, Ezekiel 14:9

[1068] See glossary for more details, and notes on 3:51, 6:153, 19:36, 36:61, and 43:64 on what the straight path is, here and in verses 87, 126, and 161.

[1069] Injil, Revelation 14:7

[1070] Zabur, Psalms 119:67,71

[1071] Tawrah, Genesis 3:5,6

[1072] Injil, Luke 12:16-21; the word for despair is from the same root as devil.

[1073] It is masculine, whereas if the intention was sight and hearing, the word would be feminine.

[1074] or do you[MS] think you[MP]

[1075] Injil, Revelation 9:5-6, Tawrah, 1 Samuel 16:14, Jeremiah 26:13

[1076] Or transgression or immorality, here and in verses 121 and 145.

## Chapter 6

warn those who fear being gathered to their Lord: they have no protector or intercessor besides him, so let them be reverent. (51) Do not expel^MS those who pray to their Lord early in the morning and at night, desiring his face. You^MS are not at all responsible to reckon with them, nor are they responsible to reckon with you^MS for anything. If you^MS expel them, you^MS are wicked. (52) Thus we tempted some of them by others, to say, "Are they the ones among us to whom Allah has given?" Does Allah not know best who gives thanks? (53) If believers in our signs come to you^MS, say "Peace be upon you^MP." You^MP Lord has prescribed mercy for himself, so that if any of you^MP does evil ignorantly, then repents and does good, Allah is forgiving[1077] and merciful.[1078] (54) Thus we explain the signs, so you^MS can clarify the path of wrongdoers. (55) Say^MS, "I have been forbidden to worship those you^MP pray to besides Allah." Say^MS, "I do not follow your^MP desires, or else I would go astray and not be guided." (56) Say^MS, "I [trust in][1079] a miracle from my Lord, and you^MP have rejected him. I cannot bring about what you^MP are in a hurry for. Judgment is Allah's. He relates the truth and explains best." (57) Say^MS, "If I could do what you^MP are in a hurry for, the matter would have been judged between me and you^MP. Allah well knows the wicked." (58) 7B2 He has the keys of the unseen. No one but he knows it. He knows what is on land and sea. Not even a leaf falls that he does not know about.[1080] Every seed in the dark places of the earth, whether green or dry, is [written] in a clear book. (59) He makes you^MP die at night, and he knows what you^MP do[1081] in the daytime. Then he resurrects you^MP in it so that the stated period of time would be completed. Then you^MP will return to him,[1082] and he will tell you^MP your^MP deeds. (60) He is victorious over his servants, and sends protectors[1083] over you^MP, so that when one of you^MP approaches death, our messengers make him die. They are not negligent. (61) Then they were returned to Allah, their true Master. Is judgment not his? He is the

---

[1077] Here and in verses 145 and 165, see Zabur, Psalms 103:3, 130:4, Tawrah, Isaiah 43:25, Exodus 34:7, Injil, Acts 26:18.

[1078] Here and in verses 133, 145, and 165, see glossary for more details on "merciful."

[1079] or stand upon

[1080] Injil, Matthew 10:29-30

[1081] or wound

[1082] Injil, Romans 14:12

[1083] or memorizers (to record deeds)

swiftest in reckoning. (62) Say<sup>MS</sup>, "Who will rescue you<sup>MP</sup> from the darkness of land and sea?" You<sup>MP</sup> pray to him humbly and in secret: "If he rescues us from this, we will definitely give thanks." (63) Say<sup>MS</sup>, "Allah will rescue you<sup>MP</sup> from it, and from every distress, and then you<sup>MP</sup> will worship other gods." (64) Say<sup>MS</sup>, "He can send torment upon you<sup>MP</sup> from above you<sup>MP</sup>, or beneath your<sup>MP</sup> feet, or he can confuse you<sup>MP</sup> in sects and make some of you<sup>MP</sup> taste the misery of others. See how we explain signs so that they may understand. (65)

\*\*\*

Your<sup>MS</sup> people rejected him,[1084] though he is the truth. Say<sup>MS</sup>, "I am not responsible for you<sup>MP</sup>." (66)

\*\*\*

For every message, there is a place where it settles, and you<sup>MP</sup> will know. (67) If you<sup>MS</sup> see those who engage in [discussing] our signs, turn away from them until they engage in another topic. Satan will definitely make you<sup>MS</sup> forget, so do not sit with wicked people after the reminder. (68) Those who are reverent are not responsible for their reckoning at all.[1085] [That is] a reminder, so that they may be reverent. (69) Leave<sup>MS</sup> those who take their religion as a sport and amusement. This world has deceived them. Remind<sup>MS</sup> [them] with it that souls will be turned over to perdition, as they deserve. They will have no helper or intercessor besides[1086] Allah. Though they pay any ransom, it will not be accepted from them.[1087] They are the ones delivered to perdition, as they deserve. They will drink boiling water and have painful torment for their disbelief. (70) Say<sup>MS</sup>, "Shall we pray to something besides Allah? It cannot help us or harm us,[1088] and we will be turned back on our heels after Allah guided us, like one who was infatuated with devils,[1089] distracted on the ground. His companions call him to guidance: Come to us. Say<sup>MS</sup>, "Allah's guidance is [real] guidance.

---

[1084] Or it (the torment). If the meaning is a person, this might refer to Isa. Injil, John 14:6.
[1085] It is unclear whether the meaning is that the reverent are not responsible for the reckoning of others (the unreverent) or their own. If the latter, see Injil, John 5:24
[1086] Some translations have "from"
[1087] Zabur, Psalms 49:7,8
[1088] Zabur, Psalms 115:4-7, Tawrah, Isaiah 44:20
[1089] Arabic /shayatin/ here and in verses 112 and 121. See glossary for more details.

## Chapter 6

We were commanded to submit to the Lord of the universe, (71) to perform[MP] prayers, and to fear[MP] him. You[MP] will be gathered to him. (72)

\*\*\*

He created the heavens and the earth in truth. When he says, "Be," it will be.[1090] His saying is true, and the kingdom is his. On the day the trumpet is blown, [he] knows the unseen and the seen.[1091] He is wise and aware. (73) **7B3**

\*\*\*

When Ibrahim[1092] told his father, Azar,[1093] "Do you[MS] take idols for gods? I think you[MS] and your[MS] people are clearly led astray." (74) Thus we showed Ibrahim the kingdom of the heavens and the earth, so that he would be certain. (75) When night covered him, he saw a planet.[1094] He said, "This is my Lord." When it set, he said, "I do not like things that set." (76) When he saw the moon rising, he said, "This is my Lord." When it set, he said, "If my Lord does not guide me, I will be one of the people who have gone astray." (77) When he saw the sun rising, he said, "This is my Lord. It is bigger." When it set, he said, "My people, I am innocent of the gods you[MP] worship. (78) I have set my face to the creator of the heavens and the earth as a monotheist. I am not a polytheist." (79) His people disputed with him. He said, "Do you[MP] dispute with me about Allah, who has guided me? I do not fear the gods you[MP] worship instead of him, unless my Lord wills it. My Lord's knowledge covers everything. Do you[MP] not remember? (80) How should I fear the gods you[MP] worship? You[MP] do not fear worshiping gods other than Allah that he has not authorized for you[MP]. Which of the parties[D] is more worthy of protection, if you[MP] know? (81) Believers who do not cloak their faith with wickedness are secure and guided. (82) This is the argument that we gave Ibrahim for his people. We raise in rank those we will. Your[MS] Lord is wise and all-knowing. (83) We gave him Ishaq[1095] and Yaqub,[1096] we guided

---

[1090] Tawrah, Genesis 1:3-28

[1091] or testimony

[1092] Abraham here and in verses 75, 83, and 161. See glossary for more details.

[1093] Terah

[1094] or star

[1095] Isaac. See glossary for more details.

[1096] Jacob. See glossary for more details.

## Chapter 6

them all. We guided Nuh[1097] before them, and of his seed, Dawud,[1098] Sulayman,[1099] Ayyub,[1100] Yusuf,[1101] Musa,[1102] and Harun.[1103] Thus we reward the generous. (84) Also, Zakariyya,[1104] Yahya,[1105] Isa,[1106] and Ilyas.[1107] All of them were righteous. (85) Also, Ismail,[1108] Alyasa,[1109] Yunus,[1110] and Lut.[1111] We preferred each over [the rest of] mankind.[1112] (86) Some of their ancestors, descendants, and brothers we chose and guided on the straight path. (87) That is Allah's guidance. He guides the servants he wills with it. If they had been idolaters, their works would have perished. (88) Those are the ones we gave the book, judgment, and prophethood. If they disbelieve in it, we will entrust it to other people who are not disbelievers.[1113] (89) Allah guided them, so follow[MS] their guidance. Say[MS], "I do not ask you[MP] for payment. It is only a reminder to mankind." (90) They did not give Allah the honor he deserves, for they said, "Allah has not revealed anything to men." Say[MS], "Who revealed the book which Musa brought as light and guidance to men?[1114] You[MP] make it sheets of paper to show off, and you[MP] hide much, and were taught much that neither you[MP] nor your[MP] fathers knew." Say[MS], "Allah." Then let them play in their discussions. (91) This is a blessed book we revealed, confirming[1115] what is in in his possession.[1116] Warn the mother of

---

[1097] Noah. See glossary for more details.
[1098] David. See glossary for more details.
[1099] Solomon. See glossary for more details.
[1100] Job. See glossary for more details.
[1101] Joseph, son of Jacob. See glossary for more details.
[1102] Moses, here and in verses 91 and 154. See glossary for more details.
[1103] Aaron. See glossary for more details.
[1104] Zechariah. See glossary for more details.
[1105] John the Baptist. See glossary for more details.
[1106] Jesus. See glossary for more details.
[1107] Elijah. See glossary for more details.
[1108] Ishmael. See glossary for more details.
[1109] Elisha. See glossary for more details.
[1110] Jonah. See glossary for more details.
[1111] Lot. See glossary for more details.
[1112] or the universe
[1113] Injil, Matthew 21:43.
[1114] See 5:44
[1115] The Qur'an confirms the previous books many times (2:41,89,91,97,101, 3:3,81, 4:47, 5:48, 6:92, 35:31, 46:12,30)

## Chapter 6

villages and those around it. Believers in the hereafter believe in him[1117] and keep doing their prayers. (92) Who is more wicked than him who invents lies about Allah or says, "I was inspired," when he was not inspired at all,[1118] or him who says, "I will reveal something similar to what Allah revealed." If only you[MS] could see the wicked as they suffer the pangs of death, when the angels stretch out their hands: "Expel[MP] your[MP] souls. Today you[MP] will be paid back with contemptuous torment for your[MP] false sayings about Allah. You[MP] were arrogant toward his signs. (93) You[MP] have come to us individually, as we created you[MP] the first time, and you[MP] left what we bestowed on you[MP] behind your[MP] backs. We do not see your[MP] intercessors with you[MP], those whom you[MP] claimed were your[MP] partners. What you[MP] claimed has been cut off from you[MP], and gone astray from you[MP]. (94) 7B4 Allah splits the seed and the date pit. He brings forth the living from among the dead[1119] and brings forth the dead from among the living. That is Allah. How can you[MP] lie? (95) He makes the morning break, makes the night quiet, and [makes] the sun and moon a reckoning.[1120] This is decreed by the strong,[1121] all-knowing one. (96) He makes stars to guide you[MP] in the darkness of land and seas. We have explained our signs to people who know. (97) He made you[MP] from one soul, as a fixed dwelling and storehouse.[1122] We have explained our signs to people who understand. (98) He sent rain[1123] down from the sky, and with it we brought forth all kinds of plants. By it we brought forth green herbs. By it, we bring forth heaps of seeds. From the palm buds, date clusters hanging low, and gardens of grapes, olives, and pomegranates, both similar and dissimilar. Look at their fruit when it comes forth and ripens.

---

[1116] Or "in his hands," or "in front of him" or "before it." Allah does not have a physical body or hands, but like the Injil and Tawrah, the Qur'an uses anthropomorphisms to talk about Allah. Hands covey the idea of possessing.
[1117] or it (the book)
[1118] Tawrah, Jeremiah 23:28-29
[1119] Injil, Luke 24:5-7
[1120] Tawrah, Genesis 1:14-17
[1121] Tawrah, Job 9:4, Zabur Psalms 24:8, Injil, Ephesians 6:10, Revelation 18:8
[1122] the meaning here could be the womb
[1123] Tawrah, Deuteronomy 28:12, Job 5:10, Joel 2:23, Zabur, Psalms 68:9, Injil, Matthew 5:45

## Chapter 6

Those are signs for people who believe. (99) They made jinns[1124] equal to Allah, though he created them, and falsely claim he has sons and daughters, though they do not know. May he be glorified and exalted above what they describe! (100) He is the creator of the heavens and the earth. How could he have a boy, since he has no girlfriend?[1125] He created everything, and knows everything. (101) He is Allah, your[MP] Lord. He is the only god, the creator of everything. So worship him. He is in charge of all things. (102) No eye sees him, but he sees them. He is kind and aware. (103) Insights from your[MP] Lord have come to you[MP]. He who sees benefits himself, and he who is blind harms himself. I am not your[MP] keeper. (104) Thus we explain signs, so they will say, "You[MS] have studied," and so we will explain them to people who know. (105) Follow[MS] what was inspired to you[MS] by your Lord. He is the only god. Turn[MS] away from idolaters. (106)

\*\*\*

If Allah had willed, they would not have been idolaters, and we would not have made you[MS] their keeper.[1126] You[MS] are not responsible for them. (107)

\*\*\*

Do not swear[MP] at those who pray to other gods beside Allah,[1127] lest they swear at Allah maliciously and unknowingly. Thus we made every nation's works seem pleasing to them. Then they will return to their Lord, who will tell them what they did. (108) They swear strong oaths by Allah that if a sign comes to them, they will believe in it. Say[MS], "The signs are Allah's." What will make you[MP] realize that if one comes, they will not believe. (109) We turn over their hearts and their sight, just as they have not believed in him[1128] the first time. We leave them to wander about in their transgression. (110) 8A1 If we had sent angels down on them, if

---

[1124] Or demons, here and in verses 112, 128, and 130. See glossary for more details.

[1125] i.e. sexual partner. All the books reject the idea of Allah having sexual relations with a woman.

[1126] Tawrah, Genesis 4:9.

[1127] Or, at the gods they pray to besides Allah.

[1128] This word is masculine and nothing in the immediate context fits as a masculine noun. The word sight is feminine. Reference is probably to Allah.

## Chapter 6

the dead had spoken to them,[1129] and if we had gathered everything facing against them, they would not have believed except if Allah had willed. But most of them are ignorant. (111) Thus we made an enemy for every prophet: devils among men and jinns, who inspire each other with fancy sayings [130] to tempt. If your<sup>MS</sup> Lord had not willed it, they would not have done so. Leave them and their lies. (112) Let the hearts of those who do not believe in the hereafter listen and please him, and let them continue to commit the same sins.[1131] (113) Do I want a judge other than Allah? He revealed the book to you<sup>MP</sup> in detail. Those whom we gave the book know that it is revealed from your<sup>MS</sup> Lord in truth. Do not doubt. (114) And the word of your<sup>MS</sup> Lord was fulfilled in truth and justice. There is no substituter of his words,[1132] and he hears all and knows all. (115) If you<sup>MS</sup> obey most of those on earth, they will cause you<sup>MS</sup> to go astray from Allah's path. They are following mere conjecture. They merely guess. (116) Your<sup>MS</sup> Lord knows best who has gone astray from his path, and he knows best those who are guided. (117) So eat<sup>MP</sup> what has had Allah's name mentioned over it, if you<sup>MP</sup> believe Allah's signs. (118) What is wrong with you<sup>MP</sup>? Why do you<sup>MP</sup> not eat what has had Allah's name mentioned over it? He has explained to you<sup>MP</sup> what he has forbidden to you<sup>MP</sup> except in cases of necessity.[1133] Many unknowingly lead others astray by their desires. Your<sup>MS</sup> Lord knows best who are the wicked. (119) Forsake<sup>MP</sup> both obvious and hidden guilt.[1134] Those who are guilty will be repaid, as they deserve. (120) Do not eat what has not had Allah's name mentioned over it. It is unbelief. Devils inspire their supporters to dispute with you<sup>MP</sup>. If you<sup>MP</sup> obey them, you<sup>MP</sup> are idolaters. (121)

\*\*\*

Is someone who was dead, whom we made alive and gave light to walk among people, like someone still in darkness? Thus we made disbelievers' works seem pleasing to them. (122) Thus we

---

[1129] It is unclear who the dead people are that spoke to them. Isa is the only one named in the Qur'an who spoke after his death (5:117).
[1130] Or traditions
[1131] Injil, Revelation 22:11
[1132] For being impossible to change or corrupt Allah's words, see also 18:27, 6:34, 10:64.
[1133] The foods that are forbidden are permitted if starvation is the only other option.
[1134] Zabur, Psalms 19:12,13

appointed major wrongdoers in every village to plot in it. They plot only against themselves, and they do not realize it. (123) If a sign comes to them, they say, "We will not believe until we receive something like Allah's messengers brought." Allah knows best where to put his message. Vileness before Allah will afflict wrongdoers, and harsh torment for their plots. (124) If Allah wants to guide someone, he opens his heart to submit, and if he wants to lead someone astray, he tightens and narrows his heart, as if he were ascending in the sky. Thus Allah puts an abomination on those who do not believe. (125) This is your[MS] Lord's straight path. We explain our signs to people who remember. (126) 8A2 They will have the house of peace[1135] with their Lord. He is their protector in what they did. (127) On the day he gathers them all, legion[1136] of jinns, you have influenced[1137] mankind a lot. Their helpers among people said, "Our Lord, we have enjoyed each other. We have reached the end of our lives as you[MS] determined for us." He said, "Your[MP] dwelling is hellfire, where you[MP] will be forever, except as Allah wills. Your[MS] Lord is wise and all-knowing." (128) Thus we set some of the wicked over others, as they deserve. (129) Legion[1138] of jinns and men, have messengers from among you[MP] not come to you[MP], relating our signs and warning you[MP] of this day of meeting? They said, "We testify against ourselves. The world enticed us." They testified against themselves that they were disbelievers. (130) That is because your[MS] Lord did not wickedly destroy the villages while their people were unaware. (131) All have their own degree of what they have done. Your[MS] Lord is aware of what they do. (132) Your[MS] Lord is self-sufficient and merciful. If he wills, he does away with you[MP] and makes whom he wants your[MP] successors, just as he established you[MP] from the seed of other people. (133) What you[MP] have been promised is coming. You[MP] cannot stop it. (134) Say,[MS] "My people, do according to your[MP] situation. I am doing so, and you[MP] will know who has the reward of heaven."[1139] The wicked do not prosper. (135) They set aside a portion of their fields and cattle, and claim, "This is for Allah, and this is for our partners." Their partners' portion does not reach Allah, and what

---

[1135] Injil, John 14:1-3, 27
[1136] Here and in verse 130, see Injil, Mark 5:9.
[1137] i.e. by seducing them
[1138] the meaning may be, "You who have been close to..."
[1139] or the house

was Allah's goes to their partners. Their judgment is evil. (136) Their partners make many idolaters pleased with killing their children, in order to destroy them and obscure their religion to them. If Allah had willed, they would not have done it, so let them and their lies alone. (137) They claim, "These cattle and fields are forbidden as food. None may eat them unless we wish it." The backs of the cattle are forbidden, and they do not mention Allah's name over them. They lie to him, and he will punish them for their lies. (138) They said, "What is in the wombs of these cattle is specifically for our men[1140] and it is forbidden to our women." If it is dead,[1141] they share it. He will punish them for their description. He is wise and all-knowing. (139) Those who killed their children are lost, foolish and unknowing. They have forbidden what Allah provided, lying to Allah. They have gone astray, and were not guided. (140) 8A3

\*\*\*

He planted trellised and untrellised gardens, palm trees, and differing plants for food: olives, pomegranates, similar yet dissimilar. Eat their fruit when it ripens, and pay for it on harvest day. Do not waste it. He does not love wasters.[1142] (141) Some cattle are beasts of burden or for slaughter. Eat what Allah has provided you[MP], and do not follow Satan's steps; he is your[MP] clear enemy. (142) Eight pair: two of sheep, and two of goats. Say[MS], "Are the two males forbidden or the two females? Or what the two females bear in their wombs? Tell[MP] me clearly, if you[MP] are telling the truth." (143) Two camels and two oxen. Say[MS], "Are the two males forbidden or the two females? Or what the two females bear in their wombs? Were you[MP] witnesses when Allah commanded you[MP] about this? Who is more wicked than him who invents lies about Allah to lead people without knowledge astray? Allah does not guide wicked people." (144) Say[MS], "I find in what has been inspired to me no food that is forbidden to eat except for carcasses, poured out blood, or pork, which is an abomination, or meat slaughtered in the name of other gods in unbelief. If someone is desperate, unwillingly and unintentionally, Allah is forgiving and merciful." (145) We have forbidden everything with claws[1143] to

---

[1140] Tawrah, Numbers 18:10

[1141] The word "it is" is masculine, but "dead" is feminine. Possibly another meaning is intended.

[1142] Zabur, Psalms 5:4-5, 11:5, Tawrah, Proverbs 6:16-19

[1143] Tawrah, Leviticus 11:27

the Jews,[1144] as well as the fat of the oxen and sheep,[1145] except for on their backs or intestines, or what is mixed with bone. That is because we paid them back for their wrongdoing, and we are telling the truth. (146) If they reject you[MS], say, "Your[MP] Lord's mercy is broad, and his vengeance will not be turned back from people who do wrong." (147)

\*\*\*

Idolaters will say, "If Allah had willed, we and our ancestors would not have been idolaters, and we would not have forbidden anything. This is how those before them rejected, so they tasted our vengeance." Say[MS], "If you[MP] know anything, show us. You[MP] are following mere conjecture. You[MP] merely guess." (148) Say[MS], "Allah's argument is conclusive. If he had willed, he would have guided you[MP] all." (149) Say[MS], "Bring[MP] witnesses who will testify that Allah forbade this." If they testify, do not testify[MS] with them. Do not follow[MS] the desires of those who reject our signs and those who do not believe in the hereafter, as they make other gods equal to their Lord. (150) 8A4 Say[MS], "Come[MP] and I will read[1146] what your[MP] Lord has forbidden for you[MP]: do not have other gods beside him,[1147] do good to your parents,[1148] do not kill your children because of poverty – we provide for you[MP] and them, – stay away from promiscuity,[1149] whether it is obvious or hidden, and do not kill someone, which Allah has forbidden, except in justice. He commanded you[MP] that, so that you[MP] may comprehend. (151) Stay away from an orphan's money, except fairly, until he reaches adulthood, and have just weights and balances.[1150] We never give anyone more than he can handle.[1151] If you[MP] say something, be just about it, even in the case of a relative. Keep Allah's covenant. This is what he has commanded you[MP], so that you[MP] may

---

[1144] Or those who repented and turned back to the truth. This refers to the Jews, probably when they repented after worshiping the golden calf idol (2:54, 92, 7:138, 148-150, Tawrah, Exodus 32).
[1145] Tawrah, Leviticus 3:14-16.
[1146] Or recite or tell
[1147] Tawrah, Exodus 20:3
[1148] Tawrah, Exodus 20:12
[1149] Or lewdness, adultery or abomination, see Tawrah, Exodus 20:14
[1150] Tawrah, Leviticus 19:36
[1151] Injil, 1 Corinthians 10:13

## Chapter 6

remember. (152) This is my straight path,[1152] so follow it, and do not follow [other] paths, lest you[MP] scatter from his path. He commanded you[MP] that, so that you[MP] may be reverent." (153) Then we gave Musa the book, complete for him who does good, an explanation of everything, guidance, and mercy, so that they may believe in a meeting with their Lord. (154) And this is a blessed book which we revealed, so follow[MP] it and be reverent, so that you[MF] may receive mercy, (155) lest you[MP] say, "The book was revealed to two groups before us and we were unaware of their studying,"[1153] (156) or say, "If the book had been revealed to us, we would have been better guided than they," since a miracle, guidance, and mercy has come to you[MP] from your[MP] Lord. Who is more wicked than one who rejects Allah's signs, and turns from them? We will repay those who turn from our signs with awful torment because of their turning away. (157) Do they expect that the angels will come to them, or that your[MS] Lord will come, or that some of your[MS] Lord's signs will come? When some of your[MS] Lord's signs come, faith will not help them since they did not believe beforehand or gain any good from their faith. Say[MS], "Wait. We are waiting." (158) You[MS] are not one of those who cause divisions and sects in their religion at all. Their issue is with Allah, and he will tell them what they did. (159) He who does a good deed will be credited ten times, and he who does a bad deed will only be punished once. They will not be wronged. (160) Say[MS], "My Lord has guided me to a straight path, a right religion, the spiritual path[1154] of Ibrahim, monotheism. He was not a polytheist." (161) Say[MS], "My prayers, devotion, life and death are Allah's;[1155] he is the Lord of the universe. (162) He has no partner. This is what I was commanded. I am the first one to submit." (163) Say[MS], "Do I want a lord other than Allah? He is the Lord of everything. Each soul gets only what it deserves. No one carries

---

[1152] See glossary for more details, and notes on 3:51, 6:153, 19:36, 36:61, and 43:64 on what the straight path is. From the context, some infer that the straight path involves keeping Allah's commandments, possibly the Ten Commandments that Musa was given by Allah (Tawrah, Exodus 20:1-17, Deuteronomy 5:6-21).

[1153] In other words, Muslims should be aware of the former books by studying them.

[1154] Arabic /millah/. See glossary.

[1155] Philippians 1:20-25

## Chapter 6

another's burden.[1156] Then to your[MP] Lord you[MP] will return, and he will inform you[MP] about your[MP] differences. (164) He appointed you[MP] as regents of the earth.[1157] He raised some of you[MP] to a higher rank than others, to test you[MP] through what he gave you[MP]." Your[MS] Lord is quick to punish. He is forgiving and merciful. (165)[1158]

---

[1156] Injil, Galatians 6:5
[1157] Tawrah, Genesis 1:28
[1158] The verses in this chapter that rhyme are put together in paragraphs, separated by ***.

# Chapter 7 Al-Aaraf[1159]

8B1 In the name of Allah, the most merciful and Gracious.[1160] ALMS.[1161] (1) A book was revealed to you[MS], so do not let there be any difficulty in your[MS] heart because of it, so you[MS] may warn with it. [It is] a reminder for believers. (2) Follow[MP] what was revealed to you[MP] from your[MP] Lord, and do not follow[MP] any helpers beside him. You[MP] remember little. (3) How many villages we destroyed! Thus our vengeance came upon them at night or napping. (4) Their only prayer, when our vengeance came to them, was that they said, "We were wicked." (5) We will certainly ask those who were sent to them, and we will certainly ask the messengers. (6) We will relate knowledge to them, and we were not absent. (7) The weighing that day is the truth. Those whose weight[1162] is heavy are successful. (8) Those whose weight is light will lose their souls, because they were wicked regarding our signs.[1163] (9) We established you[MP] on the earth and we gave you[MP] provision. How little you[MP] give thanks. (10) We created you[MP], then formed you[MP], then told the angels, "Bow[MP] down[1164] to Adam."[1165] All except Iblis[1166] bowed down; he did not bow down. (11) He[1167] said, "What kept you[MS] from bowing down, since I commanded you[MS]?" He said, "I am better than he is. You[MS] created me from fire, and you[MS] created him from clay." (12) He[1168] said, "Go down[MS] from

---

[1159] Dividing wall between heaven and hell; other possibilities are "The Heights", "Faculties of Discernment," or "The Customs."

[1160] Zabur, Psalms 103:8, 145:8. See glossary for more details.

[1161] Here and at the beginning of many chapters there are unvowelled letters of unknown meaning. Numerous theories have been proposed, but there is no agreement on the subject. These letters are not related to the word alms in English.

[1162] Here and in verse 9, the weight of good deeds.

[1163] Arabic /ayat/ here and in verses 36, 37, 40, 51, 64, 72, 146 (three times), 147, 176, 177, and 182. See glossary for more details.

[1164] Zabur, Psalms 97:7, Injil, Hebrews 1:6

[1165] For Adam here and in verses 19, 26, 27, 31, 35, and 172, see glossary for more details.

[1166] The devil. See glossary for more details.

[1167] i.e. Allah

[1168] i.e. Allah

## Chapter 7

it.[1169] You[MS] have no right to be proud in it. So go[MS] out. You[MS] are contemptible." (13) He said, "Reprieve[MS] me until the day they are resurrected."[1170] (14) He[1171] said, "You[MS] are reprieved." (15) He said, "Since you[MS] have led me astray, I will sit[MS] in ambush for them on your[MS] straight path.[1172] (16) Then I will come to them[M] in front of them, behind them, on their right and on their left. You'll[MS] find most of them do not give thanks." (17) He[1173] said, "Go out[MS] of it, despised and rejected." I will fill hell with you[MP]: you[MS] and those among them who follow you[MS]. (18) Adam, you[MS] and your[MS] wife, live[D] in the heavenly garden,[1174] and eat[D] wherever you[D] want.[1175] Do not come[D] near this tree, or you'll[D] be[D] wicked."[1176] (19) Satan whispered[1177] to them[D] to show them[D] their[D] hidden shame;[1178] he said, "Your[D] Lord only forbade this tree to you[D] lest you be angels or immortal."[1179] (20) He[1180] swore to them[D], "I am your[D] advisor."[1181] (21) So he guided them[D] in temptation, and when they[D] tasted the tree,[1182] their[D] shame was apparent[1183] to them[D] and they began[D] to sew[D] leaves of the heavenly garden[1184] upon themselves[D]. Their Lord called them[D], "Did I not forbid you[D] from that tree[1185] and tell you[D], Satan is truly a clear enemy to you[D]?" (22) They[D] said, "Our Lord, we have wronged ourselves, and if you[MS] do not forgive us[1186] and have mercy on us, we will

---

[1169] Injil, Revelation 12:9

[1170] Injil, John 5:21, Acts 5:30, 2 Corinthians 4:14, 1 Peter 1:21

[1171] i.e. Allah

[1172] See glossary for more details, and notes on 3:51, 6:153, 19:36, 36:61, and 43:64 on what the straight path is.

[1173] i.e. Allah

[1174] Arabic /jannah/ here and in verses 22, 27, 40, and 50. See glossary for more details.

[1175] Tawrah, Genesis 2:16

[1176] Tawrah, Genesis 2:17

[1177] Tawrah, Genesis 3:1

[1178] Tawrah, Genesis 3:10

[1179] Tawrah, Genesis 3:4-5

[1180] i.e. Satan

[1181] Tawrah, Genesis 3:4

[1182] Tawrah, Genesis 3:6

[1183] Tawrah, Genesis 3:10

[1184] Tawrah, Genesis 3:7

[1185] Tawrah, Genesis 3:11

[1186] The belief that all prophets and messengers are sinless is not supported by the Qur'an. For instances of prophets or messengers asking

## Chapter 7

certainly be lost." (23) He said, "Go down[MP],[1187] each of you[MP] an enemy to each other.[1188] You have the earth to settle on,[1189] and enjoy for a while." (24) He said, "On it, you[MP] will live and die, then be brought[MP] forth from it.[1190] (25) Children of Adam, we have sent down upon you[MP] clothing and feathers to hide your[MP] shame.[1191] The clothing of reverence[1192] is the best." This is one of Allah's signs,[1193] so that they[MP] may remember. (26) Children of Adam, do not let Satan tempt you[MP] as he expelled your[MP] ancestors[D] from the heavenly garden, stripping their[D] clothing[1194] from them[D] to show them their[D] shame. He and his tribe see you[MP] from where you[MP] do not see them[MP]." We have made devils[1195] helpers of those who do not believe. (27) If they[MP] commit promiscuity,[1196] they say, "We found our fathers doing it and Allah has commanded us to do it too." Say[MS], "Allah does not command promiscuity. Do you[MP] say what you[MP] do not know about Allah?" (28) Say[MS], "My Lord has commanded justice. Set your[MP] faces straight at every place of worship, and pray to[MP] him with sincere religion. As he created[1197] you[MP], you[MP] will return." (29) One group he guided and another group deserved to stray.[1198] They[MP] took

---

forgiveness or committing sins, see 7:23, 20:121 (Adam), 11:47, 71:28 (Nuh), 26:82, 14:41 (Ibrahim), 28:15-16 (Musa), 7:151, 20:93 (Musa and Harun), 38:24 (Dawud), 38:32,35 (Sulayman), 21:87, 37:142 (Yunus), 48:2, 47:19, 40:55, 4:79,106, 9:43, 13:30, 80:1-2, 110:3, 94:2, 23:118, 66:1, 33:37, 8:67, and 9:117 (Muhammad (s).

[1187] Here and in verse 27, see Tawrah, Genesis 3:24. The command to go down is in the plural, not the dual, so it includes Adam, Eve, and Iblis.
[1188] Tawrah, Genesis 3:15-16
[1189] Tawrah, Genesis 3:23
[1190] Tawrah, Genesis 3:19
[1191] Tawrah, Genesis 3:21
[1192] Tawrah, Isaiah 61:10, Injil, Ephesians 6:14
[1193] The clothing Allah provided for the children of Adam and the clothing of reverence are a sign or symbol that is expanded upon in the Qur'an.
[1194] This may be figurative, referring to their innocence, since before they disobeyed Allah they were righteous, which is described in verse 26 as clothing.
[1195] Arabic /shayatin/ here and in verse 30. See glossary for more details.
[1196] Or lewdness, adultery or abomination, here twice and in verses 33 and 80.
[1197] Or began.
[1198] Deserve is masculine and error is feminine. There may be a special meaning.

## Chapter 7

devils as helpers besides Allah, and imagine that they are guided. (30) ßB2 Children of Adam, take<sup>MP</sup> your<sup>MP</sup> apparel at every place of worship, eat<sup>MP</sup> and drink<sup>MP</sup>, but do not waste<sup>MP</sup>. He does not love the wasteful.[1199] (31) Say<sup>MS</sup>, "Who forbids Allah's adornment, which he brought forth for his servants,[1200] and the good things of the provision?" Say<sup>MS</sup>, "It is for the believers in this world, ready on the day of resurrection."[1201] Thus we explain signs for people who know. (32) Say<sup>MS</sup>, "My Lord has forbidden both public and private promiscuity, guilt, unlawful oppression, belief in other gods besides Allah, for which he has not given authority, and saying things you<sup>MP</sup> do not know about Allah." (33) Every nation has its lifespan, and when their time comes, they cannot delay it or advance it by one hour."[1202] (34) Children of Adam, messengers will come to you<sup>MP</sup> telling you<sup>MP</sup> our signs. Those who are reverent and make amends[1203] shall not fear or grieve. (35) Those who reject our signs and are proud against them will go to hellfire, where they will be forever. (36) Who is more wicked than him who invents a lie about Allah or who rejects his signs? They will receive their portion from[1204] the book. Even when our messengers come to them to make them die, they say, "Where are the gods you<sup>MP</sup> prayed to besides Allah?" They said, "They have strayed from us. They witness against themselves that they were disbelievers." (37) He said, "Enter among the nations of jinns[1205] and people that have passed away before you<sup>MP</sup> into hellfire." Every time a nation enters, they curse their sister nations, until they are all overtaken in it. Then the last will tell the first, "Our Lord, these made us go astray, so give them double[1206] the torment[1207] in hellfire." He said, "All will get double, but you<sup>MP</sup> do not know." (38) Then the first told the last, "You<sup>MP</sup> have no more

---

[1199] Zabur, Psalms 5:4-5, 11:5, Tawrah, Proverbs 6:16-19

[1200] See glossary for "servant" here and in verse 194.

[1201] For "day of resurrection" here and in verses 167 and 172, see Tawrah, Daniel 12:2 Injil, Acts 24:15, 1 Corinthians 15:52-54, Revelation 20:11-15

[1202] Injil, Matthew 6:27, Luke 12:25

[1203] Or do good or reconcile.

[1204] Or of

[1205] Or demons here and in verse 179. See glossary for more details.

[1206] Tawrah, Isaiah 40:2, Injil, Romans 2:9,10

[1207] Here and in verses 39, 59, 73, 156, 164, and 165, see Tawrah, Isaiah 50:11, Injil, Matthew 18:34, 25:41,46, Luke 16:23-28, Revelation 20:15.

## Chapter 7

grace than we do, so taste the torment you<sup>MP</sup> deserve. (39) Heaven's doors will not be opened to those who reject our signs and are proud against them, and they will not enter the heavenly garden until a camel goes through the eye of a tailor's needle."[1208] Thus we repay wrongdoers. (40) Their abode is hell, and they will be covered. Thus we repay the wicked. (41) We do not burden believers who do righteous deeds[1209] with more than what they can bear.[1210] They will go to the heavenly garden and be there forever. (42) We tore out the enmity from their hearts, and made rivers flow underneath them. They said: Praise be to Allah, who guided us to this. We would not have been guided unless Allah had guided us. Messengers of our Lord came with truth, and they were told, "This is the heavenly garden. You<sup>MP</sup> have inherited it for your<sup>MP</sup> deeds." (43) Heaven's inhabitants called to the inhabitants of hellfire, "We found what our Lord promised to be true. Have you<sup>MP</sup> found what your<sup>MP</sup> Lord promised to be true?" They said, "Yes." A caller among them called, "Allah's curse[1211] is on the wicked, (44) who block others from Allah's path[1212] and want it[1213] crooked.[1214] They disbelieve in the hereafter." (45) Between them is a curtain,[1215] and over the dividing wall are men who are all known by their mark.[1216] They called the inhabitants of heaven, "Peace be upon you<sup>MP</sup>." They have not entered it as they desired. (46) 8B3 If their gaze is averted towards the inhabitants of hellfire, they said, "Our Lord, do not put us with wicked people." (47) Those on the dividing wall called men they knew by their mark. They said, "Your<sup>MP</sup> hoarding did not benefit you<sup>MP</sup>, nor your<sup>MP</sup> pride. (48) Are those the ones you<sup>MP</sup> swore about: Allah will not reach them with mercy?" Enter the heavenly garden, neither fearing or grieving. (49) The inhabitants of hellfire called to the inhabitants of the heavenly garden, "Pour<sup>MP</sup> on us some extra water

---

[1208] Injil, Matthew 19:24, Mark 10:25, Luke 18:25

[1209] Injil, 1 Corinthians 3:8, James 2:14-17, Revelation 19:8

[1210] Injil, 1 Corinthians 10:13

[1211] Injil, 1 Corinthians 16:22

[1212] Injil, Matthew 23:13, Luke 11:52.

[1213] "It" is feminine and "path" is masculine. Possibly "it" refers to the curse of the previous verse.

[1214] Here and in verse 86, see Injil, Acts 13:10.

[1215] Injil, Luke 16:26

[1216] Injil, Revelation 14:9-11

## Chapter 7

or whatever Allah has provided you[MP]."[1217] They said, "Allah has forbidden both of them to disbelievers."[1218] (50) Today we will forget those who take their religion as an amusement and a game, whom this world has tempted, just as they forgot the meeting on their day with them. This is because they deny our signs. (51) We brought them a book which we explained according to knowledge as guidance and mercy to people who believe. (52) They only wait for its interpretation. When its interpretation comes, those who forgot it beforehand will say, "Messengers of our Lord came with truth. Do we have intercessors to intercede for us, or will we be returned and do differently than what we used to do? They have lost their souls, and what they lied about has strayed from them. (53) Your[MP] Lord is Allah, who created the heavens and the earth[1219] in six days,[1220] then sat down on the throne.[1221] He covers the night with the day, following it quickly. The sun,[1222] moon and stars are subject to his command.[1223] Does he not have creation and a command? Blessed be Allah, Lord of the universe. (54) Pray to your[MP] Lord in supplication and in secret. He does not love transgressors.[1224] (55) Do not cause destruction on the earth after it has been made right. Pray to him in fear and desire. Allah's mercy[1225] is near to those who do good. (56) He sent the winds bearing good news in front of[1226] his mercy, until it bears heavy clouds, which we brought upon a dead land, sent rain[1227] down from it, and brought forth by it all kinds of fruit. This is how we bring forth the dead, so that you[MP] may remember. (57) The good land[1228] brought forth its plants with its Lord's permission, and the evil one brings forth only little. Thus we explain the signs to

---

[1217] Injil, Luke 16:23-24
[1218] Injil, Luke 16:25
[1219] Tawrah, Genesis 1:1, Isaiah 42:5, 45:18
[1220] Tawrah, Genesis 1:1-31
[1221] Tawrah, Genesis 2:2
[1222] Zabur, Psalms 136:8
[1223] Zabur, Psalms 136:9
[1224] Zabur, Psalms 5:4-5, 11:5, Tawrah, Proverbs 6:16-19
[1225] "Mercy" has a different spelling here and in 6 other places. See glossary.
[1226] Or, "between the hands of" or "before."
[1227] Tawrah, Deuteronomy 28:12, Job 5:10, Joel 2:23, Zabur, Psalms 68:9, Injil, Matthew 5:45
[1228] Or country or place

## Chapter 7

people who give thanks. (58) We sent Nuh[1229] to his people. He said, "My people, worship Allah. He is your[MP] only god.[1230] I fear that you[MP] will suffer the torment of a great day." (59) The nobility of his people said, "We think you[MS] are clearly led astray." (60) He said, "My people, I have not gone astray, but I am a messenger from the Lord of the universe. (61) I bring you[MP] my Lord's messages, and I advise you[MP]. I know things from Allah that you[MP] do not. (62) Are you[MP] amazed that the reminder[1231] came to you[MP] from your[MP] Lord by a man from among you[MP] to warn you[MP], so that you[MP] would be reverent and receive mercy." (63) So they rejected him, and we rescued him along with those who were with him in the ark. We drowned those who rejected our signs. They were blind people. (64) 8B4 To Aad[1232] [we sent] their brother Hud. He said, "My people, worship Allah. He is your[MP] only god[1233]. Are you[MP] not reverent?" (65) The disbelieving nobility of his people said, "We think you[MS] are silly. We think you[MS] are a liar." (66) He said, "My people, I am not silly, but I am a messenger from the Lord of the universe. (67) I bring you[MP] messages from my Lord, and I am a faithful advisor. (68) Do you[MP] like it that a reminder has come from your[MP] Lord to a man from among you[MP] to warn you[MP]. Remember when he made you[MP] regents after Nuh's people, and he increased your[MP] stature[1234] among the creation, so remember[MP] Allah's benefits so that you[MP] may prosper. (69) They said, "Have you[MS] come to us so that we would worship only Allah and leave what our fathers worshiped? Bring[MS] on what you[MS] promise us if you[MS] are telling the truth." (70) He said, "Abomination and anger has fallen on you[MP] from your[MP] Lord. Do you[MP] argue with me about names you[MP] and your[MP] fathers gave, about which Allah has not revealed authority? So wait. I am waiting with you[MP]. (71) So we rescued him and those who were with him by our mercy. So we cut off the stragglers[1235] of those who rejected our signs. They were not believers. (72) And

---

[1229] Noah here and verse 69. See glossary for more details.
[1230] Arabic /ilah/ here and in verses 73, 85, 127, 138 (twice), 140, and 158. See glossary for more details.
[1231] Arabic /dhikr/ here and in verse 69. See glossary for more details. Here the reminder is what was given to Nuh.
[1232] Aad (here and verse 74) and Thamud were names of tribes.
[1233] Arabic /ilah/. See glossary for more details.
[1234] Or excellence
[1235] Or extremities. See Tawrah, Deuteronomy 25:17-18

## Chapter 7

[we sent] Thamud their brother Salih.[1236] He said, "My people, worship Allah. He is your[MP] only god. A miracle has come to you[MP] from your[MP] Lord: this female camel of Allah's is a sign for you[MP]. Let her eat on Allah's land, and do not touch[MP] her with evil, or painful torment will seize you[MP]. (73) Remember when he made you[MP] regents after Aad. He settled you[MP] in the land, where you[MP] made palaces of its plains and carved mountains into houses. Remember Allah's benefits and do no evil, causing destruction on the earth. (74) The proud nobility of his people told the believers who were weakened, "Do you[MP] know that Salih is a messenger from his Lord?" They said, "We believe his message." (75) The proud said, "We disbelieve what you[MP] believe." (76) They hamstrung the female camel and were insolent against their Lord's command, and said, "Salih, bring on what you[MS] promised us if you[MS] are a messenger." (77) Trembling[1237] overtook them and in the morning,[1238] they were face-down in their houses. (78) He turned away from them, and said, "My people, I told you[MP] my Lord's message and advised you[MP], but you[MP] do not like advisors." (79) And [remember] Lut,[1239] when he told his people, "Do you[MP] commit promiscuity[1240] that no one in the world before you[MP] has ever done? (80) You[MP] go after men in lust instead of women.[1241] and further, you[MP] are dissipated[1242] people. (81) His people's only answer was, "Expel[MP] them from your[MP] village. They are people who purify themselves." (82) And we rescued him and his family,[1243] except for his wife,[1244] who delayed. (83) And we rained upon them.[1245] See how the punishment of wrongdoers was![1246] (84) And to Midian,[1247] [we sent] their brother Shuaib.[1248]

---

[1236] Methuselah here and in verses 75 and 77. See glossary for more details. Tawrah, Genesis 5:21-27, 1 Chronicles 1:3, Injil, Luke 3:37
[1237] Or earthquake
[1238] Or they became
[1239] Lot. See glossary for more details.
[1240] In this case, male homosexuality.
[1241] Tawrah, Genesis 19:5, Injil, Romans 1:24-27
[1242] Or wasteful. Tawrah, Ezekiel 16:49
[1243] Tawrah, Genesis 19:29
[1244] Tawrah, Genesis 19:26
[1245] Tawrah, Genesis 19:24
[1246] Here and in verse 86, "was" (masculine) does not match "punishment" (feminine). There may be another meaning.
[1247] Tawrah, Exodus 18:1-12

He said, "My people, worship Allah. He is your[MP] only god. A miracle has come to you[MP] from your[MP] Lord, so use[MP] a just measure and scale,[1249] and do not lessen[MP] people's things, nor cause[MP] destruction in the land after it has been made right. That is better for you[MP], if you[MP] are believers. (85) Do not sit[MP] on every path, threatening and blocking believers in Allah from his path, desiring to make it crooked. Remember when you[MP] were few and he multiplied you[MP], and see how the punishment of the corrupt was. (86) If one group of you[MP] believed[1250] in my message and another group did not believe, endure[1251] until Allah judges among us. He is the best judge. (87) 9A1 The proud nobility of his people said, "Shuaib, we will expel you[MP] and those who believed with you[MS] from our village unless you[MP] return to our spiritual path."[1252] He said, "Even if we hate it? (88) We would be lying about Allah to return to your[MP] spiritual path[1253] after Allah rescued us from it. We cannot return to it except if Allah, our Lord, wills. Our Lord knows everything. We trust in Allah." Our Lord, give true victory[1254] between us and our people in truth. You[MS] are the best victor. (89) The disbelieving nobility of his people said, "If you[MP] follow Shuaib, you[MP] will be lost." (90) Trembling overtook them and in the morning they were face-down on the ground in their houses. (91) It was as if those who rejected Shuaib did not dwell in it. Those who rejected Shuaib were lost. (92) So he turned away from them and said, "My people, I have delivered my Lord's messages to you[MP], and advised you[MP]. How could I be sad about disbelieving people?" (93) Every time we sent a prophet to a village, we afflicted them with misfortune and harm, so that they would humble themselves. (94) Then we replaced the bad with goodness until they abounded, and they said, "Harm and joy touched our fathers. We seized them suddenly. They did not realize it. (95) If only the inhabitants of the village had believed

---

[1248] Jethro here and in verses 88, 90, and 92 (twice). See glossary for more details.

[1249] Tawrah, Leviticus 19:36

[1250] The lack of agreement between the verb (masculine) and the subject (group) is because the word group is considered as a plural consisting of several people.

[1251] See "endure" in glossary here and in verses 126, 128, and 137.

[1252] Arabic /millah/. See glossary.

[1253] Arabic /millah/. See glossary.

[1254] Tawrah, Isaiah 25:8, Injil, 1 Corinthians 15:57, 1 John 5:4

## Chapter 7

and feared Allah, we would have poured blessings upon them from heaven and earth. But they rejected, so we took them, as they deserved. (96) Did the village people feel safe that our affliction would [not] come to them by night while they slept? (97) Did the village people feel safe from our affliction coming to them in the morning as they played? (98) Did they feel safe from Allah's deceiving? Only people who are lost feel safe from Allah's deception.[1255] (99) Did he[1256] not guide those who inherited the land from its inhabitants?[1257] If we willed, we would have punished them for their sins. We seal their hearts, so they do not hear. (100) We tell you[MS] the news about those villages. Their messengers came to them with miracles, and they would not have believed in what they rejected beforehand. Thus Allah seals the hearts of the disbelievers. (101) We did not find a covenant with most of them. We found most of them unbelievers.[1258] (102) Then we sent Musa[1259] after them with our signs to Pharaoh[1260] and his nobility, and they[1261] were wicked regarding them.[1262] See the punishment[1263] of the corrupt? (103) Musa[1264] said, "Pharaoh, I am a messenger from the Lord of the universe. (104)

\*\*\*

It is fitting that I say nothing except the truth about Allah. I have brought you[MP] a miracle from your[MP] Lord, so send[MS] the people of Israel with me."[1265] (105)

\*\*\*

He said, "If you[MS] are going to bring a sign, then bring[MS] it on if you[MS] are telling the truth." (106) So he threw down his staff, and it

---

[1255] Here and in verses 178 and 186, see Injil, 2 Thessalonians 2:11, Tawrah, 2 Samuel 22:27, 1 Kings 22:20-23, Ezekiel 14:9
[1256] Or was it
[1257] Tawrah, Numbers 33:54
[1258] Or transgressors or immoral, here and in verses 145, 163, and 165.
[1259] Moses here and in verses 104, 115, 117, 122, 127, 128, 131, 134, 138, 142 (twice), 143 (twice), 1444, 148, 150, 154, 155, 159, and 160. See glossary for more details.
[1260] Tawrah, Exodus 3:10
[1261] The people
[1262] The signs
[1263] The verb and noun do not match here. Maybe the punishment is seen as a person who punishes.
[1264] Moses. See glossary for more details.
[1265] Tawrah, Exodus 5:1

## Chapter 7

was clearly a serpent.[1266] (107) He took out his hand and it was white to those who saw it.[1267] (108) The nobility of Pharaoh's people said, "This is a learned magician. (109) He wants to expel you[MP] from your[MP] land. What do you[MP] command?" (110) They said, "Put him and his brother off, and send assemblers to the cities, (111) who will bring you[MS] every learned magician."[1268] (112) The magicians came to Pharaoh and said, "We get a fee if we are victorious." (113) He said, "Yes. And you[MP] will be brought close." (114) They said, "Musa, either you[MS] throw first, or we will." (115) He said, "Throw[MP]." When they threw, they magically tricked people's eyes and terrified them with the great magic they brought. (116) 9A2 We inspired Musa, "Throw your[MS] staff. It will swallow[1269] their lies."[1270] (117) Then the truth came forth[1271] and what they did was in vain. (118) They were defeated there and were overthrown, humiliated. (119) So the magicians fell down, bowing down on the ground. (120) They said, "We believe in the Lord of the universe,[1272] (121) the Lord of Musa and Harun."[1273] (122) Pharaoh said, "Have you[MP] believed before I gave you[MP] permission? This is a deceitful thing you[MP] have done in the city, in order to expel its inhabitants. You[MP] shall know. (123) I will cut off your[MP] hands and feet on opposite sides, then crucify all of you[MP]." (124) They said, "We will return to our Lord, (125) and you[MS] are only taking revenge on us because we believed in the signs of our Lord when we saw them. Our Lord, give us endurance and let us die submitted."[1274] (126) The nobility of Pharaoh's people said, "Will you[MS] let Musa and his people go to cause destruction in the land, while he forsakes you[MS] and your[MS] gods?" He said, "We will slaughter their sons and let their women live.[1275] We will be victorious over them." (127) Musa told his people, "Ask Allah for

---

[1266] Tawrah, Exodus 7:10. See note at 7:133

[1267] Musa is the only one in the Qur'an who does this. Tawrah, Exodus 4:6. See note at 7:133

[1268] Tawrah, Exodus 7:11

[1269] Or grab

[1270] Tawrah, Exodus 7:12

[1271] Or fell

[1272] Tawrah, Exodus 8:19

[1273] Aaron here and in verse 142. See glossary for more details.

[1274] Injil, James 4:7. For "submitted," some translators do not translate this. See glossary for more details.

[1275] The words translated "let" and "forsake" are the same word in Arabic. Tawrah, Exodus 1:17

## Chapter 7

help and endure. The land is Allah's[1276] and he gives it to those of his servants he wills. The reverent will be rewarded." (128) They said, "We were hurt before you[MS] came to us and after you[MS] came to us." He said, "Your[MP] Lord may destroy your[MP] enemy and cause you[MP] to be regents over the land. He watches your[MP] deeds. (129) We afflicted Pharaoh's family for years with lack of fruit[1277] so that they may remember. (130) When something good happened to them, they said, "This is ours." When something bad happened to them, they said it was an evil omen of Musa and those with him." Actually, they were blaming Allah, but most of them do not know. (131) They said, "You[MS] bewitch us with every sign you[MS] bring us, so we will not believe in you[MS]." (132) We sent upon them the flood[1278], the locusts,[1279] the lice,[1280] the frogs,[1281] and the blood,[1282] detailed signs.[1283] But they were proud, and were wrongdoers. (133)

\*\*\*

When the plague fell upon them, they said, "Musa, pray to your[MS] Lord by the covenant he made with you[MS].[1284] If you[MS] lift the plague from us, we will believe in you[MS], and will send you[MS] off with the people of Israel.[1285] (134)

\*\*\*

Then we lifted the plague from them for a time and they got what they wanted. Then they broke their oaths.[1286] (135) So we took revenge upon them, and drowned them in the sea[1287] because they

---

[1276] Zabur, Psalms 24:1
[1277] Tawrah, Genesis 47:13, Exodus 9:13-10:20. See note at 7:133
[1278] Some commentators believe this word refers to plagues, which would include the plagues described in Tawrah, Exodus 9:3,12,15, 12:29
[1279] Tawrah, Exodus 10:12,13
[1280] Tawrah, Exodus 8:16
[1281] Tawrah, Exodus 8:2-13
[1282] Tawrah, Exodus 12:29-31
[1283] 79:20 talks about the greatest sign. 17:101 mentions nine, which makes a total of ten. This corresponds to the ten signs mentioned in Tawrah, Exodus 7-12. In the Qur'an, this verse and verses 7:107,108, and 130 describe many of these signs. The last sign, probably the same as the "greatest sign" mentioned both here and in Tawrah, Exodus 11:4-5, 12:23,24,29,30 is the blood. The Exodus passages gives the details.
[1284] Tawrah, Exodus 9:28
[1285] Tawrah, Exodus 10:28, 12:31
[1286] Tawrah, Exodus 8:28-32
[1287] Tawrah, Exodus 14:27-28, Isaiah 43:17

## Chapter 7

rejected our signs and ignored them. (136) Then we made the people who were weak inherit the east and the west of the land we blessed,[1288] and the best word of your[MS] Lord was fulfilled to the people of Israel because they endured. We destroyed what Pharaoh and his people had made and built. (137) We made the people of Israel pass through the sea,[1289] and they came to people worshiping their idols.[1290] They said, "Musa, make us a god like the gods they have."[1291] He said, "You[MP] are ignorant people. (138) What they are involved in will be destroyed and their works will be vain." (139) He said: "Shall I seek a god for you[MP] other than Allah, who preferred you[MP] above all mankind?" (140) When we rescued you[MP] from Pharaoh's family who afflicted you[MP] with torment,[1292] slaughtering your[MP] sons[1293] and letting your[MP] women live, that was a great plague from your[MP] Lord. (141) **9A3** We made an appointment with Musa for thirty days, and we completed them with ten more, so the total amount of time he was with his Lord was forty nights.[1294] Musa told his brother Harun, "Take my place with my people and do good.[1295] Do not follow the path of the corrupt." (142) When Musa came to our appointment and his Lord spoke to him, he said, "My Lord, show me how to look to you[MS]."[1296] He said, "You[MS] will not see me, but look at the mountain.[1297] If it remains in its place, you[MS] will see me." When his Lord appeared to the mountain, he pulverized it to powder. Musa fainted. When he revived, he said, "May you[MS] be glorified! I repent to you[MS], and am the first believer." (143) He said, "Musa, I have chosen you[MS] to be over the people[1298] with my message and my words. Take what I gave you[MS] and give[MS] thanks." (144) So we wrote everything for him on the tablets[1299] as an admonition and explanation of everything. Take it firmly and command your[MS]

---

[1288] Tawrah, Exodus 6:8
[1289] Tawrah, Exodus 14:1-22
[1290] Tawrah, Exodus 34:12-16
[1291] Tawrah, Exodus 32
[1292] Tawrah, Exodus 5:6-15
[1293] Tawrah, Exodus 1:16
[1294] Tawrah, Exodus 24:18
[1295] Tawrah, Exodus 24:14
[1296] Tawrah, Exodus 33:18
[1297] Tawrah, Exodus 33:21-22
[1298] Tawrah, Exodus 3:10
[1299] Tawrah, Exodus 24:12, 31:18

people to take the best of it. I will show you<sup>MP</sup> the house of the unbelievers. (145) I will turn those who are unjustly proud on the earth away from my signs. Even if they see every sign, they will not believe in them. If they see the path of guidance, they will not take it. If they see the path of wrong, they'll take it. That is because they rejected our signs and neglected them. (146) The works of those who disbelieve in our signs and in an appointment with the hereafter will be in vain. Will they not be paid back for their deeds? (147) After him, Musa's people took their jewelry[1300] [to make] the body of a calf[1301] that mooed. Did they not see that it did not speak to them or guide them on a path? They took it and were wicked. (148) When it fell from their hands, and they saw that they had gone astray, they said, "If our Lord does not have mercy on us and forgive us, we will definitely be lost." (149) When Musa returned to his people, angry[1302] and sad, he said, "You<sup>MP</sup> sure did a dreadful job in my place after I left. Were you<sup>MP</sup> in a hurry[1303] regarding your<sup>MP</sup> Lord's command?" He[1304] threw down the tablets[1305] and grabbed his brother by his head, dragged him to himself. He[1306] said, "Son of my mother, the people weakened me[1307] and almost killed me, so do not make my enemies rejoice over me, and do not put me with wicked people." (150) He said, "Lord, forgive[1308] me and my brother[1309] and make us enter your<sup>MS</sup> mercy. You<sup>MS</sup> are the most merciful of all."[1310]

---

[1300] Tawrah, Exodus 32:2,3
[1301] Tawrah, Exodus 32:4
[1302] Tawrah, Exodus 32:19
[1303] Tawrah, Exodus 32:1
[1304] Musa
[1305] Tawrah, Exodus 32:19
[1306] Harun
[1307] Tawrah, Exodus 32:22,23
[1308] The belief that all prophets and messengers are sinless is not supported by the Qur'an. For instances of prophets or messengers asking forgiveness or committing sins, see 7:23, 20:121 (Adam), 11:47, 71:28 (Nuh), 26:82, 14:41 (Ibrahim), 28:15-16 (Musa), 7:151, 20:93 (Musa and Harun), 38:24 (Dawud), 38:32,35 (Sulayman), 21:87, 37:142 (Yunus), 48:2, 47:19, 40:55, 4:79,106, 9:43, 13:30, 80:1-2, 110:3, 94:2, 23:118, 66:1, 33:37, 8:67, and 9:117 (Muhammad (s)).
[1309] Tawrah, Numbers 20:11,12
[1310] Here and in verses 153 and 167, see glossary for more details on "merciful."

## Chapter 7

(151) Those who chose the calf[1311] will receive their Lord's anger, as well as humiliation in this world. Thus we repay liars. (152) Your[MS] Lord is forgiving and merciful toward those who do bad deeds and later repent and believe. (153) When Musa's anger subsided, he took the tablets.[1312] There was guidance and mercy in its copy for those who are in awe of their Lord. (154) Musa chose from his people seventy men[1313] to meet us. When they began trembling,[1314] he said, "My Lord, if you[MS] willed, you[MS] could have destroyed them and me beforehand. Do you[MS] destroy us because of deeds of the foolish ones among us? That is only your[MS] trial, in which you lead astray those you[MS] will and guide those you[MS] will.[1315] You[MS] are our protector, so forgive us and have mercy on us. You[MS] are the best forgiver. (155) 9A4 Record a good deed for us in this world and in the hereafter. We have returned to you[MS]." He said, "I afflict those I will with my torment, and my mercy embraces everything.[1316] I will write it for those who are reverent, pay the poor-tax, and believe in our signs." (156) Those who follow the messenger, the Gentile[1317] prophet,[1318] whom they find

---

[1311] i.e. as a god, Tawrah, Exodus 32:4,8

[1312] Tawrah, Exodus 34:1

[1313] Tawrah, Exodus 24:1

[1314] Tawrah, Exodus 20:18

[1315] Tawrah, Exodus 33:19, Injil, Romans 9:15,18

[1316] Injil, Romans 9:18-22

[1317] Here and in verse 158, some translations render this as "illiterate", but that does not fit with what the rest of the Qur'an says about Muhammad (s), for instance in 17:106, where he is told by Allah to read /yaqra'/ the Qur'an to the people, in 16:98, where he is told to seek Allah's protection from Satan when he reads /yaqra'/ it, as well as in 17:45. There are a number of instances where Muhammad (s) is told to read/recite /yatlu/, a different Arabic word (5:27, 7:175, 10:71, 18:27, 26:69, 27:92, 29:45), but the word used in this verse and 16:98, 17:45, and 17:106, translated "read," can only mean "read." Since Muhammad (s) was a businessman before he received the Qur'an, he was probably literate. In either case, illiteracy is not inconsistent with a high level of language. Homer, for example, was blind (hence illiterate), but is considered the best of all Greek writers.

[1318] Here and in 7:158 are the only references to a Gentile (non-Jewish) prophet. Most prophets were Jews, however Adam, Salih, Nuh, Ibrahim, Ismail, Ishaq, and Ya'qub were pre-Jewish.

## Chapter 7

written about[1319] in the Tawrah[1320] and Injil.[1321] He promotes virtue, prevents vice,[1322] allows good things for them, forbids evil things,[1323] and takes away their burden and the chains that bound them. Those who believed in him, strengthened him, saved him, and followed the light that descended with him are successful. (157) Say[MS], "People, I am Allah's messenger[1324] to you[MP]. The kingdom of the heavens and the earth are his.[1325] He is the only god. He gives life and causes death,[1326] so believe in Allah and his messenger, the Gentile prophet who believes in Allah and his words. Follow him so you[MP] may be guided." (158) Among Musa's people are a nation who guides and acts justly with the truth. (159) We split them up into twelve tribes[1327] or nations, and inspired Musa, when his people asked him for drink,[1328] "Strike[MS] the rock with your[MS] staff."[1329] Twelve springs of water sprang forth from it. All the people knew where they were to drink and we overshadowed them with the cloud,[1330] and sent manna[1331] and quails[1332] down upon them. Eat[MP] of the good things we have provided for you[MP]. They did not wrong us, but they wronged themselves.[1333] (160) They were told, "Live[MP] in this village and

---

[1319] According to this verse, followers of the prophet see things in the former books that refer to him. In general, followers of the former books do not think that those verses refer to him.

[1320] The Law. See glossary for more details.

[1321] Gospel. See glossary for more details.

[1322] or commands what is right/kind and forbids what is wrong

[1323] Some think that this verse refers to Isa. See 3:49, 5:110

[1324] The ones specifically called Allah's messenger in the Qur'an are Muhammad (s) 48:29, 7:158, 33:21,40,53, etc., Musa 61:5, Thamud's messenger 91:13, and Isa 4:157,171, 61:6.

[1325] Tawrah, Isaiah 45:12, Zabur, Psalms 24:1, 89:11, Injil, Hebrews 1:10

[1326] Tawrah, 1 Samuel 2:6, Deuteronomy 32:39

[1327] Tawrah, Genesis 49:28

[1328] Tawrah, Exodus 15:24, 17:2

[1329] Tawrah, Exodus 17:6

[1330] Tawrah, Exodus 13:21

[1331] Tawrah, Exodus 16:4,8,14-31

[1332] Tawrah, Exodus 16:13

[1333] For here and in verse 177, the injustice/wickedness, disbelief/ungratefulness, evil, unrighteousness/sin, or lostness of mankind is mentioned in a number of verses in the Qur'an as well as in the previous books. Injustice or wickedness: 2:57, 3:117,135, 4:64,97, 7:160,177, 9:70, 10:44, 11:101, 14:34,45, 16:33,61,118, 29:40, 30:9, 33:72, 34:19, 35:32, 43:76, 65:1, Tawrah, Genesis 6:5, Job 25:4, Injil,

## Chapter 7

eat<sup>MP</sup> in it wherever you<sup>MP</sup> want. Say<sup>MP</sup>: Forgiveness. Enter<sup>MP</sup> the door bowing down, and we will forgive your<sup>MP</sup> faults. We will increase those who do good." (161) The wicked among them substituted a different saying for what they had been told, and we sent a plague upon them from heaven for their wickedness. (162) Ask them about the village by the sea, when they broke the sabbath,[1334] when their whales appeared clearly to them on their sabbath, and when they did not rest, they did not come. Thus we try them for their unbelief. (163) One nation among them said, "Why do you<sup>MP</sup> preach to people Allah will destroy or torment severely?" They said, "As an excuse to their Lord, that they may be reverent." (164)When they forgot what they had been reminded of, we rescued those who forbade wrong, and seized the wicked in miserable torment for their unbelief. (165) When they were insolent in what they were forbidden, we told them, "Be driven away like apes."[1335] (166) Your<sup>MS</sup> Lord proclaimed, "Those who will punish them with wicked punishment will seek them until the day of resurrection." Your<sup>MS</sup> Lord is swift in punishment, forgiving and merciful. (167) We split them up in the land as nations.[1336] Some of them were righteous and others less so. We tried them with good deeds and bad deeds so that they may return. (168) A succeeding generation followed them and inherited the book. They take this world's goods and say, "It will be forgiven for us." If similar goods come to them, they take them. Was the book's covenant not made with them, to say only the truth about Allah? They studied its contents.[1337] The abode of the hereafter is better for the reverent. Do you<sup>MP</sup> not comprehend? (169) Those who hold the book tightly and perform prayers are righteous, and we will not

---

Acts 3:26, disbelief or ungratefulness: 14:34, 17:67, 22:66, 42:48, 43:15, 80:17, Injil, Hebrews 3:19, Evil: 12:53, Tawrah, Jeremiah 17:9, Injil, Matthew 15:19, Mark 7:21, unrighteousness or sin: 91:8, Tawrah, 1 Kings 8:46, Ecclesiastes 7:20, Injil, Romans 3:9-19, 5:12, lostness: 103:2, Tawrah, Jeremiah 50:6, Injil, Luke 19:10, Romans 3:23, 6:23

[1334] Here twice, see Tawrah, Exodus 20:8-11, 31:13; Isaiah 56:6,7, 58:13,14, 66:22,23; Ezekiel 20:20, Injil, Mathew 12:8, 24:20; Mark 2:27; Luke 23:56.

[1335] The adjective "driven away" is in the form for thinking beings, not animals, so it is probable that the being turned into apes is metaphorical and not literal. See 2:65, 5:60, as well as Injil, Matthew 7:6, where some people are compared to pigs.

[1336] Tawrah, Numbers 34:17, Joshua 13:7

[1337] Injil, John 5:39

# Chapter 7

lose their reward. (170) **9B1** We shook the mountain above them as if it were a covering, and they thought it would fall on them. Take<sup>MP</sup> what we have given you<sup>MP</sup> firmly and remember what is in it so that you<sup>MP</sup> may be reverent. (171) Your<sup>MS</sup> Lord made a covenant with the children of Adam and their seed after them, and made them swear against themselves: Am I not your<sup>MP</sup> Lord? They said, "Yes, you are."[1338] We testify that you<sup>MP</sup> will say on the day of resurrection, "We were unaware of this," (172) Or you<sup>MP</sup> will say, "Our fathers were idolaters beforehand, and we were their seed after them. Will you<sup>MS</sup> destroy us because of vain people's deeds?" (173) Thus we explain signs so that they may return. (174) Read[1339] them the story of him who received our signs, and he cast them off, so Satan followed him and he went astray. (175) If we wanted, we would have raised him up with them, but he inclined toward the earth and followed his passions. He is like a dog: if you<sup>MS</sup> attack him, he hangs his tongue out, or if you<sup>MS</sup> leave him alone, he hangs his tongue out. This is what people who reject our signs are like. Tell the stories, so that they may consider. (176) People who rejected our signs are a bad example. They wronged themselves. (177) If Allah guides someone, he is guided. If he leads people astray, they are lost. (178) We have destined many jinns and people to hell. They have hearts, but they do not understand with them.[1340] They have eyes, but they do not see with them. They have ears, but they do not hear with them.[1341] They are like cattle, but even further astray. They are unaware. (179) Allah has the best names, so pray to him with them. Leave alone those that blaspheme[1342] his names. They will be repaid for their deeds. (180) Some of those we created are a nation who guide and judge with truth. (181) We will gradually draw those who reject our signs toward destruction from places they do not know. (182) I will give them more time. My plan[1343] is firm. (183) Do they not consider? What about their companion? Is he demonized?[1344] He is only a clear warner. (184) Have they not seen the kingdom of the heavens and the earth, and everything Allah created? Perhaps their

---

[1338] Tawrah, Joshua 24:1-26
[1339] Or recite or tell. See note at 7:157.
[1340] Zabur, Psalms 32:9
[1341] Tawrah, Isaiah 6:10, Injil, Matthew 13:15
[1342] Or are atheists with respect to
[1343] Or trick or plot
[1344] Or jinned (crazy). See glossary for more details.

## Chapter 7

time is near. What saying will they believe in after it? (185) If Allah leads someone astray, no one can guide him. He leaves them wandering in their transgression. (186) They ask you[MS] about the hour,[1345] "When is it fixed?" Say[MS], "My Lord knows. No one but he will reveal it until its time.[1346] It is heavy in the heavens and the earth. It will only come to you[MP] suddenly.[1347] They ask you[MS] as if you[MS] were well-acquainted with it. Say[MS], "Knowledge of it belongs to Allah."[1348] Most people do not know this. (187) Say[MS], "I cannot help or harm myself except as Allah wills. If I knew the unseen,[1349] I would make great use of the good, and evil would not touch me. I am only a warner and bearer of good news for believing people." (188) 9B2 He created you[MP] from one soul,[1350] and made from him[1351] his wife to live with her. When he had sex with her, she became pregnant.[1352] Her pregnancy was light, and she passed by it. When it got heavier, they[D] prayed to Allah, their[D] Lord, "If you[MS] bring us a righteous [boy], we will give thanks." (189) When he brought them a righteous [boy],[1353] they worshiped other gods for what he had brought them. May Allah be exalted above the gods they worship. (190) Will they worship as gods what does not create anything, despite their being created? (191) They cannot save them, or even save themselves. (192) If you[MP] call them to guidance, they do not follow you[MP], whether you[MP] pray to them or are silent. (193) Those whom you[MP] pray to other than Allah are servants like you[MP], so pray[MP] to them, and let them answer you[MP], if you[MP] are telling the truth. (194) Do they have legs they walk with, or hands they grab with, or eyes they see with, or ears they hear with? Say[MS], "Pray to your[MP] other gods, and plot against me. Do not wait for me." (195) My protector is Allah, who revealed the book, and he is responsible for the righteous. (196) Those other than Allah to whom you[MP] pray cannot save you[MP] or even save themselves. (197) If you[MP] pray to them for guidance, they will not hear. You[MS] will see them looking at you[MS],

---

[1345] Injil, Revelation 14:7
[1346] Injil, Matthew 24:36, Mark 13:32, 1 Thessalonians 5:1-3.
[1347] Injil, 1 Thessalonians 5:2,3
[1348] See 43:61, where Isa has knowledge of the last hour as well.
[1349] Only Isa knows the unseen (3:49,52, Injil, Matthew 9:4, 12:25)
[1350] Tawrah, Genesis 2:7
[1351] Tawrah, Genesis 2:21-22
[1352] Tawrah, Genesis 4:1
[1353] Tawrah, Genesis 4:2, Injil, 1 John 3:12

## Chapter 7

and they do not see. (198) Take<sup>MS</sup> a pardon, command<sup>MS</sup> a benefit, and turn<sup>MS</sup> away from the ignorant. (199) If Satan incites you<sup>MS</sup> with an evil suggestion, ask<sup>MS</sup> for Allah's protection. He hears all and knows all.[1354] (200) The reverent remember when they are touched by an appearance from Satan, and they see. (201) Their[1355] brothers make them increase in error, then will not desist. (202) When you<sup>MS</sup> do not bring them a sign, they say, "If only you<sup>MS</sup> brought it." Say<sup>MS</sup>, "I just follow what is inspired to me by my Lord. This is evidence,[1356] guidance, and mercy from your<sup>MP</sup> Lord for believing people. (203) When the Qur'an[1357] is read, listen<sup>MP</sup> to it and be silent, so that you<sup>MP</sup> may receive mercy. (204) Remember your<sup>MS</sup> Lord in your<sup>MS</sup> soul in supplication and fear, and do not be public in speaking morning or evening. Do not be<sup>MS</sup> unaware. (205) Those with your<sup>MS</sup> Lord are not too proud to worship him. They glorify him and bow down to him." (206)[1358]

---

[1354] Tawrah, Job 37:16, Isaiah 40:14, Zabur, Psalms 33:13-15, Injil, 1 John 3:20

[1355] The reference may be to other appearances from Satan.

[1356] The word "this" is masculine, and "evidence" is feminine. There may be a different meaning.

[1357] Or recitation. See glossary for more details.

[1358] The verses in this chapter that rhyme are put together in paragraphs, separated by ***.

# Chapter 8 Al-Anfal[1359]

9B3 In the name of Allah, the most gracious and merciful.[1360] They ask you[MS] about spoils. Say[MS], "Spoils belong to Allah and his messenger, so fear Allah,[1361] reconcile among yourselves[MP], and obey[MP] Allah and his messenger if you[MP] are believers." (1) Truly believers are those who when Allah is mentioned, their[MP] hearts tremble, and when his signs[FP] are recited[1362] to them[MP], they[MP] make their[MP] faith increase, and they[MP] trust in[1363] their Lord. (2) They perform the prayers and donate from what we have provided them. (3) They are true believers, and they have higher position, forgiveness, and generous provision with their Lord. (4) As your[MS] Lord truly expelled you[MS] from your[MS] house, some believers hate it. (5) They argue with you[MS] about truth after it became clear, as if they are being driven to death as they watch.[1364] (6) When Allah promises you[MP] one of the two parties will be yours[MP], you[MP] wish that the unarmed one would be yours[MP]. Allah wants to fulfill the truth with his words, and root[1365] out disbelievers, (7) to fulfill the truth and nullify what is vain, even though wrongdoers hate it. (8) For you[MP] ask your[MP] Lord for help and he answers you[MP], "I will provide you[MP] with a thousand angels[1366] following one another." (9) Allah has made it all good news, so that your[MP] hearts will be at rest. Salvation is only from Allah.[1367] Allah is mighty[1368] and wise.[1369] (10)

\*\*\*

---

[1359] Spoils (of raiding or war)

[1360] Zabur, Psalms 103:8, 145:8. See glossary for more details.

[1361] For "fear Allah" here and in verses 29 and 48, see Tawrah, Deuteronomy 10:12, Isaiah 29:13, Injil, 1 Peter 2:17, Revelation 14:7.

[1362] Or read or told, here and in verse 31.

[1363] Or depend on

[1364] Tawrah, Proverbs 24:11

[1365] Or cut off the remnant or back or edges

[1366] Tawrah, Daniel 7:10, Zabur, Psalms 68:17, Injil, Matthew 26:53, Revelation 5:11

[1367] Injil, Revelation 19:1

[1368] Injil, Revelation 18:8, Tawrah, Isaiah 60:16, Zabur, Psalms 93:4

[1369] For "wise" here and in verses 49, 63, 67, and 71, see Tawrah, Job 9:4, Proverbs 2:6, Jeremiah 9:23-24, Injil, 1 Corinthians 1:21-25, Romans 16:27.

## Chapter 8

When drowsiness covers you<sup>MP</sup> as security from him, and he sends you<sup>MP</sup> rain[1370] from the sky, it is to purify you<sup>MP</sup>, send away Satan's abomination from you<sup>MP</sup>, bond your<sup>MP</sup> hearts, and make your<sup>MP</sup> feet strong.[1371] (11) Your<sup>MS</sup> Lord inspired the angels, "I am with you<sup>MP</sup>. Make<sup>MP</sup> the believers firm. I will cast terror into the hearts of disbelievers, so strike<sup>MP</sup> above their necks and strike their fingertips." (12) That was because they contended with Allah and his messenger. Allah is severe in punishment[1372] to those who contend with Allah and his messenger. (13) So taste<sup>MP</sup> it. Disbelievers will have the torment[1373] of hellfire. (14) Believers, if you<sup>MP</sup> meet disbelievers marching, do not flee from them. (15) \*\*\*

He who flees from them, unless it is to turn aside to fight or to retreat to a group, will receive Allah's wrath. His abode will be hell, a dreadful destiny. (16)
\*\*\*

You<sup>MP</sup> did not kill them, but Allah killed them. You<sup>MS</sup> did not throw when you<sup>MS</sup> threw, but Allah threw.[1374] He did it to test the believers well by it. Allah hears all and knows all.[1375] (17) Thus Allah weakens disbelievers' plots. (18) If you<sup>MP</sup> seek victory, you<sup>MP</sup> will have it, and if you<sup>MP</sup> desist, it will be better for you. If you<sup>MP</sup> return, we will return, and your<sup>MP</sup> group will not help you<sup>MP</sup> at all, even if they are many. Allah is with believers. (19) Believers, obey Allah and his messenger. Do not turn away from him as you<sup>MP</sup> hear. (20) Do not be like those who said, "We hear" when they do not hear. (21) 9B4 The most evil living creatures to Allah are the deaf and dumb who do not comprehend.[1376] (22) If Allah had known any good in them, he would have made them hear. If he

---

[1370] Tawrah, Deuteronomy 28:12, Job 5:10, Joel 2:23, Zabur, Psalms 68:9, Injil, Matthew 5:45

[1371] Zabur, Psalms 40:2

[1372] Here and in verses 25, 48, and 52, see Tawrah, Ezekiel 25:17, Injil, Matthew 8:12, 13:42,50, 22:13, 24:51, 25:30, Mark 9:48, Luke 13:28, 19:27.

[1373] For "torment" here and in verses 32,35,50, and 68, see Tawrah, Isaiah 50:11, Injil, Matthew 18:34, 25:41,46, Luke 16:23-28, Revelation 20:15

[1374] The meaning here is not that they did not kill or throw, but that Allah is sovereign over all.

[1375] Here and in verses 42, 43, 53, 61, and 71, see Tawrah, Job 37:16, Isaiah 40:14, Zabur, Psalms 33:13-15, Injil, 1 John 3:20.

[1376] Injil, Matthew 13:15, Tawrah, Isaiah 6: 9-10. This verse is probably spiritual deafness - see verse 55.

## Chapter 8

had made them hear, they would have turned away and rejected. (23) Believers, respond to Allah and his messenger when he calls you[MP] to what gives you[MP] life,[1377] and know that Allah passes between a person and his heart. You[MP] will be gathered to him.[1378] (24)

\*\*\*

Fear a trial that will not afflict only the wicked among you[MP]. Know that Allah is severe in punishment. (25)

\*\*\*

Remember when you[MP] were few and weak in the land, fearing that people would carry you[MP] off. He gave you[MP] refuge, aided you with his salvation, and provided you[MP] with good things, so that you[MP] might give thanks. (26) Believers, do not betray[MP] Allah and the messenger, and thus knowingly betray your[MP] trusts. (27) Know that your[MP] money and your[MP] children[1379] are tests, and that there is a great reward with Allah.[1380] (28) Believers, if you[MP] fear Allah, he will give you[MP] discernment, propitiate[1381] your[MP] bad deeds, and forgive you[MP]. Allah has great grace. (29) Disbelievers were crafty against you[MS] to keep you[MS] in bonds, kill you[MS], or expel you[MS]. They are crafty, and Allah is crafty, and Allah is the craftiest.[1382] (30) When our signs are recited to them, they say, "We hear. If we wanted to, we would have said something like this. Those are only ancient legends." (31) They said, "Allah, if this is truth from you[MS], rain[MS] stones upon us from heaven or give[MS] us painful torment." (32) Allah would not torment them while you[MS] were among them, nor would he torment them while they were asking forgiveness. (33) But why should Allah not torment them, when they bar the way to the sacred place of worship?[1383] They were not its protectors. The reverent are its protectors, but most of them do not know. (34) Their prayer at the sanctuary was only whistling and clapping. Taste torment for your[MP] disbelief. (35) Disbelievers donate their money to blocking Allah's path. They will donate it

---

[1377] Tawrah, Deuteronomy 30:19-20
[1378] Here and in verse 36, see Tawrah, Joel 3:11-14, Zephaniah 3:8, Injil, Matthew 25:32, John 15:6, Revelation 16:16.
[1379] or sons
[1380] Zabur, Psalms 127:3
[1381] Tawrah, Isaiah 27:9, Injil, Romans 3:25, Hebrews 2:17, 1 John 2:2, 4:10
[1382] See 3:54
[1383] Injil, John 4:20-24, Hebrews 8:1-2, 9:24, 10:19-22.

## Chapter 8

and it will make them sigh. They will be defeated, and disbelievers will be gathered to hell. (36) Allah will distinguish between the evil and the good, and set the evil on top of each other and pile them all up and send them to hell. They are lost. (37) Tell[MS] the disbelievers, "If they stop, they will be forgiven for what is past. If they return, the traditions of the ancients are gone." (38)

\*\*\*

Fight them until there is no more sedition, and all religion is Allah's.[1384] If they stop, Allah sees what they do. (39) If they turn away, know that Allah, your[MP] Lord is a wonderful Lord and a wonderful savior.[1385] (40) 10A1 Know that a fifth of your[MP] booty is for Allah, the messenger, relatives, orphans,[1386] the poor, and travelers. Give this if you[MP] believe in Allah and in what we revealed to our servant[1387] on the day of distinction, the day the two groups met. Allah can do anything.[1388] (41)

\*\*\*

You[MP] were on the near side of the valley and they were on the far side and the caravan was below you[MP]. If you[MP] had made an appointment, you[MP] would have differed about the time. Allah predestined a matter, and it was done, and he will destroy those he will based on a miracle, and give life to whom he wills[1389] based on a miracle. Allah hears all and knows all. (42)

\*\*\*

Allah will show them to you[MS] as few in your[MS] dream. If he showed them to you[MS] as many, you[MP] would have failed and disagreed about the matter, but Allah gave peace. He knows what is in the heart. (43) He showed them to you[MP] as few when you[MP] met, and made you[MP] seem few in their eyes. Allah predestined a matter, and it was done. Matters return to Allah. (44)

\*\*\*

---

[1384] Or, "religion is each person's before Allah," or "there is freedom of religion for all with Allah."

[1385] Tawrah, Hosea 13:4, Zabur, Psalms 106:21, Injil, Luke 1:47, Titus 1:3

[1386] Tawrah, Job 29:12, Zabur, Psalms 82:3, Injil, James 1:27

[1387] See glossary for "servant" here and in verse 51.

[1388] Tawrah, Job 42:2, Isaiah 14:27, Daniel 4:35, Injil, Matthew 19:26, Mark 10:27, Luke 1:37

[1389] Injil, Romans 9:18

## Chapter 8

Believers, if you[MP] meet a party, stand firm[MP] and remember[MP] Allah frequently, so that you[MP] may be successful.[1390] (45) Obey[MP] Allah and his messenger, and do not quarrel[MP],[1391] lest you[MP] fail and your[MP] power fail. Endure, for Allah is with those who endure.[1392] (46)

\*\*\*

Do not be like those who went out of their homes in insolence and hypocrisy toward people, blocking Allah's path.[1393] Allah is aware of what they do. (47)

\*\*\*

Satan made their deeds seem fair to them, and said, "No one will defeat you[MP] today. I am your[MP] neighbor." When the two parties saw each other, he retreated on his heels, and said, "I am innocent towards you[MP]. I see what you[MP] do not. I fear Allah, and Allah is severe in punishment." (48)

\*\*\*

The hypocrites and those with sick hearts[1394] say, "Their religion has deceived them." Allah is mighty[1395] and wise to those who trust in Allah. (49)

\*\*\*

If you[MS] see when the angels cause the disbelievers to die, they beat their faces and their backs. "Taste the torment of the fire." (50)

\*\*\*

That is because of their deeds. Allah does not wrong the servants.[1396] (51)

\*\*\*

They disbelieved in Allah's signs[1397] as did Pharaoh's family and those before them, so Allah seized them for their sins. Allah is strong,[1398] and is severe in punishment. (52)

\*\*\*

---

[1390] Tawrah, 2 Chronicles 20:17, Zabur, Psalms 1:2-3
[1391] Injil, 2 Timothy 2:24-26
[1392] For "endure" here twice, in verses 65, and in 66 twice, see glossary.
[1393] Injil, Matthew 23:13, Luke 11:52.
[1394] Tawrah, Jeremiah 8:18, 17:9-10
[1395] Injil, Revelation 18:8, Tawrah, Isaiah 60:16, Zabur, Psalms 93:4
[1396] This verse is one of only five verses where the plural form /abid/ is used. All five use the same phrase. This word can also be translated "slaves." The other verses are 3:182, 22:10, 41:46, and 50:29.
[1397] Arabic /ayat/. See glossary for more details.
[1398] Tawrah, Job 9:4, Zabur, Psalms 24:8, Injil, Ephesians 6:10, Revelation 18:8

Chapter 8

That is because Allah would not change his blessings toward people[1399] until they change what is within them. Allah hears all and knows all. (53) They rejected their Lord's signs like Pharaoh's family[1400] and those before them, so we destroyed them for their sins and drowned Pharaoh's family.[1401] They were all wicked. (54) The most evil living creatures to Allah are the disbelievers. They do not believe. (55) Those with whom you[MS] made a treaty break it all the time and are not reverent. (56) If you[MS] meet them in war, use them to disperse[MS] those behind them, so that they may remember. (57) If you[MS] fear treachery from people, reject[MS] them[1402] as well. Allah does not love traitors.[1403] (58) Let the disbelievers not think that they have won. They cannot frustrate [them][1404]. (59) Prepare as much as you[MP] can against them – forces and horses tethered – to terrify[1405] Allah's enemy and yours[MP], and others besides them whom you[MP] do not know. Allah knows them. Whatever you[MP] spend in Allah's path will be repaid to you[MP], and you[MP] will not be wronged.[1406] (60) 10A2 If they incline to peace, incline[MS] to it.[1407] Trust[MS] Allah. He hears all and knows all. (61) If they want to deceive you[MS], Allah is adequate for you[MS]. He aids you[MS] with his salvation and with the believers. (62) He united their hearts.[1408] If you[MS] were to donate everything on earth, you[MS] would not unite their hearts, but Allah united them. He is mighty[1409] and wise. (63) Prophet, Allah is adequate for you[MS] and the believers who follow you[MS]. (64) Prophet, exhort[MS] the believers to the battle.[1410] If there are twenty who endure, they will defeat two hundred, and if there are a hundred of you[MP], they will defeat a thousand disbelievers,[1411] for they are people who do not understand. (65) Allah has lightened it for you[MP]. He knows that there is weakness among you[MP]. If there are a hundred who endure,

---

[1399] Injil, Hebrews 13:8, James 1:17
[1400] Tawrah, Exodus 4:23
[1401] Tawrah, Exodus 14:27-28, 15:4, Isaiah 43:17
[1402] the direct object of "the treaty with them" is understood here
[1403] Zabur, Psalms 5:4-5, 11:5, Tawrah, Proverbs 6:16-19
[1404] or Allah. The object is not mentioned in the text.
[1405] Tawrah, Genesis 35:5, Exodus 15:16, 23:27.
[1406] Tawrah, Proverbs 19:17
[1407] Peace is masculine and it is feminine. The reference of "it" is unclear.
[1408] Injil, John 17:21-24
[1409] Injil, Revelation 18:8, Tawrah, Isaiah 60:16, Zabur, Psalms 93:4
[1410] Tawrah, 1 Samuel 14:24
[1411] Tawrah, Leviticus 26:8, Judges 7:1-12.

## Chapter 8

they will defeat two hundred, and if there are a thousand, they will defeat two thousand with Allah's permission. Allah is with those who endure. (66) The prophet should never have taken prisoners unless there was a great slaughter in the land. You[MP] want this world's goods, and Allah wants the hereafter. Allah is strong and wise. (67) If not for a previous book from Allah, you[MP] would have been touched by great torment for what you[MP] took. (68) Eat[MP] of the booty you[MP] have taken. It is allowed and good. Fear[MP] Allah. Allah is forgiving[1412] and merciful[1413] (69) Prophet, say to those you[MP] took as prisoners, "Allah knows of good in your[MP] hearts, he will give you[MP] good for what was taken from you[MP]. Allah will forgive you[MP]. He is forgiving and merciful." (70) If they want to betray you[MS], they have betrayed Allah previously, so this is possible from them. Allah is all-knowing and wise. (71)

\*\*\*

Those who believed, emigrated, and struggled in Allah's path with their money and themselves, and those who sheltered and delivered are friends of each other. You[MP] are to have no friendship with believers who did not emigrate until they do so. If they ask you[MP] for help in religion, you[MP] must help them, except for people with whom you[MP] have a treaty. Allah sees your[MP] deeds. (72)

---

[1412] Here and in verse 70, see Zabur, Psalms 103:3, 130:4, Tawrah, Isaiah 43:25, Exodus 34:7, Injil, Acts 26:18.
[1413] Here and in verse 70, see glossary for more details on "merciful."

Disbelievers are friends with each other. If you<sup>MP</sup> do not do this, there will be strife and great destruction in the land. (73)

\*\*\*

Believers who emigrated and struggled in Allah's path and those who sheltered and delivered are true believers.[1414] They have forgiveness and a generous provision. (74) Those who believed later, emigrated and struggled with you<sup>MP</sup> are some of your<sup>MP</sup> own, and blood relatives are closer to each other in Allah's book. Allah knows everything. (75)[1415]

---

[1414] Injil, James 1:27
[1415] The verses in this chapter that rhyme are put together in paragraphs, separated by \*\*\*.

# Chapter 9: Al-Tawbah[1416] or Al-Baraah[1417]

**10A3** [There is] blamelessness from Allah and his messenger toward those idolaters with whom you^MP made a covenant, (1) so travel^MP in the land four months. Know^MP that you^MP cannot block Allah, and that Allah will shame the disbelievers. (2) [There is] a proclamation from Allah and his messenger for people on the day of the great hajj,[1418] that Allah is guiltless toward the idolaters. Also his messenger.[1419] If you^MP repent, it is better for you^MP, and if you^MP turn away, know^MP that you^MP cannot frustrate Allah. Give good news[1420] of painful torment[1421] to the disbelievers. (3) The exception is the idolaters with whom you^MP made a covenant, and who fulfilled all their obligations towards you^MP and who did not assist anyone against you^MP. Fulfill your^MP covenant with them until it expires. Allah loves the reverent. (4) And when the sacred months are finished, kill the idolaters wherever you^MP find them;[1422] take^MP them, surround^MP them, and set^MP all sorts of ambushes against them. If they repent and perform their prayers

---

[1416] Repentance. This chapter is the only chapter that does not begin with "In the name of Allah, the most gracious and Merciful." For this reason, some think that is was originally the second part of chapter 8.

[1417] Immunity

[1418] pilgrimage. See glossary for more details.

[1419] The connection of messenger to another word here is uncertain, since messenger is nominative, whereas Allah is accusative and disbelievers is genitive.

[1420] This is probably sarcastic, here and in verse 34, as the news is bad news.

[1421] For "torment" here and in verses 34, 61, 66, 68, 74, 79, 90, 101, and 106, see Tawrah, Isaiah 50:11, Injil, Matthew 18:34, 25:41,46, Luke 16:23-28, Revelation 20:15.

[1422] The Qur'an has four verses that command killing others (2:191, 4:89,91, and 9:5), but none of these apply today. Similarly, the Tawrah has many verses that refer to killing others (Exodus 23:23-24,28-30, 32:27, Numbers 21:35, 31:2,7-8,17, Deuteronomy 7:2,16, 9:3-4, Joshua 6:17-21, 8:2, Judges 21:11, 1 Samuel 15:3, 27:9,11, 2 Chronicles 15:13) and none of them apply today either.

## Chapter 9

and pay the poor-tax, let them go. Allah is forgiving[1423] and merciful.[1424] (5) If a polytheist seeks refuge with you[MS], grant him asylum so that[1425] he can hear Allah's word. Then take[MS] him to a place of safety. This is because they are people who do not know. (6) How can idolaters have a covenant with Allah[1426] and with his messenger, except for those with whom you[MP] made a covenant at the sacred place of worship?[1427] As long as they are upright with you[MP], be upright with them. Allah loves the reverent. (7) And what if they get the better of you[MP] and respect neither relationship nor treaty? They please you[MP] with their mouths while their hearts reject. Most of them are unbelievers.[1428] (8) They sold Allah's verses[1429] for a small price and block the path to him.[1430] Their deeds were evil. (9) They respect neither relationship nor treaty with a believer. They are the aggressors. (10) If they repent, perform prayers, and pay the poor-tax, [they are] your[MP] brothers in religion. We give detailed signs for people who know. (11) If they break their oaths after making a covenant, and speak evil of your[MP] religion, fight[MP] the leaders[1431] of disbelief - they have no oaths - that they may cease. (12) Will you[MP] not fight people who break their oaths, plot to expel the messenger, and attacked you first? Do you[MP] fear them? Allah is the one you[MP] ought to fear if you[MP] are believers.[1432] (13) Fight[MP] them. Allah will torment them with your[MP] hands,[1433] shame them, give you[MP] victory over them, heal the hearts[1434] of believing people, (14) and remove the wrath of their hearts. Allah accepts repentance from whoever he wills.

---

[1423] For "forgiving" here and in verses 27,91,99, and 102, see Zabur, Psalms 103:3, 130:4, Tawrah, Isaiah 43:25, Exodus 34:7, Injil, Acts 26:18.

[1424] Here and in verses 27, 91, 99, 102, 104, 117, 118, and 128, see glossary for more details on "merciful."

[1425] Or until

[1426] Injil, 2 Corinthians 6:14-17

[1427] For "sacred place of worship here and in verss 19 and 28, see Injil, John 4:20-24, Hebrews 8:1-2, 9:24, 10:19-22.

[1428] Or transgressors or immoral, here and in verses 24, 53, 67, 80, 84, and 96.

[1429] or signs

[1430] Or his path. Injil, Matthew 23:13, Luke 11:52.

[1431] Or imams

[1432] Tawrah, Proverbs 29:25

[1433] Injil, Romans 16:20

[1434] Or chests or breasts.

## Chapter 9

Allah is all-knowing[1435] and wise.[1436] (15) Or do you[MP] think that you[MP] will be abandoned, since Allah knows those of you[MP] who struggled and did not choose as confidants other than Allah, his messenger, or the believers? Allah is aware of your[MP] deeds. (16) Idolaters would not build Allah's places of worship, while witnessing to their own disbelief. Their works are in vain, and they will remain in hellfire forever. (17) Those who build Allah's places of worship are those who believe in Allah and the last day, perform prayer, pay the poor-tax, and fear Allah[1437] alone. They might be guided. (18) 10A4 Do you[MP] make someone who gives water[1438] to a pilgrim[1439] and builds the sacred place of worship equal to someone who believes in Allah and the last day and who struggles in Allah's path? They are not equal in Allah's eyes. Allah does not guide wicked people. (19) Truly those who believed, emigrated and struggled in Allah's path with their money and their lives are higher in rank with Allah. They are the winners. (20) Their Lord gives them good news of mercy and good pleasure from him and of heavenly gardens[1440] of permanent pleasure for them, (21) where they will remain forever. Allah's reward is great. (22) Believers, do not take your[MP] fathers and brothers as protectors if they prefer disbelief over belief. Those of you[MP] who take them are wicked. (23) Say[MS], "If you[MP] love your fathers, sons, brothers, wives, tribes, the money you[MP] have gained, the goods you[MP] fear will become stagnant, and the homes you[MP] desire more than Allah,[1441] his messenger, and struggling in his path, then watch out lest Allah bring his command. Allah does not guide unbelieving people." (24) Allah has given you[MP] victory in many lands. On the day of Hunayn, when you[MP] were pleased with your[MP] numbers, they did not help you[MP]. The land was not big enough for you[MP]

---

[1435] For "all-knowing" here and in verse 28, 60, 97, 98, 103, 106, 110, and 115, see Tawrah, Job 37:16, Isaiah 40:14, Zabur, Psalms 33:13-15, Injil, 1 John 3:20

[1436] For "wise" here and in verses 28, 40, 60, 71, 97, 106, and 110, see Tawrah, Job 9:4, Proverbs 2:6, Jeremiah 9:23-24, Injil, 1 Corinthians 1:21-25, Romans 16:27.

[1437] Tawrah, Deuteronomy 10:12, Isaiah 29:13, Injil, 1 Peter 2:17, Revelation 14:7

[1438] Injil, Matthew 10:42

[1439] pilgrimage. See glossary for more details.

[1440] Arabic /jannah/ here and in verses 72 (twice), 89, 100, and 111. See glossary for more details.

[1441] Injil, Luke 14:26, Matthew 10:37

## Chapter 9

despite its breadth. Then you[MP] turned away and fled. (25) Then Allah revealed his presence[1442] to his messenger and the believers, and he sent down hosts you[MP] have not seen,[1443] and tormented the disbelievers. That is the disbelievers' reward. (26) Then Allah will accept repentance from whoever he wills. Allah is forgiving and merciful. (27) Believers, idolaters are unclean.[1444] They are not to approach the sacred place of worship after this year of theirs. If you[MP] fear poverty, Allah by his grace will enrich you[MP] if he wills. Allah is all-knowing and wise. (28) Fight[MP] those who were given the book who do not believe in Allah or the last day, do not forbid what Allah and his messenger have forbidden, and do not profess the religion of truth until they pay reparations by hand in subjection. (29) The Jews said, "Ezra is the son of Allah,"[1445] and the Christians[1446] said: "The Messiah[1447] is the son of Allah.[1448]" That is the saying of their mouths, resembling the sayings of disbelievers beforehand.[1449] Allah fought them. How they lie! (30)

---

[1442] Here and in verse 40, this word /sakeenah/ can mean either Shekinah (an Arabized word from Hebrew, meaning Allah's presence) or tranquility. Since true tranquility comes from Allah's presence, the two meanings are not contradictory. It is used in 2:248, 9:26,40, 48:4,18,26. In 2:248 it clearly refers to Allah's presence. Tawrah, Numbers 7:89

[1443] Here and in verse 40, see Tawrah, 2 Kings 6:16,17.

[1444] For idolatry and other sins' connection with uncleanness, see Tawrah, Numbers 6:9-11, Ezekiel 44:27.

[1445] The Jewish veneration and glorification of Ezra is noted in Louis Feldman, "Josephus' Portrait of Ezra," *Vestus Testamentum* 43, no. 2 (1993): 192-193: Ezra is said (Koheleth Rabbah 1.4) by the rabbis to have had such stature that he would have been high priest even if Aaron himself were then alive. Furthermore, we are told (Yoma 69b) that he reached such a level of holiness that he was able to pronounce the divine name "as it is written". Indeed, he is one of five men whose piety is especially extolled by the rabbis (Midrash Psalms on cv 2). ... In short, it is not surprising that this glorification of Ezra reached such proportions that ... the Koran (Sura 9.30) ... accuses the Jews of regarding Ezra as the veritable son of God."

[1446] For /nasara/ (Christian), see glossary for more details.

[1447] Or Christ, here and in verse 31. Arabic Al-Masih. See glossary for more details.

[1448] Apparently these Christians believed that Christ was biologically or sexually the son of Allah. This idea, which has no basis in the Injil, is rightly rejected.

[1449] The disbelievers beforehand may refer to the Greeks and Romans, who believed in many gods, some of which they believed had come to

## Chapter 9

They made their priests and monks gods to the exclusion of Allah[1450] and the Messiah, the son of Mariam.[1451] They were only commanded[1452] to worship one god,[1453] and he is the only god. May he be glorified above the gods they worship! (31) They want to extinguish Allah's light[1454] with their mouths, and Allah rejected this and perfected his light, even though the disbelievers hate it. (32) He sent his messenger with guidance and the religion of truth to clarify all religion,[1455] even though the idolaters hate it.[1456] (33) 10B1 Believers, many priests and monks vainly steal people's money, and obstruct Allah's path. They hoard gold and silver and do not spend it in Allah's path. Give them good news of painful torment (34) on a day when it[1457] will be heated in the fire of hell, and their foreheads, sides, and backs will be ironed with it. "This is what you[MP] have hoarded for yourselves[MP], so taste[MP] what you[MP] have hoarded." (35) The number of months in Allah's eyes is twelve months, in Allah's book on the day he created the heavens and the earth.[1458] Four months[FP] are sacred[MP]. This is

---

earth and had sexual relations with women. The Tawrah, Zabur, Injil, and Qur'an all agree that this is false.

[1450] Apparently the people referred to here left the clear teaching of Allah and the Messiah, of both the Tawrah and the Injil, "Hear, O Israel: the LORD our God is one LORD" (Tawrah, Deuteronomy 6:4, quoted in Injil, Mark 12:29 by Isa); "There is no Allah but One" (Injil, 1 Corinthians 8:4, 1 Timothy 2:5). Nowhere in the Tawrah or Injil does it say that Allah is not one. Those who substitute human teaching for Allah's word have truly gone astray. See "Allah" and "god" in glossary for more details.

[1451] Mary, mother of Jesus. See glossary for more details. This verse is understood by some to mean "They made their priests, monks, and the Messiah, the son of Mariam, gods to the exclusion of Allah." Another possible translation is "They made their priests and monks gods and the Messiah to the exclusion of Allah."

[1452] Injil, Matthew 23:9,10

[1453] Arabic /ilah/ here twice and in verse 129. See glossary for more details.

[1454] Injil, John 1:4-9, 3:19-21, 8:12, 9:5, 12:35-36, 2 Corinthians 4:4-6, Ephesians 5:14, 1 John 1:5, Revelation 21:23-24, 22:5

[1455] Submission to Allah is at the core of true religion, whether that of the Qur'an, Injil, Tawrah, or Zabur. See 2:62, 5:69.

[1456] Injil, John 1:10-11

[1457] probably referring back to the gold and silver. See Injil, James 5:1-6.

[1458] Tawrah, Genesis 1:1, Isaiah 42:5, 45:18

straight religion, so do not wrong^MP yourselves^MP in them^FP,^1459 and fight^MP all^1460 idolaters as they all fight you^MP. Know that Allah is with the godfearers. (36) Postponing the month is an increase in disbelief and leads disbelievers astray. They allow it for a year and forbid it for a year, to conform to the number Allah has forbidden and so permit what Allah has forbidden. The evil of their works looks pleasing to them, and Allah does not guide disbelieving people. (37)

\*\*\*

Believers, what is wrong with you^MP? When you^MP are told, "Go^MP forth in Allah's path," you^MP become heavy [and fall] to the ground? Are you^MP pleased with this life more than the hereafter? This life's enjoyment is nothing compared to the hereafter. (38)

\*\*\*

If you^MP do not go forth, he will torment you^MP painfully, and replace you^MP with other people;^1461 you^MP will not hurt him at all. Allah can do anything.^1462 (39)

\*\*\*

If you^MP do not help him, Allah will help him, for the disbelievers expelled him like the second of two who were in the cave. He told his companion, "Do not grieve! Allah is with us." Then Allah sent down his presence on him and aided him with his hosts, which you^MP have not seen. He made the word of the disbelievers lower and Allah's word is the highest. Allah is strong and wise. (40) Go forth, lightly or heavily [armed], and struggle with your^MP money and your^MP souls in Allah's path. That is better for you^MP, if you^MP really knew. (41) If there were quick worldly gain and an easy^1463 trip, they would have followed you^MS, but the distance^1464 was too far for them. They will swear by Allah, "If we had been able to, we would have gone out with you^MP." They destroy themselves, and Allah knows that they are liars. (42) May Allah forgive

---

^1459 The word "sacred" is for masculine thinking beings, the word "them" is for feminine thinking beings, and "months" are masculine. This may allude to the months being holy and almost living beings.
^1460 Or fight in every place.
^1461 Injil, Matthew 21:43
^1462 Tawrah, Job 42:2, Isaiah 14:27, Daniel 4:35, Injil, Matthew 19:26, Mark 10:27, Luke 1:37
^1463 Or intentional
^1464 or difficulty

## Chapter 9

you<sup>MS</sup>!<sup>1465</sup> Why did you<sup>MS</sup> permit them, before it was clear to you<sup>MS</sup> who were sincere and you<sup>MS</sup> knew who were liars. (43) Believers in Allah and the last day do not ask your<sup>MS</sup> permission to struggle with their money and their souls. Allah knows the godfearers. (44) It is the disbelievers in Allah and the last day who ask your<sup>MS</sup> permission. Their hearts doubt. They are in doubt and hesitant. (45) 10B2 If they had wanted to go out, they would have prepared provisions for it, but Allah hated sending them so he made them slothful, and it was said, "Sit down along with the others who are sitting." (46) If they had gone out among you<sup>MP</sup>, they would have only hindered you<sup>MP</sup> and hurried about.<sup>1466</sup> They want you<sup>MP</sup> to have strife. Some of you<sup>MP</sup> would have listened to them. Allah knows who is wicked. (47) They previously wanted strife, and turned matters upside down for you<sup>MS</sup> until the truth came and Allah's command became apparent, while they hated it. (48) Some of them say, "Give me permission and do not tempt me." Did they not fall in temptation?<sup>1467</sup> Hell surrounds the disbelievers. (49) If something good happens to you<sup>MS</sup>, they think evil of it, and if something evil happens to you<sup>MS</sup>, they say, "We ordered our matter previously." Then they turn away happily. (50) Say<sup>MS</sup>, "Nothing will happen to us except what Allah has ordained. He is our master, so let the believers trust in him." (51) Say<sup>MS</sup>, "Are you<sup>MP</sup> waiting for us to receive one of the two best things? We are waiting for Allah to afflict you<sup>MP</sup> with torment, either himself or by our hands. So wait<sup>MP</sup>, and we are waiting with you<sup>MP</sup>." (52) Say<sup>MS</sup>, "Donate<sup>MP</sup> willingly or unwillingly, and it will not be accepted from you<sup>MP</sup>. You<sup>MP</sup> have been unbelieving people." (53) What prevented them from their donations being received is only their disbelief in Allah and his messenger, their not attending prayers except lazily, and their unwillingness to donate. (54) Do not be

---

<sup>1465</sup> The belief that all prophets and messengers are sinless is not supported by the Qur'an. For instances of prophets or messengers asking forgiveness or committing sins, see 7:23, 20:121 (Adam), 11:47, 71:28 (Nuh), 26:82, 14:41 (Ibrahim), 28:15-16 (Musa), 7:151, 20:93 (Musa and Harun), 38:24 (Dawud), 38:32,35 (Sulayman), 21:87, 37:142 (Yunus), 48:2, 47:19, 40:55, 4:79,106, 9:43, 13:30, 80:1-2, 110:3, 94:2, 23:118, 66:1, 33:37, 8:67, and 9:117 (Muhammad (s).

<sup>1466</sup> The meaning could be "driven your camels too quickly" which could be the result of hurrying about.

<sup>1467</sup> the word here translated temptation is the same word translated strife in the previous verse.

## Chapter 9

attracted by their money or their children.[1468] Allah wants to torment[1469] them by means of it in this life, and for their souls to perish while disbelievers. (55) They swear by Allah that they belong to you<sup>MP</sup>, while they do not belong to you<sup>MP</sup>. They are fearful people. (56) If they could find a refuge, caves, or a hideaway, they would turn obstinately toward it. (57) Some of them slander you<sup>MS</sup> regarding alms for the poor. If they are given some alms, they are content, and if they are not given any, they are enraged. (58) If only they had been content with what Allah and his messenger gave them, and had said, "Allah is enough for us, and he and his messenger will give to us out of Allah's grace. We want Allah." (59) 10B3 Giving is for the poor, the needy, those who work with it, and those whose hearts are in harmony, for slaves, debtors, as gifts in Allah's path, and for travellers. This is an ordinance from Allah. Allah is all-knowing and wise. (60) Some of them harm[1470] the prophet and say, "He is an ear." Say<sup>MS</sup>, "A good ear to you<sup>MP</sup>. He believes in Allah and gives safety[1471] to the believers, and is a mercy to the believers among you<sup>MP</sup>. Those who harm Allah's messenger will have painful torment." (61) They swear to you<sup>MP</sup> by Allah in order to please you<sup>MP</sup>, whereas Allah and his messenger deserve to be pleased more, if they were believers. (62) Do they not know that those who oppose Allah and his messenger will go to the fire of hell forever? That is the great shame. (63) The hypocrites warn about a chapter being revealed to them which reveals what is in their hearts. Say<sup>MS</sup>, "Mock<sup>MP</sup>! Allah will send you<sup>MP</sup> what you<sup>MP</sup> warn against." (64) If you<sup>MS</sup> ask them, they will say, "We were talking vainly[1472] and playing."[1473] Say<sup>MS</sup>, "Were you<sup>MP</sup> mocking Allah, his signs, and his messenger?" (65) Do not apologize. You<sup>MP</sup> disbelieved after being believers. If we forgive some of you<sup>MP</sup>, we will torment others of you<sup>MP</sup> because they were wrongdoers. (66) The male and female hypocrites promote vice, prevent virtue,[1474] and clench their fists. They have

---

[1468] Or sons, here and in verses 69 and 85.

[1469] Injil, Revelation 9:5-6, Jeremiah 26:13, James 5:1-6, here and in verse 85.

[1470] Or insult.

[1471] This word is the same word as the word translated "believe" in this verse.

[1472] Some translations use "gossip" here and in verse 69

[1473] Tawrah, Proverbs 26:18,19

[1474] or kindness

forgotten Allah and he has forgotten them. Hypocrites are unbelieving. (67) Allah has promised the male and female hypocrites and the disbelievers that they will remain forever in the fires of hell. It is their just due. Allah has damned them and they will have permanent torment, (68) just like those before you[MP] who were stronger and richer than you[MP], had more children, and they enjoyed their portion. You[MP] enjoyed your[MP] portion as those before you[MP] enjoyed theirs. You[MP] were talking vainly just like they were. Their works are in vain in this world and the hereafter. They are lost. (69) Have they not received the news of those before them? The messengers to the people of Nuh,[1475] Aad[1476] and Thamud, the people of Ibrahim,[1477] the companions of Midian, Sodom and Gomorrah[1478] brought them miracles. Allah would never wrong them but they wronged themselves.[1479] (70) Male and female believers are helpers of each other. They promote virtue,[1480] prevent vice, perform prayers, pay the poor-tax, and obey Allah and his messenger. Allah will have mercy on them. Allah is strong and wise. (71) Allah has promised the male and female believers heavenly gardens with flowing rivers[1481] underneath where they will be forever, and nice dwellings in the heavenly gardens of

---

[1475] Noah. See glossary for more details.
[1476] Aad and Thamud are names of tribes.
[1477] Abraham. See glossary for more details.
[1478] Or, the cities that were overthrown. See Tawrah, Genesis 19:24-25.
[1479] The injustice/wickedness, disbelief/ungratefulness, evil, unrighteousness/sin, or lostness of mankind is mentioned in a number of verses in the Qur'an as well as in the previous books. Injustice or wickedness: 2:57, 3:117,135, 4:64,97, 7:160,177, 9:70, 10:44, 11:101, 14:34,45, 16:33,61,118, 29:40, 30:9, 33:72, 34:19, 35:32, 43:76, 65:1, Tawrah, Genesis 6:5, Job 25:4, Injil, Acts 3:26, disbelief or ungratefulness: 14:34, 17:67, 22:66, 42:48, 43:15, 80:17, Injil, Hebrews 3:19, Evil: 12:53, Tawrah, Jeremiah 17:9, Injil, Matthew 15:19, Mark 7:21, unrighteousness or sin: 91:8, Tawrah, 1 Kings 8:46, Ecclesiastes 7:20, Injil, Romans 3:9-19, 5:12, lostness: 103:2, Tawrah, Jeremiah 50:6, Injil, Luke 19:10, Romans 3:23, 6:23
[1480] or kindness
[1481] Here and in verses 89 and 100, see Injil, Revelation 22:1-2, Tawrah, Ezekiel 47:12.

## Chapter 9

Eden, and Allah's pleasure, which is more than that.[1482] That is the great victory.[1483] (72)

\*\*\*

Prophet, struggle against the disbelievers and the hypocrites and press heavily upon them. Their refuge is hell, and it is a dreadful destiny. (73) They swore by Allah that they didn't say it, but they said the word of disbelief. They disbelieved after having submitted[1484] and were concerned about what they had not received. They only disliked that Allah and his messenger had enriched them with his grace. If they repent, it will be better for them. If they turn away, Allah will torment them with painful torment in this life[1485] and the hereafter. They will have no helper or savior on earth. (74) 10B4

\*\*\*

Some of them promise Allah, "If he brings us some of his grace, we will give alms and be righteous." (75) When he brought them some of his grace, they were stingy, and turned away in aversion. (76) So he made hypocrisy follow them in their hearts until the day they meet him, because they did not do what they had promised Allah, but were liars. (77)

\*\*\*

Do they not know that Allah knows their secrets and private counsels? Allah knows what is invisible. (78)

\*\*\*

They slander and mock the believing volunteers in their alms and those who find only their own labor [to offer]. May Allah mock them. They will have painful torment. (79) It does not matter if you ask forgiveness[MS] for them or do not ask. Even if you[MS] ask forgiveness for them seventy times, Allah will not forgive them.[1486] That is because they disbelieve in Allah and his messenger. Allah does not guide unbelieving people. (80) Those who were left behind rejoiced in their sitting in opposition to

---

[1482] Zabur, Psalms 16:11

[1483] For "victory" here and in verses 89, 100, and 111, see Tawrah, Isaiah 25:8, Injil, 1 Corinthians 15:57, 1 John 5:4.

[1484] Injil, James 4:7. For "submitted," some translators do not translate this. See glossary for more details.

[1485] Injil, Revelation 9:5-6, Tawrah, 1 Samuel 16:14, Jeremiah 26:13

[1486] Here the Qur'an makes it clear that Muhammad (s) is not an intercessor, contrary to popular beliefs. If Allah decides to torment someone, Muhammad's (s) intercession does not help.

Allah's messenger, and they hated to struggle in Allah's path with their money and souls. They said, "Do not go out in the heat." Say^MS, "The fire of hell is hotter, if they only understood." (81) Let them laugh a little and cry a lot for what they deserve. (82) If Allah returns you^MS to a group of them, and they ask you^MS to go out, say^MS, "You^MP will never go out with me nor fight an enemy with me.[1487] You^MP were happy to sit the first time, so sit^MP with the rest of those who sit behind. (83) Do not pray^MS for any of them who dies, and do not stand^MS over his grave. They disbelieved in Allah and his messenger and died in their unbelief. (84) Do not be attracted by their money or their children. Allah wants to torment them by means of them in this world, and for them to die disbelievers. (85) And if a chapter is revealed saying, believe in Allah and struggle with his messenger, the wealthy among them ask permission of you^MS saying, "Allow^MS us to sit." (86) They want to be with those who stay behind. Their hearts are sealed, and they do not understand. (87) But the messenger and those who believed with him struggled with their money and their souls. They will have good things and they are prosperous. (88) Allah has prepared heavenly gardens for them with flowing rivers underneath where they will be forever. That is the great victory. (89) Then those desert nomads[1488] who had excuses came to ask permission. Those who rejected Allah and his messenger sat down. Painful torment will afflict the disbelievers among them. (90) Those who are weak[1489] or sick or have nothing to donate should not be embarrassed if they are faithful[1490] to Allah and his messenger. Those who do good have no other way. Allah is forgiving and merciful. (91) Nor should those who come to you^MS to be carried, when you^MS say, "I have nothing to carry you^MP on. Go^MP back." Their eyes overflow with tears in sorrow that they have nothing to donate. (92) 11A1 The way is truly against the rich who ask permission of you^MS and want to stay behind sitting. Allah has sealed their hearts, so they do not know it. (93) They apologize to you^MP when you^MP return to them. Say^MS, "Do not apologize. We will not trust you^MP. Allah has informed us of your^MP news. Allah and

---

[1487] Tawrah, 1 Samuel 29:4-7.

[1488] Or Bedouins, here and in verses 97, 98, 99, 101, and 120.

[1489] Here and in 2:266, this word has a different spelling than in 14:21 and 40:47. Some say the reason is that this one refers to those who are weak in this world.

[1490] Or if they advise

## Chapter 9

his messenger will see your<sup>MP</sup> work. Then you<sup>MP</sup> will be turned back to the knower of the invisible and the visible, and he will tell you<sup>MP</sup> your<sup>MP</sup> deeds." (94) If you<sup>MP</sup> turn back to them, they will swear by Allah to you<sup>MP</sup> to pass by them. Pass<sup>MP</sup> by them. They are an abomination. Their refuge is hell, the punishment they deserve. (95) They swear to you<sup>MP</sup> so that you<sup>MP</sup> will be pleased with them. Even if you<sup>MP</sup> are pleased with them, Allah is not pleased with unbelieving people. (96) The desert nomads are more disbelieving and hypocritical, and less deserving of knowing the limits of what Allah has revealed to his messenger. Allah is all-knowing and wise. (97) Some desert nomads consider their donations a fine, and watch you<sup>MP</sup> for cycles to come around. A cycle of evil is around them,[1491] and Allah sees all and knows all. (98) Some desert nomads believe in Allah and the last day, and consider their donations as ways to draw near to Allah and as prayers for the messenger. These really are ways for them to draw near. Allah will cause them to enter his mercy. Allah is forgiving and merciful. (99) Allah is pleased with the first emigrants and helpers who led the way, and those who followed them in giving,[1492] and they are pleased with Allah. He has prepared heavenly gardens with flowing rivers underneath for them, where they will be forever. This is the great victory. (100) Some of the desert nomads around you<sup>MP</sup> are hypocrites and some of the people of Medina[1493] are obstinate in hypocrisy. You<sup>MS</sup> do not know them, but we know them. We will torment them twice, then they will be returned to a great torment. (101) Others confess their sins and mixed righteous deeds with bad.[1494] Allah may accept their repentance. He is forgiving and merciful. (102) Take<sup>MS</sup> their money as alms that cleanse and purify them and pray for them. Your<sup>MS</sup> prayers are rest for them. Allah hears all and knows all. (103) Do they not know that Allah accepts repentance from his servants[1495] and receives alms? Allah is the merciful acceptor of repentance.[1496] (104) Say<sup>MS</sup>: "Work<sup>MP</sup>, and Allah, his messenger, and the believers will see your<sup>MP</sup> work. Then you<sup>MP</sup> will be returned to the knower of the

---

[1491] Tawrah, Genesis 6:5
[1492] or good deeds
[1493] Or, the city, here and in verse 120.
[1494] Tawrah, Proverbs 28:13, Injil, 1 John 1:9
[1495] See glossary.
[1496] For "repentance" here and in verses 106, 117 (twice), and 119 (twice), see glossary. Tawrah, Jeremiah 18:8, Joel 2:13, Jonah 3:9-4:2

## Chapter 9

invisible and the visible, and he will tell you<sup>MP</sup> your<sup>MP</sup> deeds." (105) Others are made to wait for Allah's command, whether he will torment them or accept their repentance. Allah is all-knowing and wise. (106) Those who take a place of worship for injury, disbelief, and dissension between believers, ambushing him who previously fought against Allah and his messenger, will swear, "We wanted only good." Allah is witness that they are liars. (107) Do not stand<sup>MS</sup> in it at all. A place of worship founded upon reverence from the first day is better for you<sup>MS</sup> to stand in, for it has men who love to be purified. Allah loves the purified. (108) Is he who founds his building on reverence from Allah and on pleasing [him] better, or one who founds his building on the edge of a tottering cliff, which falls with him into the fire of hell?[1497] Allah does not guide wicked people. (109) The building they built is still [a cause of] doubt in their hearts until their hearts are cut.[1498] Allah is all-knowing and wise. (110) 11A2 Allah has bought the believers' souls and money[1499] and given them the heavenly garden. They fight in Allah's path, and they kill and are killed. [This was] a true promise by him in the Tawrah,[1500] Injil,[1501] and Qur'an.[1502] Who is more faithful to fulfill his promise than Allah?[1503] So rejoice about your<sup>MP</sup> selling what you<sup>MP</sup> contracted. That is the great victory. (111) The repenters, the worshipers, the praisers, the travelers,[1504] the kneelers, those who bow down, those who promote virtue[1505] and prevent vice, those who keep Allah's limits.[1506] Give good news to the believers. (112) The prophet and the believers would not ask for forgiveness for the idolaters, even if they were relatives, after it became clear that they were going to the blazing fire. (113) Ibrahim's[1507] asking for forgiveness for his father was only because he had promised him. When it became

---

[1497] Compare Injil, Matthew 7:24-27
[1498] Injil, Hebrews 4:12, Matthew 7:24-27, Acts 2:37
[1499] see Injil, 1 Corinthians 6:19-20
[1500] The Law. See glossary for more details.
[1501] Gospel. See glossary for more details.
[1502] Or recitation. See glossary for more details.
[1503] Injil, Hebrews 6:18
[1504] probably who travel around as preachers or ascetics
[1505] or kindness
[1506] There is no verb connected with this list, but the meaning might be that these activities describe those who are true believers.
[1507] Abraham, twice here. See glossary for more details.

## Chapter 9

clear that he was an enemy of Allah, he washed his hands of him. Ibrahim was compassionate and gentle.[1508] (114) Allah would never lead people astray after having guided them to show them what they fear. Allah knows everything. (115)

\*\*\*

The kingdom of the heavens and the earth is Allah's.[1509] He gives life and causes death.[1510] You[MP] have no helper or savior apart from Allah.[1511] (116)

\*\*\*

Allah accepted the repentance of the prophet[1512] and the emigrants and the helpers who followed him in the hour of difficulty after the hearts of a group of them nearly went astray;[1513] then he accepted their repentance. He is compassionate and merciful[1514] to them. (117) And of[1515] the three who were left behind when the earth closed in around them though it was wide, and their souls closed in around them, and they thought that there was no refuge for them from Allah except toward him. Then he relented[1516] toward them so they would repent. Allah is the merciful acceptor of repentance. (118) Believers, fear Allah[1517] and be with the truthful. (119) The people of Medina and the desert nomads around them should not have remained behind Allah's messenger, nor desired themselves above him, for every time they suffer thirst, hardship, or hunger in

---

[1508] Zabur, Psalms 45:4, 145:17, Injil, Matthew 11:29, Galatians 5:22
[1509] Tawrah, Isaiah 45:12, Zabur, Psalms 24:1, 89:11, Injil, Hebrews 1:10
[1510] Tawrah, 1 Samuel 2:6, Deuteronomy 32:39
[1511] Tawrah, Hosea 13:4, Zabur, Psalms106:21, Injil, Luke 1:47, Titus 1:3
[1512] The belief that all prophets and messengers are sinless is not supported by the Qur'an. For instances of prophets or messengers asking forgiveness or committing sins, see 7:23, 20:121 (Adam), 11:47, 71:28 (Nuh), 26:82, 14:41 (Ibrahim), 28:15-16 (Musa), 7:151, 20:93 (Musa and Harun), 38:24 (Dawud), 38:32,35 (Sulayman), 21:87, 37:142 (Yunus), 48:2, 47:19, 40:55, 4:79,106, 9:43, 13:30, 80:1-2, 110:3, 94:2, 23:118, 66:1, 33:37, 8:67, and 9:117 (Muhammad (s)).
[1513] The noun here is feminine and the verb is masculine, so there may be a different meaning.
[1514] Injil, James 5:11, here and in verse128.
[1515] i.e. Allah also accepted the repentance of
[1516] Or accepted their repentance. For "repentance," see glossary. Tawrah, Jeremiah 18:8, Joel 2:13, Jonah 3:9-4:2
[1517] Tawrah, Deuteronomy 10:12, Isaiah 29:13, Injil, 1 Peter 2:17, Revelation 14:7

## Chapter 9

Allah's path, or tread anywhere that angers the disbelievers or get anything from an enemy, it will be counted as a righteous deed for them. Allah does not lose the reward of those who do good. (120) Allah will record it if they donate a small or large amount, or cross a valley, and will reward them for the best of their deeds.[1518] (121)

11A3 All the believers should not have gone forth. Rather, some from every group of them should understand religion and warn their people when they return to them, so that they may be aware. (122) Believers, fight[MP] the disbelievers who are close to[1519] you[MP]. Let them find you[MP] strong. Know[MP] that Allah is with the reverent. (123) When a chapter is revealed, some of them say, "Whose faith among you[MP] increased because of this?" But it increased the believers' faith, and they rejoiced. (124) It made those with sick hearts[1520] more abominable, and they died disbelievers. (125) Do they not see that they are beguiled once or twice a year, then they do not repent or remember? (126) When a surah is revealed, some of them look at each other. "Does anyone see you[MP]?" Then they go away. May Allah send their hearts away, because they are people without understanding. (127) A messenger has come to you[MP] from among yourselves[MP]. Your[MP] suffering is dear to him. He watches over you[MP]. He is compassionate and merciful[1521] toward the believers. (128) If they turn away, say, "Allah is enough for me. He is the only god. I have trusted in him, and he is the Lord of the great throne." (129)[1522]

---

[1518] Tawrah, Daniel 7:10, Injil, Revelation 20:12
[1519] Or possibly, soft with.
[1520] Tawrah, Jeremiah 8:18, 17:9-10
[1521] Injil, James 5:11
[1522] The verses in this chapter that rhyme are put together in paragraphs, separated by ***.

# Chapter 10 Yunus[1523]

In the name of Allah, the most gracious and merciful.[1524] ALR.[1525] Those[1526] are verses of the wise book. (1) Is it so amazing to people that we inspired a man among them? "Warn people and give believers good news: that they have an honest foot[ing] with their Lord." The disbelievers said, "This one is clearly a magician." (2) Your[MP] Lord is Allah, who created the heavens and the earth[1527] in six days,[1528] then sat down on his throne[1529] directing matters. No one can intercede except after getting his permission.[1530] That is Allah, your[MP] Lord, so worship him. Do you[MP] not remember? (3) All of you[MP] will return to him,[1531] according to Allah's true promise. He begins creation, and then brings it back to reward the believers who did righteous deeds[1532] in justice. Disbelievers will drink boiling water and have painful torment[1533] for their disbelief. (4) He made the sunshine, and the moonlight,[1534] and made its homes,[1535] so that you[MP] would know the number of years and their reckoning.[1536] Allah created everything in truth, and he explains his signs to people who know. (5) The difference[1537] between night and day and Allah's creation of the heavens and the earth are signs for reverent people. (6)

---

[1523] Jonah
[1524] Zabur, Psalms 103:8, 145:8. See glossary
[1525] Here and at the beginning of many chapters there are unvowelled letters of unknown meaning. Numerous theories have been proposed, but there is no agreement on the subject.
[1526] Since it says "those" and not "these" the reference is probably to the former books.
[1527] Here and in verse 6, see Tawrah, Genesis 1:1, Isaiah 42:5, 45:18 .
[1528] Tawrah, Genesis 1:3-28
[1529] Tawrah, Genesis 2:2,3, Injil, Revelation 4:2
[1530] 3:49, 5:110, Injil, Romans 8:34, 1 Timothy 2:5. See 2:255, 20:109, 34:23.
[1531] Injil, Romans 14:12
[1532] Here and in verse 9, see Injil, 1 Corinthians 3:8, James 2:14-17, Revelation 19:8.
[1533] Here and in verses 15, 52, 54, 70, 88, and 97, see Tawrah, Isaiah 50:11, Injil, Matthew 18:34, 25:41,46, Luke 16:23-28, Revelation 20:15.
[1534] Tawrah, Genesis 1:16
[1535] Or stages. Tawrah, Genesis 1:17
[1536] Tawrah, Genesis 1:14
[1537] Or alternation

## Chapter 10

Those who do not want to meet us, who are pleased and content with this world, who ignore our signs, (7) are going to hellfire, as they deserve. (8) Believers who do righteous deeds are guided by their Lord through faith to heavenly gardens[1538] of delight where rivers flow[1539] underneath. (9) There they cry, "Allah, may you[MS] be glorified!" Their greetings there are, "Peace!" Their final cry is, "Praise be to Allah, the Lord of the universe." (10) 11A4 If Allah made evil hasten to people as much as they would hasten good, their lifespan would be decided. We let those who do not want to meet us wander alone in their wickedness. (11) If harm touches a person, he prays to us lying on his side, sitting or standing, and when we take away the harm, he passes by as if he never called on us about the harm that touched him. Thus the works of the wasteful seem pleasing to them. (12) We have destroyed generations[1540] before you[MP] for their wickedness. Their messengers came to them with miracles and they would not believe. Thus we repay wrongdoers. (13) After them, we made you[MP] regents on the earth, so we could see how you[MP] work. (14) And when our signs are read[1541] as miracles, those who do not want to meet us say, "Bring a different recitation,[1542] or exchange it." Say[MS], "I cannot replace it by myself. I only follow what is inspired to me. I would fear the torment of a great day if I disobeyed my Lord." (15) Say[MS], "If Allah had willed, I would not have read[1543] it to you[MP] or told you[MP] of it. I remained with you[MP] a lifetime before it. Do you[MP] not comprehend? (16) Who is more wicked than one who lies about Allah or rejects our signs?[1544] Wrongdoers do not prosper." (17) They worship other gods beside Allah, who cannot harm them or help them,[1545] and they say, "These are our intercessors with Allah." Say[MS], "Do you[MP] tell Allah what he does not know in the heavens or the earth? May he be glorified and exalted above the gods they worship!" (18) People

---

[1538] Arabic /jannah/. See glossary for more details.
[1539] Injil, Revelation 22:1-2, Tawrah, Ezekiel 47:12
[1540] or centuries
[1541] Or recited or told, here and in verses 16 and 71.
[1542] Or qur'an or Qur'an, here and in verses 37 and 61. See glossary for more details.
[1543] Or recited.
[1544] Arabic /ayat/ here and in verses 21, 73, 92 (twice) and 95. See glossary for more details.
[1545] Zabur, Psalms 115:4-7, Tawrah, Isaiah 44:20, here and in verse 106.

were only one nation, and then they differed.[1546] If not for a word[1547] that went forth beforehand from your[MS] Lord, it would have been decided among them regarding their differences. (19) They say, "If only a sign were revealed[1548] to him from his Lord." Say[MS], "The unseen belongs to Allah, so wait. I will be waiting, too." (20) If we give people a taste of mercy after harm touches them, they plot against our signs. Say[MS], "Allah is faster in plotting." Our messengers write down your[MP] plots. (21) He makes you[MP] go on land and sea, even when you[MP] were in the ark. They[FP] drove them along with a pleasant wind, and they[MP] rejoiced in it. Then a strong[1549] wind came and waves from every direction,[1550] and they thought they were surrounded, so they prayed to Allah, sincere in religion, "If you[MS] rescue us from this, we will give thanks." (22) When he rescued them, they acted wrongfully and untruthfully on the land.[1551] People, you[MP] wrong yourselves[MP] in the things of this life, and then you[MP] will return to us, and we will tell you[MP] your[MP] deeds. (23) This world is like rain we sent down[1552] from the sky, which was mixed with the plants of the ground eaten by people and cattle, and when the earth is adorned and decorated, people on the earth imagine they can control it. Our command came to it by night or day, and we harvested[1553] it,[1554] as if it had not been enriched yesterday. Thus we explain our signs to people who consider. (24) Allah calls [people] to the house of

---

[1546] Injil, Acts 17:26

[1547] See 11:110, 20:129, 41:45, 42:14, where this phrase is also used. Isa is called a word (3:39,45, 4:171) so this could be referring to him. See footnotes on verses 20 and 22.

[1548] Sign is feminine and revealed is masculine, so maybe the sign referred to is a person. The only people named in the Qur'an that are referred to as signs are Pharaoh (10:92), Mariam (21:91, 23:50), and Isa (19:21, 21:91, 23:50). Given the context of verses 19 and 22, this probably refers to Isa.

[1549] The adjective "strong" here is masculine, while the adjective "pleasant" earlier in the same verse is feminine. Possibly the second wind represents a person, or Allah sending the wind.

[1550] This probably refers to the account in Injil, Mark 4:37-41. See also Tawrah, Jonah 1

[1551] Or earth

[1552] Tawrah, Deuteronomy 28:12, Job 5:10, Joel 2:23, Zabur, Psalms 68:9, Injil, Matthew 5:45

[1553] Or possibly, destroyed

[1554] Injil, Mark 4:26-29

## Chapter 10

peace and guides whom he wills to a straight path.[1555] (25) **11B1** Those who do good deeds will have a good reward and more. No blackness or humiliation will be on their faces. They will go to heaven and be there forever. (26) Those who do bad deeds will be repaid with bad deeds like them. Their faces will be humiliated. They have no defender from Allah. It is as if their faces were covered with pieces of darkness from the night.[1556] They will go to hellfire and be there forever. (27) On the day we gather[1557] them all, we will say to the idolaters, "You[MP] and your[MP] partner gods, your[MP] place."[1558] We separated them. Their partners said, "You[MP] did not worship us." (28) Allah is an adequate witness between us and you[MP]; we were unaware of your[MP] worship. (29) There every soul will be tested[1559] because of its former deeds. They will be brought back to Allah, their true Lord, and what they lied about will go astray from them. (30) Say[MS], "Who provides for you[MP] out of the sky and the earth? Who owns hearing and sight? Who brings forth the living from the dead, and the dead from the living? Who manages things?" They will say, "Allah." Say[MS], "Do you[MP] not fear god?" (31) That is Allah, your[MP] true Lord. Beyond truth is only straying. How can you[MP] have been turned away? (32) Thus the word of your[MS] Lord was fulfilled on the unbelievers,[1560] since they do not believe. (33) Say[MS], "Do any of your[MP] partner gods begin creation and then restore[1561] it?" Say[MS], "Allah begins creation and restores it. How you[MP] lie!" (34) Say[MS], "Do any of your[MP] partner gods guide toward the truth?" Say[MS], "Allah guides toward the truth. Is he who guides toward the truth more worthy of being followed or one who cannot guide until he has been guided? What is wrong with you[MP]? How do you[MP] judge?" (35) Most of them follow only suppositions. Suppositions give no truth. Allah knows what they do. (36) This recitation could not have been

---

[1555] See glossary for more details, and notes on 3:51, 6:153, 19:36, 36:61, and 43:64 on what the straight path is.
[1556] Injil, Matthew 8:12, 22:13, 25:30
[1557] Here and in verse 45, see Tawrah, Joel 3:11-14, Zephaniah 3:8, Injil, Matthew 25:32, John 15:6, Revelation 16:16
[1558] The idea is "stay at (or go to) your place"
[1559] Injil, 1 Corinthians 3:12-15
[1560] Or transgressors or immoral
[1561] Or repeat (twice in this verse)

## Chapter 10

invented[1562] without Allah, but [it is] a confirmation of what is before it[1563] and an explanation of the book of which there is no doubt, from the Lord of the universe. (37) Or do they say, "He invented it."? Say[MS], "Bring a chapter like it, and pray to whoever you[MP] can besides Allah, if you[MP] are telling the truth." (38) But they reject that of which they are ignorant, even when it is explained to them. Those before them likewise rejected. See the punishment of such wicked people! (39) Some of them believe in it and some do not. Your[MS] Lord knows best who are corrupt. (40) If they reject you[MS], say, "I have my works, and you[MP] have yours[MP]. You[MP] are innocent of what I do, and I am innocent of your[MP] deeds." (41) Some of them listen to you[MS]. Can you[MS] make the deaf hear,[1564] even when they do not comprehend? (42) Some of them look at you[MS]. Can you[MS] guide the blind,[1565] even when they do not see? (43) Allah does not wrong people at all, but they wrong themselves.[1566] (44) On the day they are gathered, it will be as if they remained only an hour of the day, getting to know each other. Those who rejected a meeting with Allah are lost. They were not guided. (45) Either we will show you[MS] some of what we promise them, or we will make you[MS] die. They will return to us, and then Allah will witness what they do. (46) Every nation has a messenger. When their messenger comes, it will be justly decided among them. They will not be wronged. (47) They will say, "When will this promise happen,[1567] if you[MP] are telling the truth?"

---

[1562] Here and in the next verse, the word elsewhere translated "to make a lie" is used.

[1563] Or, "between its (or his) hands" or "in front of it (or him)" or "in his possession"

[1564] Injil, Matthew 11:5, Mark 7:37, Luke 7:22

[1565] Injil, Romans 2:19, Isaiah 42:16

[1566] The injustice/wickedness, disbelief/ungratefulness, evil, unrighteousness/sin, or lostness of mankind is mentioned in a number of verses in the Qur'an as well as in the previous books. Injustice or wickedness: 2:57, 3:117,135, 4:64,97, 7:160,177, 9:70, 10:44, 11:101, 14:34,45, 16:33,61,118, 29:40, 30:9, 33:72, 34:19, 35:32, 43:76, 65:1, Tawrah, Genesis 6:5, Job 25:4, Injil, Acts 3:26, disbelief or ungratefulness: 14:34, 17:67, 22:66, 42:48, 43:15, 80:17, Injil, Hebrews 3:19, Evil: 12:53, Tawrah, Jeremiah 17:9, Injil, Matthew 15:19, Mark 7:21, unrighteousness or sin: 91:8, Tawrah, 1 Kings 8:46, Ecclesiastes 7:20, Injil, Romans 3:9-19, 5:12, lostness: 103:2, Tawrah, Jeremiah 50:6, Injil, Luke 19:10, Romans 3:23, 6:23

[1567] Injil, 2 Peter 3:4

## Chapter 10

(48) Say<sup>MS</sup>, "I cannot harm or help myself, except as Allah wills. Every nation has a lifespan.<sup>1568</sup> When its time comes, they cannot postpone it or advance it, even by an hour."<sup>1569</sup> (49) Say<sup>MS</sup>, "What do you<sup>MP</sup> think? If his torment comes to you<sup>MP</sup>, by night or by day, what will wrongdoers do to hasten it? (50) Then when it happens, you<sup>MP</sup> believe in it now, while you<sup>MP</sup> used to hasten it." (51) Then the wicked were told, "Taste<sup>MP</sup> eternal torment. Do you<sup>MP</sup> not deserve your<sup>MP</sup> punishment?" (52) 11B2 They ask you<sup>MS</sup> to tell them, "Is it true?" Say<sup>MS</sup>, "By my Lord, yes, it is true. You<sup>MP</sup> cannot stop it." (53) Even if every wicked soul owned everything on earth, and they offered it as ransom,<sup>1570</sup> they would secretly regret it when they see the torment. When they are judged, they will not be wronged. (54) Is everything in the heavens and the earth not Allah's?<sup>1571</sup> Is Allah's promise not true? Most of them do not know. (55) He revives and causes death.<sup>1572</sup> To him you<sup>MP</sup> will be returned. (56) People, your<sup>MP</sup> Lord has sent you<sup>MP</sup> an admonition, healing for what is in the heart, guidance and mercy to believers. (57) Say<sup>MS</sup>, "By Allah's grace and mercy." Let them rejoice at that. He is better than what they gather up. (58) Say<sup>MS</sup>, "What do you<sup>MP</sup> think? You<sup>MP</sup> have prohibited or allowed what Allah sent down to you<sup>MP</sup> as provision." Say<sup>MS</sup>, "Did Allah give you<sup>MP</sup> permission, or are you<sup>MP</sup> lying about Allah?" (59) On the day of resurrection, <sup>573</sup> what will those who lie about Allah think? That Allah will show grace to people? Most of them do not give thanks. (60) Whenever you<sup>MS</sup> do something or read<sup>MS</sup><sup>1574</sup> of it from a recitation, or you<sup>MP</sup> do a work, we are witnesses, for you<sup>MP</sup> are immersed in it. Not a speck on the earth or in the sky escapes your<sup>MS</sup> Lord, nor anything smaller or larger. It is all in a clear book. (61) Allah's helpers will not fear or grieve, (62) for they believe and are reverent. (63) They have good news in this world and in the hereafter: there is no

---

<sup>1568</sup> Injil, Acts 17:26

<sup>1569</sup> Injil, Matthew 6:27

<sup>1570</sup> Injil, Matthew 16:26

<sup>1571</sup> Here and in verses 66 and 68, see Tawrah, Isaiah 45:12, Zabur, Psalms 24:1, 89:11, Injil, Hebrews 1:10.

<sup>1572</sup> Tawrah, 1 Samuel 2:6, Deuteronomy 32:39

<sup>1573</sup> For "day of resurrection" here and in verse 93, see Tawrah, Daniel 12:2 Injil, Acts 24:15, 1 Corinthians 15:52-54, Revelation 20:11-15

<sup>1574</sup> Or recite

## Chapter 10

substitution of Allah's words.[1575] That is the great victory.[1576] (64) Do not be[MS] sad at their saying. Allah has all power. He hears all and knows all.[1577] (65) Everyone in the heavens and the earth is Allah's. Those who pray to other gods beside Allah follow only suppositions. They merely guess. (66) He makes night for you[MP] so that you[MP] can be silent in it, and daytime for seeing[MS]. Those are signs for people who hear.[1578] (67) They said, "Allah has chosen a boy." May he be glorified (above that)! He is self-sufficient, and everything in the heavens and the earth is his. Even if you[MP] have authority in this matter, do you[MP] say about Allah things you[MP] do not know about? (68) Say[MS], "Those who tell lies about Allah do not prosper. (69) They may have enjoyment in the world, but they will return to us, and then we will make them taste harsh torment for their disbelief." (70) 11B3 Read to them the story of Nuh,[1579] when he told his people, "My people, if it is a big issue to you[MP] that I stand reminding [you] of Allah's signs, I trust in Allah. Gather your[MP] matters and your[MP] partner gods, and do not let your[MP] matter bother you[MP]. Then judge[MP] me without delay. (71) If you[MP] turn away, I have not asked you[MP] for pay. My pay comes only from Allah. I was commanded to submit."[1580] (72) They rejected him and we rescued him and those with him in the ark, and we made them regents[1581] and we drowned those who rejected our signs. See what was the punishment of those who were warned? (73) After him, we sent messengers to their people, and they brought them miracles, but they would not believe what they had disbelieved in beforehand. We seal transgressors' hearts. (74) After them, we sent Musa[1582] and Harun[1583] with our signs to

---

[1575] For being impossible to change or corrupt Allah's words, see also 18:27, 6:34,115. This verse specifically says it is impossible both in this world and in the hereafter.

[1576] Tawrah, Isaiah 25:8, Injil, 1 Corinthians 15:57, 1 John 5:4

[1577] Tawrah, Job 37:16, Isaiah 40:14, Zabur, Psalms 33:13-15, Injil, 1 John 3:20

[1578] Injil, Matthew 13:43

[1579] Noah. See glossary for more details.

[1580] Injil, James 4:7. For "submit(ted)" here and in verses 84 and 90, some translators do not translate this. See glossary for more details.

[1581] Tawrah, Genesis 9:1-2

[1582] Moses, here and in verses 77, 80, 81, 83, 84, 87, and 88. See glossary for more details.

[1583] Aaron. See glossary for more details.

## Chapter 10

Pharaoh and his people, but they were proud, wrongdoing people. (75) When the truth came to them from us, they said, "This is clear magic." (76) Musa said, "Do you[MP] say of the truth that comes to you[MP]: Is this magic?" Magicians never prosper. (77) They said, "Have you[MS] come to turn us away from what we found our fathers doing,[1584] to make yourselves[D] proud in the earth? We do not believe you[D]."(78) Pharaoh said, "Bring me every knowledgeable magician. (79) When the magicians came, Musa told them, "Throw down what you[MP] throw." (80) When they threw, Musa said, "Allah will nullify the magic you[MP] have brought. Allah does not make the work of the corrupt good." (81) Allah fulfills the truth with his words, even though wrongdoers hate it. (82) Only the seed of his people believed in Musa through fear of Pharaoh and his nobles, lest they be tempted,[1585] since Pharaoh was great in the land, and he was wasteful. (83) Musa said, "My people, if you[MP] believe in Allah, trust in him, if you[MP] have submitted." (84) They said, "We have trusted in Allah. Our Lord, do not make us a temptation to wicked people. (85) Rescue us[1586] by your[MS] mercy from disbelieving people. (86) We inspired Musa and his brother, "Prepare[D] houses for your[D] people in Egypt. Let[MP] your[MP] houses be the prayer direction, perform[MP] prayers, and give[MS] good news to the believers." (87) Musa said, "Our Lord, you[MS] gave Pharaoh and his people decoration and money in this life. Our Lord, let them[1587] be led astray from your[MS] path. Lord, blow[MS] upon their money, and tighten[MS] their hearts so that they will not believe until they see painful torment." (88) He said, "Your[D] prayer has been answered, so be[D] upright[1588] and do not walk[D] on the path of those who do not know."[1589] (89) 11B4 We made the children of Israel cross the sea,[1590] and Pharaoh and his armies followed him in injustice and enmity until he was drowned.[1591] He said, "I believe that the only god[1592] is the one the people of Israel believe[1593] in, and I have

---

[1584] Tawrah, Jeremiah 11:10, Injil, Acts 7:51, Galatians 1:14, Colossians 2:20-22
[1585] Or tricked or persecuted
[1586] Injil, Matthew 6:13, 2 Thessalonians 3:2
[1587] or, so that they may
[1588] Tawrah, Proverbs 4:25, 3:6
[1589] Tawrah, Isaiah 30:21
[1590] Tawrah, Exodus 14:1-25
[1591] Tawrah, Exodus 14:26-31, 15:4, Isaiah 43:17
[1592] Arabic /ilah/. See glossary for more details.

## Chapter 10

submitted." (90) Now? You[MS] have disobeyed beforehand and were[MS] corrupt. (91) Today we will rescue you in your[MS] body so that you[MS] will be[MS] a sign[1594] to those who come after[1595] you[MS]. Many people are unaware of our signs. (92) We prepared a true dwelling for the people of Israel[1596] and provided good things for them,[1597] and they did not differ until knowledge came to them. Their Lord will judge among them on the day of resurrection about their differences. (93) So when you[MS] are in doubt about what we have revealed to you[MS], ask[MS] those who are reading the book that was before you[MS].[1598] Truth has come to you[MS] from your[MS] Lord,[1599] so do not be[MS] a doubter, (94) nor be[MS] one who denies Allah's signs, for then you[MS] will be lost. (95) Those upon whom your[MS] Lord's word was fulfilled will not believe, (96) even if every sign were to come to them, until they see painful torment. (97) No village believed and benefited from their faith except Yunus's[1600] people.[1601] When they believed, we saved them from shameful torment in this life and let them enjoy it for a time.[1602] (98) If your[MS] Lord had willed, everyone on earth would have believed – all of them. So are you[MS] trying to force people to become believers? (99) No soul can believe without Allah's permission. He makes an abomination for those who do not comprehend. (100) Say[MS], "Look at what is in heaven and on earth." Signs and warnings do not benefit people who do not believe. (101) Aren't they only waiting for days like the ones of those who passed away before them. Say[MS], "Wait. I will wait with you[MP]." (102) Then we rescue our messengers and believers. Thus we are obligated to rescue believers. (103) Say[MS], "People, if you[MP] are in doubt about my religion, I do not worship the gods you[MP]

---

[1593] The word "believe" here is feminine, while "people" is masculine. There may be a different meaning.

[1594] Tawrah, Exodus 14:4. Pharaoh, Mariam, and Isa are the only people named who are signs. See 21:91

[1595] Or are behind

[1596] Zabur, Psalms 135:12

[1597] Tawrah, Deuteronomy 31:20

[1598] Any doubts should be clarified by asking those who read the previous books, not just normal Christians and Jews. The previous books are the authority, not people who do not read it and know what it says.

[1599] Zabur, Psalms 119:160

[1600] Jonah. See glossary for more details.

[1601] Tawrah, Jonah 3:5-10

[1602] Tawrah, Jonah 3:10

## Chapter 10

worship besides Allah, but I worship Allah, who will make you[MP] die. I have been commanded to be a believer: (104) Turn your[MS] face to monotheistic religion, do not worship[MS] other gods, (105) do not pray[MS] to gods besides Allah, which do not benefit you[MS] or harm you[MS]. If you[MS] do, you[MS] will be wicked. (106) If Allah touches you[MS] with harm, there is no one except him that can take it away.[1603] If he wants good for you[MS], there is no one that can take his grace away.[1604] He gives it to those of his servants[1605] that he wills. He is forgiving[1606] and merciful."[1607] (107) Say[MS], "People, truth from your[MP] Lord has come to you[MP]. Whoever is guided is guided for his soul's benefit, and whoever goes astray, goes astray to his soul's detriment. I am not responsible for you[MP]." (108) Follow[MS] what is revealed to you[VS] and endure[MS] until Allah judges.[1608] He is the best judge. (109)

---

[1603] Injil, 2 Corinthians 12:7-9
[1604] Injil, Revelation 3:7,8
[1605] See glossary.
[1606] Zabur, Psalms 103:3, 130:4, Tawrah, Isaiah 43:25, Exodus 34:7, Injil, Acts 26:18
[1607] See glossary for more details on "merciful."
[1608] See "endure" in glossary

# Chapter 11 Hud[1609]

In the name of Allah, the most gracious and merciful.[1610] ALR.[1611] A book whose verses are firm, which are explained by one wise and experienced, (1) so that you[MP] would only worship Allah. I am a warner and bearer of good news from him to you[MP], (2) that you[MP] ask forgiveness from your[MP] Lord, then repent toward him. He will make you[MP] enjoy life well for a set lifespan, and give his grace to every person of grace. If you[MP] turn away, I fear that you[MP] will come to the torment[1612] of a great day. (3) You[MP] will return to Allah. He can do anything.[1613] (4) Do they not fold their hearts[1614] to hide from him? When they cover themselves with their clothes, he knows what they conceal and what they announce.[1615] He knows all that is in their hearts. (5)

\*\*\*

**12A1** Every living creature on earth gets its provision from Allah.[1616] He knows their habitat and hiding place. It is all in a clear book.[1617] (6) He created the heavens and the earth[1618] in six days.[1619] His throne was on the water[1620] to test you[MP] and see which of you[MP] were best in works. If you[MS] say, "You[MP] will be resurrected after death," disbelievers will say, "This is clearly magic." (7) If we postpone torment for them to a numbered, fixed term, he will say, "What is keeping it?" It is a day that will come to them, and is not averted from them. Then they were surrounded by what they had made fun of. (8)

---

[1609] Hud is a name

[1610] Zabur, Psalms 103:8, 145:8. See glossary for more details.

[1611] Here and at the beginning of many chapters there are unvowelled letters of unknown meaning. Numerous theories have been proposed, but there is no agreement on the subject.

[1612] Here and in verses 20, 26, 39, 58, 84, 93, and 103, see Tawrah, Isaiah 50:11, Injil, Matthew 18:34, 25:41,46, Luke 16:23-28, Revelation 20:15.

[1613] Tawrah, Job 42:2, Isaiah 14:27, Daniel 4:35, Injil, Matthew 19:26, Mark 10:27, Luke 1:37

[1614] or breasts or chests

[1615] See also 2:77, 14:38, 16:19,23, 27:25,74, 28:69, 36:76, 60:1, 64:4.

[1616] Zabur, Psalms 145:16

[1617] Tawrah, Job 38-41

[1618] Tawrah, Genesis 1:1, Isaiah 42:5, 45:18

[1619] Tawrah, Genesis 1:1-31

[1620] Zabur, Psalms 24:2

## Chapter 11

\*\*\*

If we make mankind taste our mercy, then take it away from him, he despairs and is ungrateful.[1621] (9) If we give him a taste of blessings after harm has touched him, he will say, "Bad things have gone[1622] away from me," and he will be joyful and boastful. (10) Those who endure[1623] and do righteous deeds are not like that. They will have forgiveness and a great reward. (11)

\*\*\*

Perhaps you[MS] have deserted some of what you[MS] were inspired with, and your[MS] heart[1624] was constricted because of it, lest they say, "If only a treasure had been revealed to him, or an angel had come with him." You[MS] are only a warner and Allah is responsible for everything. (12)

\*\*\*

Or lest they say, "He invented it." Say[MS], "Then come up with ten invented chapters like it, and pray to whoever you[MP] can besides Allah, if you[MP] are telling the truth." (13) If they do not answer you[MP], know[MP] that it was revealed with Allah's knowledge and he is the only god.[1625] So are you[MP] submitted?[1626] (14) We will repay the works of whoever wants this world and its charm; their due will not be withheld. (15) The only hereafter they will have is hellfire, and what they have done in it will be in vain. Their works are in vain. (16) Is he who has a miracle[FS] from his Lord and reads[1627] it[MS] a witness from him? The book of Musa[1628] before it[MS] was a leader and mercy.[1629] They believe in it[MS], and whoever among the parties disbelieves in it[MS] has an appointment with

---

[1621] or disbelieving
[1622] "Have gone away" is masculine and "bad things" is feminine. There may be an implied word.
[1623] See "endure" in glossary, here and in verses 49 and 115.
[1624] or breast or chest
[1625] Arabic /ilah/ here and in verses 50, 53, 54, 61, 84, and 101. See glossary for more details.
[1626] Injil, James 4:7. For "submitted," some translators do not translate this. See glossary for more details.
[1627] It is unclear what he reads. It is not the miracle, because the gender of the noun "miracle" is feminine and the pronoun "it" is masculine. "It" could refer to the Zabur, which is also masculine.
[1628] Moses. See glossary for more details.
[1629] That the book of Musa was before it is a further confirmation that the miracle that is read is the Zabur.

## Chapter 11

hellfire. So do not be<sup>MS</sup> in doubt about it<sup>MS</sup>.[1630] It is the truth from your<sup>MS</sup> Lord, but most people do not believe. (17) Who is more wicked than him who invents lies about Allah? They will be presented to their Lord, and the witnesses will say, "These are denied their Lord. Is Allah's curse not on the wicked, (18) who block Allah's path,[1631] and want it to be crooked,[1632] and who disbelieve in the hereafter?" (19) They could not frustrate[1633] [Allah] on earth, and they had no helper other than Allah. Their torment will be doubled.[1634] They could not hear or see. (20) They have lost their souls, and what they invented has gone astray from them. (21) No doubt in the hereafter they will be the most lost. (22) Believers who do righteous deeds[1635] and humble themselves[1636] before their Lord will enter heaven and remain there forever.[1637] (23) 12A2 The two groups are like the blind and deaf compared to the sighted and hearing. Are they alike? Do you<sup>MP</sup> not remember? (24) We sent Nuh[1638] to his people:[1639] "I am a clear warner to you<sup>MP</sup> (25) that you<sup>MP</sup> worship only Allah. I fear that you<sup>MP</sup> will suffer the torment of a painful day." (26) The disbelieving nobles of his people said, "We think you<sup>MS</sup> are human like us. And we do not see that anyone except the vile and opinionated among us has followed you<sup>MS</sup>. We do not think you<sup>MP</sup> are any better than we are. We think you<sup>MP</sup> are liars." (27) He said, "My people, if I have a miracle from my Lord, and he gave me his mercy and you<sup>MP</sup> are blind to it, should we compel you<sup>MP</sup> to it against your<sup>MP</sup> will? (28) My people, I do not ask you<sup>MP</sup> for money for it. My reward is from Allah. I will not expel the believers. They will meet their Lord. I think you<sup>MP</sup> are ignorant people. (29) My people, who can save me from Allah if I expel them? Do you<sup>MP</sup> not remember? (30) I do not claim that I own Allah's

---

[1630] Muhammad (s) here is told not to doubt about the book of Musa because it is true.
[1631] Injil, Matthew 23:13, Luke 11:52.
[1632] Injil, Acts 13:10, Luke 3:5
[1633] or they were not unable
[1634] Tawrah, Isaiah 40:2, Injil, Romans 2:9,10
[1635] Injil, 1 Corinthians 3:8, James 2:14-17, Revelation 19:8
[1636] Injil, James 4:10
[1637] Injil, Matthew 18:4
[1638] Noah here and in verses 32, 36, 42, 45, 46, 48, and 89. See glossary for more details.
[1639] Tawrah, Genesis 6-8

storehouses.[1640] I do not know what is unseen, and I do not claim to be an angel. I do not tell those your[MP] eyes despise that Allah will not give them any good.[1641] Allah knows best what is in their souls. I would be wicked if I [did that]." (31) They said, "Nuh, you[MS] have disputed with us greatly. Bring on what you[MS] promise us if you[MS] are telling the truth." (32) He said, "Allah will bring it upon you[MP] if he wills, and you[MP] will not be able to frustrate him. (33) My counsel will not help you[MP], if I wanted to counsel you[MP] and Allah wanted to mislead you[MP]. He is your[MP] Lord and you[MP] will return to him."[1642] (34) Or do they say, "He invented it"? Say[MS], "If I have invented it, that is my wrongdoing. But I am innocent of your[MP] wrongdoings." (35) Nuh was inspired, "No more of your[MS] people will believe. So do not grieve over what they did. (36) Make the ark under our supervision[1643] and inspiration,[1644] and do not talk to me about the wicked. They will be drowned." (37) As he made the ark, whenever the nobles of his people passed by, they made fun of him. He said, "If you[MP] mock us, we will mock you[MP] just like you[MP] are mocking. (38) You[MP] will know who will be tormented, shamed, and permanently tormented. (39)

\*\*\*

When our command came forth and the deep gushed forth,[1645] we said, "Load it up with a pair of every kind of animal, your[MS] family except the one previously mentioned, and those who believed."[1646] Only a few believed.[1647] (40) 12A3

\*\*\*

And he said, get on the boat.[1648] Its course and its harbor are in Allah's name. My Lord is forgiving[1549] and merciful.[1650] (41) As it

---

[1640] Tawrah, Job 38:22
[1641] Zabur, Psalms 85:12
[1642] Injil, Romans 14:12
[1643] or, our eyes
[1644] Tawrah, Genesis 6:14-16,21
[1645] Tawrah, Genesis 7:11
[1646] Tawrah, Genesis 7:2-3
[1647] Injil, 1 Peter 3:20
[1648] Tawrah, Genesis 7:1
[1649] Zabur, Psalms 103:3, 130:4, Tawrah, Isaiah 43:25, Exodus 34:7, Injil, Acts 26:18
[1650] Here and in verses 43 and 90, see glossary for more details on "merciful."

Chapter 11

was carrying them on waves[1651] like mountains, Nuh called his son, who was estranged, "Son, get on the boat with us, and do not be a disbeliever." (42) He said, "I will take refuge on a mountain[1652] that will protect me from the water." He said, "Nothing can protect [anyone] from Allah's command today except for those he shows mercy." Then the waves came between them and he drowned.[1653] (43) Then it was said, "Earth[FS], swallow your[FS] water. Sky[FS], desist[FS]."[1654] And the water subsided and it was so.[1655] It rested on Mount Ararat[1656] and it was said, "Away with wicked people." (44) Nuh called his Lord. He said, "My Lord, my son is part of my family, your[MS] promise is true, and you[MS] are the wisest[1657] Judge of all." (45) He said, "Nuh, he was not part of your[MS] family; it[1658] is an unrighteous deed. So do not ask[MS] me what you[MS] know nothing about. I warn you[MS] not to be ignorant." (46) He said, "My Lord, I take refuge in you[MS] for asking about what I was ignorant. If you[MS] do not forgive me[1659] and have mercy on me, I will certainly be lost." (47) It was said, "Nuh, disembark[MS] with our peace and blessings on you[1660] and on the nations[1661] with you[MS]." We will make nations enjoy life, and then touch them with painful torment. (48) We tell you[MS] this news of the unseen. Neither you[MS] nor your[MS] people knew it before. Endure[MS], for there is a reward for the reverent. (49) To Aad,[1662] [we sent] their

---

[1651] Tawrah, Genesis 7:17
[1652] Tawrah, Genesis 7:19
[1653] Tawrah, Genesis 7:21-22
[1654] Tawrah, Genesis 8:1-2
[1655] Tawrah, Genesis 8:3
[1656] or Al-Judy
[1657] Tawrah, Job 9:4, Proverbs 2:6, Jeremiah 9:23-24, Injil, 1 Corinthians 1:21-25, Romans 16:27
[1658] or he
[1659] The belief that all prophets and messengers are sinless is not supported by the Qur'an. For instances of prophets or messengers asking forgiveness or committing sins, see 7:23, 20:121 (Adam), 11:47, 71:28 (Nuh), 26:82, 14:41 (Ibrahim), 28:15-16 (Musa), 7:151, 20:93 (Musa and Harun), 38:24 (Dawud), 38:32,35 (Sulayman), 21:87, 37:142 (Yunus), 48:2, 47:19, 40:55, 4:79,106, 9:43, 13:30, 80:1-2, 110:3, 94:2, 23:118, 66:1, 33:37, 8:67, and 9:117 (Muhammad (s).
[1660] Tawrah, Genesis 8:16
[1661] Tawrah, Genesis 10
[1662] Aad (here and in verses 59 and 60 (twice)) and Thamud (verses 60, 68 (twice), and 95) are names of tribes.

## Chapter 11

brother Hud.[1663] He said, "My people, worship Allah. He is your[MP] only god. You[MP] are just inventors. (50) My people, I do not ask you[MP] for payment. My payment comes only from my creator. Do you[MP] not comprehend? (51) My people, ask[MP] your[MP] Lord's forgiveness, and repent[MP] toward him. Then he will send abundant rain[1664] upon you[MP] from the sky and increase your[MP] strength.[1665] Do not turn[MP] away and do wrong." (52) They said, "Hud, you[MS] have not brought us a miracle, and we will not leave our gods just because you[MS] say so. We do not believe you[MS]. (53) We say that some of our gods have afflicted you[MS] with evil." He said, "I call Allah as my witness. Testify[MP] that I have nothing to do with the gods you[MP] worship (54) besides him. Plot[MP] against me, all of you[MP], and give[MP] me no more time. (55) I trust in Allah, my Lord and your[MP] Lord. He takes every living creature by its forelocks. My Lord is on the straight path."[1666] (56)

\*\*\*

If they[MP] turn away,[1667] I have given you[MP] the message I was sent with for you[MP]. My Lord will make other people your[MP] successors. You[MP] will not harm him at all. My Lord protects everything." (57) When our command came, we rescued Hud and those who believed along with him by our mercy. We rescued them from severe torment. (58)

\*\*\*

That was Aad, who rejected their Lord's signs,[1668] disobeyed his messengers, and followed the commands of every stubborn, perverse person. (59) They were followed by a curse in this world, and on the day of resurrection.[1669] Aad will be disbelievers in their Lord. Is it not so? Away with Aad, Hud's people. (60) 12A4

---

[1663] Hud here and in verses 53, 58, 60, and 89 does not appear to correspond with anyone in the Tawrah, Zabur, and Injil. Some commentators say he was an Arab.

[1664] Tawrah, Deuteronomy 28:12, Job 5:10, Joel 2:23, Zabur, Psalms 68:9, Injil, Matthew 5:45

[1665] Tawrah, Isaiah 40:31

[1666] See glossary for more details, and notes on 3:51, 6:153, 19:36, 36:61, and 43:64 on what the straight path is.

[1667] Other translations assume there is a missing letter and translate "you[MP]."

[1668] Arabic /ayat/ here and in verse 103. See glossary for more details.

[1669] For "day of resurrection" here and in verses 98 and 99, see Tawrah, Daniel 12:2 Injil, Acts 24:15, 1 Corinthians 15:52-54, Revelation 20:11-15

## Chapter 11

\*\*\*

And to Thamud [we sent] their brother Salih.[1670] He said, "My people, worship[MP] Allah. He is your[MP] only god. He created you[MP] from the earth and settled you[MP] on it. So ask[MP] forgiveness from him and repent[MP] toward him. My Lord is near and he answers." (61) They said, "Salih, we had high hopes for you[MS] before this. Do you[MS] forbid us from worshiping what our fathers worshiped? We have serious doubts about what you[MS] call us to." (62)

\*\*\*

He said, "My people, what do you think? If I have a miracle from my Lord, and he gave me his mercy, who can save me from Allah if I disobey him. You[MP] would only give me greater loss. (63)

\*\*\*

My people, this is Allah's she-camel, a sign for you[MP], so let her eat in Allah's land and do not harm her, or torment will soon seize you[MP]." (64) So they hamstrung her. He said, "Enjoy[MP] yourselves in your[MP] homes for three days. That is a promise, with no lie." (65)

\*\*\*

Then our command came, and we rescued Salih and those who believed along with him from the shame of that day by our mercy. Your[MS] Lord is strong[1671] and mighty.[1672] (66)

\*\*\*

Then the cry overtook[1673] the wicked, and they bowed down in their homes, (67)

\*\*\*

as if they had never flourished in it. Truly Thamud disbelieved in their Lord.
Away with Thamud! (68)

\*\*\*

Our messengers came to Ibrahim[1674] with good news.[1675] They said, "Peace!" He said, "Peace!" He did not delay, but brought a grilled calf.[1676] (69)

---

[1670] Methuselah here and in verses 62, 66, and 89. See glossary for more details. Tawrah, Genesis 5:21-27, 1 Chronicles 1:3, Injil, Luke 3:37
[1671] Tawrah, Job 9:4, Zabur, Psalms 24:8, Injil, Ephesians 6:10, Revelation 18:8
[1672] Injil, Revelation 18:8, Tawrah, Isaiah 60:16, Zabur, Psalms 93:4
[1673] the word cry here is feminine and the verb is masculine. There may be a reference to the cry being brought by angels.

## Chapter 11

\*\*\*

When he saw that their hands did not reach out to it, he denied[1677] them and was afraid of them. They said, "Do not be afraid. We were sent to Lut's[1678] people."[1679] (70)

\*\*\*

His wife was standing and she laughed.[1680] So we gave her good news of Ishaq,[1681] and through Ishaq, Yaqub.[1682] (71) She said, "Woe is me. Shall I give birth when I am old and barren, and my master[1683] is an old man?[1684] This is strange. (72)

\*\*\*

They said, "Do you[FS] think Allah's command is strange?[1685] May Allah's mercy[1686] and blessings be upon you,[MP] the household. He is praiseworthy and glorious." (73)

\*\*\*

When the fear had gone from Ibrahim and the good news had come to him, he argued with him about Lut's people.[1687] (74)

\*\*\*

Ibrahim was gentle, compassionate, and repentant. (75)

\*\*\*

"Ibrahim, turn[MS] away from this. Your[MS] Lord's command has come. I will bring them torment that cannot be turned back."[1688] (76)

---

[1674] Abraham here and in verses 74, 75, and 76. See glossary for more details.
[1675] Tawrah, Genesis 18:1-2,10
[1676] Tawrah, Genesis 18:7-8
[1677] translators have put a wide range of meanings for this word, from "become uneasy" to "mistrust", but the base meaning is "deny"
[1678] Lot, nephew of Abraham here and in verses 74, 77, 81, and 89. See glossary for more details.
[1679] Tawrah, Genesis 18:16-22
[1680] Tawrah, Genesis 18:12-15
[1681] Isaac here twice. See glossary for more details. Tawrah, Genesis 18:10
[1682] Jacob. See glossary for more details.
[1683] Injil, 1 Peter 3:6
[1684] Tawrah, Genesis 18:12
[1685] Tawrah, Genesis 18:13,14
[1686] "Mercy" has a different spelling here and in 6 other places. See glossary.
[1687] Tawrah, Genesis 18:23-33
[1688] Tawrah, Genesis 18:32

Chapter 11

\*\*\*
When our messengers came[1689] to Lut, he was sad for them and could not
protect them[MP]. He said, "This is a grievous day." (77) His people came rushing toward him.[1690] They had previously done bad deeds. He said, "My people, these are my daughters[1691] and they[FP] are purer for you[MP]. Fear[MP] Allah and do not shame[MP] me in front of my guest.[1692] Is there no guided man among you[MP]?" (78) They said, "You[MS] know we have no right to your[MS] daughters. You[MS] know what we want."[1693] (79) He said, "If only I could overpower you[MP] or take refuge in a strong place." (80) They said,[1694] "Lut, we are messengers from your[MS] Lord. They will not get you[MS]. Take[MS] your[MS] family quickly at night,[1695] and none of you[MP] turn back,[1696] except your[MS] wife.[1697] She will be afflicted by what afflicts them.[1698] Their appointment is morning. Is morning not near?"[1699] (81)
\*\*\*
When our command came, we made its high parts low and rained stones of baked clay piled up on it, (82)
\*\*\*
marked by your[MS] Lord. They are not far from the wicked. (83)
12B1 [We sent] their brother Shuaib[1700] to Midian.[1701] He said, "My people, worship Allah. He is your[MP] only god. Do not lessen[MP] the measure and the scale.[1702] I see you[MP] prosper, and I fear you[MP] will suffer the torment of a day that surrounds. (84)
\*\*\*

---

[1689] Tawrah, Genesis 19:1
[1690] Tawrah, Genesis 19:4
[1691] Tawrah, Genesis 19:8
[1692] Tawrah, Genesis 19:7-8
[1693] Tawrah, Genesis 19:5
[1694] Tawrah, Genesis 19:10-13
[1695] Tawrah, Genesis 19:12-13
[1696] Tawrah, Genesis 19:17
[1697] Tawrah, Genesis 19:26
[1698] Tawrah, Genesis 19:17
[1699] Tawrah, Genesis 19:15,24
[1700] Jethro here and in verses 87, 91, and 94. See glossary for more details.
[1701] Tawrah, Exodus 3:1, 4:18
[1702] Tawrah, Deuteronomy 25:15 here and in verse 85

## Chapter 11

My people, keep<sup>MP</sup> the measure and the scale just, and do not lessen<sup>MP</sup> people's things, nor be evil and destructive in the land. (85)

\*\*\*

Allah's remnant is better for you<sup>MP</sup>, if you<sup>MP</sup> are believers. I am not your<sup>MP</sup> keeper."[1703] (86)

\*\*\*

They said, "Shuaib, does your<sup>MS</sup> prayer command you<sup>MS</sup> that we leave what our
fathers worshiped, or to do what we want with our money? You<sup>MS</sup> are gentle[1704] and guided." (87)

\*\*\*

He said, "My people, what do you<sup>MP</sup> think? If I have a miracle from my Lord and he provided for me well through it, I do not want to oppose you<sup>MP</sup> in what I forbid you<sup>MP</sup>. I only want whatever reconciliation I can do. Only Allah can give me success. I trust him and repent toward him. (88)

\*\*\*

My people, do not let contending with me make you<sup>MP</sup> do wrong so you are afflicted like Nuh's people or Hud's people or Salih's people. Lut's people are not far from you<sup>MP</sup>. (89) Ask forgiveness from your<sup>MP</sup> Lord, and repent<sup>MP</sup> toward him. My Lord is merciful and loving." (90)

\*\*\*

They said, "Shuaib, we do not understand much of your<sup>MS</sup> sayings, and we think you<sup>MS</sup> are weak among us. If not for your<sup>MS</sup> clan, we would have stoned you<sup>MS</sup>. You<sup>MS</sup> are no stronger than we are." (91)

\*\*\*

He said, "My people, is my clan stronger against you<sup>MP</sup> than Allah? Have you<sup>MP</sup> put him behind you<sup>MP</sup>? My Lord is aware of your<sup>MP</sup> deeds. (92)

\*\*\*

My people, act according to your<sup>MP</sup> status! I will act, and you<sup>MP</sup> will know who will be tormented, shamed, and shown to be a liar. Watch me, for I am watching with you<sup>MP</sup>." (93)

\*\*\*

When our command came, we rescued Shuaib and those who believed along with him by our mercy. The cry overtook the wicked, and they bowed down in their houses, (94)

---

[1703] Tawrah, Genesis 4:9
[1704] Zabur, Psalms 45:4, 145:17, Injil, Matthew 11:29, Galatians 5:22

## Chapter 11

\*\*\*

as if they had not flourished in them. Away with Midian, as with Thamud. (95)

\*\*\*

We sent Musa,[1705] with our signs and clear authority, (96)

\*\*\*

to Pharaoh[1706] and his nobles, and they followed Pharaoh's command, which was not guided. (97) He will lead his people on the day of resurrection, and make them enter hellfire, a dreadful place to enter. (98) They were followed in this by a curse, and on the day of resurrection it will be a dreadful gift given. (99) That is news of the villages that we relate to you[MS]. Some are standing and others are reaped.[1707] (100)

\*\*\*

We did not wrong them, but they wronged themselves.[1708] The gods they prayed to besides Allah did not benefit them at all. When your[MS] Lord's command came, the only thing they got more of was loss. (101)

\*\*\*

That is the way your[MS] Lord seized, when he seized the wicked villages. When he seizes, it is painful and harsh. (102) That is a sign for him who fears the torment of the hereafter. That is a day when people are gathered.[1709] It is a day that will be witnessed. (103) We do not delay it except for a numbered time. (104) On that day, no soul will speak except with his permission. Some of them will be miserable and others happy. (105)

---

[1705] Moses here and in verse 110. See glossary for more details.

[1706] Tawrah, Exodus 3:10

[1707] Injil, Revelation 14:6

[1708] The injustice/wickedness, disbelief/ungratefulness, evil, unrighteousness/sin, or lostness of mankind is mentioned in a number of verses in the Qur'an as well as in the previous books. Injustice or wickedness: 2:57, 3:117,135, 4:64,97, 7:160,177, 9:70, 10:44, 11:101, 14:34,45, 16:33,61,118, 29:40, 30:9, 33:72, 34:19, 35:32, 43:76, 65:1, Tawrah, Genesis 6:5, Job 25:4, Injil, Acts 3:26, disbelief or ungratefulness: 14:34, 17:67, 22:66, 42:48, 43:15, 80:17, Injil, Hebrews 3:19, Evil: 12:53, Tawrah, Jeremiah 17:9, Injil, Matthew 15:19, Mark 7:21, unrighteousness or sin: 91:8, Tawrah, 1 Kings 8:46, Ecclesiastes 7:20, Injil, Romans 3:9-19, 5:12, lostness: 103:2, Tawrah, Jeremiah 50:6, Injil, Luke 19:10, Romans 3:23, 6:23

[1709] Tawrah, Joel 3:11-14, Zephaniah 3:8, Injil, Matthew 25:32, John 15:6, Revelation 16:16

## Chapter 11

\*\*\*

The miserable will be in hellfire, where there will be sobbing and sighing, (106)

\*\*\*

being in it forever, as long as the heavens and the earth remain,[1710] except as your[MS] Lord wills. Your[MS] Lord is effective in what he wants. (107) **12B2**

\*\*\*

The happy are in the heavenly garden[1711] forever, as long as the heavens and the earth remain, except as your[MS] Lord wills, an uninterrupted gift. (108)

\*\*\*

Do not doubt what these [people] worship. They only worship what their fathers worshiped beforehand. We will repay them with their destiny in full. (109)

\*\*\*

We gave Musa the book, and people differed about it. If not for a word[1712] which came previously[1713] from your[MS] Lord, he would have judged between them. They are in serious doubt about it. (110)

\*\*\*

Your[MS] Lord will repay every one of them for their works. He knows what they do. (111) So be[MS] upright, as you[MS] were commanded, along with those who repent with you[MS]. Do not transgress[MP]. He sees your[MP] deeds. (112)

\*\*\*

Do not depend[MP] on the wicked, lest hellfire reach you[MP] and you[MP] have no helpers apart from Allah. Then you[MP] will not be saved. (113) Perform[MS] the prayers at both ends of the day and the first part of the night. Good deeds drive away bad deeds.[1714] That is something to remember. (114) Endure[MS], for Allah does not lose the reward of those who do good. (115) If only there were a

---

[1710] Injil, Matthew 24:35

[1711] Arabic /jannah/. See glossary for more details.

[1712] This word might be Isa, who came previously (3: 45,39, 4:171), or it might be a previous book (Tawrah, Zabur, or Injil). If "previously" refers to the book of Musa, then Genesis in the Tawrah may be what is intended.

[1713] See 10:19, 20:129, 41:45, 42:14 where this phrase is also used.

[1714] Tawrah, Proverbs 10:12, Injil, 1 Peter 4:8, Ezekiel 18:21

## Chapter 11

remnant[1715] in the generations before you[MP] who forbade destruction in the land, except for a few of them whom we rescued. The wicked followed the good things of the world and were wrongdoers. (116) Your[MS] Lord would not have destroyed the villages unjustly while they were mending their ways. (117) If your[MS] Lord had willed, he would have made people all one nation.[1716] They all continue to differ, (118) except for those your[MS] Lord showed mercy. That is why he created them. Your[MS] Lord's word was fulfilled: "I will fill hell with jinns[1717] and people all together." (119) We relate all this news of messengers to you[MS] to make your[MS] heart firm. Truth, an admonition,[1718] and reminder has come to you[MS] in this. (120) Say[MS] to those who do not believe, "Act according to your[MP] status. We are acting. (121) Wait[MP]. We are waiting." (122) The unseen things of the heavens and the earth are Allah's. The whole matter returns to him, so worship[MS] him and trust him. Your[MS] Lord is aware of your[MP] deeds. (123)[1719]

---

[1715] Injil, Romans 9:27, 11:5.
[1716] Injil, Acts 17:26,27
[1717] Or demons. See glossary for more details.
[1718] In addition to the Qur'an, the Tawrah 7:145 and the Injil 5:46 are called an admonition.
[1719] The verses in this chapter that rhyme are put together in paragraphs, separated by ***.

# Chapter 12 Yusuf[1720]

In the name of Allah, the most gracious and merciful.[1721] ALR.[1722] Those[1723] are signs of the clear book. (1) We revealed it as an Arabic recitation,[1724] so that you[MP] might comprehend. (2) We relate to you[MS] the best stories, as we have inspired you[MS] with this recitation, since you[MS] were previously ignorant. (3) Yusuf[1725] told his father, "Father, I saw eleven stars, the sun, and the moon bowing down to me."[1726] (4) He said, "My son, do not tell your[MS] vision[1727] to your[MS] brothers,[1728] or they'll plot against you[MS]. Satan is a clear enemy to mankind. (5) Thus your[MS] Lord chooses you[MS] and teaches you[MS] how to interpret stories, and he completes his blessings on you[MS] and on the family of Yaqub,[1729] as he completed them on your[MS] fathers Ibrahim[1730] and Ishaq[1731] beforehand. Your[MS] Lord is all-knowing[1732] and wise."[1733] (6) **12B3** There were signs regarding Yusuf and his brothers to those who ask. (7) They

---

[1720] Joseph (son of Jacob)

[1721] Zabur, Psalms 103:8, 145:8. See glossary for more details.

[1722] Here and at the beginning of many chapters there are unvowelled letters of unknown meaning. Numerous theories have been proposed, but there is no agreement on the subject.

[1723] Since it says "those" and not "these," the reference is probably to the former books.

[1724] Or Qur'an or qur'an here and in verse 3. The emphasis seems to be that the Qur'an reveals the same signs (or verses) that are in the former book, but in Arabic. In the context of the story of Yusuf, this probably means the Tawrah, which recorded the story of Yusuf more than two thousand years before the Qur'an. See glossary for more details.

[1725] Joseph (son of Jacob) here and in verses 7, 8, 9, 10, 11, 17, 21, 23, 29, 46, 51, 56, 58, 69, 76, 77, 80, 84, 85, 87, 89, 90, 94, and 99. See glossary for more details.

[1726] Tawrah, Genesis 37:9

[1727] Injil, Matthew 17:9

[1728] Tawrah, Genesis 37:10

[1729] Jacob here and in verses 38 and 68. See glossary for more details.

[1730] Abraham here and in verse 38. See glossary for more details.

[1731] Isaac here and in verse 38. See glossary for more details.

[1732] Tawrah, Job 37:16, Isaiah 40:14, Zabur, Psalms 33:13-15, Injil, 1 John 3:20

[1733] Tawrah, Job 9:4, Proverbs 2:6, Jeremiah 9:23-24, Injil, 1 Corinthians 1:21-25, Romans 16:27

## Chapter 12

said "Our father loves Yusuf and his brother more than us,[1734] though we are a large group. Our father is clearly astray. (8) Kill[MP] Yusuf[1735] or throw[MP] him on the ground and you[MP] will get your father's favor. After that, you[MP] will be righteous people." (9) One of them said,[1736] "Do not kill[MP] Yusuf. If you[MP] want to do something, throw[MP] him in the bottom of a cistern,[1737] and some passers-by will take him out." (10) They said, "Our father, what is wrong with you[MS] that you[MS] do not entrust Yusuf to us? We are his advisors. (11) Send him with us tomorrow to enjoy himself and play. We will protect him." (12) He said, "It would sadden me for you[MP] to go with him. I fear that wolves might eat him while you[MP] are not paying attention to him." (13) They said, "If wolves eat him though we are a large group, we are lost." (14) When they went with him and agreed unanimously to put him in the bottom of a cistern, we inspired him, "You[MS] will inform them of this matter of theirs, when they do not realize it." (15) They came to their father in the evening,[1738] crying. (16) They said, "Our father, we went racing and left Yusuf with our equipment, and wolves ate him. You[MS] will not believe us even if we are telling the truth." (17) They put false blood on his shirt.[1739] He said, "Rather, your[MP] souls have contrived a matter. Patient endurance.[1740] I seek Allah's help against what you[MP] describe." (18) A caravan passed by[1741] and they sent one of them to draw water. When he let down his bucket. He said, "Good news! Here is a boy." They hid him as merchandise. Allah knows what they did. (19) They bought[1742] him cheaply, for a few coins.[1743] They thought little of him. (20) The Egyptian who bought him[1744] said to his wife,[1745] "Honor[FS] his dwelling. He may benefit us or we could adopt him." Thus we made Yusuf firm in the land,[1746] so we could teach him to interpret

---

[1734] Tawrah, Genesis 37:11
[1735] Tawrah, Genesis 37:18
[1736] Reuben - Tawrah, Genesis 37:21
[1737] Tawrah, Genesis 37:20,22,24
[1738] Tawrah, Genesis 37:32
[1739] Tawrah, Genesis 37:31
[1740] See "endure" in glossary, here and in verses 83 and 90.
[1741] Tawrah, Genesis 37:25
[1742] or sold
[1743] Tawrah, Genesis 37:26-28
[1744] Tawrah, Genesis 37:28,36, 39:1
[1745] Or, "bought him for his wife said":
[1746] Tawrah, Genesis 39:2

## Chapter 12

stories. Allah was victorious over his circumstances,[1747] but most people do not know. (21) When he was full-grown, we gave him rulership[1748] and knowledge. Thus we reward those who do good. (22) The woman of the house Yusuf was in wanted to have sex with him,[1749] locked the doors, and said, "Come here!" He said, "Allah forbid. He is my lord, who has given me a fine dwelling. The wicked do not prosper." (23) She was thinking about him, and he would have thought about her, if he had not seen a proof from his Lord.[1750] Thus we keep evil and promiscuity[1751] away. He was one of our sincere servants.[1752] (24) They[D] raced for the door, and she tore his shirt[1753] from behind. They[D] met her master at the door.[1754] She said, "What should be the punishment of one who wanted evil for your[MS] family?" "Either prison or painful torment." (25) He said, "She wanted to have sex with me." A witness from her family said, "If his shirt is torn in front, she is honest and he is a liar. (26) If his shirt is torn from behind, she is a liar and he is telling the truth." (27) When he saw that his shirt was torn from behind, he said, "This is one of your[FP] tricks. Your[FP] guile is great." (28) "Yusuf, turn[MS] away from this." "Ask[FS] forgiveness for your[FS] sin. You[FS] were at fault." (29) 12B4 Women from the city said,[1755] "The powerful man's[1756] wife wanted to have sex with her young man. She fell in love with him. We think she has clearly gone astray." (30) When she heard of their[FP] deceit, she sent to them and prepared them[FP] a banquet, and gave every one[F] of them [FP] a knife. She said, "Come[MS] out to them[FP]." When they saw him, they praised him and cut their hands and said, "Allah forbid. This is not a human. He is a noble angel.'"[1757] (31) She said, "That is the one you[FP] blamed me about. I wanted to have sex with him and he abstained. If he does not do what I command him, let him be

---

[1747] Tawrah, Genesis 50:20
[1748] Tawrah, Genesis 39:2-4
[1749] Tawrah, Genesis 39:7
[1750] Tawrah, Genesis 39:10
[1751] Or lewdness, adultery or abomination
[1752] See glossary.
[1753] Tawrah, Genesis 39:12
[1754] Tawrah, Genesis 39:16-18
[1755] "Said" is masculine but "women" is feminine. There may be another meaning.
[1756] This is a title, not a name. In verses 78 and 88, it is used of Joseph.
[1757] Tawrah, Genesis 39:6

## Chapter 12

imprisoned and despised." (32) He said, "My Lord, I prefer prison to what they call me to. If you[MS] do not foil their plot against me, I will desire them[FP] and be ignorant." (33) His Lord answered him and foiled their[F] plot. He hears all and knows all.[1758] (34) After they[MP] had seen the signs, it seemed best to them[MP] to imprison him[1759] for a while. (35) Two young men entered the prison with him.[1760] One of them said, "I saw myself pressing wine."[1761] The other said, "I saw myself carrying bread on my head, and birds were eating from it. Tell us what it means. We think you[MS] do good."[1762] (36) He said, "Before your[D] next meal, I will tell you[D] its interpretation.[1763] Before it comes to you[D], my Lord will teach me. I left the spiritual path[1764] of people who do not believe in Allah and disbelieve in the hereafter. (37) I follow the spiritual path of my fathers Ibrahim, Ishaq, and Yaqub. We could not believe in other gods besides Allah. That is by Allah's grace to us and to mankind. Most people do not give thanks. (38)
\*\*\*

My fellow inmates[MD], are scattered lords better, or the one victorious Allah? (39)
\*\*\*

The gods you[MP] worship besides him are only names that you[MP] and your[MP] fathers have called. Allah has not given them any authority. Allah is the only ruler. He has commanded: Do not worship any gods beside him. That is straight religion, but most people do not know. (40)
\*\*\*

My fellow inmates[MD], One[M] of you[D] will pour his lord[1765] wine, but the other will be crucified and birds will eat his head.[1766] The matter about which you[D] seek a decision has been decreed." (41)
\*\*\*

---

[1758] Tawrah, Job 37:16, Isaiah 40:14, Zabur, Psalms 33:13-15, Injil, 1 John 3:20
[1759] Tawrah, Genesis 39:20
[1760] Tawrah, Genesis 40:1-3
[1761] Tawrah, Genesis 40:9-11
[1762] Tawrah, Genesis 40:16-17
[1763] Tawrah, Genesis 40:18
[1764] Arabic /millah/ here and in verse 38. See glossary.
[1765] Or Lord. There is no capitalization in Arabic.
[1766] Tawrah, Genesis 40:18-19

## Chapter 12

He told the one[M] of them[P] whom he thought would be rescued, "Remember me with your[MS] lord."[1767] But Satan made him forget to mention it to his lord, so he remained in prison several years.[1768] (42) The king said, "I see seven fat[1769] cows[1770] being eaten by[1771] seven skinny ones,[1772] and seven green heads of grain,[1773] and others that are withered.[1774] Nobles, explain my vision to me if you[MP] can interpret a vision."[1775] (43) They said, "Confused dreams! We do not know how to interpret dreams."[1776] (44) The one of them[P] that was rescued, having remembered after a fixed term,[1777] said, "I will tell you[MP] its meaning. Send[MP] me." (45) "Yusuf, most truthful, what is the meaning of seven fat cows being eaten by seven skinny ones, and seven green heads of grain and other withered ones, so that I can return to the people so that they may know?"[1778] (46) He said, "For seven years, you[MP] will sow as usual. What grain you[MP] harvest, leave[MP] in its heads, except for a little, which you[MP] can eat. (47) After that there will be seven harsh ones, which will eat[1779] up what you[MP] have prepared beforehand for them,[1780] except for a little you[MP] store up.[1781] (48) After that will come a year when people will be rescued, and press grapes." (49) The king said, "Bring him to me." When the messenger came to him, he said, "Return[MS] to your[MS] lord and ask[MS] him: what was the intent of the women who cut their hands? My Lord knows all about their[FP]

---

[1767] Tawrah, Genesis 40:14
[1768] Tawrah, Genesis 41:1
[1769] All the adjectives for cows and heads of grain are used for thinking beings. The meaning might be that the cows and heads of grain symbolize something else.
[1770] Tawrah, Genesis 41:1-2
[1771] Tawrah, Genesis 41:4
[1772] Tawrah, Genesis 41:3
[1773] Tawrah, Genesis 41:5
[1774] Tawrah, Genesis 41:6-7
[1775] Tawrah, Genesis 41:8
[1776] Tawrah, Genesis 41:8
[1777] or long time or nation. Tawrah, Genesis 41:9
[1778] Tawrah, Genesis 41:17-24
[1779] The verb used here and the word "them" later in this verse are used for thinking beings. Possibly the meaning is the years will eat the stored grain like a person eats.
[1780] Tawrah, Genesis 41:25-32
[1781] Tawrah, Genesis 41:33-36

Chapter 12

plan." (50) He said, "What do you^FP say, since you wanted to have sex with Yusuf?" They^FP said, "Allah forbid! We know no evil about him." The powerful man's wife said, "Now the truth is out in the open. I wanted to have sex with him and he was telling the truth. (51) This was so that he would know that I did not betray him unseen. Allah does not guide the plots of traitors. (52) 13A1 I do not justify myself. The soul is prone to evil,[1782] except when my Lord is merciful.[1783] My Lord is forgiving[1784] and merciful." (53) The king said, "Bring him to me.[1785] I will take him into my service."[1786] When he spoke to him, he said, "Today [you have] a firm, faithful position with us."[1787] (54) He said, "Put me in charge of the storehouses of the land. I will be a knowledgeable keeper."[1788] (55) Thus we made Yusuf firm in the land, to take possession of it wherever he willed.[1789] We give our mercy to those we will, and we do not lose the reward of those who do good. (56) The wages of the hereafter are better for reverent believers. (57) Yusuf's brothers came and entered before him,[1790] and he recognized them, though they did not know him.[1791] (58) When he prepared them with their equipment,[1792] he said, "Bring

---

[1782] The injustice/wickedness, disbelief/ungratefulness, evil, unrighteousness/sin, or lostness of mankind is mentioned in a number of verses in the Qur'an as well as in the previous books. Injustice or wickedness: 2:57, 3:117,135, 4:64,97, 7:160,177, 9:70, 10:44, 11:101, 14:34,45, 16:33,61,118, 29:40, 30:9, 33:72, 34:19, 35:32, 43:76, 65:1, Tawrah, Genesis 6:5, Job 25:4, Injil, Acts 3:26, disbelief or ungratefulness: 14:34, 17:67, 22:66, 42:48, 43:15, 80:17, Injil, Hebrews 3:19, Evil: 12:53, Tawrah, Jeremiah 17:9, Injil, Matthew 15:19, Mark 7:21, unrighteousness or sin: 91:8, Tawrah, 1 Kings 8:46, Ecclesiastes 7:20, Injil, Romans 3:9-19, 5:12, lostness: 103:2, Tawrah, Jeremiah 50:6, Injil, Luke 19:10, Romans 3:23, 6:23

[1783] Here twice and in verses 64, 92, and 98, see glossary for more details on "merciful."

[1784] Here and in verse 98, see Zabur, Psalms 103:3, 130:4, Tawrah, Isaiah 43:25, Exodus 34:7, Injil, Acts 26:18.

[1785] Tawrah, Genesis 41:14

[1786] Tawrah, Genesis 41:46

[1787] Tawrah, Genesis 41:40-44

[1788] Tawrah, Genesis 41:33-36

[1789] Tawrah, Genesis 41:40

[1790] Tawrah, Genesis 42:3-6

[1791] Tawrah, Genesis 42:7-8

[1792] or provision, Tawrah, Genesis 42:25

## Chapter 12

me a brother of yours<sup>MP</sup> from your<sup>MP</sup> father.[1793] Do you<sup>MP</sup> not know that I give a full measure, and am the best host?[1794] (59) If you<sup>MP</sup> do not bring him to me, you'll<sup>MP</sup> have no measure from me, nor shall you<sup>MP</sup> approach me."[1795] (60) They said, "We will make his father desire that. We will do it." (61) He told his servants, "Put their money in their saddlebags,[1796] that they may know it when they return to their families. That way, they may return. (62) When they returned to their father, they said, "Our father, our measure was forbidden. Send our brother with us so we can get our measures.[1797] We will protect him." (63) He said, "Shall I trust you<sup>MP</sup> with him like I trusted you<sup>MP</sup> with his brother previously?[1798] Allah is the best protector[1799] and the most merciful of all." (64)

\*\*\*

When they opened their goods, they found their money had been returned to them.[1800] They said, "Father, what do we seek? Our money has been returned to us. We will provide food for our families and protect our brother and get another camel load.[1801] That is an easy measure." (65)

\*\*\*

He said, "I will not send him with you<sup>MP</sup> until you<sup>MP</sup> come to me with a promise sworn by Allah,[1802] that you<sup>MP</sup> will return him to me unless you<sup>MP</sup> are surrounded. When they brought him their promise sworn by Allah, he said, "Allah is responsible for our saying."[1803] (66)

\*\*\*

He said, "My son, do not enter<sup>MP</sup> through one door. Enter through separate doors. I cannot provide anything for you<sup>MP</sup> against Allah. Allah is the only ruler. I trust in him.[1804] Let those who trust trust in him, too. (67) They entered as their father had commanded

---

[1793] Benjamin, who was not with the other brothers, Tawrah, Genesis 42:15-20.
[1794] Tawrah, Genesis 42:25-27
[1795] Tawrah, Genesis 43:3, 44:26
[1796] Tawrah, Genesis 42:25
[1797] Tawrah, Genesis 43:4
[1798] Tawrah, Genesis 42:36
[1799] Tawrah, Genesis 43:11-14
[1800] Tawrah, Genesis 42:27,35
[1801] Tawrah, Genesis 43:4-10
[1802] Tawrah, Genesis 42:37, 43:8-9
[1803] Tawrah, Genesis 43:8-9
[1804] Tawrah, Genesis 43:14

## Chapter 12

them,[1805] though there was nothing they could do against Allah. It was just a need in Yaqub's soul that was fulfilled. He knew what we taught him. Most people do not know. (68) When they entered before Yusuf, he received his brother.[1806] He said, "I am your[MS] brother,[1807] so do not despair of what they did. (69) When he prepared them with their equipment,[1808] he put the drinking cup in the saddlebags of his brother,[1809] and then someone called out, "You[MP] caravan of thieves[1810]!" (70) They said as they came to them, "What have you[MP] lost?" (71) They said, "We lost the king's cup,[1811] whoever brings it gets a camel's load. I guarantee it." (72) They said, "By Allah, you[MP] know we did not come to cause destruction in the land. We are not thieves."[1812] (73) They said, "What is the punishment if you[MP] are liars?" (74) They said, "He in whose saddlebags it was found will be punished."[1813] Thus we repay the wicked. (75) He began in their vessels before his brother's sack,[1814] then took it out of his brother's sack. Thus we plotted for Yusuf. He could not have taken his brother to the king's judgment, except that Allah willed. We raise in rank those we will. The all-knowing[1815] is above every knowledgeable one. (76) 13A2 They said, "If he stole, one of his brothers stole previously. Yusuf kept this hidden in his soul, and did not reveal it to them. He said, "You[MP] are in an evil position.[1816] Allah knows what you[MP] describe." (77) They said, "Powerful one, his father is very old. Take one of us instead of him.[1817] We think you[MS] do good. (78) He said, "Allah forbid that we should take anyone other than the one with whom we found our goods. We would thus be wicked."[1818] (79) When they had lost hope about him, they

---

[1805] Tawrah, Genesis 43:15
[1806] Tawrah, Genesis 43:16,29
[1807] Tawrah, Genesis 45:1-4
[1808] or provisions
[1809] Tawrah, Genesis 44:2
[1810] Tawrah, Genesis 44:4-6
[1811] Tawrah, Genesis 44:5
[1812] Tawrah, Genesis 44:7-8
[1813] Tawrah, Genesis 44:9
[1814] Tawrah, Genesis 44:12
[1815] For "all-knowing" here and in verse 83 and 100, see Tawrah, Job 37:16, Isaiah 40:14, Zabur, Psalms 33:13-15, Injil, 1 John 3:20
[1816] Tawrah, Genesis 44:15-16
[1817] Tawrah, Genesis 44:33
[1818] Tawrah, Genesis 44:17

## Chapter 12

conferred privately. The oldest said, "Do you[MP] not know that your[MP] father has made you[MP] swear by Allah? Previously you[MP] were negligent with Yusuf. I will not leave the land until my father gives me permission, or until Allah gives judgment for me. He is the best judge." (80) Return to your[MP] father and say[MP], "Our father, your[MS] son stole, and we did not testify except what we knew. We are not keepers of the unseen. (81) Ask the village we were in, and the caravan we traveled with. We are telling the truth." (82) He said, "Rather your[MP] souls contrived a matter. Patient endurance. Allah may bring all of them to me. He is all-knowing and wise."[1819] (83) He turned away from them and said, "How great is my grief over Yusuf. His eyes turned white from sadness as he grieved.[1820] (84) They said, "By Allah, will you[MS] not cease remembering Yusuf until you[MS] are sick or dead?" (85) He said, "I complain to Allah of my sorrow and sadness. I know something from Allah that you[MP] do not. (86) My sons, go[MP] and make[MP] inquiries about Yusuf and his brother. Do not despair of Allah's spirit. Only disbelieving people despair of Allah's spirit." (87) When they entered before him, they said, "Powerful one, we and our family have been harmed, and we have come with little money. Give us what this buys, and be charitable. Allah rewards the charitable." (88) He said, "Do you[MP] know what you[MP] did to Yusuf and his brother, when you[MP] were ignorant?" (89) They said, "Are you[MP] Yusuf?" He said, "I really am Yusuf,[1821] and this is my brother. Allah has been gracious to us. Allah does not lose the reward of those who are reverent, enduring, and charitable." (90) They said, "By Allah, Allah has chosen you[MS] over us. We were at fault." (91) He said, "There is no blame for you[MP] today.[1822] Allah will forgive you[MP].[1823] He is the most merciful of all. (92) Take[MP] my shirt[1824] and throw[MP] it on the face of my father, and he will be able to see again. Then bring your[MP] whole family."[1825] (93) When the caravan departed, their father said, "I sense Yusuf's smell, though you[MP] think me senile." (94) They said, "By Allah, you[MS]

---

[1819] Here and in verse 100, see Tawrah, Job 9:4, Proverbs 2:6, Jeremiah 9:23-24, Injil, 1 Corinthians 1:21-25, Romans 16:27.
[1820] Tawrah, Genesis 42:36
[1821] Tawrah, Genesis 45:2-4
[1822] Tawrah, Genesis 50:20
[1823] Tawrah, Genesis 45:7-8
[1824] Tawrah, Genesis 45:22-23
[1825] Tawrah, Genesis 45:18-19

## Chapter 12

are straying the same old way." (95) When the bearer of good news had come, he threw it on his face, and he could see again.[1826] He said, "Did I not tell you[MP] that I knew something from Allah that you[MP] did not?" (96) They said, "Our father, ask Allah's forgiveness for our faults. We did wrong." (97) He said, "I will ask my Lord's forgiveness for you[MP]. He is forgiving and merciful. (98) When they entered before Yusuf, he gave his parents refuge[1827] and said, "Enter Egypt in safety,[1828] if Allah wills." (99) He raised his parents on the throne and they[MP] bowed down to him.[1829] He said, "Father, this is the interpretation of my previous vision. Allah has fulfilled it. He has done me good by getting me out of prison,[1830] and has brought you[MP] from the desert[1831] after Satan incited evil between me and my brothers.[1832] My Lord is kind in what he wills. He is all-knowing and wise. (100) 13A3 My Lord, you[MS] have given me a kingdom and taught me to interpret events. Creator of the heavens and the earth,[1833] you[MS] are my protector in this world and the hereafter. Let me be submitted[1834] when I die, and let me be righteous." (101) That is news of the unseen which we inspire to you[MS]; you[MS] were not with them when they unanimously decided to conspire. (102) Most people are not believers, however much you[MS] desire it![1835] (103) You[MS] do not ask them for payment. It is only a reminder[1836] to mankind. (104) How many signs[1837] there are in the heavens and the earth which they pass by and turn away from! (105) Most of

---

[1826] Tawrah, Genesis 45:27
[1827] Tawrah, Genesis 46:29, 47:12
[1828] Tawrah, Genesis 47:6-11
[1829] Tawrah, Genesis 42:6,9 Those who bowed were plural, not dual, so either the rest of the family is intended or the parents and the rest of the family. Since Joseph's vision (verse 4), of which this was the fulfillment, had the sun and moon and 11 stars bowing to Joseph, the latter is more probable.
[1830] Tawrah, Genesis 41:14
[1831] Tawrah, Genesis 47:1
[1832] Tawrah, Genesis 37:18-20
[1833] Tawrah, Genesis 1:1, Isaiah 42:5, 45:18
[1834] Injil, James 4:7. For "submitted," some translators do not translate this. See glossary for more details.
[1835] Injil, Matthew 22:14
[1836] Arabic /dhikr/. It is not clear whether the Qur'an or the Tawrah is meant here. See glossary for more details.
[1837] Arabic /ayah/. See glossary for more details.

## Chapter 12

them do not believe in Allah except as one of many gods. (106) Are they safe from Allah's torment[1838] covering them, or the hour[1839] coming suddenly upon them without their realizing it?[1840] (107) Say[MS], "This is my path. I along with those who follow me pray to Allah with insight. May Allah be glorified! I am not a polytheist." (108) Those we sent before you[MS] were only men we inspired from among people of the villages. Did they not walk in the land and see what was the end of those before them? The hereafter is better for the reverent. Do you[MP] not comprehend? (109) Even when the messengers lost hope and thought lies were told about them, our salvation came to them. We rescue those we will. Misery from us will overtake wrongdoing people. (110) There was a moral in their stories for thinkers. It was not an invented saying, but a confirmation of what is in his possession,[1841] an explanation of everything, guidance,[1842] and mercy to believing people. (111)[1843]

---

[1838] Tawrah, Isaiah 50:11, Injil, Matthew 18:34, 25:41,46, Luke 16:23-28, Revelation 20:15

[1839] Injil, Revelation 14:7

[1840] Injil, 1 Thessalonians 5:1-4, Revelation 3:3

[1841] Or, "between his hands" or "in front of him."

[1842] The Tawrah (5:44), Injil (5:46), and Qur'an (here) all contain guidance.

[1843] The verses in this chapter that rhyme are put together in paragraphs, separated by ***.

# Chapter 13 Al-Raad[1844]

In the name of Allah, the most gracious and merciful.[1845] ALMR.[1846] Those[1847] are verses[1848] of the book. What was revealed to you[ms] from your[ms] Lord is truth, but most people do not believe. (1) Allah raised up the heavens[1849] without visible pillars, then sat on the throne[1850] and made the sun and moon both go for a certain period.[1851] He directs the matter. He explains signs so that you[mp] may be certain of a meeting with your[mp] Lord. (2) He stretched out[1852] the earth and made mountains and rivers in it,[1853] and pairs[1854] of every fruit. He makes the night cover the day.[1855] Those are signs for people who consider. (3) In the earth there are sections next to each other, vineyards, crops, and double- and single-palm trees, all irrigated by the same water, but some taste better than others. Those are signs for people who comprehend. (4) If you[ms] are amazed at all, be amazed at their saying: "When we are dust, will we be re-created?"[1856] They are disbelievers in their Lord. There will be chains around their necks. They are headed to hellfire, where they will be forever. (5)

\*\*\*

They want you[ms] to hasten bad deeds before good deeds. Examples of punishment have gone before them. Your[ms] Lord is forgiving[1857]

---

[1844] Thunder
[1845] Zabur, Psalms 103:8, 145:8. See glossary for more details.
[1846] Here and at the beginning of many chapters there are unvowelled letters of unknown meaning. Numerous theories have been proposed, but there is no agreement on the subject.
[1847] Since it says "those" and not "these," the reference is probably to the former books.
[1848] Or signs. Arabic /ayat/ here and in verses 2, 4, 7, 27, and 38.
[1849] Tawrah, Isaiah 40:22
[1850] This is an anthropomorphism for Allah's rule, and it does not mean that Allah has a physical body. Zabur, Psalms 123:1
[1851] Tawrah, Genesis 1:14
[1852] Tawrah, Isaiah 44:24
[1853] Tawrah, Isaiah 41:18
[1854] the reference may be to male and female plants
[1855] see Zabur, Psalms 19:2, 74:16, Tawrah, Amos 5:8
[1856] Injil, Revelation 21:5.
[1857] Zabur, Psalms 103:3, 130:4, Tawrah, Isaiah 43:25, Exodus 34:7, Injil, Acts 26:18

## Chapter 13

of people's injustice, but your<sup>MS</sup> Lord is severe in punishment.[1858] (6)

\*\*\*

Disbelievers say, "If only his Lord had given him a sign[1859] from heaven[1860]!" You<sup>MS</sup> are only a warner. Every people has its own guide. (7)

\*\*\*

Allah knows what every female carries, and how long or short the wombs have left.[1861] Everything he has is measured. (8)

\*\*\*

[He] knows the unseen and the seen. He is great and exalted. (9)

\*\*\*

It is the same whether one of you<sup>MP</sup> hides a statement or says it, whether he tries to hide at night or goes out freely in the daytime;[1862] (10)

\*\*\*

he has a line of those who are in front of him[1863] and behind him,[1864] who guard him by Allah's command. Allah does not change what is in people until they change what is in themselves. If Allah wants evil for people, nothing can hold it back. They have no protector besides him. (11) He shows you<sup>MP</sup> lightning that both frightens and brings hope,[1865] and makes heavy clouds. (12) Thunder and the angels glorify and praise him[1866] out of fear of him, and he sends thunderbolts and afflicts those he wills with them.[1867] They argue about Allah, and he is mighty[1868] in power. (13) The only true prayer is to him, and those they pray to besides him do not answer them at all. That is like someone stretching out his hands to water to reach his mouth, and not reaching it.

---

[1858] Tawrah, Ezekiel 25:17, Injil, Matthew 8:12, 13:42,50, 22:13, 24:51, 25:30, Mark 9:48, Luke 13:28, 19:27.

[1859] The verb here is masculine and "sign" is feminine. The meaning might refer to someone who brought him a sign. Alternatively, it might be a direct quotation of disbelievers who spoke Arabic ungrammatically.

[1860] Injil, Luke 11:16, Mark 8:11, Matthew 16:1

[1861] or how the wombs expand and contract

[1862] Zabur, Psalms 139:11-12

[1863] Or, "between his hands."

[1864] this may refer to angels, Zabur, Psalm 139:5

[1865] Tawrah, Jeremiah 10:13

[1866] Tawrah, Job 37:2, Zabur, Psalm 29

[1867] Tawrah, Isaiah 29:6

[1868] Injil, Revelation 18:8, Tawrah, Isaiah 60:16, Zabur, Psalms 93:4

## Chapter 13

Disbelievers' prayers are straying. (14) Everything in heaven and earth will bow down to Allah, either willingly or unwillingly,[1869] just like their shadows morning and evening. (15)

\*\*\*

Say[MS], "Who is Lord of the heavens and the earth?" Say[MS], "Allah." Say[MS], "Have you[MP] chosen helpers beside him, who cannot benefit or harm themselves?" Say[MS], "Is the blind like the sighted? Are darkness and light alike? Have they chosen partners to Allah, who created things like he did? Thus creation is alike to them." Say[MS], "Allah created everything. He is the one victor." (16)

\*\*\*

He sent rain down[1870] from the sky, and it flowed in the valleys,[1871] each according to its size. The roaring water foams with a foam like the dross when they melt ore in the fire to make jewelry or utensils. Thus Allah sets forth truth and vanity. As for the foam, it goes away, but what benefits people remains on earth. Thus Allah gives parables. (17)

\*\*\*

Those who respond to their Lord have a good reward. Even if those who do not respond to him owned everything on earth twice over and offered it as a ransom, they would have an evil reckoning. They will be in hell, a dreadful abode. (18)

\*\*\*

**13B1** Is he who knows that truth has been revealed to you[MS] from your[MS] Lord like one who is blind? Thinkers remember. (19)

\*\*\*

They keep Allah's covenant and do not break the treaty. (20)

\*\*\*

They join what Allah commands to be joined, fear their Lord, and are afraid of an evil reckoning. (21)

\*\*\*

They endure,[1872] seek their Lord's face, perform the prayers, and donate from what we provide them, both secretly and openly. They drive away bad deeds with good deeds.[1873] Their reward is heaven, (22)

---

[1869] Injil, Philippians 2:10
[1870] Tawrah, Deuteronomy 28:12, Job 5:10, Joel 2:23, Zabur, Psalms 68:9, Injil, Matthew 5:45
[1871] Or dry river beds or wadis.
[1872] See "endure" in glossary, here and in verse 24
[1873] Injil, Romans 12:21, 1 Peter 4:8

## Chapter 13

\*\*\*

heavenly gardens[1874] of Eden[1875] they will enter, along with the righteous among their ancestors, spouses, and descendants. Angels will enter upon them
from every door, (23)

\*\*\*

"Peace to you[ms] for your[ms] endurance." The reward of heaven is wonderful. (24) Those who break Allah's covenant after it is confirmed and sever what Allah commanded to be joined and cause destruction on the earth are damned,[1876] and are going to the worst place. (25)

\*\*\*

Allah extends provision to those he wills,[1877] and he is able. They rejoice in this world. This world is just amusement[1878] compared to the hereafter. (26)

\*\*\*

Disbelievers say, "If only a sign had been revealed[1879] to him by his Lord." Say[ms], "Allah leads astray[1880] those he wills and guides those who repent to him."[1881] (27) Believers' hearts are at rest[1882] when they remember Allah. It is only in remembering Allah that the heart can rest.[1883] (28) Blessed are believers who do righteous deeds.[1884] They have a good place to return. (29) Thus we sent you[ms] to a nation before which other nations had passed away so that you[ms] would read[1885] to them what we inspired you[ms] with, and they disbelieve in the most gracious. Say[ms], "He is my Lord. He is

---

[1874] Arabic /jannah/ here and in verse 35. See glossary for more details.
[1875] Tawrah, Genesis 2:15
[1876] Tawrah, Ezekiel 17:19
[1877] Zabur, Psalms 145:15-16
[1878] Injil, 1 John 2:15-16
[1879] "Sign" is feminine and "revealed" is masculine. This may be a quotation of people who did not speak Arabic well.
[1880] Here and in verse 33, see Injil, 2 Thessalonians 2:11, Tawrah, 2 Samuel 22:27, 1 Kings 22:20-23, Ezekiel 14:9.
[1881] Tawrah, Exodus 33:19, Injil, Romans 9:15,18
[1882] Injil, Colossians 2:2
[1883] Tawrah, Isaiah 26:3, Injil, Philippians 4:6-7, 1 Peter 5:7, Zabur, Psalms 119:165
[1884] Injil, 1 Corinthians 3:8, James 2:14-17, Revelation 19:8
[1885] Or recite

the only god.[1886] I have trusted in him and repent[1887] toward him." (30)

\*\*\*

If only there had been a recitation[1888] that moved mountains[1889] or split the earth, or spoke to the dead! The command is totally Allah's. Do believers not despair, since if Allah had willed, he would have guided all mankind? Adversity still afflicts disbelievers[1890] for what they made,[1891] or it will afflict them soon from their houses, until Allah's promise is fulfilled. Allah does not break promises.[1892] (31)

\*\*\*

Messengers before you[MS] were mocked.[1893] I gave disbelievers an opportunity, then grabbed them. What kind of punishment did I give? (32)

\*\*\*

Who stands over every soul regarding what it deserves? Yet they choose other gods in addition to Allah![1894] Say[MS], "Name them!" Or do you[MP] tell him what he does not know on earth? Or have a clear saying? Deceit seems pleasing to disbelievers, and they are blocked from the path. If Allah leads someone astray,[1895] no one can guide him. (33)

\*\*\*

---

[1886] Arabic /ilah/. See glossary for more details.

[1887] The belief that all prophets and messengers are sinless is not supported by the Qur'an. For instances of prophets or messengers asking forgiveness or committing sins, see 7:23, 20:121 (Adam), 11:47, 71:28 (Nuh), 26:82, 14:41 (Ibrahim), 28:15-16 (Musa), 7:151, 20:93 (Musa and Harun), 38:24 (Dawud), 38:32,35 (Sulayman), 21:87, 37:142 (Yunus), 48:2, 47:19, 40:55, 4:79,106, 9:43, 13:30, 80:1-2, 110:3, 94:2, 23:118, 66:1, 33:37, 8:67, and 9:117 (Muhammad (s).

[1888] Or Qur'an or qur'an. See glossary for more details.

[1889] Injil, Matthew 17:20, 21:21, Mark 11:23, 1 Corinthians 13:2

[1890] Tawrah, Isaiah 13:11

[1891] Tawrah, Isaiah 10:11

[1892] Tawrah, 1 Kings 8:56, Numbers 23:19, Injil, Hebrews 6:13

[1893] Tawrah, 2 Chronicles 30:10, 36:16, Zabur, Psalms 35:16, Injil, Matthew 20:19, 27:29,31,41, Mark 15:20,31, Luke 18:32, 22:63, 23:11,36

[1894] Tawrah, Deuteronomy 7:4

[1895] Injil, 2 Thessalonians 2:11, Tawrah, 2 Samuel 22:27, 1 Kings 22:20-23, Ezekiel 14:9

They will have torment in this world,[1896] and the torment[1897] of the hereafter is worse. No one can protect them from Allah. (34)
\*\*\*

13B2 The heavenly garden, which the reverent are promised, which has flowing rivers underneath, and [1898] whose food and shade are permanent, is like...[1899] That is the reward of the reverent, and the punishment of disbelievers is hellfire.[1900] (35)
\*\*\*

Those we gave the book rejoice at what was revealed to you[MS]. Some of the factions deny some of it. Say[MS], "I was commanded to serve Allah and not other gods.[1901] I pray to him,[1902] and will return to him."[1903] (36)
\*\*\*

Thus we revealed it as an Arabic judgment.[1904] If you[MS] follow their desires after knowledge has come to you[MS], you[MS] have no help or protection from Allah. (37)
\*\*\*

We have sent messengers before you[MS], and we gave them spouses and descendants. No messenger brought a sign except with Allah's permission. There is a book for every time. (38) Allah erases[1905] or confirms what he wills,[1906] and he has the master[1907] book. (39) What we show you[MS] is part of what we promise them, or we will make you[MS] die. Your[MS] responsibility is to proclaim, and our responsibility is to reckon. (40) Have they not seen that we come

---

[1896] Injil, Revelation 9:5-6, Tawrah, 1 Samuel 16:14, Jeremiah 26:13
[1897] Tawrah, Isaiah 50:11, Injil, Matthew 18:34, 25:41,46, Luke 16:23-28, Revelation 20:15
[1898] Injil, Revelation 22:1-2, Tawrah, Ezekiel 47:12
[1899] The sentence does not have a predicate.
[1900] Injil, Mark 9:43
[1901] Tawrah, Exodus 20:3
[1902] or I invite [people] to him
[1903] Injil, Romans 14:12
[1904] In 5:43, the Tawrah contains Allah's judgment, and here, the Qur'an is an Arabic judgment.
[1905] Injil, Revelation 3:5
[1906] Injil, Romans 9:18
[1907] Or "mother of the book" or "essence of the book." Based on the context, the meaning might be the book of life or the book of works. Injil, Revelation 20:12

to the land and diminish its borders?[1908] Allah judges.[1909] There is nothing following his sentence. He is swift to reckon. (41)

\*\*\*

Those before them were deceitful. All deceit is Allah's. He knows what each soul deserves.[1910] Disbelievers will know who goes to heaven. (42)

\*\*\*

Disbelievers say, "You[MS] are not a messenger." Say[MS], "Allah and those that know the book are adequate witnesses between me and you[MP]." (43) [1911]

---

[1908] compare Tawrah, Exodus 34:24, Isaiah 26:15
[1909] Tawrah, Genesis 16:5
[1910] Injil, Matthew 16:27
[1911] The verses in this chapter that rhyme are put together in paragraphs, separated by \*\*\*.

# Chapter 14 Ibrahim[1912]

In the name of Allah, the most gracious and merciful.[1913] ALR.[1914] We revealed a book to you[MS] so you[MS] could lead people out of darkness to light[1915] with their Lord's permission, to the path of the powerful, praiseworthy one, (1) Allah. Everything in the heavens and the earth is his.[1916] Woe to disbelievers for a harsh torment.[1917] (2) They prefer this world to the hereafter, block Allah's path,[1918] and want it crooked.[1919] They have gone far astray. (3) Every messenger we sent spokein the language of his people to make things clear to them. Allah leads astray those he wills[1920] and guides those he wills.[1921] He is powerful and wise.[1922] (4)
\*\*\*

We sent Musa[1923] with our signs: "Get my people out of darkness into light,[1924] and remind them of Allah's days."[1925] Those are signs for everyone who endures[1926] and gives thanks. (5)
\*\*\*

Musa told his people, "Remember Allah's blessings to you[MP], when he rescued you[MP] from Pharaoh's family, who subjected

---

[1912] Abraham

[1913] Zabur, Psalms 103:8, 145:8. See glossary for more details.

[1914] Here and at the beginning of many chapters there are unvowelled letters of unknown meaning. Numerous theories have been proposed, but there is no agreement on the subject.

[1915] Zabur, Psalms 112:4, Isaiah 9:2, Colossians 1:13-14

[1916] Tawrah, Isaiah 45:12, Zabur, Psalms 24:1, 89:11, Injil, Hebrews 1:10

[1917] For "torment" here and in verses 7, 17, 21, 22, and 44, see Tawrah, Isaiah 50:11, Injil, Matthew 18:34, 25:41,46, Luke 16:23-28, Revelation 20:15

[1918] Injil, Matthew 18:7, 23:13

[1919] Injil, Acts 13:10, Philippians 2:15

[1920] Here and in verse 27, see Injil, 2 Thessalonians 2:11, Tawrah, 2 Samuel 22:27, 1 Kings 22:20-23, Ezekiel 14:9.

[1921] Tawrah, Exodus 33:19, Injil, Romans 9:15,18

[1922] Tawrah, Job 9:4, Proverbs 2:6 Jeremiah 9:23-24, Injil, 1 Corinthians 1:21-25, Romans 16:27

[1923] Moses here and in verses 6 and 8. See glossary for more details.

[1924] Tawrah, 2 Samuel 22:29, Isaiah 58:10, Zabur, Psalms 18:28, 112:4, Injil, Matthew 4:16, John 8:12, 12:46, Ephesians 5:8, 1 Peter 2:9

[1925] Tawrah, Deuteronomy 4:15, Isaiah 13:6-9

[1926] See "endure" in glossary, here and in verses 12 and 21.

you<sup>MP</sup> to evil torment,[1927] slaughtering your<sup>MP</sup> sons and sparing your<sup>MP</sup> daughters."[1928] That was a great trial from your<sup>MP</sup> Lord. (6)
\*\*\*

And when your<sup>MP</sup> Lord announced, "If you<sup>MP</sup> give thanks, I will multiply[1929] you<sup>MP</sup>, and if you<sup>MP</sup> are unthankful,[1930] my torment is harsh." (7)
\*\*\*

Musa said, "If you<sup>MP</sup> and everyone else on earth disbelieve, Allah is self-sufficient and praiseworthy."[1931] (8)
\*\*\*

Have you<sup>MP</sup> not heard about those before you<sup>MP</sup> – the people of Nuh,[1932] Aad,[1933] Thamud and those after them. No one knows them except Allah. Their messengers brought them miracles, and they responded by putting their hands in their mouths. They said, "We disbelieve in what you<sup>MP</sup> brought and we seriously doubt what you<sup>MP</sup> call us to." (9) 13B3
\*\*\*

Their messengers[1934] said, "Is there doubt about Allah, the creator of the heavens and the earth,[1935] who calls you<sup>MP</sup> in order to forgive you<sup>MP</sup> your<sup>MP</sup> sins, and reprieve you<sup>MP</sup> for a named period?"[1936] They said, "You<sup>MP</sup> are only people like us. You<sup>MP</sup> want to block us from what our fathers worshiped. Bring us clear authority." (10) Their messengers said, "We are people like you<sup>MP</sup>, but Allah gives gifts[1937] to those of his servants that he wills. We could not bring you<sup>MP</sup> clear authority except with Allah's permission. Let the believers trust in Allah. (11) We cannot do other than to trust in

---

[1927] Tawrah, Exodus 1:11
[1928] Tawrah, Exodus 1:16
[1929] Tawrah, Genesis 26:24, Injil, Matthew 13:12, Luke 19:26
[1930] or disbelieving
[1931] Zabur, Psalms 18:3
[1932] Noah. See glossary for more details.
[1933] Aad and Thamud are names of tribes.
[1934] Here, the verb form used for inanimate objects is used for messengers. Possibly some of the messengers here were angels, as angels are sometimes referred to with an inanimate verb and sometimes an animate one.
[1935] Here and in verses 19 and 32, see Tawrah, Genesis 1:1, Isaiah 42:5, 45:18.
[1936] Zabur, Psalms 91:16
[1937] Injil, 1 Corinthians 12:4-12

## Chapter 14

Allah, who has guided us on our paths.[1938] We will endure the harm you[MP] have done us. Let those who trust, trust in Allah." (12) The disbelievers told their messengers, "We will expel you[MP] from our land unless you[MP] return to our spiritual path."[1939] Their Lord inspired them, "We will destroy the wicked (13)

***

and make you[MP] dwell in their land after them. That is for those who fear my position and fear my threat." (14) They sought Allah's help and every proud, stubborn one was disappointed. (15) Hell is behind him and he will be given boiling[1940] water to drink. (16)

***

He will sip it but barely swallow it, and death will come to him from everywhere, yet he will not die. Behind him,[1941] there will be severe torment. (17)

***

The works of disbelievers in their Lord are like ashes blown by the wind on a stormy day.[1942] They can do nothing against what they deserve. That is going far astray. (18) Do you[MS] not see that Allah truly created the heavens and the earth?[1943] If he wants to, he can do away with you[MP] and bring a new creation.[1944] (19)

***

That is not difficult to Allah. [1945] (20)

***

They all appeared before Allah. The weak[1946] told the proud, "We were your[MP] followers. Can you[MP] protect us in anything from Allah's torment?" They said, "If Allah had guided us, we would have guided you[MP]. It is the same whether we are endure or not; there will be no escape."[1947] (21)

---

[1938] Zabur, Psalms 23:2
[1939] Arabic /millah/. See glossary.
[1940] Or putrid, like pus
[1941] Or after that
[1942] Zabur, Psalms 1:4, Injil, Revelation 21:1
[1943] Tawrah, Genesis 1:1, Isaiah 42:5, 45:18
[1944] Tawrah, Isaiah 65:17, 66:22
[1945] Injil, Luke 1:37
[1946] Here and in 40:47, this word has a different spelling than in 2:266 and 9:91. Some say the reason is that this one refers to those who are weak in the hereafter.
[1947] Tawrah, Jeremiah 48:8, Injil, Romans 2:3, 1 Thessalonians 5:3

Chapter 14

\*\*\*

Satan said, "When the matter was decreed, Allah promised you<sup>MP</sup> truly and I promised you<sup>MP</sup> and broke my promise[1948] to you<sup>MP</sup>. I had no authority over you<sup>MP</sup>.[1949] I merely called you<sup>MP</sup> and you<sup>MP</sup> responded to me. Do not blame<sup>MP</sup> me. Blame yourselves<sup>MP</sup>. I cannot help you<sup>MP</sup> and you<sup>MP</sup> cannot help me. I rejected[1950] your<sup>MP</sup> worship of me beforehand." The wicked will have painful torment. (22)

\*\*\*

The believers who did righteous deeds[1951] will be brought in to heavenly gardens[1952] with flowing rivers underneath,[1953] where they will dwell forever by their Lord's permission. Their greeting there is "Peace." (23)

\*\*\*

Have you<sup>MS</sup> not seen how Allah tells parables? A good word is like a good tree[1954] Its root is firm[1955] and its branches are in the sky.[1956] (24)

\*\*\*

It gives its food at all times by its Lord's permission.[1957] Allah tells parables to people so that they may remember.[1958] (25)

\*\*\*

A rotten word is like a rotten tree[1959] torn up on the ground.[1960] It has no abode. (26) Allah establishes the believers[1961] with a firm saying in this world and in the hereafter, and Allah leads the wicked astray. Allah does what he wills.[1962] (27) **13B4**

\*\*\*

---

[1948] Injil, John 8:44
[1949] Injil, Matthew 28:18, Mark 6:7, Luke 10:19, John 19:11
[1950] Or "disbelieved in." Injil, James 2:19
[1951] Injil, 1 Corinthians 3:8, James 2:14-17, Revelation 19:8
[1952] Arabic /jannah/. See glossary for more details.
[1953] Injil, Revelation 22:1-2, Tawrah, Ezekiel 47:12
[1954] Zabur, Psalms 1:3, Injil, Matthew 7:17-18, Luke 13:18,19, Tawrah, Jeremiah 17:7-8
[1955] Tawrah, Proverbs 12:3
[1956] Tawrah, Daniel 4:10-20
[1957] Zabur, Psalms 1:3, Injil, Revelation 22:2, Tawrah, Jeremiah 17:7-8
[1958] Injil, Matthew 13:35
[1959] Injil, Matthew 7:17-19
[1960] Injil, Jude 12, Injil, Matthew 15:13
[1961] Injil, 1 Thessalonians 3:13
[1962] Tawrah, Exodus 33:19, Injil, Romans 9:15,18

## Chapter 14

Have you[MS] not seen those who exchange Allah's blessings for disbelief,[1963] and allowed their people to go to perdition? (28) They will be roasted in hell, a dreadful abode. (29) They made rivals to Allah, to lead others astray from the path. Say[MS], "Enjoy yourselves[MP]. Your[MP] destiny is hellfire." (30)

\*\*\*

Tell[MS] my servants[1964] who believe to perform prayers,[1965] and donate from what we have provided, both in secret[1966] and in public, before a day comes in which there is no buying[1967] or friendship. (31)

\*\*\*

Allah is the creator of the heavens and the earth, and he sent down rain[1968] from the sky, brought forth fruits from it as provision for you[MP], and made ships subject[1969] to you[MP] so they can travel on the sea by his command, and he made the rivers subject to you[MP]. (32) He made the sun and moon faithful in their work and subject to you[MP], and he made night and day subject to you[MP]. (33) He gave you[MP] everything you[MP] asked.[1970] If you[MP] were to count[1971] Allah's blessings, you[MP] would not be able. Mankind are wicked disbelievers.[1972] (34)

\*\*\*

---

[1963] or ingratitude
[1964] See glossary.
[1965] Injil, Matthew 6:5-15
[1966] Injil, Matthew 6:1-4
[1967] Zabur, Psalms 49:8-9
[1968] Tawrah, Deuteronomy 28:12, Job 5:10, Joel 2:23, Zabur, Psalms 68:9, Injil, Matthew 5:45
[1969] Zabur, Psalms 107:23-29
[1970] Injil, John 11:22, 14:13
[1971] Zabur, Psalms 139:18
[1972] For here and in verse 45, the injustice/wickedness, disbelief/ungratefulness, evil, unrighteousness/sin, or lostness of mankind is mentioned in a number of verses in the Qur'an as well as in the previous books. Injustice or wickedness: 2:57, 3:117,135, 4:64,97, 7:160,177, 9:70, 10:44, 11:101, 14:34,45, 16:33,61,118, 29:40, 30:9, 33:72, 34:19, 35:32, 43:76, 65:1, Tawrah, Genesis 6:5, Job 25:4, Injil, Acts 3:26, disbelief or ungratefulness: 14:34, 17:67, 22:66, 42:48, 43:15, 80:17, Injil, Hebrews 3:19, Evil: 12:53, Tawrah, Jeremiah 17:9, Injil, Matthew 15:19, Mark 7:21, unrighteousness or sin: 91:8, Tawrah, 1 Kings 8:46, Ecclesiastes 7:20, Injil, Romans 3:9-19, 5:12, lostness: 103:2, Tawrah, Jeremiah 50:6, Injil, Luke 19:10, Romans 3:23, 6:23

## Chapter 14

Ibrahim[1973] said, "Lord, make this place safe, and keep me and my sons from worshipping idols. (35)

\*\*\*

Lord, they[1974] have led many people astray. Whoever follows me is mine. Whoever disobeys me, you[ms] are forgiving[1975] and merciful.[1976] (36) Our Lord, I have made some of my seed live in a barren valley[1977] near your sacred house.[1978] Our Lord, may they perform the prayers! Make some people's hearts love them, and provide them with fruit, so that they may give thanks. (37)

\*\*\*

Our Lord, you[ms] know what we conceal and what we announce."[1979] Nothing is hidden from Allah,[1980] either on earth or in heaven. (38) Praise be to Allah, who gave me Ismail[1981] and Ishaq[1982] in my old age.[1983] My Lord hears prayer. (39) My Lord, make me and some of my seed[1984] perform prayers. Lord, accept my prayer.[1985] (40)

\*\*\*

Our Lord, forgive me[1986] and my parents and the believers on the day of reckoning.[1987] (41)

---

[1973] Abraham. See glossary for more details.

[1974] the idols. The pronoun used here is for thinking beings, so maybe the meaning is the demons behind the idols. Injil, 1 Corinthians 10:20

[1975] Zabur, Psalms 103:3, 130:4, Tawrah, Isaiah 43:25, Exodus 34:7, Injil, Acts 26:18

[1976] See glossary for more details on "merciful."

[1977] Tawrah, Genesis 13:10-11

[1978] Zabur, Psalms 79:1

[1979] See also 2:77, 11:5, 16:19,23, 27:25,74, 28:69, 36:76, 60:1, 64:4.

[1980] Zabur, Psalms 69:5, 139:15

[1981] Ishmael. See glossary for more details. Tawrah, Genesis 16:15

[1982] Isaac. See glossary for more details. Tawrah, Genesis 21:3

[1983] Tawrah, Genesis 16:16, 21:5

[1984] Tawrah, Genesis 22:8, Injil, Galatians 3:16-19

[1985] Tawrah, 2 Chronicles 6:20

[1986] Tawrah, Genesis 20:9, Zabur, Psalms 103:3. The belief that all prophets and messengers are sinless is not supported by the Qur'an. For instances of prophets or messengers asking forgiveness or committing sins, see 7:23, 20:121 (Adam), 11:47, 71:28 (Nuh), 26:82, 14:41 (Ibrahim), 28:15-16 (Musa), 7:151, 20:93 (Musa and Harun), 38:24 (Dawud), 38:32,35 (Sulayman), 21:87, 37:142 (Yunus), 48:2, 47:19, 40:55, 4:79,106, 9:43, 13:30, 80:1-2, 110:3, 94:2, 23:118, 66:1, 33:37, 8:67, and 9:117 (Muhammad (s).

[1987] Tawrah, Isaiah 2:12

## Chapter 14

\*\*\*

Do not consider<sup>MS</sup> that Allah is unaware of deeds of the wicked.<sup>1988</sup> He gives them time until a day there will be staring, (42)

\*\*\*

running with heads lifted up in horror. Their sight will not return to them, and their hearts will be empty.<sup>1989</sup> (43)

\*\*\*

Warn people of a day when they will be tormented. The wicked say, "Our Lord, give us a little more time. Then we will respond to your<sup>MS</sup> call and follow the messengers." Have you<sup>MP</sup> not sworn previously that you<sup>MP</sup> would never pass away? (44) You<sup>MP</sup> lived in the dwellings of those who wronged themselves, <sup>1990</sup> and it was clear to you<sup>MP</sup> what we did to them. We told you<sup>MP</sup> parables. (45) They deceived with their deceit, and their deceit is known to Allah, even they could make mountains disappear their deceit.<sup>1991</sup> (46)

\*\*\*

Do not consider<sup>MS</sup> that Allah will break his promise to his messengers.<sup>1992</sup> Allah is powerful and avenging.<sup>1993</sup> (47)

\*\*\*

On that day, the earth and the heavens will be replaced,<sup>1994</sup> and they will appear to Allah, the one victor. (48)

\*\*\*

You<sup>MS</sup> will see the wrongdoers on that day, bound with fetters, (49) with garments of tar and fire covering their faces. (50)

\*\*\*

Thus Allah will repay each soul as it deserves.<sup>1995</sup> Allah is swift in reckoning.<sup>1996</sup> (51) This is a message to people, to be warned and know that he is one god.<sup>1997</sup> Let thinkers remember. (52)<sup>1998</sup>

---

[1988] Tawrah, Job 37:16, Isaiah 40:14, Zabur, Psalms 33:13-15, Injil, 1 John 3:20
[1989] Tawrah, Isaiah 21:4
[1990] 2:57, 3:117,135, 4:64,97,7:160,177, 9:70, 11:101, 16:33,118, 29:40, 30:9, 34:19, 35:32, 43:76, 65:1, Injil, Revelation 2:23.
[1991] Injil, Matthew 21:21
[1992] Injil, Hebrews 6:18
[1993] Tawrah, Deuteronomy 32:35, Ezekiel 25:17, Injil, Romans 12:19, Hebrews 10:30
[1994] Injil, Revelation 21:1
[1995] Injil, Revelation 22:12

Chapter 14

---

[1996] Tawrah, Isaiah 19:1, Malachi 3:5, Zabur, Psalms 147:15, Injil, 2 Peter 2:1, Revelation 22:12
[1997] Arabic /ilah/. See glossary for more details.
[1998] The verses in this chapter that rhyme are put together in paragraphs, separated by ***.

# Chapter 15 Al-Hijr[1999]

**14A1** In the name of Allah, the most gracious and merciful.[2000] ALR.[2001] Those[2002] are verses of the book[2003] and of a clear recitation.[2004] (1) Disbelievers may wish they were submitted.[2005] (2) Let them eat and enjoy themselves[2006] and let their hope entertain them. They will know. (3) We have never destroyed a village except if it had a known book. (4) No nation can advance its set time or postpone it.[2007] (5) They[2008] said, "You[MS] who received the reminder[2009] are crazy.[2010] (6) If only you[MS] would bring us angels, if you[MS] are telling the truth." (7) We only send angels with truth. In that case, they would not have been given more time.[2011] (8) We ourselves revealed[2012] the reminder,[2013] and we are its protectors. (9) We sent before you[MS] those of the party of the men of old, (10) and whenever a messenger came to them, they

---

[1999] A dam, wall, or something forbidden
[2000] Zabur, Psalms 103:8, 145:8. See glossary for more details.
[2001] Here and at the beginning of many chapters there are unvowelled letters of unknown meaning. Numerous theories have been proposed, but there is no agreement on the subject.
[2002] Since it says "those" and not "these,' the reference is probably to the former books.
[2003] i.e. the former book
[2004] Or Qur'an or qur'an. See glossary for more details.
[2005] Injil, James 4:7. For "submitted," some translators do not translate this. See glossary for more details.
[2006] Injil, 1 Corinthians 15:32, Matthew 24:37-38
[2007] Injil, Acts 17:26
[2008] "They" here probably refers to the last-mentioned group, those of the villages Allah destroyed who received a book.
[2009] Arabic /dhikr/ here and in verse 9. See glossary for more details. Here the reminder is given to former nations.
[2010] or demon-possessed. Apparently this was a common event for those peoples who received the book of remembrance.
[2011] In their being judged.
[2012] Tawrah, Exodus 31:18
[2013] The reminder, or book of remembrance, referred to here in context is the one that was given to the peoples mentioned in verses 4-8. This agrees with 21:7,48,105.

## Chapter 15

mocked him.[2014] (11) Thus we make it go into the hearts of wrongdoers. (12) They do not believe in him,[2015] though the traditions of the men of old have passed away. (13) Even if we opened a door in the sky, that they could keep going up through, (14) they would have said, "Our sight was drunken; rather, we were bewitched people." (15) We made constellations[2016] in the sky and decorated them for people to look at. (16) We protected them from every damned devil, (17) except for the ones that eavesdropped and were followed clearly by a flame.[2017] (18) We stretched out the earth[2018] and set mountains in it, and caused everything to sprout in balance. (19) In it, we made a livelihood for you[MP] as well as for those you[MP] do not provide for.[2019] (20) We have treasuries of everything,[2020] and we only send it down in known quantities. (21) We sent the wind to pollinate, and sent rain[2021] down from the sky and quenched your[MP] thirst with it. You[MP] do not store it up. (22) We give life and take it, and we give inheritances.[2022] (23) We knew who among you[MP] would press forward and who would lag behind. (24) Your[MS] Lord himself will gather[2023] them. He is wise[2024] and all-knowing.[2025] (25) We created mankind of clay, from mud formed into shape. (26) We created jinns[2026] previously from the fire of scorching wind. (27) Your[MS] Lord told the angels, "I am creating humans from clay, from mud formed into shape, (28) so when I have formed him and

---

[2014] Tawrah, 2 Chronicles 30:10, 36:16, Zabur, Psalms 35:16, Injil, Matthew 20:19, 27:29,31,41, Mark 15:20,31, Luke 18;32, 22:63, 23:11,36

[2015] or it

[2016] Or towers or the zodiac. Tawrah, Job 38:31,32.

[2017] Or meteor.

[2018] Tawrah, Isaiah 44:24

[2019] Zabur, Psalms 145:15-16, Tawrah, Genesis 3:19

[2020] Tawrah, Job 38:22, Jeremiah 51:16, Zabur, Psalms 33:7

[2021] Tawrah, Deuteronomy 28:12, Job 5:10, Joel 2:23, Zabur, Psalms 68:9, Injil, Matthew 5:45

[2022] Literally, "we are heirs."

[2023] Tawrah, Joel 3:11-14, Zephaniah 3:8, Injil, Matthew 25:32, John 15:6, Revelation 16:16

[2024] Tawrah, Job 9:4, Proverbs 2:6, Jeremiah 9:23-24, Injil, 1 Corinthians 1:21-25, Romans 16:27

[2025] Tawrah, Job 37:16, Isaiah 40:14, Zabur, Psalms 33:13-15, Injil, 1 John 3:20

[2026] Or demons. See glossary for more details.

## Chapter 15

breathed of my spirit into him,[2027] fall down and bow down[2028] before him." (29) So the angels all bowed down, (30) except for Iblis,[2029] who refused to bow down. (31) He said, "Iblis, what is wrong that you[MS] do not bow down?" (32) He said, "I should not bow down to humans. You[MS] created him from clay, from mud formed into shape." (33) He said, "Leave it.[2030] You[MS] are damned. (34) You are damned until the day of judgment." (35) He said, "My Lord, give me more time, until the day they are resurrected." (36) He said, "You[MS] have more time, (37) until the day of a known time." (38) He said, "My Lord, since you[MS] have led me astray, I will make things on earth desirable for them, and lead them all astray, (39) except for your[MS] sincere servants[2031] among them." (40) He said, "This is a straight path[2032] for me. (41) You[MS] have no authority over my servants,[2033] except for those who follow you[MS] as they are led astray." (42) Hell is promised to all of them. (43) It has seven doors, each one of which has a specified portion. (44) The reverent will be in a heavenly garden[2034] among springs. (45) "Enter it in peace and safety." (46) We took enmity from their hearts, [and they will be] brothers on couches facing each other. (47) They will not be tired, and will not be expelled from it. (48) 14A2 Tell my servants that I am forgiving[2035] and merciful,[2036] (49) and that my torment[2037] is really painful. (50) Tell them about Ibrahim's[2038] guests.[2039] (51) They came to him and said, "Peace."

---

[2027] Adam (here in 15:29, 38:72, and 32:9) and Isa (21:91 and 66:12) are the only ones into whom Allah breathed his spirit.

[2028] Zabur, Psalms 97:7, Injil, Hebrews 1:5

[2029] The devil here and in verse 32. See glossary for more details.

[2030] there is no reference in the passage for "it". The meaning is probably heaven. Injil, Revelation 12:9, Isaiah 14:12,19

[2031] See glossary for "servant" here and in verses 42 and 49.

[2032] See glossary for more details, and notes on 3:51, 6:153, 19:36, 36:61, and 43:64 on what the straight path is.

[2033] Injil, John 14:30,19:11, Matthew 28:18, Mark 6:7, Luke 10:19, Hebrews 2:14-15, 1 John 4:4

[2034] Arabic /jannah/. See glossary for more details.

[2035] Zabur, Psalms 103:3, 130:4, Tawrah, Isaiah 43:25, Exodus 34:7, Injil, Acts 26:18

[2036] See glossary for more details on "merciful."

[2037] Tawrah, Isaiah 50:11, Injil, Matthew 18:34, 25:41,46, Luke 16:23-28, Revelation 20:15

[2038] Abraham. See glossary for more details.

[2039] Tawrah, Genesis 18:1-2

## Chapter 15

He said, "We are afraid of you^MP."²⁰⁴⁰ (52) They said, "Do not be afraid. We bring you^MS good news of a knowledgeable boy."²⁰⁴¹ (53) He said, "Have you^MP brought me good news despite my old age?²⁰⁴² What exactly are you^MP giving me good news about?" (54) They said, "We give you^MS good news in truth. Do not despair^MS.²⁰⁴³ (55) Only those who go astray despair of their Lord's mercy." (56) He said, "Then what is your^MP message, messengers?"²⁰⁴⁴ (57) They said, "We have been sent to wrongdoing people,²⁰⁴⁵ (58) except for Lut's²⁰⁴⁶ family. We will rescue every one of them²⁰⁴⁷ (59) except for his wife.²⁰⁴⁸ We have destined that she would lag behind." (60) When the messengers came to Lut's family, (61) he said, "You^MP people are strangers."²⁰⁴⁹ (62) They said, "Rather we have brought you^MS what they doubted, (63) we have brought you^MS truth, and we are telling the truth. (64) So take your^MS family during the night, and follow^MS behind them.²⁰⁵⁰ None of you^MP should turn around.²⁰⁵¹ Go^MP where you^MP are commanded." (65) We decreed that command to him, that their remnant would be cut off by morning.²⁰⁵² (66) The people of the city came seeking good news.²⁰⁵³ (67) He said, "These are my guests.²⁰⁵⁴ Do not scandalize me.²⁰⁵⁵ (68) Fear Allah²⁰⁵⁶ and do not shame me." (69) They said, "Did we not forbid you^MS from dealing with other people?"²⁰⁵⁷ (70)

---

²⁰⁴⁰ See Tawrah, Genesis 18:2
²⁰⁴¹ Tawrah, Genesis 18:9-10
²⁰⁴² Tawrah, Genesis 18:11
²⁰⁴³ Tawrah, Genesis 18:12-14
²⁰⁴⁴ Tawrah, Genesis 18:17
²⁰⁴⁵ Tawrah, Genesis 18:21
²⁰⁴⁶ Lot, nephew of Abraham here and in verse 61. See glossary for more details.
²⁰⁴⁷ Tawrah, Genesis 19:15
²⁰⁴⁸ Tawrah, Genesis 19:26
²⁰⁴⁹ Or disavowed or denied or unknown. Tawrah, Genesis 19:1-2
²⁰⁵⁰ Tawrah, Genesis 19:12-13
²⁰⁵¹ Tawrah, Genesis 19:17
²⁰⁵² Tawrah, Genesis 19:17,22,23
²⁰⁵³ Or rejoicing. Tawrah, Genesis 19:5
²⁰⁵⁴ Tawrah, Genesis 19:8
²⁰⁵⁵ Tawrah, Genesis 19:7
²⁰⁵⁶ Tawrah, Deuteronomy 10:12, Isaiah 29:13, Injil, 1 Peter 2:17, Revelation 14:7
²⁰⁵⁷ Tawrah, Genesis 19:9

## Chapter 15

He said, "These are my daughters, if you^MP must do something."[2058] (71) By your^MS life, they are wandering as if drunk.[2059] (72) The cry overtook them at sunrise.[2060] (73) We turned them upside down,[2061] and rained upon them stones of dried clay.[2062] (74) That is a sign for the observant. (75) They[2063] are in a permanent path. (76) That is a sign for believers. (77) The people of the woods were wicked, (78) so we took revenge on them. They both are in a clear pattern. (79) The people of the chamber[2064] rejected the messengers, (80) and we brought them our signs, and they turned away from them. (81) They carved safe homes out of the mountains, (82) but the cry overtook them in the morning. (83) What they gained[2065] did not help them. (84)

\*\*\*

We truly created the heavens and the earth[2066] and what is between them.[2067] The hour[2068] is coming,[2069] so pardon graciously. (85)

\*\*\*

Your^MS Lord is the all-knowing[2070] creator. (86) We have given you^MS seven doubles[2071] and the great Qur'an.[2072] (87) Do not envy^MS[2073] the pleasure we give some couples and do not grieve^MS over them. Lower your^MS wing for the believers. (88) Say^MS, "I myself am the clear warner." (89) We also revealed to the dividers, (90) who made the Qur'an[2074] separate parts. (91) By your^MS Lord, we will question them all (92) about what they have done. (93) Expound what you^MS have been commanded, and turn^MS

---

[2058] Tawrah, Genesis 19:8
[2059] Tawrah, Genesis 19:11
[2060] Tawrah, Genesis 19:23-24
[2061] Tawrah, Genesis 19:25
[2062] Tawrah, Genesis 19:24
[2063] The signs
[2064] or wall, or dam, or the forbidding people
[2065] Or earned
[2066] Tawrah, Genesis 1:1, Isaiah 42:5, 45:18
[2067] Tawrah, Genesis 1
[2068] Injil, Revelation 14:7
[2069] Injil, John 5:25-28
[2070] Tawrah, Job 37:16, Isaiah 40:14, Zabur, Psalms 33:13-15, Injil, 1 John 3:20
[2071] some other translations put "oft-repeated" instead of "doubles"
[2072] Or recitation. See glossary for more details.
[2073] or stretch your eyes toward
[2074] Or recitation. See glossary for more details.

Chapter 15

away from the idolaters. (94) We are adequate for you[MS] against the scoffers (95) who make another god[2075] besides Allah. They will know. (96) We knew that your[MS] heart is tightened by what they say, (97) so glorify and praise your[MS] Lord, and bow[MS] down. (98) Worship your[MS] Lord until you[MS] are certain. (99) [2076]

---

[2075] Arabic /ilah/. See glossary for more details.
[2076] The verses in this chapter that rhyme are put together in paragraphs, separated by ***.

# Chapter 16 Al-Nahl[2077]

**14A3** In the name of Allah, the most gracious and merciful.[2078] Allah's command will[2079] come, so do not hasten it. May he be glorified and exalted above the gods they worship! (1) He sends the angels down[2080] with the spirit from his command to those servants[2081] he wills, "Warn[MP] [people] that I am the only god,[2082] so fear[MP] me." (2) He truly created the heavens and the earth.[2083] May he be exalted above the gods they worship. (3) He created humans from a sperm, and he is clear opponent. (4) [He created] cattle for you[MP], to give warmth, benefits, and food. (5) You[MP] have beauty from them when you[MP] bring [them] home and send[MP] [them] to pasture. (6) They carry your[MP] loads to places you[MP] could not reach except by great effort. Your[MP] Lord is compassionate and merciful.[2084] (7) [He created] horses, mules, and donkeys to ride and as decoration. He creates things you[MP] do not know about. (8) Allah's path is right and [some] turn away from it. If he had willed it, he would have guided all of you[MP]. (9) He sent you[MP] rain from the sky,[2085] some to drink, some for trees among which you[MP] can send flocks to pasture. (10) He sprouts crops, olives, palm trees, grapes, and all fruits. That is a sign[2086] for people who consider. (11) He made night and day,[2087] the sun, moon, and stars[2088] subject to you[MP] by his command. Those are signs for people who comprehend. (12) What he created on earth is of differing colors. That is a sign for people who remember. (13) He subjected the

---

[2077] Bees, or bee
[2078] Zabur, Psalms 103:8, 145:8. See glossary for more details.
[2079] Or has
[2080] Injil, Acts 10:22
[2081] See glossary.
[2082] Arabic /ilah/ here and twice in verse 22. See glossary for more details.
[2083] Tawrah, Genesis 1:1, Isaiah 42:5, 45:18
[2084] Injil, James 5:11. Here and in verses 18, 47, 110, 115, and 119, see glossary for more details on "merciful."
[2085] Tawrah, Deuteronomy 28:12, Job 5:10, Joel 2:23, Zabur, Psalms 68:9, Injil, Matthew 5:45
[2086] Arabic /ayat/ here and in verses 12, 13, 79, 104, and 105. See glossary for more details.
[2087] Zabur, Psalms 19:2
[2088] Zabur, Psalms 148:3

## Chapter 16

sea[2089] to you[MP], so you[MP] could eat fresh meat from it and get[MP] ornaments to wear from it. You[MS] see[2090] the ships plow through its waves,[2091] so you[MP] would desire his grace, and so you[MP] would give thanks. (14) He put mountains on the earth, lest[2092] it should move with you[MP]; rivers and paths, so that you[MP] may be guided; (15) and signals. They are guided by the stars. (16) Is one who creates like one who does not? Do you[MP] not remember? (17) If you[MP] tried to count Allah's blessings, you[MP] would not be able to.[2093] Allah is forgiving[2094] and merciful. (18) Allah knows what you[MP] conceal and what you[MP] announce.[2095] (19) Those they pray to besides Allah do not create anything.[2096] In fact, they are created (20) dead, not alive, and they do not realize when they will be resurrected. (21) Your[MP] god is one god, and those who do not believe in the hereafter have hearts that deny, and they are proud. (22) No doubt Allah knows what they conceal and what they announce. He does not love the proud.[2097] (23) When they are asked, "What did your[MP] Lord reveal?" they say, "Ancient legends." (24) Thus they will fully bear their burdens on the day of resurrection,[2098] and some burdens of those who unknowingly lead them astray. Is that not an evil burden? (25) Those before them were deceitful, and Allah came against their building from the foundations and the ceiling fell upon them from above.[2099] Torment came upon them from places they did realize. (26) Then, on the day of resurrection, he will shame them and say, "Where are my partner gods about which you[MP] contended?" Those who were given knowledge will say, "Shame and evil will come today

---

[2089] Zabur, Psalms 8:8

[2090] or "and so that you see"

[2091] Zabur, Psalms 107:23

[2092] Or so

[2093] Zabur, Psalms 139:17,18

[2094] Here and in verses 110, 115, and 119, see Zabur, Psalms 103:3, 130:4, Tawrah, Isaiah 43:25, Exodus 34:7, Injil, Acts 26:18 for "forgiving."

[2095] Here and in verse 23, see also 2:77, 11:5, 14:38, 27:25,74, 28:69, 36:76, 60:1, 64:4.

[2096] Tawrah, Isaiah 46:7

[2097] Zabur, Psalms 5:4-5, 11:5, Tawrah, Proverbs 6:16-19

[2098] For "day of resurrection" here and in verses 27, 92, and 124, see Tawrah, Daniel 12:2, Injil, Acts 24:15, 1 Corinthians 15:52-54, Revelation 20:11-15

[2099] Tawrah, Judges 16:30

## Chapter 16

upon the disbelievers (27) whom the angels cause to die while they were wronging themselves." They will ask for a amnesty, "We were not doing evil." "Yes, [you were]. Allah knows your<sup>MP</sup> deeds. (28) Enter the doors of hell and remain there forever." The place of the proud is dreadful." (29) 14A4 The reverent will be asked, "What did your<sup>MP</sup> Lord reveal?" They will say, "Good; good for those who do good deeds in this world, and the hereafter is better.[2100] How wonderful is the abode of the reverent.[2101] (30) They will enter heavenly gardens[2102] of Eden with flowing rivers underneath.[2103] They will have whatever they want in them. This is how Allah rewards the reverent (31) whom the angels cause to die when they are good. They will say, "Peace be upon you<sup>MP</sup>. Enter<sup>MP</sup> the heavenly garden for your<sup>MP</sup> deeds."[2104] (32) What do they expect, besides the angels coming to them, or their Lord's command coming? Those before them did that. Allah did not wrong them, but they wronged themselves. (33) Then their evil deeds overtook them[2105] and what they mocked surrounded them. (34) The idolaters said, "If Allah had willed, we and our ancestors would not have worshiped anything besides him, nor would we have sanctified[2106] anything besides him. Those before them did that. Are messengers responsible for anything beyond clear proclamation?[2107] (35) We sent every nation a messenger, "Worship Allah, and avoid[2108] false gods."[2109] Allah guided some of them, and some of them deserved to go astray. Walk<sup>MP</sup> through the land and see<sup>MP</sup> the punishment of the rejectors.[2110] (36) If you<sup>MS</sup> desire to guide them, Allah does not guide those he leads astray.[2111] They will have no savior.[2112] (37) They swore<sup>M</sup> by Allah

---

[2100] Injil, Mark 10:30, Luke 18:29-30
[2101] Injil, Matthew 25:34-40
[2102] Arabic /jannah/ here and in verse 32. See glossary for more details.
[2103] Injil, Revelation 22:1-2, Tawrah, Ezekiel 47:12
[2104] Injil, Matthew 25:34-40
[2105] Tawrah, Deuteronomy 28:15
[2106] or forbidden
[2107] Tawrah, Ezekiel 33:6-9
[2108] Injil, 1 John 5:21
[2109] Arabic /Al-Taghut/. See glossary for more details.
[2110] The verb is masculine and the subject feminine. There may be another meaning.
[2111] For "misleads" here and in verse 93, see Injil, 2 Thessalonians 2:11, Tawrah, 2 Samuel 22:27, 1 Kings 22:20-23, Ezekiel 14:9.
[2112] Tawrah, Isaiah 43:11, Hosea 13:4, Injil, Hebrews 10:26

## Chapter 16

with their most-binding oaths, "Allah will not resurrect those who die."[2113] Oh yes, he will! It is his true promise,[2114] which most people do not know, (38) so that he may clarify to them what they differed about, and so that disbelievers may know that they were liars. (39) When we want something, we merely say to it, "Be[2115]!" and it is. (40) We will give a good dwelling in this world to those who emigrated for Allah's sake after being wronged. The reward of the hereafter is greater, if they only knew.[2116] (41) Those who endure[2117] and trust in their Lord.[2118] (42) Those we sent before you[MS] were men we inspired, so ask[MP] the people of the reminder[2119] if you[MP] do not know (43) about the miracles and psalms.[2120] We reveal the reminder[2121] to you[MS] so you[MS] could show people clearly what has been revealed to them, and so that they may consider. (44) Are those who schemed bad deeds safe from Allah making the earth swallow them,[2122] from torment coming to them from places they do not realize (45) or overtaking them unstoppably in their going to and fro,[2123] (46) or from overtaking them in fear? Your[MP] Lord is compassionate and merciful. (47) Have they not seen that Allah has created things whose shadows turn to the right and left, bowing down humbly to Allah? (48) All the living creatures and angels in the heavens and the earth will bow down to Allah.[2124] They will not be proud. (49) They fear their Lord above them and they do as they are commanded. (50) **14B1** Allah said, "Do not choose two gods. He is one god,[2125] so be in awe of me."

---

[2113] Injil, 1 Corinthians 15:12
[2114] Injil, 1 Corinthians 15:20
[2115] Tawrah, Genesis 1
[2116] Injil, Mark 10:30, Luke 18:29-30
[2117] See "endure" in glossary
[2118] There is no predicate in this sentence. It may refer to the people in the previous verse.
[2119] Arabic /dhikr/ here and in verse 44. See glossary for more details. See 21:7. Here followers of the Qur'an are told to ask people of the reminder if they do not know. Thus the reminder here is not the Qur'an. 21:48,105 clarify this, and refer to the Tawrah as the reminder.
[2120] Or books
[2121] here, the Qur'an
[2122] Tawrah, Numbers 16:32, 26:10, Deuteronomy 11:6, Zabur, Psalms 106:17
[2123] Or their business. Zabur, Psalms 121:8
[2124] Injil, Philippians 2:9-11, Romans 14:11
[2125] Arabic /ilah/. See glossary for more details.

## Chapter 16

(51) Everything in the heavens and the earth is his.[2126] The day of judgment[2127] is his forever. Will you[MP] fear anyone besides Allah?[2128] (52) Any blessing you[MP] have is from Allah.[2129] Then if any harm comes to you[MP], you[MP] supplicate him with groans. (53) Then, if he removes the harm from you[MP], a group of you[MP] worship gods other than their Lord, (54) thereby disbelieving in[2130] what came to them. So enjoy yourselves[MP]. You[MP] will know. (55) They give a portion of what we provided them to what they do not know. By Allah, you[MP] will be questioned about your[MP] invention. (56) They claim Allah has daughters! May he be glorified (above that)! They will get what they lust for. (57) If one of them is given good news of a daughter, his face will be dark as he grieves. (58) He will hide from his people because of the evil news he received. Should he keep it in shame or bury[2131] it in the ground? Is their judgment not evil? (59) Those who do not believe in the hereafter have a bad example, and Allah has the highest example. He is mighty and wise.[2132] (60) If Allah were to punish men for their wickedness, he would not leave any living creature on it, [2133] but he gives them a specified lifespan. When their lifespan is up, they cannot postpone or advance it even one hour.[2134] (61) They ascribe what they hate to Allah, and their tongues describe a lie, that they have the best reward. No doubt they will hasten to hellfire. (62) By

---

[2126] Tawrah, Isaiah 45:12, Zabur, Psalms 24:1, 89:11, Injil, Hebrews 1:10

[2127] Or Religion

[2128] Tawrah, Joshua 24:14, 1 Samuel 12:23-24

[2129] Injil, James 1:17

[2130] Or being ungrateful for

[2131] or hide

[2132] Tawrah, Job 9:4, Proverbs 2:6, Jeremiah 9:23-24, Injil, 1 Corinthians 1:21-25, Romans 16:27

[2133] The injustice/wickedness, disbelief/ungratefulness, evil, unrighteousness/sin, or lostness of mankind is mentioned in a number of verses in the Qur'an as well as in the previous books. Injustice or wickedness: 2:57, 3:117,135, 4:64,97, 7:160,177, 9:70, 10:44, 11:101, 14:34,45, 16:33,61,118, 29:40, 30:9, 33:72, 34:19, 35:32, 43:76, 65:1, Tawrah, Genesis 6:5, Job 25:4, Injil, Acts 3:26, disbelief or ungratefulness: 14:34, 17:67, 22:66, 42:48, 43:15, 80:17, Injil, Hebrews 3:19, Evil: 12:53, Tawrah, Jeremiah 17:9, Injil, Matthew 15:19, Mark 7:21, unrighteousness or sin: 91:8, Tawrah, 1 Kings 8:46, Ecclesiastes 7:20, Injil, Romans 3:9-19, 5:12, lostness: 103:2, Tawrah, Jeremiah 50:6, Injil, Luke 19:10, Romans 3:23, 6:23

[2134] Injil, Matthew 6:27, Luke 12:25

## Chapter 16

Allah, we have sent messengers to nations before you[MS], and Satan made their deeds seem fair to them. He is their helper today. They will have painful torment.[2135] (63) We only revealed the book to you[MS] to clarify to them what they differed about, and as guidance and mercy to believing people. (64) Allah sent rain[2136] down from the sky, and with it revived the earth[2137] after it had died. That is a sign for people who hear. (65) There is a lesson for you[MP] in the cattle. We quench your[MP] thirst with what is in their[2138] bellies, between the feces and the blood: pure milk,[2139] delicious to those who drink. (66) From the fruit of the palm tree and grapes, you[MP] get intoxicants[2140] and good provision. That is a sign for people who comprehend. (67) Your[MS] Lord inspired the bees[MS], "Make[FS][2141] houses in the mountains, trees and what they build. (68) Eat[FS] from all the fruits, and walk[FS] in the easy paths of your[FS] Lord." He will make drinks of differing kinds come from their bellies which heal people.[2142] That is a sign for people who consider. (69)
\*\*\*

Allah created you[MP], then will make you[MP] die. Some of you[MP] will be returned to the worst part of life, so that they do not know anything any more. Allah is all-knowing[2143] and all-powerful.[2144] (70)
\*\*\*

Allah prefers some of you[MP] over others in provision. Those he prefers do return their provision to the slaves they[MP] own and thus make them equal. Do they deny Allah's blessings? (71) Allah

---

[2135] For "torment" here and in verses 85, 88, 94, 104, 106, and 117, see Tawrah, Isaiah 50:11, Injil, Matthew 18:34, 25:41,46, Luke 16:23-28, Revelation 20:15.

[2136] Tawrah, Deuteronomy 28:12, Job 5:10, Joel 2:23, Zabur, Psalms 68:9, Injil, Matthew 5:45

[2137] Tawrah, Isaiah 55:10

[2138] Cattle" is feminine in Arabic and "their" is masculine. There may be a different meaning.

[2139] Tawrah, Exodus 3:8

[2140] Tawrah, Ecclesiastes 2:3

[2141] "Bees" is masculine and "Make" is feminine. There may be a different meaning.

[2142] Tawrah, Exodus 3:8, Proverbs 24:13

[2143] Tawrah, 1 Samuel 16:7, 1 Chronicles 28:9, Zabur, Psalms 44:21, Injil, Luke 16:15, Romans 8:27, Acts 15:8, 1 John 3:20

[2144] Tawrah, Job 42:2

## Chapter 16

made spouses from yourselves[MP],[2145] and made children[2146] and grandchildren[2147] for you[MP] from your[MP] spouses.[2148] He gave you[MP] good things. Will they believe in what is vain, and be ungrateful[2149] for Allah's blessings? (72) They worship other gods besides Allah, which cannot give any provision from the heavens or the earth. They are unable.[2150] (73) Do not make proverbs about Allah. Allah knows and you[MP] do not know.[2151] (74) **14B2** Allah makes a proverb of a slave who is owned and cannot do anything. Another person we provided for well, and he donates from it in secret[2152] and in public. Are they the same? Praise be to Allah. Most of them do not know. (75) Allah gives a proverb of two men. One of them is dumb and can do nothing; he is totally dependant on his master; wherever he sends him, he gets nothing. Is he equal to one who promotes justice[2153] and is on the straight path?[2154] (76)
\*\*\*

The unseen things of the heavens and the earth are Allah's,[2155] and the hour[2156] is a twinkling of an eye[2157] or less. Allah can do anything.[2158] (77)
\*\*\*

Allah brought you[MP] forth from your[MP] mothers' wombs,[2159] knowing nothing. He gave you[MP] hearing, sight, and hearts, so that you[MP] may give thanks.[2160] (78) Do they not see the birds,[2161]

---

[2145] Tawrah, Genesis 2:21-22
[2146] or sons
[2147] Zabur, Psalms 128:6
[2148] Injil, Acts 17:26
[2149] Or disbelieving.
[2150] Tawrah, Isaiah 45:20, Zabur, Psalms 115:4-7
[2151] Tawrah, Ecclesiastes 5:2, Isaiah 55:8-9
[2152] Injil, Matthew 6:1-4
[2153] Injil, Luke 12:42-46
[2154] Here and in verse 121, see glossary for more details, and notes on 3:51, 6:153, 19:36, 36:61, and 43:64 on what the straight path is.
[2155] Tawrah, Isaiah 45:12, Zabur, Psalms 24:1, 89:11, Injil, Hebrews 1:10
[2156] Injil, Revelation 14:7
[2157] Injil, 1 Corinthians 15:52
[2158] Tawrah, Job 42:2, Isaiah 14:27, Daniel 4:35, Injil, Matthew 19:26, Mark 10:27, Luke 1:37
[2159] Zabur, Psalms 139:13-14
[2160] Injil, 1 Thessalonians 5:18
[2161] Injil, Matthew 6:26

whose domain is the air of the sky.[2162] Only Allah can catch them.[2163] Those are signs for people who believe. (79) Allah made your[MP] houses dwellings, and made animal skins houses that you[MP] carry lightly the day you[MP] emigrate and the day you[MP] dwell,[2164] and of their wool, camel fur, and animal hair, furniture and household goods[2165] for a while. (80) Out of what Allah created for you[MP], he made shade, shelters in the mountains, garments to protect you[MP] from the heat,[2166] garments to protect you[MP] in battle. Thus he completes his blessings on you[MP], so that you[MP] may submit.[2167] (81) If they turn away, your[MS] [only] responsibility is to proclaim clearly. (82) They know Allah's blessings, yet deny them.[2168] Most of them are disbelievers.[2169] (83) On the day we send a witness from every nation, disbelievers will not be given permission or received favorably.[2170] (84) When the wicked see the torment, it will not be lightened for them, nor will they be given more time.[2171] (85) When the idolaters see the gods they worshiped, they will say, "Our Lord, these are the ones we used to pray to besides you[MS]." They countered, "You[MP] are liars." (86) They will ask for amnesty with Allah on that day, and what they invented will go astray from them. (87) We will greatly increase the torment of disbelievers who blocked Allah's path[2172] for their corruption. (88) On that day, we'll send a witness against every nation from among them. We brought you[MS] as a witness against these. We revealed the book to you[MS] as an explanation for everything, guidance, mercy, and good news for those who submit. (89) **14B3** Allah commands justice, good deeds, and giving to relatives. He forbids promiscuity,[2173] vice, and

---

[2162] Tawrah, Proverbs 30:19
[2163] Them is for thinking beings. Possibly the birds are being considered representatives of creation.
[2164] Or the day you travel and the day you set up tents
[2165] Or enjoyment
[2166] Tawrah, Isaiah 25:4
[2167] Injil, James 4:7. For "submit" here and in verses 89 and 102, some translators do not translate this. See glossary for more details.
[2168] Injil, Romans 1:21
[2169] or unthankful
[2170] or be given a chance to repent
[2171] Injil, Matthew 25:41
[2172] Here and in verse 94, see Injil, Matthew 23:13, Luke 11:52.
[2173] Or lewdness, adultery or abomination

## Chapter 16

prostitution.[2174] He warns you[MP] so that you[MP] may remember. (90) Keep Allah's covenant when you[MP] make it and do not break your oaths after, you[MP] confirm them.[2175] You[MP] make Allah your[MP] guarantor. Allah knows your[MP] deeds. (91) Do not be like the woman who breaks her thread into fibers after it has been strongly spun. You[MP] take your[MP] oaths falsely among yourselves[MP], because one nation is more numerous than another nation. Allah tests you[MP] with this, and will clarify your[MP] differences for you[MP] on the day of resurrection. (92) If Allah had willed, he would have made you[MP] one nation, but he leads astray those he wills and guides those he wills. You[MP] will be questioned about your[MP] deeds. (93) Do not swear falsely among yourselves[MP], or a foot may slip[2176] after being firm, and you[MP] would taste evil for blocking Allah's path, and get great torment. (94) Do not sell[MP] Allah's covenant for a small price. What Allah has is better for you[MP], if you[MP] only knew. (95) Your[MP] possessions will vanish,[2177] and what Allah has is eternal. We will reward those who endure[2178] for the best of what they did. (96) We will revive every male or female believer who does righteous deeds to a good life and reward them for the best of what they did. (97) When you[MS] read[2179] the Qur'an,[2180] ask[MS] Allah's protection from damned Satan.[2181] (98) He has no authority over believers who trust in their Lord.[2182] (99) His authority is over those who have turned to him as a helper, and the idolaters. (100) If we replace one sign[2183] instead of another sign, Allah knows what he

---

[2174] Or insolence

[2175] Tawrah, Numbers 30:2

[2176] Zabur, Psalms 94:18, 119:133

[2177] Injil, 2 Corinthians 4:16-18, Matthew 6:19-21

[2178] See "endure" in glossary, here and in verses 110, 126 twice, and 127 twice.

[2179] This word can mean only read, not recite. It is in the masculine singular, referring to Muhammad (ﷺ), and is one of the clearest of many verses that show that he could read.

[2180] Or recitation. See note at 7:157. See glossary for more details.

[2181] Contrary to using "In the name of Allah, the most gracious and Merciful," before reading the Qur'an, as some do, the Qur'an here clearly tells what people should say before they read the Qur'an: "I seek protection from damned Satan."

[2182] Injil, John 14:30,19:11, Matthew 28:18, Mark 6:7, Luke 10:19, Hebrews 2:14-15, 1 John 4:4

[2183] Or verse, here and in verses 104 and 105. Arabic /ayat/. See glossary for more details.

## Chapter 16

reveals. They said, "You<sup>MS</sup> are an inventor." Most of them do not know. (101) Say<sup>MS</sup>, "The Holy Spirit truly revealed it from your<sup>MS</sup> Lord to establish the believers, and as guidance and good news to those who submit. (102) We know that they say, "A human being taught him." The language of the one they wickedly refer to is foreign, and this is a clear Arabic language. (103) Allah does not guide those who do not believe in Allah's signs. They will have painful torment. (104) Those who do not believe in Allah's signs invent lies. They are liars. (105) Those who disbelieve in Allah after believing in him, except those whose hearts are at peace in faith but are compelled, and freely proclaim disbelief will have Allah's wrath and great torment. (106) That is because they loved this world more than the hereafter. Allah does not guide disbelieving people. (107) Allah has sealed their hearts, their hearing, and their sight. They are unaware.[2184] (108) No doubt in the hereafter, they will be lost. (109) And then your<sup>MS</sup> Lord, to those who emigrated after they were tested, then struggled and endured, your<sup>MS</sup> Lord will be forgiving and merciful. (110) **14B4** On that day, every soul will dispute on its own behalf. Every soul will be repaid for its deeds. They will not be wronged. (111) Allah gives a parable. There was a village that was safe and at peace, and it had bountiful provision from everywhere. They were ungrateful[2185] for Allah's blessings, so Allah made it taste a garment of hunger and fear for their deeds. (112) A messenger from among themselves came to them, and they rejected him, so torment overtook them[2186] for their wickedness. (113) So eat<sup>MP</sup> what we provided you<sup>MP</sup> that is permitted and delicious. Give<sup>MP</sup> thanks for Allah's blessings if you<sup>MP</sup> worship him. (114) Animal carcasses, blood, pork, and food offered to idols are forbidden[2187] to you<sup>MP</sup>. If anyone is compelled unwillingly and not maliciously, Allah is forgiving and merciful. (115) Do not lie in your<sup>MP</sup> tongues' description by saying, "This is permitted, and this is forbidden," in order to invent lies about Allah. Those who invent lies about Allah do not prosper. (116) They get a little enjoyment, but will have painful torment. (117) We forbade what we told you to the

---

[2184] Tawrah, Isaiah 6:10, Injil, Matthew 13:14-15
[2185] or unthankful
[2186] Tawrah, 1 Samuel 16:14
[2187] Injil, Acts 15:29

## Chapter 16

Jews[2188] beforehand. We did not wrong them, but they wronged themselves. (118) And then your[MS] Lord, to those who did evil in ignorance and later repented and made amends, your[MS] Lord will be forgiving and merciful. (119) Ibrahim[2189] was a nation devout[2190] to Allah and monotheistic. He was not a polytheist. (120) He gave thanks for his blessings. He chose him and guided him to the straight path. (121) We gave him good deeds in this world. He will be righteous in the hereafter. (122) Then we inspired you[MS], "Follow[MS] Ibrahim's spiritual path[2191] as a monotheist. He was not a polytheist. (123) The sabbath[2192] was made for those[2193] who differed about it. Your[MS] Lord will judge among them on the day of resurrection regarding their differences. (124) Invite[MS] [people] to your[MS] Lord's path with wisdom, good admonition, and argue politely with them. Your[MS] Lord knows well who has gone astray from his path, and who is guided. (125) If you[MP] punish, punish[MP] as you[MP] were punished. But if you[MP] endure it, that is better.[2194] (126) Endure[MS]. Your[MS] endurance is only from Allah. Do not grieve[MS] over them, and do not be[MS] troubled about their scheming. (127) Allah is with the reverent and those who do good. (128)[2195]

---

[2188] Or those who repented and turned back to the truth. This refers to the Jews, probably when they repented after worshiping the golden calf idol (2:54, 92, 7:138, 148-150, Tawrah, Exodus 32).

[2189] Abraham here and in verse 123. See glossary for more details.

[2190] nation is feminine and devout is masculine. The meaning may be "a nation and he was devout"

[2191] Arabic /millah/. See glossary.

[2192] Tawrah, Exodus 20:8-11, 31:13; Isaiah 56:6,7, 58:13,14, 66:22,23; Ezekiel 20:20, Injil, Mathew 12:8, 24:20; Mark 2:27; Luke 23:56

[2193] Injil, Mark 2:27

[2194] Injil, Matthew 10:22, 24:13

[2195] The verses in this chapter that rhyme are put together in paragraphs, separated by ***.

Chapter 17

# Chapter 17 Al-Isra[2196] or Banu Israil[2197]

15A1 In the name of Allah, the most gracious and merciful.[2198] Glory be to him who took his servant by night[2199] from the sacred place of worship[2200] to the farthest place of worship, around which we blessed,[2201] to show him our signs. He hears all and sees all. (1)
***
We gave Musa[2202] the book[2203] and made it[2204] guidance to the people of Israel: "Do not choose any other guardian besides me,[2205] (2) you seed of those we carried along with Nuh.[2206] He was a servant[2207] who gave thanks."[2208] (3) We decreed in the book[2209] for the people of Israel, "You[MP] will cause destruction twice in the land, and you[MP] will be greatly exalted."[2210] (4) When the first [of the destructions][D] happened, we sent against you[MP] our very strong servants,[2211] and they searched through the houses,[2212] as a fulfillment of a promise.[2213] (5) Then we turned things around

---

[2196] Causing of night travel

[2197] The people of Israel. This was the common name of the chapter before 1948.

[2198] Zabur, Psalms 103:8, 145:8. See glossary for more details.

[2199] Injil, Revelation 17:3, Tawrah, Ezekiel 11:1

[2200] Injil, John 4:20-24, Hebrews 8:1-2, 9:24, 10:19-22.

[2201] Zabur, Psalms 65:4

[2202] Moses here and in verse 101 (twice). See glossary for more details.

[2203] Tawrah, Exodus 31:18

[2204] Or him.

[2205] Tawrah, 2 Kings 17:7-18, Jeremiah 25:6, Exodus 20:1-2

[2206] Noah here and in verse 17. See glossary for more details. Tawrah, Genesis 11:10-32, Exodus 32:18

[2207] See glossary.

[2208] Tawrah, Exodus 14:31

[2209] Tawrah, Deuteronomy 28:36-41

[2210] Tawrah, Numbers 24:7

[2211] See glossary for "servant" here and in verses 5, 17, 30, 53, 65, and 96.

[2212] Tawrah, 2 Kings 17:20.

[2213] This may refer to the destruction of Jerusalem in 586 B.C. by the Babylonians, Tawrah, 2 Kings 24:10-16, Jeremiah 44:1-30 25:1-11. The northern part of the people of Israel were taken captive in 722 B.C. by the Assyrians, Tawrah, 2 Kings 17:5-18. The other possibility is that the first destruction is the Babylonian captivity Tawrah, Jeremiah 2:15,

## Chapter 17

against them, and gave you[MP] money and children,[2214] and made you[MF] a more-numerous host.[2215] (6) If you[MP] do good, then you[MP] do good for your[MP] souls',[2216] and if you[MP] do evil, then[2217] for them also. When the promised of the latter happened,[2218] it was that they would vex your[MP] faces, and to enter the place of worship as they entered it the first time,[2219] and utterly destroy what they were proud about.[2220] (7) Perhaps your[MP] Lord will have mercy on you[MP]. If you[MP] return, we will return.[2221] We have made hell a prison for disbelievers.[2222] (8) This recitation[2223] guides to what is straighter, and gives good news to believers who do righteous deeds:[2224] that they have a great reward.[2225] (9) We have prepared painful torment[2226] for those who do not believe in the hereafter. (10) People pray for evil the same way they pray for good. People are in a hurry. (11) We made the night and the day signs[D],[2227] and we erased the sign of the night, and made the sign of the day visible,[2228] so that you[MP] would seek grace from your[MP] Lord, and know the number of the years and the reckoning. We have explained everything in detail. (12) We attached every man's evil

---

3:2,9, 12:11, and the second destruction is the destruction of the temple foretold in Injil, Matthew 24:15, 23:34-36, Mark 13:14.

[2214] Or sons, here and in verse 64.

[2215] Tawrah, Jeremiah 29:6, 10-14.

[2216] Tawrah, Jeremiah 29:5-7.

[2217] i.e. then you do evil

[2218] This probably refers to the destruction of Jerusalem in 70 A.D. by the Romans. Injil, Luke 21:20.

[2219] Tawrah, 2 Chronicles 36:17-19.

[2220] Injil, Matthew 24:15,21, Mark 13:14, Luke 21:20-24

[2221] Tawrah, Zechariah 1:3, Jeremiah 15:19. The meaning could either be returning in repentance, and Allah returning to them, or returning to their sins, in which case, Allah would return to punishing them.

[2222] Injil, Matthew 25:41

[2223] Or qur'an or Qur'an. See glossary for more details.

[2224] Injil, 1 Corinthians 3:8, James 2:14-17, Revelation 19:8

[2225] Injil, Hebrews 10:35

[2226] For "torment" here and in verses 54, 57 (twice), and 58, see Tawrah, Isaiah 50:11, Injil, Matthew 18:34, 25:41,46, Luke 16:23-28, Revelation 20:15.

[2227] Arabic /ayat/. For "sign(s)" here (three times) and in verses 59 (twice) and 98, see glossary.

[2228] Tawrah, Genesis 1:14

## Chapter 17

omen[2229] to his neck, and we will bring out a book[2230] for him on the day of resurrection,[2231] which he will receive opened up. (13) "Read your[MS] book. Your[MS] own soul[2232] is an adequate reckoner against you[MS] today." (14) Whoever is guided is guided for his own soul's gain, and whoever strays, strays to its own loss. No soul carries another's burden.[2233] We would not torment until we sent a messenger. (15) If we had wanted to destroy a village, we would have commanded their rich, and they would have been unbelieving[2234] in it. Then the saying was fulfilled against them, and we destroyed them totally. (16) How many generations we destroyed since Nuh, and your[MS] Lord is adequately aware of and sees his servants' sins. (17) We hastened what is transient to those who want it, giving what we will in it for those we want. Then we put him in hell, roasted, disgraced, and rejected. (18) The efforts of those who want the hereafter and strive toward it rightly as believers will be gratefully accepted. (19) We will assist all of them with some of your[MS] Lord's gift. Your[MS] Lord's gift is not restricted. (20) Look[MS] how we preferred some of them over others.[2235] The hereafter is greater in degree and greater in preference. (21) Do not take another god[2236] with Allah, or you[MS] will be disgraced and forsaken. (22) **15A2** Your[MS] Lord decreed that you[MP] should not worship anyone but him, and to do good to parents,[2237] whether one or both of them grow old with you[MS]. Do not grumble[MS] at them[2238] and do not rebuke them,[2239] but speak to them graciously.[2240] (23) Be humble[2241] to them in mercy, and say,

---

[2229] This word is of uncertain meaning. It literally means flier or bird. Other translations include deeds or actions, fate or destiny, augury, omen, or bird of omen.
[2230] Injil, Revelation 20:15. Probably a book of his works.
[2231] For "day of resurrection" here and in verses 58, 62, and 97, see Tawrah, Daniel 12:2 Injil, Acts 24:15, 1 Corinthians 15:52-54, Revelation 20:11-15
[2232] or You yourself
[2233] Tawrah, Ezekiel 18:20
[2234] Or transgressing or immoral
[2235] Tawrah, Deuternomy 10:15
[2236] Arabic /ilah/ here and in verse 42. See glossary for more details.
[2237] Tawrah, Deuteronomy 5:16
[2238] Injil, Philippians 2:14
[2239] Tawrah, Isaiah 3:5, Injil, 1 Timothy 5:19
[2240] Injil, Ephesians 4:29-32
[2241] Or lower the wing of humility. Injil, 1 Peter 5:5

## Chapter 17

"My Lord, have mercy on them, since they brought me up since childhood." (24) Your[MP] Lord knows what is in your[MP] souls,[2242] if you[MP] are righteous. He is forgiving[2243] to the repentant. (25) Give[MS] relatives, the poor and the sojourners their rights, but do not be wasteful. (26) The wasteful are brothers to devils.[2244] Satan was ungrateful[2245] to his Lord. (27) If you[MS] turn away from them, seeking and hoping for your[MS] Lord's mercy, speak[MS] gently to them. (28) Do not keep your[MS] hand chained[2246] to your[MS] neck, but do not spread it out completely either,[2247] or you[MS] will be blameworthy and destitute. (29) Your[MS] Lord spreads forth or withholds provision to those he wills.[2248] He is aware of and sees his servants. (30) Do not kill[MP] your[MP] children[2249] for fear of poverty. We provide[2250] for them and for you[MP]. Killing them is a grave fault. (31) Stay far from adultery.[2251] It is promiscuity[2252] and a wrong path. (32) Do not kill[MP] anyone[2253] Allah has forbidden, except in truth. We have given authority to the helper[2254] of anyone murdered unjustly,[2255] but let him not be excessive in killing. He will be[2256] aided. (33) Stay far[MP] from an orphan's money until he comes of age, except with the best motives.[2257] Be faithful[MP] to covenants.[2258] Covenants involve responsibility. (34) Give[MP] a full measure when you[MP] measure it,

---

[2242] Tawrah, 1 Samuel 16:7, 1 Chronicles 28:9, Zabur, Psalms 44:21, Injil, Luke 16:15, Romans 8:27, Acts 15:8, 1 John 3:20

[2243] Here and in verse 44, see Zabur, Psalms 103:3, 130:4, Tawrah, Isaiah 43:25, Exodus 34:7, Injil, Acts 26:18.

[2244] Arabic /shayatin/. See glossary for more details. Tawrah, Proverbs 18:9

[2245] Or disbelieving

[2246] i.e. as a miser

[2247] i.e. wastefully

[2248] Zabur, Psalms 111:5, 145:16

[2249] Or sons

[2250] Tawrah, Genesis 45:11

[2251] Tawrah, Exodus 20:14, Injil, 1 Corinthians 6:18.

[2252] Or lewdness, adultery or abomination

[2253] Tawrah, Exodus 20:13

[2254] Or, "the avenger of blood."

[2255] Tawrah, Numbers 35:12-27

[2256] or, "it is" (aided by the law)

[2257] Tawrah, Exodus 22:22

[2258] Tawrah, Leviticus 19:12, Numbers 30:2, Deuteronomy 23:21, Ecclesiastes 5:4-5

## Chapter 17

and weigh<sup>MP</sup> with a just balance.[2259] That is better and the best explanation. (35) Do not follow<sup>MS</sup> what you<sup>MS</sup> know nothing about. Hearing, sight, and the heart are responsibilities.[2260] (36) Do not walk<sup>MS</sup> insolently in the land. You<sup>MS</sup> will not pierce the earth, nor will you<sup>MS</sup> be as tall as the mountains. (37) Your<sup>MS</sup> Lord hates the evil of all of those.[2261] (38) That is part of the wisdom your<sup>MS</sup> Lord has inspired you<sup>MS</sup> with. Do not take<sup>MS</sup> another god[2262] in addition to Allah,[2263] or you<sup>MS</sup> will go to hell, blameworthy and rejected. (39) Has your<sup>MP</sup> Lord preferred you<sup>MP</sup> by giving you<sup>MP</sup> sons, while he chose female angels? Your<sup>MP</sup> saying is serious. (40) We have explained in this recitation,[2264] so that they would remember, and it only makes them flee further. (41) Say<sup>MS</sup>, "If only he had other gods with him, as they say, they would have sought the path of the owner of the throne.[2265] (42) May he be glorified and highly exalted[2266] above what they say! (43) The seven heavens, the earth, and all in them glorify him.[2267] Everything glorifies and praises him, but you<sup>MP</sup> do not understand their glorifying. He is gentle[2268] and forgiving." (44) When you<sup>MS</sup> read the Qur'an,[2269] we make a curtain and a covering between you<sup>MS</sup> and those who do not believe in the hereafter. (45) We have put a veil over their hearts,[2270] lest[2271] they should understand, and have plugged their ears.[2272] When you<sup>MS</sup> remember your<sup>MS</sup> Lord in the Qur'an[2273] alone, they

---

[2259] Tawrah, Deuteronomy 25:15, Proverbs 11:1
[2260] literally, asked about
[2261] Tawrah, Proverbs 6:16-17
[2262] Arabic /ilah/. See glossary for more details.
[2263] Tawrah, Exodus 20:3
[2264] Or Qur'an or qur'an here and in verses 78 (twice), 88, and 89. See glossary for more details.
[2265] Zabur, Psalms 9:4,7, 11:4, 47:8
[2266] Zabur, Psalms 57:5,11
[2267] Zabur, Psalms 148:1-14
[2268] Zabur, Psalms 45:4, 145:17, Injil, Matthew 11:29, Galatians 5:22
[2269] Or recitation here and in verses 46, 60, 82, and 106. See note at 7:157. The word "read" here means only read, not recite. This clearly shows Muhammad (s) could read. See glossary for more details.
[2270] Injil, 2 Corinthians 3:15
[2271] Or so
[2272] Tawrah, Isaiah 6:10
[2273] Or recitation. See glossary for more details.

turn their backs, fleeing.²²⁷⁴ (46) We know very well how they listen when they listen to you^MS, and their secret conspiracies. The wicked say, "You^MP are merely following a bewitched man." (47) See how they tell you^MS proverbs and go astray. They will not be able to reach the path. (48) They say, "When we are bones and dust, will we be resurrected as a new creation?²²⁷⁵ (49) 15A3 Say^MS, "Be rocks, iron, (50) or something worse in your^MP hearts."²²⁷⁶ They will say, "Who will restore us?" Say^MS, "He who created you^MP the first time." They will wag their heads at you^MS and say, "When will that be?" Say^MS, "It may be soon,²²⁷⁷ (51) on a day he calls you^MP, and you^MP will answer with his praise. You^MP will imagine that you^MP remained only a short time." (52) Tell my servants to say what is better. Satan incites evil among them.²²⁷⁸ Satan is a clear enemy to man.²²⁷⁹ (53) Your^MP Lord knows you^MP best. If he wills, he will have mercy on you^MP, and if he wills, he will torment you^MP.²²⁸⁰ We did not send you^MS to be responsible for them. (54) Your^MS Lord knows everyone in the heavens and the earth. We preferred some prophets above others,²²⁸¹ and we brought Dawud²²⁸² the Zabur.²²⁸³ (55) Say^MS, "Pray^MP to those you^MP claim besides him, but who cannot protect you^MP from evil, or turn it away."²²⁸⁴ (56) Those they pray to want to be close to their Lord. Which of them is closer? They hope for his mercy, and fear his torment. Your^MS Lord's torment is fearsome.²²⁸⁵ (57) We will destroy every village before the day of resurrection, or torment it severely. That is written in the book. (58) What is to prevent us from sending signs, except that the ancient peoples rejected them? We brought Thamud²²⁸⁶ the female camel visibly, and they mistreated it. We send all signs to frighten. (59) When we tell

---

²²⁷⁴ Injil, Titus 1:14
²²⁷⁵ Injil, 1 Corinthians 15:42-54, 2 Corinthians 5:17
²²⁷⁶ Injil, Mark 8:17
²²⁷⁷ Injil, Revelation 22:7
²²⁷⁸ Tawrah, 1 Chronicles 21:1
²²⁷⁹ Injil, Revelation 12:9
²²⁸⁰ Injil, Romans 9:18
²²⁸¹ Injil, Luke 1:70. Here Allah prefers some prophets over others. See 2:136, which talks about distinguishing.
²²⁸² David. See glossary for more details.
²²⁸³ Psalms. See glossary for more details.
²²⁸⁴ Tawrah, 1 Kings 18:21-40, Zabur, Psalms 115:6-8, 135:15-17
²²⁸⁵ Tawrah, Isaiah 2:10, 19, 21
²²⁸⁶ A name of a tribe

## Chapter 17

you[MS] that your[MS] Lord surrounds people, we only made the vision we showed you[MS] and the damned tree[2287] in the Qur'an also a test for people. We frighten them, but it only makes them transgress more. (60) When we told the angels, "Bow down[2288] to Adam,"[2289] they bowed down, except for Iblis.[2290] He said, "Should I bow down to one you[MS] made out of clay?"[2291] (61) He said, "What do you[MS] think? You[MS] honored this one more than me. If you[MS] give me more time, until the day of resurrection, I will master all but a few of his seed."[2292] (62) He said, "Go. You[MS] and those of them that follow you[MS] will have hell as your[MP] full reward.[2293] (63) Stir up those of them you[MS] can with your[MS] voice, bring your[MS] horses and foot-soldiers against them, share[MS] money and children with them, and give[MS] them promises." What Satan promises them is deceitful. (64) You[MS] have no authority[2294] over my servants. Your[MS] Lord is an adequate guardian. (65) Your[MP] Lord propels ships on the sea[2295] for you[MP] so you[MP] would seek his grace. He is merciful[2296] to you[MP]. (66) If harm touches you[MP] on the sea, those you[MP] pray to besides him go astray.[2297] When he rescues you[MP] and gets you[MP] to land,[2298] you[MP] turn away. Man is ungrateful.[2299] (67)

---

[2287] Tawrah, Genesis 3:17, Injil, Mark 11:21, Galatians 3:13
[2288] Zabur, Psalms 97:7, Injil, Hebrews 1:6
[2289] For Adam here and in verse 70, see glossary for more details.
[2290] The devil. See glossary for more details.
[2291] Tawrah, Genesis 2:7
[2292] Injil, Matthew 22:14
[2293] Injil, Matthew 25:41
[2294] Injil, John 14:30,19:11, Matthew 28:18, Mark 6:7, Luke 10:19, Hebrews 2:14-15, 1 John 4:4
[2295] Tawrah, Proverbs 30:19
[2296] See glossary for more details on "merciful."
[2297] Tawrah, Jonah 1:5
[2298] Zabur, Psalms 107:23-28
[2299] The injustice/wickedness, disbelief/ungratefulness, evil, unrighteousness/sin, or lostness of mankind is mentioned in a number of verses in the Qur'an as well as in the previous books. Injustice or wickedness: 2:57, 3:117,135, 4:64,97, 7:160,177, 9:70, 10:44, 11:101, 14:34,45, 16:33,61,118, 29:40, 30:9, 33:72, 34:19, 35:32, 43:76, 65:1, Tawrah, Genesis 6:5, Job 25:4, Injil, Acts 3:26, disbelief or ungratefulness: 14:34, 17:67, 22:66, 42:48, 43:15, 80:17, Injil, Hebrews 3:19, Evil: 12:53, Tawrah, Jeremiah 17:9, Injil, Matthew 15:19, Mark 7:21, unrighteousness or sin: 91:8, Tawrah, 1 Kings 8:46, Ecclesiastes 7:20, Injil, Romans 3:9-19, 5:12, lostness: 103:2, Tawrah, Jeremiah 50:6, Injil, Luke 19:10, Romans 3:23, 6:23

## Chapter 17

Are you[MP] safe from him swallowing you[MP] up by the shore or sending a sand storm against you[MP]? Then you[MP] would find no helper for yourselves[MP]. (68) Or are you[MP] safe from his returning you[MP] in it again, and him sending a gale-force wind against you[MP], and drowning you[MP] for your[MP] disbelief? Then you[MP] would find no helper for yourselves[MP] from us.[2300] (69) 15A4 We honor the sons of Adam, carry them on land and sea, provide them with good things, and definitely prefer them over much of what we created.[2301] (70) On that day, we will call all people with their leaders. Those who are given their books in their right hands will read their books and will not be wronged at all. (71) Those in this [world] who are blind[2302] will be blind in the hereafter, and further gone astray from the path. (72) They almost tempted you[MS] away from what we inspired you[MS] with, in order to invent another one against us. Then they would have taken you[MS] as a friend. (73) If we had not made you[MS] firm, you[MS] would almost have trusted in them a little. (74) Then we would have made you[MS] taste twice the life and twice the death.[2303] Then you[MS] would have found no savior from us.[2304] (75) They almost incited you[MS] away from the land, to expel you[MS] from it. Then they would only have remained a little while after you[MS], (76) as the custom of our messengers we sent before you[MS], and you[MS] will not find any change in our customs. (77) Perform the prayers as the sun declines until the beginning of night, and the recitation of the dawn. The recitation of the dawn is witnessed. (78) Get[MS] up at night with it as something beyond your[MS] duty.[2305] Your[MS] Lord may resurrect you[MS] to a praised position. (79) Say[MS], "My Lord, make me enter righteously,[2306] and make me go out righteously.[2307] Give me saving authority from yourself[MS]." (80) Say[MS], "Truth has come and vanity has vanished. Vanity is perishable."[2308] (81) The part of the

---

[2300] Tawrah, Job 14:13
[2301] Tawrah, Genesis 1:26-28
[2302] This probably refers to spiritual blindness. Tawrah, Isaiah 6:9-10, Injil, Matthew 13:14-15
[2303] Tawrah, Isaiah 40:2
[2304] Tawrah, Isaiah 43:11, Hosea 13:4, Injil, Hebrews 10:26
[2305] Zabur, Psalms 119:62, 164, Injil, Matthew 26:41
[2306] Injil, 2 Peter 1:11
[2307] Zabur, Psalms 121:8
[2308] Tawrah, Ecclesiastes 1:14

## Chapter 17

Qur'an we reveal[2309] is healing and mercy to believers, and it gives the wicked only loss. (82) If we give blessings to people, they turn away and go aside.[2310] If evil touches them, they despair. (83) Say[MS], "Everyone works in his own way. Your[MP] Lord knows very well who is best guided on the path." (84)

\*\*\*

They ask you[MS] about the spirit. Say[MS], "The spirit is by my Lord's command.[2311] You[MP] were given only a little knowledge. (85) If we willed, we would take away what we revealed to you[MS]. Then you[MS] would not find anything in it to protect yourself[MS] from us (86) except for mercy from your[MS] Lord. His grace toward you[MS] was great. (87) If mankind and the jinns[2312] joined together to produce a recitation like this one, they would not be able to bring one like it, even if they helped each other. (88) We have explained every proverb to people[2313] in this recitation. Most people refused everything except disbelief. (89) They said, "We will not believe you[MS] until you[MS] cause a spring to break forth from the ground,[2314] (90) or until you[MS] have a garden of dates and grapes, and you[MS] make rivers break forth through it, (91) or until you[MS] make part of the sky fall, as you[MS] claimed, or until you[MS] bring Allah and the angels as guarantors, (92) or until you[MS] have an embellished house, or until you[MS] ascend to the sky. We will not believe in your[MS] ascent until you[MS] bring us a book we can read." Say[MS], "May my Lord be glorified! Am I something besides a man as a messenger?" (93) What prevents people from believing when guidance has come to them, except that they said, "Has Allah sent a man as a messenger?" (94) Say[MS], "If there were angels walking peacefully on the earth, we would have sent an angel down from heaven to them as a messenger." (95) Say[MS], "Allah is an adequate witness between me and you[MP]. He is aware of and sees his servants." (96) He whom Allah guides is guided,[2315] and you[MS] will

---

[2309] This seems to mean that the whole Qur'an is with Allah, and he revealed part of it to Muhammad (s).
[2310] Injil, Luke 16:19-31
[2311] The meaning could be, "The spirit is my Lord's business." Injil, John 14:26
[2312] Or demons. See glossary for more details.
[2313] Tawrah, Proverbs 1:2-6
[2314] Tawrah, Exodus 17:6
[2315] Tawrah, Isaiah 48:17

## Chapter 17

not find any helpers for those he leads astray[2316] besides him. We will gather[2317] them on the day of resurrection, blind, deaf and dumb on their faces. Their abode will be hell. Whenever it dies down, we will increase the burning fire for them. (97) That is their payment, for they disbelieved in our signs[2318] and said, "If we are bones and dust, will we be resurrected in a new creation?" (98) **15B1** Have they not seen that Allah, who created the heavens and the earth,[2319] is able to create similar ones and give them an undoubtable lifespan. The wicked refuse everything except disbelief. (99) Say[MS], "If you[MP] owned storehouses of my Lord's mercy, you[MS] would have held back for fear of overspending." People are stingy. (100) We gave Musa[2320] nine miraculous signs,[2321] so ask the people of Israel, because he came to them. Pharaoh told him, "I think you[MS] are bewitched, Musa."[2322] (101) He said, "You[MS] know that only the Lord of the heavens and the earth has revealed these as evidence. Pharaoh, I think you[MS] are lost." (102) He wanted to provoke them out of the land, so we drowned him and everyone that was with him.[2323] (103) We told the people of Israel after him, "Dwell in the land. When the promise of the hereafter comes, we will bring the whole crowd of you[MP].[2324] (104) We truly revealed it; it was truly revealed. We sent you[MS] only as a bearer of good news and a warner. (105) We divided[2325] the Qur'an so that you[MS] could read[2326] it to people

---

[2316] Injil, 2 Thessalonians 2:11, Tawrah, 2 Samuel 22:27, 1 Kings 22:20-23, Ezekiel 14:9

[2317] Tawrah, Joel 3:11-14, Zephaniah 3:8, Injil, Matthew 25:32, John 15:6, Revelation 16:16

[2318] Arabic /ayat/ here and in verse 101. See glossary for more details.

[2319] Tawrah, Genesis 1:1, Isaiah 42:5, 45:18

[2320] Moses. See glossary for more details.

[2321] 79:20 talks about the greatest sign, which would make a total of ten. This corresponds to the ten signs mentioned in the Tawrah, Exodus 7-12. In the Qur'an, 7:107,108, 130, and 133 describe many of these signs. The last sign, probably the same as the "greatest sign" mentioned both in 7:133 and in the Tawrah, Exodus 11:4-5, 12:23,24,29,30 is the blood. The Exodus passages gives the details.

[2322] Tawrah, Exodus 7-8

[2323] Tawrah, Exodus 14:26-28

[2324] Injil, Romans 11:26

[2325] Or explained

[2326] Contrary to common beliefs, the Qur'an here clearly affirms that Muhammad (s) could read. There are a number of instances where

slowly. We truly revealed it. (106) Say<sup>MS</sup>, "Believe in it or do not believe in it. Those who have been given knowledge before it fall down, bowing down on their faces when it is read to them." (107) They say, "May our Lord be glorified! Our Lord's promise is fulfilled." (108) They fall down on their faces, weep, and it makes them more humble. (109) Say<sup>MS</sup>, "Pray to Allah, or pray to the most gracious. Whatever you<sup>MP</sup> call him, he has the beautiful names. Do not perform your<sup>MS</sup> prayers too loudly, and do not whisper<sup>MS</sup> them. Aim<sup>MS</sup> for a path between them." (110) Say<sup>MS</sup>, "Praise be to Allah, who has not chosen a boy,[2327] and who has no partner in his kingdom. He has no helper in humility. Exalt him greatly!" (111)

---

Muhammad (s) is told to read/recite, using a different Arabic word (5:27, 7:175, 10:71, 18:27, 26:69, 27:92, 29:45), but the word used in this verse and 16:98, 17:45, and 17:106, translated "read," can only mean "read." For a discussion of the verses usually misinterpreted to mean he was illiterate, see the note on 7:157.

[2327] The Qur'an, Tawrah, and Injil all reject the idea that Allah chose a human to be a son to him.

# Chapter 18 Al-Kahf[2328]

In the name of Allah, the most gracious and merciful.[2329] Praise be to Allah, who revealed the book to his servant, and did not make it crooked, (1) [but][2330] straight,[2331] to warn of severe vengeance from him, to give good news to believers who do righteous deeds,[2332] that they have a good reward,[2333] (2) where they will remain forever,[2334] (3) and to warn those who say, "Allah has chosen a boy."\[2335] (4) They and their ancestors have no knowledge of him. A grievous word came out of their mouths. They say only lies. (5) You[MS] may fret yourself[MS] with sorrow, following them, if they do not believe in this saying. (6) We made everything on earth as ornaments[2336] for it, to test which of them has better works. (7) We will make everything on it dry ground.[2337] (8) Have you[MS] considered that those in the cave[2338] with the tablet[2339] were one of our wondrous signs?[2340] (9) The young men took refuge in the cave. They said, "Our Lord, give us your[MS] mercy, and prepare us right guidance in our matter." (10) So we struck[2341] their ears in the cave for many years. (11) Then we resurrected them, so we would know which of the parties[p] could better figure how long they had remained. (12) We tell you[MS] their

---

[2328] the cave
[2329] Zabur, Psalms 103:8, 145:8. See glossary for more details.
[2330] or, " It is"
[2331] Zabur, Psalms 19:9
[2332] Injil, 1 Corinthians 3:8, James 2:14-17, Revelation 19:8
[2333] Injil, Matthew 25:21-23
[2334] Injil, Matthew 25:46
[2335] The Qur'an, Tawrah, and Injil all reject the idea that Allah chose a human to be a son to him.
[2336] Tawrah, Genesis 1:1-31
[2337] Tawrah, Genesis 1:9-10
[2338] The location of this cave is supposed to be in the city of Efes (ancient Ephesus), in what is now Turkey. Injil, Ephesians 5:14 also mentions a sleeper being raised from the dead.
[2339] There is no general agreement about the meaning of this word. It is from the same root word as "number" but may be the name of the mountain, or some other meaning.
[2340] Arabic /ayat/ here and in verses 17, 105, and 106. See glossary for more details.
[2341] Or "covered" or some other meaning. Arabic /daraba/. See the note on

news in truth. They were young men who believed in their Lord, and we gave them more guidance. (13) We tied up their hearts when they stood up, and they said, "Our Lord is Lord of the heavens and the earth.[2342] We will not pray to any god[2343] except him." That would be saying a lie. (14) They, our people, chose other gods besides him. If only they would bring clear authority for them! Who is more wicked than those who invent lies about Allah?[2344] (15) When you[MP] have separated yourselves from them and from the gods they worship besides Allah, take refuge in the cave, and your[MP] Lord will spread out his mercy and prepare you[MP] comfortably for your[MP] matter. (16) **15B2** You[MS] see the sun when it has risen, rising over their cave on the right, and when it sets, it turns away from them on the left. They are in a gap of it.[2345] That is one of Allah's signs. Those Allah guides are guided,[2346] and those he leads astray[2347] will never find a helper to guide them. (17) You'd[MS] think they were awake, but they were sleeping, and we turn them over on their right and left. Their dog stretches out his legs over the threshold. If you[MS] had looked at them, you[MS] would have turned away from them and fled from them, full of terror. (18) So we resurrected them[2348] so they would question each other. One of them said, "How long did you[MP] remain?" They said, "We remained a day, or part of a day." They said, "Your[MP] Lord knows[2349] exactly how long you[MP] remained. Now send[MP] one of you[MP] with this money of yours[MP] to the city, and let him see what food is the purest, and bring you[MP] provision of it. Let him be kind, and do not let anyone know about you[MP]. (19) If they know about you[MP], they will stone you[MP] or return you[MP] to their spiritual path,[2350] and then you[MP] will not succeed at all." (20) So we disclosed to them so that they would know that Allah's promise is

---

[2342] Tawrah, Deuteronomy 10:14

[2343] Arabic /ilah/ here and in verses 15 and 110 (twice). See glossary for more details.

[2344] These people of the cave were devout believers, and have been honored by Muslims for centuries.

[2345] i.e. the cave

[2346] Zabur, Psalms 73:24

[2347] Injil, 2 Thessalonians 2:11, Tawrah, 2 Samuel 22:27, 1 Kings 22:20-23, Ezekiel 14:9

[2348] Injil, Ephesians 5:14 refers to a sleeper rising from the dead.

[2349] For "knows" here and in verses 22 and 26, see Tawrah, Job 37:16, Isaiah 40:14, Zabur, Psalms 33:13-15, Injil, 1 John 3:20

[2350] Arabic /millah/. See glossary.

## Chapter 18

true, and that there is no doubt of the hour.[2351] When they disputed with each other about their matter, they said, "Build a building over them.[2352] Their Lord well knows who they are."[2353] Those who prevailed over their matter said, "Let's make a place of worship over them." (21) They say, "[They are] three, and their dog is the fourth." They will say, "Five, and their dog is the sixth." They guess at the unseen. They will say, "Seven, and their dog is the eighth." Say[MS], "My Lord knows how many they are." Only a few know of them. Do not debate[MS] about[2354] them, except outwardly. Do not ask[MS] any of them for a religious ruling about them. (22) Do not say[MS] regarding anything, "I will do it tomorrow," (23) but rather: "If Allah wills."[2355] Remember[MS] your[MS] Lord when you[MS] forget, and say, "My Lord may guide me to something more rightly guided." (24) They remained in their cave 309 years.[2356] (25) Say[MS] "Allah well knows how long they remained. He knows the unseen things in the heavens and the earth. How well he sees! How well he hears! They have no protector besides him. He does not share his rule[2357] with anyone." (26) Read[MS] the part of your[MS] Lord's book that you[MS] were inspired with.[2358] There is no substituter of his words,[2359] and you[MS] will not find any refuge besides him. (27) Endure[MS][2360] along with those who pray to their Lord morning and evening, desiring his face.[2361] Do not let your[MS] eyes[D] turn from them or desire[MS] the adornment of

---

[2351] Injil, John 5:28

[2352] This seems to refer to the sanctuary that was built over the cave in Ephesus. It is mentioned by historians from A.D. 550 (72 years before the Hijrah), and is still a place of pilgrimage.

[2353] Injil, 2 Timothy 2:19

[2354] or doubt

[2355] Injil, James 4:15

[2356] Some commentators take this number figuratively, and others literally. The sleepers were probably followers of Christ who were martyred under the persecution of the Roman emperor Decius in about AD 250.

[2357] or judgment

[2358] The Qur'an here says that it (what Muhammad (s) was inspired with) is only part of Allah's book, and thus affirms the previous books.

[2359] For being impossible to change or corrupt Allah's words, see also 10:64, 6:34,115.

[2360] See "endure" in glossary, here and in verses 67, 68, 69, 72, 75, 78, and 82.

[2361] Zabur, Psalms 27:8

## Chapter 18

this world.[2362] Do not obey[MS] those whose hearts we made unaware to remember us, who follow their lusts. They are extravagant.[2363] (28) Say[MS], "Truth is from your[MP] Lord. Whoever wills to, let him believe, and whoever wills to, let him disbelieve. We have prepared hellfire for the wicked. They will be surrounded like a tent. If they call for help, they will be given water like molten brass that will scorch their faces. What an awful drink. It is a bad resting place. (29) We do not lose the reward[2364] of the believers who do well, who do righteous deeds.[2365] (30) They will have heavenly gardens[2366] of Eden, with flowing rivers underneath,[2367] where they will be adorned with gold bracelets and wear green clothes of silk and brocade, reclining in it on couches.[2368] What a wonderful reward and what a good resting place! (31) **15B3** Tell[MS] them the parable about two men. We gave one of them two grape gardens, surrounded them[D] with palms, and put crops between them. (32) Both gardens brought forth food, and the crops did not fail at all.[2369] We made a river flow through them[D], (33) so he had fruit. He told his friend, as he was discussing it with him, "I have more money and stronger people than you[MS] do."[2370] (34) He entered his garden, wronging himself, and said, "I do not think this will ever perish, (35) nor do I think that the hour is coming.[2371] If I am returned to my Lord, I will find something better in exchange for it."[2372] (36) His friend told him as he was discussing it with him, "Have you[MS] been ungrateful to[2373] him who created you[MS] from soil,[2374] then from a drop of semen, and then formed you[MS] into a man? (37) He is Allah, my Lord, and I do not believe in any other gods besides him. (38) When you[MS] entered your[MS] garden, why did you[MS] not say: What Allah has willed! There is no power

---

[2362] Injil, 1 John 2:15-17
[2363] or insolent
[2364] Injil, 2 Timothy 1:12
[2365] Injil, 1 Corinthians 3:8, James 2:14-17, Revelation 19:8
[2366] Arabic /jannah/ here and in verse 107. See glossary for more details.
[2367] Injil, Revelation 22:1-2, Tawrah, Ezekiel 47:12
[2368] or thrones. Injil, Matthew 19:28, Revelation 11:16
[2369] Injil, Luke 12:16-17
[2370] Injil, Luke 12:18
[2371] Injil, Luke 12:19
[2372] Injil, Luke 12:20
[2373] or disbelieving in
[2374] Tawrah, Genesis 2:7

Chapter 18

except in Allah?[2375] If you[MS] look at me, I have less money and fewer children[2376] than you[MS]. (39) Allah may give me a better garden than yours[MS], and send his arrows[2377] on it, and it will become[2378] slippery soil (40) or its water may become subterranean, and you[MS] will not be able to find it." (41) Then his fruit was surrounded, and he wrung his hands over what he had spent on it. It had all fallen down from its trellises. He said, "I wish I had not worshiped gods besides my Lord." (42) There was no one to save him besides Allah, and he could not defend himself. (43) Protection comes only from Allah, the true one. His rewards are better, and he gives the best success. (44) Tell[MS] them the parable of this world. It is like rain[2379] we send down from the sky. The plants on earth are mixed with it, and in the morning it is stubble[2380] that the wind scatters. Allah can do anything.[2381] (45) Money and children are the adornment of this world, but lasting[FP] righteous deeds are better to Allah, and give a better hope. (46) On the day we move the mountains and you[MS] see the earth like a plain, we will gather them, and will not leave anyone behind.[2382] (47) They will be presented to your[MS] Lord in rows. "You[MP] have come to us as we created you[MP] at first, but you[MP] claimed that we would not make this appointment with you[MP]." (48) The book will be placed, and you[MS] will see the wrongdoers in terror of what is in it. They will say, "Woe to us. What is wrong with this book that it records everything, whether small or large?"[2383] They will find all their works there. Your Lord does not wrong anyone. (49) We told the angels to bow down[2384] to Adam,[2385] and all except for Iblis[2386] bowed down; he was a jinn,[2387] and he went against his Lord's

---

[2375] Tawrah, Deuteronomy 8:16-18
[2376] Or sons, here and in verse 46.
[2377] i.e. lightning, or "accounting"
[2378] or "be in the morning"
[2379] Tawrah, Deuteronomy 28:12, Job 5:10, Joel 2:23, Zabur, Psalms 68:9, Injil, Matthew 5:45
[2380] Injil, Matthew 6:30, Zabur, Psalms 1:4
[2381] Tawrah, Job 42:2, Isaiah 14:27, Daniel 4:35, Injil, Matthew 19:26, Mark 10:27, Luke 1:37
[2382] Injil, Revelation 20:11-15
[2383] Injil, Revelation 20:12
[2384] Zabur, Psalms 97:7, Injil, Hebrews 1:6
[2385] See glossary for more details.
[2386] The devil. See glossary for more details.
[2387] Or demon. See glossary for more details.

## Chapter 18

command in unbelief.[2388] Do you[MP] choose him and his seed as helpers instead of me? They are your[MP] enemies. The wicked have made an awful exchange. (50) 15B4 I did not make them witnesses of the creation of the heavens and the earth, nor their own creation. I do not choose those who lead others astray as helpers. (51) On that day, he will say, "Call out to the other gods you[MP] claimed were my partners." They will pray to them, but [the gods] will not answer them. We will cause destruction among them. (52) The wrongdoers will see hellfire, think they will fall into it, and find no escape from it. (53) We have explained every parable to people in this recitation.[2389] Mankind is more argumentative than anything else. (54) Nothing keeps mankind from believing and asking their Lord's forgiveness when guidance has come to them, except for the traditions of the ancients[2390] coming to them or seeing torment[2391] face to face. (55) We only send the messengers as bearers of good news and warners. Disbelievers argue about vain things,[2392] in order to weaken the truth with it. They mock my signs and the warnings they received. (56) Who is more wicked than one who is reminded of his Lord's signs, and yet turns away from them and forgets what his hands have done? We have put coverings over their hearts, lest they should understand, and deafness in their ears.[2393] Even if you[MS] call them to guidance, they will never be guided. (57) Your[MS] Lord is forgiving[2394] and merciful.[2395] If he punished them as they deserve, he would hasten their torment.[2396] But they have an appointment from which they will find no escape. (58) We destroyed those villages when they were wicked[2397] and made an appointment for their destruction.[2398] (59) Musa[2399] told his servant, "I will not

---

[2388] Or transgression or immorality. Tawrah, Isaiah 14:13-14

[2389] Or qur'an or Qur'an. See glossary for more details.

[2390] Injil, Mark 7:1-12. Traditions are probably one of the biggest factors that keep people from true guidance.

[2391] For "torment" here and in verses 58 and 87, see Tawrah, Isaiah 50:11, Injil, Matthew 18:34, 25:41,46, Luke 16:23-28, Revelation 20:15.

[2392] Injil, 1 Timothy 1:6

[2393] Tawrah, Isaiah 6:10, Jeremiah 6:10

[2394] Zabur, Psalms 103:3, 130:4, Tawrah, Isaiah 43:25, Exodus 34:7, Injil, Acts 26:18

[2395] See glossary for more details on "merciful."

[2396] Zabur, Psalm 130:3

[2397] Tawrah, Genesis 19:1-24

[2398] Injil, Matthew 10:15

## Chapter 18

leave until I reach where two seas meet, or I will go on trying for ages. (60) When they⁰ got to where they met, they⁰ had forgotten about their whale, and it chose a path in the sea like a tunnel. (61) When they⁰ passed over it, he told his servant, "Bring us our lunch. We are tired from this journey." (62) He said, "What do you^MS think? When we took refuge in the rock, I forgot the whale, and only Satan made me forget to mention it. It chose an amazing path in the sea." (63) He said, "This is what we wanted." So they⁰ went back, following their⁰ tracks. (64) They⁰ found one of our servants whom we gave our mercy, and whom we had taught ourselves. (65) Musa told him, "Shall I follow you^MS, providing that you^MS teach me according to the right guidance you^MS were taught?" (66) He said, "You^MS will not be able to endure me. (67) How can you^MS endure what you^MS do not know?" (68) He said, "If Allah wills, you^MS will find me enduring, and I will not disobey you^MS at all." (69) He said, "Then if you^MS follow me, do not ask^MS about anything until I mention it to you^MS." (70) So they⁰ went off until they⁰ boarded a ship, and he made a hole in it. He said, "Did you^MS make a hole in it to drown the people on it? You^MS have done a strange thing." (71) He said, "Did I not tell you^MS that you^MS would not be able to endure me?" (72) He said, "Do not punish^MS me for forgetting. Do not make^MS my matter too hard for me." (73) So they⁰ went off until they⁰ found a boy, and he killed him. He said, "Have you^MS killed a pure soul other than in revenge? You^MS have done an awful thing." (74) 16A1 He said, "Did I not tell you^MS that you^MS would not be able to endure me?" (75) He said, "If I ask you^MS about anything further after this, do not go^MS with me any more. You^MS have had enough of my excuses." (76) So they⁰ went off until they⁰ came to people of a village. They⁰ asked the people for food, but they^MP refused to offer them⁰ any. They⁰ found a wall in it almost ready to fall down, and he set it up. He said, "If you^MS want, you^MS could get paid for that." (77) He said, "This means you^MS and I will separate. I will tell you^MS the meaning of what you^MS had to endure. (78) The ship belonged to poor people who worked at sea. I wanted to make it unserviceable because there was a king who took all ships by force. (79) The boy's parents were believers, and we feared that his transgression and disbelief would be troublesome to them, (80) and we wanted their Lord to exchange him for someone better, more holy, and more

---

[2399] Moses here and in verse 66. See glossary for more details.

## Chapter 18

affectionate. (81) The wall was owned by two orphan boys in the city, and there was a treasure of theirs[D] under it. Their father was righteous, and your[MS] Lord wanted them[D] to come of age and dig[D] up their treasure out of your[MS] Lord's mercy. I did not do it of myself. That is the meaning of what you[MS] had to endure." (82) They ask you[MS] about Dhul-Qarnayn.[2400] Say[MS], "I will recite[2401] his fame[2402] for you[MP]." (83) We made him strong on the earth and gave him a way to accomplish everything, (84) so he went his way.[2403] (85) When he reached the sunset, he found it setting in[2404] a muddy spring,[2405] and he found people nearby. We said, "Dhul-Qarnayn, you will either torment or do good to them." (86) He said, "We will torment those who are wicked, and then they will be returned to their Lord, and he will torment them horribly. (87) But believers who do righteous deeds[2406] will have a reward,[2407] the best one, and we will tell them easy commands of ours." (88) So he went his way. (89) When he came to the sunrise, he found it rising on people whom we gave no shade. (90) Thus we knew what was before him. (91) Then he went his way. (92) When he arrived between two dams,[2408] he found people below them who could barely understand what was said. (93) They said, "Dhul-Qarnayn, Yajuj and Majuj[2409] are destroying the earth. Shall we give you[MS] tribute to make a dam[2410] between us and them?" (94) He said, "What my Lord empowers me to do is better. Help me with power[2411] and I will make a wall between you[MP] and them. (95) Bring me lumps of iron." When he made it level between the

---

[2400]This has been identified with Alexander the Great or Cyrus, here and in verses 86 and 94. See glossary for more details. Tawrah, Daniel 11:3, Isaiah 45:1.

[2401] Or read or tell of

[2402] Or reminder.

[2403] Or "followed a path," here and in verses 89 and 92.

[2404] or "over"

[2405] possibly a muddy body of water to the west of the land to which he went

[2406] Here and in verses 107 and 110, see Injil, 1 Corinthians 3:8, James 2:14-17, Revelation 19:8.

[2407] Injil, John 14:1-3

[2408] or obstacles or mountains

[2409] Gog and Magog. See glossary for more details. Tawrah, Ezekiel 38:2, 39:1-6, Injil, Revelation 20:8

[2410] or "obstacle" or "mountain"

[2411] or possibly "forces"

## Chapter 18

cliffs<sup>D</sup>, he said, "Blow." When he made it fire, he said, "Bring me molten brass to pour on it." (96) They were not able to mount it or pierce it. (97) He said, "This is my Lord's mercy. When my Lord's promise comes, he will make it a flat mound. The promise of my Lord is true."[2412] (98) 16A2 On that day, we will leave some of them to roll like waves against others. The trumpet will be blown[2413] and we will gather[2414] them together. (99) On that day, we will show hell to the disbelievers, (100) whose eyes were covered from remembering me, and who could not hear.[2415] (101) Did the disbelievers think that they could take my servants as helpers instead of me? We have prepared hell as the abode of disbelievers. (102) Say<sup>MS</sup>, "Shall we tell you<sup>MP</sup> who will be the most lost in terms of deeds? (103) It is those whose efforts go astray in this world. They think that they do good. (104) The works of those who disbelieve in the signs of their Lord and in meeting him will be in vain. We will not give them any weight on the day of resurrection.[2416] (105) Hell is their reward because of their disbelief and their mocking my signs and my messengers. (106) Believers who do righteous deeds will have heavenly gardens of paradise[2417] as their abode. (107) They will be in it forever,[2418] never desiring a change from it." (108) Say<sup>MS</sup>, "If the sea were ink for the words of my Lord, the sea would run out before my Lord's words run out, even if we replaced it."[2419] (109) Say<sup>MS</sup>, "I am human like you<sup>MP</sup>, and I was inspired that your<sup>MP</sup> god is one god. Whoever wants to meet his Lord should do righteous deeds, and not worship any gods other than his Lord."[2420] (110)

---

[2412] Tawrah, 2 Samuel 22:31
[2413] Injil, 1 Corinthians 15:52
[2414] Tawrah, Joel 3:11-14, Zephaniah 3:8, Injil, Matthew 25:32, John 15:6, Revelation 16:16
[2415] Tawrah, Isaiah 6:9-10, Injil, Matthew 13:14-15
[2416] Tawrah, Daniel 12:2, Zabur, Psalms 62:9, Injil, Acts 24:15, 1 Corinthians 3:12-15,15:52-54, Revelation 20:11-15
[2417] Injil, Revelation 22:1-5, 2:7, Luke 23:43
[2418] Injil, Matthew 25:34-40
[2419] Injil, John 21:25
[2420] Injil, Mark 12:28-31, 1 Timothy 2:5

Chapter 19

# Chapter 19: Mariam[2421]

In the name of Allah, the most gracious and merciful.[2422] KHYAS.[2423] (1)

\*\*\*

A reminder[2424] of your[MS] Lord's mercy[2425] to his servant[2426] Zakariyya[2427] (2) when he called on his Lord in secret.[2428] (3) He said, "My Lord, my bones are weak and my head is gray,[2429] and I have not been disappointed in my prayer[2430] to you[MS], my Lord. (4) I am afraid of heirs[2431] after me, and my wife is barren, so give me a protector from yourself[MS] (5) who will inherit from me and from the family of Yaqub.[2432] My Lord, make him pleasing."[2433] (6) Zakariyya, we give you[MS] good news of a boy whose name is Yahya.[2434] We have not made him a namesake previously.[2435] (7) Say[MS], "Lord, how can I have a boy when my wife is barren, and I am old and decrepit?"[2436] (8) He said, "This is your[MS] Lord's saying: It is easy for me,[2437] since I have created you[MS] beforehand when you[MS] were nothing." (9) He said, "My Lord, give me a

---

[2421] Mary (mother of Jesus)
[2422] Zabur, Psalms 103:8, 145:8. See glossary for more details.
[2423] Here and at the beginning of many chapters there are unvowelled letters of unknown meaning. Numerous theories have been proposed, but there is no agreement on the subject.
[2424] Arabic /dhikr/. See glossary for more details. The Qur'an often refers to the accounts contained in the former books and expounds on them. In this case, the account of Zechariah is found in Injil, Luke 1:5-25, 56-80. Reminder here seems to mean the story of Zakariyya.
[2425] "Mercy" has a different spelling here and in 6 other places. See glossary.
[2426] See glossary.
[2427] Zechariah, here and in verse 7. See glossary for more details. Injil, Luke 1:5
[2428] Injil, Luke 1:13
[2429] Injil, Luke 1:7
[2430] Injil, Luke 1:13
[2431] or masters
[2432] Jacob. See glossary for more details.
[2433] Injil, Luke 1:17
[2434] John the Baptist, here and in verse 12. See glossary for more details.
[2435] Injil, Luke 1:61
[2436] Injil, Luke 1:18
[2437] Injil, Luke 1:37

## Chapter 19

sign."[2438] He said, "Your[MS] sign is that you[MS] will not speak to people[2439] for three complete nights."[2440] (10) So he went out to his people from the sanctuary[2441] and he gestured[2442] to them: Glorify [him] morning and evening. (11) Yahya, take the book with power. As a boy, we gave him judgment, (12) tenderness, and purity from us. He was reverent (13) and obedient to his parents. He was not arrogant or disobedient. (14) Peace be upon him the day he was born,[2443] the day he will die,[2444] and the day he will be resurrected alive.[2445] (15) Remember Mariam[2446] in the book,[2447] when she withdrew from her family to an Eastern place.[2448] (16) She placed a veil away from them; then we sent her our spirit, who appeared to her as a complete man [2449] (17) She said, "I take refuge from you[MS] in the most gracious if you[MS] fear Allah."[2450] (18) He said, "I am truly a messenger of your[FS] Lord to give you[FS] a sinless[2451] boy."[2452] (19) She said, "How can I have a boy when no man has ever touched[2453] me, and I have never been a

---

[2438] Injil, Luke 1:18,20

[2439] Injil, Luke 1:20

[2440] See appendix 1 for other ways this phrase is translated.

[2441] Injil, Luke 1:9-11, This term may refer to the inner sanctuary, the holy of holies.

[2442] or revealed. Luke 1:22

[2443] Injil, Luke 1:57

[2444] Injil, Matthew 14:10

[2445] Injil, 1 Corinthians 15:52; see Injil, Matthew 14:2.

[2446] Mary, mother of Jesus, here and in verse 27. See glossary for more details.

[2447] the account referred to here is found in Injil, Luke 1:26-56, 2:1-20

[2448] see Injil, Luke 1:39-40

[2449] Injil, Luke 1:26-27

[2450] Injil, Luke 1:29-30, Revelation 14:7, Tawrah, Deuteronomy 10:12, Isaiah 29:13

[2451] Isa is called /zakiyyan/ sinless, pure and holy, and that before his birth. In verse 13, Yahya is given purity (related word) sometime after his birth. See Injil, Hebrews 4:15, Luke 1:28-31.

[2452] This begins a section that refers to a number of uniquenesses of Isa. Isa is the only prophet or messenger in the Qur'an who: is sinless (verse 19), was born of a virgin (20), is a sign (21), spoke as an infant (30), was a prophet from birth (30), is blessed /mubarak/ (31), and pronounces peace upon himself (33). For more information about this subject, see notes at 3:36, 4:158, 5:46,110, 43:59.

[2453] i.e. sexually

## Chapter 19

prostitute?"[2454] (20) He said, "This is your[FS] Lord's saying: It is easy for me,[2455] so we will make him a sign[2456] for people, and a mercy from us.[2457] This was a predestined[2458] matter." (21) **16A3** So she became pregnant with him[2459] and went with him to a far place.[2460] (22) Her birth pangs came upon her by a palm tree trunk. She said, "I wish I had died before this and had been totally forgotten." (23) He[2461] called to her[2462] from beneath her, "Do not grieve[FS]. Your[FS] Lord has made a stream underneath you[FS]. (24) Shake[FS] the palm tree trunk toward you[FS], and ripe dates will fall on you[FS] as a harvest. (25) So eat[FS], drink[FS] and be comforted[FS]. If you[FS] see anyone, say[FS]: I have vowed to the most gracious to fast,[2463] and will not speak to anyone today." (26) Then she brought him to her people, carrying him. They said, "Mariam, you[FS] have done something unprecedented. (27) Sister of Harun,[2464] your father was not a bad man, nor was your[FS] mother a prostitute."[2465] (28) So she pointed to him. They said: "How can we talk to a little boy in a

---

[2454] Here and in verse 28, most translations have "unchaste," but the Arabic word is actually much stronger than that. Injil, Luke 1:34. See note on verse 19.

[2455] Injil, Luke 1:37

[2456] See note at verse 19.

[2457] Injil, Luke 1:35

[2458] this word /maqdiy/ "predestined" is used only twice in the Qur'an (19:21,71). The two predestined things are Isa being mercy from Allah and a sign for all men (21) and hellfire (71). Since mercy and hellfire are opposites, it seems the Qur'an is giving men a choice.

[2459] Injil, Luke 1:38

[2460] Injil, Luke 1:39

[2461] He who called is almost certainly the newborn Isa, since she was alone in a far place. Also, it seems Mariam knew he could speak, since she points to him to defen her (vs 29).

[2462] The Qur'an lists other of his miracles in 3:49,52, 5:110,112, 19:19,20, 30-33. Most of the miracles Isa does that are mentioned in the Injil, with the stories behind them, are in the Injil, Matthew 8-11, 14-15,17,21, Mark 1-9,11, Luke 2,4-9,22, John 2,4-6,9,11.

[2463] It seems she was fasting (abstaining) from speaking to people.

[2464] Aaron. See glossary for more details. It is uncertain whether Harun the brother of Musa is meant here. See Injil, Luke 1:36, where Mary is called a relative of Elizabeth, and Injil, Luke 1:5, where Elizabeth is said to be descended from Harun. It is also possible that Harun was the name of her brother as well.

[2465] Injil, Matthew 1:18-19

## Chapter 19

cradle?" (29) He[2466] said,[2467] "I am Allah's servant.[2468] He has given me the book and made me a prophet.[2469] (30) He made me blessed[2470] wherever I am, and commanded me to pray and pay the poor-tax as long as I remain alive,[2471] (31) and to honor my mother. He did not make me arrogant and naughty.[2472] (32) Peace be upon me[2473] the day I was born, the day I will die,[2474] and the day I will be resurrected[2475] alive!" (33)
\*\*\*

This is Isa[2476] the son of Mariam,[2477] the saying of truth, about whom they are doubting. (34) Allah would not take[2478] a son. May he be glorified (above that)! If he determines a matter, He only says to it: "Be,[2479]" and it is. (35) Truly Allah is my Lord and

---

[2466] Isa

[2467] Here Isa speaks as a newborn baby. The Qur'an lists some other miracles of Isa in 3:52, 5:110,112, 19:19,20,24,30-33. In the Injil, most of the stories of the miracles that Isa does are mentioned in Matthew 8-12, 14-15, 17, 20, Mark 1-10, Luke 1, 4-9, 11, 14, 17-18, 22, John 2, 4-6, 9, 11. See note at verse 19/

[2468] See glossary.

[2469] See note at verse 19.

[2470] The word /mubarak/ (blessed) is only used once of a person in the Qur'an. See note at verse 19.

[2471] 3:55 and 5:117 say that Allah made Isa die. This verse confirms that Isa died, for if he did not die, then he would have to be giving money to poor people in heaven, where he is now (4:58). In the heavenly garden, there is no need of a poor tax. There are no poor people in heaven. This verse shows that Isa must have died before being raised to Allah in heaven, where he has now been brought near to Allah. (3:45)

[2472] Or miserable

[2473] A person who pronounces peace upon himself must have authority to do so.

[2474] Abdullah Yusuf Ali's footnote 2485 on this verse contains "those who believe that [Christ] never died should ponder over this verse."

[2475] Injil, Matthew 28:1-15, Luke 24:1-48, Acts 2:30-32, 5:30, 10:39-40, Romans 6:4

[2476] Jesus. See glossary for more details.

[2477] Mary, mother of Jesus. See glossary for more details.

[2478] Or choose. Apparently there were people who taught that Allah had chosen a son from among people.

[2479] Allah is able to create anything from nothing. In the case of Isa's conception, Allah breathed of his spirit into Mary (21:91, 66:12) and through that, Allah created a sperm or chromosomes or something from nothing.

## Chapter 19

your<sup>MP</sup> Lord,[2480] therefore worship him; this is a straight path.[2481] (36) And the various parties differed among themselves. Woe to those who disbelieve that they will see a great day. (37) Make<sup>MS</sup> them hear of and see[2482] the day they will come to us. But the wicked today are clearly astray. (38) Warn<sup>MS</sup> them of a day of sorrow, since the matter has been predestined, they are unaware of it, and they do not believe. (39) We will inherit the earth and those in it,[2483] and they will return to us. (40)

\*\*\*

Remember Ibrahim[2484] in the book.[2485] He was a righteous prophet. (41) He told his father, "Father, why do you<sup>MS</sup> worship what does not hear or see or benefit you<sup>MS</sup>? (42) Father, knowledge came to me that did not come to you<sup>MS</sup>, so follow me and I will guide you<sup>MS</sup> on a straight path.[2486] (43) Father, do not worship<sup>MS</sup> Satan. Satan was truly disobedient to the most gracious. (44) Father, I fear that torment will overtake you<sup>MS</sup> from the most gracious, and you<sup>MS</sup> will be Satan's helper." (45) He said, "Do you<sup>MS</sup> dislike my gods,[2487]

---

[2480] See Injil, Mark 12:29, John 20:17

[2481] The straight path is mentioned often in the Qur'an (1:7 and 37:118 as "the straight path", 7:16 as "your straight path," 6:126 as "your Lord's straight path," 6:153 as "my straight path," and 2:108,142,213, 3:51,101, 4:68,175, 5:12,16,60,77, 6:39,87,161, 10:25, 11:56, 15:41, 16:76, 121, 19:36,43, 20:135, 22:54, 23:73, 24:46, 28:22, 36:4,61, 38:22, 42:52, 43:43,61,64, 46:30, 48:2,20, 60:1, 67:22 as "a straight path.") However, only 3:51, 6:153, 19:36, 43:61,64, and 36:61 say what the straight path is. This passage is one of the most complete in its explanation, and we can conclude that the straight path includes (from verses 19-36) 1) believing that Isa is sinless, 2) that his mother was a virgin, 3) that Isa is a sign and mercy that were predestined, 4) that Isa is Allah's servant, 5) that Allah gave Isa a book and made him a prophet, 6) that he blessed him and commanded him to pray, give alms, and respect his mother, 7) that he was not proud or disobedient, 8) that the days of his birth, death and resurrection were blessed, 9) that he was the statement of truth, 10) that Allah would never choose a boy, 11) that Allah says "Be" when he decrees something, 12) believing in the one Allah, who is Isa's and our Lord, and 13) worshiping Allah. See notes on the other four passages.

[2482] or, How well will they see and hear

[2483] See Zabur, Psalms 24:1, Injil, Matthew 5:5

[2484] Abraham here and in verse 46. See glossary for more details.

[2485] See Tawrah, Genesis 11:26 – Genesis 25:8

[2486] See glossary for more details, and notes on 3:51, 6:153, 19:36, 36:61, and 43:64 on what the straight path is.

[2487] Arabic /ilah/. See glossary for more details.

## Chapter 19

Ibrahim? If you[MS] do not stop, I will certainly stone you[MS]. Leave[MS] me for a long time." (46) He said, "Peace be upon you[MS]. I will ask my Lord to forgive you[MS]. He has received me warmly. (47) I will isolate myself from you[MP] and the gods you[MP] pray to instead of Allah, and will pray to my Lord. I hope that I will not be disappointed[2488] in praying to my Lord." (48) So when he had isolated himself from them and what they worship instead of Allah, we gave him Ishaq[2489] and Yaqub,[2490] and we made them[P] prophets,[2491] (49) and gave them some of our mercy and a high and true renown.[2492] (50) Remember Musa[2493] in the book. He was a sincere messenger and prophet. (51) We called him from the right side of the mountain and brought him close and intimate (52) and gave him his brother Harun[2494] as a prophet[2495] out of our mercy. (53) Remember Ismail[2496] in the book. He kept his promise and was a messenger and prophet. (54) He commanded his family[2497] to perform prayers and pay the poor-tax, and he was pleasing to his Lord. (55) Remember Idris[2498] in the book. He was a righteous[2499] prophet (56) and we raised him to a high place.[2500] (57) These are the prophets whom Allah blessed, from the seed of Adam,[2501] from those we carried with Nuh,[2502] from the seed of Ibrahim[2503] and Israel, and from those we guided and chose. If the signs of the most gracious are read to them, they fall down, bowing down and weeping. (58) **16A4** Successors followed after them who made the prayers vanish and followed lust. They will

---

[2488] or disobedient or miserable
[2489] Isaac. See glossary for more details.
[2490] Jacob. See glossary for more details.
[2491] See 37:112
[2492] Or tongue
[2493] Moses. See glossary for more details. See Tawrah, Exodus 2:10 – Deuteronomy 34:5
[2494] Aaron. See glossary for more details.
[2495] Tawrah, Exodus 4:14-27
[2496] Ishmael. See glossary for more details. Tawrah, Genesis 16:11-25:17
[2497] Compare Tawrah, Genesis 18:19.
[2498] Enoch. See glossary for more details. Tawrah, Genesis 5:18-24, Injil, Hebrews 11:5.
[2499] Injil, Hebrews 11:5
[2500] Tawrah, Genesis 5:24, Hebrews 11:5
[2501] See glossary for more details.
[2502] Noah. See glossary for more details.
[2503] Abraham. See glossary for more details.

## Chapter 19

meet destruction, (59) except for those who repent, believe, and do righteous deeds;[2504] they will enter the heavenly garden,[2505] and will not be wronged at all. (60) [Those are] the heavenly gardens of Eden in the unseen world which the most gracious has promised to his servants.[2506] His promise will be fulfilled. (61) They will not hear vain words there, only "Peace." They'll have their provision there morning and evening. (62) This is the heavenly garden which our reverent servants[2507] will inherit. (63) We[2508] will not descend except by command of your[MS] Lord. He owns what is in front of us, behind us, and in between.[2509] Your[MS] Lord is not forgetful. (64) Worship the Lord of the heavens, the earth, and what is between them. Endure[2510] in worshiping him. Do you[MS] know a namesake for him?[2511] (65) Man says: "If I die, will I be brought forth alive?" (66) Does man not remember that we created him beforehand, when he was nothing? (67) [I swear] by your[MS] Lord, we will certainly gather[2512] them and the devils,[2513] and bring them kneeling around hell. (68) Then we will take away the most rebellious against the most gracious from each sect. (69) Then we know best who among them most deserves to be roasted[2514] in it. (70) Every one of you[MP] shall come to it.[2515] This is a predestined[2516] certainty for your[MS] Lord. (71) Then we will rescue the reverent and leave the wicked kneeling in it." (72) If our signs

---

[2504] Here and verse 96, see Injil, 1 Corinthians 3:8, James 2:14-17, Revelation 19:8.

[2505] Arabic /jannah/ here, in verse 61 and verse 63). See glossary for more details.

[2506] See glossary.

[2507] See glossary.

[2508] The we of this verse is probably the angels. Their statement continues through verse 71, or possibly verse 76.

[2509] Or our future, past and present.

[2510] See "endure" in glossary

[2511] Tawrah, Isaiah 45:6

[2512] Tawrah, Joel 3:11-14, Zephaniah 3:8, Injil, Matthew 25:32, John 15:6, Revelation 16:16

[2513] Arabic /shayatin/. See glossary for more details.

[2514] Or broiled or burned

[2515] hell

[2516] this word "predestined" /maqdiy/ is used only twice in the Qur'an (19:21,71). The two predestined things are Isa as mercy from Allah and a sign for all men (21) and hellfire (71). Since mercy and hellfire are opposites, it seems the Qur'an is giving men a choice.

## Chapter 19

are read to them as miracles, the disbelievers will say to the believers, "Which of the two parties has a nicer place to live and better companions?" (73) How many wealthier and better-looking generations have we destroyed before them! (74) Say^MS, "May the most gracious extend the time of him who goes astray, so that when they see what they have been promised, whether torment or the hour,[2517] they will know who is in an more evil place with a weaker host. (75) Allah will increase the guidance of those who are guided. Lasting^FP righteous deeds[2518] have better rewards and a better return. (76) Have you^MS seen him who disbelieves in our signs[2519] and says, "I will be given money and a son."?[2520] (77) Is he familiar with the invisible, or has he made a covenant with the most gracious? (78) No! We will write down what he says, and extend his torment for him, (79) and we will inherit what he says from him, and he will come to us alone. (80) They chose gods[2521] beside Allah for power. (81) No! They will disbelieve in worshipping them and they will be against them. (82) Have you^MS not seen that we have sent devils[2522] to the disbelievers to incite them? (83) Do not be^MS in haste over them. We will surely count out for them (84) on the day when we gather the reverent to the most gracious in a group (85) and we will herd the wrongdoers to hell.[2523] (86) They have no intercession except for those who make a covenant with the most gracious. (87) They said, "The most gracious has chosen[2524] a boy."[2525] (88) You^MP have brought something grievous. (89) The heavens almost split and the earth is almost broken, and the mountains fall down in utter ruin over it:

---

[2517] Injil, Revelation 14:7
[2518] or remaining righteous women
[2519] Arabic /ayat/. See glossary for more details.
[2520] the meaning here is probably children, but the singular is used to make the rhyme
[2521] Arabic /ilah/. See glossary for more details.
[2522] Arabic /shayatin/. See glossary for more details.
[2523] some translations, for the idea of "in a herd", have "thirsty" or "weary".
[2524] The Qur'an strongly rejects the idea of Allah choosing or adopting a son. This probably refers to the ancient doctrine, rejected by early Christians, called adoptionism, or dynamic monarchianism. The Ebionites believed this doctrine, and may have tried to convince Muhammad (ص) of it.
[2525] All the books reject the idea that Allah needs anything, including a son. The idea that Allah chose a son is against all the books.

Chapter 19

(90) They ascribe a boy[2526] to the most gracious! (91) The most gracious does not need to take a boy. (92) Everything in the heavens and the earth worships[2527] the most gracious.[2528] (93) He has counted them and numbered them exactly. (94) Each of them will come alone to him on the day of resurrection.[2529] (95) The most gracious will give love to the believers who do righteous deeds. (96) We have made it easy in your[MS] tongue so you[MS] can give good news about it to the reverent and warn contentious people. (97) How many generations we destroyed before them! Do you[MS] perceive any of them or hear even a whisper from them? (98)[2530]

---

[2526] This word means a physical son, here and in the next verse. None of the books support the idea of physical procreation between Allah and a woman.
[2527] See glossary under servant.
[2528] Zabur, Psalms 119:91
[2529] Tawrah, Daniel 12:2 Injil, Acts 24:15, 1 Corinthians 15:52-54, Revelation 20:11-15
[2530] The verses in this chapter that rhyme are put together in paragraphs, separated by ***.

Chapter 20

# Chapter 20: Taha[2531]

**16B1** In the name of Allah, the most gracious and merciful.[2532] TH.[2533] (1)
\*\*\*

We did not reveal the Qur'an[2534] to you[ms] so that you[ms] would be miserable, (2) but rather as a reminder to those who fear, (3) revealed by him who created the earth and the heavens above. (4) The most gracious sat down[2535] on the throne. (5) He has everything in the heavens, the earth, between them, and under the earth. (6) If you[ms] make public a saying, he knows the secret and hides it.[2536] (7) Allah is the only god;[2537] he has the beautiful names. (8) Have you[ms] received the story of Musa?[2538] (9) When he saw a fire, he told his family, "Wait here! I notice a fire. I may bring you[mp] a coal from it or find guidance on it."[2539] (10) When he came to it, he was called: "Musa![2540] (11) It is I, your[ms] Lord, so take off your[ms] shoes.[2541] You[ms] are in the holy[2542] valley of Tuwa, (12) and I have chosen you[ms],[2543] so listen to what is inspired. (13)
\*\*\*

It is I, Allah.[2544] I am the only god,[2545] so worship me and perform the prayers to remember me. (14)

---

[2531] This title may have a hidden meaning. It is composed of two letters, T and H.
[2532] Zabur, Psalms 103:8, 145:8. See glossary for more details.
[2533] Here and at the beginning of many chapters there are unvowelled letters of unknown meaning. Numerous theories have been proposed, but there is no agreement on the subject.
[2534] Or recitation. See glossary for more details.
[2535] Sitting down does not mean that Allah has a physical body, but anthropomorphic expressions are used in all the books and are not to be taken literally.
[2536] Or, and [that which] is more hidden
[2537] Arabic /ilah/. See glossary for more details.
[2538] Moses. See glossary for more details.
[2539] Tawrah, Exodus 3:3
[2540] Moses. See glossary for more details.
[2541] Tawrah, Exodus 3:5
[2542] Tawrah, Exodus 3:5
[2543] Tawrah, Exodus 3:10
[2544] Tawrah, Exodus 3:6, 14
[2545] Arabic /ilah/. See glossary for more details.

## Chapter 20

\*\*\*

The hour[2546] is truly coming. I almost hide it so that every soul would be rewarded for what it strives for. (15) Do not let^MS those who disbelieve in it block you^MS from it, make you^MS follow[2547] his desire, and so perish^MS. (16) What is that in your^MS right hand,[2548] Musa?[2549] (17) He said, "It is my staff,[2550] which I lean on and bear down fodder for my sheep,[2551] among other things." (18) He said, "Throw it down,[2552] Musa."[2553] (19) So he threw it down, and it actually became a snake crawling.[2554] (20) He said, "Take it[2555] and do not be afraid. We will restore it to its former state.[2556] (21) Put your^MS hand in your^MS armpit,[2557] and it will come out white, but unharmed as another sign,[2558] (22) so that we may show you^MS some of our greater signs.[2559] (23) Go^MS to Pharaoh. He has been a tyrant.[2560]" (24)

\*\*\*

He said, "Lord, open my heart, (25) and make my task easier, (26) and untie the knot in my tongue (27) so they understand what I say.[2561] (28) Give me an aide from my family,[2562] (29) Harun[2563] my brother. (30) Support me through him.[2564]" (31) Let him share my task[2565] (32)

\*\*\*

---

[2546] Injil, Revelation 14:7
[2547] or, he follows his desire
[2548] Tawrah, Exodus 4:2
[2549] Moses. See glossary for more details.
[2550] Tawrah, Exodus 4:2
[2551] or guide my sheep or shoo flies from my sheep or bear branches for my sheep
[2552] Tawrah, Exodus 4:3
[2553] Moses. See glossary for more details.
[2554] Tawrah, Exodus 4:3
[2555] Tawrah, Exodus 4:4
[2556] Tawrah, Exodus 4:5
[2557] or wing
[2558] Tawrah, Exodus 4:6-7
[2559] Tawrah, Exodus 4:8-9
[2560] Tawrah, Exodus 3:10
[2561] Tawrah, Exodus 4:10-12
[2562] Tawrah, Exodus 4:13
[2563] Aaron. See glossary for more details.
[2564] Tawrah, Exodus 4:14
[2565] Tawrah, Exodus 4:15-16

so that we may glorify you^MS often, (33) and remember you^MS frequently. (34) You^MS see us.^2566" (35) He said, "You^MS have obtained your^MS request,^2567 Musa,^2568 (36) and we granted you^MS a favor another time, (37) when we inspired your^MS mother with an inspiration:^2569 (38)

\*\*\*

Cast^FS him in the ark,^2570 and throw^FS it into the water,^2571 that the water may cast him onto the shore and an enemy of mine and of his will take him.^2572 I cast my love upon you^MS that you^MS might be formed under my watch-care, (39)

\*\*\*

when your^MS sister was walking and said: Shall I guide you^MP to someone who will take care of him?^2573 And we restored you^MS to your^MS mother^2574 so that her eyes would be refreshed and not grieve. And you^MS killed a man^2575 and we rescued you^MS from distress,^2576 and tested you^MS with trials. You^MS remained years among the people of Midian.^2577 Then you^MS came by destiny,^2578 Musa.^2579 (40)

\*\*\*

I made you^MS for myself. (41) You^MS and your^MS brother go with my signs^2580 and do not neglect^D to remember me. (42)

\*\*\*

Go^D to Pharaoh;^2581 he is a tyrant. (43) Speak^D gently to him. Perhaps he will remember or fear. (44) They^D said, "Our Lord, we

---

[2566] Tawrah, Genesis 16:13
[2567] Tawrah, Exodus 4:14-16
[2568] Moses. See glossary for more details.
[2569] see Injil, Hebrews 11:23
[2570] the word "ark" here is the same word used for the ark of the covenant, which was a box, but not the one used for Noah's ark, which was a boat. Tawrah, Exodus 2:3
[2571] Tawrah, Exodus 2:3
[2572] Tawrah, Exodus 2:5,6
[2573] Tawrah, Exodus 2:7
[2574] Tawrah, Exodus 2:8,9
[2575] Tawrah, Exodus 2:12
[2576] Tawrah, Exodus 2:15
[2577] Tawrah, Exodus 2:15-23, 7:7
[2578] Tawrah, Exodus 3:14
[2579] Moses. See glossary for more details.
[2580] Tawrah, Exodus 4:9-30
[2581] Tawrah, Exodus 3:10, 4:21, 6:12

## Chapter 20

fear that he would be insolent or tyrannical with us." (45) He said, "Do not fear<sup>D</sup>; I am with you<sup>D</sup>. I hear and see. (46) So go<sup>D</sup> to him and say<sup>D</sup>, "We are messengers<sup>D</sup> of your<sup>MS</sup> Lord. Send<sup>MS</sup> the people of Israel and do not torment<sup>MS</sup> them.[2582] We have come to you<sup>MS</sup> with a sign from your<sup>MS</sup> Lord. Peace be upon those who follow guidance. (47) It has been revealed to us that whoever rejects and turns away will be tormented."[2583] (48) He said, "Who is your<sup>D</sup> Lord, Musa?"[2584] (49) He said, "Our Lord created and guided everything." (50) He said, "Then what about the former generations?"[2585] (51) He said, "That knowledge is with my Lord in a book. My Lord does not go astray or forget. (52) He made the earth as a cradle for you<sup>MP</sup>, made paths for you<sup>MP</sup>, sent rain[2586] from the sky, and made all kinds of plants." (53) Eat<sup>MP</sup> and tend your<sup>MP</sup> cattle. Those are signs for those who understand. (54) **16B2** We created you<sup>MP</sup> from it, and we will return you<sup>MP</sup> into it,[2587] and from it we will bring you<sup>MP</sup> out at another time. (55) We showed him all our signs[2588] and he rejected and refused them.[2589] (56) He said, "Musa,[2590] Have you<sup>MS</sup> come to expel us from our land with magic?[2591] (57) We will bring you<sup>MS</sup> similar magic.[2592] Set an appointment between us and you<sup>MS</sup> in a suitable place. We will not be late, nor should you<sup>MS</sup>." (58) He said, "Your<sup>MP</sup> appointment is on the feast[2593] day. Let the people be gathered in the morning." (59) So Pharaoh turned away and finalized[2594] his plot. Later, he came. (60) Musa[2595] told them, "Woe to you<sup>MP</sup>. Do not tell lies about Allah, or he will destroy you<sup>MP</sup> with torment.[2596] Liars will be

---

[2582] Tawrah, Exodus 4:22,23, 5:1
[2583] Tawrah, Exodus 4:23
[2584] Moses. See glossary for more details. Tawrah, Exodus 5:2
[2585] or centuries
[2586] Tawrah, Deuteronomy 28:12, Job 5:10, Joel 2:23, Zabur, Psalms 68:9, Injil, Matthew 5:45
[2587] Tawrah, Genesis 3:19
[2588] Tawrah, Exodus 7:11,12
[2589] Tawrah, Exodus 7:13 – 11:10
[2590] Moses. See glossary for more details.
[2591] Tawrah, Exodus 7:13,22
[2592] Tawrah, Exodus 7:11,12,22
[2593] or decoration
[2594] or gathered
[2595] Moses. See glossary for more details.
[2596] For "torment" here and in verses 71 and 127, see Tawrah, Isaiah 50:11, Injil, Matthew 18:34, 25:41,46, Luke 16:23-28, Revelation 20:15.

disappointed. (61) So they disputed with each other about the matter, and concealed their private discussion. (62) They said, "These[MD] are magicians[MD] who want[MD] to expel[MD] you[MP] from your[MP] land with their[MD] magic and make your[MP] exemplary ways vanish[MD]. (63) So make your[MP] plot, and come[MP] in a line. Whoever is higher today will prosper. (64) They said, "Musa,[2597] either you[MS] cast first, or we will." (65) He said, "Cast[MP]. Their ropes and staffs seemed to him to run by their magic.[2598] (66) Musa's[2599] soul was afraid. (67) We said, "Do not fear[MS]. You[MS] are superior.[2600] (68) Cast down what is in your[MS] right hand and it will swallow what they did. They made a plot of magic. Magicians will not prosper anywhere. (69) The magicians fell down, bowed down and said, "We believe in the Lord of Harun[2601] and Musa."[2602] (70) He said, "You[MP] believed in him before I gave you[MP] permission. He is your[MP] superior, who taught you[MP] magic. I will cut off your[MP] hands and feet on opposite sides and crucify you[MP] on palm tree trunks. You[MP] will know who is harsher and more permanent in torment. (71) They said, "We will not prefer you[MS] over the miracles that have come to us and him who created us. Decree whatever you[MS] want. Your[MS] decrees only affect this life. (72) We believe in our Lord so that he will forgive us our faults and the magic you[MS] imposed on us. Allah is better and more lasting. (73) He who comes to his Lord as a wrongdoer will go to hell, where he will neither die nor live. (74) Those who come as believers who did righteous deeds[2603] will be exalted to the highest ranks: (75) heavenly gardens[2604] of Eden with flowing rivers[2605] underneath, where they will be forever. That is the reward of those who are purified. (76) We inspired Musa,[2606] "Take my servants[2607] and

---

[2597] Moses. See glossary for more details.
[2598] Tawrah, Exodus 7:10-12
[2599] Moses. See glossary for more details.
[2600] See Tawrah, Exodus 7:12
[2601] Aaron. See glossary for more details.
[2602] Moses. See glossary for more details. Tawrah, Exodus 8:19
[2603] Here and in verse 82, see Injil, 1 Corinthians 3:8, James 2:14-17, Revelation 19:8
[2604] Arabic /jannah/. See glossary for more details.
[2605] Injil, Revelation 22:1-2, Tawrah, Ezekiel 47:12
[2606] Moses. See glossary for more details.
[2607] See glossary.

Chapter 20

strike[2608] a dry[2609] path for them in the sea. Do not fear being caught from behind. Do not be afraid.[2610] (77)

\*\*\*

And Pharaoh followed them with his army,[2611] and some of the water covered them.[2612] (78)

\*\*\*

So Pharaoh led his people astray and did not guide. (79) People of Israel, we rescued you[MP] from your[MP] enemy and made an appointment with you[MP] on the right side of the mountain. We sent down upon you[MP] manna and quail. (80) Eat[MP] the good things we have provided you[MP] and do not transgress[MP] in them, or my anger will come upon you[MP]. If my anger comes upon anyone, he will fall. (81) I am most forgiving[2613] to him who repents, believes, does righteous deeds, and then is guided. (82) **16B3** Musa,[2614] what made you[MS] hurry in front of your[MS] people? (83) He said, "They are following me and I hastened to you[MS], Lord, so you[MS] would be pleased." (84)

\*\*\*

He said, "We have tempted your[MS] people after you[MS], and the Samaritan has led them astray."[2615] (85) Musa[2616] returned to his people angry and sorrowful.[2617] He said, "My people, did your[MP] Lord not give you[MP] a good promise? Did the time grow too long for you[MP],[2618] or did you[MP] want your[MP] Lord's anger to come upon you[MP]?[2619] Is that why you[MP] broke my promise?" (86) They said, "We did not break your[MS] promise intentionally. But we had to carry the burdens of the finery[2620] of the people. So we threw it, as did the Samaritan,[2621] (87) and he brought out a body of a calf[2622]

---

[2608] Tawrah, Exodus 14:16,21
[2609] Tawrah, Exodus 14:22
[2610] Tawrah, Exodus 14:13-14
[2611] Tawrah, Exodus 14:23-25
[2612] Tawrah, Exodus 14:26-28
[2613] Zabur, Psalms 103:3, 130:4, Tawrah, Isaiah 43:25, Exodus 34:7, Injil, Acts 26:18
[2614] Moses. See glossary for more details.
[2615] Tawrah, Exodus 32:7
[2616] Moses. See glossary for more details.
[2617] Tawrah, Exodus 32:15
[2618] Tawrah, Exodus 32:1
[2619] Tawrah, Exodus 32:10
[2620] or ornaments or jewelry. Tawrah, Exodus 32:2,3
[2621] Tawrah, Exodus 32:24

## Chapter 20

that mooed. They said, "This is your[MP] god,[2623] and Musa's[2624] god,"[2625] and he forgot. (88)
\*\*\*

Do they not see that it will not speak back to them, and that it cannot harm them or help them?[2626] (89)
\*\*\*

Harun[2627] told them beforehand, "My people, you[MP] were tempted with it, and your[MP] Lord is the most gracious. So follow[MP] me and obey[MP] my command."[2628] (90)
\*\*\*

They said, "We will not stop worshiping it until Musa[2629] comes back. (91)
\*\*\*

He said, "Harun,[2630] what prevented you[MS] when you[MS] saw them going astray?[2631]" (92) "Do you[MS] not follow me? Have you[MS] thus disobeyed[2632] my command?[2633]" (93) He said, "Blood brother, do not take[MS] me by the beard or the head.[2634] I feared that you[MS] would say: You[MS] made a division among the people of Israel, and did not

---

[2622] Tawrah, Exodus 32:24

[2623] Arabic /ilah/. See glossary for more details.

[2624] Moses. See glossary for more details.

[2625] Arabic /ilah/. See glossary for more details.

[2626] Zabur, Psalms 115:4-7, Tawrah, Isaiah 44:20

[2627] Aaron. See glossary for more details.

[2628] Several prophets tell the people specifically, "obey me." (Nuh 26:108,110, 71:3, Hud 26:126,131, Salih 26:144,150, Lut 26:163, Shuaib 26:179, Harun 20:90, and Isa 3:50, 43:63) Isa is the only one who commands obedience in the context of the straight path. Several verses command people to obey "the messenger" (3:32,132, 4:59, 5:92, 8:1,19,46, 24:54,56, 47:33, 58:13, 64:12) , most of which probably refer to Muhammad (s).

[2629] Moses. See glossary for more details.

[2630] Aaron. See glossary for more details.

[2631] Tawrah, Exodus 32:21

[2632] The belief that all prophets and messengers are sinless is not supported by the Qur'an. For instances of prophets or messengers asking forgiveness or committing sins, see 7:23, 20:121 (Adam), 11:47, 71:28 (Nuh), 26:82, 14:41 (Ibrahim), 28:15-16 (Musa), 7:151, 20:93 (Musa and Harun), 38:24 (Dawud), 38:32,35 (Sulayman), 21:87, 37:142 (Yunus), 48:2, 47:19, 40:55, 4:79,106, 9:43, 13:30, 80:1-2, 110:3, 94:2, 23:118, 66:1, 33:37, 8:67, and 9:117 (Muhammad (s).

[2633] Tawrah, Exodus 32:21

[2634] Tawrah, Exodus 32:22

## Chapter 20

observe[MS] my saying." (94) He said, "What's the matter with you[MS], Samaritan?"[2635] (95) He said, "I saw what they did not see, and grabbed a handful[2636] from the messengers footsteps and threw it. It seemed good to me. (96)
***
He said, "Go[MS]. In this life, you[MS] must say: Untouchable. You[MS] have an appointment you[MS] cannot miss. Look at your[MS] god[2637] that you[MS] kept worshipping. We will burn it and scatter its ashes in the water.[2638] (97) Your[MP] god[2639] is Allah. He is the only god. He knows everything." (98) Thus we relate to you[MS] some events that happened beforehand. We have given you[MS] a reminder[2640] from us. (99) He who turns away from it will carry a burden on the day of resurrection[2641] (100) forever. It will be an evil burden to them on the day of resurrection. (101) On that day a trumpet will be blown and we will gather[2642] the wrongdoers on that day. They will turn blue (102) and speak softly among themselves, "You[MP] remained only ten."[2643] (103) We know better what they say, for the most distinguished among them in the way will say, "You[MP] stayed only a day." (104) They ask you[MP] about the mountains. Say[MS], "My Lord will crush them to powder (105) and leave them on a level plain (106) on which you[MS] see nothing crooked or curved." (107) On that day, they will follow the caller in whom there is nothing crooked, and voices will humble themselves before the most gracious. You[MS] will hear nothing but whispers. (108) On that day, intercession will not help, except for him who has the most

---

[2635] some think that "the Samaritan" is a negative title given to Harun, and others that the Samaritan is a separate person.
[2636] probably of soil
[2637] Arabic /ilah/. See glossary for more details.
[2638] Tawrah, Exodus 32:20
[2639] Arabic /ilah/ twice in this verse. See glossary for more details.
[2640] Arabic /dhikr/. See glossary for more details.
[2641] For "day of resurrection" here and in verses 100 and 124, see Tawrah, Daniel 12:2 Injil, Acts 24:15, 1 Corinthians 15:52-54, Revelation 20:11-15
[2642] Here and in verses 124-125, see Tawrah, Joel 3:11-14, Zephaniah 3:8, Injil, Matthew 25:32, John 15:6, Revelation 16:16
[2643] The Arabic does not state the noun that ten modifies. Some commentators suggest "centuries" and others have "days." Since 29:14 states that Noah lived 950 years, centuries is more probable. See Injil, 2 Peter 3:8 and Tawrah, Genesis 5.

## Chapter 20

merciful's permission,[2644] and whose statement[2645] he is pleased with. (109) He knows what is in front of them and behind them,[2646] and they do not know about him. (110) 16B4 Faces will humbled before the Living, Eternal One.[2647] He that carries injustice will be disappointed. (111) A believer who does righteous deeds[2648] will not fear being cheated or wronged. (112) Thus we revealed an Arabic recitation[2649] and explained threats in it, that they may beware or be reminded. (113) Exalted be Allah, the True King. Do not hurry[MS] with the Qur'an[2650] before its inspiration is decreed to you[MS]. Say[MS], "Lord, give[MS] me more knowledge." (114) And we made a covenant with Adam[2651] beforehand, but he forgot, and we found no determination in him. (115)

\*\*\*

When we told the angels, "Bow down[2652] to Adam,"[2653] all except for Iblis[2654] bowed down. He refused. (116) So we said, "Adam, he is an enemy to you[MS] and your[MS] wife, so do not let him expel you[D] from the heavenly garden and you[MS] be miserable. (117) You[MS] have the privilege of not being hungry or naked in it, (118) nor will you[MS] thirst in it, nor be exposed to the sun." (119) Satan whispered to him, saying, "Adam, shall I guide you[MS] to the tree of eternity and a kingdom that lasts forever?" (120) And they[D] ate of it and their[D] shame[2655] was apparent to them, and they began sewing on themselves leaves of the heavenly garden.[2656] Adam

---

[2644] See 2:255, 10:3, 34:23, 43:86

[2645] The only person in the Qur'an called a statement is Isa (19:34), who is called the statement of truth. It is also said of him in the Qur'an six times that Allah gave him permission (5:110 (four times), and 3:49 (twice)). See Injil, 1 Timothy 2:5

[2646] This could refer to Allah (see 21:28) or to the intercessor. 3:49 says something similar about Isa.

[2647] This word could also mean Self-Subsistent One or Resurrector.

[2648] Injil, 1 Corinthians 3:8, James 2:14-17, Revelation 19:8

[2649] Or Qur'an or qur'an. See glossary for more details.

[2650] Or recitation. See glossary for more details.

[2651] See glossary for more details.

[2652] Zabur, Psalms 97:7, Injil, Hebrews 1:6

[2653] See glossary for more details on the name Adam here and in verses 117, 120, 121.

[2654] The devil. See glossary for more details.

[2655] Or nakedness Tawrah, Genesis 3:7

[2656] Arabic /jannah/ here and in verse 117. See glossary for more details. Tawrah, Genesis 3:7

# Chapter 20

disobeyed[2657] his Lord and went astray.[2658] (121) Then his Lord chose him, accepted his repentance, and guided him. (122) He said, "Go down[D] from it, everyone of you[MP] an enemy to the others.[2659] If guidance comes from me to you[MP], whoever follows my guidance will not go astray or be miserable. (123) But he who turns away from remembering me has a narrow life, and on the day of resurrection we will gather him blind." (124)

\*\*\*

He will say, "My Lord, why have you[MS] gathered me blind, when I used to be sighted?" (125)

\*\*\*

He said, "Thus it is. Our signs came to you[MS] and you[MS] forgot them, so today you[MS] will be forgotten. (126) Thus we repay the wasteful one who did not believe in his Lord's signs.[2660] The torment of the hereafter is harsher and more permanent." (127) Has he not guided them how many generations before them we destroyed as they walk in their dwellings? Those are signs for those who understand. (128) If a word from your[MS] Lord and a fixed period of time had not come previously,[2661] judgment would have come. (129) So endure[MS][2662] what they say, and glorify your[MS] Lord before sunrise,[2663] before sunset, and in the night. Thus glorify and praise him at the borders of the daytime, so that you[MS] might be pleased. (130) Do not let your[MS] eyes envy[2664] the kinds we have let them enjoy.[2665] They are the flower of this life, so that we can try them by them. Your[MS] Lord's provision is better and

---

[2657] The belief that all prophets and messengers are sinless is not supported by the Qur'an. For instances of prophets or messengers asking forgiveness or committing sins, see 7:23, 20:121 (Adam), 11:47, 71:28 (Nuh), 26:82, 14:41 (Ibrahim), 28:15-16 (Musa), 7:151, 20:93 (Musa and Harun), 38:24 (Dawud), 38:32,35 (Sulayman), 21:8, 37:142 (Yunus), 48:2, 47:19, 40:55, 4:79,106, 9:43, 13:30, 80:1-2, 110:3, 94:2, 23:118, 66:1, 33:37, 8:67, and 9:117 (Muhammad (s).

[2658] Tawrah, Genesis 3:11-12

[2659] The phrase "to the others" is in the plural, not the dual. The meaning is probably that not only were Adam and his wife enemies, but Satan was an enemy to both of them.

[2660] Arabic /ayat/. See glossary for more details.

[2661] See 10:19, 11:110, 41:45, 42:14 where this phrase is also used.

[2662] See "endure" in glossary, here and in verse 132.

[2663] Zabur, Psalms 5:3, 143:8-10

[2664] Or stretch toward

[2665] Tawrah, Exodus 20:17

more lasting. (131) Command your<sup>MS</sup> family to perform prayers and endure it. We do not ask you<sup>MS</sup> for provision. We give you<sup>MS</sup> provision. Rewards are for the reverent. (132) They said, "If only he would give us a sign from his Lord." Has a miracle of what was in the earliest books not come to them? (133) If we had destroyed them with torment before him[2666], they would have said, "Our Lord, if only you<sup>MS</sup> had sent us a messenger, we would have followed your<sup>MS</sup> signs before we were humbled and ashamed." (134) Say<sup>MS</sup>, "Everyone is waiting, so you<sup>MP</sup> wait, too. You<sup>MP</sup> will know who is on the straight path,[2667] and who is guided." (135)[2668]

---

[2666] or it. It is unclear what the reference is
[2667] See glossary for more details, and notes on 3:51, 6:153, 19:36, 36:61, and 43:64 on what the straight path is.
[2668] The verses in this chapter that rhyme are put together in paragraphs, separated by ***.

# Chapter 21 Al-Anbiya'[2669]

17A1In the name of Allah, the most gracious and merciful.[2670] People's reckoning has come near, though they are unaware and turn away. (1) Whenever an updated reminder[2671] of their Lord comes, they listen to it while they play. (2) Their hearts are entertained and the wicked[2672] secretly conceal. "Is this not just a man like you[MP]? Will you[MP] bring magic while you[MP] watch?" (3) He said, "My Lord knows what is said in heaven and earth. He hears all and knows all. (4) But they say, "Confused dreams. He invented it. He is a poet. Let him bring on a sign, like the early messengers. (5) No village we destroyed before them believed. Will they believe? (6) All we sent before you[MS] were men whom we inspired, so ask[MP] the people of the reminder[2673] if you[MP] do not know. (7) We did not give them bodies that did not eat food, nor were they immortal. (8) Then we fulfilled the promise made to them and rescued them and those we willed, and we destroyed the wasteful. (9) We have revealed to you[MP] a book in which is your[MP] reminder.[2674] Do you[MP] not comprehend? (10) How many wicked villages we shattered, and raised up other people after them. (11) When they sensed our power, they ran from it. (12) Do not run[MP] away, but return to the riches you[MP] were given and to your[MP] dwellings, that you[MP] may be questioned. (13) They said, "Woe to us. We were wicked." (14) That was their cry[2675] until we destroyed and extinguished them. (15) We did not create heaven and earth and what is between them in play.[2676] (16) If we had wanted amusement, we would have done it ourselves, if at all. (17) Rather we throw the truth against what is vain and destroy it, so it vanishes. Woe to you[MP] for your[MP] description. (18) Everyone in the

---

[2669] prophets
[2670] Zabur, Psalms 103:8, 145:8. See glossary for more details.
[2671] Arabic /dhikr/. See glossary for more details.
[2672] There may be a missing word implied, because the verb here precedes the noun, yet is plural, against the rule.
[2673] Arabic /dhikr/. See glossary for more details. See 16:43. Here followers of the Qur'an are told to ask people of the reminder if they do not know. Thus the reminder here is not the Qur'an. Verses 48 and 105 clarify this, and refer to the Tawrah as the reminder.
[2674] Arabic /dhikr/. See glossary for more details.
[2675] Or case (as in a court)
[2676] Tawrah, Isaiah 45:18

## Chapter 21

heavens and the earth is his, and those with him are not too proud or tired to worship him.[2677] (19) They glorify him night and day and do not grow weary.[2678] (20) Or have they taken gods[2679] from the earth who resurrect? (21) If there were gods[2680] in either of them[2681] besides Allah, they would have decayed. May Allah, Lord of the throne, be glorified above what they describe! (22) He will not be asked about what he does, but they will. (23) Have they chosen gods[2682] beside him? Say[MS], "Bring on your[MP] proofs.[2683] This is a reminder[2684] of him who is with me, and a reminder[2685] of him who was before me."[2686] Most of them do not know the truth, so turn away. (24) Every messenger we sent before you[MS] we inspired: "I am the only god,[2687] so worship me." (25) They said, "The most gracious has chosen a boy." May he be glorified (above that)! Rather, honored servants (26) do not say things before he does, and they do what he commands. (27) He knows what is in front of them and what is behind them, and they only intercede for him who is pleasing. They are in terror and fear of him. (28) 17A2 We will repay any of them who says, "I am a god[2688] besides him" with hell. That is how we repay the wicked. (29) Do disbelievers not know that the heavens and the earth were one mass[2689] and we split them[2690] and made every living thing from water.[2691] Do they not believe? (30) We made firm mountains lest it move with them and we made mountain passes as paths, so that they may be guided. (31) We made the sky a preserved roof, yet they turn away from its signs. (32) He created night and day,[2692]

---

[2677] Injil, Revelation 4:8
[2678] Injil, Revelation 7:15
[2679] Arabic /ilah/. See glossary for more details.
[2680] Arabic /ilah/. See glossary for more details.
[2681] The dual pronoun here probably refers to the heavens and the earth.
[2682] Arabic /ilah/. See glossary for more details.
[2683] Tawrah, Isaiah 45:21
[2684] Arabic /dhikr/. See glossary for more details.
[2685] Arabic /dhikr/. See glossary for more details.
[2686] Injil, Revelation 1:8
[2687] Arabic /ilah/. See glossary for more details.
[2688] Arabic /ilah/. See glossary for more details.
[2689] Tawrah, Genesis 1:6,7
[2690] Tawrah, Genesis 1:8,9
[2691] Tawrah, Genesis 1:6-12
[2692] Tawrah, Genesis 1:5

## Chapter 21

the sun and the moon,[2693] each swimming in its orbit.[2694] (33) We gave immortality to no one before you[MS]. If you[MP] die, will they be immortal? (34) Every soul will taste death. We will test you[MP] with evil and good as a trial and you[MP] will return to us. (35) If the disbelievers see you[MS], they will make fun of you[MS], "Is this the one that mentioned your[MP] gods?"[2695] They disbelieve at the mention of the most gracious. (36) Man was created out of haste.[2696] I will show you[MP] my signs, so do not be in a hurry. (37) They say, "When will this promise be, if you[MP] are telling the truth?" (38) If only disbelievers knew the time they will not be able to keep hellfire from their faces or backs, nor be saved! (39) It will come upon them suddenly, astounding them. They will not be able to repel it, and they will have no more time. (40) Messengers before you[MS] were mocked,[2697] and those who made fun of them were surrounded by what they had made fun of. (41) Say[MS], "Who will keep you[MP] safe by night and day from the most gracious?" But they turn away from the reminder[2698] of their Lord.[2699] (42) Do they have gods[2700] besides us that will prevent them? They are not able to save themselves, nor be protected from us. (43) But we made them and their fathers enjoy things until they grew old. Do they not see that we come to the land and lessen it on its edges? Are they victors? (44) Say[MS], "I warn you[MP] by inspiration." But the deaf do not hear the call when they are warned. (45) If the breath of your[MS] Lord's torment touches them, they will say, "Woe to us! We were wicked." (46) We set up just scales for the day of resurrection.[2701] Not a soul will be wronged at all. We will bring even the weight of a mustard seed.[2702] We are sufficient reckoners.

---

[2693] Tawrah, Genesis 1:14-16
[2694] Tawrah, Genesis 1:17-18, see Zabur, Psalms 19:4-5
[2695] Arabic /ilah/. See glossary for more details.
[2696] This probably refers to man's hastiness. The word also means precipitation, and in that meaning it could mean similar to verse 30.
[2697] Tawrah, 2 Chronicles 30:10, 36:16, Zabur, Psalms 35:16, Injil, Matthew 20:19, 27:29,31,41, Mark 15:20,31, Luke 18;32, 22:63, 23:11,36
[2698] Or mentioning
[2699] Injil, 2 Timothy 4:1-4, Tawrah, Isaiah 30:8-11
[2700] Arabic /ilah/. See glossary for more details.
[2701] Tawrah, Daniel 12:2, Injil, Acts 24:15, 1 Corinthians 15:52-54, Revelation 20:11-15
[2702] Injil, Matthew 13:31, 17:20

## Chapter 21

(47) We gave Musa[2703] and Harun[2704] the criterion, shining, and reminder[2705] to the reverent, (48) who fear their Lord in the unseen world, and are in terror of the hour.[2706] (49) And this is a blessed reminder[2707] we revealed. Do you[MP] deny it? (50) 17A3 We gave Ibrahim[2708] his guidance beforehand,[2709] and we knew him. (51) He told his father and his people, "What are these statues you[-IP] are devoted to?" (52) They said, "We found our fathers worshipping them."(53) He said, "You[MP] and your[MP] fathers have clearly gone astray. (54) They said, "Have you[MS] brought truth to us, or are you[MS] playing?" (55) He said, "Your[MP] Lord is Lord of the heavens and the earth, which[2710] he created,[2711] and I testify to that."(56) By Allah, I will plot against your[MP] idols after you[MP] turn and go away. (57) He shattered them, except for a big one they had, so that they would return to him.[2712] (58) They said, "Who did this[2713] to our gods?[2714] He is wicked." (59) They said, "We heard a young man named Ibrahim[2715] mentioning them." (60) They said, "Bring him before the people, so that they may witness.[2716] (61) They said, "Did you[MS] do this to our gods,[2717] Ibrahim?"[2718] (62) He said, "Rather this big one did it to them. Ask them, if they speak." (63) They turned back to themselves, and said, "You[MP] are wicked." (64) Then they were turned upside down. "You[MS] know that these do not speak." (65) He said, "Do you[MP] worship what cannot help you[MP] or harm[2719] you[MP] instead of Allah?" (66) Shame on you[MP] and

---

[2703] Moses. See glossary for more details.
[2704] Aaron. See glossary for more details.
[2705] Arabic /dhikr/. See glossary for more details. Here the reminder is given to Musa and Harun, i.e. the Tawrah
[2706] Injil, Revelation 14:7
[2707] Arabic /dhikr/. See glossary for more details.
[2708] Abraham. See glossary for more details.
[2709] Tawrah, Genesis 12:1
[2710] The word which used here is for thinking beings, so possibly the heavens and earth are viewed as active servants of Allah.
[2711] Tawrah, Genesis 1:1, Isaiah 42:5, 45:18
[2712] Or it (the big idol)
[2713] See Tawrah, Judges 6:29
[2714] Arabic /ilah/. See glossary for more details.
[2715] Abraham. See glossary for more details.
[2716] Tawrah, Judges 6:30
[2717] Arabic /ilah/. See glossary for more details.
[2718] Abraham. See glossary for more details.
[2719] Zabur, Psalms 115:4-7, Tawrah, Isaiah 44:20

Chapter 21

what you<sup>MP</sup> worship other than Allah! Do you<sup>MP</sup> not comprehend? (67) They said, "Burn<sup>MP</sup> him and rescue<sup>MP</sup> your<sup>MP</sup> gods,[2720] if you<sup>MP</sup> do anything." (68) We said, "Fire, be coldness and peace[2721] to Ibrahim."[2722] (69) They wanted to plot against him, so we made them the most lost. (70) We rescued him[2723] and Lut[2724] [and brought them] to a land we blessed for all mankind. (71) We gave him Ishaq[2725] and Yaqub[2726] in our bounty; both we made righteous. (72) We made them leaders[2727] who guided people by our command. We inspired them to do good deeds, perform[2728] the prayers, and pay the poor-tax, and they worshiped us. (73) We gave Lut[2729] judgment and knowledge and rescued him from the village that did wickedness.[2730] They were bad, unbelieving[2731] people.[2732] (74) We made him enter our mercy. He was righteous.[2733] (75) Nuh,[2734] beforehand, called and we answered him and rescued him and his family from the great distress.[2735] (76) We saved him from people who rejected our signs.[2736] They were bad people, and we drowned them all.[2737] (77) Dawud[2738] and Sulayman[2739] judged about a field where the people's sheep strayed. We were witness of their judgment. (78) We made Sulayman[2740] understand it, and we gave both judgment and

---

[2720] Arabic /ilah/. See glossary for more details.
[2721] Tawrah, Daniel 3:19-28
[2722] Abraham. See glossary for more details.
[2723] Tawrah, Genesis 19:29, 13:14-15
[2724] Lot, nephew of Abraham. See glossary for more details.
[2725] Isaac. See glossary for more details.
[2726] Jacob. See glossary for more details.
[2727] or imams
[2728] this word is missing a letter, but we assume the meaning given.
[2729] Lot, nephew of Abraham. See glossary for more details.
[2730] Tawrah, Genesis 19:29
[2731] Or transgressing or immoral
[2732] Tawrah, Genesis 13:13
[2733] Injil, 2 Peter 2:7
[2734] Noah. See glossary for more details.
[2735] Tawrah, Genesis 7-8
[2736] Arabic /ayat/. See glossary for more details.
[2737] Tawrah, Genesis 7:21
[2738] David. See glossary for more details.
[2739] Solomon. See glossary for more details.
[2740] Solomon. See glossary for more details.

## Chapter 21

knowledge.[2741] With Dawud.[2742] we made the mountains[2743] and the birds[2744] praise.[2745] We did that. (79) We taught him to make garments for you[MP], to protect you[MP] from your[MP] misery. Do you[MP] give thanks? (80) We made the wind blow at Sulayman's[2746] command[2747] on the land we blessed. We knew everything. (81) Some devils[2748] dived for him and did other work, too. We protected them. (82) 1744 Ayyub[2749] called to his Lord, "Harm has touched me, and you[MS] are the most merciful of all."[2750] (83) We answered him and took away the harm,[2751] and brought him his family[2752] and others in addition as our mercy and a reminder for those who worship. (84) Ismail,[2753] Idris,[2754] and Dhu-Al-Kifl[2755] endured.[2756] (85) We made them enter our mercy.[2757] They were righteous. (86) Dhu-Al-Nun[2758] went[2759] angrily,[2760] thinking we were not more powerful than he. He called from the darkness,[2761] "You[MS] are the only god.[2762] May you[MS] be glorified! I was wicked."[2763] (87) We answered him and rescued him from the

---

[2741] Tawrah, 1 Kings 3:9-14
[2742] David. See glossary for more details.
[2743] Zabur, Psalms 148:9
[2744] Zabur, Psalms 148:10
[2745] Zabur, Psalms 148:13 The word praise is used of thinking beings, and it seems the mountains and birds are considered as giving praise voluntarily. See Injil, Luke 19:40
[2746] Solomon. See glossary for more details.
[2747] Tawrah, Ecclesiastes 1:6
[2748] Arabic /shayatin/. See glossary for more details.
[2749] Job, the prophet known for patience. See glossary for more details.
[2750] Tawrah, Job 2:7-10
[2751] Tawrah, Job 42:10
[2752] Tawrah, Job 42:13-14
[2753] Ishmael. See glossary for more details. Tawrah, Genesis 16:11-25:16
[2754] Enoch. See glossary for more details. Tawrah, Genesis 5:18-24, Injil, Hebrews 11:5.
[2755] Ezekiel?. See glossary for more details. Tawrah, Ezekiel 1-48
[2756] See "endure" in glossary.
[2757] Tawrah, Genesis 5:21-24
[2758] Jonah. See glossary under Yunus for more details.
[2759] Tawrah, Jonah 1:3
[2760] Tawrah, Jonah 4:1
[2761] Tawrah, Jonah 2:1-9
[2762] Arabic /ilah/. See glossary for more details.
[2763] Tawrah, Jonah 2:9. The belief that all prophets and messengers are sinless is not supported by the Qur'an. For instances of prophets or

darkness.[2764] Thus we rescue believers. (88) Zakariyya[2765] called to his Lord, "My Lord, do not leave me without an heir.[2766] You are the best giver of inheritance."[2767] (89) We answered him and gave him Yahya.[2768] We made his wife fertile to him.[2769] They[MP] tried[2770] to outdo each other in good deeds,[2771] and in praying to us in desire and awe.[2772] They were humble. (90) We breathed of our spirit[2773] into her[2774] who guarded her chastity,[2775] and made her and her son a sign[2776] for all the universe.[2777] (91) This nation of yours[MP] is one nation. I am your[MP] Lord, so worship[MP] me. (92) But they split up the matter among them. All will return to us. (93) The efforts of any believer who does righteous deeds[2778] will not be denied. We will write them down for him. (94) Any city we have destroyed is forbidden. They will not return (95) until Yajuj and Majuj[2779] are loosed[2780] and hasten from every hill (96) and the true promise approaches. Disbelievers' eyes will stare, "Woe to us! We were unaware of this, and were wicked." (97) You[MP] and

---

messengers asking forgiveness or committing sins, see 7:23, 20:121 (Adam), 11:47, 71:28 (Nuh), 26:82, 14:41 (Ibrahim), 28:15-16 (Musa), 7:151, 20:93 (Musa and Harun), 38:24 (Dawud), 38:32,35 (Sulayman), 21:87, 37:142 (Yunus), 48:2, 47:19, 40:55, 4:79,106, 9:43, 13:30, 80:1-2, 110:3, 94:2, 23:118, 66:1, 33:37, 8:67, and 9:117 (Muhammad (s).

[2764] Tawrah, Jonah 2:10
[2765] Zechariah. See glossary for more details.
[2766] or alone.
[2767] Literally, "the best heir." Injil, Luke 1:13
[2768] John the Baptist. See glossary for more details.
[2769] Injil, Luke 1:13,24
[2770] the plural, not the dual is used here, refering to Zechariah, his wife, and John
[2771] Injil, Romans 12:10
[2772] Injil, Luke 1:6
[2773] Injil, Luke 1:35. Isa and Adam are the only ones who came about through Allah's spirit. See 32:9, 15:29, 38:72 for Adam, and here and 66:12 for Isa.
[2774] Mary, the mother of Jesus
[2775] literally vulva or genitals
[2776] Injil, Luke 1:34. Many messengers had signs, but Mariam and Isa are the only believers who <u>were</u> themselves signs. See 23:50.
[2777] Injil, Matthew 28:18
[2778] Injil, 1 Corinthians 3:8, James 2:14-17, Revelation 19:8
[2779] Gog and Magog. See glossary for more details. Tawrah, Ezekiel 38:2, 39:1-6, Injil, Revelation 20:8
[2780] Or are defeated

## Chapter 21

the gods you<sup>MP</sup> worship besides Allah are fuel for hell, and you<sup>MP</sup> are going there. (98) If they were gods,[2781] they would not have entered it. All will remain in it forever. (99) In it, they will sob and not hear. (100) Those to whom we did good are far away. (101) They hear no sound and they will be where their souls desired forever. (102) The great terror does not make them grieve,[2782] and the angels receive them,[2783] "This is your<sup>MP</sup> day you<sup>MP</sup> were promised."[2784] (103) It is the day we roll up the heavens like a scroll,[2785] just like we began creation at first, we promise we will restore it,[2786] and we will do it. (104) We have written in the Zabur[2787] after the reminder,[2788] "My righteous servants will inherit the earth."[2789] (105) This is an announcement to people who worship. (106) We sent you<sup>MS</sup> only as a mercy to mankind. (107) Say<sup>MS</sup>, "I received inspiration that your<sup>MP</sup> god[2790] is one god.[2791] Are you submitted?"[2792] (108) If they turn away, say<sup>MS</sup>, "I have proclaimed to you<sup>MP</sup> all alike, even though I do not know whether what you<sup>MP</sup> have been promised is near or far. (109) He knows what is said publicly, and he knows what you<sup>MP</sup> hide. (110) For all I know, it might be a trial for you<sup>MP</sup>, and enjoyment for a while. (111) He said, "My Lord, judge truly. Our Lord is the most gracious, whose help is sought against what you<sup>MP</sup> describe." (112)

---

[2781] Arabic /ilah/. See glossary for more details.
[2782] Injil, Revelation 2:11, 20:6
[2783] Injil, Matthew 13:39
[2784] Injil, John 14:1-3
[2785] Injil, Hebrews 1:10-12
[2786] Injil, Revelation 21:5
[2787] Psalms. See glossary for more details.
[2788] Arabic /dhikr/. See glossary for more details. Here the reminder refers to the book before the Zabur, i.e. the Tawrah.
[2789] Zabur, Psalms 24:1
[2790] Arabic /ilah/. See glossary for more details.
[2791] Arabic /ilah/. See glossary for more details.
[2792] Injil, James 4:7. For "submitted," some translators do not translate this. See glossary for more details.

# Chapter 22 Al-Hajj[2793]

**17B1** In the name of Allah, the most gracious and merciful.[2794] People, fear your[MP] Lord. The earthquake of the hour is severe.[2795] (1)

On the day you[MP] see it, every nursing mother will forget her nursing child, and every pregnant woman will give birth.[2796] You[MS] will see people acting drunk when they are not drunk.[2797] Allah's torment[2798] is severe. (2) Some people ignorantly argue about Allah.[2799] They follow every rebellious devil, (3)

about whom it is written that he leads astray everyone who chooses him as a helper,[2800] and guides him into the torment of burning fire. (4)

People, if you[MP] doubt the resurrection,[2801] we created you[MP] from soil,[2802] then from a drop of semen, then from a blood clot, then from a bit of flesh,[2803] well-formed and not well-formed,[2804] to clarify to you[MP]. We confirm what we will in the wombs[2805] for a specific timespan. Then we deliver you[MP] as children, and then you[MP] grow up. Some of you[MP] die and some are returned to the worst part of life, senile.[2806] You[MS] see the barren ground. If we

---

[2793] Pilgrimage
[2794] Zabur, Psalms 103:8, 145:8. See glossary for more details.
[2795] Injil, Revelation 11:13
[2796] Injil, Matthew 24:19
[2797] Tawrah, Isaiah 51:21
[2798] For "torment" here and in verses 4, 9, 18, 25, 47, 55, and 57, see Tawrah, Isaiah 50:11, Injil, Matthew 18:34, 25:41,46, Luke 16:23-28, Revelation 20:15.
[2799] Injil, 2 Timothy 2:16-18
[2800] Injil, 2 Timothy 2:25-26
[2801] Injil, 1 Corinthians 15:12-21, 2 Timothy 2:18
[2802] Tawrah, Genesis 2:7
[2803] Tawrah, Job 10:10, Zabur, Psalms 139:13-16
[2804] Tawrah, Job 10:11
[2805] Tawrah, Isaiah 49:5
[2806] Tawrah, Ecclesiastes 12:1-6

Chapter 22

send rain down on it,[2807] it shakes, swells, and sprouts all kinds of delicious plants.[2808] (5)
\*\*\*

That is because Allah is true, and he gives life to the dead. He can do anything.[2809] (6) The hour is coming. There is no doubt of it. Allah will resurrect those in the graves.[2810] (7) Some people argue ignorantly about Allah,[2811] with no guidance or enlightening book.[2812] (8)
\*\*\*

He turns aside to lead [people] astray from the path of Allah. He will have shame in this world, and on the day of resurrection,[2813] we will make him taste the torment of the fire.[2814] (9)
\*\*\*

That is because of your[MS] deeds. Allah does not wrong his servants.[2815] (10)
\*\*\*

Some people worship Allah on the fence.[2816] When good happens, they are secure, but when testing comes, they turn on their faces.[2817] They are lost both in this world and the hereafter. That is clearly a loss. (11)
\*\*\*

They pray to gods besides Allah that cannot harm them or help them.[2818] That is going far astray. (12)

---

[2807] Tawrah, Deuteronomy 28:12, Job 5:10, Joel 2:23, Zabur, Psalms 68:9, Injil, Matthew 5:45

[2808] Tawrah, Isaiah 55:10

[2809] Tawrah, Job 42:2, Isaiah 14:27, Daniel 4:35, Injil, Matthew 19:26, Mark 10:27, Luke 1:37

[2810] Injil, Revelation 20:5, John 5:25

[2811] Injil, 2 Corinthians 10:5

[2812] See 31:20, 35:25, 3:184, the last two of which indicate that it refers to the previous books. Zabur, Psalms 119:130, 105, 19:8

[2813] Here and in verses 17 and 69, for "day of resurrection," see Tawrah, Daniel 12:2 Injil, Acts 24:15, 1 Corinthians 15:52-54, Revelation 20:11-15

[2814] Injil, Philippians 3:19

[2815] This verse is one of only five verses where the plural form /abid/ is used. All five use the same phrase. This word can also be translated "slaves." The other verses are 3:182, 8:51, 41:46, and 50:29.

[2816] Injil, Revelation 3:16

[2817] Injil, Matthew 13:21

[2818] Tawrah, Isaiah 41:23

# Chapter 22

\*\*\*

They pray to a god[2819] that is more likely to harm them than to help them. What an awful master! What an awful companion! (13)

\*\*\*

Allah causes believers who do righteous deeds[2820] to enter heavenly gardens[2821] with rivers underneath.[2822] Allah does whatever he wants. (14)

\*\*\*

If anyone thinks that Allah will not save him in this world and the hereafter, let him stretch a connection to heaven and then let him cut off.[2823] Let him see if his plot gets rid of what causes rage. (15)

\*\*\*

Thus we have revealed miraculous signs.[2824] Allah guides those he wants to. (16) Allah will separate between the believers the Jews,[2825] the Sabeans,[2826] the Christians,[2827] the magi,[2828] and the

---

[2819] Arabic /ilah/. See glossary for more details.

[2820] Injil, 1 Corinthians 3:8, James 2:14-17, Revelation 19:8

[2821] Arabic /jannah/. See glossary for more details.

[2822] Tawrah, Genesis 2:10

[2823] It is unclear what he is to cut off. From the context, one meaning is "worship of other gods."

[2824] Arabic /ayat/ See glossary.

[2825] Or those who repented and turned back to the truth. This refers to the Jews, probably when they repented after worshiping the golden calf idol (2:54, 92, 7:138, 148-150, Tawrah, Exodus 32).

[2826] Sabeans are only mentioned three times in the Qur'an (here, 2:62, and in 5:69). They may be followers of John the Baptizer, as some by that name still exist in Iraq today, or a tribe of Christians in northern Arabia who were known for praying 7 times a day, or this may refer to the Mandeans. Whoever they are, they seem to be monotheists.

[2827] For /nasara/ (Christian) here and in verses 113 (twice) and 120, see glossary for more details.

[2828] The magus (commonly known as wise men or magi, but who were not kings, as is sometimes thought) are also mentioned in the Injil, Matthew 2:1-12, and were experts in astronomy. They saw the star that announced the birth of the Messiah and came from a far place (probably Arabia, judging from the direction (Injil, Matthew 2:1) and the gifts they brought (Injil, Matthew 2:11, Isaiah 60:6,7), which were and still are products of the Arabian peninsula) to give homage to the Messiah, who was appointed by Allah as prophet (19:30, 3:49, Injil, Matthew 13:57, 21:11,46), priest (3:55, 5:117, 37:107, 2:255, 3:49, 5:110, 19:19, 3:45,

## Chapter 22

idolaters on the day of resurrection. Allah witnesses everything. (17)

\*\*\*

Have you<sup>MS</sup> not seen that everything in the heavens and on the earth bows down to Allah: the sun, the moon, the stars, the mountains, the trees, the living creatures, and many people?<sup>2829</sup> Many others deserve torment. Those Allah dishonors will not be honored by anyone. Allah does what he wills.<sup>2830</sup> (18) 1 7B2

\*\*\*

There<sup>MD</sup> were<sup>MD</sup> two who argued<sup>MP2831</sup> about their<sup>MP</sup> Lord. Disbelievers will have garments of fire cut out for them, and boiling water will be poured over their heads, (19)

\*\*\*

making their organs and their skin dissolve. (20) They will have iron hooks. (21)

\*\*\*

Whenever they want to get out of it<sup>2832</sup> in their anguish, they will be put back
into it. "Taste the torment of the fire."<sup>2833</sup> (22)

\*\*\*

Allah will cause the believers who do righteous deeds<sup>2834</sup> to enter heavenly gardens<sup>2835</sup> with rivers underneath,<sup>2836</sup> where they will be adorned with golden bracelets, pearls, and silk clothing. (23)

\*\*\*

They will be guided to good speech and guided to the path of the praiseworthy one. (24)

\*\*\*

We will make disbelievers who block<sup>2837</sup> Allah's path<sup>2838</sup> and the sacred place of worship<sup>2839</sup> we made for all people taste painful

---

Injil, Hebrews 6:20), and king (hints in 3:50-51, 43:61-64, Injil, Revelation 17:14).

<sup>2829</sup> Zabur, Psalms 148:1-13

<sup>2830</sup> Zabur, Psalms 115:3

<sup>2831</sup> The subject is dual, and the verb is plural. There may be another meaning.

<sup>2832</sup> Injil, Revelation 3:16

<sup>2833</sup> Injil, Revelation 18:7, 20:10, Matthew 25:41,46

<sup>2834</sup> Injil, 1 Corinthians 3:8, James 2:14-17, Revelation 19:8

<sup>2835</sup> Arabic /jannah/. See glossary for more details.

<sup>2836</sup> Tawrah, Genesis 2:10

<sup>2837</sup> Or, "hinder [people] from"

<sup>2838</sup> Injil, Matthew 23:13, Luke 11:52.

## Chapter 22

torment, whether they stay there, appear there, or want to wickedly deviate in it. (25)

\*\*\*

We settled Ibrahim[2840] at the sanctuary, "Do not worship anything besides me. Purify my sanctuary[2841] for those who go around it, and for those who stand, kneel, and bow down. (26)

\*\*\*

Proclaim hajj[2842] to people, those who come to you[MS] on foot, those who come on every thin beast from every deep crevice, (27)

\*\*\*

so that they may see benefits for themselves, and mention Allah's name on specific[2843] days over the beasts of the cattle he provided them." Eat[MP] of them and feed the needy and the poor. (28)

\*\*\*

Then let them get rid of their uncleanness, pay their vows, and go around the ancient sanctuary. (29)

\*\*\*

Thus it is better with their Lord for those who honor the sacred things of Allah. Cattle are allowed for you[MP], except what is read[2844] to you[MP]. Avoid the abomination of idols[2845] and avoid false sayings, (30)

\*\*\*

as monotheists who believe in Allah and no other gods. When someone worships other gods besides Allah, it is as if he falls down from heaven,[2846] and a bird catches him or the wind blows him far away.[2847] (31)

\*\*\*

But whoever thus honors Allah's ordinances does so from reverence in heart. (32) You[MP] have benefit in it for a span of time, and then its place of sacrifice will be the ancient sanctuary. (33)

\*\*\*

---

[2839] Injil, John 4:20-24, Hebrews 8:1-2, 9:24, 10:19-22.
[2840] Abraham. See glossary for more details.
[2841] Tawrah, Ezekiel 43:26
[2842] pilgrimage. See glossary for more details.
[2843] The adjective is for thinking beings. There may be another meaning.
[2844] Or recited or told
[2845] Tawrah, Deuteronomy 7:25
[2846] Injil, Luke 10:18
[2847] Zabur, Psalms 1:4

Every nation has its own place of sacrifice, so that they would mention Allah's name over the beasts of the cattle Allah provided them. Your^MP god[2848] is one god.[2849] Submit[2850] to him, and give good news to the humble (34) whose hearts tremble when Allah is mentioned,[2851] as well as to those who endure[2852] in tribulation,[2853] and those who perform prayers and donate out of what we have provided. (35) We have made sacrificed camels part of Allah's ordinances for you^MP. There is good in them, so mention Allah's name over them as they are lined up for sacrifice. When they fall down dead on their sides, eat of them and feed beggars and the poor. Thus we have made them subject to you^MP, so that you^MP may give thanks. (36) Their flesh and blood will not be acceptable to Allah, but righteousness[2854] from you^MP will be acceptable to him. Thus we have made them subject to you^MP, so that you^MP would magnify Allah for how he has guided you^MP.[2855] Give^MS good news to those who do good deeds. (37)
***

**17B3** Allah defends the believers. Allah does not love any disbelieving traitors.[2856] (38) Those who were wronged may fight. Allah is able to save them. (39)
***

They were wrongfully expelled from their homes. All they did was say, "Our Lord is Allah." If Allah had not pushed the people into each other, monasteries, churches, places of prayer, and places of worship, where Allah's name is remembered frequently, would have been destroyed. Allah will save those who help[2857] him.[2858] Allah is strong[2859] and mighty. (40)
***

---

[2848] Arabic /ilah/. See glossary for more details.
[2849] Arabic /ilah/. See glossary for more details.
[2850] Injil, James 4:7. For "submit," some translators do not translate this. See glossary for more details.
[2851] Zabur, Psalms 114:7
[2852] See "endure" in glossary
[2853] Injil, Romans 12:12, 5:2-5
[2854] Injil, Hebrews 2:11
[2855] Zabur, Psalms 78:52,72
[2856] Zabur, Psalms 5:4-5, 11:5, Tawrah, Proverbs 6:16-19
[2857] Or save.
[2858] Tawrah, Isaiah 50:5-10
[2859] Tawrah, Job 9:4, Zabur, Psalms 24:8, Injil, Ephesians 6:10, Revelation 18:8

If we make them firm in the land, they perform prayers, pay the poor-tax, promote virtue,[2860] and prevent vice. The end of the matter is Allah's. (41)

\*\*\*

If they reject you[MS], the people of Nuh,[2861] Aad,[2862] and Thamud rejected[2863] beforehand, (42)

\*\*\*

as well as Ibrahim's[2864] people, Lut's[2865] people,[2866] (43)

\*\*\*

and those of Midian.[2867] Musa[2868] was rejected, too. I gave disbelievers more
time, then overtook them. How was my punishment? (44)

\*\*\*

How many wicked villages we destroyed![2869] They are ruined down to their foundations, a neglected well, and a lofty[2870] palace. (45)

\*\*\*

Have they not walked in the land, and comprehended with their hearts or ears that hear? Their sight is not blind, but their hearts inside of them are blind.[2871] (46)

\*\*\*

They desire you[MS] to hasten the torment. Allah will not break his promise.[2872] A day with your[MS] Lord is as a thousand years as you[MP] count them.[2873] (47)

\*\*\*

How many villages have I given more time,[2874] though they were wicked? Then I overtook them. I am [man's] destiny. (48)

---

[2860] or kindness
[2861] Noah. See glossary for more details. Tawrah, Genesis 6:1-12
[2862] Aad and Thamud are names of tribes.
[2863] The verb is feminine here and the noun is masculine. There may be another meaning.
[2864] Abraham. See glossary for more details.
[2865] Lot, nephew of Abraham. See glossary for more details.
[2866] Tawrah, Genesis 19:9
[2867] Tawrah, Numbers 22:7
[2868] Moses. See glossary for more details.
[2869] Tawrah, Deuteronomy 2:21-22, 7:22-23
[2870] or plastered
[2871] Tawrah, Isaiah 29:9, 6:10
[2872] Tawrah, Numbers 23:19
[2873] Injil, 2 Peter 3:8

Chapter 22

\*\*\*

Say[MS], "People, I am clearly a warner to you[MP]." (49) Believers who do righteous deeds[2875] will have forgiveness and a generous provision.[2876] (50) Those who seek to nullify our signs[2877] are inmates of the blazing fire. (51) Whenever we sent a messenger or prophet before you[MS], and he wished anything, Satan threw forth a suggestion about what he wished. Allah nullifies what Satan throws forth. Then Allah makes his signs firm. Allah is all-knowing[2878] and wise.[2879] (52)

\*\*\*

That is in order to make what Satan threw forth a temptation[2880] for the sick-hearted or hard-hearted. The wicked are in great dissension. (53)

\*\*\*

It is also so that the knowledgeable will know that it is the truth from your[MS] Lord, will believe in it, and their hearts be humble toward him.[2881] Allah guides those who believe[2882] to the straight path.[2883] (54) Disbelievers will still be in doubt about it until the hour comes upon them suddenly,[2884] or until the torment of a grievous[2885] day comes upon them.[2886] (55) On that day, the kingdom will be Allah's,[2887] and he will judge between them. Believers who do righteous deeds will be in heavenly gardens[2888]

---

[2874] Injil, Acts 17:30
[2875] Here and in verse 56, see Injil, 1 Corinthians 3:8, James 2:14-17, Revelation 19:8.
[2876] Injil, James 2:14-26
[2877] Arabic /ayat/. See glossary for more details.
[2878] For "all-knowing" here and in verse 59, see Tawrah, Job 37:16, Isaiah 40:14, Zabur, Psalms 33:13-15, Injil, 1 John 3:20
[2879] Tawrah, Job 9:4, Proverbs 2:6, Jeremiah 9:23-24, Injil, 1 Corinthians 1:21-25, Romans 16:27
[2880] Injil, James 1:13
[2881] Or it.
[2882] Zabur, Psalms 23:3
[2883] See glossary for more details, and notes on 3:51, 6:153, 19:36, 36:61, and 43:64 on what the straight path is.
[2884] Injil, Luke 21:34
[2885] Or barren
[2886] Injil, 1 Thessalonians 5:2-3
[2887] Injil, Revelation 11:15
[2888] Arabic /jannah/. See glossary for more details.

Chapter 22

of delight (56) and disbelievers who rejected our signs[2889] will have shameful torment. (57) Those who emigrated in Allah's path and then are killed or died will be well-provided for by Allah. Allah is the best provider.[2890] (58) He will cause them to enter by a gate that pleases them.[2891] Allah is all-knowing and gentle.[2892] (59)

17B4

\*\*\*

Thus when anyone punishes as he was punished, and then is transgressed against, Allah will save him. Allah is pardoning and forgiving.[2893] (60) That is because Allah makes the night enter the day and the day enter the night. Allah hears all and sees all. (61) That is because Allah is true, and those gods they pray to are false. Allah is most high and great. (62) Have you[MS] not seen that Allah sends rain from the sky[2894] and the ground becomes green? Allah is kind and aware. (63)

\*\*\*

Everything in the heavens and the earth is his.[2895] Allah is self-sufficient and praiseworthy. (64)

\*\*\*

Have you[MS] not seen that Allah has subjected everything on earth to you[MP]? The ship sails on the sea by his command. He grasps the sky, lest it fall on the earth without his permission. Allah is compassionate and merciful[2896] to people. (65)

\*\*\*

He is the one that gives you[MP] life, then makes you[MP] die, then will revive you[MP]. Man is disbelieving.[2897] (66)

---

[2889] Arabic /ayat/. See glossary for more details.
[2890] Injil, Matthew 6:26
[2891] Injil, 2 Peter 1:11
[2892] Zabur, Psalms 45:4, 145:17, Injil, Matthew 11:29, Galatians 5:22
[2893] Zabur, Psalms 103:3, 130:4, Tawrah, Isaiah 43:25, Exodus 34:7, Injil, Acts 26:18
[2894] Tawrah, Deuteronomy 28:12, Job 5:10, Joel 2:23, Zabur, Psalms 68:9, Injil, Matthew 5:45
[2895] Tawrah, Isaiah 45:12, Zabur, Psalms 24:1, 89:11, Injil, Hebrews 1:10
[2896] Injil, James 5:11. See glossary for more details on "merciful."
[2897] The injustice/wickedness, disbelief/ungratefulness, evil, unrighteousness/sin, or lostness of mankind is mentioned in a number of verses in the Qur'an as well as in the previous books. Injustice or wickedness: 2:57, 3:117,135, 4:64,97, 7:160,177, 9:70, 10:44, 11:101, 14:34,45, 16:33,61,118, 29:40, 30:9, 33:72, 34:19, 35:32, 43:76, 65:1, Tawrah, Genesis 6:5, Job 25:4, Injil, Acts 3:26, disbelief or

## Chapter 22

\*\*\*

We have given every nation their own place of sacrifice for them to use. Do not let them dispute with you[MS] about the matter. Pray to your[MS] Lord. You[MS] have straight guidance.[2898] (67) If they argue with you[MS], say[MS], "Allah well knows your[MP] deeds. (68) Allah will judge between you[MP] on the day of resurrection about your[MP] differences." (69)

\*\*\*

Do you[MS] not know that Allah knows everything in heaven and earth? That is in a book. That is easy for Allah. (70) They worship gods besides Allah who have not been authorized, and of which they have no knowledge. The wicked have no savior.[2899] (71) If our signs and miracles are read to them, you[MS] will know disbelievers by their faces because of what they deny. They almost attack those who read our signs to them. Say[MS], "Shall I tell you[MP] of something more evil than that? Allah has promised hellfire to the disbelievers. It is an awful destiny." (72)

\*\*\*

People, here is a proverb. Listen to it. Those gods you[MP] pray to besides Allah will never create a fly, even if they all work together. And if a fly robs them of anything, they will not rescue it from him. Both those who ask and those who are asked are weak. (73)

\*\*\*

They do not honor Allah as he deserves. Allah is strong[2900] and mighty. (74)

\*\*\*

Allah chooses some angels and people as messengers. Allah hears all and sees all. (75) He knows what is before them and behind them.[2901] All matters return to Allah. (76)

---

ungratefulness: 14:34, 17:67, 22:66, 42:48, 43:15, 80:17, Injil, Hebrews 3:19, Evil: 12:53, Tawrah, Jeremiah 17:9, Injil, Matthew 15:19, Mark 7:21, unrighteousness or sin: 91:8, Tawrah, 1 Kings 8:46, Ecclesiastes 7:20, Injil, Romans 3:9-19, 5:12, lostness: 103:2, Tawrah, Jeremiah 50:6, Injil, Luke 19:10, Romans 3:23, 6:23

[2898] Zabur, Psalms 25:10

[2899] Tawrah, Isaiah 43:11, Hosea 13:4, Injil, Hebrews 10:26

[2900] Tawrah, Job 9:4, Zabur, Psalms 24:8, Injil, Ephesians 6:10, Revelation 18:8

[2901] Or "what is in front of them and behind them" or "what is between their hands and behind them" or "their future and their past."

Chapter 22

\*\*\*

Believers, kneel<sup>MP</sup>, bow<sup>MP</sup> down, and worship<sup>MP</sup> your<sup>MP</sup> Lord, and do<sup>MP</sup> good, so that you<sup>MP</sup> may prosper. (77)

\*\*\*

Struggle in Allah with the struggle he deserves.[2902] He has chosen you<sup>MP</sup> and has not made anything in religion embarrassing for you<sup>MP</sup>. According to the spiritual path[2903] of your<sup>MP</sup> father Ibrahim,[2904] he has called you<sup>MP</sup> submitted[2905] beforehand. May the messenger be a witness against you<sup>MP</sup> in this, and may you<sup>MP</sup> be witnesses against the people. So perform<sup>MP</sup> the prayers and pay<sup>MP</sup> the poor-tax. Take refuge in Allah.[2906] He is your<sup>MP</sup> master,[2907] the best of masters, and the best of saviors. (78)[2908]

---

[2902] Tawrah, 2 Samuel 22:4
[2903] Arabic /millah/. See glossary.
[2904] Abraham. See glossary for more details.
[2905] Injil, James 4:7. For "submitted," some translators do not translate this. See glossary for more details.
[2906] Zabur, Psalms 46:1
[2907] Injil, Colossians 4:1
[2908] The verses in this chapter that rhyme are put together in paragraphs, separated by \*\*\*.

# Chapter 23 Al-Muminun[2909]

18A1 In the name of Allah, the most gracious and merciful.[2910] Happy[2911] are the believers, (1) who are humble[2912] in performing prayers, (2) turn away from vanity,[2913] (3) pay the poor-tax, (4) and protect their chastity[2914] (5) from all except their spouses or their slaves, for they are blameless. (6) Those who desire more than that are transgressors. (7) Those who observe their pledges and covenants (8) and those who observe the performance of prayers (9) are the heirs.[2915] (10) They will inherit paradise, and remain there forever.[2916] (11) We created mankind from an extract of clay.[2917] (12) Then we made him a sperm in a secure, fixed place. (13) Then we created the sperm as a blood clot, and created the blood clot as tissue, and created the tissue as bones, and adorned the bones with meat,[2918] then produced another creation. Blessed be Allah,[2919] the best of the creators.[2920] (14) After that, you'll[MP] be dead. (15) Then, on the day of resurrection,[2921] you'll[MP] be resurrected.[2922] (16) We created seven paths,[2923] and were not ignorant of the creation. (17) We sent rain down from the sky[2924] by decree,[2925] and made it remain in the ground. We can take it away. (18) With it, we made heavenly gardens[2926] for you[MP], with

---

[2909] The believers
[2910] Zabur, Psalms 103:8, 145:8. See glossary for more details.
[2911] Or blessed or successful or prosperous
[2912] Injil, Matthew 5:3
[2913] Zabur, Psalms 1:1
[2914] Or genitals.
[2915] Injil, Matthew 5:5
[2916] Injil, Matthew 5:10
[2917] Tawrah, Genesis 2:7
[2918] Zabur, Psalms 139:13-16
[2919] Zabur, Psalms 103:1
[2920] It is unclear what is intended by the use of the plural "creators."
[2921] Here and in verse 100, for "day of resurrection," see Tawrah, Daniel 12:2 Injil, Acts 24:15, 1 Corinthians 15:52-54, Revelation 20:11-15
[2922] Injil, John 11:24
[2923] Probably a reference to heavens
[2924] Tawrah, Deuteronomy 28:12, Job 5:10, Joel 2:23, Zabur, Psalms 68:9, Injil, Matthew 5:45
[2925] Or measure
[2926] Arabic /jannah/. See glossary for more details.

Chapter 23

palms and grapes for you<sup>MP</sup>.[2927] There are many fruits in it that you<sup>MP</sup> can eat, (19) as well as a tree that comes out of Mount Sinai,[2928] that produces oil and sauce[2929] to eat. (20) There is a moral for you<sup>MP</sup> in cattle. We give you<sup>MP</sup> drink from what is in their bellies, they give you<sup>MP</sup> many benefits, and you<sup>MP</sup> can eat them. (21) They and ships can also carry you<sup>MP</sup>. (22) We sent Nuh[2930] to his people.[2931] He said, "My people, worship<sup>MP</sup> Allah. He is the only god[2932] you<sup>MP</sup> have. Will you<sup>MP</sup> not be reverent?" (23) The disbelieving nobles of his people said, "This is only a man like you<sup>MP</sup>. He wants to be superior to you<sup>MP</sup>. If Allah had willed, he would have sent down angels. We have not heard of this from[2933] our ancestors. (24) He is only a man with a jinn.[2934] Watch him for awhile." (25) He said, "My Lord, save me from their rejecting me." (26) So we inspired him, "Make the ship under our supervision and inspiration.[2935] When our command comes and the deep gushes forth,[2936] sail in it with a couple of every kind and your family,[2937] except for him who was mentioned previously.[2938] Do not speak to me about the wicked. They will be drowned."[2939] (27) When you<sup>MS</sup> and those that are with you<sup>MS</sup> have boarded the ship,[2940] say<sup>MS</sup>, "Praise be to Allah, who rescued us from wicked people." (28) Say<sup>MS</sup>, "My Lord, set me down[2941] on a blessed place. You<sup>MS</sup> are the best at setting down." (29) Those are signs, and we were testing."[2942] (30) Then we produced another generation after them, (31) and sent them a messenger of their own, "Worship Allah.[2943] He is the only god you<sup>MP</sup> have. Will you<sup>MP</sup> not be

---

[2927] Tawrah, Isaiah 55:10
[2928] Injil, Acts 7:30
[2929] many translations have "relish"
[2930] Noah. See glossary for more details.
[2931] Injil, 2 Peter 2:5
[2932] Arabic /ilah/, here and in verse 32. See glossary for more details.
[2933] Or about
[2934] Or demon. See glossary for more details.
[2935] Tawrah, Genesis 6:14
[2936] Tawrah, Genesis 7:11
[2937] Tawrah, Genesis 6:19
[2938] Tawrah, Genesis 6:17
[2939] Tawrah, Genesis 7:21
[2940] Tawrah, Genesis 7:7
[2941] Tawrah, Genesis 8:4
[2942] Or proving
[2943] Tawrah, Exodus 20:1-3

## Chapter 23

reverent?" (32) The disbelieving nobles of his people who rejected the appointment of the hereafter, though we had given them the riches in this world, said, "This is only a man like you[MP]. He eats what you[MP] eat, and drinks what you[MP] drink. (33) If you[MP] obey a man like yourselves[MP], you[MP] are lost. (34) Does he promise you[MP] that when you[MP] die and are soil and bones, you[MP] will be brought forth? (35) 18A2 Away with it[2944]! Away with what you[MP] are promised. (36) This world is all that there is. We will die and live, and we will not be resurrected. (37) He is only a man who invented a lie about Allah. We will not believe him." (38) He said, "My Lord, save me from their rejecting me." (39) He said, "They will regret it soon." (40) Then the cry rightly overtook them, and we made them scum. Away with wicked people. (41) Then we produced other generations after them. (42) No nation can hasten or delay their lifespan.[2945] (43) Then we sent our messengers, one after another. Whenever their messenger came to a nation, they rejected him,[2946] so we made them follow each other. We made them tales. Away with people that do not believe. (44) Then we sent[2947] Musa[2948] and his brother Harun,[2949] with our signs and clear authority,[2950] (45) to Pharaoh and his nobles, but they were proud, haughty people.[2951] (46) They said, "Shall we believe in men[D] like us, while their[D] people are our slaves?" (47) So they[MP] rejected them[D] and were[MP] destroyed.[2952] (48) We gave Musa the book[2953] so that they might be guided. (49) We made the son[2954] of Mariam[2955] and his mother a sign,[2956] and we gave them[D] refuge on a secure hill with a spring. (50) "Messengers[MP], eat[MP] of the good things and do[MP] righteous deeds. I know your[MP] deeds. (51) This nation of yours[MP] is one nation. I am your[MP] Lord, so fear[MP] me."

---

[2944] Other translations have "far," "far-fetched," or "impossible."
[2945] Injil, Matthew 6:27, Acts 17:26
[2946] Injil, Matthew 21:42
[2947] Tawrah, Exodus 4:14
[2948] Moses, here and in verse 49. See glossary for more details.
[2949] Aaron. See glossary for more details.
[2950] Tawrah, Exodus 4:21
[2951] Tawrah, Exodus 5:2
[2952] Injil, Hebrews 11:29
[2953] Tawrah, Exodus 31:18
[2954] Injil, Mark 6:3
[2955] Mary, mother of Jesus. See glossary for more details.
[2956] Isa and Mariam are the only believers in the Qur'an to be called signs. See 21:91.

## Chapter 23

(52) But they divided up the matter among them as sects.²⁹⁵⁷ Every party was happy with what they had. (53) Leave^MS them in their confusion for awhile. (54) Do they consider that we provide them²⁹⁵⁸ with money and children?²⁹⁵⁹ (55) We hasten to them with good, but they do not realize it. (56) Those who fear their Lord are afraid. (57) They believe in the signs of their Lord. (58) They do not worship other gods besides their Lord. (59) They pay [the poor-tax] on what they are given, while their hearts tremble that they will return to their Lord. (60) They hasten to good, and get there first. (61) We do not give any soul a burden beyond what it can bear.²⁹⁶⁰ We have a book that speaks the truth, and they will not be wronged.²⁹⁶¹ (62) Their hearts are confused by this, and they have other deeds that they have done. (63) Even if we seize their wealthy people with torment, they will groan in prayer. (64) Do not groan in prayer today. You^MP will not be saved from us. (65) My signs were read to you^MP, and you^MP retreated backwards, (66) proudly talking nonsense about it²⁹⁶² at night. (67) Do they not reflect on the saying, or have they received what their ancestors did not? (68) Did they not know their messenger when they denied him? (69) Or do they say, "He has a jinn."?²⁹⁶³ Rather he brought them truth, and most of them hate the truth. (70) If truth had followed their desires, the heavens and the earth would have been spoiled, along with everyone in them. But we brought them their reminder,²⁹⁶⁴ and they turned away from their reminder. (71) Do you^MS ask them for tribute? Your^MS Lord's tribute is better, and he is the best provider.²⁹⁶⁵ (72) You^MS call them²⁹⁶⁶ to the straight path.²⁹⁶⁷ (73) Those who do not believe in the hereafter turn aside from the path. (74) 18A3 If we had had mercy on them, and had taken away the harm they have, they would have

---

²⁹⁵⁷ Or "with scriptures"
²⁹⁵⁸ Zabur, Psalms 65:9
²⁹⁵⁹ Or sons
²⁹⁶⁰ Injil, 1 Corinthians 10:13
²⁹⁶¹ Injil, Revelation 19:2
²⁹⁶² or him. "It" is masculine while "signs" is feminine. The closest masculine noun is "torment" in verse 64.
²⁹⁶³ Or demon. See glossary for more details.
²⁹⁶⁴ Arabic /dhikr/. See glossary for more details.
²⁹⁶⁵ Zabur, Psalms 145:15,16
²⁹⁶⁶ Zabur, Psalms 23:3
²⁹⁶⁷ See glossary for more details, and notes on 3:51, 6:153, 19:36, 36:61, and 43:64 on what the straight path is.

## Chapter 23

wandered around obstinately in their transgressions. (75) We seized them with torment, but they did not abase themselves before their Lord or pray humbly. (76) Even when we opened the door of severe torment to them, they were overcome with despair. (77) He produced hearing, sight, and hearts for you[MP]. How little you[MP] give thanks! (78) He multiplies you[MP] on the earth,[2968] and you[MP] will be gathered[2969] to him.[2970] (79) He gives life and causes death,[2971] and the difference[2972] of night and day is his. Do you[MP] not comprehend? (80) No. They said what the ancient peoples said. (81) They said, "When we die and are soil and bones, will we be resurrected? (82) This is what we and our ancestors were promised beforehand. These are only legends of the earliest people. (83) Say[MS], "Who owns the earth and its contents,[2973] if you[MP] know?" (84) They will say, "Allah." Say[MS], "Do you[MP] not remember?" (85) Say[MS], "Who is Lord of the seven heavens[2974] and Lord of the great throne?"[2975] (86) They will say, "They are Allah's." Say[MS], "Will you[MP] not fear Allah?"[2976] (87) Say[MS], "Who holds the kingdom of all things in his hand,[2977] who protects and is not protected, if you[MP] know?" (88) They will say, "Allah." Say[MS], "How are you[MP] bewitched?" (89) No, we brought them the truth, and they are liars. (90) Allah has not chosen a boy,[2978] and there was no other god[2979] with him.[2980] Otherwise, every other god[2981] would have taken what he created and some would have been higher than others. May Allah be glorified above what they

---

[2968] Tawrah, Isaiah 9:3
[2969] Tawrah, Joel 3:11-14, Zephaniah 3:8, Injil, Matthew 25:32, John 15:6, Revelation 16:16
[2970] Injil, Matthew 25:32
[2971] Tawrah, 1 Samuel 2:6, Deuteronomy 32:39
[2972] Or "alternation." Tawrah, Genesis 1:16-18, 8:22
[2973] Tawrah, Deuteronomy 10:14
[2974] Tawrah, Genesis 24:3
[2975] Injil, Revelation 4:9
[2976] Tawrah, Deuteronomy 10:12, Isaiah 29:13, Injil, 1 Peter 2:17, Revelation 14:7
[2977] Injil, 1 Timothy 6:15
[2978] The idea of Allah choosing or adopting a boy is rejected in all the books.
[2979] Arabic /ilah/. See glossary for more details.
[2980] Here the Qur'an clearly rejects the idea of Allah choosing a boy as his son, or there being other gods.
[2981] Arabic /ilah/. See glossary for more details.

## Chapter 23

describe! (91) [He] knows the unseen and the seen. May he be exalted above the other gods they worship. (92) Say<sup>MS</sup>, "My Lord, please show me what they are promised. (93) My Lord, do not make me one of[2982] the wicked people." (94) We are able to show you<sup>MS</sup> what we promise them. (95) Repel<sup>MS</sup> bad deeds with what is better.[2983] We well know what they describe. (96) Say<sup>MS</sup>, "My Lord, I take refuge in you<sup>MS</sup> from the evil suggestions of devils.[2984] (97) I take refuge in you<sup>MS</sup>, my Lord, from their coming to me." (98) When death comes to any of them, he will say, "My Lord, return<sup>MP</sup> me, (99) so that I may do righteous deeds among what I left behind." No. It is a word that he says. Behind him is a barrier[2985] until the day of resurrection. (100) When the trumpet is blown, there are no relatives among them on that day, nor will they wonder. (101) Those with heavy scales will be prosperous, (102) while those with light scales have lost their souls, and will remain in hell forever. (103) Hellfire will scorch their faces and they will scowl in it. (104) "Were my signs[2986] not read to you<sup>MP</sup>, and you<sup>MP</sup> rejected them?" (105) They will say, "Our Lord, our misery has defeated us, and we were people who went astray. (106) Our Lord, get us out of it. Then if we still return, we'd really be wicked." (107) He said, "Be driven away in it, and do not speak to me." (108) There was a group of my servants who said, "Our Lord, we believe. Forgive us and have mercy on us. You<sup>MS</sup> are the most merciful."[2987] (109) You<sup>MP</sup> made fun of them until they made you<sup>MP</sup> forget to remember[2988] me, and you<sup>MP</sup> laughed at them. (110) I have repaid them today for what they endured,[2989] and they are the winners. (111) He said, "How long did you<sup>MP</sup> remain on the earth in years?" (112) They said, "We remain a day or part of a day. Ask those who counted." (113) He said, "You<sup>MP</sup> remained only a short while, if you<sup>MP</sup> only knew. (114) Do you<sup>MP</sup> think that we created you<sup>MP</sup> in vain,[2990] and that you<sup>MP</sup> will not be returned to

---

[2982] Or "in the midst of"
[2983] Injil, Romans 12:21
[2984] Arabic /shayatin/. See glossary for more details. Injil, Matthew 4:9
[2985] Injil, Luke 16:26
[2986] Arabic /ayat/. See glossary for more details.
[2987] Here and in verse 118, see glossary for more details on "merciful."
[2988] Or mention
[2989] See "endure" in glossary
[2990] Tawrah, Isaiah 45:18

us?" (115) May Allah, the True King,[2991] be exalted. He is the only god,[2992] the Lord of the noble throne.[2993] (116) Those who pray to a god[2994] besides Allah, about which there is no proof, will have a reckoning[2995] with their Lord. He does not make disbelievers prosper. (117) Say[MS], "My Lord, forgive[2996] and have mercy! You[MS] are the most merciful." (118)

---

[2991] Tawrah, Jeremiah 10:10, Injil, Revelation 15:3

[2992] Arabic /ilah/. See glossary for more details.

[2993] Injil, Revelation 20:11

[2994] Arabic /ilah/. See glossary for more details.

[2995] Tawrah, Genesis 9:5

[2996] The belief that all prophets and messengers are sinless is not supported by the Qur'an. For instances of prophets or messengers asking forgiveness or committing sins, see 7:23, 20:121 (Adam), 11:47, 71:28 (Nuh), 26:82, 14:41 (Ibrahim), 28:15-16 (Musa), 7:151, 20:93 (Musa and Harun), 38:24 (Dawud), 38:32,35 (Sulayman), 21:87, 37:142 (Yunus), 48:2, 47:19, 40:55, 4:79,106, 9:43, 13:30, 80:1-2, 110:3, 94:2, 23:118, 66:1, 33:37, 8:67, and 9:117 (Muhammad (s).

Chapter 24

# Chapter 24 Al-Noor[2997]

18𐤀4 In the name of Allah, the most gracious and merciful.[2998] A chapter we revealed and imposed. We revealed miraculous signs[2999] in it, so that you[MP] may remember. (1) Whip[MP] both the adulteress[3000] and the adulterer[3001] with 100 lashes.[3002] Do not have compassion on them in Allah's religion,[3003] if you[MP] believe in Allah and the last day. Let a group of believers witness their[D] torment. (2) An adulterer should only marry an adulteress[3004] or a polytheist[FS] and an adulteress should only marry an adulterer or a polytheist[MS]. That is forbidden for believers. (3) Whip[MP] the unbelieving[3005] people who throw [accusations] at chaste married women, and then cannot bring four witnesess, with 80 lashes, and thereafter do not accept their testimony at all,[3006] for they are unbelieving. (4) The exception is those who later repent and make amends. Allah is forgiving[3007] and merciful.[3008] (5) Those who throw [accusations] at their wives,[3009] and do not have witnesses besides themselves shall testify by Allah four times that he is telling the truth, (6) and must take a fifth oath that Allah's curse be upon him if he is lying. (7) Her torment will be averted if she testifies four times that he is lying, (8) and a fifth oath that Allah be angry with her if he is telling the truth. (9) If Allah's grace and mercy had not been on you[MP], and if Allah had not been the wise[3010] acceptor of repentance …[3011] (10) A group of you[MP] lied.

---

[2997] light
[2998] Zabur, Psalms 103:8, 145:8. See glossary for more details.
[2999] or "verses"
[3000] or "female fornicator," also twice in verse 3.
[3001] or "fornicator," also twice in verse 3.
[3002] Tawrah, Leviticus 20:10
[3003] or "judgment"
[3004] compare Tawrah, Hosea 1:2
[3005] Or transgressing or immoral
[3006] Tawrah, Deuteronomy 19:16-21
[3007] Here and in verses 22, 33, and 62, see Zabur, Psalms 103:3, 130:4, Tawrah, Isaiah 43:25, Exodus 34:7, Injil, Acts 26:18.
[3008] Here and in verses 20, 22, 33, 62, and 70, see glossary for more details on "merciful."
[3009] Tawrah, Numbers 5:11-31
[3010] Tawrah, Job 9:4, Proverbs 2:6, Jeremiah 9:23-24, Injil, 1 Corinthians 1:21-25, Romans 16:27

## Chapter 24

Do not think<sup>MP</sup> that it is evil for you<sup>MP</sup>. It is better for you<sup>MP</sup>. Every man of them will pay for his guilt.³⁰¹² Those who take upon themselves a greater part of it will have great torment.³⁰¹³ (11) When you<sup>MP</sup> had heard it, why did the male and female believers not think well of themselves, and say, "This is clearly a lie." (12) Why did they not bring four witnesses? Since they did not bring witnesses, they are liars in Allah's eyes. (13) If Allah's grace and mercy had not been on you<sup>MP</sup> in this world and the hereafter, you<sup>MP</sup> would have been touched by great torment for your<sup>MP</sup> exaggeration, (14) since you<sup>MP</sup> received it on your<sup>MP</sup> tongues and speak what you<sup>MP</sup> know nothing about with your<sup>MP</sup> mouths. You<sup>MP</sup> think it is easy, but it is a serious matter with Allah. (15) When you<sup>MP</sup> heard it, why did you<sup>MP</sup> not say, "We cannot speak of this. May you<sup>MS</sup> be glorified! This is serious slander." (16) Allah warns you<sup>MP</sup> not to repeat such a thing ever again, if you<sup>MP</sup> are believers. (17) Allah makes his signs clear to you<sup>MP</sup>. Allah is all-knowing³⁰¹⁴ and wise.³⁰¹⁵ (18) Those who like promiscuity³⁰¹⁶ to be spread among³⁰¹⁷ believers will have painful torment in this world and the hereafter.³⁰¹⁸ Allah knows, and you<sup>MP</sup> do not know. (19) If Allah's grace and mercy had not been on you<sup>MP</sup>, and Allah had not been compassionate and merciful³⁰¹⁹… (20) 18B1 Believers, do not follow Satan's footsteps. Satan commands those who follow his footsteps to do promiscuous, immoral things. If Allah's grace and mercy had not been on you<sup>MP</sup>, none of you<sup>MP</sup> would ever be pure,³⁰²⁰ but Allah purifies³⁰²¹ those he wills. Allah hears all and knows all. (21) Do

---

³⁰¹¹ Verse 10 and 20 do not seem to be connected with either the sentence before or after it.
³⁰¹² Tawrah, Ezekiel 18:20
³⁰¹³ Injil, Luke 12:47, Matthew 25:41,46, Revelation 20:10
³⁰¹⁴ For "all-knowing" and "knows all" here and in verses 21 and 32, see Tawrah, Job 37:16, Isaiah 40:14, Zabur, Psalms 33:13-15, Injil, 1 John 3:20
³⁰¹⁵ Tawrah, Job 9:4, Proverbs 2:6, Jeremiah 9:23-24, Injil, 1 Corinthians 1:21-25, Romans 16:27
³⁰¹⁶ Or lewdness, adultery or abomination, here and in verse 21
³⁰¹⁷ Or, "who like rumors of promiscuity to be spread about"
³⁰¹⁸ For "torment" here and in verse 23, see Tawrah, Isaiah 50:11, Injil, Matthew 18:34, 25:41,46, Luke 16:23-28, Revelation 20:15.
³⁰¹⁹ Injil, James 5:11
³⁰²⁰ Tawrah, Ecclesiastes 7:20, Proverbs 20:9, Isaiah 64:6
³⁰²¹ Tawrah, Malachi 3:3, Zabur, Psalms 19:8, 119:9,140, Injil, Acts 15:8,9, 1 Peter 2:2, Titus 2:14, Hebrews 1:3

not let those among you^MP who have grace^3022 and have the ability swear off giving to their relatives, the poor, and the sojourners in Allah's path. Let them pardon and forgive. Do you^MP not want Allah to forgive you^MP? Allah is forgiving and merciful. (22) Those who throw [accusations] at unaware, believing, chaste married women are damned in this world and the hereafter. They will have great torment (23) on the day their tongues, their hands, and their feet testify against them because of their deeds. (24) On that day, Allah will repay them their true debt,^3023 and they will know that Allah is the Clear Truth. (25) Impure women^3024 are for impure men and impure men are for impure women. Pure women are for pure men, and pure men are for pure women. They^MP are innocent of what they say. They^MP will have forgiveness and a generous provision. (26) Believers, do not enter houses that are not your^MP houses before you^MP ask permission and greet^MP the family in them. That is better for you^MP, so that you^MP may remember. (27) If you^MP do not find anyone in them, do not enter them before being given permission. If you^MP are told, "Go^MP back!" then go^MP back. It is purer for you^MP. Allah knows your^MP deeds. (28) It is not wrong for you^MP to enter uninhabited houses that you^MP have goods in. Allah knows what you^MP show and what you^MP hide. (29) Tell^MS believers^MP to lower their^MP gaze^3025 and guard their chastity.^3026 That is holier for them. Allah is aware of what they do. (30) Tell^MP believers^FP to lower their^FP gaze and guard their^FP chastity, and not to show their beauty,^3027 except for what is evident. Let them draw their coverings over their cleavage^3028 and not show their beauty except to their^FP husbands, their^FP fathers, their^FP fathers-in-law, their^FP sons, their^FP step-sons, their^FP brothers, the sons of their^FP brothers or sisters, their^FP women, their^FP slaves, servants^MP who are eunuchs,^3029 or a child who^MP 3030 does not know about women's nakedness. Let

---

3022 Or, "those to whom Allah has been gracious"
3023 Tawrah, Isaiah 59:18
3024 Or, "deeds," here and in the rest of the verse when feminine.
3025 Tawrah, Proverbs 4:25
3026 Or genitals, here and in the next verse. Injil, 1 Corinthians 6:18
3027 Or, "ornaments"
3028 literally, "pockets." The word could also include the genital area. This verse cannot be used as a justification for covering the face, however.
3029 Or, "who have no desire"
3030 The word "who" is plural, so the meaning may be "menservants without sexual desire and children, who"

themᶠᴾ not stomp their feet, to make known what adornment theyᶠᴾ hide. All believers, repentᴹᴾ toward Allah so that youᴹᴾ may succeed. (31) Marryᴹᴾ off the unmarried among youᴹᴾ and the righteous female and male slaves. If theyᴹᴾ are poor, Allah will enrich themᴹᴾ with his grace. Allah is omnipresent[3031] and all-knowing. (32) Let thoseᴹᴾ who do not find the means to marry remain pure until Allah enriches themᴹᴾ with his grace. As for those who want to betroth yourᴹᴾ slaves, legally free them if youᴹᴾ see something good in them, and give them some of the money Allah has given youᴹᴾ. If yourᴹᴾ girls[3032] want to remain pure, do not force themᶠᴾ into prostitution so that youᴹᴾ can seek temporal goods of this world.[3033] As for those who compel them, Allah is forgiving and merciful after the compulsion. (33) We have revealed to youᴹᴾ signs, clear things, a parable from those who passed away before youᴹᴾ, and an admonition to the reverent. (34) 18B2 Allah is the light of the heavens and the earth.[3034] His light is like a lamp[3035] in a niche in the wall. The lamp is in a glass container, and the container is like a shining star, lit by a blessed olive tree[3036] that is neither eastern nor western. Its oil would almost shine even without fire touching it. [It is] light upon light.[3037] Allah guides those he wills to his light.[3038] Allah tells parables to people,[3039] and Allah knows everything. (35) Allah's name is remembered in houses of worship he has permitted to be built. He is praised there morning and evening. (36) Business or sales do not distract [those] men from remembering Allah, performing[3040] prayers, and paying the poor-tax. They fear a day when hearts and sight will be changed (37) so that Allah may reward them better for the best of their works,[3041] and increase his

---

[3031] Zabur, Psalms 139:7-12
[3032] the meaning could be daughters or servant girls
[3033] Injil, 1 Corinthians 7:32-38
[3034] Injil, 1 John 1:5
[3035] Zabur, Psalms 119:105
[3036] Tawrah, Zechariah 4:3-14
[3037] Tawrah, Exodus 35:14
[3038] Tawrah, 2 Samuel 22:29, Isaiah 58:10, Zabur, Psalms 18:28, 112:4, Injil, Matthew 4:16, John 8:12, 12:46, Ephesians 5:8, 1 Peter 2:9
[3039] Injil, Matthew 13:13-14
[3040] The word form is different from the usual one with this meaning by the lack of a letter. There may be a different meaning.
[3041] Injil, Luke 14:14

## Chapter 24

grace to them. Allah provides bountifully to those he wills.[3042] (38) The works of disbelievers are like a mirage on a flat plain, which a thirsty person thinks is water until he gets to it and does not find anything. There he finds Allah, who repays him his reckoning. Allah is swift in reckoning.[3043] (39)

\*\*\*

Or they are like the deep sea darkness, covered by waves upon waves, above which are clouds. There are layers of darkness above others. If he puts his hand forth, he will barely see it.[3044] He whom Allah does give light does not have any light.[3045] (40)

\*\*\*

Have you[MS] not seen how everything in heaven and earth praises Allah? The birds are lined up, every one knowing its own prayer and glorifying. Allah knows what they do. (41)

\*\*\*

The kingdom of the heavens[3046] and earth is Allah's, and Allah is their destiny. (42)

\*\*\*

Have you[MS] not seen that Allah drives the clouds, then joins them together, then heaps them up, and you[MS] see rain coming through them.[3047] He sends down hail[3048] from mountains in the sky, and afflicts those he wills with it,[3049] keeping it away from those he wills.[3050] The splendor of his lightning is almost blinding.[3051] (43) Allah turns over the night and the day.[3052] There is a lesson for those who can see. (44)

\*\*\*

---

[3042] Zabur, Psalms 145:15,16
[3043] Tawrah, Isaiah 19:1, Malachi 3:5, Zabur, Psalms 147:15, Injil, 2 Peter 2:1, Revelation 22:12
[3044] Injil, Matthew 8:12, 22:13, 25:30
[3045] Injil, John 1:9
[3046] Injil, Matthew 4:17
[3047] Tawrah, Deuteronomy 28:12, Job 5:10, Joel 2:23, Zabur, Psalms 68:9, Injil, Matthew 5:45
[3048] Tawrah, Job 38:22
[3049] Tawrah, Exodus 9:22
[3050] Tawrah, Exodus 9:26
[3051] Tawrah, Daniel 10:6
[3052] Tawrah, Genesis 1:14-18

Allah created every living creature from water.[3053] Some of them walk on their bellies, some walk on two legs, and some walk on four. Allah creates what he wills. Allah can do anything.[3054] (45)
\*\*\*

We revealed signs and clear things. Allah guides[3055] those he wills to a straight path.[3056] (46) They say, "We believe in and obey Allah and the messenger." Then later a group of them turns away. They are not believers. (47) If they are called to Allah and his messenger, to be judged among them, a group of them turn away. (48) If they are in the right, they come to him submissively. (49) Do they have sick hearts?[3057] Do they doubt? Or are they afraid Allah and his messenger will wrong them? They are the wrongdoers.[3058] (50) When they were called to Allah and his messenger to be judged among them, the believers said, "We hear and obey." They are successful. (51) Those who obey Allah and his messenger, are afraid of Allah, and fear him,[3059] will be the winners. (52) 18B3 Swear$^{MP}$ serious oaths by Allah.[3060] If you$^{MS}$ command them to go out, say$^{MS}$, "Do not swear$^{MP}$. Obedience is a favor.[3061] Allah knows your$^{MP}$ deeds." (53) Say$^{MS}$, "Obey$^{MP}$ Allah and obey$^{MS}$ the messenger." If they$^{MP}$ turn away, he has his burden, and you$^{MP}$ have your$^{MP}$ burden.[3062] If you$^{MP}$ obey him, you$^{MP}$ will be guided. The messenger is only responsible to proclaim clearly. (54) Allah promises to make believers among you$^{MP}$ who do righteous deeds[3063] become regents on earth[3064] as he made those before them regents,[3065] to strengthen their religion, which pleases him, and to replace their fear with safety. They worship me, and worship nothing else. Those who disbelieve after that are

---

[3053] Tawrah, Genesis 1:20
[3054] Tawrah, Job 42:2, Isaiah 14:27, Daniel 4:35, Injil, Matthew 19:26, Mark 10:27, Luke 1:37
[3055] Zabur, Psalms 23:3
[3056] See glossary for more details, and notes on 3:51, 6:153, 19:36, 36:61, and 43:64 on what the straight path is.
[3057] Tawrah, Jeremiah 8:18, 17:9-10
[3058] Tawrah, Proverbs 29:27
[3059] Tawrah, Ecclesiastes 12:13
[3060] Tawrah, Deuteronomy 6:13
[3061] Or, "Do not swear. Kind obedience [is what is required]."
[3062] Injil, Galatians 6:5
[3063] Injil, 1 Corinthians 3:8, James 2:14-17, Revelation 19:8
[3064] Injil, Matthew 25:21,23, Luke 19:17,19
[3065] Tawrah, Genesis 1:28

unbelieving.³⁰⁶⁶ (55) Perform^MP prayers, pay^MP the poor-tax, and obey^MP the messenger so that you^MP may be shown mercy.³⁰⁶⁷ (56) \*\*\*

Do not consider^MS that disbelievers can be frustraters on earth, since their abode will be hellfire, an awful destiny. (57) \*\*\*

Believers, your^MP slaves and those who have not reached puberty should ask your^MP permission³⁰⁶⁸ on three occasions: before the dawn prayers, and when you^MP put off your^MPclothes from midday heat, and after evening prayers, the three times of nakedness. Besides these, you^MP and they will not be blamed when you^MP go around each other. Thus Allah clarifies the signs to you^MP. Allah is all- knowing³⁰⁶⁹ and wise.³⁰⁷⁰ (58) When the children³⁰⁷¹ among you^MP reach puberty, let them ask permission as those before them did. Thus Allah clarifies his signs to you^MP. Allah is all-knowing and wise. (59) Post-menopausal women who have no hope of marriage are not to be blamed when they take off their clothes, not showing adornment. To be chaste is better for them.³⁰⁷² Allah hears all and knows all. (60) It is not wrong for the blind, the lame, the sick, or yourselves^MP that you^MP eat in your^MP houses, your^MP fathers' houses, your^MP mother's houses, your^MP brothers' houses, your^MP sisters' houses, your^MP paternal uncles' houses, your^MP paternal aunts' houses, your^MP maternal uncles' houses, your^MP maternal aunts' houses, or houses you^MP own the keys to, or your^MP friend's house.³⁰⁷³ It is not wrong for you^MP to eat together or apart. If you^MP enter houses, greet^MP each other with Allah's blessed, good greeting. Thus Allah clarifies his signs to you^MP, so that you^MP may comprehend. (61) Believers are those who believe in Allah and his messenger. If they are with him on a common matter, let them not go away until they ask permission. Those who ask permission are

---

³⁰⁶⁶ Or transgressing or immoral

³⁰⁶⁷ Injil, Matthew 5:7

³⁰⁶⁸ i.e. before they come into your presence

³⁰⁶⁹ For "all-knowing" and "knows all" here and in verses 59, 60, and 64, see Tawrah, Job 37:16, Isaiah 40:14, Zabur, Psalms 33:13-15, Injil, 1 John 3:20

³⁰⁷⁰ For "wise" here and in verse 59, see Tawrah, Job 9:4, Proverbs 2:6, Jeremiah 9:23-24, Injil, 1 Corinthians 1:21-25, Romans 16:27

³⁰⁷¹ or sons

³⁰⁷² Injil, 1 Corinthians 7:8-9,39,40

³⁰⁷³ Injil, 1 Corinthians 10:27

## Chapter 24

those who believe in Allah and his messenger. If they ask you$^{MS}$ permission about some matter of theirs, give permission to those of them you$^{MS}$ want, and ask$^{MS}$ Allah's forgiveness for them. Allah is forgiving and merciful. (62) Do not call$^{MP}$ the messenger as you$^{MP}$ call each other. Allah knows those of you$^{MP}$ who sneak toward shelter. Let those who disobey his command beware lest temptation strike them, or they be afflicted with painful torment. (63) Is not everything in the heavens and the earth Allah's?[3074] He may[3075] know what state you$^{MP}$ are in. On that day, they will return to him and he will tell them what they did. Allah is all-knowing. (64)[3076]

---

[3074] Tawrah, Isaiah 45:12, Zabur, Psalms 24:1, 89:11, Injil, Hebrews 1:10
[3075] Most translators assume this means He (Allah) knows. Possibly the meaning is the messenger may know.
[3076] The verses in this chapter that rhyme are put together in paragraphs, separated by ***.

# Chapter 25 Al-Furqan[3077]

**18B4** In the name of Allah, the most gracious and merciful.[3078] Blessed be he who revealed the criterion to his servant,[3079] so that he would be a warner to all people. (1) The kingdom of the heavens and the earth is his.[3080] He has not chosen a boy,[3081] and he has no partner in his kingdom. He created everything.[3082] He has measured[3083] it precisely. (2) They have chosen other gods[3084] besides him, though they did not create anything, but rather were created, and cannot either harm or help.[3085] They have no power over death, life, or resurrection. (3) Disbelievers said, "This is only a lie he has created, and other people helped him. They have brought injustice[3086] and lies." (4) They said, "They are ancient legends he had written, which were dictated to him morning and night." (5) Say[MS], "He who knows the secrets of the heavens and the earth[3087] revealed it. He is forgiving[3088] and merciful."[3089] (6) They said, "What is wrong with this messenger? He eats food[3090] and walks in the markets. If only an angel had been sent down to him,[3091] so that he would be a warner with him, (7) or a treasure had been given to him, or he had a garden to eat from." The wicked said, "You[MP] only follow a bewitched man." (8) Look[MS]

---

[3077] Criterion. 21:48 says that the criterion was given to Musa and Harun, i.e. the Tawrah.
[3078] Zabur, Psalms 103:8, 145:8. See glossary for more details.
[3079] See glossary. Since the "criterion" according to 2:53 and 21:48 refers to the Tawrah, and in 2:185 it refers to the Qur'an, this could refer to either Muhammad (s) or Musa.
[3080] Tawrah, Isaiah 45:12, Zabur, Psalms 24:1, 89:11, Injil, Hebrews 1:10
[3081] All the books reject the idea of Allah choosing a boy.
[3082] Tawrah, Isaiah 45:7-8,12
[3083] or estimated
[3084] Arabic /ilah/. See glossary for more details.
[3085] here and verse 55, see Zabur, Psalms 115:4-7, Tawrah, Isaiah 44:15-20, Jeremiah 10:5
[3086] Or, wickedness
[3087] Tawrah, Daniel 2:47
[3088] Here and in verse 70, see Zabur, Psalms 103:3, 130:4, Tawrah, Isaiah 43:25, Exodus 34:7, Injil, Acts 26:18.
[3089] Here and in verse 70, see glossary for more details on "merciful."
[3090] Injil, Luke 4:2
[3091] Injil, Mathew 4:11

Chapter 25

how they tell proverbs to you[MS], then go astray. They cannot find a path. (9) Blessed is he who gives you[MS] better than that when he wills, heavenly gardens[3092] with flowing rivers underneath. He makes you[MS] palaces. (10) Rather, they reject the hour.[3093] We have prepared a burning fire for those who reject the hour.[3094] (11) When it sees him from afar, they hear it roaring in fury. (12) When they are chained and cast into a narrow place of it, they pray for destruction.[3095] (13) Today, do not pray for one destruction. Pray[MS] for much destruction. (14) Say[MS], "Is that better, or an eternal heavenly garden promised to the reverent as their reward and destiny? (15) In it, they have what they want, and they will be there forever." This is a promise your[MS] Lord is responsible for. (16)
\*\*\*

The day he gathers them[3096] along with what they worship besides Allah, he will say, "Did you[MP] lead these servants[3097] of mine astray or did they go astray from the path themselves?" (17)
\*\*\*

They will say, "May you[MS] be glorified! We should not choose others as protectors besides you[MS], and you[MS] made them and their fathers enjoy life, until they forgot the reminder.[3098] Those people perished." (18) They will reject you[MP] for your[MP] sayings, and you[MP] cannot avert it or be saved from it. We will make the wicked among you[MP] taste great torment.[3099] (19) All the messengers we sent before you[MS] ate food[3100] and walked in the markets. We made some of you[MP] a trial to others, if you[MP] would endure.[3101] Your[MS] Lord sees all. (20) 19A1 Those who do not hope to meet us said, "If only angels had been sent to us, or we could see our Lord!" They are proud in themselves and are very insolent. (21) On the

---

[3092] Arabic /jannah/, also in verse 15. See glossary for more details.
[3093] Injil, Revelation 14:7
[3094] Injil, Revelation 14:7
[3095] Injil, Revelation 9:11.
[3096] Here and in verse 34, see Tawrah, Joel 3:11-14, Zephaniah 3:8, Injil, Matthew 25:32, John 15:6, Revelation 16:16.
[3097] See glossary.
[3098] Arabic /dhikr/. See glossary for more details. Here the reminder refers to what people and their ancestors received.
[3099] For "torment" here and in verses 37, 42, and 65, see Tawrah, Isaiah 50:11, Injil, Matthew 18:34, 25:41,46, Luke 16:23-28, Revelation 20:15.
[3100] Injil, Matthew 4:2
[3101] See "endure" in glossary, here and in verses 42 and 75.

## Chapter 25

day they see the angels, on that day there will be no good news for wrongdoers. They will say, "It is strictly forbidden!"[3102] (22) We came to the deeds they did and scattered them like dust. (23) On that day, those who are going to heaven[3103] have a better dwelling, a better place to rest. (24) On the day the sky is split by clouds and the angels are sent down, (25) the most gracious will own the true kingdom,[3104] and it will be a hard day for disbelievers. (26) On that day, the wicked will bite their hands,[3105] saying, "I wish I had chosen the messenger's path. (27) Woe is me! I wish I had not chosen such a one as a friend. (28) He led me astray from the reminder after it came to me. Satan betrays people." (29) The messenger said, "My Lord, my people take this recitation[3106] as nonsense." (30) We have given a wrongdoing enemy to every prophet.[3107] Your[MS] Lord is an adequate guide and savior. (31) Disbelievers said, "If only the Qur'an[3108] had been revealed to him all at once." This way, we can make your[MS] heart firm, and we have arranged[3109] it well. (32) Whenever they bring you[MS] a proverb, we give you[MS] truth and a better explanation. (33) Those who are gathered on their faces in hell are in a more evil place and further astray from the path. (34) We gave Musa[3110] the book and made his brother Harun[3111] a minister with him. (35) We said, "Go[D] to people who have rejected our signs,"[3112] and we destroyed them. (36)

\*\*\*

When Nuh's[3113] people rejected the messengers, we drowned them[3114] and made them a sign to all people. We prepared painful torment for the wicked. (37)

\*\*\*

---

[3102] or a sealed room
[3103] Injil, Revelation 21:1-6
[3104] Zabur, Psalms 145:11-13
[3105] Injil, Matthew 25:30
[3106] Or Qur'an or qur'an. See glossary for more details.
[3107] Injil, Luke 6:26
[3108] Or recitation. See glossary for more details.
[3109] or chanted
[3110] Moses. See glossary for more details.
[3111] Aaron. See glossary for more details.
[3112] Arabic /ayat/. See glossary for more details.
[3113] Noah. See glossary for more details.
[3114] Tawrah, Genesis 7:18

## Chapter 25

As for Aad,[3115] Thamud, the people of Al-Rass, and the many generations between them, (38) we have made proverbs of each of them, and destroyed them all. (39) They came to the city that had gotten an evil rain.[3116] Did they not see it? They do not hope for resurrection. (40) When they see you[MS], they mock you[MS], "Is this the messenger Allah has sent? (41) He almost led us astray from our gods,[3117] if we had not endured for them!"[3118] When they witness the torment, they will know who is further astray. (42) Have you[MS] seen him who made his desire his god?[3119] Are you[MS] responsible for him? (43) Or do you[MS] think that most of them hear or think? They are like cattle, except more astray from the path. (44) Have you[MS] not seen how your[MS] Lord stretched out the shadow? If he had willed, he would have made it stationary,[3120] then made the sun a guide for it, (45) then grasped it[3121] to us lightly. (46) He made the night for your[MP] clothing, sleep for rest, and the day for rising. (47) He sent the winds as good news before[3122] his mercy. We sent pure rain[3123] down from the sky, (48) to revive a dead town[3124] and we irrigate with it many cattle and people we have created. (49) We distributed it[3125] among them so they would remember, and they refused. Most people are ungrateful. (50) If we had willed, we would have sent a warner to every village. (51) Do not obey the disbelievers, but struggle greatly against them with it.[3126] (52) 19A2 He loosens both seas. One is sweet and fresh,[3127] and the other is salty and bitter. He put a barrier and a dividing wall between them.[3128] (53) He created

---

[3115] Aad and Thamud are names of tribes.
[3116] probably a reference to Sodom and Gomorrah, the cities of Lot which were destroyed by fire.
[3117] Arabic /ilah/. See glossary for more details.
[3118] The gods
[3119] Injil, Philippians 3:19
[3120] or "quiet" or "still." Tawrah, Joshua 10:13
[3121] i.e. the shadow
[3122] Or, "between the hands of" or "in front of."
[3123] Tawrah, Deuteronomy 28:12, Job 5:10, Joel 2:23, Zabur, Psalms 68:9, Injil, Matthew 5:45
[3124] "Dead" is masculine and "town" is feminine. There may be another meaning.
[3125] i.e. the rain
[3126] possibly the warning, implied from the previous verse
[3127] or, like the Euphrates
[3128] Zabur, Psalms 104:6-9

## Chapter 25

man from water,³¹²⁹ and gave him relatives and in-laws. Your^MS Lord is all-powerful.³¹³⁰ (54) They worship gods instead of Allah, who cannot help them nor harm them. The disbeliever is a helper against his Lord. (55) We sent you^MS only as a bearer of good news and a warner. (56) Say^MS, "I do not ask you^MP for a wage, except for him who wills to choose the path to his Lord." (57) Trust in the living one who does not die, and glory in his praise. He is adequately aware of the sins of his servants.³¹³¹ (58) He created the heavens, the earth, and what is between them in six days,³¹³² and then sat down³¹³³ on the throne. He is most gracious, so ask anyone who is aware of him. (59) When they are told, "Bow^MP down to the most gracious," they say, "What is the most gracious? Should we bow down to what you^MS command us?" It makes them more repulsed. (60) Blessed is he who made constellations in the sky, and a shining moon³¹³⁴ as a lamp in it. (61) He made night and day³¹³⁵ follow each other for those who want³¹³⁶ to remember or give thanks. (62)

\*\*\*

The servants³¹³⁷ of the most gracious walk on the earth modestly and say, "Peace," when ignorant people address them. (63) They spend the night bowing down and standing before their Lord. (64) They say, "Our Lord, keep hell's torment away from us. Its torment is continuous. (65) It is an evil dwelling and abode." (66) They are not wasteful or stingy,³¹³⁸ but spend moderately. (67) They do not pray to another god³¹³⁹ besides Allah, and they do not kill souls that Allah has forbidden, except in truth, nor do they commit adultery.³¹⁴⁰ Whoever does those is guilty; (68) he will have double torment³¹⁴¹ on the day of resurrection,³¹⁴² and he will then be shamed forever, (69)

---

³¹²⁹ Tawrah, Genesis 1:20-27
³¹³⁰ Tawrah, Job 42:2
³¹³¹ See glossary.
³¹³² Tawrah, Genesis 1:31 – 2:1
³¹³³ Tawrah, Genesis 2:2
³¹³⁴ Tawrah, Genesis 1:14-15
³¹³⁵ Tawrah, Genesis 1:14
³¹³⁶ or, "he wants"
³¹³⁷ See glossary.
³¹³⁸ Tawrah, Proversb 28:22
³¹³⁹ Arabic /ilah/. See glossary for more details.
³¹⁴⁰ Injil, Galatians 5:19
³¹⁴¹ Tawrah, Isaiah 40:2, Injil, Romans 2:9,10

## Chapter 25

\*\*\*

except for those who repent, believe, and do righteous deeds.[3143] For them, Allah will exchange their bad deeds for good deeds.[3144] Allah is forgiving and merciful. (70)

\*\*\*

Those who repent and do righteous deeds, repent toward Allah. (71)

\*\*\*

They do not give false testimony, and when they encounter vain talk, they pass by honorably. (72)

\*\*\*

When they are reminded of their Lord's signs, they do not fall down deaf and blind. (73)

\*\*\*

They say, "Our Lord, give us delight from our wives and our descendants, and make us leaders for the reverent." (74) They will be paid back with the room[3145] for their endurance, and in it they will be given greetings and peace. (75) They will remain there forever. It is a good dwelling and abode. (76) Say[MS], "My Lord would not be pleased with you[MP] except for your[MP] prayers. You[MP] have rejected [it], and it will be fixed."[3146] (77)

---

[3142] Tawrah, Daniel 12:2 Injil, Acts 24:15, 1 Corinthians 15:52-54, Revelation 20:11-15

[3143] Here and in verse 71, see Injil, 1 Corinthians 3:8, James 2:14-17, Revelation 19:8.

[3144] Injil, 2 Corinthians 5:21, 1 John 2:2

[3145] or, "a drink of water" or "a high room." Injil, John 14:2

[3146] or "permanent" (punishment)

# Chapter 26 Al-Shuara[3147]

**19A3** In the name of Allah, the most gracious and merciful.[3148] TSM.[3149] (1) Those are signs[3150] of the clear book. (2) Your^MS grief may be killing you^MS because[3151] they are not believers. (3) If we will it, we will reveal a heavenly sign to[3152] them, so their necks would remain subjected to it. (4) Every time a renewed reminder[3153] comes to them from the most gracious, they turn away from it. (5) They have rejected, so news of what they made fun of will come to them. (6) Have they not seen how many agreeable kinds we made to sprout on the earth? (7) That is a sign, but most of them were not believers. (8) Your^MS Lord is mighty[3154] and merciful.[3155] (9) Your^MS Lord called Musa,[3156] "Go to wicked people, (10) Pharaoh's people.[3157] Will they not be reverent?" (11) He said, "My Lord, I fear they will reject me,[3158] (12) and my heart will be constrained, and my tongue tied.[3159] Send Harun.[3160] (13) They hold a sin against me, and I fear they will kill me."[3161] (14) He said, "No. Go^D with our signs.[3162] We will be listening with you^MP.[3163] (15) Go^D to Pharaoh, and say^D: We are a messenger[3164] of the Lord of the universe.[3165] (16)

---

[3147] Poets

[3148] Zabur, Psalms 103:8, 145:8. See glossary for more details.

[3149] Here and at the beginning of many chapters there are unvowelled letters of unknown meaning. Numerous theories have been proposed, but there is no agreement on the subject.

[3150] or verses

[3151] or "You may be fretting yourself to death because"

[3152] or send down upon

[3153] Arabic /dhikr/. See glossary for more details.

[3154] Injil, Revelation 18:8, Tawrah, Isaiah 60:16, Zabur, Psalms 93:4

[3155] Here and in verses 68, 104, 122, 140, 159, 175, 191, and 217, see glossary for more details on "merciful."

[3156] Moses. See glossary for more details.

[3157] Tawrah, Exodus 3:10

[3158] Tawrah, Exodus 3:11

[3159] Tawrah, Exodus 4:10

[3160] Aaron. See glossary for more details. Tawrah, Exodus 4:13

[3161] Tawrah, Exodus 2:12-15

[3162] Tawrah, Exodus 4:17

[3163] Tawrah, Exodus 4:11-12

[3164] The singular is used here, but the meaning could be "delegation."

[3165] Tawrah, Exodus 3:10,14

## Chapter 26

\*\*\*
Send the people of Israel with us."[3166] (17)
\*\*\*

He said, "Did we not raise you[ms] among us since you[ms] were a child,[3167] and did you[ms] not spend many years of your[ms] life with us?[3168] (18) And you[ms] did the deed you[ms] did,[3169] and you[ms] are a disbeliever."[3170] (19) He said, "I went astray when I did that, (20) and I fled[3171] from you[mp] when I feared you[mp],[3172] and my Lord gave me judgment and made me a messenger.[3173] (21)
\*\*\*

That is a blessing you[ms] reproach me with, since you[ms] enslaved the people of Israel!"[3174] (22)
\*\*\*

Pharaoh said, "What is the Lord of the universe?"[3175] (23) He said, "The Lord of the heavens, the earth, and what is between them, if you[mp] are certain." (24) He told those around him, "Do you[mp] not hear?" (25) He said, "Your[mp] Lord and the Lord of your[mp] ancestors." (26) He said, "Your[mp] messenger who was sent to you[mp] is crazy."[3176] (27) He said, "Lord of the sunrise and the sunset[3177] and what is between them, if you[mp] comprehend."(28) He said, "If you[ms] choose any god[3178] besides me, I will put you[ms] in prison." (29) He said, "Even if I bring you[ms] something clear?" (30) He said, "Bring it on if you[ms] are telling the truth."[3179] (31) So he threw down his staff, and it was clearly a serpent.[3180] (32) Then he took away his hand and it was white to those who saw it.[3181] (33) He

---

[3166] Tawrah, Exodus 3:18
[3167] Tawrah, Exodus 2:5-10
[3168] Tawrah, Exodus 2:11
[3169] This probably refers to Moses' killing a man, mentioned in 28:15, 19, and 33. Tawrah, Exodus 2:11-12.
[3170] the word also has the connotation of "ungrateful" in this context
[3171] Tawrah, Exodus 2:15
[3172] Tawrah, Exodus 2:14
[3173] Tawrah, Exodus 3:10
[3174] Tawrah, Exodus 3:9
[3175] Tawrah, Exodus 5:2
[3176] or demon-possessed
[3177] or the east and the west
[3178] Arabic /ilah/. See glossary for more details.
[3179] Tawrah, Exodus 7:9
[3180] Tawrah, Exodus 7:10
[3181] Tawrah, Exodus 4:6

## Chapter 26

told the nobles around him, "This is a learned magician (34) who wants to expel you$^{MP}$ from your$^{MP}$ land by his magic. What do you$^{MP}$ command?" (35) They said, "Put him and his brother off and send gatherers to the cities, (36) to bring you$^{MS}$ every learned magician." (37) So the magicians were assembled³¹⁸² for an appointment of a known day, (38) and the people were asked, "Are you$^{MP}$ assembled?" (39) "We may follow the magicians if they are victorious." (40) When the magicians came, they told Pharaoh, "Will we get paid if we are victorious?" (41) He said, "Yes. You$^{MP}$ will also be brought close." (42) Musa³¹⁸³ told them, "Throw down what you$^{MP}$ will throw." (43) So they threw down their ropes and staffs³¹⁸⁴ and said, "By the might of Pharaoh, we are victorious." (44) Then Musa threw down his staff, and it swallowed up what they had falsely done.³¹⁸⁵ (45) Then the magicians fell down and bowed down.³¹⁸⁶ (46) They said, "We believe in the Lord of the universe,³¹⁸⁷ (47) the Lord of Musa and Harun."³¹⁸⁸ (48) He said, "Have you$^{MP}$ believed in him before I give you$^{MP}$ permission?³¹⁸⁹ He is your$^{MP}$ chief who taught you$^{MP}$ magic. You$^{MP}$ will know. I will cut off your$^{MP}$ hands and feet on opposite sides, and crucify you$^{MP}$ all." (49) They said, "There is no harm in that. We will return to our Lord. (50) We hope that he will forgive our faults, since we are the first believers." (51) **19A4** We inspired Musa, "Go³¹⁹⁰ by night³¹⁹¹ with my servants.³¹⁹² You$^{MP}$ will be followed."³¹⁹³ (52) So Pharaoh sent recruiters³¹⁹⁴ to the cities, (53) "They are a small band, (54) who have made us angry, (55) and we are all wary." (56) Thus we expelled them from gardens, springs, (57) treasures,³¹⁹⁵ and a noble status, (58)

---

³¹⁸² Tawrah, Exodus 7:11
³¹⁸³ Moses, here and in verses 45, 48, 52, 61, 63, and 65. See glossary for more details.
³¹⁸⁴ Tawrah, Exodus 7:12
³¹⁸⁵ Tawrah, Exodus 7:10,12
³¹⁸⁶ Tawrah, Exodus 8:18-19
³¹⁸⁷ Tawrah, Exodus 8:19
³¹⁸⁸ Aaron. See glossary for more details.
³¹⁸⁹ Tawrah, Exodus 8:19
³¹⁹⁰ Tawrah, Exodus 3:10
³¹⁹¹ Tawrah, Exodus 12:31
³¹⁹² Or worshipers. See glossary.
³¹⁹³ Tawrah, Exodus 14:4
³¹⁹⁴ or gatherers
³¹⁹⁵ Tawrah, Exodus 12:31

\*\*\*
and gave it as an inheritance to the people of Israel. (59)
\*\*\*

So they followed them at sunrise.[3196] (60) When both groups saw each other, Musa's companions said, "We have been overtaken."[3197] (61) He said, "No. My Lord is with me. He will guide me."[3198] (62) We inspired Musa, "Strike the sea with your[MS] staff."[3199] It was divided,[3200] and each part was like the great mountain."[3201] (63) We brought the others there[3202] (64) and rescued Musa and all that were with him.[3203] (65) Then we drowned the others.[3204] (66) That is a sign, though most of them did not believe. (67) Your[MP] Lord is mighty[3205] and merciful. (68) Recite[3206] them the news of Ibrahim,[3207] (69) when he told his father and his people, "What do you[MP] worship?" (70) They said, "We worship idols,[3208] and we will continue to be devoted to them." (71) He said, "Do they hear you[MP] when you[MP] pray?[3209] (72) Or do they benefit you[MP] or harm you[MP]?"[3210] (73) They said, "We found our fathers doing thus."(74) He said, "Have you[MP] seen what you[MP] used to worship, (75) you[MP] and your[MP] ancestors?[3211] (76) They are enemies to me, except for the Lord of the universe, (77) who created me. He guides me, (78) and he gives me food and drink. (79) When I get sick, he heals me.[3212] (80) He makes me die and then gives me life.[3213] (81) I hope he will forgive me[3214] my

---

[3196] Tawrah, Exodus 14:5-8
[3197] Tawrah, Exodus 14:9-12
[3198] Tawrah, Exodus 14:13-14
[3199] Tawrah, Exodus 14:15-16
[3200] Tawrah, Exodus 14:21
[3201] Tawrah, Exodus 14:22
[3202] Tawrah, Exodus 14:23
[3203] Tawrah, Exodus 14:29-30
[3204] Tawrah, Exodus 14:26-31, 15:4, Isaiah 43:17
[3205] Injil, Revelation 18:8, Tawrah, Isaiah 60:16, Zabur, Psalms 93:4
[3206] Or read or tell. See note at 7:157.
[3207] Abraham. See glossary for more details.
[3208] Tawrah, Joshua 24:2
[3209] Zabur, Psalms 115:6
[3210] Zabur, Psalms 115:4-7, Tawrah, Isaiah 44:20
[3211] Tawrah, Deuteronomy 32:15-18
[3212] Zabur, Psalms 103:3
[3213] Zabur, Psalms 103:4

sin³²¹⁵ on the Day of Judgment. (82) My Lord, give me judgment,³²¹⁶ and join me with the righteous.³²¹⁷ (83) Give me an honest tongue³²¹⁸ among the others. (84) Make me an heir of the heavenly garden³²¹⁹ of delight. (85) Forgive my father. He has gone astray. (86) Do not shame me on the day when they are resurrected, (87) the day when neither money nor children³²²⁰ will benefit, (88) except for him who comes to Allah with a sound heart."³²²¹ (89) The heavenly garden has come close to the reverent. (90) The blazing fire has been made obvious to those who went astray. (91) It will be told them, "Where are the gods you^MP worshiped (92) besides Allah? Will they save you^MP or themselves?" (93) Then they were thrown in it, both they, those who went astray, (94) and all the hosts³²²² of Iblis.³²²³ (95) They said while fighting within it, (96) "By Allah, we were clearly astray (97) when we made you^MP equal to the Lord of the universe.³²²⁴ (98) Only the wrongdoers made us go astray. (99) We have no intercessors (100) or close friends. (101) If we could return, we would be believers." (102) That is a sign, but most of them are not believers. (103) Your^MS Lord is mighty³²²⁵ and merciful. (104) Nuh's³²²⁶ people rejected the messengers.³²²⁷ (105)

---

³²¹⁴ The belief that all prophets and messengers are sinless is not supported by the Qur'an. For instances of prophets or messengers asking forgiveness or committing sins, see 7:23, 20:121 (Adam), 11:47, 71:28 (Nuh), 26:82, 14:41 (Ibrahim), 28:15-16 (Musa), 7:151, 20:93 (Musa and Harun), 38:24 (Dawud), 38:32,35 (Sulayman), 21:87, 37:142 (Yunus), 48:2, 47:19, 40:55, 4:79,106, 9:43, 13:30, 80:1-2, 110:3, 94:2, 23:118, 66:1, 33:37, 8:67, and 9:117 (Muhammad (s).
³²¹⁵ Ibrahim's sin is also referred to in 14:41. See Tawrah, Genesis 20:9, Zabur, Psalms 103:3.
³²¹⁶ Zabur, Psalms 101:1
³²¹⁷ Zabur, Psalms 103:17-18
³²¹⁸ Zabur, Psalms 101:2-3
³²¹⁹ Arabic /jannah/, here and in verse 90. See glossary for more details.
³²²⁰ Or sons
³²²¹ Zabur, Psalms 24:3-5. "Sound" can also mean pure, whole, healthy, or right.
³²²² Injil, Revelation 20:10,14,15
³²²³ The devil. See glossary for more details.
³²²⁴ Injil, Luke 16:19-31
³²²⁵ Injil, Revelation 18:8, Tawrah, Isaiah 60:16, Zabur, Psalms 93:4
³²²⁶ Noah, here and in verses 106 and 116. See glossary for more details.
³²²⁷ Tawrah, Genesis 6:12

## Chapter 26

Their brother Nuh told them, "Will you[MP] not be reverent? (106) I am a faithful messenger[3228] to you[MP]. (107) So fear Allah[3229] and obey me.[3230] (108) I do not ask you[MP] for wages for this. My wages come from the Lord of the universe. (109) So fear Allah and obey me." (110) 19B1 They said, "Should we believe in you[MS] when only the vilest people follow you[MS]?" (111) He said, "What do I know of what they did? (112) Their reckoning is only with my Lord, if you[MP] only realized. (113) I would never drive out believers. (114) I am only a clear warner."[3231] (115) They said, "Nuh, if you[MS] do not stop, you[MS] will be stoned." (116) He said, "Lord, my people have rejected me. (117) Open a rift between me and them, and rescue me along with the believers that are with me." (118) And we rescued him and those who were with him in a loaded ark.[3232] (119) Then we drowned the rest.[3233] (120) That is a sign, but most of them were not believers. (121) Your[MS] Lord is mighty[3234] and merciful. (122) Aad[3235] rejected the messengers. (123) Their brother Hud told them, "Will you[MP] not be reverent? (124) I am a faithful messenger to you[MP]. (125) Fear Allah and obey me. (126) I do not ask you[MP] for wages for this. My wages come from the Lord of the universe. (127) Do you[MP] build a sign on every high hill in vain (128) and choose buildings so that you[MP] may be immortal? (129) And when you[MP] attack, you[MP] attack powerfully.[3236] (130) Fear Allah and obey me. (131) Fear[MP] him who gave you[MP] your[MP] knowledge. (132) He gave you[MP] cattle and

---

[3228] Tawrah, Genesis 6:8

[3229] For "fear Allah" here and in verses 110, 126, 131, 144, and 151, see Tawrah, Deuteronomy 10:12, Isaiah 29:13, Injil, 1 Peter 2:17, Revelation 14:7.

[3230] Regarding "obey me" here and in verses 110, 126, 131, 144, 150, 163, and 179, several prophets tell the people specifically, "obey me." (Nuh 26:108,110, 71:3, Hud 26:126,131. Salih 26:144,150, Lut 26:163, Shuaib 26:179, Harun 20:90, and Isa 3:50, 43:63) Isa is the only one who commands obedience in the context of the straight path. Several verses command people to obey "the messenger" (3:32,132, 4:59, 5:92, 8:1,19,46, 24:54,56, 47:33, 58:13, 64:12), most of which probably refer to Muhammad (s).

[3231] Injil, 2 Peter 2:5. Muhammad is also called a clear warner (46:9).

[3232] Tawrah, Genesis 7:23

[3233] Tawrah, Genesis 7:22-23

[3234] Injil, Revelation 18:8, Tawrah, Isaiah 60:16, Zabur, Psalms 93:4

[3235] Aad here and Thamud (verse 141) are names of tribes.

[3236] or powerful ones

## Chapter 26

children,[3237] (133) gardens and springs. (134) I fear torment[3238] of a great day for you[MP]." (135) They said, "Whether or not you[MS] preach to us, (136) this is only a habit of the men of old. (137) We will not be tormented." (138) So they rejected him and we destroyed them. That is a sign, but most of them were not believers. (139) Your[MS] Lord is mighty[3239] and merciful. (140) Thamud rejected the messengers. (141) Their brother Salih[3240] told them, "Will you[MP] not be reverent? (142) I am a faithful messenger to you[MP]. (143) Fear Allah and obey me. (144) I do not ask you[MP] for wages for this. My wages will come from the Lord of the universe. (145) Will you[MP] be left secure here (146) among gardens, springs, (147) fields and palm trees with slender sprouts, (148) while you[MP] cleverly carve out homes from the mountains? (149) Fear Allah and obey me. (150) Do not obey the command of the wasteful, (151) who cause destruction in the land and do not amend it."[3241] (152) They said, "You[MS] are bewitched. (153) You[MS] are only a human like us. Bring on a sign if you[MS] are telling the truth." (154) He said, "This female camel has a time to drink, and you[MP] will have a time to drink on a known day. (155) Do not harm her, or torment of a great day will overcome you[MP]." (156) They hamstrung her, and in the morning[3242] regretted it. (157) Then torment seized them. That is a sign, but most of them were not believers. (158) Your[MS] Lord is mighty[3243] and merciful. (159) Lut's[3244] people rejected the messengers.[3245] (160) Their brother Lut told them, "Will you[MP] not be reverent?[3246] (161) I am a faithful messenger[3247] to you[MP]. (162) Fear[MP] Allah and obey me. (163) I do not ask you[MP] for wages for this. My wages come from the Lord of

---

[3237] Or sons

[3238] For "torment" here and in verses 156, 189, 201, 213, see Tawrah, Isaiah 50:11, Injil, Matthew 18:34, 25:41,46, Luke 16:23-28, Revelation 20:15.

[3239] Injil, Revelation 18:8, Tawrah, Isaiah 60:16, Zabur, Psalms 93:4

[3240] Methuselah. See glossary for more details. Tawrah, Genesis 5:21-27, 1 Chronicles 1:3, Injil, Luke 3:37

[3241] or do good or reconcile.

[3242] Or then

[3243] Injil, Revelation 18:8, Tawrah, Isaiah 60:16, Zabur, Psalms 93:4

[3244] Lot, nephew of Abraham, here and in verses 161 and 167. See glossary for more details.

[3245] Tawrah, Genesis 19:9

[3246] Tawrah, Genesis 18:20-21

[3247] Injil, 2 Peter 2:7-8

the universe. (164) Do you[MP] go to men for sex[3248] (165) and leave the wives your[MP] Lord created for you[MP]? You[MP] are transgressing people." (166) They said, "Lut, if you[MS] do not stop, you[MS] will be expelled."[3249] (167) He said, "I hate your[MP] works. (168) Lord, rescue me and my family from what they do." (169) So we rescued him and all his family,[3250] (170) except for an old woman who delayed.[3251] (171) Then we destroyed the others,[3252] (172) and rained down a rain upon them. The rain[3253] of those who were warned was awful. (173) That is a sign, but most of them were not believers.[3254] (174) Your[MS] Lord is mighty[3255] and merciful. (175) Those of the forest rejected the messengers. (176) Shuaib[3256] told them, "Will you[MP] not be reverent? (177) I am a faithful messenger[3257] to you[MP]. (178) Fear God[MP] and obey me. (179) I do not ask you[MP] for wages for this. My wages come from the Lord of the universe. (180) 19B2 Pay the measure and do not cause loss. (181) Weigh with a straight balance.[3258] (182) Do not withhold things that are due people, and do not do evil and destroy in the land. (183) Fear him who created both you[MP] and the ancient generations." (184) They said, "You[MS] are bewitched. (185) You[MS] are only a human like us and we think you[MS] are a liar. (186) Make pieces fall from the sky if you[MS] are telling the truth." (187) He said, "My Lord well knows your[MP] deeds." (188) So they rejected him and the torment of a day of covering[3259] overtook them. It was the torment of a great day. (189) That is a sign, but most of them were not believers. (190) Your[MS] Lord is mighty[3260] and merciful. (191) It is a revelation of the Lord of the universe. (192) The faithful spirit brought it down (193) on your[MS] heart, so that you[MS] would be a warner (194) in a clear Arabic tongue. (195) It[3261] is in

---

[3248] Injil, Jude 7, Romans 1:27
[3249] Tawrah, Genesis 19:29, 13:14-15
[3250] Tawrah, Genesis 19:29
[3251] Injil, Luke 17:32
[3252] Injil, Luke 17:29
[3253] Tawrah, Genesis 19:24
[3254] Tawrah, Genesis 18:19-33
[3255] Injil, Revelation 18:8, Tawrah, Isaiah 50:16, Zabur, Psalms 93:4
[3256] Jethro. See glossary for more details.
[3257] Tawrah, Exodus 4:18, 18:1-27
[3258] Tawrah, Leviticus 19:36, Ezekiel 45:10
[3259] or shadow
[3260] Injil, Revelation 18:8, Tawrah, Isaiah 50:16, Zabur, Psalms 93:4
[3261] The Qur'an (or its contents).

Chapter 26

the books³²⁶² of the men of old.³²⁶³ (196) Was it not a sign to them that the scholars of the people of Israel know it? (197) If we had revealed it to some foreigners, (198) and he read it to them, they would not have believed in it. (199) Thus we made it go into the hearts of the wrongdoers. (200) They will not believe in it until they see the painful torment. (201) It will come to them suddenly,³²⁶⁴ when they do not realize it. (202) They will say, "Will we be given more time?" (203) Are they in a hurry for our torment? (204) What do you[MS] think? If we let them enjoy themselves for years, (205) and then what they were promised comes to them, (206) what good will their enjoyment do them? (207) We never destroyed a village without its having warners (208) as a reminder. We were not wicked. (209) The devils³²⁶⁵ did not reveal it. (210) They should not do it, nor are they able. (211) They are isolated from hearing. (212) Do not pray to[MS] another god³²⁶⁶ besides Allah, or you[MS] will be tormented. (213) Warn your[MS] clan and relatives. (214) Put your[MS] wing³²⁶⁷ down for those believers who follow you[MS]. (215) If they disobey you[MS], say, "I am innocent of your[MP] deeds." (216) Trust[MS] in the strong,³²⁶⁸ merciful one, (217) who sees you[MS] when you[MS] get up,³²⁶⁹ (218) and your[MS] turning about among those who bow down. (219) He hears all and knows all.³²⁷⁰ (220) Shall I tell you[MP] about those on whom the devils³²⁷¹ come down?³²⁷² (221) They³²⁷³ come down on every guilty liar. (222) They listen, and most of them are liars. (223) Poets are followed by those who go astray. (224) Have you[MS] not seen that they wander in every valley?³²⁷⁴ (225) They say what

---

³²⁶² Or psalms
³²⁶³ See 41:43, which affirms the unity of the content of the books.
³²⁶⁴ Injil, 1 Thessalonians 5:2-3
³²⁶⁵ Arabic /shayatin/. See glossary for more details.
³²⁶⁶ Arabic /ilah/. See glossary for more details.
³²⁶⁷ This is a metaphor. Muhammad (ص) did not have wings. The meaning is probably "be kind" or "protect"
³²⁶⁸ Tawrah, Job 9:4, Zabur, Psalms 24:8, Injil, Ephesians 6:10, Revelation 18:8
³²⁶⁹ Zabur, Psalms 139:2-3
³²⁷⁰ Tawrah, Job 37:16, Isaiah 40:14, Zabur, Psalms 33:13-15, Injil, 1 John 3:20
³²⁷¹ Arabic /shayatin/. See glossary for more details.
³²⁷² Injil, Ephesians 4:26-27
³²⁷³ or you (MS)
³²⁷⁴ Or wadi (dry stream bed)

## Chapter 26

they do not do.[3275] (226) Except for believers who do righteous deeds[3276] and remember Allah frequently, and are victorious after they were wickedly treated. Those who treated them wickedly will know how they will be overthrown. (227)[3277]

---

[3275] Injil, Matthew 23:3
[3276] Injil, 1 Corinthians 3:8, James 2:14-17, Revelation 19:8
[3277] The verses in this chapter that rhyme are put together in paragraphs, separated by ***.

Chapter 27

# Chapter 27 Al-Naml[3278]

**19B3** In the name of Allah, the most gracious and merciful.[3279] TS.[3280] Those are verses of the Qur'an[3281] and of a clear book,[3282] (1) as guidance[3283] and good news to believers, (2) who perform prayers and pay the poor-tax, and are certain of the hereafter.[3284] (3) We made the works of those who do not believe in the hereafter seem fair to them, and they wander.[3285] (4) They will have evil torment[3286] and they will be the most lost in the hereafter. (5) You[MS] have received the Qur'an[3287] from the wise,[3288] all-knowing[3289] one. (6) Musa[3290] told his family, "I noticed a fire.[3291] I will bring you[MP] news from it, or a lighted fire, so that you[MP] may be warm." (7) When he came to it, he was called, "Blessed be he who is in the fire, and he who is around it. May Allah, the Lord of the universe, be glorified! (8) Musa, it is I,[3292] Allah, mighty[3293]

---

[3278] Ants

[3279] Zabur, Psalms 103:8, 145:8. See glossary for more details.

[3280] Here and at the beginning of many chapters there are unvowelled letters of unknown meaning. Numerous theories have been proposed, but there is no agreement on the subject.

[3281] Or recitation. See glossary for more details.

[3282] The previous book here is called "a clear book." See 28:2, Tawrah, Exodus 24:7, Joshua 1:8.

[3283] Zabur, Psalms 119:105

[3284] The Qur'an refers to people who are certain of the hereafter here and in 2:4 and 31:4. All three passages seem to have a reference to the previous books. Injil, John 5:24

[3285] Injil, 2 Thessalonians 2:11, Tawrah, 2 Samuel 22:27, 1 Kings 22:20-23, Ezekiel 14:9

[3286] Tawrah, Isaiah 50:11, Injil, Matthew 18:34, 25:41,46, Luke 16:23-28, Revelation 20:15

[3287] Or recitation. See glossary for more details.

[3288] Tawrah, Job 9:4, Proverbs 2:6, Jeremiah 9:23-24, Injil, 1 Corinthians 1:21-25, Romans 16:27

[3289] Tawrah, Job 37:16, Isaiah 40:14, Zabur, Psalms 33:13-15, Injil, 1 John 3:20

[3290] Moses, here and in verses 9 and 10. See glossary for more details.

[3291] Tawrah, Exodus 3:3-4

[3292] Tawrah, Exodus 3:6,14

[3293] Injil, Revelation 18:8, Tawrah, Isaiah 60:16, Zabur, Psalms 93:4

Chapter 27

and wise.³²⁹⁴ (9) Cast down your[MS] staff."³²⁹⁵ When he saw it shaking like a jinn,³²⁹⁶ he turned, fled, and did not go back.³²⁹⁷ "Musa, do not fear.³²⁹⁸ Messengers do not fear around me, (10) except for those who have done wrong,³²⁹⁹ then replaced evil with good. I am forgiving³³⁰⁰ and merciful.³³⁰¹ (11) Put your[MS] hand in your[MS] pocket. It will come out white, though unharmed,³³⁰² among the nine signs for Pharaoh³³⁰³ and his people.³³⁰⁴ They are unbelieving³³⁰⁵ people." (12) When our signs came to them visibly, they said, "This is clearly magic."³³⁰⁶ (13) They wickedly and pridefully³³⁰⁷ rejected them, though their souls believed in them firmly. See[MS] the punishment of the corrupt. (14) We gave Dawud³³⁰⁸ and Sulayman³³⁰⁹ knowledge.³³¹⁰ They said, "Praise be

---

³²⁹⁴ Tawrah, Job 9:4, Proverbs 2:6, Jeremiah 9:23-24, Injil, 1 Corinthians 1:21-25, Romans 16:27

³²⁹⁵ Tawrah, Exodus 4:2-3

³²⁹⁶ Or demon. See glossary for more details.

³²⁹⁷ Tawrah, Exodus 4:4-5

³²⁹⁸ Tawrah, Exodus 4

³²⁹⁹ The Qur'an here makes it clear that at least some messengers do wrong. The Qur'an does not say that all messengers are sinless. For instances of prophets or messengers asking forgiveness or committing sins, see 7:23, 20:121 (Adam), 11:47, 71:28 (Nuh), 26:82, 14:41 (Ibrahim), 28:15-16 (Musa), 7:151, 20:93 (Musa and Harun), 38:24 (Dawud), 38:32,35 (Sulayman), 21:87, 37:142 (Yunus), 48:2, 47:19, 40:55, 4:79,106, 9:43, 13:30, 80:1-2, 110:3, 94:2, 23:118, 66:1, 33:37, 8:67, and 9:117 (Muhammad (s).

³³⁰⁰ Zabur, Psalms 103:3, 130:4, Tawrah, Isaiah 43:25, Exodus 34:7, Injil, Acts 26:18.

³³⁰¹ See glossary for more details on "merciful."

³³⁰² Tawrah, Exodus 4:6

³³⁰³ 79:20 talks about the greatest sign, which would make ten. This corresponds to the ten signs mentioned in the Tawrah, Exodus 7-12. In the Qur'an, 7:107,108, 130, and 133 describe many of these signs. The last sign, probably the same as the "greatest sign" mentioned both in 7:133 and in the Tawrah, Exodus (11:4-5, 12:23,24,29,30) is the blood. The Exodus passages gives the details.

³³⁰⁴ Tawrah, Exodus 7-12

³³⁰⁵ Or transgressing or immoral

³³⁰⁶ Tawrah, Exodus 7-8

³³⁰⁷ Tawrah, Exodus 8:32

³³⁰⁸ David. See glossary for more details.

³³⁰⁹ Solomon, here and in verses 16, 17, and 18. See glossary for more details.

## Chapter 27

to Allah, who preferred us over many of his believing servants."[3311] (15) Sulayman was Dawud's[3312] heir. He said, "People, we were taught the speech[3313] of birds, and were given some of everything. This is clearly grace." (16) Sulayman's army of jinns,[3314] people, and birds was gathered to him in rows, (17) until they came to the valley of the ants. A female ant said, "Ants, enter your[MP] dwellings, so that Sulayman and his army will not crush you[MP] without realizing it." (18) He smiled and laughed at its saying, and said, "My Lord, make me give you[MS] thanks for your[MS] blessings which you[MS] gave me and my parents, and do righteous deeds pleasing to you. By your[MS] mercy, make me one of your[MS] righteous servants." (19) He checked on the birds, and said, "What is wrong with me that I do not see the hoopoe?[3315] Or is it missing? (20) I will torment it severely or slaughter it if it does not bring me a clear excuse."[3316] (21) It remained not far off,[3317] and said, "I know things you[MS] do not know. I have come to you[MS] from Yemen[3318] with sure news. (22) I found a woman ruling them who has some of everything.[3319] She has a great throne. (23) I found her and her people bowing down to the sun instead of Allah, and Satan made their deeds seem fair to them,[3320] and blocked them from the path. They are not guided. (24) They do not bow down to Allah, who makes what is hidden in the heavens and the earth come forth.[3321] He knows what you[MP] conceal and what you[MP] announce.[3322] (25) Allah! He is the only god,[3323] the Lord of the great throne."[3324] (26) 19B4 He said, "We will wait to see if you[MS]

---

[3310] Tawrah, 1 Kings 4:32
[3311] See glossary.
[3312] David. See glossary for more details.
[3313] literally, logic. See Tawrah, 1 Kings 4:33
[3314] Or demons. See glossary for more details.
[3315] The hoopoe is still a common bird in Palestine and Yemen, as well as elsewhere in Eurasia and Africa.
[3316] or authority or authorization
[3317] or a short time
[3318] Or Sheba
[3319] Tawrah, 1 Kings 10, 2 Chronicles 9
[3320] Injil, Revelation 20:10
[3321] Injil, Luke 12:3
[3322] Here and in verse 74, see also 11:5, 14:38, 16:19,23, 28:69, 36:76, 60:1, 64:4.
[3323] Arabic /ilah/. See glossary for more details.
[3324] Injil, Revelation 20:11

## Chapter 27

are truthful or a liar. (27) Go with this letter[3325] of mine, and give it[3326] to them, then turn away from them, and wait to see what they return." (28) She said, "Nobles, an honorable letter[3327] has been given to me. (29) It is from Sulayman,[3328] and it says: In the name of Allah, the most gracious and merciful.[3329] (30) Do not exalt[MP] yourselves[MP] over me, but come[MP] to me submitted[MP]."[3330] (31) She said, "Nobles, give[MP] me an opinion about my matter. I will not firmly decide on the matter until you[MP] witness to me." (32) They said, "We are powerful, strong, and forceful. The matter is yours[FS] to decide. Look how you[FS] will command." (33) She said, "When kings enter a village, they destroy it, and abase the leading citizens. They do that. (34) I will send them a gift[3331] and wait and see what the messengers bring back." (35) When it came to Sulayman, he said, "Will you[MP] give me money? What Allah has given me is better than what you[MP] brought. Yet you[MP] rejoice in your[MP] gift. (36) Return to them, and we will bring them an unprecedented army and expel them from it, abased and contemptible." (37) He said, "Nobles, which of you[MP] will bring me her throne before they come submitted to me?" (38) A jinn[3332] sprite said, "I will bring it to you[MS] before you[MS] can stand up from your[MS] place. I am strong and faithful." (39) The one with knowledge from the book said, "I will bring it to you before you[MS] can blink."[3333] When he saw it resting by him, he said, "This is by the grace of my Lord, to test me, whether I will give thanks or disbelieve.[3334] He who gives thanks gives thanks for his own good. As for him who is disbelieving, my Lord is self-sufficient and generous. (40) He said, "Make her throne's image appear to her, and we will wait and see whether she will be guided or not." (41) When she came, it was said, "Is your[FS] throne like this?" She said, "It looks like it." We were given knowledge of it before her, and

---

[3325] Or book
[3326] The Arabic word can mean "throw it" or "speak it out."
[3327] Or book
[3328] Solomon, here and in verse 36. See glossary for more details.
[3329] Zabur, Psalms 103:8, 145:8. See glossary for more details.
[3330] Injil, James 4:7. For "submitted" here and in verses 38, 42, and 44, some translators do not translate this. See glossary for more details.
[3331] Tawrah, 2 Chronicles 9:9, 1 Kings 10:10
[3332] Or demonic. See glossary for more details.
[3333] Tawrah, 1 Kings 22:21-22, 2 Chronicles 18:20-21
[3334] Or ungrateful

## Chapter 27

we were submitted. (42) What she used to worship instead of Allah blocked her. She was from disbelieving people. (43) It was said, "Enter the palace. When she saw it, she thought it was a lake, and exposed her legs. He said, "It is a smooth palace of glass. She said, "My Lord, I wronged myself, and I have submitted with Sulayman[3335] to Allah, the Lord of the universe.[3336] (44) We sent their brother Salih[3337] to Thamud,[3338] "Worship Allah." They were two groups quarreling. (45) He said, "My people, why are you<sup>MP</sup> hastening bad deeds before good deeds? If only you<sup>MP</sup> would ask Allah's forgiveness, so that you<sup>MP</sup> may receive mercy. (46) They said, "We have an evil omen about you<sup>MS</sup> and those who are with you<sup>MS</sup>." He said, "Your evil omen is with Allah, and you<sup>MP</sup> people who are being led into temptation." (47) There were nine men of a family who were destructive in the land, and who did not do good. (48) They said, "Swear by Allah with each other, that we may attack him and his family by night. Then we will say to his helper, "We did not witness his family's destruction, and we are telling the truth." (49) They were crafty, and we were crafty[3339] without them realizing it. (50) See the punishment of their craftiness. We destroyed them and all their people. (51) Their homes were empty because of their wickedness. That is a sign for people who know. (52) We rescued the reverent believers. (53) Lut[3340] told his people, "Do you<sup>MP</sup> commit promiscuity[3341] knowingly?[3342] (54) You<sup>MP</sup> go to men lustfully instead of women. You<sup>MP</sup> are ignorant people." (55) **20A1** His people's answered only, "Expel Lut's family from your<sup>MP</sup> village.[3343] They are purified." (56) So we rescued him and his family,[3344] all except for his wife, whom we destined to lag behind.[3345] (57) Then we rained a rain upon them,

---

[3335] Solomon. See glossary for more details.
[3336] Tawrah, 1 Kings 10:1-6
[3337] Methuselah. See glossary for more details. Tawrah, Genesis 5:21-27, 1 Chronicles 1:3, Injil, Luke 3:37
[3338] A name of a tribe.
[3339] See 3:54 for a similar phrase.
[3340] Lot, nephew of Abraham, here and in verse 56. See glossary for more details.
[3341] Or lewdness, adultery or abomination
[3342] Tawrah, Genesis 19:5-7
[3343] Tawrah, Genesis 19:12-17
[3344] Tawrah, Genesis 19:15-22
[3345] Injil, Luke 17:32, Tawrah, Genesis 19:26

and those who were warned got an evil rain.[3346] (58) Say[MS], "Praise be to Allah, and peace to his chosen[3347] servants."[3348] What is better? Allah or the other gods you[MP] worship? (59) Who created the heavens and the earth[3349] and sent rain[3350] from the sky and made delightful gardens sprout whose trees you[MP] could not make sprout? Is there another god[3351] besides Allah? They are people who equate Allah to other gods.[3352] (60) Who made the earth a stable place to live,[3353] with rivers through it,[3354] mountains,[3355] and a barrier between the two seas? Is there another god besides Allah?[3356] Most of them do not know. (61) Who answers the one in need when he prays to him,[3357] keeps evil away,[3358] and makes them regents over the earth?[3359] Is there another god besides Allah?[3360] They remember infrequently. (62) Who guides you[MP] in the darkness of land and sea?[3361] Who sends winds as good news before[3362] his mercy? Is there another god[3363] besides Allah?[3364] May Allah be exalted far above the gods they worship![3365] (63) Who began creation,[3366] and then restored it?[3367] Who provides for you[MP] from heaven and earth?[3368] Is there another god[3369] besides

---

[3346] Tawrah, Genesis 19:24
[3347] Injil, Luke 2:14
[3348] See glossary.
[3349] Tawrah, Genesis 1:1, Isaiah 42:5, 45:18
[3350] Tawrah, Deuteronomy 28:12, Job 5:10, Joel 2:23, Zabur, Psalms 68:9, Injil, Matthew 5:45
[3351] Arabic /ilah/, here and in verses 61 and 62. See glossary for more details.
[3352] or deviate. Tawrah, Isaiah 44:6,8, 45:5,6,18,22
[3353] Zabur, Psalms 24:1-2
[3354] Tawrah, Genesis 2:10-14, Isaiah 41:18
[3355] Zabur, Psalms 30:7
[3356] Tawrah, Isaiah 44:6,8, 45:5,6,18,22
[3357] Injil, Matthew 6:8, Mark 11:24
[3358] Injil, Matthew 6:13
[3359] Tawrah, Genesis 1:28
[3360] Tawrah, Isaiah 44:6,8, 45:5,6,18,22
[3361] Zabur, Psalms 23:3
[3362] Or, "between the hands of" or "in front of."
[3363] Arabic /ilah/. See glossary for more details.
[3364] Tawrah, Isaiah 44:6,8, 45:5,6,18,22
[3365] Zabur, Psalms 108:5, Isaiah 33:5
[3366] Tawrah, Genesis 1:1
[3367] Tawrah, Genesis 1:3-31
[3368] Zabur, Psalms 145:15,16

Allah?³³⁷⁰ Say^MS, "Show your^MP proof³³⁷¹ if you^MP are telling the truth!" (64) Say^MS, "No one besides Allah in the heavens and the earth knows what is unseen."³³⁷² They do not realize when they will be resurrected.³³⁷³ (65) Their knowledge of the hereafter has failed. They are in doubt of it! In fact, they are blind of it! (66) Disbelievers said, "When we and our ancestors become soil, will we be brought forth? (67) We and our ancestors have been promised this beforehand. This is nothing more than an ancient legend." (68) Say^MS, "Walk around the land and see what was the punishment of the wrongdoers."³³⁷⁴ (69) Do not grieve over them, and do not be upset about how they deceive. (70) They say, "When will this promise be,³³⁷⁵ if you^MP are telling the truth?" (71) Say^MS, "Some of what you^MP were hastening may be following you^MP." (72) Your^MS Lord is gracious to people, but most of them do not give thanks. (73) Your^MS Lord knows what their hearts conceal, and what they announce. (74) Everything hidden in the heaven and the earth is in a clear book. (75) This recitation³³⁷⁶ relates to the people of Israel most of what they differ about. (76) It is guidance and mercy to the believers. (77) Your^MS Lord will pronounce his judgment between them. He is mighty³³⁷⁷ and all-knowing.³³⁷⁸ (78) Trust^MS in Allah. You^MS are standing on clear truth. (79) You^MS will not make the dead hear or make the deaf hear your^MS call if they turn their backs and flee. (80) You^MS are not a guide to the blind who go astray. You^MS only make those who believe in our signs hear. They are submitted.³³⁷⁹ (81) **20A2** If the saying falls on them, we will make a living creature from the earth

---

³³⁶⁹ Arabic /ilah/. See glossary for more details.

³³⁷⁰ Tawrah, Isaiah 44:6,8, 45:5,6,18,22

³³⁷¹ Tawrah, Isaiah 45:21

³³⁷² Tawrah, Isaiah 66:18, Injil, Matthew 24:36. However, 3:49 states that Isa told people what they ate and what they stored in their houses, which was a sign for believers.

³³⁷³ Injil, 2 Timothy 2:18

³³⁷⁴ "Punishment" is feminine and "was" is masculine. There may be another meaning or an implied word. 1 Peter 4:17

³³⁷⁵ Injil, 2 Peter 3:4

³³⁷⁶ Or Qur'an or qur'an. See glossary for more details.

³³⁷⁷ Injil, Revelation 18:8, Tawrah, Isaiah 60:16, Zabur, Psalms 93:4

³³⁷⁸ Tawrah, Job 37:16, Isaiah 40:14, Zabur, Psalms 33:13-15, Injil, 1 John 3:20

³³⁷⁹ Injil, James 4:7. For "submitted" here and in verse 91, some translators do not translate this. See glossary for more details.

Chapter 27

come out and speak[3380] to them, because people were not certain of our signs (82) on the day we gather[3381] groups who rejected our signs[3382] from every nation and march them out.[3383] (83) When they have come, he will say, "Have you[MP] rejected my signs when you[MP] did not know about them, or what did you[MP] do?" (84) The saying will fall on them for their wickedness, and they will not speak. (85) Have they not seen that we made night for them to rest and the day to see? Those are signs for believing people. (86) On the day when the trumpet is blown, those in the heavens and the earth will be terrified,[3384] except for those Allah wills. All will come to him,[3385] humbled. (87) You[MS] see the mountains, which you[MS] thought were firm, passing on like clouds.[3386] This is the handiwork of Allah, who does all things excellently.[3387] He is aware of your[MP] deeds. (88) Everyone who does good deeds will get better than that, and they will be safe from terror on that day. (89) Everyone who does bad deeds will be thrown face-down into hellfire.[3388] Will you[MP] be repaid for anything other than your[MP] deeds?[3389] (90) I was commanded to worship the Lord of this town, who sanctified it. He owns everything. I was commanded to be submitted, (91) and to read[3390] the Qur'an.[3391] Whoever is guided benefits himself by being guided. As for those who go astray, say, "I am a warner." (92) Say[MS], "Praise be to Allah." He will show you[MP] his signs, and you[MP] will know them. Your[MS] Lord is not unaware of your[MP] deeds.[3392] (93)

---

[3380] Injil, Revelation 13:11. Other living creatures that spoke in the Tawrah are a serpent, Tawrah, Genesis 3:1, and a donkey, Tawrah, Numbers 22:28,30.
[3381] Tawrah, Joel 3:11-14, Zephaniah 3:8, Injil, Matthew 25:32, John 15:6, Revelation 16:16
[3382] Arabic /ayat/, here and in verse 84. See glossary for more details.
[3383] Injil, Matthew 25:32
[3384] Injil, Revelation 11:13, 1 Corinthians 15:52
[3385] Injil, Matthew 25:32
[3386] Injil, Revelation 16:20
[3387] Injil, Mark 7:37
[3388] Injil, Matthew 25:46
[3389] Injil, Matthew 16:27
[3390] Or recite. See note at 7:157.
[3391] Or recitation. See glossary for more details.
[3392] Tawrah, Job 37:16, Isaiah 40:14, Zabur, Psalms 33:13-15, Injil, 1 John 3:20

# Chapter 28 Al-Qasas[3393]

In the name of Allah, the most gracious and merciful.[3394] TSM.[3395] (1) Those[3396] are signs[3397] of a clear book. (2) We recite to you[MS] some of the news of Musa[3398] and Pharaoh[3399] truly for believing people. (3) Pharaoh exalted himself in the land[3400] and made its people into parties who ill-treated a group of them[3401] by slaughtering their sons and keeping their women alive.[3402] He was destructive. (4) We want to be gracious to those who are weak in the land, make them leaders and heirs, (5) fortify them in the land, and show Pharaoh, Haman,[3403] and their[D] armies what they dreaded from them. (6) We inspired Musa's mother, "Nurse him.[3404] When[3405] you[FS] fear for him, cast him in the water.[3406] Do not fear or grieve. We will return[3407] him to you[FS] and make him a messenger."[3408] (7) Pharaoh's family took him,[3409] so that he could be an enemy and a cause of grief to them. Pharaoh, Haman,[3410] and

---

[3393] story

[3394] Zabur, Psalms 103:8, 145:8. See glossary for more details.

[3395] Here and at the beginning of many chapters there are unvowelled letters of unknown meaning. Numerous theories have been proposed, but there is no agreement on the subject.

[3396] The Qur'an here says "those" and not "these" so the reference is probably to the previous book. The book given to Musa and Harun is called a similar name in 37:117, so this may be the book referred to. See 27:1 where the phrase is used of a book different from the Qur'an.

[3397] or verses

[3398] Moses, here and in verses 7, 10, 15,18,19,and 20. See glossary for more details.

[3399] Tawrah, Exodus 5-12

[3400] Tawrah, Exodus 5:2

[3401] Tawrah, Exodus 3:7

[3402] Tawrah, Exodus 1:16-20

[3403] Tawrah, Esther 3-9 tells the story of a wicked man named Haman, but this may refer to a different Haman.

[3404] Tawrah, Exodus 2:1-3

[3405] Tawrah, Exodus 2:3

[3406] Tawrah, Exodus 2:3

[3407] Tawrah, Exodus 2:7-9

[3408] Tawrah, Exodus 3:10

[3409] Tawrah, Exodus 2:10

[3410] Tawrah, Esther 3-9 tells the story of one Haman, but this may refer to a different Haman.

## Chapter 28

theirᴰ armies were sinners. (8) Pharaoh's wife said, "The apple of my eye and yoursᴹˢ.³⁴¹¹ Do not killᴹᴾ him. He might benefit us, or we could take him as a son.³⁴¹² They did not realize. (9) Musa's mother's heart became³⁴¹³ empty and almost showed him,³⁴¹⁴ if we had not bound up her heart so she would believe.³⁴¹⁵ (10) She told his sister, "Followᶠˢ him."³⁴¹⁶ She watched him from the side, while they did not realize. (11) **20A3** We forbade him from nursing³⁴¹⁷ beforehand, and she said, "Shall I show youᴹᴾ a family who will take care of him for you and advise him?"³⁴¹⁸ (12) So we returned him to his mother,³⁴¹⁹ so that her heart³⁴²⁰ would be delighted and not grieve, and so she would know that Allah's promise is true.³⁴²¹ Most of them do not know. (13) When he grew strong and tall,³⁴²² we gave him judgment and knowledge.³⁴²³ Thus we reward those who do good. (14) He entered the city when its inhabitants did not expect it, and found two men fighting.³⁴²⁴ The first was from his party and the second was his enemy.³⁴²⁵ The one from his party cried out for help from his enemy, and Musa struck him and killed him.³⁴²⁶ He said, "This is a work of Satan. He is an enemy who clearly leads astray." (15) He said, "My Lord, I have wronged myself. Forgive me!"³⁴²⁷ So he forgave him. He is

---

³⁴¹¹ Tawrah, Exodus 2:5-6
³⁴¹² Tawrah, Exodus 2:6-10, Hebrews 11:24
³⁴¹³ or in the morning was
³⁴¹⁴ Tawrah, Exodus 2:3
³⁴¹⁵ Injiil, Hebrews 11:23
³⁴¹⁶ Tawrah, Exodus 2:4
³⁴¹⁷ or the breasts
³⁴¹⁸ Tawrah, Exodus 2:7
³⁴¹⁹ Tawrah, Exodus 2:8-9
³⁴²⁰ or her eye
³⁴²¹ Injiil, Hebrews 11:23
³⁴²² Tawrah, Exodus 2:11
³⁴²³ Injiil, Acts 7:22
³⁴²⁴ Tawrah, Exodus 2:11
³⁴²⁵ Tawrah, Exodus 2:11
³⁴²⁶ Tawrah, Exodus 2:12. This is probably the crime Pharaoh refers to in 26:19, which is here referenced in verses 28:15, 19, and 33.
³⁴²⁷ The belief that all prophets and messengers are sinless is not supported by the Qur'an. For instances of prophets or messengers asking forgiveness or committing sins, see 7:23, 20:121 (Adam), 11:47, 71:28 (Nuh), 26:82, 14:41 (Ibrahim), 28:15-16 (Musa), 7:151, 20:93 (Musa and Harun), 38:24 (Dawud), 38:32,35 (Sulayman), 21:87, 37:142 (Yunus),

forgiving³⁴²⁸ and merciful.³⁴²⁹ (16) He said, "My Lord, since you^MS have blessed me, I will never help wrongdoers." (17) He became³⁴³⁰ fearful³⁴³¹ and watchful in the city, and when he who had asked for his help the previous day asked his assistance, Musa told him, "You^MS are clearly in the wrong."³⁴³² (18) When he wanted to attack their^D enemy, he said, "Musa, do you^MS want to kill me like you^MS killed a soul yesterday?³⁴³³ You^MS just want to be powerful³⁴³⁴ in the land. You^MS do not want to do good."³⁴³⁵ (19) A man came running from the furthest part of the city. He said, "Musa, the nobles are plotting against you to kill you.³⁴³⁶ I advise you^MS to leave."³⁴³⁷ (20) So he left them, fearful and watchful. He said, "My Lord, save me from wicked people." (21)

\*\*\*

When he headed for Midian,³⁴³⁸ he said, "Maybe my Lord will guide me on a straight path."³⁴³⁹ (22)

\*\*\*

When he entered the waters of Midian,³⁴⁴⁰ he found a nation of people drawing water, and found besides them two women³⁴⁴¹ driving away [their flocks]. He said, "What is your^D story?" They^DF said, "We will not water our flocks until the shepherds send [theirs] away,³⁴⁴² and our father is very old. (23) So he watered

---

48:2, 47:19, 40:55, 4:79,106, 9:43, 13:30, 80:1-2, 110:3, 94:2, 23:118, 66:1, 33:37, 8:67, and 9:117 (Muhammad (s).

³⁴²⁸ Zabur, Psalms 103:3, 130:4, Tawrah, Isaiah 43:25, Exodus 34:7, Injil, Acts 26:18.

³⁴²⁹ See glossary for more details on "merciful."

³⁴³⁰ Or "in the morning, he was"

³⁴³¹ Tawrah, Exodus 2:14

³⁴³² Tawrah, Exodus 2:13

³⁴³³ See verses 15 and 33, and 26:19.Tawrah, Exodus 2:14

³⁴³⁴ Tawrah, Exodus 2:14

³⁴³⁵ or reconcile

³⁴³⁶ Tawrah, Exodus 2:15

³⁴³⁷ Tawrah, Exodus 2:14

³⁴³⁸ Tawrah, Exodus 2:15

³⁴³⁹ See glossary for more details, and notes on 3:51, 6:153, 19:36, 36:61, and 43:64 on what the straight path is.

³⁴⁴⁰ Tawrah, Exodus 2:15

³⁴⁴¹ Tawrah, Exodus 2:16-17

³⁴⁴² Tawrah, Genesis 29:8

them for them[D],[3443] then turned away to the shade. He said, "My Lord, I need the good things you[MS] have sent down to me." (24)
\*\*\*

One of them[DF] came walking to him bashfully, and said, "My father invites you[MS] in order to repay you[MS] for watering for us.[3444] When he came to him, he told him the story. He said, "Do not fear[MS]. You[MS] have escaped from wicked people." (25) One of them said, "Father, hire[MS] him. The best one you[MS] can hire is strong and faithful." (26) He said, "I want to marry you[MS] to one[F] of these[D] daughters[D] of mine, provided you[MS] work for me for hire eight hajjs.[3445] If you[MS] finish ten, that is your[MS] choice. I do not want to be hard on you[MS]. You[MS] will find me righteous, if Allah wills. (27)
\*\*\*

He said, "That is between me and you[MS]. Whichever of the two I complete, there will be no enmity against me. Allah is responsible for my saying." (28) 20A4
\*\*\*

When Musa[3446] had completed the time, and walked[3447] with his family,[3448] he noticed a fire next to the mountain.[3449] He told his family, "Stay[MP] here. I noticed a fire.[3450] Either I will bring you[MP] news from it, or a coal from the fire to warm you[MP]."[3451] (29) When he came to it, he was called from the right bank of the valley, in the tree's blessed spot,[3452] "Musa, I am Allah, the Lord of the universe.[3453] (30) Cast down your[MS] staff."[3454] When he saw it shaking like it was a jinn,[3455] he turned, fled, and did not follow it.[3456] "Musa, approach it and do not be afraid. You[MS] are safe.[3457]

---

[3443] Tawrah, Exodus 2:19, Genesis 29:10
[3444] Tawrah, Exodus 2:20
[3445] Pilgrimages, i.e. years. Tawrah, Exodus 2:21. See glossary for more details.
[3446] Moses, here and in verses 30, 31, 36, 37, and 38. See glossary for more details.
[3447] or traveled
[3448] Tawrah, Exodus 3:1
[3449] Tawrah, Exodus 3:2
[3450] Tawrah, Exodus 3:3
[3451] Tawrah, Exodus 3:3
[3452] Tawrah, Exodus 3:4
[3453] Tawrah, Exodus 3:4-6
[3454] Tawrah, Exodus 4:2-3
[3455] Or demon. See glossary for more details.
[3456] Tawrah, Exodus 4:3

## Chapter 28

(31) Put your[MS] hand in your[MS] pocket and it will come out white, but unharmed.[3458] Pull[MS] your[MS] arm back so you do not fear. These[D] are proofs from your[MS] Lord to Pharaoh and his nobles.[3459] They are unbelieving[3460] people. (32) He said, "My Lord, I killed one of them,[3461] and fear they will kill me. (33) My brother Harun[3462] is more eloquent in speech than I am. Send him with me as a helper to confirm me. I fear they will reject me."[3463] (34) He said, "We will strengthen your[MS] arms with your[MS] brother,[3464] and give you[D] authority. With our signs,[3465] they will not get to you[D]. You[D] and those who follow you[D] will be victorious." (35) When Musa came to them with our signs as miracles, they said, "This is only invented magic.[3466] We did not hear of this among our ancestors." (36) Musa said, "My Lord knows best who brought his guidance, and who will go to heaven. The wicked do not prosper." (37) Pharaoh said, "Nobles, I know no other god[3467] for you[MP] besides me. Haman,[3468] light a fire for me on the clay, and make a tower so that I can go up to Musa's god.[3469] I think he is a liar." (38) So he and his army were unjustly proud in the land, thinking that they would not return to us. (39) So we seized him and his army, and left them in the water.[3470] See the punishment of the wicked! (40) We made them leaders who call to hellfire, and on the day of resurrection,[3471] they will not be saved. (41) We made a curse follow them in this world, and on the day of resurrection, they will

---

[3457] Tawrah, Exodus 4:4
[3458] Tawrah, Exodus 4:6
[3459] Tawrah, Exodus 4:8
[3460] Or transgressing or immoral
[3461] Tawrah, Exodus 4:8. See verses 15 and 19, and 26:19 for details of Moses killing the Egyptian.
[3462] Aaron. See glossary for more details.
[3463] Tawrah, Exodus 4:10-16
[3464] Tawrah, Exodus 4:15-16
[3465] Tawrah, Exodus 4:12,17
[3466] Tawrah, Exodus 7:10-12
[3467] Arabic /ilah/. See glossary for more details.
[3468] Tawrah, Esther 3-9 tells the story of one Haman, but this may refer to a different Haman.
[3469] Arabic /ilah/. See glossary for more details.
[3470] Tawrah, Exodus 14:26-31
[3471] Here and in verses 42, 61, 71, and 72, for "day of resurrection," see Tawrah, Daniel 12:2 Injil, Acts 24:15, 1 Corinthians 15:52-54, Revelation 20:11-15

## Chapter 28

be loathed.[3472] (42) After we destroyed the first generations, we gave Musa[3473] the book[3474] as insight to men, guidance, and mercy, so that they may remember."[3475] (43) You[MS] were not on the west side when we decreed the commandment[3476] to Musa, and you[MS] were not a witness. (44) But we raised up generations, and they grew old. You[MS] did not live in Midian to recite our signs to them, but we sent messengers. (45) You[MS] were not beside the mountain when we called, but as a mercy from your[MS] Lord, you[MS] warn people. No warner before you[MS] has come to them, so that they may remember. (46) Otherwise, when a disaster strikes them because of their deeds, they would say, "Our Lord, if only you[MS] had sent us a messenger, we would have followed your[MS] signs and been believers." (47) When truth from us came to them, they said, "If only he had been given what Musa was given[3477]! Did they not disbelieve in what Musa was given beforehand? They said, "Two kinds of magic support[D] each other." They said, "We disbelieve in them." (48) Say[MS], "Bring a book from Allah that is better-guided than these[D] [kinds of magic] and I will follow it, if you[MP] are telling the truth." (49) If they do not respond to you[MS], know[MS] that they follow their desires. Who is further astray than those who follow their desires without Allah's guidance. Allah does not guide wicked people. (50) **20B1** We have brought them the saying so that they may remember. (51) Those whom we brought the book before it believe in it.[3478] (52) When it is read[3479] to them, they say, "We believe in it. It is the truth from our Lord. We were submitted[3480] before it." (53) They will be given their reward twice, for enduring[3481] and driving away bad deeds with good deeds. They donate out of what we provide them. (54) When they hear vanity, they turn away from it and say, "We have our works

---

[3472] or abhorred or ugly
[3473] Moses, here and in verses 44 and 48 twice. See glossary for more details.
[3474] Tawrah, Exodus 31:18
[3475] Tawrah, Deuteronomy 4:39
[3476] or matter. The reference might be to the ten commandments.
[3477] Tawrah, Exodus 31:18
[3478] the reference is unclear – probably the saying of the previous verse, but possibly the book of this verse.
[3479] Or recited or told
[3480] Injil, James 4:7. For "submitted," some translators do not translate this. See glossary for more details.
[3481] See "endure" in glossary, here and in verse 80.

and you<sup>MP</sup> have your<sup>MP</sup> works. Peace be upon you<sup>MP</sup>. We do not desire ignorant people." (55) You<sup>MS</sup> do not guide those you<sup>MS</sup> love, but Allah guides those he wills. He knows best who are guided. (56) They said, "If we follow guidance with you<sup>MS</sup>, we will be snatched from our land." Have we not made them a safe sanctuary for them? Fruits of everything are brought[3482] as tribute to it as provision from us, but most of them do not know. (57) How many villages that were insolent about their livelihood have we destroyed! Most of their dwellings were not lived in after them. We were heirs. (58) Your<sup>MS</sup> Lord did not destroy suburbs[3483] until he sent a messenger to their city to recite our signs to them. We would not have destroyed the villages unless their people were wicked. (59) Whatever you<sup>MP</sup> were given was of this world and its adornment. What Allah has is better and more lasting. Do you<sup>MP</sup> not comprehend? (60) Is he who receives the good we promise like him whom we let enjoy the things of this world, who is then arraigned on the day of resurrection? (61) On the day he calls them, he will say, "Where are the gods you<sup>MP</sup> supposed were my partners?" (62) Those on whom the saying was fulfilled said, "Our Lord, we led astray the ones we did just as we went astray. We are innocent before you<sup>MS</sup>. They were not worshiping us." (63) It will be said, "Pray to your<sup>MP</sup> other gods." They will call on them, but they will not respond to them, and they will see torment. If only they had been guided. (64) On the day he calls them, he will say, "How did you<sup>MP</sup> answer the messengers?" (65) They will be blind to the news that day, and they will not ask each other. (66) But he who repents, believes, and does righteous deeds[3484] may be successful. (67) Your<sup>MS</sup> Lord creates and chooses what he wills. They cannot choose. May Allah be glorified and exalted above the gods they worship! (68) Your<sup>MS</sup> Lord knows what their hearts conceal and what they announce.[3485] (69) He is Allah. He is the only god.[3486] He is praised in this world and the hereafter.

---

[3482] The verb is masculine and the noun is feminine. Possibly the fruits referred to here are people who come on pilgrimage.

[3483] Or villages. "City" in this verse would then be equivalent to the county seat or the nearest major city.

[3484] Here and in verse 80, see Injil, 1 Corinthians 3:8, James 2:14-17, Revelation 19:8.

[3485] See also 2:77, 11:5, 14:38, 16:19,23, 27:25,74, 36:76, 60:1, 64:4.

[3486] Arabic /ilah/, here and in verses 71 and 72. See glossary for more details.

## Chapter 28

Judgment is his, and you[MP] will return to him.[3487] (70) Say[MS], "What do you[MP] think? If Allah makes it eternal night over you[MP] until the day of resurrection, what other god besides Allah can bring light? Do you[MP] not hear?" (71) Say[MS], "What do you[MP] think? If Allah makes it eternal day over you[MP] until the day of resurrection, what other god besides Allah can bring you[MP] night you[MP] can rest in? Do you[MP] not see?" (72) Out of his mercy, he made night and day[3488] for you[MP], so that you[MP] can rest in it and desire his grace, and so that you[MP] may give thanks. (73) On the day he calls them, he will say, "Where are the gods you[MP] supposed were my partners?" (74) We brought out a witness from every nation and said, "Bring on your[MP] proofs."[3489] They knew that Allah was right, and what they invented went astray from them. (75) **20B2** Korah was of Musa's[3490] people and he desired to rule them.[3491] We gave him treasures so great[3492] that their keys would be too heavy for a group of strong men. His people told him, "Do not exult.[3493] Allah does not like those who exult."[3494] (76) Along with what Allah has given you[MS], desire the abode of the hereafter, and do not forget[MS] your portion in this world. Do[MS] good, as Allah has done good to you[MS].[3495] Do not desire[MS] destruction on earth. Allah does not like destroyers." (77) He said, "What I have been given is because of knowledge I have." What did he think? Did he not know that Allah had destroyed generations before him of those who were stronger and more numerous than he? Wrongdoers will not be questioned about their sins. (78) He went out to his people in his adornment.[3496] Those who want this world[3497] said, "If only we had something like Korah was given. He is very lucky." (79) Those who had been given knowledge said, "Woe to you[MP]! Allah's reward for those who believe and do righteous deeds is better.

---

[3487] Injil, Romans 14:12
[3488] Tawrah, Genesis 1:14-19
[3489] Tawrah, Isaiah 45:21
[3490] Moses. See glossary for more details.
[3491] Tawrah, Numbers 16:1-3. Other translations have "betrayed" or "oppressed" or "was insolent."
[3492] Tawrah, Numbers 16:6-7
[3493] (in your riches) Tawrah, Jeremiah 9:23-24
[3494] Injil, 1 Peter 5:5-6, Matthew 23:12, James 4:6, Zabur, Psalms 138:6, Tawrah, Isaiah 66:1-2
[3495] Injil, 1 Timothy 6:17-18
[3496] Tawrah, Numbers 16:19
[3497] Injil, 1 Timothy 6:9

## Chapter 28

Only those who endure will get it."[3498] (80) We made the earth swallow him and his house.[3499] He had no group to save him apart from Allah, so he was not saved. (81) Those who had wanted to be in his place the previous day started to say, "Aha! Allah spreads out or withholds his provision to his servants[3500] that he wills. If Allah had not been gracious to us, he would have swallowed us up.[3501] Aha! Disbelievers do not prosper." (82) That is the abode of the hereafter, which we assign to those who do not want a high position or destruction on earth. This reward is for the reverent. (83) Whoever does a good deed gets something better from it.[3502] As for those who do bad deeds, those who do bad deeds will only be repaid for their deeds.[3503] (84) He who imposed the Qur'an[3504] upon you[MS] will restore you[MS] to a place to return. Say[MS], "My Lord knows best who brought guidance and who has clearly gone astray. (85) You[MS] did not hope that the book would be cast down to you[MS] except as a mercy from your[MS] Lord. Do not help[MS] the disbelievers. (86) Do not let them block you[MS] from Allah's signs after they were revealed to you[MS]. Invite [others] to your[MS] Lord and do not be[MS] a polytheist. (87) Do not pray[MS] to another god[3505] besides Allah. He is the only god. Everything will be destroyed except his face. Judgment is his, and you[MP] will return to him.[3506] (88)[3507]

---

[3498] Injil, Matthew 24:13
[3499] Tawrah, Numbers 16:31-33
[3500] See glossary.
[3501] Tawrah, Numbers 16:34
[3502] Injil, Matthew 10:41-42, 19:27-30, Mark 10:28-31, Luke 18:28-30
[3503] Injil, Colossians 3:25
[3504] Or recitation. See glossary for more details.
[3505] Arabic /ilah/, here and later in this verse. See glossary for more details.
[3506] Injil, Romans 14:12
[3507] The verses in this chapter that rhyme are put together in paragraphs, separated by ***.

# Chapter 29 Al-Ankabut[3508]

**20B3** In the name of Allah, the most gracious and merciful.[3509] ALM.[3510] (1) Do people think that they will be left alone on saying, "We believe," without being tested? (2) We tested those who were before them.[3511] Allah well knows who is honest, and he well knows who is a liar. (3) Do those who do bad deeds think that they will beat us? They judge badly. (4) Allah's timespan is coming for those who hope to meet Allah. He hears all and knows all. (5) Whoever struggles, struggles for his own benefit. Allah has no need of anything from anyone. (6) We will expiate the bad deeds of believers[3512] who do righteous deeds,[3513] and reward them for the best of what they did.[3514] (7) We commanded people to do good to their parents.[3515] But if they[D] struggle[3516] to make you[MS] worship gods other than me,[3517] of which you[MS] have no knowledge, do not obey them. You[MP] will return to me, and I will tell you[MP] your[MP] deeds. (8) We will cause believers who do righteous deeds to be admitted among the righteous.[3518] (9) Some people say, "We believe in Allah." If he is harmed for Allah's sake, he makes people's testing like Allah's torment. When salvation from your[MS] Lord comes, he will say, "We were with you[MP]." Does Allah not know best what is in the heart[3519] of all mankind? (10) Allah know who believes and who is a hypocrite.

---

[3508] spider
[3509] Zabur, Psalms 103:8, 145:8. See glossary for more details.
[3510] Here and at the beginning of many chapters there are unvowelled letters of unknown meaning. Numerous theories have been proposed, but there is no agreement on the subject.
[3511] Injil, 1 Corinthians 10:13
[3512] Tawrah, Isaiah 27:9, Injil, Romans 3:25, Hebrews 2:17, 1 John 2:2, 4:10
[3513] Here and in verse 9, see Injil, 1 Corinthians 3:8, James 2:14-17, Revelation 19:8.
[3514] Injil, Hebrews 11, especially verse 6.
[3515] Tawrah, Exodus 20:12
[3516] This word is the verbal form of the noun /jihad/, and this usage shows that the true meaning in the Qur'an is "struggle," and not "holy war."
[3517] Tawrah, Exodus 20:3
[3518] Injil, James 2:24
[3519] Injil, Luke 6:8,16:15, John 2:25, Romans 8:27, Acts 15:8, 1 John 3:20, Tawrah, 1 Samuel 16:7, 1 Chronicles 28:9, Zabur, Psalms 44:21

(11) The disbelievers tell the believers, "Follow our path, and we will bear your$^{MP}$ guilt." They cannot even bear their own guilt. They are liars. (12) They will bear their own burdens[3520] in addition to other burdens along with them. They will be questioned on the day of resurrection[3521] for their inventions. (13) We sent Nuh[3522] to his people, and he remained with them fifty years short of a thousand years.[3523] The flood overtook them while they were wicked,[3524] (14) but we rescued him and the others on the ship.[3525] We made it a sign for mankind.[3526] (15) And when Ibrahim[3527] told his people, "Worship$^{MP}$ and fear Allah.[3528] That is better for you$^{MP}$, if you$^{MP}$ only knew. (16) You$^{MP}$ worship idols instead of Allah,[3529] and you$^{MP}$ create lies. Other gods you$^{MP}$ worship besides Allah cannot provide for you$^{MP}$. Seek your$^{MP}$ provision from Allah,[3530] worship$^{MP}$ him and give$^{MP}$ him thanks. You$^{MP}$ will be returned to him. (17) If you$^{MP}$ reject [him], nations before you$^{MP}$ rejected. The only responsibility of a messenger is clear proclamation." (18)

\*\*\*

Have they not seen how Allah began the creation, then renewed it? That is easy for Allah. (19) Say$^{MS}$, "Walk$^{MP}$ through the land and see$^{MP}$ how he began the creation. Then Allah establishes the latter establishment. Allah can do anything.[3531] (20)

\*\*\*

He torments those he wills and has mercy on those he wills.[3532] You$^{MP}$ will be returned to him. (21)

\*\*\*

---

[3520] Injil, Galatians 6:5
[3521] Here and in verse 25, for "day of resurrection," see Tawrah, Daniel 12:2 Injil, Acts 24:15, 1 Corinthians 15:52-54, Revelation 20:11-15
[3522] Noah. See glossary for more details.
[3523] Tawrah, Genesis 9:29
[3524] Tawrah, Genesis 7:23
[3525] Tawrah, Genesis 8:18
[3526] Tawrah, Genesis 9:12
[3527] Abraham. See glossary for more details. Tawrah, Genesis 12:1-3
[3528] Tawrah, Deuteronomy 10:12, Isaiah 29:13, Injil, 1 Peter 2:17, Revelation 14:7
[3529] Tawrah, Joshua 24:14
[3530] Zabur, Psalms 145:15, 34:10, 81:9-10, Injil, Matthew 6:33
[3531] Tawrah, Job 42:2, Isaiah 14:27, Daniel 4:35, Injil, Matthew 19:26, Mark 10:27, Luke 1:37
[3532] Injil, Romans 9:18

## Chapter 29

You[MP] cannot hinder anything in the earth or in heaven. You[MP] have no helper or savior besides Allah.[3533] (22)

\*\*\*

Those who disbelieve in Allah's signs[3534] and in meeting him will despair of Allah's mercy. They will have painful torment."[3535] (23) His people's answer was merely this they said, "Kill him or burn him." But Allah rescued him from the fire. Those are signs for believing people. (24) He said, "You[MP] have chosen idols instead of Allah because you[MP] are fond of each other in this world. On the day of resurrection, you[MP] will disbelieve in each other, and curse[MP] each other. Your[MP] abode will be hellfire, and you[MP] will have no savior."[3536] (25) 20B4 Lut[3537] believed in him, and said, "I will flee[3538] to my Lord.[3539] He is mighty and wise."[3540] (26) We gave him Ishaq[3541] and Yaqub,[3542] and gave some of his seed prophethood[3543] and the book.[3544] We gave him his reward in this world, and in the hereafter,[3545] he will be righteous. (27) And Lut[3546] told his people, "You[MP] commit unprecedented promiscuity.[3547] (28) You[MP] have sex with men, and are highway robbers,[3548] doing wrong in your[MP] council." His people's response was merely, "Then bring Allah's torment on us if you[MS] are telling the truth." (29) He said, "My Lord, give me victory over corrupt

---

[3533] Tawrah, Hosea 13:4, Zabur, Psalms 106:21, Injil, Luke 1:47, Titus 1:3
[3534] Arabic /ayat/. See glossary for more details.
[3535] For "torment" here and in verses 53, 54, and 55, see Tawrah, Isaiah 50:11, Injil, Matthew 18:34, 25:41,46, Luke 16:23-28, Revelation 20:15.
[3536] Tawrah, Isaiah 43:11, Hosea 13:4, Injil, Hebrews 10:26
[3537] Lot, nephew of Abraham. See glossary for more details.
[3538] Or emigrate
[3539] Tawrah, Genesis 19:20
[3540] Tawrah, Job 9:4, Proverbs 2:6, Jeremiah 9:23-24, Injil, 1 Corinthians 1:21-25, Romans 16:27
[3541] Isaac. See glossary for more details. Tawrah, Genesis 21:3
[3542] Jacob. See glossary for more details. Tawrah, Genesis 25:26
[3543] Tawrah, Exodus 7:1, Deuteronomy 34:10, 1 Samuel 3:20
[3544] Tawrah, Exodus 24:12
[3545] Injil, Hebrews 11:8-13
[3546] Lot, nephew of Abraham, here and in verses 32 and 33. See glossary for more details.
[3547] Or lewdness, adultery or abomination See Tawrah, Genesis 19:5
[3548] Tawrah, Ezekiel 16:49-50

people." (30) When our messengers came to Ibrahim³⁵⁴⁹ with good news,³⁵⁵⁰ they said, "We will destroy the inhabitants of this village.³⁵⁵¹ They are wicked." (31) He said, "Lut is in it." They said, "We well know who is in it. We will rescue him and his family, all except his wife, who lags behind." (32) When our messengers came to Lut, he was vexed for them³⁵⁵² and unable to help them. They said, "Do not be afraid or grieve. We will rescue you^MS and your^MS family, all except your^MS wife, who lags behind." (33) We will send punishment from heaven down on this village for their unbelief."³⁵⁵³ (34) We left behind a miraculous sign from it for people who comprehend. (35) And Shuaib³⁵⁵⁴ their brother [was sent] to Midian.³⁵⁵⁵ He said, "My people, worship Allah. Hope for the last day, and do not do evil and destruction on the earth." (36) They rejected him and an earthquake overtook them, and in the morning they were lying on their faces in their houses. (37) And it was clear to you^MP from Aad and Thamud's³⁵⁵⁶ dwellings. Satan made their works seem fair to them,³⁵⁵⁷ and he diverted them from the path, though they were insightful. (38) Musa³⁵⁵⁸ brought Korah,³⁵⁵⁹ Pharaoh,³⁵⁶⁰ and Haman³⁵⁶¹ miracles. They were proud in the land, but did not beat him. (39) Each of them we seized from his sin. Against some, we sent a sandstorm,³⁵⁶² some were seized by the cry, some we made the earth swallow,³⁵⁶³ and some we drowned.³⁵⁶⁴ Allah would never wrong them; they wronged themselves.³⁵⁶⁵ (40) Those who choose

---

[3549] Abraham. See glossary for more details.
[3550] Tawrah, Genesis 18:10
[3551] Tawrah, Genesis 18:20-21
[3552] Injil, 2 Peter 2:8.
[3553] Or immorality or transgression. Tawrah, Genesis 19:13
[3554] Jethro. See glossary for more details.
[3555] Tawrah, Exodus 3:1
[3556] Aad and Thamud were tribes.
[3557] Tawrah, Deuteronomy 11:16
[3558] Moses. See glossary for more details.
[3559] Tawrah, Numbers 16
[3560] Tawrah, Exodus 3-14
[3561] Tawrah, Esther 3-9. Possibly another Haman is meant.
[3562] or a violent storm or a storm of stones
[3563] Tawrah, Numbers 16:31-35
[3564] Tawrah, Exodus 14:28
[3565] The injustice/wickedness, disbelief/ungratefulness, evil, unrighteousness/sin, or lostness of mankind is mentioned in a number of

## Chapter 29

helpers besides Allah are like the spider, which[3566] chooses a house. The spider's house is the frailest house of all, if they only knew. (41) Allah knows everything they pray to besides him. He is mighty and wise.[3567] (42) We tell those proverbs to people, but only the knowledgeable comprehend them.[3568] (43) Allah truly created the heavens and the earth. That is a sign for believers. (44) Recite[3569] the part of the book you[MS] were inspired with, and perform prayers. Performing prayers hinders promiscuity[3570] and vice. Remembering Allah is greater. Allah knows your[MP] deeds. (45) 21A1 Do not argue[MP] with the people of the book but [speak] in a fair manner,[3571] except with the wicked among them. Say[MP], "We believe in what was revealed to us and what was revealed to you[MP]. Our god[3572] and your[MP] god is one,[3573] and we submit[3574] to him." (46) Thus we revealed the book to you[MS]. Those to whom we gave the book believe in it.[3575] Some of them believe in it, and only the disbelievers reject our signs.[3576] (47) Before it, you[MS] did not recite any book, nor write[MS] one with your[MS] right hand. Otherwise, those who frustrate it would doubt. (48) It is

---

verses in the Qur'an as well as in the previous books. Injustice or wickedness: 2:57, 3:117,135, 4:64,97, 7:160,177, 9:70, 10:44, 11:101, 14:34,45, 16:33,61,118, 29:40, 30:9, 33:72, 34:19, 35:32, 43:76, 65:1, Tawrah, Genesis 6:5, Job 25:4, Injil, Acts 3:26, disbelief or ungratefulness: 14:34, 17:67, 22:66, 42:48, 43:15, 80:17, Injil, Hebrews 3:19, Evil: 12:53, Tawrah, Jeremiah 17:9, Injil, Matthew 15:19, Mark 7:21, unrighteousness or sin: 91:8, Tawrah, 1 Kings 8:46, Ecclesiastes 7:20, Injil, Romans 3:9-19, 5:12, lostness: 103:2, Tawrah, Jeremiah 50:6, Injil, Luke 19:10, Romans 3:23, 6:23

[3566] "spider" is masculine and "which" is feminine. There may be a different meaning.
[3567] Tawrah, Job 9:4, Proverbs 2:6, Jeremiah 9:23-24, Injil, 1 Corinthians 1:21-25, Romans 16:27
[3568] Injil, Matthew 13:13-17
[3569] Or read or tell. See note at 7:157.
[3570] Or lewdness, adultery or abomination
[3571] or "in a better way" or "politely"
[3572] For "god" twice here, see glossary for more details. Arabic /ilah/.
[3573] Tawrah, Deuteronomy 6:4, Injil, Mark 12:29, 1 Timothy 2:5
[3574] Injil, James 4:7. For "submit," some translators do not translate this. See glossary for more details.
[3575] "It" here could refer to the former book or to the Qur'an.
[3576] Arabic /ayat/ here and in verse 49. See glossary for more details.

## Chapter 29

miraculous signs[3577] in the hearts of those who have been given knowledge, and only the wicked reject our signs. (49) They said, "If only signs had been revealed[3578] to him by his Lord." Say[MS], "Signs are from Allah. I am a clear warner." (50) Is it not enough for them that we revealed to you[MS] the book that is read[3579] to them? That is mercy and a reminder for believing people. (51) Say[MS], "Allah is an adequate witness between me and you[MP]. He knows what is in the heavens and the earth. Those who believe in vain things and disbelieve in Allah are lost. (52) They desire you[MS] to hasten the torment. If it did not have a specified timespan,[3580] torment would have already come to them. It will come upon them suddenly while they do not realize it.[3581] (53) They desire you[MS] to hasten the torment. Hell surrounds the disbelievers. (54) On the day they are covered with torment from above and beneath their feet, he will say, "Taste your[MP] deeds." (55) "My believing servants, my land is broad, so worship[MP] me. (56) Every soul will taste death. Then you[MP] will be returned to us."[3582] (57) We will prepare dwellings for believers who do righteous deeds[3583] in the heavenly garden,[3584] apartments with flowing rivers underneath, where they will remain forever. How nice is the reward[3585] of the workers (58) who endure[3586] and trust in their Lord. (59) How many living creatures cannot even carry their own provision! Allah provides for them and for you[MP].[3587] He hears all and knows all. (60) If you[MS] ask them who created the heavens and the earth, and subjected the sun and the moon,[3588] they will say, "Allah." So how do they lie? (61) Allah extends or withholds his provision to those of his servants he wills. Allah knows everything. (62) If

---

[3577] The subject is masculine and the complement is feminine. There may be a different meaning.
[3578] The subject is feminine and the verb is masculine. There may be a different meaning.
[3579] Or recited or told
[3580] Injil, Revelation 14:15
[3581] Injil, 1 Thessalonians 5:3
[3582] Injil, Hebrews 9:27
[3583] Injil, 1 Corinthians 3:8, James 2:14-17, Revelation 19:8
[3584] Arabic /jannah/. See glossary for more details.
[3585] Injil, 1 Corinthians 3:12-15
[3586] See "endure" in glossary
[3587] Injil, Matthew 6:25-34
[3588] Tawrah, Genesis 1

you[MS] ask them who sends the rain down,[3589] reviving the dead ground, they will say, "Allah." Say[MS], "Praise be to Allah." Most of them do not comprehend. (63) This world is only amusement and play.[3590] The hereafter is real life, if they only knew.[3591] (64) When they board a ship, they pray in sincere religion to Allah. When he rescues them and gets them back to shore, they worship other gods, (65) thus being ungrateful for our gifts to them, and enjoy [life]. They will know. (66) Have they not seen that we made a safe sanctuary, while all around them, people are snatched? Do they believe in vanity, and are they ungrateful for Allah's blessings? (67) Who is more wicked than those who invent lies about Allah or disbelieves in the truth that comes to him?[3592] Is hell not the abode of the disbelievers? (68) We will guide those who struggle in us in our paths. Allah is with[3593] those who do good.[3594] (69)[3595]

---

[3589] Tawrah, Deuteronomy 28:12, Job 5:10, Joel 2:23, Zabur, Psalms 68:9, Injil, Matthew 5:45
[3590] Injil, 2 Corinthians 4:18
[3591] Injil, 1 Timothy 6:19
[3592] Injil, Romans 1:18
[3593] Injil, Romans 8:32
[3594] Tawrah, Proverbs 15:9
[3595] The verses in this chapter that rhyme are put together in paragraphs, separated by ***.

Chapter 30

# Chapter 30 Al-Roum[3596]

21A2 In the name of Allah, the most gracious and merciful.[3597] ALM.[3598] (1) May the Greeks be[3599] defeated[3600] (2) in the nearest part of the land. After they were defeated,[3601] they will be victorious (3) in a few years. It is Allah's command,[3602] both before and afterwards. On that day, the believers will rejoice (4) in Allah's victory. Allah gives victory to those he wills.[3603] He is mighty and merciful.[3604] (5) As for Allah's promise, Allah does not break his promise,[3605] but most people do not know it. (6) They know this world superficially, but they are totally unaware of the hereafter. (7) Have they not considered within themselves? Allah created the heavens, the earth,[3606] and what is in between them in truth, for a stated period of time.[3607] Most people disbelieve in an appointment with their Lord.[3608] (8) Have they not walked in the land and seen what was the end of those before them? They were stronger than them, ploughed the earth, and built on it more than they built on it. Their messengers came[3609] to them with miracles. Allah would never wrong them but they wronged themselves.[3610]

---

[3596] Greeks (Byzantines)

[3597] Zabur, Psalms 103:8, 145:8. See glossary for more details.

[3598] Here and at the beginning of many chapters there are unvowelled letters of unknown meaning. Numerous theories have been proposed, but there is no agreement on the subject.

[3599] Or, "The Greeks were"

[3600] Tawrah, Daniel 11:2-4

[3601] Or "victorious"

[3602] or matter

[3603] Tawrah, Proverbs 21:31

[3604] See glossary for more details on "merciful."

[3605] Injil, Hebrews 6:17-18, Tawrah, Numbers 23:19

[3606] Tawrah, Genesis 1:1

[3607] Injil, Acts 17:26, Ecclesiastes 3:11

[3608] Injil, Romans 14:10

[3609] The verb used here is for non-thinking creatures, so possibly "messengers" here includes other things Allah sent with miracles (instead of or in addition to people).

[3610] The injustice/wickedness, disbelief/ungratefulness, evil, unrighteousness/sin, or lostness of mankind is mentioned in a number of verses in the Qur'an as well as in the previous books. Injustice or wickedness: 2:57, 3:117,135, 4:64,97, 7:160,177, 9:70, 10:44, 11:101, 14:34,45, 16:33,61,118, 29:40, 30:9, 33:72, 34:19, 35:32, 43:76, 65:1,

## Chapter 30

(9) Then the end of the evildoers was evil, since they rejected and made fun of Allah's signs.[3611] (10) Allah begins the creation, and then restores it, and then you[MP] will be returned to him. (11) On the day the hour comes,[3612] wrongdoers will be confused.[3613] (12) None of their gods will intercede for them, and they will disbelieve in their gods. (13) On the day the hour comes, on that very day, they will be divided.[3614] (14) Believers who did righteous deeds[3615] will be delighted in a meadow. (15) Disbelievers who rejected our signs and their appointment with the hereafter will be brought into torment.[3616] (16) May Allah be glorified in your[MP] evening and morning![3617] (17) Praise be to him in the heavens and the earth, at night and at your[MP] noon. (18) He brings forth the living from the dead and the dead from the living. He revives the dead ground. In the same way, you[MP] will be brought forth. (19) One of his signs was that he created you[MP] from soil,[3618] and then you[MP] became human, and spread[MP] abroad.[3619] (20) One of his signs is that he created spouses for you[MP] from yourselves[MP],[3620] to dwell with them.[3621] He caused love and mercy between you[MP].[3622] Those are signs for people who consider. (21) Other signs of his are creating the heavens and the earth and the differences in your[MP] tongues[3623] and colors.[3624] Those are signs for

---

Tawrah, Genesis 6:5, Job 25:4, Injil, Acts 3:26, disbelief or ungratefulness: 14:34, 17:67, 22:66, 42:48, 43:15, 80:17, Injil, Hebrews 3:19, Evil: 12:53, Tawrah, Jeremiah 17:9, Injil, Matthew 15:19, Mark 7:21, unrighteousness or sin: 91:8, Tawrah, 1 Kings 8:46, Ecclesiastes 7:20, Injil, Romans 3:9-19, 5:12, lostness: 103:2, Tawrah, Jeremiah 50:6, Injil, Luke 19:10, Romans 3:23, 6:23

[3611] Arabic /ayat/ here and in verse 16. See glossary for more details.
[3612] Injil, John 5:28
[3613] or dressed
[3614] Injil, Matthew 25:32
[3615] Injil, 1 Corinthians 3:8, James 2:14-17, Revelation 19:8
[3616] Or "torture." Tawrah, Isaiah 50:11, Injil, Matthew 18:34, 25:41,46, Luke 16:23-28, Revelation 20:15
[3617] Or, when you go to bed and when you get up.
[3618] Tawrah, Genesis 2:7
[3619] Tawrah, Genesis 11:8
[3620] Tawrah, Genesis 2:21-24
[3621] The word "them" is used for unthinking beings, so there may be an alternate meaning. Injil, 1 Peter 3:8
[3622] Injil, Ephesians 5:25-28, Titus 2:4
[3623] Tawrah, Genesis 10:1-31

## Chapter 30

all beings. (22) Another sign is your[MP] sleep at night[3625] and day,[3626] and your[MP] desire for his grace. Those are signs for people who hear. (23) One of his signs is showing you[MP] lightning,[3627] which makes you[MP] both fear and hope, and he makes rain fall from the sky,[3628] and revives the dead ground.[3629] Those are signs for people who comprehend. (24) One of his signs is that heaven and earth stand by his command.[3630] Then when he calls you[MP] forth from the earth, you[MP] will go out. (25) Everything in the heavens and the earth is his.[3631] Everything obeys him.[3632] (26) He begins creation and then renews it, and that it easy for him. He has the highest example[3633] in the heavens and the earth.[3634] He is mighty and wise.[3635] (27) He made a proverb for you[MP] from among yourselves[MP]. Are any of the slaves we provided you[MP] equal partners in our provision for you[MP], and you[MP] fear them as you[MP] fear yourselves[MP]?[3636] Thus we explain signs to people who comprehend. (28) Disbelievers follow their desires unknowingly.[3637] Who can guide those Allah has led astray?[3638] They have no savior.[3639] (29) Set your[MS] face toward religion as a monotheist, which is the instinct Allah gave people.[3640] There is no substituting Allah's creation. That is straight religion, but most people do not know it (30) 21A3 as they turn toward him. Fear[MP]

---

[3624] Tawrah, Genesis 10:1-31
[3625] Injil, 1 Thessalonians 5:7, Zabur, Psalms 16:7
[3626] i.e. a nap/siesta in the hot afternoon
[3627] Tawrah, Job 37:11
[3628] Tawrah, Deuteronomy 28:12, Job 5:10, Joel 2:23, Zabur, Psalms 68:9, Injil, Matthew 5:45
[3629] Tawrah, Isaiah 44:3
[3630] Zabur, Psalms 119:89-90
[3631] Tawrah, Isaiah 45:12, Zabur, Psalms 24:1, 89:11, Injil, Hebrews 1:10
[3632] Zabur, Psalms 119:91
[3633] Or proverb
[3634] Zabur, Psalms 47:9
[3635] Tawrah, Job 9:4, Proverbs 2:6, Jeremiah 9:23-24, Injil, 1 Corinthians 1:21-25, Romans 16:27
[3636] Or "each other"
[3637] Injil, Romans 8:7
[3638] Injil, 2 Thessalonians 2:11, Tawrah, 2 Samuel 22:27, 1 Kings 22:20-23, Ezekiel 14:9
[3639] Tawrah, Isaiah 43:11, Hosea 13:4, Injil, Hebrews 10:26
[3640] Injil, Romans 1:19-20

## Chapter 30

him, perform<sup>MP</sup> prayers, and do not became<sup>MP</sup> idolaters,[3641] (31) who divided up their religion and were a sect.[3642] Every party is happy about what they have. (32) If people are touched by harm, they pray to their Lord, and turn to him. Then if he gives them a taste of his mercy, some of them worship gods other than their Lord, (33) being ungrateful for our gifts to them. Enjoy! You<sup>MP</sup> will know. (34) Or did we give them authority that speaks of the gods they worship?[3643] (35) If we gave people a taste of mercy, they are happy for it, but if something bad happens to them, because of what they have done, they despair. (36) Have they not seen that Allah spreads forth and withholds[3644] provision to those he wills?[3645] Those are signs for believing people. (37) Give<sup>MS</sup> relatives, the poor, and travelers their due.[3646] That is good for those who seek Allah's face.[3647] They will be successful. (38) The profit you make on the usury[3648] you<sup>MP</sup> charge people will not get any interest with Allah if you give it. The poor-tax you<sup>MP</sup> pay, seeking Allah's face, they[3649] are the ones who double it.[3650] (39) Allah created you<sup>MP</sup> and provided for you<sup>MP</sup>.[3651] Then he makes you<sup>MP</sup> die and revives you<sup>MP</sup>.[3652] Do any of your<sup>MP</sup> gods do any of that?[3653] May he be glorified and exalted above the gods they worship![3654] (40) Destruction shows up on land and seas because of what people do,[3655] and he gives them a taste of some of what they did, so that they may return. (41) Say<sup>MS</sup>, "Walk<sup>MP</sup> through the land and see<sup>MP</sup> what happened to those beforehand. Most of them were idolaters." (42) Set your<sup>MS</sup> face toward right religion before a day comes from Allah which cannot be turned back. On that day,

---

[3641] Injil, 1 John 5:21
[3642] Injil, Jude 19
[3643] Tawrah, Isaiah 44:8
[3644] in some translations, this word is translate "and is able"
[3645] Tawrah, 1 Samuel 2:7
[3646] Tawrah, Deuteronomy 24:14
[3647] Zabur, Psalms 27:8
[3648] Tawrah, Exodus 22:24, Leviticus 25:35-37, Deuteronomy 23:20-21, Zabur, Psalms 15:5
[3649] The pronoun changes here in Arabic.
[3650] Tawrah, Proverbs 19:17
[3651] Injil, Matthew 6:25-26
[3652] Injil, Revelation 20:12
[3653] Tawrah, Isaiah 41:21-23
[3654] Tawrah, Isaiah 41:24
[3655] Tawrah, Isaiah 24:5

## Chapter 30

they will be split in two.[3656] (43) The disbelief of disbelievers will be held against them, but those who do righteous deeds make provision for themselves,[3657] (44) so he will repay believers who do righteous deeds[3658] out of his grace.[3659] He does not love disbelievers.[3660] (45) One of his signs is that he send the winds with good news,[3661] to give you[MP] a taste of his mercy, to make ships sail by his command,[3662] so that you[MP] would desire his grace, and so that you[MP] may give thanks. (46) We sent messengers before you[MS] to their peoples, and they brought miracles. We took revenge on the wrongdoers, but we were obliged to save the believers. (47) Allah sends the wind and it forms clouds, which he spreads in the sky as he wills. Then he makes them break up, and you[MS] see the rain come out through them.[3663] When he makes it fall on those of his servants he wills,[3664] they rejoice, (48) even if they had despaired before it fell on them. (49)

\*\*\*

Look[MS] at the result of Allah's mercy,[3665] how he revives the dead ground.[3666] This is what reviving the dead is like. He can do anything.[3667] (50)

\*\*\*

Even if we send a wind they see as yellow, they will remain disbelievers. (51) You[MS] do not make the dead hear, nor make[MS] the deaf hear the call when they turn their back and go away. (52)

---

[3656] Injil, Matthew 25:32
[3657] Injil, John 5:29, 2 Timothy 1:12
[3658] Injil, 1 Corinthians 3:8, James 2:14-17, Revelation 19:8
[3659] Injil, James 2:22
[3660] Zabur, Psalms 5:4-5, 11:5, Tawrah, Proverbs 6:16-19
[3661] Injil, John 3:8
[3662] Zabur, Psalms 107:23
[3663] Tawrah, Deuteronomy 28:12, Job 5:10, Joel 2:23, Zabur, Psalms 68:9, Injil, Matthew 5:45
[3664] Injil, Matthew 5:45
[3665] "Mercy" has a different spelling here and in 6 other places. See glossary.
[3666] Tawrah, Job 5:10
[3667] Tawrah, Job 42:2, Isaiah 14:27, Daniel 4:35, Injil, Matthew 19:26, Mark 10:27, Luke 1:37

## Chapter 30

You[MS] are not a guide to the blind[3668] in their lostness. You[MS] only make believers in our signs hear, and they submit.[3669] (53)

\*\*\*

21A4 Allah created you[MP] in weakness, then after weakness gave strength, then after strength, weakness and gray hair.[3670] He creates whatever he wills. He is all-knowing[3671] and all-powerful.[3672] (54)

\*\*\*

On the day the hour comes, wrongdoers will swear they only remained an hour. Thus they will be overthrown. (55) Those who have been given knowledge and faith will say, "You[MP] remained in Allah's book[3673] until the day of resurrection.[3674] This is the day of resurrection, but you[MP] did not know." (56) On that day, their excuses will not help disbelievers, and they will not be allowed favor.[3675] (57) We have made some of every proverb in this recitation.[3676] If you[MS] bring them a sign, disbelievers will say, "You[MP] deal only in vanity." (58) Thus Allah seals the hearts of those who do not know.[3677] (59) So endure;[3678] Allah's promise is true. Do not let those who are not certain make fun of you[MS]. (60)[3679]

---

[3668] Injil, Romans 2:19
[3669] Injil, James 4:7. For "submit," some translators do not translate this. See glossary for more details.
[3670] Tawrah, Ecclesiastes 12:2-7
[3671] Tawrah, Job 37:16, Isaiah 40:14, Zabur, Psalms 33:13-15, Injil, 1 John 3:20
[3672] Tawrah, Job 42:2
[3673] Zabur, Psalms 139:16
[3674] Tawrah, Daniel 12:2 Injil, Acts 24:15, 1 Corinthians 15:52-54, Revelation 20:11-15
[3675] Injil, Revelation 20:12-13
[3676] Or Qur'an or qur'an. See glossary for more details.
[3677] Injil, Romans 9:18
[3678] See "endure" in glossary
[3679] The verses in this chapter that rhyme are put together in paragraphs, separated by \*\*\*.

Chapter 31

# Chapter 31 Luqman[3680]

In the name of Allah, the most gracious and merciful.[3681] ALM.[3682] (1) Those are verses of the wise book,[3683] (2) guidance and mercy to those who do good, (3) who perform prayers and pay the poor-tax, and are certain of the hereafter.[3684] (4) They are guided by their Lord, and they are successful.[3685] (5) Some people buy entertaining talk that unknowingly leads astray from Allah's path, and they mock it. They will have shameful torment.[3686] (6) If our signs[3687] are read[3688] to them, they turn proudly away as if they have not heard it, as if their ears are deaf. Give them their good news: painful torment. (7) Believers who do righteous deeds[3689] will have heavenly gardens[3690] of delight, (8) where they will remain forever,[3691] according to Allah's true promise. He is mighty[3692] and wise.[3693] (9) He created the heavens without visible supports,[3694] and put mountains on the earth so that it would not move you^MP, and he sent every living creature onto it.[3695] We sent

---

[3680] Luqman is a name

[3681] Zabur, Psalms 103:8, 145:8. See glossary for more details.

[3682] Here and at the beginning of many chapters there are unvowelled letters of unknown meaning. Numerous theories have been proposed, but there is no agreement on the subject.

[3683] The use of the word "those" and not "these" in this verse seems to refer to the previous books. Thus "wise book "is probably a title for the previous books. See 3:58, 5:46, Tawrah, Proverbs 1:2-6

[3684] The Qur'an refers to people who are certain of the hereafter here and in 2:4 and 27:3. All three passages seem to have a reference to the previous books. Injil, John 5:24

[3685] Tawrah, Joshua 1:8

[3686] For "torment" here and in verses 21 and 24, see Tawrah, Isaiah 50:11, Injil, Matthew 18:34, 25:41,46, Luke 16:23-28, Revelation 20:15.

[3687] or verses

[3688] Or recited or told

[3689] Injil, 1 Corinthians 3:8, James 2:14-17, Revelation 19:8

[3690] Arabic /jannah/. See glossary for more details.

[3691] Injil, John 4:14

[3692] Tawrah, Joshua 22:22

[3693] Tawrah, Job 9:4, Proverbs 2:6, Jeremiah 9:23-24, Injil, 1 Corinthians 1:21-25, Romans 16:27

[3694] Tawrah, Job 9:8, Proverb 3:19, Isaiah 40:22, 42:5, 44:24, Zabur, Psalms 33:6, 89:11, 119:89

[3695] Tawrah, Genesis 1:20-25

rain from the sky,[3696] to make every generous kind of plant sprout.[3697] (10) This is Allah's creation. Show me what others beside him have created. The wicked have clearly gone astray. (11)

\*\*\*

We gave Luqman wisdom, "Give thanks to Allah.[3698] Whoever gives thanks gives thanks to his own benefit, and as for those who are unthankful,[3699] Allah is self-sufficient and praiseworthy." (12)

\*\*\*

When Luqman told his son as he admonished him, "My son, do not worship gods besides Allah. Worshiping other gods is great wickedness." (13)

\*\*\*

We commanded people to take care of their parents. Their mothers bore them in weakness,[3700] and weaned them after two years. Give[MS] thanks to me and your[MS] parents. I am [your] destiny. (14)

\*\*\*

If they[D][3701] struggle[3702] to make you[MS] worship gods besides me that you[MS] do not know, do not obey[MS] them.[3703] Accompany[MS] them[D] kindly in this world and follow[MS] the path of those who repent toward me. Then you[MP] will return to me, and I will tell you[MP] your[MP] deeds. (15)

\*\*\*

My son, even if it[3704] is a mustard seed's[3705] weight within a rock or in the heavens or on earth, Allah will bring it. Allah is kind[3706] and aware. (16) My son, perform[MS] the prayers, promote[MS] virtue[3707]

---

[3696] Tawrah, Deuteronomy 28:12, Job 5:10, Joel 2:23, Zabur, Psalms 68:9, Injil, Matthew 5:45

[3697] Tawrah Deuteronomy 11:14, 1 Kings 8:36, Job 5:10, Isaiah 44:14, Jeremiah 14:22, Hosea 6:6, Zabur, Psalms 68:9

[3698] Zabur, Psalms 105:1-3, 1 Chronicles 16:8-10

[3699] Or disbelieves

[3700] Tawrah, Proverbs 23:25

[3701] i.e. the parents

[3702] This word is the verbal form of jihad, and shows that jihad means struggle, not holy war.

[3703] Injil, Ephesians 6:1

[3704] Probably referring to a deed in the previous verse

[3705] Injil, Mark 4:31, Luke 17:6, 13:18-19

[3706] Injil, Romans 11:22

[3707] or kindness

## Chapter 31

and prevent[MS] vice. Endure[MS] what afflicts you[MS].[3708] That is from determination regarding matters. (17) Do not turn[MS] your[MS] cheek away scowling[3709] at people, and do not walk[MS] insolently[3710] in the land. Allah does not like anyone who is arrogant[3711] and boastful. (18) Take[MS] a moderate[3712] course[3713] in your[MS] walking, and cover your[MS] voice. The most disagreeable sound is the donkey's. (19) Have you[MP] not seen that Allah has subjected everything in the heavens and the earth to you[MP] and has made his blessings, both obvious and hidden, abound to you[MP]? Some people argue about Allah without knowledge,[3714] guidance, or the enlightening book.[3715] (20) If they are told, "Follow[MP] what Allah has revealed," they say, "Rather we will follow what we found our fathers doing,"[3716] even if Satan was calling them to the torment of burning fire. (21) 21B1 He who submits[3717] his face to Allah and does good has laid hold of the firmest handle. The results of matters are Allah's. (22) Do not let disbelievers' disbelief sadden you[MS]. They will return to us and we will tell them what they did. Allah knows what is in their hearts.[3718] (23)
\*\*\*

We make them enjoy life for a little while, then we will compel them to go to heavy torment. (24)
\*\*\*

If you[MS] ask them, "Who created the heavens and the earth," they will say, "Allah." Say[MS], "Praise be to Allah." Most of them do not know. (25)
\*\*\*

---

[3708] See "endure" in glossary, here and in verse 31.
[3709] Injil, Matthew 5:39
[3710] or cheerfully, or proudly ignoring
[3711] Tawrah, Proverbs 6:16-17
[3712] Injil, Philippians 4:5
[3713] or be intentional
[3714] Tawrah, Job 38:2
[3715] See 22:8, 35:25, 3:184, the last two of which indicate that it refers to the previous books. Zabur, Psalms 119:130, 105, 19:8
[3716] Tawrah, Jeremiah 11:10, Injil, Acts 7:51, Galatians 1:14, Colossians 2:20-22
[3717] Injil, James 4:7. For "submits," some translators do not translate this. See glossary for more details.
[3718] Tawrah, 1 Samuel 16:7, 1 Chronicles 28:9, Zabur, Psalms 44:21, Injil, Luke 16:15, Romans 8:27, Acts 15:8, 1 John 3:20

Chapter 31

Everything in the heavens and the earth is Allah's.[3719] He is rich[3720] and praiseworthy. (26)

\*\*\*

If all the trees on earth were pens and the seas were extended by seven seas of ink, Allah's words would not finish.[3721] Allah is mighty[3722] and wise.[3723] (27) Both your[MP] creation and your[MP] resurrection[MP] are as one soul. Allah hears all and sees all. (28) Have you[MS] not seen that Allah makes the night merge into day and the day merge into night? He has subjected the sun and the moon, and both move until a stated lifespan. Allah is aware of your[MP] deeds. (29) That is because Allah is true,[3724] and what they pray to besides him is vain. Allah is most high[3725] and great.[3726] (30) Have you[MS] not seen how the ship goes through the sea[3727] by Allah's blessing, to show you[MP] some of his signs? Those are signs to everyone who endures and gives thanks. (31) When waves cover them like shade, they pray to Allah sincerely and religiously.[3728] When he rescues them, and they reach land, some of them waver.[3729] No one except an ungrateful[3730] traitor denies our signs.[3731] (32) People, fear your[MP] Lord, and fear the day when no father can pay for his son's deeds, nor a son for his father's.[3732] Allah's promise is true, so do not let[MS] this world deceive you[MP],[3733] nor let[MS] the deceiver[3734] deceive you[MP].[3735] (33) Allah knows the

---

[3719] Tawrah, Isaiah 45:12, Zabur, Psalms 24:1, 89:11, Injil, Hebrews 1:10
[3720] i.e. he does not need anything from people.
[3721] Injil, John 21:25
[3722] Zabur, Psalms 50:1, 99:4
[3723] Tawrah, Job 9:4, Proverbs 2:6, Jeremiah 9:23-24, Injil, 1 Corinthians 1:21-25, Romans 16:27
[3724] Injil, John 14:6, John 17:3, Tawrah, 2 Chronicles 15:3, Jeremiah 10:10
[3725] Tawrah, Genesis 14:20, Daniel 3:26, Zabur, Psalms 47:2
[3726] Tawrah, 2 Samuel 7:23, Zabur, Psalms 70:4
[3727] Tawrah, Proverbs 30:19
[3728] Zabur, Psalms 107:23-29
[3729] Or have good intentions. Zabur, Psalms 78:32
[3730] or disbelieving
[3731] Arabic /ayat/. See glossary for more details.
[3732] Tawrah, Ezekiel 18:1-35
[3733] Injil, 1 John 2:15-16
[3734] i.e. Satan. Injil, 2 John 7, Revelation 12:9
[3735] Injil, 2 Corinthians 11:2-3

hour,[3736] and he sends down rain.[3737] He knows what is in the womb.[3738] No one knows what he will gain tomorrow,[3739] nor does anyone know what land he will die in. Allah is all-knowing[3740] and aware. (34)[3741]

---

[3736] Injil, Mark 13:32
[3737] Tawrah, Deuteronomy 28:12, Job 5:10, Joel 2:23, Zabur, Psalms 68:9, Injil, Matthew 5:45
[3738] Zabur, Psalms 139:13
[3739] Injil, James 4:13-14
[3740] Tawrah, Job 37:16, Isaiah 40:14, Zabur, Psalms 33:13-15, Injil, 1 John 3:20
[3741] The verses in this chapter that rhyme are put together in paragraphs, separated by ***.

# Chapter 32 Al-Sajdah[3742]

In the name of Allah, the most gracious and merciful.[3743] ALM.[3744] (1) There is no doubt in the revelation of the book from the Lord of the universe. (2) Do they say, "He invented it."? It is truth from your[MS] Lord, so that you[MS] may warn people who have had no warner before you[MS], and they be guided. (3) Allah created the heavens, the earth, and everything between them in six days.[3745] Then he sat down on the throne.[3746] You[MP] have no protector nor intercessor besides him.[3747] Do you[MP] not remember? (4) He arranges the matter from the sky to the earth, then it[3748] ascends to him[3749] on a day whose length is 1000 years[3750] as you[MP] count them. (5) He knows the unseen and the seen, is mighty and merciful,[3751] (6) and does all things well[3752] in creating them. He began the creation of man with clay.[3753] (7) Then he made his descendants of a stream of despised water. (8) Then he formed him and breathed into him of his spirit,[3754] and he gave you[MP] hearing, sight and hearts. How little you[MP] give thanks! (9) They said, "If we go astray on earth, will we have a new creation?"[3755] They disbelieve that they will meet their Lord. (10) **21B2** Say[MS], "The angel of death will make you[MP] die. He is responsible for you[MP]. Then you[MP] will be returned to your[MP] Lord." (11) If only

---

[3742] bowing down (prostration)
[3743] Zabur, Psalms 103:8, 145:8. See glossary for more details.
[3744] Here and at the beginning of many chapters there are unvowelled letters of unknown meaning. Numerous theories have been proposed, but there is no agreement on the subject.
[3745] Tawrah, Genesis 1:1-31
[3746] Tawrah, Genesis 2:1-2
[3747] Tawrah, 1 Samuel 2:25, Injil, 1 Timothy 2:5; see other verses in the Qur'an and the previous books that tell of an intercessor between Allah and man. (2:255, 10:3, 20:109, 34:23, and 43:86)
[3748] or he
[3749] Injil, Acts 1:9-11, Ephesians 4 8-10
[3750] Injil, 2 Peter 3:8, Revelation 20:6,7
[3751] See glossary for more details on "merciful."
[3752] Injil, Mark 7:37, Tawrah, Genesis 1:4,10,12,18,21,25,31
[3753] Tawrah, Genesis 2:7, here and in the next verse
[3754] Adam (here in 32:9, 38:72, and 15:29) and Isa (21:91 and 66:12) are the only ones into whom Allah breathed his spirit.
[3755] Injil, 2 Corinthians 5:17

## Chapter 32

you[MS] could see the wrongdoers hanging their heads in front of their Lord. "Our Lord, we have seen and heard, so let us return and do righteous deeds. We are certain." (12) If we had willed, we would have given guidance to every soul, but the saying from me is true: "I will fill hell with jinns[3756] and men all together.[3757] (13) Taste the meeting of this day of yours[MP] because of what you[MP] forgot. We have forgotten[3758] you[MP], so taste[MP] eternal torment[3759] because of your[MP] deeds." (14) Believers bow down and praise their Lord when they are reminded of our signs, and they are not proud. (15) They are far from sleep as they pray to their Lord in fear and desire,[3760] and they donate from what we have provided them.[3761] (16) No souls know what delight is hidden for them[3762] in reward for their deeds. (17) Is a believer equal to an unbeliever? They are not the same. (18) Believers who do righteous deeds[3763] will have heavenly gardens[3764] of refuge as an abode prepared[3765] because of their deeds. (19) But the abode of the unbelievers[3766] will be hellfire. Every time they want to get out of it, they will be put back in. They will be told, "Taste the torment of hellfire, which you[MP] denied."[3767] (20) We will make them taste the near torment[3768] before the greater torment, so that they may return. (21) Who is more wicked than one who is reminded of the signs of his Lord, and then turns away from them? We will take revenge on wrongdoers. (22) We gave Musa[3769] the book, so do not be[MS] in doubt of meeting it.[3770] We made it guidance for the people of Israel. (23) We made some of them leaders, guiding by our

---

[3756] Or demons. See glossary for more details.
[3757] Tawrah, Proverbs 30:15-16
[3758] Zabur, Psalms 103:12, 42:9
[3759] For "torment" here and in verses 20 and 21, see Tawrah, Isaiah 50:11, Injil, Matthew 18:34, 25:41,46, Luke 16:23-28, Revelation 20:15.
[3760] Zabur, Psalms 119:62
[3761] Injil, 1 Timothy 6:18
[3762] Injil, 1 Corinthians 2:9
[3763] Injil, 1 Corinthians 3:8, James 2:14-17, Revelation 19:8
[3764] Arabic /jannah/. See glossary for more details.
[3765] Injil, John 14:1-3
[3766] Or transgressors or immoral.
[3767] Or, "called a lie."
[3768] Injil, Revelation 9:5-6, Tawrah, 1 Samuel 16:14, Jeremiah 26:13
[3769] Moses. See glossary for more details.
[3770] Or "him." The reference is unclear.

## Chapter 32

command when they endured[3771] and were certain of our signs. (24) Your[MS] Lord will distinguish among them on the day of resurrection[3772] concerning what they differed over. (25) Did he not guide them as to how many generations before them we destroyed while they[3773] were walking in their dwellings? Those are signs. Do they not hear? (26) Do they not see that we send the rain[3774] to the dry ground, and cause plants to sprout so that they and their cattle can eat? Do they not see? (27) They say, "When will this victory be, if you[MP] are telling the truth?" (28) Say[MS], "On the day of victory, disbelievers' faith will not help them, and they will get no more time." (29) So turn[MS] away from them and wait[MS]. They are waiting, too. (30)[3775]

---

[3771] See "endure" in glossary

[3772] Tawrah, Daniel 12:2 Injil, Acts 24:15, 1 Corinthians 15:52-54, Revelation 20:11-15

[3773] it is unclear whether the former generations or the people being spoken of are intended.

[3774] Tawrah, Deuteronomy 28:12, Job 5:10, Joel 2:23, Zabur, Psalms 68:9, Injil, Matthew 5:45

[3775] The verses in this chapter that rhyme are put together in paragraphs, separated by ***.

Chapter 33

# Chapter 33 Al-Ahzab[3776]

**21B3** In the name of Allah, the most gracious and merciful.[3777] Prophet, fear[MS] Allah and do not obey[MS] the disbelievers and hypocrites. Allah is all-knowing[3778] and wise.[3779] (1) Follow[MS] your[MS] Lord's inspiration to you[MS]. Allah is aware of your[MP] deeds. (2) Trust in Allah. Allah is an adequate guardian. (3)

\*\*\*

Allah did not give any man two hearts in his chest, and he did not make the wives you[MP] divorce[3780] into your[MP] mothers. He did not make your[MP] adopted sons your[MP] real sons. Those [only] your[MP] sayings with your[MP] mouths. Allah speaks the truth, and guides on the path.[3781] (4)

\*\*\*

Call[MP] them[3782] by their[MP] fathers' names. That is more just to Allah. If you[MP] do not know their fathers, [call them] your[MP] brothers in religion[3783] and your[MP] relatives. You[MP] are not to blame if you[MP] at fault in this unless you[MP] did it intentionally. Allah is forgiving[3784] and merciful.[3785] (5) The prophet is closer to the believers than their[MP] own souls, and his wives are their[MP] mothers. Blood relatives[MP] are closer to each other in Allah's book than believers and emigrants. However, you[MP] should treat your[MP] friends kindly. That is written in the book.[3786] (6) We made a covenant with the prophets, as well as with you.[3787] We made a strong covenant[3788]

---

[3776] Groups or parties.
[3777] Zabur, Psalms 103:8, 145:8. See glossary for more details.
[3778] Tawrah, Job 37:16, Isaiah 40:14, Zabur, Psalms 33:13-15, Injil, 1 John 3:20
[3779] Tawrah, Job 9:4, Proverbs 2:6, Jeremiah 9:23-24, Injil, 1 Corinthians 1:21-25, Romans 16:27
[3780] A common formula for divorce was, "Be as my mother's back."
[3781] Zabur, Psalms 23:3
[3782] i.e. the adopted sons
[3783] Injil, Matthew 23:9
[3784] Here and in verses 24, 50, 59, and 73, see Zabur, Psalms 103:3, 130:4, Tawrah, Isaiah 43:25, Exodus 34:7, Injil, Acts 26:18.
[3785] Here and in verses 24, 43, 50, 59, and 73, see glossary for more details on "merciful."
[3786] Injil, Matthew 7:12
[3787] Thsi phrase could belong to the following sentence.
[3788] Injil, 1 Corinthians 11:23-26, Hebrews 7:22, 8:6-13

with Nuh,[3789] Ibrahim,[3790] Musa,[3791] and Isa[3792] son of Mariam,[3793] (7) so that he may ask truthful people about their truthfulness. He prepared painful torment[3794] for the disbelievers. (8) Believers, remember Allah's blessings to you[MP], when troops came against you[MP] and we sent a wind against them, as well as troops you[MP] did not see.[3795] Allah sees your[MP] deeds. (9) They came upon you[MP] from above you[MP] and below you[MP],[3796] sight became dim and hearts were in throats. You[MP] imagined wrong thoughts about Allah.[3797] (10) There the believers were tested and shaken with a severe earthquake.[3798] (11) The hypocrites and those with sick hearts[3799] said, "Allah and his messenger promised us only vain hopes." (12) One group of them said, "People of Yathrib,[3800] you[MP] have no place, so go[MP] back." Another group of them asked the prophet's permission. They said, "Our houses[F][3801] are exposed," whereas they[F] were not exposed. They[MP] only want to flee. (13) If they[MP] were attacked from their[F] sides, and they[MP] were asked to defect, they[MP] would have come to them[F] and not remained[MP] long. (14) They[MP] had promised Allah beforehand that they would not turn back. Promises to Allah are a responsibility.[3802] (15) Say[MS], "Fleeing will not help you[MP], if you[MP] flee death or murder.[3803] Otherwise, you[MP] would only enjoy it for a while." (16) Say[MS], "Who can preserve you[MP] from Allah, whether he wants to do bad things to you[MP] or have mercy on you[MP]?" They will find no helper

---

[3789] Noah. See glossary for more details. Tawrah, Genesis 9:9-17

[3790] Abraham. See glossary for more details. Tawrah, Genesis 15:18, 17:1-21

[3791] Moses here and in verse 69. See glossary for more details. Tawrah, Exodus 19:1-5, 24:7-8

[3792] Jesus. See glossary for more details. Injil, Matthew 3:16

[3793] Mary, mother of Jesus. See glossary for more details.

[3794] For "torment" here and in verses 24 and 73, see Tawrah, Isaiah 50:11, Injil, Matthew 18:34, 25:41,46, Luke 16:23-28, Revelation 20:15.

[3795] Tawrah, 2 Kings 6:17

[3796] Zabur, Psalms 118:10-12

[3797] Here and in verses 66 and 67, there is an extra letter added here for the sake of the rhyme.

[3798] Injil, Matthew 27:54, Revelation 11:13

[3799] Tawrah, Jeremiah 8:18, 17:9-10

[3800] The old name of Medinah

[3801] The feminine words in this verse and the next refer to the houses.

[3802] Tawrah, Ecclesiastes 5:4

[3803] Zabur, Psalms 139:7-10

or savior besides Allah.³⁸⁰⁴ (17) **21B4** Allah surely knows the hinderers among you^(MP), and those who tell their brothers, "Come to us." They rarely come to fight, (18) being greedy of you^(MP). When fear comes upon them, you^(MS) see them looking to you^(MS). Their eyes roll like someone fainting on the verge of death. When fear goes away, they abuse you^(MS) with sharp tongues, greedy^(MP) for good things. They do not believe, and Allah has made their works vain. That is easy for Allah. (19) They think that the groups have not gone, and when the groups come, they wish that they were desert nomads,³⁸⁰⁵ asking about your^(MP) news. Even if they had been among you^(MP), they would only have fought a little. (20) You^(MP) have a good example in Allah's messenger³⁸⁰⁶ for those who hope in Allah and the last day, and who remember Allah frequently. (21) When the believers saw the groups, they said, "This is what Allah and his messenger promised us. Allah and his messenger were right." This caused them to increase in faith and submission.³⁸⁰⁷ (22) Some believing men are honest in what they promise Allah, some of them fulfill their vows,³⁸⁰⁸ and some of them wait, and do not change at all. (23) May Allah reward the honest for their honesty, and torment the hypocrites if he wills,³⁸⁰⁹ or accept their repentance.³⁸¹⁰ Allah is forgiving and merciful. (24) Allah sends disbelievers back, furious because they got no spoils. Allah is sufficient for the believers in battle.³⁸¹¹ Allah is strong³⁸¹² and mighty. (25) Allah cast down from their castles the people of the book who assisted them, and put fear in their hearts. Some of them you^(MP) kill, and some of them you^(MP) take as prisoners. (26) He made

---

³⁸⁰⁴ Injil, Jude 25, Hosea 4
³⁸⁰⁵ Or Bedouins.
³⁸⁰⁶ Injil, 1 Corinthians 11:1. The ones specifically called Allah's messenger in the Qur'an are Muhammad (s) 48:29, 7:158, 33:21,40,53, etc., Musa 61:5, Thamud's messenger 91:13, and Isa 4:157,171, 61:6. /uswa hasana/ (good example) is said about Allah's messenger here and in 60:4-6 about Ibrahim and those with him.
³⁸⁰⁷ Injil, James 4:7. For "submission" and "submit" here and in verse 35, some translators do not translate this. See glossary for more details.
³⁸⁰⁸ i.e. by dying
³⁸⁰⁹ Injil, Romans 9:18
³⁸¹⁰ For "repentance," here and in verse 73, see glossary. Tawrah, Jonah 3:10
³⁸¹¹ Or, "spared the believers from battle."
³⁸¹² Tawrah, Job 9:4, Zabur, Psalms 24:8, Injil, Ephesians 6:10, Revelation 18:8

## Chapter 33

you^MP inherit their lands, houses and money,^3813 a land you^MP had not set foot upon. Allah can do anything.^3814 (27) Prophet, tell your^MS wives, "If you^FP want this world and its glamor,^3815 come^FP. I will provide for you^FP and divorce you^FP graciously. (28) But if you^FP want Allah, his messenger and the hereafter, Allah has prepared a great reward for those of you^FP who do good." (29) Wives of the prophet, if one of you^FP commits promiscuity^3816 clearly, she will have double the torment.^3817 That is easy for Allah. (30) **22A1** We will give a double reward^3818 to those among you^FP who are devout in obedience to Allah and his messenger, and do righteous deeds.^3819 We have prepared a generous provision for them. (31) Wives of the prophet, you^FP are not like another^MS 3820 woman.^3821 If you^FP are reverent, do not use^FP coarse speech,^3822 or someone with a sick heart may desire. Speak^FP kindly.^3823 (32) Sit^FP quietly in your^FP houses,^3824 and do not dress up^FP as in the days of former ignorance.^3825 Perform^FP prayers, pay^FP the poor-tax, and obey^FP Allah and his messenger. Household, Allah wants to put abominations far from you^MP and purify^3826 you^MP. (33) Remember^FP Allah's signs and wisdom that are read^3827 in your^FP houses.^3828 Allah is kind and aware. (34) Allah has prepared forgiveness and a great reward for men and women who submit, men and women^3829 believers, devout men and women, truthful men and women, men

---

3813 Tawrah, Deuteronomy 6:10-11
3814 Tawrah, Job 42:2, Isaiah 14:27, Daniel 4:35, Injil, Matthew 19:26, Mark 10:27, Luke 1:37
3815 Injil, 1 John 2:15-16
3816 Or lewdness, adultery or abomination
3817 Tawrah, Isaiah 40:2, Injil, Romans 2:9,10
3818 Tawrah, Isaiah 61:7
3819 Injil, 1 Timothy 5:10
3820 It is unknown why a masculine pronoun is used here.
3821 Injil, 1 Peter 3:1-4
3822 Injil, 1 Timothy 4:12
3823 Injil, Colossians 4:6
3824 Injil, Titus 2:5
3825 Injil, 1 Peter 1:14, Acts 17:30
3826 Tawrah, Malachi 3:3, Zabur, Psalms 19:8, 119:9,140, Injil, Acts 15:8,9,1 Peter 2:2, Titus 2:14, Hebrews 1:3
3827 Or recited
3828 Tawrah, Deuteronomy 6:7
3829 Or, "male and female" throughout this verse.

Chapter 33

and women who endure,[3830] humble men and women, men and women who give alms, men and women who fast, men and women who guard their chastity,[3831] and men and women who mention Allah frequently. (35) No believing man or woman has a choice in their matter once Allah and his messenger have decreed a matter. Whoever disobeys Allah and his messenger has clearly gone astray. (36) When you[MS] told the one blessed by Allah and blessed by you[MS],[3832] "Keep your[MS] wife and fear[MS] Allah," you[MS] hid in your[MS] soul what Allah had shown and feared[MS] people.[3833] Allah is more worthy of being feared. When Zayd had done what was necessary for her, we married you[MS] to her, so that believers would be blameless regarding the wives of their adopted sons if they do what is required for them[FP]. Allah's order was carried out. (37) The prophet is not to be blamed regarding Allah's commands, regarding the custom of those who passed away beforehand. Allah's command is a determined decree. (38) Those who deliver Allah's messages fear him, and fear no one else besides Allah.[3834] Allah is a sufficient reckoner. (39) Muhammad[3835] was not the father of any of your[MP] men, but Allah's messenger, and the seal[3836] of the prophets. Allah knows everything. (40) Believers, remember Allah frequently. (41) Worship him morning and evening.[3837] (42) He and his angels bless[3838] you[MP], to bring you[MP] out of darkness into the light.[3839] He is merciful to believers. (43) The greeting they will be given on the day they meet him is "Peace." He has prepared a generous reward for them. (44) Prophet, we sent you[MS] as a witness, a bearer of good news, a

---

[3830] See "endure" in glossary
[3831] Or their genitals.
[3832] i.e. Zayd, whom Muhammad had adopted as his son.
[3833] Tawrah, Proverbs 29:25
[3834] Injil, Matthew 4:10
[3835] Muhammad (s) is mentioned by name here and in three other verses (3:144, 47:2, and 48:29). In addition, he is often referred to, but he is never to be worshiped; he pointed people to Allah. There is no basis in the Qur'an to call Muslims Mohammedans.
[3836] Arabic /khatam/ Probably one who confirms the prophets (as a seal of confirmation, or a signet ring). The other possibility is "the last prophet who received divine revelation," though this would usually be spelled /khatim/. Muhammad (s) is the only one who is called this.
[3837] Zabur, Psalms 55:17
[3838] Or, "pray over," here and twice in verse 56.
[3839] Injil, 1 John 2:9,10, Colossians 1:13-14

## Chapter 33

warner, (45) a caller to Allah by his permission, and a shining lamp.[3840] (46) Give believers the good news that they have Allah's great grace. (47) Do not obey[MS] disbelievers and hypocrites. Ignore[MS] their harm, and trust[MS] in Allah. Allah is a sufficient protector. (48) Believers, if you[MP] marry believing women and then divorce them[FP] before you[MP] have sex with them[FP],[3841] there is no time period you[MP] have to wait.[3842] Make provision for them[FP] and divorce them[FP] graciously. (49) Prophet, we have allowed you[MS] to marry your[MS] wives when you[MS] have paid their[FP] dowry,[3843] as well as slave girls you[MS] own from spoils Allah has given you[MS], as well as any daughters of your[MS] paternal uncles and aunts, daughters of your[MS] maternal uncles and aunts who emigrated with you[MS], or any believing woman who gives herself to the prophet, if the prophet wants to marry her. This is a special privilege for you[MS], and not for the believers. We know what we decreed for them[MP] about their[MP] wives and the slave girls they own, so that you[MS] would be blameless. Allah is forgiving and merciful. (50) 22A2 You[MS] can put away[3844] those you[MS] want, and bring to yourself[MS] those you[MS] wish. If you[MS] want one of them that you[MS] have sent away, you[MS] are blameless.[3845] That way, it is more likely to comfort them[FP], so that they[FP] would not sorrow,[3846] but rather be pleased[FP] with your[MS] gift to each of them[FP]. Allah knows what is in your[MP] hearts.[3847] Allah is all-knowing[3848] and gentle.[3849] (51) Beyond that, women are not allowed for you[MS], nor can you[MS] exchange them[FP] for other wives,[3850] even if their[FP] beauty pleases you[MS], except for slave girls you[MS] own. Allah watches over everything. (52) Believers, do not go into the houses of the prophet until you[MP] have been given permission to eat, without looking[MP] for a convenient

---

[3840] Injil, John 5:35. Muhammad (s) is the only one in the Qur'an who is called this.
[3841] Literally, touch them. See Injil, 1 Corinthians 7:1
[3842] i.e. to ensure they are not pregnant. Injil, Matthew 1:19
[3843] Or "wages"
[3844] Tawrah, Ezra 10:3
[3845] Injil, 1 Corinthians 7:11
[3846] Injil, Philippians 2:27
[3847] Tawrah, 1 Samuel 16:7, 1 Chronicles 28:9, Zabur, Psalms 44:21, Injil, Luke 16:15, Romans 8:27, Acts 15:8, 1 John 3:20
[3848] Tawrah, Job 37:16, Isaiah 40:14, Zabur, Psalms 33:13-15, Injil, 1 John 3:20
[3849] Zabur, Psalms 45:4, 145:17, Injil, Matthew 11:29, Galatians 5:22
[3850] Tawrah, Deuteronomy 22:29

## Chapter 33

opportunity.³⁸⁵¹ If you^MP are invited, enter^MP, and when you^MP have finished eating, disperse^MP, not asking^MP permission to speak.³⁸⁵² That would harm³⁸⁵³ the prophet and he would be ashamed of you^MP.³⁸⁵⁴ Allah is not ashamed of the truth. If you^MP ask them^FP³⁸⁵⁵ for something, ask^MP them^FP from behind a curtain.³⁸⁵⁶ That is purer for your^MP hearts and their^FP hearts. You^MP should not harm Allah's messenger, or ever marry^MP his wives after him.³⁸⁵⁷ That would be a great sin to Allah. (53) Whether you^MP reveal something or hide^MP it, Allah knows everything. (54) There is no blame for them^FP in front of their^FP fathers, their^FP sons, their^FP brothers, their^FP brothers' or sisters' sons, their^FP maidservants or their^FP slaves. Fear^FP Allah, for Allah is witness of everything. (55) Allah and his angels bless the prophet. Believers, bless him and greet him. (56) Those who harm Allah and his messenger are damned by Allah in this world and the hereafter.³⁸⁵⁸ He has prepared shameful torment for them. (57) Those who harm men and women believers undeservingly have taken slander and clear guilt upon themselves. (58) Prophet, tell your^MS wives, your^MS daughters, and the believers' wives to draw^FP their^FP robes around them^FP,³⁸⁵⁹ so that it would be more likely that they^FP would be known and not harmed^FP. Allah is forgiving and merciful. (59) 22A3 If the hypocrites, those with sick hearts,³⁸⁶⁰ and those who cause commotion in the city do not stop, we will incite you^MS against them^MP. Then they^MP will live nearby you^MS in it only for a short while, (60) damned.³⁸⁶¹ Wherever they are found, they will be seized and slaughtered, (61) as is Allah's custom regarding those who passed away beforehand. You^MS will find no change in Allah's customs. (62) People ask you^MS about the hour. Say^MS, "Only Allah knows about it."³⁸⁶² He does not tell you^MS about it, because the hour might be soon.³⁸⁶³

---

³⁸⁵¹ Tawrah, Proverbs 23:2
³⁸⁵² Or, "a story" or "news"
³⁸⁵³ Or "bother," here and in verses 57, 58, 59 and 69
³⁸⁵⁴ i.e. to ask you to leave
³⁸⁵⁵ i.e. wives of the prophet
³⁸⁵⁶ Tawrah, Proverbs 4:23,25
³⁸⁵⁷ i.e. after he divorces them
³⁸⁵⁸ Injil, Hebrews 6:8
³⁸⁵⁹ Injil, 1 Timothy 2:9
³⁸⁶⁰ Tawrah, Jeremiah 8:18, 17:9-10
³⁸⁶¹ Injil, 2 Peter 2:14
³⁸⁶² Injil, Matthew 24:36
³⁸⁶³ Injil, Revelation 22:20

## Chapter 33

(63) Allah has damned the disbelievers and prepared a burning fire for them,[3864] (64) where they will be forever. They will not find a helper or savior (65) on the day their faces are turned over in hellfire. They will say, "If only we had obeyed Allah and obeyed the messenger." (66) They said, "Our Lord, we obeyed our masters and leading men, and they led us astray from the way. (67) Our Lord, give them twice as much torment,[3865] and damn them greatly. (68) Believers, do not be like those who harmed Musa, though Allah vindicated[3866] him from what they said. He was highly exalted[3867] with Allah."[3868] (69) Believers, fear Allah[3869] and speak[MP] an opportune saying.[3870] (70) He will make your[MP] deeds good and forgive your[MP] sins. Whoever obeys Allah and his messenger has won the great victory.[3871] (71) We offered a trust for safekeeping[3872] to the heavens, the earth, and the mountains, and they refused to bear it, and feared it. Mankind took it, and they were unjust and foolish,[3873] (72) so Allah will torment men and women hypocrites and men and women idolaters, but will accept

---

[3864] Injil, Matthew 25:41
[3865] Tawrah, Isaiah 40:2
[3866] Injil, 1 Timothy 3:16
[3867] Only Musa and Isa are called "highly exalted." Musa here is called "highly exalted with Allah," and in 3:45, Isa is called, "highly exalted in this world and in the hereafter."
[3868] Tawrah, Numbers 16:3
[3869] Tawrah, Deuteronomy 10:12, Isaiah 29:13, Injil, 1 Peter 2:17, Revelation 14:7
[3870] Injil, Colossians 4:6, Tawrah, Proverbs 15:23
[3871] Tawrah, Isaiah 25:8, Injil, 1 Corinthians 15:57, 1 John 5:4
[3872] Tawrah, Genesis 1:28
[3873] The injustice/wickedness, disbelief/ungratefulness, evil, unrighteousness/sin, or lostness of mankind is mentioned in a number of verses in the Qur'an as well as in the previous books. Injustice or wickedness: 2:57, 3:117,135, 4:64,97, 7:160,177, 9:70, 10:44, 11:101, 14:34,45, 16:33,61,118, 29:40, 30:9, 33:72, 34:19, 35:32, 43:76, 65:1, Tawrah, Genesis 6:5, Job 25:4, Injil, Acts 3:26, disbelief or ungratefulness: 14:34, 17:67, 22:66, 42:48, 43:15, 80:17, Injil, Hebrews 3:19, Evil: 12:53, Tawrah, Jeremiah 17:9, Injil, Matthew 15:19, Mark 7:21, unrighteousness or sin: 91:8, Tawrah, 1 Kings 8:46, Ecclesiastes 7:20, Injil, Romans 3:9-19, 5:12, lostness: 103:2, Tawrah, Jeremiah 50:6, Injil, Luke 19:10, Romans 3:23, 6:23

Chapter 33

the repentance of men and women believers. Allah is forgiving and merciful. (73)[3874]

---

[3874] The verses in this chapter that rhyme are put together in paragraphs, separated by ***.

# Chapter 34 Saba[3875]

In the name of Allah, the most gracious and merciful.[3876] Praise be to Allah. Everything in the heavens and the earth is his.[3877] He will be praised in the hereafter. He is wise[3878] and aware. (1) He knows what enters the ground, what comes out of it, what comes down from heaven, and what goes up to it.[3879] He is merciful[3880] and forgiving.[3881] (2)

\*\*\*

Disbelievers say, "The hour will not come upon us." Say[MS], "Yes it will. [I swear] by my Lord, the knower of the unseen, it will come upon you[MP]. Not a speck is hidden from him in the heavens and the earth. No, not even something smaller or larger than that. It is all in a clear book."[3882] (3) This is so that he can reward the believers who do righteous deeds.[3883] They will have forgiveness and a generous provision.[3884] (4) Those who try to hinder our signs[3885] will have torment[3886] of painful impurity. (5)

\*\*\*

Those who are knowledgeable think[3887] that what was revealed to you[MS] from your[MS] Lord is true, and guides to the path of the Mighty, Praiseworthy One. (6) Disbelievers say, "Shall we guide you[MP] to a man who will tell you[MP] that when you[MP] are torn in pieces,[3888] you[MP] will be a new creation?"[3889] (7) Did he invent a lie

---

[3875] Sheba
[3876] Zabur, Psalms 103:8, 145:8. See glossary for more details.
[3877] Tawrah, Isaiah 45:12, Zabur, Psalms 24:1, 89:11, Injil, Hebrews 1:10
[3878] Tawrah, Job 9:4, Proverbs 2:6, Jeremiah 9:23-24, Injil, 1 Corinthians 1:21-25, Romans 16:27
[3879] Injil, Ephesians 4:9-10
[3880] See glossary for more details on "merciful."
[3881] Here and in verse 15, see Zabur, Psalms 103:3, 130:4, Tawrah, Isaiah 43:25, Exodus 34:7, Injil, Acts 26:18.
[3882] Zabur, Psalms 139:16
[3883] Injil, 1 Corinthians 3:8, James 2:14-17, Revelation 19:8
[3884] Injil, James 2:14-26
[3885] Arabic /ayat/. See glossary for more details.
[3886] Here and in verses 8, 12, 14, 33, 38, 42 and 46, see Tawrah, Isaiah 50:11, Injil, Matthew 18:34, 25:41,46, Luke 16:23-28, Revelation 20:15
[3887] Or see
[3888] Zabur, Psalms 50:22, Injil, Acts 23:10
[3889] Injil, 2 Corinthians 5:17, 1 Corinthians 15:44

## Chapter 34

about Allah? Or is he demonized?[3890] No, but those who do not believe in the hereafter will be in torment and far astray. (8)

\*\*\*

Have they not seen what is in front of them and behind them in heaven and earth? If we want, we will make the earth swallow them up,[3891] or make part of the sky fall on them.[3892] That is a sign for every servant who turns. (9) 22A4

\*\*\*

We gave Dawud[3893] grace from us, "Mountains, sing Allah's praises with him and the birds."[3894] We made iron soft for him.[3895] (10)

\*\*\*

"Make[MS] coats of mail and measure[MS] the chains." Do[MP] righteous deeds. I see your[MP] deeds. (11) To Sulayman[3896] [we subjected] the wind. Its morning is a month, and its evening is a month.[3897] We made a fountain of brass flow[3898] for him. Some jinns[3899] worked in front of[3900] him by his Lord's permission. We make those who deviate from our command taste the torment of burning fire. (12) They made what he willed[3901] for him: holy places,[3902] statues,[3903] large dishes like cisterns,[3904] and fixed pots.[3905] Family of Dawud,[3906] work to give thanks. Few of my servants give thanks. (13)

\*\*\*

---

[3890] Or jinned (crazy). See glossary for more details.
[3891] Tawrah, Numbers 16:32-34
[3892] Tawrah, Genesis 19:12-26
[3893] David. See glossary for more details.
[3894] Zabur, Psalms 148:9,10,13
[3895] David. See glossary for more details.
[3896] Zabur, Psalms 107:16
[3897] Some commentators believe the meaning is the wind blows as far as a person can walk in a month.
[3898] Tawrah, 1 Kings 7:14-16
[3899] Or demons. See glossary for more details.
[3900] Or, "between his hands."
[3901] Tawrah, 1 Kings 7:40-44
[3902] Tawrah, 1 Kings 7:45-50
[3903] Tawrah, 1 Kings 7:15-22
[3904] Tawrah, 1 Kings 7:23-26
[3905] Tawrah, 1 Kings 7:27-37
[3906] David. See glossary for more details.

## Chapter 34

When we determined he would die, only an animal crawling on the ground showed them that he was dead when it ate his staff. When he fell down, the jinns[3907] saw clearly that if they had known the unseen, they would not have remained in shameful torment. (14)

\*\*\*

There was a sign[3908] for Sheba[3909] in their dwellings: two gardens, on the right
and left. "Eat of the provision of your^MP Lord, and give him thanks." A good town and a forgiving Lord.[3910] (15)

\*\*\*

But they turned away, so we sent against them the flood of viciousness[3911] and replaced their gardens^D with two gardens of bitter food, tamarisks, and a few lote trees. (16)

\*\*\*

Thus we repaid them for their disbelief. Do we punish any except disbelievers? (17)

\*\*\*

Between them and the villages we blessed, we made obvious villages, and measured how far it was to walk. "Walk^MP among them nights and days in safety." (18)

\*\*\*

They said, "Our Lord, make^MS our journeys farther apart." They wronged themselves,[3912] and we made stories of them, and tore

---

[3907] Or demons. See glossary for more details.

[3908] The verb is masculine while the subject is feminine. There may be an alternate meaning.

[3909] A country in modern Yemen or its people. Tawrah, 1 Kings 10:1

[3910] There is no predicate to this phrase. Possibly the intention is "What a...."

[3911] Or "Of Arim". The word may be a proper noun.

[3912] The injustice/wickedness, disbelief/ungratefulness, evil, unrighteousness/sin, or lostness of mankind is mentioned in a number of verses in the Qur'an as well as in the previous books. Injustice or wickedness: 2:57, 3:117,135, 4:64,97, 7:160,177, 9:70, 10:44, 11:101, 14:34,45, 16:33,61,118, 29:40, 30:9, 33:72, 34:19, 35:32, 43:76, 65:1, Tawrah, Genesis 6:5, Job 25:4, Injil, Acts 3:26, disbelief or ungratefulness: 14:34, 17:67, 22:66, 42:48, 43:15, 80:17, Injil, Hebrews 3:19, Evil: 12:53, Tawrah, Jeremiah 17:9, Injil, Matthew 15:19, Mark 7:21, unrighteousness or sin: 91:8, Tawrah, 1 Kings 8:46, Ecclesiastes 7:20, Injil, Romans 3:9-19, 5:12, lostness: 103:2, Tawrah, Jeremiah 50:6, Injil, Luke 19:10, Romans 3:23, 6:23

# Chapter 34

them in pieces.[3913] Those are signs for everyone who endures[3914] and gives thanks. (19)

\*\*\*

Iblis[3915] confirmed his thought to them, and all but a group of believers followed him. (20)

\*\*\*

He had no authority over them.[3916] It was only so that we would know those who had doubted from those who believe in the hereafter. Your[MS] Lord keeps everything. (21)

\*\*\*

Say[MS], "Pray[MP] to those you[MP] claimed were gods besides Allah." They do not even control as much as a speck in the heavens and the earth.[3917] They have no other gods in them[D], and he has no helper in them[MP]. (22) No one's intercession will help with him except the one he gave permission to.[3918] When their hearts are free from fear, they will say, "What did your[MP] Lord say?" They said, "The truth. He is most high and great." (23) **22B1**

\*\*\*

Say[MS], "Who provides for you[MP] from the heavens and the earth?"[3919] Say[MS], "Allah. Either you[MP] or we are guided, and the other is clearly lost." (24) Say[MS], "You[MP] will not be questioned about our wrongdoing, and we will not be questioned about your[MP] deeds."[3920] (25) Say[MS], "Our Lord will gather us together, and then give victory[3921] between us in truth. He is victorious and all-knowing."[3922] (26) Say[MS], "Show[MP] me the gods you[MP] have added to him. No! Allah is mighty and wise[3923]." (27) We sent you[MS] to all people only as a bearer of good news and a warner, but most people do not know it. (28) They will say, "When is this

---

[3913] Zabur, Psalms 50:22
[3914] See "endure" in glossary
[3915] The devil. See glossary for more details. Injil, Revelation 20:10,14,15
[3916] Injil, John 14:30,19:11, Matthew 28:18, Mark 6:7, Luke 10:19, Hebrews 2:14-15, 1 John 4:4
[3917] Injil, 1 Corinthians 8:4
[3918] See 2:255, 10:3, 20:109, 43:86. Injil, 1 Timothy 2:5.
[3919] Tawrah, Genesis 1:30
[3920] Tawrah, Deuteronomy 24:16
[3921] Tawrah, Isaiah 25:8, Injil, 1 Corinthians 15:57, 1 John 5:4
[3922] Tawrah, Job 37:16, Isaiah 40:14, Zabur, Psalms 33:13-15, Injil, 1 John 3:20
[3923] Tawrah, Job 9:4, Proverbs 2:6, Jeremiah 9:23-24, Injil, 1 Corinthians 1:21-25, Romans 16:27

## Chapter 34

promise,³⁹²⁴ if you^MP are telling the truth?" (29) Say^MS, "You^MP have an appointment on a certain day³⁹²⁵ and you^MP cannot advance it or postpone it one hour."³⁹²⁶ (30) Disbelievers said, "We will not believe in this recitation,³⁹²⁷ nor in what is in front of³⁹²⁸ it."³⁹²⁹ What if you^MS saw the wicked brought to stand before their Lord?³⁹³⁰ Some of them will speak to others. The weak will tell the proud, "If not for you^MP, we would have been believers." (31) The proud will tell the weak, "Did we block you^MP from guidance after it came to you^MP? No. You^MP are wrongdoers." (32) The weak will tell the proud, "No. It was [your] plotting by night and day, since you^MP commanded us to disbelieve in Allah and take rival gods to him." They will be secretly remorseful when they witness the torment, when we put chains around the disbelievers' necks. Are they being repaid for anything besides their deeds?³⁹³¹ (33) Whenever we sent a warner to a village, the wealthy there said, "We disbelieve in your^MP message." (34) They said, "We have more wealth and more children,³⁹³² and we will not be tormented."³⁹³³ (35) Say^MS, "My Lord gives and withholds provision from those he wills, but most people do not know. (36) Neither your^MP wealth nor your^MP children³⁹³⁴ can bring you^MP closer to us.³⁹³⁵ Only believers who do righteous deeds³⁹³⁶ will have a double reward for their deeds,³⁹³⁷ and they will be safe in rooms³⁹³⁸ [above]. (37) Those who strive to nullify our signs³⁹³⁹ will be summoned to torment." (38) Say^MS, "My Lord gives to and withholds provision from those servants of his as he wills.³⁹⁴⁰

---

³⁹²⁴ Injil, 2 Peter 3:4
³⁹²⁵ Injil, 2 Timothy 4:8
³⁹²⁶ Injil, Matthew 6:27
³⁹²⁷ Or Qur'an or qur'an. See glossary for more details.
³⁹²⁸ Or, "between its hands."
³⁹²⁹ Probably a reference to the former books.
³⁹³⁰ Injil, Romans 14:10
³⁹³¹ Injil, Revelation 22:12
³⁹³² Or sons
³⁹³³ Injil, Luke 16:25
³⁹³⁴ Or sons
³⁹³⁵ Zabur, Psalms 49:8
³⁹³⁶ Injil, 1 Corinthians 3:8, James 2:14-17, Revelation 19:8
³⁹³⁷ Injil, Revelation 18:6, Zechariah 9:12
³⁹³⁸ Or apartments or dwellings. Injil, John 14:1-3
³⁹³⁹ Arabic /ayat/. See glossary for more details.
³⁹⁴⁰ Tawrah, 1 Samuel 2:7

## Chapter 34

When you<sup>MP</sup> donate<sup>3941</sup> anything, he will restore it.<sup>3942</sup> He is the best provider. (39) On the day he gathers<sup>3943</sup> them all, he will say to the angels, "Did these people worship you<sup>MP</sup>?" (40) They will say, "May you<sup>MS</sup> be glorified (above that)! You<sup>MS</sup> are our master, not them. They worshiped<sup>3944</sup> jinns.<sup>3945</sup> Most of them believed in them." (41) Today, one group of you can not help or harm another. We will tell the wicked, "Taste the torment of hellfire, which you<sup>MP</sup> denied." (42) When our signs and miracles are recited to them, they say, "This is only a man who wanted to block you<sup>MP</sup> from what our ancestors worshiped."<sup>3946</sup> They say, "This is only an invented lie." When truth came to the disbelievers, they said, "It is clearly only magic." (43)

\*\*\*

We did not bring them books to study and we sent no warner before you<sup>MS</sup> to them. (44) Those before them rejected, and they did not get a tenth of what we brought them. They rejected my messengers. What will my denial be like? (45) **22B2** Say<sup>MS</sup>, "I preach one thing to you<sup>MP</sup>. Stand before Allah in pairs and individually, and then consider. Your<sup>MP</sup> companion is not demonized.<sup>3947</sup> He is only a warner to you<sup>MP</sup> before<sup>3948</sup> severe torment." (46) Say<sup>MS</sup>, "I have not asked you<sup>MP</sup> for a wage. Keep it. My wages are from Allah. He is a witness over everything." (47)

\*\*\*

Say<sup>MS</sup>, "My Lord casts forth truth.<sup>3949</sup> He knows well all that is unseen." (48)

\*\*\*

Say<sup>MS</sup>, "The truth came. Falsehood cannot create or restore." (49)

\*\*\*

Say<sup>MS</sup>, "If I go astray, I go astray against myself. If I am guided, it is because of

---

<sup>3941</sup> Or spend
<sup>3942</sup> Tawrah, Proverbs 19:17
<sup>3943</sup> Tawrah, Joel 3:11-14, Zephaniah 3:8, Injil, Matthew 25:32, John 15:6, Revelation 16:16
<sup>3944</sup> Tawrah, 2 Kings 21:21, Injil, Revelation 9:20
<sup>3945</sup> Or demons. See glossary for more details.
<sup>3946</sup> Tawrah, Judges 2:19
<sup>3947</sup> Or jinned (crazy). See glossary for more details.
<sup>3948</sup> Or, "between the hands of" or "in front of."
<sup>3949</sup> Zabur, Psalms 147:18

## Chapter 34

what my Lord inspired to me.[3950] He hears all, and he is near. (50) If only you[MS] could see when they will be terrified. There is no escape. They will be seized from near by. (51)

\*\*\*

They said, "We believed in him."[3951] How can they receive it from far away? (52) They disbelieved in it beforehand, and cast away the unseen from far away. (53)

\*\*\*

They will be kept away from what they desired, as happened to those of their sects[3952] beforehand. They were in serious doubt. (54)[3953]

---

[3950] Injil, 2 Corinthians 5:13
[3951] Or it (the truth?)
[3952] Or "those like them"
[3953] The verses in this chapter that rhyme are put together in paragraphs, separated by \*\*\*.

## Chapter 35 Fatir[3954] or Al-Malaika[3955]

In the name of Allah, the most gracious and merciful.[3956] Praise be to Allah the creator of the heavens and the earth,[3957] him who made the angels messengers[3958] with wings, two, three, and four.[3959] He increases what he wills of his creation. Allah can do anything.[3960] (1) When Allah opens[3961] mercy to people, no one can restrain it. If he withholds it, no one afterwards can send it forth. He is mighty and wise.[3962] (2) People, remember[MP] Allah's blessings to you[MP].[3963] Is there any other creator besides Allah?[3964] He provides for you[MP] from heaven and earth. He is the only god.[3965] How you[MP] lie! (3)

\*\*\*

They reject you[MS]. Messengers before you[MS] were rejected. Matters are returned to Allah. (4) People, Allah's promise is true,[3966] so do not let this world beguile you[MP]. Nor let beguilements beguile you[MP] against Allah. (5) Satan is an enemy to you[MP]; make him your[MP] enemy.[3967] He calls his party to go to the burning fire. (6) Disbelievers will suffer severe torment,[3968] while believers who do righteous deeds[3969] will receive forgiveness and a great reward.[3970] (7)

---

[3954] Creator
[3955] Angels
[3956] Zabur, Psalms 103:8, 145:8. See glossary for more details.
[3957] Tawrah, Genesis 1:1
[3958] Injil, Hebrews 1:14
[3959] Tawrah, Isaiah 6:2, Injil, Revelation 4:8
[3960] Tawrah, Job 42:2, Isaiah 14:27, Daniel 4:35, Injil, Matthew 19:26, Mark 10:27, Luke 1:37
[3961] The meaning may be "opens [the door of]"
[3962] Tawrah, Job 9:4, Proverbs 2:6, Jeremiah 9:23-24, Injil, 1 Corinthians 1:21-25, Romans 16:27
[3963] Zabur, Psalms 105:5
[3964] Tawrah, Isaiah 44:8
[3965] Arabic /ilah/. See glossary for more details.
[3966] Zabur, Psalms 18:30
[3967] Injil, Ephesians 6:10-17
[3968] Here and in verses 10 and 36, see Tawrah, Isaiah 50:11, Injil, Matthew 18:34, 25:41,46, Luke 16:23-28, Revelation 20:15.
[3969] Injil, 1 Corinthians 3:8, James 2:14-17, Revelation 19:8

## Chapter 35

\*\*\*

As for those whose bad deeds seem good to them, Allah leads astray those he wills[3971] and guides those he wills. Do not let your[MS] soul sigh over them. Allah knows what they do. (8)

\*\*\*

Allah sends winds and they form clouds. We sent them to a dead town and revived the dead ground. That happens in the resurrection.[3972] (9) Whoever wants power, all power belongs to Allah. Good words ascend to him, and he raises righteous deeds. Those who plot bad deeds will have severe torment. Their plots will perish.[3973] (10) Allah created you[MP] from soil,[3974] then [later] from semen, then we made wives for you[MP].[3975] No woman conceives or gives birth except with his knowledge.[3976] No one grows old or has their life cut short except if it is in a book.[3977] That is easy for Allah. (11)

\*\*\*

The two seas are not equal. One is sweet, fresh[3978] and pleasant to drink. The other is salty[3979] and bitter.[3980] You[MP] eat fresh meat[3981] and can extract ornaments you[MP] can wear[3982] from both of them. You[MS] see ships plow through the waves[3983] so that you[MP] may seek his grace, and so that you[MP] may give thanks.[3984] (12)

\*\*\*

He makes the night merge into the day and the day merge into the night, and he subjected the sun and the moon [to himself].[3985] Both move for a specific time span.[3986] That is Allah, your[MP] Lord. The

---

[3970] Injil, Luke 6:35
[3971] Injil, Romans 9:18, 2 Thessalonians 2:11
[3972] Injil, 1 Corinthians 15:42
[3973] Zabur, Psalms 2:1
[3974] Tawrah, Genesis 2:7
[3975] Tawrah, Genesis 2:22
[3976] Zabur, Psalms 139:13-15
[3977] Zabur, Psalms 139:16
[3978] Or, "like the Euphrates."
[3979] Injil, James 3:10-11
[3980] Or, "like Ujaj."
[3981] e.g. fish
[3982] e.g. pearls
[3983] Injil, James 3:4
[3984] Injil, Colossians 3:15, 1 Thessalonians 5:18
[3985] Tawrah, Genesis 1:14-18
[3986] Zabur, Psalms 72:5

Chapter 35

kingdom belongs to him.[3987] Those you[MP] pray to besides him do not own even a date pit's skin. (13) If you[MP] pray to them, they will not hear your[MP] prayer.[3988] Even if they were to hear, they would not answer you[MP],[3989] and on the day of resurrection,[3990] they will disavow your[MP] other gods. No one will predict it like one aware. (14) **22B3**

\*\*\*

People, you[MP] are needy of Allah,[3991] but Allah is self-sufficient and praiseworthy.[3992] (15) If he wills, he will get rid of you[MP] and bring a new creation.[3993] (16)

\*\*\*

That is not a mighty thing to Allah. (17)

\*\*\*

No one can bear the load of another.[3994] If one calls out about his load, nothing of it will be carried, even if he is a relative. You[MS] warn those who fear their Lord of the unseen, and they perform the prayers. Whoever purifies himself benefits from being purified.[3995] Allah is [man's] destiny. (18) The blind and the sighted are not equal, (19) nor are darkness and light,[3996] (20) nor shadow and hot wind. (21) The living are not all equal, nor are the dead. Allah makes those he wills hear. You[MS] cannot make those in the grave hear. (22) You[MS] are only a warner. (23) We sent you[MS] truly as a bearer of good news and a warner. Every nation has had a warner come to them.[3997] (24) If they reject you[MS], those before you[MS] also rejected. Their messengers brought them miracles, books[3998] and the enlightening book.[3999] (25) Then I overtook the disbelievers. How severe was my denial. (26)

---

[3987] Injil, Matthew 6:33
[3988] Zabur, Psalms 135:17
[3989] Tawrah, Isaiah 46:7
[3990] Tawrah, Daniel 12:2 Injil, Acts 24:15, 1 Corinthians 15:52-54, Revelation 20:11-15
[3991] Injil, Matthew 5:3
[3992] Injil, Revelation 4:11
[3993] Injil, Matthew 3:9, Luke 3:8, 20:16-19
[3994] Injil, Galatians 6:5
[3995] Injil, 2 Timothy 2:21
[3996] Injil, 2 Corinthians 6:14
[3997] Or, "die in it."
[3998] Or psalms, Zabur, Psalms 3:1
[3999] See 22:8, 31:20, 3:184. This phrase here and in 3:184 refer to the previous books. Zabur, Psalms 119:130, 105, 19:8

## Chapter 35

\*\*\*

Have you<sup>MS</sup> not seen how Allah sent rain down from the sky,[4000] and by it we brought forth fruits[4001] of different kinds?[4002] And from the mountains, white, red, and black[4003] mountain paths of different colors.[4004] (27)

\*\*\*

There are different colors[4005] of people, living creatures, and cattle. The scholars of his servants fear Allah.[4006] Allah is mighty and forgiving.[4007] (28) Those who read Allah's book, perform prayers, and donate out of what we have provided them, both in secret[4008] and in public, hope in an imperishable reward. (29) He will pay them their wages and increase his grace to them. He is forgiving and grateful. (30) What we inspired you<sup>MS</sup> with out of the book is true, confirming[4009] what is in his possession.[4010] Allah is aware and seeing of his servants. (31) Then we made our servants that we chose[4011] inherit the book from them. Some of them wronged themselves,[4012] some had good intentions,[4013] and some competed

---

[4000] Zabur, Psalms 68:9

[4001] Tawrah, Deuteronomy 33:14

[4002] Or, "colors."

[4003] These words may refer to colors of grapes.

[4004] Or "kinds"

[4005] Or "kinds"

[4006] Tawrah, Deuteronomy 10:12, Isaiah 29:13, Injil, 1 Peter 2:17, Revelation 14:7

[4007] Here and in verses 30, 34, and 41, see Zabur, Psalms 103:3, 130:4, Tawrah, Isaiah 43:25, Exodus 34:7, Injil, Acts 26:18.

[4008] Injil, Matthew 6:1-4

[4009] The Qur'an confirms the previous books many times (2:41,89,91,97,101, 3:3,81, 4:47, 5:48, 6:92, 35:31, 46:12,30)

[4010] Or, "between his/its hands" or "in front of it."

[4011] Tawrah, Amos 3:2

[4012] The injustice/wickedness, disbelief/ungratefulness, evil, unrighteousness/sin, or lostness of mankind is mentioned in a number of verses in the Qur'an as well as in the previous books. Injustice or wickedness: 2:57, 3:117,135, 4:64,97, 7:160,177, 9:70, 10:44, 11:101, 14:34,45, 16:33,61,118, 29:40, 30:9, 33:72, 34:19, 35:32, 43:76, 55:1, Tawrah, Genesis 6:5, Job 25:4, Injil, Acts 3:26, disbelief or ungratefulness: 14:34, 17:67, 22:66, 42:48, 43:15, 80:17, Injil, Hebrews 3:19, Evil: 12:53, Tawrah, Jeremiah 17:9, Injil, Matthew 15:19, Mark 7:21, unrighteousness or sin: 91:8, Tawrah, 1 Kings 8:46, Ecclesiastes 7:20, Injil, Romans 3:9-19, 5:12, lostness: 103:2, Tawrah, Jeremiah 50:6, Injil, Luke 19:10, Romans 3:23, 6:23

## Chapter 35

in good deeds by Allah's permission. That is great grace. (32) They will enter heavenly gardens[4014] of Eden, where they will be adorned with golden bracelets, pearls, and silk clothing. (33) They will say, "Praise be to Allah, who has taken sorrow away from us.[4015] Our Lord is forgiving and grateful. (34)

\*\*\*

He has made us dwell in the eternal abode[4016] by his grace. We will feel no fatigue in it, nor will we feel weary. (35)

\*\*\*

Disbelievers are headed to the fires of hell, where they will never be killed or die,[4017] nor will their torment ever be lightened. This is how we repay every disbeliever." (36) They will cry aloud in it, "Our Lord, get us out of here. We will do righteous deeds besides the ones we did." Did we not give you[MP] a life long enough to remember for anyone who wanted to remember? A warner came to you[MP], so taste[MP] it.[4018] The wicked will have no savior.[4019] (37) Allah knows the unseen things in the heavens and the earth.[4020] He knows what is in the heart.[4021] (38)

\*\*\*

He made you[MP] regents in the earth,[4022] so those who disbelieve will suffer for their disbelief. The disbelief of the disbelievers will not get them anything but more hatred with their Lord. The disbelief of the disbelievers will not get them anything but more loss. (39) Say[MS], "What do you[MP] think? Show[MP] me what the gods you[MP] pray to besides Allah have created on earth. Do they have other gods[4023] in the heavens? Did we give them a book in which they have a miracle? The wicked promise each other vain hopes.[4024] (40) **22B4** Allah holds the heavens[4025] and the earth

---

[4013] Or "were lukewarm"
[4014] Arabic /jannah/. See glossary for more details.
[4015] Injil, Revelation 21:4
[4016] Injil, Revelation 21:3
[4017] Injil, Matthew 25:46
[4018] i.e. the torment of hellfire
[4019] Tawrah, Isaiah 43:11, Hosea 13:4, Injil, Hebrews 10:26
[4020] Zabur, Psalms 139:1-10
[4021] Tawrah, 1 Samuel 16:7, 1 Chronicles 28:9, Zabur, Psalms 44:21, Injil, Luke 16:15, Romans 8:27, Acts 15:8, 1 John 3:20
[4022] Tawrah, Genesis 1:28
[4023] Or a share
[4024] Tawrah, 1 Samuel 12:21
[4025] Zabur, Psalms 89:2

## Chapter 35

firm, so they do not disappear.[4026] When they disappear, no one will grasp them after him. He is gentle[4027] and forgiving. (41) They swore strong oaths by Allah that when a warner came to them, that they would be better guided than any of the nations. But when a warner came to them, they only ran away more, (42) being proud on the earth and plotting bad things. Plotting bad things only hems in those who do it.[4028] Do they expect anything besides the law[4029] of the ancients? You[MS] will not find any substituting Allah's laws, nor will you[MS] find any changing of Allah's laws. (43)

\*\*\*

Did they not walk through the land and see the end of those before them, though they were stronger than they are? Nothing in the heavens or the earth can hinder Allah.[4030] He is all-knowing[4031] and all-powerful. (44) If Allah were to count what people deserve against them, he would not leave any living creature on earth.[4032] But he gives them more time. When their time comes, Allah sees his servants.[4033] (45) [4034]

---

[4026] Injil, Matthew 5:18, 24:35
[4027] Zabur, Psalms 45:4, 145:17, Injil, Matthew 11:29, Galatians 5:22
[4028] Tawrah, Proverbs 26:27
[4029] Or "punishment" or "habit" or "tradition", also in the rest of this verse.
[4030] Tawrah, 1 Samuel 14:6
[4031] Tawrah, Job 37:16, Isaiah 40:14, Zabur, Psalms 33:13-15, Injil, 1 John 3:20
[4032] Zabur, Psalms 130:3
[4033] Zabur, Psalms 34:22
[4034] The verses in this chapter that rhyme are put together in paragraphs, separated by \*\*\*.

# Chapter 36

# Chapter 36 Ya Sin[4035]

In the name of Allah, the most gracious and merciful.[4036] YS.[4037] (1) [I swear] by the wise Qur'an,[4038] (2) you[MS] are a messenger (3) on a straight path,[4039] (4) a[4040] revelation from the mighty, merciful[4041] one, (5) so you[MS] can warn people whose fathers were not warned, so they are unaware. (6) The saying is true for most of them, since they do not believe. (7) We put shackles around their necks up to their chins, and their heads are forced up. (8) We made a dam in front of them and a dam behind them, and we covered them so they do not see. (9) Whether or not you[MS] warn them, they will not believe. (10) You[MS] only warn those who follow the reminder[4042] and fear the most gracious in the unseen world. Give good news to them that they will have forgiveness and a great reward.[4043] (11) We give life to the dead[4044] and write what they sent on beforehand and what they left behind. We counted everything in a clear book of guidance.[4045] (12) Tell them a proverb: There were people in a village when messengers came to it. (13) We sent two to them, and they rejected them. We reinforced them with a third, and they said, "We are messengers to you[MP]." (14) They said, "You[MP] are only men like us, and the most gracious has not revealed anything. You[MP] are liars." (15) They said, "Our Lord knows that we are messengers to you[MP]. (16) Our only responsibility is clear proclamation." (17) They said, "You[MP] are an evil omen to us. If you[MP] do not stop, we will stone you[MP], and torment you[MP] painfully." (18) They said, "Your[MP] evil

---

[4035] The letters Y and S.
[4036] Zabur, Psalms 103:8, 145:8. See glossary for more details.
[4037] Here and at the beginning of many chapters there are unvowelled letters of unknown meaning. Numerous theories have been proposed, but there is no agreement on the subject.
[4038] Or recitation. See glossary for more details.
[4039] See glossary for more details, and notes on 3:51, 6:153, 19:36, 36:61, and 43:64 on what the straight path is.
[4040] This phrase has no subject. It is probably a continuation of verse 2.
[4041] Here and in verse 58, see glossary for more details on "merciful."
[4042] Arabic /dhikr/ here and in verse 69. See glossary for more details.
[4043] Injil, Matthew 10:42, 6:4, etc.
[4044] Injil, Romans 4:17
[4045] Injil, Revelation 20:12, Tawrah, Daniel 7:10

## Chapter 36

omen[4046] is with you[MP], if you[MP] remember. But you[MP] are wasteful people." (19) A man came quickly from the furthest part of the city. He said, "My people, follow the messengers. (20) Follow those who do not ask you[MP] for wages, and who are guided. (21) I cannot but worship my creator.[4047] You[MP] will be returned to him. (22) Should I choose gods[4048] besides him? If the most gracious wants to harm me, their intercession does not benefit me, nor can they rescue me.[4049] (23) I would thus have clearly gone astray. (24) I have believed in your[MP] Lord, so hear[MP] me." (25) He was told, "Enter[MS] the heavenly garden."[4050] He said, "I wish that my people knew (26) that my Lord has forgiven me and honored me."[4051] (27) 23A1 We did not send down a host of heaven on his people after him. We would not send them down. (28) It was only a single cry, and then they were extinct. (29) Too bad for the worshippers. Every time a messenger came to them, they made fun of him.[4052] (30) Have they not seen how many generations before them we destroyed? They will not return to them. (31) All of them will be summoned to us. (32) And a sign for them is the dead ground: we revived it, and from it we brought forth grain they could eat.[4053] (33) We made palm gardens in it and vineyards, and made springs gush forth, (34) so that they could eat of its fruit, and their hands did not make it. Will not they give thanks? (35) Glory be to him who created all kinds of things the earth brings forth, of themselves, and of what they do not know. (36) Another sign for them is the night. With it we make the day pass away, and they are in darkness.[4054] (37) The sun goes down to its resting place. This is the decree of the mighty[4055] all-knowing[4056] one. (38) And we decreed phases for the moon, until it returned like an old, dry, date

---

[4046] Or bird. See 3:49
[4047] Injil, Romans 1:25
[4048] Arabic /ilah/. See glossary for more details.
[4049] Tawrah, Isaiah 45:20
[4050] Arabic /jannah/. See glossary for more details.
[4051] Injil, John 12:26
[4052] Tawrah, 2 Chronicles 30:10, 36:16, Zabur, Psalms 35:16, Injil, Matthew 20:19, 27:29,31,41, Mark 15:20,31, Luke 18:32, 22:63, 23:11,36
[4053] Tawrah, Isaiah 55:10
[4054] Zabur, Psalms 44:19
[4055] Tawrah, Isaiah 49:26, Zabur, Psalms 50:1, Injil, Luke 1:49
[4056] Tawrah, Job 37:16, Isaiah 40:14, Zabur, Psalms 33:13-15, Injil, 1 John 3:20

## Chapter 36

stalk. (39) The sun should not catch the moon, nor should the night beat the day. They all swim in their orbits.[4057] (40) Another sign for them is that we carried their descendants in a loaded ship.[4058] (41) We created others like it that they could board. (42) When we will, we drown them, and they will have no helper, nor will they be saved, (43) except by our mercy, to enjoy life for a while. (44) When they are told, "Beware of what is in front of you[MP] and behind you[MP],[4059] so that you[MP] maybe shown mercy," (45) whenever one of their Lord's signs comes to them, they turn away from it. (46) When they are told, "Donate some of what Allah has provided you[MP]," disbelievers tell believers, "Shall we feed those that Allah could have fed if he had willed? You[MP] have clearly gone astray." (47) They say, "When is this promise, if you[MP] are telling the truth?" (48) They only wait for one cry that will seize them while they are disputing. (49) They will not have a chance to make a will, and they will not return to their families. (50) The trumpet will be blown,[4060] and they will be brought hastily from their graves to their Lord. (51) They will say, "Woe is us. Who resurrected us from our beds? This is the promise of the most gracious; the messengers were right." (52) With merely one cry, they were all summoned before us. (53) No soul will be wronged today, and you[MP] will be repaid[4061] only for your[MP] deeds. (54) Those in heaven today are joyfully employed.[4062] (55) They and their wives are in shade, reclining on couches. (56) They have fruits there, and whatever they desire. (57) "Peace" is what a merciful Lord says. (58) Be separated today, wrongdoers![4063] (59) 23A2 Sons of Adam,[4064] did I not covenant with you[MP]? Do not worship Satan. He is a clear enemy to you[MP]. (60) Worship me. This is a straight path.[4065] (61) He led astray great multitudes of

---

[4057] Zabur, Psalms 19:5
[4058] Tawrah, Genesis 7:17
[4059] Or "your present and past."
[4060] Injil, 1 Corinthians 15:52
[4061] Injil, Luke 14:14
[4062] Or "busy in rejoicing." See Injil, Luke 19:17, Revelation 20:4,6
[4063] Injil, Matthew 25:32
[4064] See glossary for more details.
[4065] The straight path is mentioned often in the Qur'an (1:7 and 37:118 as "the straight path", 7:16 as "your straight path," 6:126 as "your Lord's straight path," 6:153 as "my straight path," and 2:108,142,213, 3:51,101, 4:68,175, 5:12,16,60,77, 6:39,87,161, 10:25, 11:56, 15:41, 16:76, 121, 19:36,43, 20:135, 22:54, 23:73, 24:46, 28:22, 36:4,61, 38:22, 42:52,

you^MP. Did you^MP not comprehend? (62) This is hell, as you^MP were promised. (63) Be roasted in it today because of your^MP disbelief. (64) Today we will seal their mouths, and their hands will speak to us. Their feet will witness what they deserve. (65) If we had willed, we would have destroyed their eyes, and they would have raced toward the path. How do they see? (66) If we had willed, we would have fixed them at their places,[4066] and they would not have been able to leave or return. (67) We make the bodies of those we give a long life bend over.[4067] Do they not comprehend? (68) We did not teach him poetry, and it is not necessary for it.[4068] It is only a reminder and a clear recitation,[4069] (69) to warn the living, and fulfill the saying against the disbelievers. (70) Have they not seen that we created with our hands cattle[4070] that they own for them^MP? (71) We have subjected them^F to them^MP. Some of them they ride, and some they eat. (72) They have benefits in them and things to drink. Will they not give thanks? (73) They chose gods[4071] besides Allah, so that they might be saved. (74) They could not save them, as an army summoned. (75) Does not their saying grieve you^MS? We know what they keep secret,[4072] and what they announce.[4073] (76) Has mankind not seen that we created him from a sperm drop? He is clearly an opponent. (77) He told us a proverb and forgot his creation. He said, "Who gives life to bones that are rotten?"[4074] (78) Say^MS, "He who created it in the beginning gives them life.[4075] He knows every creature." (79) He gives you^MP fire

---

43:43,61,64, 46:30, 48:2,20, 60:1, 67:22 as "a straight path.") However, only 3:51, 19:36, 43:61,64, and 36:61 say what the straight path is. This passage is the least complete in its explanation, but from it we can conclude that the straight path includes (from verses 60-61) 1) not worshiping Satan, and 2) worshiping Allah. See notes on the other four passages.

[4066] Or "their purpose," or "their intention." The meaning may be "according to their ability." (see 6:135)
[4067] Tawrah, Ecclesiastes 12:3
[4068] Or "him."
[4069] Or Qur'an or qur'an. See glossary for more details.
[4070] Tawrah, Genesis 1:24
[4071] Arabic /ilah/. See glossary for more details.
[4072] Injil, Luke 8:17
[4073] See also 2:77, 11:5, 14:38, 16:19,23, 27:25,74, 28:69, 60:1, 64:4.
[4074] Tawrah, Ezekiel 37:1-14
[4075] Injil, Romans 4:17

## Chapter 36

from a green tree[4076] when you[MP] kindle it. (80) Is the creator of the heavens and the earth not able to create [people] like them?[4077] Yes he is. He is the all-knowing[4078] creator.[4079] (81) Whenever he wants something, his command is, "Be," and it is. (82) May he who holds the kingdom of everything in his hand[4080] be glorified! You[MP] will return to him.[4081] (83)

---

[4076] Injil, Luke 23:31
[4077] The Arabic pronoun is for thinking beings.
[4078] Tawrah, Job 37:16, Isaiah 40:14, Zabur, Psalms 33:13-15, Injil, 1 John 3:20
[4079] Tawrah, Isaiah 40:28
[4080] Zabur, Psalms 103:19
[4081] Tawrah, Ecclesiastes 12:7

# Chapter 37: Al-Saffat[4082]

In the name of Allah, the most gracious and merciful.[4083] [I swear] by those[4084] arrayed[FP] in ranks (1) and those[FP] who drive forth[4085] (2) and those[FP] who follow the reminder:[4086] (3)

\*\*\*

"Truly your[MP] god[4087] is one, (4)

\*\*\*

Lord of the heavens, the earth, and everything between them, Lord of the sunrises."[4088] (5)

\*\*\*

We truly decorated the lower sky[4089] with the stars,[4090] (6)

\*\*\*

as protection from all rebellious devils. (7)

\*\*\*

They[MP][4091] do not listen to the highest hosts and are expelled from every side. (8) Driven away, they will have torment[4092] forever, (9) except for those who snatch by stealth and are pursued by shining fire. (10) Ask[MS] them[MP] if they are stronger[4093] than those we created. We created them from sticky clay. (11)

\*\*\*

You[MS] were amazed, and they mock. (12) If they are reminded, they will not remember it. (13) If they see a sign, they ridicule. (14) They say, "This is clearly nothing but magic. (15) If we die and are soil and bones, will we be resurrected? (16) And our forefathers, too?" (17) Say[MS], "Yes, even though you[MP] are vile."

---

[4082] This name means "arrayed in ranks."
[4083] Zabur, Psalms 103:8, 145:8. See glossary for more details.
[4084] The reference in these first five verses is probably to angels.
[4085] The implied object might be "demons"
[4086] Arabic /dhikr/. See glossary for more details.
[4087] Arabic /ilah/. See glossary for more details.
[4088] Or East.
[4089] Or heaven. Just as in the other books, the same word means sky and heaven.
[4090] In all the books, angels are connected with stars. See Tawrah, Judges 5:20, Injil, Revelation 9:1, 12:4
[4091] i.e. the devils
[4092] For "torment" here and in verses 33, 38, and 176, see Tawrah, Isaiah 50:11, Injil, Matthew 18:34, 25:41,46, Luke 16.23-28, Revelation 20:15.
[4093] or possibly, harder to create.

## Chapter 37

(18) It is one cry,[4094] and then they will see. (19) They will say, "Woe to us. It is the day of judgment." (20) This is the day of separation, which you[MP] denied. (21) **23A3** Gather[4095] the wicked with their wives and what they worshiped (22) instead of Allah, and guide them on the path of the blazing fire, (23) and stop them. They will be asked, (24) "What is wrong with you[MP] that you[MP] do you not aid each other?" (25) Today they have surrendered. (26) Some of them approached each other discussing. (27) They said, "You[MP] used to come to us on the right."[4096] (28) They said, "But you[MP] were not believers. (29) We had no power over you[MP], and you[MP] were transgressing people." (30) So our Lord's saying was fulfilled. We will taste it. (31) We beguiled you[MP]. We were beguiled[MP].[4097] (32) They will share in torment on that day. (33) This is what we do to wrongdoers. (34) If they were told, "Allah is the only god,"[4098] they became proud (35) and said, "Should we leave our gods for a demonized[4099] poet?" (36) But he came with truth and confirmed[4100] the messengers. (37) You[MP] will truly taste painful torment. (38) You[MP] will be repaid only for your[MP] deeds. (39) But as for Allah's sincere servants,[4101] (40) they will have a clear provision: (41) fruits and honor (42) in heavenly gardens[4102] of delight, (43) facing each other on couches, (44) with a cup from a fountain passed around. (45) [It is] a clear[4103] cup and a delight for those who drink. (46) It neither causes drunkenness nor does it become empty. (47) They[MP] will have low-hanging sparkling ones[FP][4104] (48) like hidden eggs. (49) Some of them approached

---

[4094] The reference is to the final judgment. See 1 Thessalonians 4:16
[4095] Tawrah, Joel 3:11-14, Zephaniah 3:8, Injil, Matthew 25:32, John 15:6, Revelation 16:16
[4096] This may mean to oppress from a position of power, or to tempt.
[4097] Tawrah, Genesis 3:13
[4098] Arabic /ilah/ here and in verse 36. See glossary for more details.
[4099] Or jinned (crazy). See glossary for more details.
[4100] Or believed.
[4101] For "servants" here and in verses 74,81,128,132,160,169, and 171, see glossary.
[4102] Arabic /jannah/. See glossary for more details.
[4103] Or white
[4104] Most translations translate this verse "modest spouses with beautiful eyes." However, the verse has no word for spouse, and instead of /'ain/ (eye), it has /'in/ (wild ox, or sparkling). The word usually translated "modest" also means "low" or "short." Thus, the translation "low-hanging ones." (see 6:99, 76:14 where fruits are said to be hanging low) This is

## Chapter 37

others and wondered. (50) One[M] of them said, "I had a partner[M]."[4105] (51) He said, "Do you[MS] believe it? (52) If we die and are soil and bones, will we be judged?" (53) He said, "Are you[MP] looking?" (54) They looked and saw him in the middle of the blazing fire. (55) He said, "By Allah, you[MS] almost destroyed me. (56) If not for my Lord's blessings, I would have been brought [there]. (57) So are we not dead, (58) except for the first death,[4106] and we are not to be tormented? (59) This is the great victory."[4107] (60) Let the workers work for such as this. (61) Is this better as a dwelling place, or the bitter almond[4108] tree, (62) which we made a trial for the wicked? (63) It is a tree with roots from the bottom of the blazing fire. (64) Its pods[4109] are like devils'[4110] heads. (65) They eat it and fill their bellies with it, (66) then drink a mixture of boiling water, (67) and then return to the blazing fire. (68) They found their forefathers going astray, (69) yet they raced after them. (70) Most of the men of old before them went astray. (71) We sent warners to them. (72) See what was the end of those who were warned.[4111] (73) But not our sincere servants. (74) Nuh called out to us.[4112] How wonderful are the responders! (75) We rescued him and his family from great distress.[4113] (76) Then we made his seed remain,[4114] (77) and left this [blessing] upon him for later ages: (78) "Peace be upon Nuh among men."[4115] (79) Thus we reward those who do good. (80) He is one of our believing[4116] servants. (81) Then we drowned the rest.[4117] (82) **23A4** Truly among those

---

more probable given the context of food and drink. The following verse compares these to eggs, which is more apt if comparison is by shape.

[4105] The reference may be to a spirit.
[4106] Injil, Revelation 20:6
[4107] Tawrah, Isaiah 25:8, Injil, 1 Corinthians 15:57, 1 John 5:4
[4108] or Zaqquum
[4109] or fruit
[4110] Arabic /shayatin/. See glossary for more details.
[4111] The word for end is feminine and the verb "was" is masculine. There may be another meaning.
[4112] Noah here and in verse 79. See glossary for more details. Tawrah, Genesis 6:13
[4113] Tawrah, Genesis 8:18
[4114] See Tawrah, Genesis 10
[4115] Or the worlds.
[4116] Injil, Hebrews 11:7
[4117] See Tawrah, Genesis 6-9

Chapter 37

of his sect was Ibrahim,[4118] (83) who came to his Lord with a sound heart, (84) when he told his father and his people, "What are you[MP] worshipping? (85) Do you[MP] want a lie: gods[4119] besides Allah? (86) What do you[MP] think about the Lord of the universe? (87) So he took a look at the stars. (88) Then he said, "I am sick."(89) So they turned away from him and went away. (90) So he turned to their gods and said, "Will you[MP] not eat? (91) Why do you[MP] not speak?"[4120] (92) So he turned upon them, striking them with his right hand, (93) and they came to him quickly. (94) He said, "Do you[MP] worship what you[MP] engrave (95) when Allah created you[MP] and everything you[MP] make?" (96) They said, "Build him a building and throw him in the blazing fire." (97) They wanted to trick him, but we humiliated them. (98) And he said, "I am going to my Lord. He will guide me. (99) Lord, give me someone righteous,"(100) so we gave him good news of a gentle son.[4121] (101) When he[4122] could walk, he[4123] said, "Son, I saw in a dream that I will sacrifice you[MS].[4124] Look;[4125] what do you[MS] see?" He said, "Father, do as you[MS] have been commanded. If Allah wills, you[MS] will find I endure."[4126] (102) When they had both submitted, and he had laid him face down, (103) we called, "Ibrahim, (104) you[MS] have fulfilled the vision."[4127] Thus we reward those who do good. (105) This was a clear test.[4128] (106) And we ransomed him with a great sacrifice[4129] (107) and left [this blessing] upon him for later ages:[4130] (108) "Peace be upon

---

[4118] Abraham here and in verses 104 and 109. See glossary for more details. Tawrah, Genesis 15:18, 17:1-21

[4119] Arabic /ilah/ here and in verse 91. See glossary for more details. Tawrah, Joshua 24:2

[4120] See Zabur, Psalms 135:16-17

[4121] See Tawrah, Genesis 18:10

[4122] The son

[4123] Abraham

[4124] See Tawrah, Genesis 22:1-2

[4125] In verse 105 it is called a vision, and here it is called a dream. Abraham's son could not see Abraham's dream, so it must have been a vision.

[4126] See "endure" in glossary

[4127] Tawrah, Genesis 22:11-12

[4128] Injil, Hebrews 11:17

[4129] See Tawrah, Genesis 22:13-14

[4130] Injil, John 8:56, Acts 7:17, 13:26, Romans 4:11-12, Galatians 3:7-9, 14-18, Hebrews 11:12

Ibrahim." (109) Thus we reward those who do good. (110) He is one of our believing servants.[4131] (111) And we gave him good news of Ishaq's[4132] prophethood and righteousness,[4133] (112) and we blessed him and Ishaq.[4134] Some of their descendants are good, and some clearly wrong themselves. (113) We gave blessing to Musa[4135] and Harun[4136] (114) and rescued[4137] them[D] and their[D] people from great distress (115) and gave them[P] victory;[4138] they[P] were the winners. (116) We gave them[P] the clear book, (117) guided them on the straight path,[4139] (118) and left upon them[D] for later ages: (119) "Peace be upon Musa and Harun." (120) Thus we reward those[MP] who do good. (121) They[D] are some of our believing servants. (122) Ilyas[4140] was one of the messengers. (123) He told his people, "Are you[MP] not reverent?" (124) Do you[MP] pray to Baal and leave the best of creators?[4141] (125) Allah is your[MP] Lord and the Lord of your[MP] ancestors.[4142] (126) They rejected him, and they are summoned. (127) But not our sincere servants. (128) and left this upon him for later ages: (129) "Peace be upon Ilyasin."[4143] (130) Thus we reward those[P] who do good. (131) He is one of our believing servants. (132) Lut[4144] was a messenger. (133) We rescued him and all his family[4145] (134) except for an old woman who lagged behind.[4146] (135) Then we destroyed the rest.[4147] (136) and you[MP] pass by them in the morning

---

[4131] Tawrah, Genesis 15:6, Hebrews 11:17
[4132] Isaac, here and in verse 113. See glossary for more details.
[4133] or Ishaq as a righteous prophet.
[4134] Tawrah, Genesis 12:2, 26:12
[4135] Moses here and in verses 117 and 120. See glossary for more details.
[4136] Aaron here and in verse 120. See glossary for more details.
[4137] Tawrah, Exodus 14:22
[4138] See Tawrah, Exodus 14:26
[4139] See glossary for more details, and notes on 3:51, 6:153, 19:36, 36:61, and 43:64 on what the straight path is.
[4140] Elijah. See glossary for more details.
[4141] See Tawrah, 1 Kings 18. It is unknown why the plural "creators" is used.
[4142] Tawrah, 1 Kings 18:36
[4143] The name for Elijah is different here, in a plural form. It may mean, "Those like Elijah." Injil, Matthew 11:14 See glossary for more details.
[4144] Lot, nephew of Abraham. See glossary for more details.
[4145] See Tawrah, Genesis 19
[4146] Tawrah, Genesis 19:26
[4147] Tawrah, Genesis 19:24

# Chapter 37

(137) and at night. Do you<sup>MP</sup> not comprehend? (138) Yunus$^{4148}$ was a messenger;$^{4149}$ (139) he fled to the laden ship.$^{4150}$ (140) He cast lots and was condemned. (141) So the whale swallowed him while he was blameworthy.$^{4151}$ (142) If he had not praised [Allah],$^{4152}$ (143) he would have remained in its belly until the day they are resurrected.$^{4153}$ (144) **23B1** So we expelled him,$^{4154}$ naked$^{4155}$ and sick, (145) and made a squash tree sprout over him,$^{4156}$ (146) and we sent him to a hundred thousand people or more.$^{4157}$ (147) They believed, so we let them enjoy$^{4158}$ for a time.$^{4159}$ (148) So ask<sup>MS</sup> them<sup>MP</sup>, "Does your<sup>MS</sup> Lord have daughters and they<sup>MP</sup> have sons? (149) Or did we create angels female as they watched? (150) But they falsely say, (151) Allah has begotten.$^{4160}$ They lie. (152) "He chose daughters over sons."$^{4161}$ (153) What is wrong with you<sup>MP</sup>? How do you<sup>MP</sup> judge? (154) Do you<sup>MP</sup> not remember? (155) Or do you<sup>MP</sup> have clear authority? (156) Bring forth your<sup>MP</sup> book if you<sup>MP</sup> are telling the truth. (157) They claim kinship between him and the jinns,$^{4162}$ even though the jinns know that they will be summoned. (158) May Allah be glorified above what they describe, (159) except for Allah's sincere servants! (160) You<sup>MP</sup> and the gods you<sup>MP</sup>

---

$^{4148}$ Jonah. See glossary for more details.

$^{4149}$ Tawrah, Jonah 1:1

$^{4150}$ Tawrah, Jonah 1:3

$^{4151}$ Tawrah, Jonah 1:16 The belief that all prophets and messengers are sinless is not supported by the Qur'an. For instances of prophets or messengers asking forgiveness or committing sins, see 7:23, 20:121 (Adam), 11:47, 71:28 (Nuh), 26:82, 14:41 (Ibrahim), 28:15-16 (Musa), 7:151, 20:93 (Musa and Harun), 38:24 (Dawud), 38:32,35 (Sulayman), 21:87, 37:142 (Yunus), 48:2, 47:19, 40:55, 4:79,106, 9:43, 13:30, 80:1-2, 110:3, 94:2, 23:118, 66:1, 33:37, 8:67, and 9:117 (Muhammad (s).

$^{4152}$ Tawrah, Jonah 2:1-9.

$^{4153}$ Tawrah, Jonah 2:9-10

$^{4154}$ Tawrah, Jonah 2:10

$^{4155}$ Or possibly, on the naked shore

$^{4156}$ Tawrah, Jonah 4:6

$^{4157}$ Tawrah, Jonah 3:2, 4:11

$^{4158}$ The object is not stated, but implied is "life" or "more time."

$^{4159}$ Tawrah, Jonah 3:6-10

$^{4160}$ The idea that Allah had sexual relations with a woman and impregnated her is repulsive to all true believers. This false idea has no support in any of the books.

$^{4161}$ This may be a continuation of the false sayings of the disbelievers.

$^{4162}$ Or demons here twice. See glossary for more details.

## Chapter 37

worship (161) will not seduce[MP] (162) anyone except those roasting in the blazing fire. (163) All of us[4163] have a known position (164) and we are arrayed[MP] in ranks. (165) We are praisers. (166) They would have said, (167) "If only we had a reminder[4164] from the men of old, (168) we would be Allah's sincere servants." (169) They disbelieved in it,[4165] and they will know. (170) We previously sent our word to our servants the messengers. (171) They are the saved ones.[4166] (172) Our winning forces are theirs.[4167] (173) So turn[MS] away from them for a while (174) and see them. They will see. (175) So will they hasten our torment? (176) If it descends on their yard,[4168] it will be a bad morning for those who were warned. (177) So turn[MS] away from them for a while (178) and see. They will see. (179) May your[MP] Lord, the Lord of power, be glorified above all they describe! (180) Peace be upon the messengers. (181) Praise be to Allah, the Lord of the Universe. (182)[4169]

---

[4163] The reference here is probably to the angels.

[4164] Arabic /dhikr/. See glossary for more details. Here the reminder is given to the men of old, probably Musa and Harun (21:48).

[4165] Or him. This probably refers to the remembrance.

[4166] Tawrah, Isaiah 25:8, Injil, 1 Corinthians 15:57, 1 John 5:4

[4167] Allah's angels often help prophets. See Tawrah, 2 Kings 6:16-17, Daniel 10:10-21, Injil, Matthew 26:53, Acts 12:7-17

[4168] or (town) square or arena, etc.

[4169] The verses in this chapter that rhyme are put together in paragraphs, separated by ***.

# Chapter 38: Sad[4170]

In the name of Allah, the most gracious and merciful.[4171] S.[4172] [I swear] by the Qur'an,[4173] which has a reminder.[4174] (1)
\*\*\*

But disbelievers are proud and divided. (2) How many generations[4175] we destroyed, and they called, but there was no time to escape. (3) They were amazed that a warner had come to them from among themselves, and the disbelievers said, "This is a lying magician. (4) Has he made the gods into one god?[4176] This is strange." (5) Their nobility went off, "Go off and endure[4177] your[MP] gods. This is something desired. (6) We did not hear about this in the last spiritual path.[4178] This is just invented. (7) Was the reminder[4179] revealed to him among us?" They are in doubt about my reminder, but they have not tasted my torment.[4180] (8) Do they have storehouses of your[MS] strong, giving Lord's mercy? (9) Do they own the kingdom of the heavens and the earth, and what is between them? Let them ascend by the ropes. (10) There is a defeated army of the parties. (11)
\*\*\*

The people of Nuh,[4181] Aad,[4182] and Pharaoh of the pyramids[4183] rejected, (12) \*\*\*

---

[4170] A letter in the alphabet, s.

[4171] Zabur, Psalms 103:8, 145:8. See glossary for more details.

[4172] Here and at the beginning of many chapters there are unvowelled letters of unknown meaning. Numerous theories have been proposed, but there is no agreement on the subject.

[4173] Or recitation. See glossary for more details.

[4174] Arabic /dhikr/, here, in verses 8 (twice), 48, and 87. See glossary for more details.

[4175] Or centuries

[4176] Arabic /ilah/ twice in this verse and in verse 6. See glossary for more details.

[4177] Or, "wait for."

[4178] Arabic /millah/. See glossary.

[4179] This reminder seems to have been revealed to former people (verse 3).

[4180] For "torment" here and in verses 26 and 61, see Tawrah, Isaiah 50:11, Injil, Matthew 18:34, 25:41,46, Luke 16:23-28, Revelation 20:15

[4181] Noah. See glossary for more details.

[4182] Aad and Thamud are names of tribes.

## Chapter 38

as did Thamud, Lut's[4184] people, and the owners of the Aika. Those are the parties. (13) Each of them rejected the messengers and my punishment was fulfilled. (14) They wait only for one cry, which will not be delayed. (15) They said, "Our Lord, hasten our sentence before the day of reckoning." (16) Endure [MS] [4185] what they say. Remember our servant[4186] Dawud,[4187] who was mighty.[4188] He was penitent.[4189] (17) We made the mountains subject with him,[4190] to give[4191] praise[FP] in the evening and at sunrise.[4192] (18) The birds were gathered, and each was penitent to him.[4193] (19) We established his kingdom, and gave him wisdom and sound judgment in legal matters. (20) **23B2** Have you[MS] heard the story of the adversaries who climbed over the wall of the sanctuary? (21) They entered in upon Dawud and he was afraid of them. They[MP] said, "Do not be afraid. Two adversaries, one of us wronged the other, so judge truthfully between us and do not be unjust. Guide us on the straight path.[4194] (22) This my brother has ninety-nine ewes, and I have one. He said, "Entrust me with it," and he convinced me by his speech.[4195] (23) He said, "He was unjust to you[MS] in asking for your[MS] ewe, and taking it to his ewes. Many of those who mix things up are unjust to each other, except for believers who do righteous deeds,[4196] and those are rare. Dawud thought that we had tried him, and he asked his Lord for

---

[4183] or tent-pegs. The meaning of this word is something pointed. It is used elsewhere in the Qur'an of mountains (78:7), and since the only "mountains" Pharaoh was around would have been the pyramids, this is probable. "Tent-pegs" makes no sense as an epithet of Pharaoh.

[4184] Lot, nephew of Abraham. See glossary for more details.

[4185] See "endure" in glossary, here and in verse 44.

[4186] For "servant" here and in verses 30,44.45, and 83, see glossary.

[4187] David. See glossary for more details.

[4188] Tawrah, here and in verses 22, 24, 26, and 30. 1 Samuel 16:18

[4189] See Zabur, Psalms 32, 51

[4190] Zabur, Psalms 148:9,13

[4191] The plural used here is for thinking beings. Possibly the intent is to ascribe volition to the mountains in praising Allah.

[4192] Zabur, Psalms 55:17

[4193] Zabur, Psalms 148:10,13

[4194] See glossary for more details, and notes on 3:51, 6:153, 19:36, 36:61, and 43:64 on what the straight path is.

[4195] Tawrah, 2 Samuel 12:1-4

[4196] Here and in verse 28, see Injil, 1 Corinthians 3:8, James 2:14-17, Revelation 19:8.

forgiveness⁴¹⁹⁷ and bowed down in repentance.⁴¹⁹⁸ (24) So we forgave him for it, and he has nearness and a good place of return to us. (25) Dawud, we have made you^MS a regent⁴¹⁹⁹ on earth, so judge⁴²⁰⁰ truthfully among men and do not follow passion,⁴²⁰¹ or it will lead you^MS astray from Allah's path. Those who are led astray from Allah's path will have severe torment on the day of reckoning because of what they forgot.⁴²⁰² (26) We did not create heaven and earth and what is between them in vain.⁴²⁰³ Disbelievers imagine that. Woe to disbelievers concerning hellfire! (27) Should we treat believers who do righteous deeds like those who cause destruction on the earth, or should we treat the reverent like the unrighteous? (28) We revealed a blessed book to you^MS, so they would reflect on his⁴²⁰⁴ signs and so thinkers would remember. (29) We gave Dawud Sulayman,⁴²⁰⁵ who was a wonderful, penitent servant. (30) He was offered swift horses^FS in the evening,⁴²⁰⁶ (31) and said, "I have loved the good things^MS more than remembering my Lord, so they^FS were hidden behind the curtain. (32) Return them to me." He began rubbing their legs and necks. (33) We tried Sulayman and put a body on his chair, then he repented. (34) He said, "Lord, forgive me, and give me a kingdom the likes of which no one after me will have.⁴²⁰⁷ You^MS are the giver."⁴²⁰⁸ (35) We made the wind subject to him, a mild wind blowing wherever he wished at his command, (36) in

---

⁴¹⁹⁷ The belief that all prophets and messengers are sinless is not supported by the Qur'an. For instances of prophets or messengers asking forgiveness or committing sins, see 7:23, 20:121 (Adam), 11:47, 71:28 (Nuh), 26:82, 14:41 (Ibrahim), 28:15-16 (Musa), 7:151, 20:93 (Musa and Harun), 38:24 (Dawud), 38:32,35 (Sulayman), 21:87, 37:142 (Yunus), 48:2, 47:19, 40:55, 4:79,106, 9:43, 13:30, 80:1-2, 110:3, 94:2, 23:118, 66:1, 33:37, 8:67, and 9:117 (Muhammad (s).

⁴¹⁹⁸ Tawrah, 2 Samuel 12:13

⁴¹⁹⁹ See 2:30, where Adam is made a regent. These two are the only ones specifically named as regents.

⁴²⁰⁰ Or rule

⁴²⁰¹ See Tawrah, 2 Samuel 11:2-12:25

⁴²⁰² Or, they will have severe torment for forgetting the day of judgment.

⁴²⁰³ Tawrah, Isaiah 45:18

⁴²⁰⁴ Or its.

⁴²⁰⁵ Solomon here and in verse 34. See glossary for more details.

⁴²⁰⁶ Tawrah, 1 Kings 4:26

⁴²⁰⁷ Tawrah, 1 Kings 3:5-14

⁴²⁰⁸ Injil, Matthew 7:11, James 1:5

## Chapter 38

addition to the devils[4209] – every builder and diver, (37) and others, bound[4210] together with cords. (38) This was our gift, to give bountifully or withhold. (39) He has nearness and a good place of return to us. (40) Remember our servant Ayyub,[4211] who called to his Lord, "Satan touched me with plunder and torment." (41) Run with your[MS] leg. This is a cold place for washing and drinking. (42) We gave him his family,[4212] and others with them as mercy from us and a reminder for thinkers. (43) Take a handful of mixed herbs, travel with it, and do not be false[MS]. We found him enduring, a wonderful servant, and penitent. (44) Remember our servants Ibrahim,[4213] Ishaq,[4214] and Yaqub,[4215] strong visionaries.[4216] (45) We certainly purified[4217] them with a reminder of heaven. (46) They were choice, chosen ones of ours. (47) Remember Ismail,[4218] Alyasa,[4219] and Dhu-Al-Kifl,[4220] each of whom were choice. (48) This is a reminder,[4221] and a good return for the reverent: (49) heavenly gardens[4222] of Eden with open doors to them, (50) reclining in it, calling for much fruit and drink. (51) 23B3 They[MP] will have low-hanging juicy ones.[4223] (52) You[MP] are promised this

---

[4209] Arabic /shayatin/. See glossary for more details.
[4210] On devils being bound, see Injil, Matthew 16:19, 18:18, 12:29, Mark 3:27
[4211] Job, the prophet known for patience. See glossary for more details.
[4212] Tawrah, Job 42:13
[4213] Abraham. See glossary for more details.
[4214] Isaac. See glossary for more details.
[4215] Jacob. See glossary for more details.
[4216] Or, those with hands and sight
[4217] Tawrah, Malachi 3:3, Zabur, Psalms 19:8, 119:9,140, Injil, Acts 15:8,9,1 Peter 2:2, Titus 2:14, Hebrews 1:3
[4218] Ishmael. See glossary for more details.
[4219] Elisha. See glossary for more details.
[4220] Ezekiel. See glossary for more details.
[4221] The prophets in the previous verse seem to be connected with the reminder here.
[4222] Arabic /jannah/. See glossary for more details.
[4223] Most translations translate this verse "modest spouses of similar age." However, the verse has no word for spouse. The word usually translated "modest" also means "low" or "short." Thus, the translation "low-hanging ones." (See 6:99, 76:14, where fruits are said to be hanging low) This is more probable given the context of food and drink (verse 51), and verse 54, which talks about provision [usually of food]. Recent linguistic research on /atrab/ (usually translated "of similar age") suggests the meaning "juicy."

## Chapter 38

for the day of reckoning. (53) This is our provision, and it will never vanish. (54) However, transgressors have an evil return. (55) They will be roasted in hell, an awful dwelling, (56) with boiling water, putridity, (57) and similar things. (58) Here is a group rushing with you[MP]; they will not be welcomed, but roasted in hellfire. (59) They said, "But you[MP] were not welcomed; you[MP] presented it to us, an evil decision[4224]." (60) They said, "Our Lord, who presented this to us? Give him twice[4225] as much torment in hellfire." (61) They said, "What is wrong with us? We do not see men we thought were evildoers. (62) We made fun of them, or has our sight missed them. (63) This is truth. The inhabitants of hellfire fight each other. (64) I am a warner, and the only god[4226] is the one, victorious Allah, (65) Lord of the heavens and the earth and what is between them, the strong[4227] forgiver. (66)

\*\*\*

Say[MS], "It is great news (67) you[MP] turned away from." (68) I had no knowledge of the higher nobility striving. (69) I have been inspired that I am only a clear warner. (70) So your[MS] Lord told the angels, "I am creating a man from clay (71) and when I have formed him and breathed into him of my spirit,[4228] fall down and bow down before him." (72) So all the angels bowed down, (73) except for Iblis,[4229] who was proud and was a disbeliever. (74) He said, "Iblis, what kept you[MS] from bowing[MS] down in front of what I created with my own hands? Were you[MS] proud, or were you[MS] haughty?" (75) He said, "I am better than he is; you[MS] created me from fire, and you[MS] created him from clay." (76) He said, "Go[MS] out of it. You[MS] are damned. (77) You[MS] have my curse until the day of judgment." (78) He said, "My Lord, Give me more time until the day they are resurrected." (79) He said, "You[MS] have more time (80) until the known day and time." (81) He said, "By your[MS] power, I will lead them all astray (82) except for those of them that are your[MS] sincere servants." (83)

---

[4224] Or dwelling
[4225] Tawrah, Isaiah 40:2
[4226] Arabic /ilah/. See glossary for more details.
[4227] Tawrah, Job 9:4, Zabur, Psalms 24:8, Injil, Ephesians 6:10, Revelation 18:8
[4228] Adam (here in 38:72, 32:9, and 15:29) and Isa (21:91 and 66:12) are the only ones into whom Allah breathed his spirit.
[4229] The devil here and in verse 75. See glossary for more details. Injil, Revelation 20:10,14,15

## Chapter 38

\*\*\*

He said, "Truly, truly I say,[4230] (84)

\*\*\*

I will fill hell with you[MS] and with all those of them that follow you[MS]." (85) Say[MS], "I do not ask you[MP] for wages for it. I am not a troublemaker." (86) It is only a reminder to people. (87) You[MS] will certainly know his news later. (88)[4231]

---

[4230] See, e.g. Injil, John 5:24

[4231] The verses in this chapter that rhyme are put together in paragraphs, separated by \*\*\*.

Chapter 39

# Chapter 39 Al-Zumar[4232]

In the name of Allah, the most gracious and merciful.[4233] A revelation of the book from[4234] the Mighty, Wise[4235] Allah. (1) We revealed the book to you<sup>MS</sup> in truth, so worship<sup>MS</sup> Allah in sincere religion. (2) Is pure religion not Allah's?[4236] Those who choose protectors beside him: "We worship them only so that they would bring us near to Allah." Allah will judge among them concerning their differences. Allah does not guide disbelieving liars.[4237] (3) If Allah had wanted to choose a boy, he would have chosen what he willed from what he created.[4238] May he be glorified (above that)! He is the one, conquering[4239] Allah. (4) He created the heavens and the earth in truth,[4240] making the night merge into the day and the day merge into the night.[4241] He subjected the sun and the moon so that each would run for a specified length of time.[4242] Is he not mighty and forgiving?[4243] (5)
\*\*\*

He created you<sup>MP</sup> from one soul,[4244] then made its spouse from it,[4245] and sent down eight pairs of cattle. He creates you<sup>MP</sup> in your<sup>MP</sup> mothers' bellies after a creation in three darknesses.[4246] That is

---

[4232] Droves or crowds
[4233] Zabur, Psalms 103:8, 145:8. See glossary for more details.
[4234] Or, "is from"
[4235] Tawrah, Job 9:4, Proverbs 2:6, Jeremiah 9:23-24, Injil, 1 Corinthians 1:21-25, Romans 16:27
[4236] Or, "Is pure freedom of religion not Allah's" or "Is pure religion not between each person and Allah?"
[4237] Injil, 2 Thessalonians 2:11, Tawrah, 2 Samuel 22:27, 1 Kings 22:20-23, Ezekiel 14:9
[4238] Apparently some people thought that Allah had chosen a human being and made him his son.
[4239] Tawrah, Isaiah 40:10, Zephaniah 3:17-19
[4240] Tawrah, Genesis 1:1
[4241] Zabur, Psalms 139:12
[4242] Zabur, Psalms 104:19
[4243] Here and in verse 53, see Zabur, Psalms 103:3, 130:4, Tawrah, Isaiah 43:25, Exodus 34:7, Injil, Acts 26:18.
[4244] Tawrah, Malachi 2:10
[4245] Tawrah, Genesis 2:22
[4246] Zabur, Psalms 139:13-16

## Chapter 39

Allah, your^MP Lord. The kingdom is his.^4247 He is the only god.^4248 How you^MP turn away! (6)

\*\*\*

If you^MP disbelieve, Allah does not need you^MP,^4249 but he is not pleased with disbelief in his servants.^4250 If you^MP give thanks, this pleases him about you^MP. No bearer can carry another's burden.^4251 Then you^MP will return to your^MP Lord^4252 and he will tell you^MP your^MP deeds. He knows what is in the heart.^4253 (7) **23B4**

\*\*\*

If a person is harmed, he prays to his Lord, and turns to him. Then if he bestows his blessings on him, he forgets what he had prayed beforehand to him, and makes rivals to Allah,^4254 to lead [others] astray from the path. Say^MS, "Enjoy your^MS disbelief for a while; you^MS are going to hellfire,^4255 (8) compared to one who is devout through the night,^4256 bowing down and standing, fearing the hereafter, and hoping for his Lord's mercy.^4257 Say^MS, "Are those who know and those who do not know equal?" Thinkers remember. (9) Say^MS, "Believing servants, fear your^MP Lord. Those who do good deeds in this world will have good, and Allah's land is wide.^4258 Those who endure^4259 will be paid their wages bountifully." (10)

\*\*\*

Say^MS, "I was commanded to worship Allah sincerely in religion, (11) and I was commanded to be the first of those who submit.^4260

---

^4247 Injil, Matthew 13:43
^4248 Arabic /ilah/. See glossary for more details.
^4249 Zabur, Psalms 50:12
^4250 Romans 11:20
^4251 Injil, Galatians 6:5
^4252 Tawrah, Ecclesiastes 12:7
^4253 Tawrah, 1 Samuel 16:7, 1 Chronicles 28:9, Zabur, Psalms 44:21, Injil, Luke 16:15, Romans 8:27, Acts 15:8, 1 John 3:20
^4254 Tawrah, Isaiah 46:9
^4255 Tawrah, Isaiah 50:11
^4256 Zabur, Psalms 88:1
^4257 Zabur, Psalms 33:18
^4258 Injil, Mark 10:30
^4259 See "endure" in glossary
^4260 Injil, James 4:7. For "submit" here and in verses 22 and 54, some translators do not translate this. See glossary for more details.

## Chapter 39

(12) Say[MS], "I fear the torment[4261] of a great day if I disobey my Lord."[4262] (13)

\*\*\*

Say[MS], "I worship Allah sincerely in my religion. (14)

\*\*\*

Worship[MP] whatever you[MP] want besides him." Say[MS], "The clearly lost are those who have lost their souls[4263] and their families on the day of resurrection,[4264] are they not? (15) They have coverings of hellfire above them and coverings below them. Allah thus frightens his servants. "My servants, fear me." (16)

\*\*\*

Those who avoid worshiping false gods[4265] and turn to Allah will have good

news. Give good news to my servants (17) who listen to the saying and follow what is better. Allah has guided them. They are thinkers. (18) Will you[MS] rescue those who deserve the word[4266] about torment from hellfire?[4267] (19) But those who fear their Lord will have rooms with other rooms built above them,[4268] with rivers flowing underneath[4269] as Allah's promise. Allah does not break his promise.[4270] (20) Have you[MS] not seen that Allah sends rain down from the sky,[4271] makes it flow in fountains on the earth, brings forth different kinds[4272] of plants,[4273] and then they

---

[4261] For "torment" here and in verses 19, 24, 26, 40, 47, 54, 55, 58, and 71, see Tawrah, Isaiah 50:11, Injil, Matthew 18:34, 25:41,46, Luke 16:23-28, Revelation 20:15.

[4262] Injil, Hebrews 3:18

[4263] Injil, Matthew 16:26

[4264] Here and in verses 24, 31, 47, and 60, for "day of resurrection," see Tawrah, Daniel 12:2 Injil, Acts 24:15, 1 Corinthians 15:52-54, Revelation 20:11-15.

[4265] Arabic /Al-Taghut/. See glossary for more details.

[4266] The subject is feminine and the verb is masculine. There may be an implied word or a different meaning.

[4267] Tawrah, Proverbs 24:11

[4268] Injil, John 14:2

[4269] Injil, Revelation 22:1-2, Tawrah, Ezekiel 47:12

[4270] Injil, Hebrews 6:17

[4271] Tawrah, Deuteronomy 28:12, Job 5:10, Joel 2:23, Zabur, Psalms 68:9, Injil, Matthew 5:45

[4272] Or colors

[4273] Tawrah, Isaiah 55:10

## Chapter 39

wither.[4274] You[MS] see them turn yellow, and then he makes them stubble.[4275] That is a reminder for thinkers. (21)

\*\*\*

If Allah opens a person's heart to submit, he has light from his Lord. Woe to those whose hearts are hardened[4276] to remembering Allah. They have clearly gone astray. (22)

\*\*\*

Allah has revealed the best story, a similar book that is repeated.[4277] The skin of those who fear their Lord tingles at it, and then their skin and hearts soften to remember Allah. This is Allah's guidance, with which he guides those he wills.[4278] Those Allah leads astray have no guide.[4279] (23)

\*\*\*

Who will beware of the terrible torment on the day of resurrection with his face? The wicked will be told, "Taste what you[MP] deserve." (24) Those before them rejected, and torment came upon them without their realizing it.[4280] (25) Allah will make them taste shame[4281] in this life, and the torment of the hereafter is greater, if they only knew. (26) We have given every kind of proverb to people in this recitation,[4282] so that they may remember, (27) as an Arabic recitation that is not crooked, so that they may beware.[4283] (28) Allah gave a proverb: There was a man owned by partners who disagreed about him, and another man who was captive to one man. Are the two proverbs the same? Praise be to Allah! No, but most of them do not know. (29) You[MS] will be dead and they will be dead. (30) Then on the day of resurrection, you[MP] will dispute before your[MP] Lord. (31) **24A1** Who is more wicked than those who lie about Allah and reject the truth when it comes to them. Is hell not the abode of the disbelievers?[4284] (32) Those that

---

[4274] Tawrah, Isaiah 40:7,8
[4275] Injil, Mathew 6:30
[4276] Tawrah, Exodus 7:13
[4277] Or, "doubled."
[4278] Zabur, Psalms 32:8
[4279] Injil, 2 Thessalonians 2:11, Tawrah, 2 Samuel 22:27, 1 Kings 22:20-23, Ezekiel 14:9
[4280] Injil, 1 Thessalonians 5:3
[4281] Injil, 1 Peter 2:6
[4282] Or Qur'an or qur'an here and in verse 28. See glossary for more details.
[4283] Or, "be reverent."
[4284] Injil, Matthew 25:41

## Chapter 39

bring truth and believe in[4285] it are the reverent. (33) They will have whatever they want from their Lord. That is the reward for those who do good, (34) and so Allah expiates[4286] their worst deeds and rewards them for their best deeds.[4287] (35)
\*\*\*

Is Allah not adequate for his servant? They make you[MS] afraid of other gods besides him. Those Allah leads astray have no one to guide them.[4288] (36) Those Allah guides have no one to lead them astray. Is Allah not mighty and avenging?[4289] (37)
\*\*\*

If you[MS] ask them who created the heavens and the earth,[4290] they will say, "Allah." Say[MS], "What do you[MP] think? If Allah wants to harm me, can those you[MP] pray to besides Allah protect from his harm?[4291] Or if he wants to show mercy to me, can they hold back his mercy?" Say[MS], "Allah is enough for me. Let those who trust, trust in him."[4292] (38) Say[MS], "My people, work according to your[MP] abilities.[4293] I am working. You[MP] will know." (39) Those who receive torment will be shamed, and permanent torment will come upon them. (40)
\*\*\*

We have truly revealed the book to you[MS] for people. Those who are guided will benefit their souls, and those who go astray will lead their own souls astray. You[MS] are not responsible for them.[4294] (41)
\*\*\*

Allah causes people[4295] to die at their time of death, and those who have not died, during their sleep. Allah holds those decreed for death, and sends forth the others for a specific lifespan.[4296] Those

---

[4285] Or, "confirm."
[4286] Tawrah, Isaiah 27:9, Injil, Romans 3:25, Hebrews 2:17, 1 John 2:2, 4:10
[4287] Injil, 1 Corinthians 3:12-15
[4288] Injil, 2 Thesalonians 2:11
[4289] Tawrah, Deuteronomy 32:35, Ezekiel 25:17, Injil, Romans 12:19, Hebrews 10:30
[4290] Tawrah, Genesis 1:1
[4291] Zabur, Psalms 115:4-8
[4292] Tawrah, Proverbs 3:5,6, Zabur, Psalms 37:5, 62:8
[4293] Or positions
[4294] Tawrah, Ezekiel 2:5
[4295] Injil, 1 Peter 4:19, Luke 23:46
[4296] Zabur, Psalms 139:16

## Chapter 39

are signs for people who consider. (42) Have they chosen intercessors besides Allah?[4297] Say[MS], "Even if they cannot do anything, and do not comprehend?"[4298] (43) Say[MS], "All intercession is Allah's. The kingdom of the heavens and the earth is his.[4299] Then you[MP] will be returned to him." (44) If Allah alone is mentioned, the hearts of those that do not believe in the hereafter are horrified. If those gods besides him are mentioned, they rejoice. (45) Say[MS], "Allah, creator of the heavens and the earth, knower of the unseen[4300] and the seen, you[MS] judge between your[MS] servants[4301] concerning their differences. (46) If the wicked had everything in the earth twice over, they would offer it as ransom for themselves[4302] from the awful torment of the day of resurrection. What they had not taken into account will appear to them from Allah. (47)The bad deeds they did will appear to them, and what they made fun of will surround them. (48) If harm comes to a person, he prays to us. Then when we give him our blessings, he says, "I was given this knowingly." Rather, it is a test, though most of them do not know. (49) This is what those before them said. What they deserved[4303] did not help them. (50) They were afflicted by the bad deeds they did. The wicked among them will also be afflicted by the bad deeds they did, and they will not be able to stop it. (51) Do they not know that Allah stretches forth or withholds provision for those he wills?[4304] Those are signs for people who believe. (52) 24A2 Say[MS], "My servants who have been wasteful against their souls, do not despair of Allah's mercy! Allah forgives all sins.[4305] He is forgiving and merciful.[4306] (53) Turn to your[MP] Lord and submit to him before torment comes upon you[MP] and you[MP] cannot be saved. (54) Follow[MP] the best of your[MP] Lord's revelation to you[MP] before torment suddenly comes upon you[MP] without you[MP] realizing it,[4307] (55) lest a soul say, "Woe is me

---

[4297] Injil, 1 Timothy 2:5
[4298] Zabur, Psalms 115:6-8
[4299] Tawrah, Isaiah 45:12, Zabur, Psalms 24:1, 89:11, Injil, Hebrews 1:10
[4300] Injil, 2 Corinthians 4:18
[4301] Tawrah, Genesis 18:25
[4302] Zabur, Psalms 49:7,8
[4303] Or earned
[4304] Zabur, Psalms 11:5, 84:11
[4305] Injil, Mark 3:28
[4306] See glossary for more details on "merciful."
[4307] Injil, 1 Thessalonians 5:3

for the duties I have neglected toward Allah. I mocked," (56) or say, "If Allah had guided me, I would have been reverent," (57) or say, when seeing torment, "If I could return, I would do good."[4308] (58) Rather, my signs[4309] came to you[MS], you[MS] rejected them, and were proud and disbelieving." (59) On the day of resurrection, you[MS] will see the blackened[4310] faces of those who lied about Allah. Is hell not the abode of the proud? (60) Allah rescues the reverent in their place of refuge. No evil will touch them, nor will they grieve.[4311] (61) Allah is the creator of everything and he is responsible for everything.[4312] (62)

\*\*\*

He has the keys of the heavens and the earth.[4313] Disbelievers in Allah's signs will be lost. (63) Say[MS], "You[MP] ignorant, do you[MP] command me to worship other than Allah?" (64) You[MS] and those before you[MS] were inspired, "If you[MS] worship other gods, your[MS] work will be in vain, and you[MS] will be lost." (65) Worship Allah, and give thanks.[4314] (66) They did not make a right estimation of Allah. All the earth is just a handful to him,[4315] and he will roll up the heavens in his right hand.[4316] May he be glorified and exalted[4317] above the gods they worship! (67) The trumpet will be blown,[4318] and those in the heavens and on the earth will be stunned and they will stand looking.[4319] (68) The light of the Lord of the earth will rise upon it,[4320] and a book will be placed,[4321] and prophets and witnesses will be brought. They will be judged justly, and they will not be wronged. (69) Every soul will be paid back for its deeds.[4322] He knows well what they did. (70) Disbelievers

---

[4308] Injil, Luke 16:24
[4309] Arabic /ayat/ here and in verse 63. See glossary for more details.
[4310] Or, "embarrassed" or "shamed."
[4311] Injil, Revelation 21:4
[4312] Zabur, Psalms 103:19
[4313] Injil, Matthew 16:19
[4314] Zabur, Psalms 136:1
[4315] Tawrah, Isaiah 40:12
[4316] Injil, Hebrews 1:12
[4317] Zabur, Psalms 47:9, 40:16
[4318] Injil, 1 Thessalonians 4:16
[4319] Injil, Luke 21:27-28
[4320] Tawrah, Isaiah 60:1, 9:2, Injil, Revelation 21:23, 22:5
[4321] Tawrah, Daniel 7:10, Injil, Revelation 20:12
[4322] Injil, Revelation 22:12

will be taken to hell in droves,[4323] and when they get there, its doors will be opened. Its keepers will say to them, "Did messengers from among yourselves[MP] not come to you[MP] reciting your[MP] Lord's signs to you[MP] and warning you[MP] of the appointment of this day of yours[MP]? They will say, "Yes, but the word of torment is fulfilled upon the disbelievers." (71) It will be said, "Enter[MP] the doors of hell, and remain there forever.[4324] It is an awful abode for the proud." (72) Those who feared their Lord will be taken to the heavenly garden[4325] in droves, and when they get there, and the doors are opened, its keepers will say to them, "Peace to you[MP]. You[MP] have done well, so enter[MP] it and remain[MP] forever."[4326] (73) They will say, "Praise be to Allah, who kept his promise and gave us the earth as an inheritance.[4327] We will dwell in the heavenly garden wherever we want. How sweet is the reward of those who work." (74) You[MS] will see the angels surrounding the throne worshiping and praising their Lord.[4328] They will be judged justly, and it will be said, "Praise be to Allah, the Lord of the universe."[4329] (75)[4330]

---

[4323] Injil, Matthew 7:13,14
[4324] Injil, Matthew 25:46
[4325] Arabic /jannah/ here and in verse 74. See glossary for more details.
[4326] Injil, 2 Peter 1:11
[4327] Injil, Matthew 5:5
[4328] Injil, Revelation 4:4-8, 5:11-12
[4329] Injil, Revelation 4:11, 5:12
[4330] The verses in this chapter that rhyme are put together in paragraphs, separated by ***.

## Chapter 40 Al-Ghafir[4331] or Al-Mu'min[4332]

**24A3** In the name of Allah, the most gracious and merciful.[4333] HM.[4334] (1) The revelation of the book from the mighty, all-knowing[4335] one, (2)

\*\*\*

the forgiver of sin,[4336] accepter of repentance,[4337] severe in punishment,[4338] powerful.[4339] He is the only god,[4340] and he is [man's] destiny.[4341] (3)

\*\*\*

Only disbelievers argue about Allah's signs. Do not let their turning around in the lands deceive you[ms]. (4) Before them, Nuh's[4342] people[4343] rejected, as well as the parties after them, and every nation plotted to seize their messenger. They argued with vain arguments[4344] to weaken the truth with them, and I seized them. What a punishment it was! (5) Thus the word of your[ms] Lord will be fulfilled against the disbelievers, when they go to hellfire. (6)

\*\*\*

---

[4331] Forgiver
[4332] Believer or faithful
[4333] Zabur, Psalms 103:8, 145:8. See glossary for more details.
[4334] Here and at the beginning of many chapters there are unvowelled letters of unknown meaning. Numerous theories have been proposed, but there is no agreement on the subject.
[4335] Tawrah, Job 37:16, Isaiah 40:14, Zabur, Psalms 33:13-15, Injil, 1 John 3:20
[4336] Tawrah, Exodus 34:7
[4337] Injil, Acts 26:20, Jonah 3:10
[4338] Here and in verse 22, see Tawrah, Ezekiel 25:17, Injil, Matthew 8:12, 13:42,50, 22:13, 24:51, 25:30, Mark 9:48, Luke 13:28, 19:27.
[4339] Or "rich"
[4340] Arabic /ilah/. See glossary for more details.
[4341] Injil, 2 Corinthians 5:10
[4342] Noah. See glossary for more details.
[4343] Tawrah, Genesis 6:5
[4344] Injil, 1 Timothy 1:6

## Chapter 40

Those who carry the throne and those around it worship and praise their Lord.[4345] They believe in him and ask his forgiveness for the believers: "Our Lord, you[MS] have made your[MS] mercy and knowledge reach everything;[4346] forgive those who repent and follow your[MS] path, and protect them from the torment[4347] of the blazing fire. (7) Our Lord, cause them to enter heavenly gardens[4348] of Eden,[4349] as you[MS] have promised them, their righteous ancestors, their spouses and their seed. You[MS] are Mighty and Wise.[4350] (8) Protect them from bad deeds.[4351] You[MS] will have mercy on that day towards those you[MS] protect from bad deeds. That is the great triumph." (9) Disbelievers will be told, "Allah's hates [you] more than you[MP] hate yourselves[MP], since you[MP] are called to faith, and yet you[MP] disbelieve." (10)

\*\*\*

They will say, "Our Lord, you[MS] have made us die twice[4352] and live twice,[4353] so we confessed our sins. Will we go forth by the path?" (11)

\*\*\*

That is because when Allah alone was prayed to, you[MP] disbelieved, and when other gods are worshiped, you[MP] believe in them. Judgment belongs to Allah, the most high and great. (12)

\*\*\*

He shows you[MP] his signs and sends provision for you[MP] from heaven.[4354] Only those who turn to him remember. (13)

\*\*\*

Pray to Allah in sincere religion, even if the disbelievers hate it. (14)

\*\*\*

---

[4345] Injil, Revelation 4:4-8
[4346] Zabur, Psalms 145:9
[4347] For "torment" here and in verse 49, see Tawrah, Isaiah 50:11, Injil, Matthew 18:34, 25:41,46, Luke 16:23-28, Revelation 20:15.
[4348] Arabic /jannah/. See glossary for more details.
[4349] Eden. Tawrah, Genesis 2:8
[4350] Tawrah, Job 9:4, Proverbs 2:6, Jeremiah 9:23-24, Injil, 1 Corinthians 1:21-25, Romans 16:27
[4351] Injil, 1 Corinthians 10:13
[4352] Here and later in the verse, another possible translation is "as two." Injil, Revelation 2:11 for the former meaning, and Injil, 1 Corinthians 7:34 for the latter.
[4353] Injil, John 3:3,5
[4354] Zabur, Psalms 78:20

## Chapter 40

He who is high in station and owner of the throne[4355] casts forth the spirit[4356] from his command on whom of his servants he wills, so he[4357] can warn of the day of meeting. (15) The day they will be plainly seen. Nothing about them will be hidden from Allah. Who has the kingdom today? The one, victorious Allah.[4358] (16) Today every soul will be repaid as it deserves.[4359] There will be no injustice today. Allah is swift in reckoning.[4360] (17) Warn them of the day that is imminent, when they will choke on their hearts in their throats. The wicked will have no friend or intercessor that will be listened to. (18)

\*\*\*

He knows those with treacherous eyes, and knows what their hearts conceal.[4361] (19) Allah judges justly.[4362] Those they pray to besides him do not judge anything. Allah hears all and sees all. (20) 24A4

\*\*\*

Have they not walked through the land and seen what was the end of those before them? They were stronger and left greater ruins behind them in the land, but Allah seized them for their sins, and no one could protect them from Allah. (21) That was because their messengers had come to them with miracles, and they disbelieved, so Allah seized them. He is strong[4363] and severe in punishment. (22)

\*\*\*

We sent Musa[4364] with our signs and clear authority (23)

\*\*\*

---

[4355] Injil, Revelation 4:2

[4356] Injil, John 16:7-11

[4357] If multiple persons were intended, this verb would have been in the plural. It is unclear who is referred to. Isa is the only one who is said to be aided by the Holy Spirit (2:87,253, 5:110), so this could be a reference to him. The other options would be the spirit or Allah himself as the warner.

[4358] Tawrah, 1 Chronicles 29:11

[4359] Injil, Luke 14:14

[4360] Tawrah, Isaiah 19:1, Malachi 3:5, Zabur, Psalms 147:15, Injil, 2 Peter 2:1, Revelation 22:12

[4361] Zabur, Psalms 44:21

[4362] Zabur, Psalms 9:4

[4363] Tawrah, Job 9:4, Zabur, Psalms 24:8, Injil, Ephesians 6:10, Revelation 18:8

[4364] Moses here and in verses 26 and 27. See glossary for more details.

## Chapter 40

to Pharaoh, Haman,[4365] and Korah,[4356] and they said, "A lying magician." (24) When he came to them with truth from us, they said, "Kill the sons of those who believe along with him, and keep their women alive.[4367] The disbelievers' plot went astray. (25) Pharaoh said, "Let me kill Musa.[4368] Let him pray to his Lord. I fear that he will replace your[MP] religion, or cause destruction on the land." (26) Musa said, "I take refuge in my Lord and your[MP] Lord from every proud person who does not believe in the day of reckoning."[4369] (27) A believing man from Pharaoh's household, who hid his faith,[4370] said, "Will you[MP] kill a man who says: My Lord is Allah, when he has come to you[MP] with your[MP] Lord's miracles? If he is a liar, then he is responsible for his lie. But if he is truthful, you[MP] will be afflicted with some of what he promises you[MP].[4371] Allah does not guide those who are wasteful liars. (28) My people, you[MP] are conspicuous in having the kingdom today on the earth. But who can save us from Allah's vengeance if it comes upon us?" Pharaoh said, "I show you[MP] only what I see, and I guide you[MP] only on the right path." (29) The believer said, "My people, I fear for you[MP] just as on the day of the parties, (30) like what happened to the people of Nuh,[4372] Aad,[4373] Thamud, and those after them. Allah does not want injustice for the servants. (31) My people, I fear for you[MP] regarding a day of mutual calling,[4374] (32) a day when you[MP] will turn back. You[MP] will have no protector from Allah. Those Allah leads astray have no guide.[4375] (33) Yusuf[4376]

---

[4365] Tawrah, Esther 3-9 mentions a man named Haman, but it might be a different person, as that Haman lived about 1000 years after Musa.
[4366] Tawrah, Numbers 16:3,32,41
[4367] Tawrah, Exodus 1:22
[4368] Tawrah, Exodus 2:15
[4369] Injil, Jude 1:6
[4370] Injil, John 19:38
[4371] Injil, Acts 5:38-39
[4372] Noah. See glossary for more details.
[4373] Aad and Thamud were tribes before the time of Musa.
[4374] There are a number of different translations of this word besides "mutual calling," including "summoning," "mutual calling between people of hell and paradise," "mutual calling and wailing," "wailing," "mutual blaming," "the summons," "calling out," and "you will cry out to one another." The Arabic is a single word, literally meaning mutual calling.
[4375] Injil, 2 Thessalonians 2:11, Tawrah, 2 Samuel 22:27, 1 Kings 22:20-23, Ezekiel 14:9

## Chapter 40

brought you[MP] miracles beforehand, and you[MP] still doubted about what he brought. When he died, you[MP] said, Allah will not send a messenger after him. This is how Allah leads astray wasteful doubters (34) who argue about Allah's signs without having been given authority. That is hateful to Allah and to believers. Thus Allah seals every proud, perverse heart."[4377] (35) Pharaoh said, "Haman, build me a tower[4378] so that I can reach the ropes, (36) the ropes of the heavens, and take a look at Musa's[4379] god.[4380] I think he is a liar." Thus Pharaoh's bad deeds were made to seem[4381] fair to him, and he was blocked from the path. Pharaoh's plot was a loss. (37) The believer said, "My people, follow[MP] me and I will guide you[MP] on the right path. (38) My people, this life is transient enjoyment,[4382] but the hereafter is the place of permanent stability.[4383] (39) Those who do bad deeds will only be punished for its equivalent, but those believers who do righteous deeds,[4384] male or female, will enter the heavenly garden,[4385] where they will be provided for bountifully." (40) 24B1 My people, what's wrong with me that I call you[MP] to rescue[4386] while you[MP] call me to hellfire? (41) You[MP] call me to disbelieve in Allah and worship other gods I know nothing about. I call you[MP] to the mighty forgiver. (42) No doubt you[MP] call me to what cannot be called in this world or the hereafter. Our return is to Allah. The wasteful are going to hellfire. (43) You[MP] will remember what I tell you[MP]. I commit my matter to Allah. Allah sees [his] servants. (44) Allah protected him from the bad deeds of what they plotted, and Pharaoh's family was surrounded by the worst torment.[4387] (45) They will be shown hellfire morning and evening, and on the day that the hour occurs, "Make Pharaoh's family enter the severest

---

[4376] Joseph (son of Jacob). See glossary for more details.
[4377] Tawrah, Exodus 9:12
[4378] Tawrah, Esther 5:14, Genesis 11:4
[4379] Moses. See glossary for more details.
[4380] Arabic /ilah/. See glossary for more details.
[4381] See for example Tawrah, Exodus 7:14
[4382] Injil, 1 John 2:17
[4383] Injil, Hebrews 12:28
[4384] Injil, 1 Corinthians 3:8, James 2:14-17, Revelation 19:8
[4385] Arabic /jannah/. See glossary for more details.
[4386] Tawrah, Proverbs 24:11
[4387] Tawrah, Exodus 7-14

## Chapter 40

torment." (46) When they argue in hellfire, the weak[4388] will say to the proud, "We followed you[MP]. Will you[MP] take for us a portion of the fire?" (47) The proud will say, "We are all in it. Allah has judged among his servants." (48) Those in hellfire will say to the keepers of hell, "Ask your[MP] Lord to lighten our torment for a day."[4389] (49) They will say, "Did your[MP] messengers not come to you[MP] with miracles?" They will say, "Yes." They will say, "Then pray[MP].[4390] The prayer[4391] of disbelievers is only astray." (50) We will save our messengers and the believers in this world and on the day when the witnesses stand up. (51) On that day, the excuses of the wicked will not help them. They will be damned[4392] and will go to the worst abode. (52) We gave Musa[4393] guidance and gave the book[4394] as an inheritance to the people of Israel, (53) guidance,[4395] and a reminder[4396] to thinkers. (54) So endure[MS],[4397] for Allah's promise is true.[4398] Ask[MS] forgiveness[4399] for your[MS] sin,[4400] and worship[MS] and praise[MS] your[MS] Lord, evening and morning.[4401] (55)

\*\*\*

---

[4388] Here and in 14:21, this word has a different spelling than in 2:266 and 9:91. Some say the reason is that this one refers to those who are weak in the hereafter.

[4389] Injil, Luke 16:24

[4390] Or, "call out."

[4391] Or, "call." Of the 14 times in the Qur'an this word is mentioned, this is the only one with a different spelling. Some believe this is because the reference here is to the hereafter.

[4392] Injil, Matthew 25:41

[4393] Moses. See glossary for more details.

[4394] Tawrah, Exodus 31:18

[4395] Tawrah, Proverbs 1:2-6

[4396] Tawrah, Deuteronomy 8:2

[4397] See "endure" in glossary, here and in verse 77.

[4398] Injil, James 5:8

[4399] The belief that all prophets and messengers are sinless is not supported by the Qur'an. For instances of prophets or messengers asking forgiveness or committing sins, see 7:23, 20:121 (Adam), 11:47, 71:28 (Nuh), 26:82, 14:41 (Ibrahim), 28:15-16 (Musa), 7:151, 20:93 (Musa and Harun), 38:24 (Dawud), 38:32,35 (Sulayman), 21:87, 37:142 (Yunus), 48:2, 47:19, 40:55, 4:79,106, 9:43, 13:30, 80:1-2, 110:3, 94:2, 23:118, 66:1, 33:37, 8:67, and 9:117 (Muhammad (ṣ)).

[4400] Injil, Romans 3:23, Tawrah, Ecclesiastes 7:20

[4401] Zabur, Psalms 55:17

Chapter 40

Those who argue about Allah's signs without having been given authority are proud at heart.[4402] They will not reach it. So take refuge in Allah. He hears all and sees all. (56)

\*\*\*

The creation of the heavens and the earth[4403] was greater than the creation of people,[4404] but most people do not know. (57) The blind and the sighted are not alike, nor are believers who do righteous deeds[4405] and those who do bad deeds. You[MP] reflect very little. (58) The hour is undoubtedly coming,[4406] but most people do not believe. (59) Your[MP] Lord said, "Call[MP] to me and I will answer you[MP].[4407] Those who are too proud to worship me will go to hell in humiliation." (60) Allah has given you[MP] the night to rest in, and the day to see in. Allah is gracious to people, but most people do not give thanks. (61) That is Allah, your[MP] Lord, creator of everything.[4408] He is the only god.[4409] How you[MP] lie! (62) Those who denied our signs[4410] lied similarly. (63) Allah has given the earth to you[MP] for stability, and the sky as a building. He formed you[MP] perfectly,[4411] and provided good things for you[MP].[4412] That is Allah, your[MP] Lord. Blessed be Allah, the Lord of the universe.[4413] (64) He is the living one,[4414] and he is the only god. Pray to him in sincere religion. Praise be to Allah, the Lord of the universe. (65)

**24B2** Say[MS], "I am forbidden to worship the gods you[MP] pray to besides Allah, since miracles from my Lord came[4415] to me and I was commanded to submit[4416] to the Lord of the universe. (66) He

---

[4402] Injil, 2 Timothy 2:23
[4403] Tawrah, Genesis 1:1-25
[4404] Tawrah, Genesis 1:26-2:22
[4405] Injil, 1 Corinthians 3:8, James 2:14-17, Revelation 19:8
[4406] Injil, John 5:25
[4407] Tawrah, Jeremiah 33:3
[4408] Injil, Revelation 4:11
[4409] Arabic /ilah/ here and in verse 65. See glossary for more details.
[4410] Arabic /ayat/. See glossary for more details.
[4411] Tawrah, Genesis 2:7,8.22, Zabur, Psalms 139:13-16
[4412] Zabur, Psalms 145:15
[4413] Injil, Acts 10:36
[4414] Injil, Revelation 1:18
[4415] "Miracles" is feminine and "came" is masculine. There may be another meaning.
[4416] Injil, James 4:7. For "submit," some translators do not translate this. See glossary for more details.

## Chapter 40

created you⁽ᴹᴾ⁾ from soil,[4417] then from a drop of sperm,[4418] then from a blood clot,[4419] then he brings you⁽ᴹᴾ⁾ forth as children, then you⁽ᴹᴾ⁾ grow up, and then you⁽ᴹᴾ⁾ grow old. Some of you⁽ᴹᴾ⁾ die before that, but you⁽ᴹᴾ⁾ will reach the specified life span,[4420] so that you⁽ᴹᴾ⁾ may comprehend. (67) He gives life and causes death.[4421] If he decrees a matter, he merely tells it, "Be," and it is.[4422] (68) Have you⁽ᴹˢ⁾ not seen how those who argue about Allah's signs turn away? (69) Those who rejected the book and what we sent our messengers with[4423] will know, (70) when with chains and shackles around their necks, they are dragged (71) through boiling water, and then burned in hellfire. (72) Then they will be asked, "Where are the gods you⁽ᴹᴾ⁾ used to worship (73) besides Allah?" They will say, "They have gone astray from us. We did not pray to anything beforehand." This is how Allah leads disbelievers astray.[4424] (74) That is for your⁽ᴹᴾ⁾ unrighteous exulting and insolence on the earth. (75) Enter⁽ᴹᴾ⁾ the doors of hell and remain there forever. It is an awful abode for the proud.[4425] (76) So endure. Allah's promise is true. Either we will show you⁽ᴹˢ⁾ some of what we promise them, or we will make you⁽ᴹˢ⁾ die, and you⁽ᴹᴾ⁾ will be returned to us. (77) We sent messengers before you⁽ᴹˢ⁾. Some of them we have told you⁽ᴹˢ⁾ about, and some we have not told you⁽ᴹˢ⁾ about. Whenever a messenger brought a sign, it was with Allah's permission. When Allah's command comes, it will be done in truth. The vain are lost. (78) Allah gave you⁽ᴹᴾ⁾ cattle.[4426] Some you⁽ᴹᴾ⁾ ride and some you⁽ᴹᴾ⁾ eat. (79) You⁽ᴹᴾ⁾ benefit from them, and you⁽ᴹᴾ⁾ can meet a need of your⁽ᴹᴾ⁾ hearts. You⁽ᴹᴾ⁾ can be carried on them and on ships. (80) He shows you⁽ᴹᴾ⁾ his signs. Which of his signs do you⁽ᴹᴾ⁾ deny? (81) Have they not walked in the land and seen what was the end of those before them? They were more numerous, stronger, and left behind them greater ruins in the land,

---

[4417] Tawrah, Genesis 2:7
[4418] Tawrah, Leviticus 15:18
[4419] Zabur, Psalms 139:13,16
[4420] Zabur, Psalms 90:10
[4421] Tawrah, 1 Samuel 2:6, Deuteronomy 32:39
[4422] Tawrah, Genesis 1:3
[4423] This refers to the former books Allah gave his messengers.
[4424] Injil, 2 Thessalonians 2:11, Tawrah, 2 Samuel 22:27, 1 Kings 22:20-23, Ezekiel 14:9
[4425] Injil, 2 Peter 2:4
[4426] Tawrah, Genesis 1:24-26

but what they had done did not help them. (82) When our messengers brought them miracles, they rejoiced with the knowledge they had, but then they were surrounded by what they had made fun of. (83) When they saw our revenge, they said, "We believe in Allah alone, and we disbelieve in the gods we worshiped." (84) Their faith did not benefit them when they saw our revenge, as was Allah's custom in the past with his servants.[4427] Those disbelievers were lost. (85)[4428]

---

[4427] Injil, Hebrews 9:27
[4428] The verses in this chapter that rhyme are put together in paragraphs, separated by ***.

# Chapter 41 Fussilat[4429], Ha Mim[4430], or Ha Mim Sajda[4431]

In the name of Allah, the most gracious and merciful.[4432] HM.[4433] (1) The revelation of the most gracious and merciful. (2) A book whose verses are explained, an Arabic recitation[4434] for people who know, (3) bearing good news and warning. Most of them turned away and do not listen. (4) They said, "Our hearts are veiled[4435] from what you^MP call us to, and our ears are deaf.[4436] There is a curtain between us and you^MS,[4437] so work. We are working." (5) Say^MS, "I am only a man like you^MP who is inspired. Your^MP god[4438] is one god, so be upright with him, and ask his forgiveness. Woe to worshipers of other gods, (6) who do not pay the poor-tax, and who do not believe in the hereafter. (7) Believers who do righteous deeds[4439] will have an undiminished reward.[4440]

(8) **24B3** Say^MS, "Do you^MP disbelieve in him who created the earth[4441] in two days,[4442] and make rival gods for him? He is the Lord of the universe,[4443] (9) and he made mountains above it,[4444]

---

[4429] It (feminine) was explained

[4430] HM – see verse 1

[4431] HM prostration

[4432] Zabur, Psalms 103:8, 145:8 here and in verse 2. See glossary for more details.

[4433] Here and at the beginning of many chapters there are unvowelled letters of unknown meaning. Numerous theories have been proposed, but there is no agreement on the subject.

[4434] Or Qur'an or qur'an here and in verses 26 and 44. See glossary for more details.

[4435] Injil, 2 Corinthians 4:3,4

[4436] Tawrah, Micah 7:16

[4437] Injil, 2 Corinthians 3:15,16

[4438] Arabic /ilah/ twice in this verse. See glossary for more details.

[4439] Injil, 1 Corinthians 3:8, James 2:14-17, Revelation 19:8

[4440] Injil, 2 John 8

[4441] Tawrah, Genesis 1:9,10

[4442] 50:38 says the earth, heavens and what is between them were created in six days. Possibly the focus is on the specific days Allah created the earth only.

[4443] Tawrah, Genesis 24:3

[4444] Tawrah, Proverbs 8:25-27

## Chapter 41

blessed it, and determined its nourishment in four days,[4445] equally to those who ask him. (10) Then he sat down in heaven,[4446] when it was smoke. He told it and to the earth, "Come[D] willingly[4447] or unwillingly." They[FD] said, "We come willingly." (11) He made them seven heavens in two days and inspired each heaven with its command. We decorated the lowest heaven with lamps[4448] and guarded it. The mighty, all-knowing[4449] one decreed that. (12)

\*\*\*

If they turn away, say[MS], "I warned you[MP] of a thunderbolt like the thunderbolt of Aad[4450] and Thamud. (13)

\*\*\*

When messengers came in front of them and behind them, "Worship only Allah," they said, "If our Lord had willed, he would have sent down angels. We disbelieve in your[MP] message." (14) Aad were unjustifiably proud in the land, and said, "Who is stronger than we are?" Have they not seen that Allah, who created them, is stronger than they are?"[4451] They denied our signs.[4452] (15) We sent a furious wind on unlucky days, to make them taste shameful torment[4453] in this world. The torment[4454] of the hereafter is more shameful, and they will not be saved. (16) As for Thamud, we guided them, but they preferred blindness to guidance, and a thunderbolt of contemptible torment seized them as they deserved, (17) while we rescued reverent believers.[4455] (18) On that day, Allah's enemies will be gathered[4456] and marched into hellfire.

---

[4445] The two days in verse 9, the four days here, and the two days in verse 12 add up to eight days, whereas 50:38 mentions six days. Possibly some of the days overlap.

[4446] Tawrah, Genesis 2:2,3

[4447] Or "obediently"

[4448] Tawrah, Genesis 1:16

[4449] Tawrah, Job 37:16, Isaiah 40:14, Zabur, Psalms 33:13-15, Injil, 1 John 3:20

[4450] Here and in verses 15 and 17, Aad and Thamud were names of tribes.

[4451] Zabur, Psalms 93:4

[4452] Arabic /ayat/ here and in verses 28 and 40. See glossary for more details.

[4453] Injil, Revelation 9:5-6

[4454] For "torment" here and in verses 27 and 50, see Tawrah, Isaiah 50:11, Injil, Matthew 18:34, 25:41,46, Luke 16:23-28, Revelation 20:15.

[4455] Injil, 2 Peter 2:6,7

[4456] Tawrah, Joel 3:11-14, Zephaniah 3:8, Injil, Matthew 25:32, John 15:6, Revelation 16:16

## Chapter 41

(19) So when they come to it, their hearing, their sight, and their skin will witness against them for their deeds. (20) They will say to their skins, "Why did you^MP witness against us?" They will say, "Allah gave us speech, just as he gave speech to everything.[4457] He created you^MP at the beginning, and you^MP will be returned to him. (21) You^MP will not be hidden from your^MP hearing, your^MP sight, and your^MP skin witnessing against you^MP. You^MP imagined that Allah does not know much about your^MP deeds.[4458] (22) The thought you^MP imagined about your^MP Lord will destroy you^MP, and you^MP will be lost." (23) If they continue, hellfire is their abode. If they beg for favor, they will not get it. (24) 24B4 We destined companions[4459] for them, and they made what was in front of them and behind them[4460] seem fair to them. The saying against those of the nations of men and jinns[4461] that passed away before them was fulfilled on them. They were lost. (25) The disbelievers said, "Do not listen to this recitation but use vain words about it, so that you^MP may be victorious." (26) We will make the disbelievers taste severe torment and repay them for the worst of what they did. (27) The penalty for Allah's enemies is hellfire.[4462] They will remain there forever as a punishment for denying our signs. (28) The disbelievers said, "Our Lord, show us the jinns or people that^D led^D us astray. We will put them^D under our feet, so that they^D will be the lowest." (29) The angels come down upon those who say, "Our Lord is Allah," and then are upright. "Do not fear and do not grieve. We give you^MP good news of the heavenly garden[4463] which you^MP were promised.[4464] (30) We are your^MP helpers in this world and the hereafter. You^MP will have whatever your^MP souls desire there. You^MP will have whatever you^MP want, (31) dwellings as a gift from a forgiving,[4465] merciful[4466] one." (32) Who is better in

---

[4457] Or possibly, "Allah spoke us into existence, just as he did everything else."
[4458] Zabur, Psalms 44:21
[4459] These companions referred to may be demons.
[4460] Or their present and past
[4461] Or demons here and in verse 29. See glossary for more details.
[4462] Injil, Jude 7
[4463] Arabic /jannah/. See glossary for more details.
[4464] Injil, Revelation 2:7
[4465] Zabur, Psalms 103:3, 130:4, Tawrah, Isaiah 43:25, Exodus 34:7, Injil, Acts 26:18.
[4466] See glossary for more details on "merciful."

## Chapter 41

speech than one who prays to Allah, does righteous deeds, and says, "I am submitted."[4467] (33) A good deed is not equal to a bad deed. Drive[MS] away with what is best,[4468] and your[MS] enemy will be like a close friend.[4469] (34) Only those who endure[4470] will be granted it.[4471] Only those with great fortune will be granted it.[4472] (35) When Satan incites you[MS] with an evil suggestion, seek protection in Allah.[4473] He hears all and knows all. (36) Among his signs are night, day, the sun and the moon.[4474] Do not bow[MP] down to the sun, or the moon.[4475] Bow down to Allah, who created them,[4476] if you[MP] worship him. (37) If they are proud, those with your[MS] Lord worship him night and day, and do not grow weary.[4477] (38)
\*\*\*

Among his signs are that you[MS] see the lowliness of the earth. If we send rain[4478] down on it, it shakes and grows. He who revives it is reviver of the dead.[4479] He can do anything.[4480] (39) Those who act profanely toward our signs[4481] are not hidden from us. Is someone who is thrown into hellfire better, then, or someone who comes

---

[4467] Injil, James 4:7. For "submitted," some translators do not translate this. See glossary for more details.

[4468] The object is not stated, but it is often understood to mean, drive away bad deeds with good deeds. For this meaning, see Injil, Romans 12:21

[4469] Tawrah, Proverbs 16:7

[4470] See "endure" in glossary

[4471] Injil, Mathew 24:13

[4472] Injil, Matthew 24:40-41

[4473] Injil, 2 Corinthians 10:5

[4474] Tawrah, Genesis 1:5,14-18

[4475] Tawrah, Deuteronomy 17:3

[4476] The word "them" is feminine plural, whereas grammatically, it would be dual masculine (assuming it referred to the sun and the moon), feminine singular (if it referred to the sun, moon, day and night), or masculine plural or dual (if human characteristics were assigned to them). Another meaning is possible.

[4477] Injil, Galatians 6:9,10, Tawrah, Isaiah 40:28-31

[4478] Tawrah, Deuteronomy 28:12, Job 5:10, Joel 2:23, Zabur, Psalms 68:9, Injil, Matthew 5:45

[4479] Injil, Romans 4:17, John 5:21

[4480] Tawrah, Job 42:2, Isaiah 14:27, Daniel 4:35, Injil, Matthew 19:26, Mark 10:27, Luke 1:37

[4481] Arabic /ayat/. See glossary for more details.

Chapter 41

safely to the day of resurrection?[4482] Do whatever you[MP] want to. He sees your[MP] deeds.[4483] (40)

\*\*\*

As for disbelievers in the reminder[4484] when it came to them, it is a mighty book; (41)

\*\*\*

nothing vain comes in front of it[4485] or behind it. [It is] a revelation from a wise,[4486] praiseworthy one. (42)

\*\*\*

Everything that is told to you[MS] was told to the messengers before you[MS].[4487] Your[MS] Lord has forgiveness and painful punishment. (43)

\*\*\*

If we had made it a foreign recitation, they would have said, "If only its signs were explained – are they foreign and Arabic?" Say[MS], "It is guidance and healing[4488] for believers. Disbelievers have deafness in their ears. It is blindness to them. They are called from afar.[4489] (44)

\*\*\*

We gave Musa[4490] the book, and it was disagreed about. And if not for a word which came previously[4491] from your[MS] Lord, it would have determined among them.[4492] They are in serious doubt about him.[4493] (45)

\*\*\*

Whoever does righteous deeds benefits his own soul, and whoever does bad deeds harms it. Your[MS] Lord does not wrong his

---

[4482] Tawrah, Daniel 12:2 Injil, Acts 24:15, 1 Corinthians 15:52-54, Revelation 20:11-15
[4483] Tawrah, Ecclesiastes 11:9
[4484] Arabic /dhikr/. See glossary for more details.
[4485] Or, "between its hands."
[4486] Tawrah, Job 9:4, Proverbs 2:6, Jeremiah 9:23-24, Injil, 1 Corinthians 1:21-25, Romans 16:27
[4487] See 26:196. This verse affirms the unity of content between all the books.
[4488] Injil, Revelation 22:2
[4489] Injil, Ephesians 2:13,17
[4490] Moses. See glossary for more details.
[4491] See 10:19, 11:110, 20:129, 42:14 where this phrase is also used.
[4492] Injil, 1 Corinthians 10:13
[4493] Or "it." The pronoun may refer to the book, Moses, your Lord, or the word (if it refers to Isa, who is called a word from Allah in 3:39,45.)

427

Chapter 41

servants.[4494] (46) **25A1** He has knowledge of the hour.[4495] No fruit comes out of the buds, or pregnant female gives birth without his knowledge.[4496] On that day, he will call to them, "Where are the gods you[MP] worshiped instead of me?" They will say, "We proclaim to you[MS] that none of us is a witness." (47)
\*\*\*
Those they previously prayed to went astray from them. They thought they had no way of escape. (48)
\*\*\* People do not grow weary[4497] of praying for good. If they are touched with evil, they utterly despair. (49)
\*\*\*
If we make them taste our mercy after harm has touched them, they will say, "This is mine. I surely do not think the hour is coming.[4498] If I am returned to my Lord, I will have a good reward." We will tell the disbelievers what they did, and make them taste harsh torment. (50)
\*\*\*
When we give someone blessings, he turns away and goes off. If evil touches him, he prays many prayers. (51)
\*\*\*
Say[MS], "What do you[MP] think? If it[4499] is from Allah and then you[MP] disbelieve in it, who is more astray than such a contentious one?" (52) We will show them our signs in the horizons and in themselves, until it is clear to them that it is truth.[4500] Is it not sufficient that your[MS] Lord is witness of everything?[4501] (53)
\*\*\*
Are they not in doubt about meeting their Lord? Does he not comprehend[4502] everything?[4503] (54)[4504]

---

[4494] This verse is one of only five verses where the plural form /abid/ is used. All five use the same phrase. This word can also be translated "slaves." The other verses are 3:182, 8:51, 22:10, and 50:29.
[4495] 43:61 says that Isa has (or is) knowledge of the hour. This may be in reference to Isa being a word from Allah (verse 45; see 3:39,45).
[4496] Injil, Matthew 10:29-31, 1 John 3:20
[4497] Injil, Galatians 6:9-10
[4498] Injil, John 5:25
[4499] Or "he"
[4500] Or that he is the truth
[4501] Tawrah, Job 28:24
[4502] Or, "surround"
[4503] Zabur, Psalms 32:7

428

# Chapter 41[4504]

---

[4504] The verses in this chapter that rhyme are put together in paragraphs, separated by ***.

# Chapter 42 Al-Shura[4505]

In the name of Allah, the most gracious and merciful.[4506] HM. (1)

***

ASQ.[4507] (2)

***

Thus the mighty,[4508] wise[4509] Allah reveals to you[MS] and to those who were before you[MS]. (3) Everything in the heavens and the earth is his.[4510] He is most high[4511] and great.[4512] (4) The heavens almost split[4513] from above, as the angels sing praises[4514] to their Lord and ask forgiveness for those on earth. Is Allah not forgiving[4515] and merciful?[4516] (5)

***

Allah keeps those who chose gods as protectors besides him; you[MS] are not responsible for them. (6)

***

Thus we inspired an Arabic recitation[4517] to you[MS] so you[MS] can warn the mother of the villages[4518] and those around them, and so you[MS] can warn about the undoubtable day of gathering.[4519] Some of them will be in heaven, and others in the burning fire. (7) If

---

[4505] counsel

[4506] Zabur, Psalms 103:8, 145:8. See glossary for more details.

[4507] Here and at the beginning of many chapters there are unvowelled letters of unknown meaning. Numerous theories have been proposed, but there is no agreement on the subject.

[4508] Tawrah, Joshua 4:24

[4509] Tawrah, Job 9:4, Proverbs 2:6, Jeremiah 9:23-24, Injil, 1 Corinthians 1:21-25, Romans 16:27

[4510] Tawrah, Isaiah 45:12, Zabur, Psalms 24:1, 89:11, Injil, Hebrews 1:10

[4511] Tawrah, Genesis 14:18-22

[4512] Zabur, Psalms 48:1

[4513] The word here is for thinking beings, so maybe the meaning is that the heavens are obedient to Allah.

[4514] Zabur, Psalms 103:20

[4515] Here and in verse 23, see Zabur, Psalms 103:3, 130:4, Tawrah, Isaiah 43:25, Exodus 34:7, Injil, Acts 26:18.

[4516] See glossary for more details on "merciful."

[4517] Or Qur'an or qur'an. See glossary for more details.

[4518] Mecca

[4519] Here and in verses 15 and 29, see Tawrah, Joel 3:11-14, Zephaniah 3:8, Injil, Matthew 25:32, John 15:6, Revelation 16:16; see glossary under "day."

## Chapter 42

Allah had willed, he would have made them one nation. He brings those he wills into his mercy. The wicked have no protector or savior. (8) Have they chosen protectors besides him? Allah is the protector. He gives life to the dead,[4520] and he can do anything.[4521] (9)
\*\*\*

Whenever you[MP] differ about him, Allah will judge. That is Allah, my Lord. I trust in him and I repent toward him. (10)
\*\*\*

The creator of the heavens and the earth[4522] made spouses for you[MP] from yourselves[MP],[4523] and spouses for cattle.[4524] This is how he multiplies you[MP].[4525] Nothing is like him.[4526] He hears all and sees all. (11)
\*\*\*

He has the keys of the heavens and the earth.[4527] He spreads forth and takes away his provision to those he wills, and he knows everything.[4528] (12) **25A2**
\*\*\*

He has appointed the religion he commanded Nuh,[4529] what we inspired you[MS] with, and what we commanded[4530] Ibrahim,[4531] Musa,[4532] and Isa:[4533] practice religion and do not be divided in it.[4534] Those who worship other gods think what you[MS] call them to

---

[4520] Injil, Romans 4:17
[4521] Tawrah, Job 42:2, Isaiah 14:27, Daniel 4:35, Injil, Matthew 19:26, Mark 10:27, Luke 1:37
[4522] Tawrah, Genesis 1:1
[4523] Tawrah, Genesis 2:22
[4524] Tawrah, Isaiah 34:15-16
[4525] Tawrah, Genesis 1:22
[4526] Tawrah, Jeremiah 10:6
[4527] Injil, Matthew 16:19, Revelation 1:18
[4528] Injil, John 16:30
[4529] Noah. See glossary for more details.
[4530] Most of what all the prophets were given came from Allah orally, and it was later written down. The exception is Musa (Tawrah, Exodus 34:28, Deuteronomy 4:13, 10:4), when Allah himself wrote them on stone tablets.
[4531] Abraham. See glossary for more details.
[4532] Moses. See glossary for more details.
[4533] Jesus. See glossary for more details.
[4534] Injil, John 17:21-23

is big.[4535] Allah chooses for himself those he wills, and guides those who repent to himself. (13) They were not divided until after knowledge had come to them, and they were insolent among themselves. If not for a word which came previously[4536] from your[MS] Lord until a specific time,[4537] they would have been judged. Those who inherited the book after them[4538] are in serious doubt about it. (14)

\*\*\*

So pray[MS] and be[MS] upright, just as you[MS] were commanded. Do not follow[MS] their desires, but say, "I believe in every book Allah revealed, and I was commanded to be just[4539] among you[MP]. Allah is our Lord and your[MP] Lord. We have our works and you[MP] have your[MP] works. There is no argument between us and you[MP]. Allah gathers us together, and he is our destiny." (15)

\*\*\*

The arguments of those who argue about Allah after he was answered have no force with their Lord. Wrath is upon them,[4540] and they will have severe torment.[4541] (16)

\*\*\*

Allah revealed the book and the scale in truth. How can you[MS] know if the hour is near?[4542] (17)

\*\*\*

Those who do not believe in it try to hasten it.[4543] Believers are afraid of it, and they know it is true. But those who doubt the hour are far astray. (18) Allah is kind to his servants. He provides for those he wills. He is strong[4544] and mighty.[4545] (19)

---

[4535] Or a big matter. A popular expression that may capture the thought is "a big deal."

[4536] See 10:19, 11:110, 20:129, 41:45 where this phrase is also used.

[4537] This may refer to specific ordinances in the Tawrah that were binding on the Jews, but not on other or later people.

[4538] This may refer to later people of the book, the people of the Gospel, who have varying viewpoints about the Tawrah.

[4539] Tawrah, Micah 6:8

[4540] Injil, John 3:36

[4541] Here and in verses 21, 26, 42, 44, and 45, see Tawrah, Isaiah 50:11, Injil, Matthew 18:34, 25:41,46, Luke 16:23-28, Revelation 20:15.

[4542] The word for hour is feminine, and the word for near is masculine, so the meaning may be different.

[4543] i.e. the hour, twice in this verse.

[4544] Tawrah, Job 9:4, Zabur, Psalms 24:8, Injil, Ephesians 6:10, Revelation 18:8

Chapter 42

\*\*\*

We will increase the fields of those who desire the fields of the hereafter. We will give those who want this world some of its goods, but they will not have a portion in the hereafter. (20)

\*\*\*

Do they have partners that they have made appointed as religion? Allah has not given permission to them. If not for the word of division, they would have been judged. The wicked will have painful torment. (21)

\*\*\*

When it happens to them, you^ms will see the wicked fearing what they deserve. Believers who do righteous deeds[4546] will be in meadows of the heavenly gardens,[4547] where they will have everything they desire from their Lord. That is the greatest grace. (22) That is the good news Allah gives to his servants who believe and do righteous deeds. Say^ms, "I do not ask you^mp for wages for it, except for love for relatives.[4548] We will increase the reward of those who do good deeds. Allah is forgiving and grateful. (23) Do they say, "He has invented lies about Allah"? If Allah had willed, he would have sealed your^ms heart. Allah erases what is vain and fulfills the truth by his words. He knows what is in the heart.[4549] (24)

\*\*\*

He accepts repentance from his servants and pardons bad deeds. He knows your^mp deeds. (25)

\*\*\*

He answers believers who do righteous deeds and increases his grace upon them. The disbelievers will have severe torment. (26)
25A3

\*\*\*

If Allah spread out his provision to his servants, they would have desired[4550] the earth, but he sends down as much as he wills. He is aware of his servants and sees them. (27)

---

[4545] Tawrah, 2 Chronicles 16:9

[4546] Here and in verses 23 and 26, see Injil, 1 Corinthians 3:8, James 2:14-17, Revelation 19:8.

[4547] Arabic /jannah/. See glossary for more details. Injil, John 5:29

[4548] Injil, Romans 13:8

[4549] Tawrah, 1 Samuel 16:7, 1 Chronicles 28:9, Zabur, Psalms 44:21, Injil, Luke 16:15, Romans 8:27, Acts 15:8, 1 John 3:20

[4550] Or "been insolent in."

## Chapter 42

\*\*\*

He sends down rain[4551] after they despair. He sends out his mercy. He is the praiseworthy protector. (28)

\*\*\*

One of his signs is the creation of the heavens, the earth, and the living creatures he sent into them. He is able to gather them when he wills.[4552] (29) The disasters that happen to you[MP] are as you[MP] deserve.[4553] He pardons much.[4554] (30) You[MP] cannot frustrate [him] on earth. You[MP] have no protector or savior besides Allah.[4555] (31)

\*\*\*

One of his signs is ships that sail on the sea like mountains. (32)

\*\*\*

If he wills, he will calm the wind,[4556] and they[4557] become still on its[4558] back. That is a sign for everyone who endures[4559] and gives thanks. (33) He may destroy them as they deserve, but he pardons much. (34)

\*\*\*

Those who argue about our signs know that they have no escape. (35)

\*\*\*

You[MP] have been given the goods of this world. What Allah has is better and most lasting for believers who trust in their Lord,[4560] (36) who avoid greater sins and promiscuity,[4561] and who forgive if they get angry. (37) They respond to their Lord and perform prayers. Their command is counsel among them, and they donate some of what we have provided them.[4562] (38) When they are

---

[4551] Tawrah, Deuteronomy 28:12, Job 5:10, Joel 2:23, Zabur, Psalms 68:9, Injil, Matthew 5:45

[4552] Tawrah, Genesis 7:8-9

[4553] Or, "what your hands have earned." Tawrah, Genesis 7:10

[4554] Tawrah, Exodus 34:7, Micah 7:18-20, here and in verse 34.

[4555] Tawrah, Hosea 13:4, Zabur, Psalms 106:21, Injil, Luke 1:47, Titus 1:3

[4556] Injil, Matthew 8:26

[4557] The reference may be to waves.

[4558] The reference is probably to the sea.

[4559] See "endure" in glossary, here and in verse 43.

[4560] Injil, Mark 8:36

[4561] Or lewdness, adultery or abomination. See Zabur, Psalms 19:12

[4562] Tawrah, 1 Chronicles 29:14

## Chapter 42

oppressed, they take revenge.[4563] (39) The penalty of a bad deed is another similar bad deed,[4564] but Allah will reward those who pardon and reconcile.[4565] He does not love the wicked.[4566] (40)

\*\*\*

Those who take revenge after wrong[4567] do not sin.[4568] (41)

\*\*\*

The path is against those who are wicked to people and are unjustifiably insolent in this world. They will have painful torment. (42)

\*\*\*

Those who endure and are forgiving are determined[4569] in matters. (43)

\*\*\*

Those Allah leads astray[4570] will have no protector after him. You[MS] will see the wicked, when they see torment. They will say, "Is there a way to return to the path?" (44)

\*\*\*

You[MS] will see them exposed to it, fearing in humiliation. They look with a hidden glance. Believers say, "Those who lose their souls and their families on the day of resurrection[4571] are truly lost. The wicked will be in permanent torment. (45)

\*\*\*

They will have no protectors besides Allah to save them. Those Allah leads astray will have no path [of escape]. (46)

\*\*\*

Respond to your[MP] Lord before the coming of a day[4572] when Allah allows no return.[4573] You[MP] will have no refuge on that day. You[MP] will not be able to deny it. (47) If they turn away, we have not sent you[MS] as a guardian. Your[MS] only responsibility is proclamation.

---

[4563] Or "are victorious."
[4564] Injil, Romans 2:9
[4565] Injil, Luke 6:37
[4566] Zabur, Psalms 5:4-5, 11:5, Tawrah, Proverbs 6:16-19
[4567] The meaning may be wrong done to him.
[4568] Injil, Romans 12:19-21
[4569] Or strong or courageous.
[4570] Injil, 2 Thessalonians 2:11, Tawrah, 2 Samuel 22:27, 1 Kings 22:20-23, Ezekiel 14:9
[4571] Tawrah, Daniel 12:2 Injil, Acts 24:15, 1 Corinthians 15:52-54, Revelation 20:11-15
[4572] Tawrah, Ecclesiastes 12:1-7. See "day" in glossary.
[4573] Or "are victorious."

## Chapter 42

When we give a man a taste of mercy,[4574] he is happy because of it. If bad things happen to him because of what his hands have done, he is ungrateful.[4575] (48) The kingdom of the heavens and the earth is Allah's.[4576] He creates what he wills. He gives females to those he wills, and give males to those he wills. (49) Or he gives them spouses, males and females and makes those he wills barren. He is all-knowing[4577] and all-powerful.[4578] (50) 25A4

\*\*\*

It is not suitable for Allah to speak to a man, except by inspiration,[4579] from behind a curtain, or by a messenger he sends, who inspires what he wills with his permission.[4580] He is most high and wise.[4581] (51) Thus we inspired you<sup>MS</sup> [with] a spirit by our command. You<sup>MS</sup> did not know the book or faith, but we made it light to guide those of our servants we will. You<sup>MS</sup> guide to a straight path,[4582] (52) Allah's path. Everything in the heavens and the earth is his. Every matter is Allah's. (53)[4583]

---

[4574] Injil, 1 Peter 2:1-3

[4575] The injustice/wickedness, disbelief/ungratefulness, evil, unrighteousness/sin, or lostness of mankind is mentioned in a number of verses in the Qur'an as well as in the previous books. Injustice or wickedness: 2:57, 3:117,135, 4:64,97, 7:160,177, 9:70, 10:44, 11:101, 14:34,45, 16:33,61,118, 29:40, 30:9, 33:72, 34:19, 35:32, 43:76, 65:1, Tawrah, Genesis 6:5, Job 25:4, Injil, Acts 3:26, disbelief or ungratefulness: 14:34, 17:67, 22:66, 42:48, 43:15, 80:17, Injil, Hebrews 3:19, Evil: 12:53, Tawrah, Jeremiah 17:9, Injil, Matthew 15:19, Mark 7:21, unrighteousness or sin: 91:8, Tawrah, 1 Kings 8:46, Ecclesiastes 7:20, Injil, Romans 3:9-19, 5:12, lostness: 103:2, Tawrah, Jeremiah 50:6, Injil, Luke 19:10, Romans 3:23, 6:23

[4576] Here and in verse 54, see Tawrah, Isaiah 45:12, Zabur, Psalms 24:1, 89:11, Injil, Hebrews 1:10.

[4577] Tawrah, Job 37:16, Isaiah 40:14, Zabur, Psalms 33:13-15, Injil, 1 John 3:20

[4578] Tawrah, Job 42:2

[4579] Injil, 2 Timothy 3:16-17, 2 Peter 1:20-21, Hebrews 1:1

[4580] Injil, Hebrews 1:1-3

[4581] Tawrah, Job 9:4, Proverbs 2:6, Jeremiah 9:23-24, Injil, 1 Corinthians 1:21-25, Romans 16:27

[4582] See glossary for more details, and notes on 3:51, 6:153, 19:36, 36:61, and 43:64 on what the straight path is.

[4583] The verses in this chapter that rhyme are put together in paragraphs, separated by \*\*\*.

Chapter 43

# Chapter 43 Al-Zukhruf[4584]

In the name of Allah, the most gracious and merciful.[4585] HM.[4586] (1) [I swear] by the clear book,[4587] (2) we have made it an Arabic recitation,[4588] so that you[MP] may comprehend. (3) It is in our master book,[4589] and is high and wise. (4) Should we turn the reminder[4590] away from you[MP] in pardon, since you[MP] are wasteful people? (5) How many prophets we sent the ancients! (6) They mocked every prophet that came to them.[4591] (7) We destroyed those who were stronger than they, and the proverb of the ancients[4592] passed away. (8) If you[MS] asked them, "Who created the heavens and the earth?", they would say, "The mighty, all-knowing[4593] one created them." (9) He made the earth a cradle for you[MP], and made paths for you[MP] in it, so that you[MP] may be guided. (10) He made rain[4594] fall from the sky by decree,[4595] and with it resurrected a dead town.[4596] Thus you[MP] will be brought out. (11) He created all species and gave you[MP] ships[4597] and cattle to ride[4598] (12) so that

---

[4584] Ornaments or embellishment
[4585] Zabur, Psalms 103:8, 145:8. See glossary for more details.
[4586] Here and at the beginning of many chapters there are unvowelled letters of unknown meaning. Numerous theories have been proposed, but there is no agreement on the subject.
[4587] The clear book here is probably the former book, since by it the next refers to the Qur'an. Swearing by the Qur'an that the Qur'an is an Arabic book would not make sense.
[4588] Or Qur'an or qur'an. See glossary for more details.
[4589] Or "mother of the book" or "essence of the book"
[4590] Arabic /dhikr/. See glossary for more details.
[4591] Tawrah, 2 Chronicles 30:10, 36:16, Zabur, Psalms 35:16, Injil, Matthew 20:19, 27:29,31,41, Mark 15:20,31, Luke 18:32, 22:63, 23:11,36
[4592] Isa is the only named person in the Qur'an called a proverb, in verse 59 of this chapter.
[4593] Tawrah, Job 37:16, Isaiah 40:14, Zabur, Psalms 33:13-15, Injil, 1 John 3:20
[4594] Tawrah, Deuteronomy 28:12, Job 5:10, Joel 2:23, Zabur, Psalms 68:9, Injil, Matthew 5:45
[4595] Or measure
[4596] "Town" is feminine and "dead" is masculine. There may be another meaning.
[4597] Tawrah, Proverbs 30:19

## Chapter 43

you would sit<sup>MP</sup> on its<sup>MS</sup> backs, and remember your<sup>MP</sup> Lord's blessings when you<sup>MP</sup> ride on it<sup>MS</sup>, and say, "May he who subjected this to us be glorified! We would not have been able to do it. (13) We will return to our Lord." (14) But they chose some of his servants[4599] [as gods] instead of him. Man is clearly ungrateful.[4600] (15) Has he chosen daughters[4601] out of what he created and chosen to give you<sup>MP</sup> sons? (16) If one of them is given good news of what they ascribe to the most gracious,[4602] his face will be sad and he will grieve. (17) Or he who was brought up with ornaments[4603] and unclear in dispute? (18) They made the angels, servants[4604] of the most gracious,[4605] females! Did they<sup>MP</sup> witness their<sup>MP</sup> creation? Their testimony will be written down,[4606] and they will be questioned. (19) They said, "If the most gracious had willed, we would not have worshiped them." They have no knowledge of that. They are merely liars. (20) Did we bring them a book before it, which they hold fast? (21) Rather they said, "We found our fathers all one nation, and we are guided by their footsteps." (22) Whenever we sent a warner before you<sup>MS</sup> to a village, its wealthy citizens said, "We found our fathers all one nation, and we will follow in their footsteps." (23) **25B1** He said, "Even if I bring you<sup>MP</sup> guidance better than what you<sup>MP</sup> found with your<sup>MP</sup> fathers?" They said, "We disbelieve in your<sup>MP</sup> message." (24) So we took revenge on them. See what was the end of the

---

[4598] Tawrah, Genesis 1:28

[4599] See glossary.

[4600] For here and verse 76, the injustice/wickedness, disbelief/ungratefulness, evil, unrighteousness/sin, or lostness of mankind is mentioned in a number of verses in the Qur'an as well as in the previous books. Injustice or wickedness: 2:57, 3:117,135, 4:64,97, 7:160,177, 9:70, 10:44, 11:101, 14:34,45, 16:33,61,118, 29:40, 30:9, 33:72, 34:19, 35:32, 43:76, 65:1, Tawrah, Genesis 6:5, Job 25:4, Injil, Acts 3:26, disbelief or ungratefulness: 14:34, 17:67, 22:66, 42:48, 43:15, 80:17, Injil, Hebrews 3:19, Evil: 12:53, Tawrah, Jeremiah 17:9, Injil, Matthew 15:19, Mark 7:21, unrighteousness or sin: 91:8, Tawrah, 1 Kings 8:46, Ecclesiastes 7:20, Injil, Romans 3:9-19, 5:12, lostness: 103:2, Tawrah, Jeremiah 50:6, Injil, Luke 19:10, Romans 3:23, 6:23

[4601] Pagan Arabs in those days worshipped goddesses.

[4602] i.e. birth of a daughter

[4603] i.e. in a wealthy environment

[4604] See glossary.

[4605] Injil, Hebrews 1:14

[4606] Injil, Revelation 20:12

## Chapter 43

rejecters.[4607] (25) Ibrahim[4608] told his father and his people, "I am innocent of the gods you[MP] worship, (26) except for my creator. He will guide me.[4609] (27) He made it a permanent word for his posterity, so that they may return."[4610] (28) But I made them and their fathers enjoy themselves until the truth and a clear messenger came to them. (29) When the truth came to them, they said, "This is magic, and we disbelieve in it." (30) They said, "If only this recitation[4611] had been revealed to a great man from the two villages." (31) Do they portion out your[MS] Lord's mercy?[4612] We portioned their living among them in this life, and raised some of them above others in position, so that some of them would make others work. The mercy of your[MS] Lord is better than what they hoard.[4613] (32) If only mankind had been one nation, we would have given disbelievers in the most gracious silver ceilings, stairs where they would appear, (33) doors for their houses, beds on which to recline, (34) and embellishment. All of those are this world's goods, but the hereafter with your[MS] Lord[4614] is for the reverent. (35) We will prepare devils[4615] as companions[4616] for those who blind themselves[4617] to remembering the most gracious. (36) They will block them from the path, while they imagine they are guided. (37) When he comes to us, he will say, "I wish I were as far from you[MS] as two sunrises." What an awful companion. (38) He will not help you[MP] today, since you[MP] were wicked. Now you[MP] will share in torment.[4618] (39) Can you[MS] make the deaf hear or guide the blind and those who are clearly astray?[4619] (40) Either

---

[4607] "End" is feminine and "was" is masculine. There may be another meaning.
[4608] Abraham. See glossary for more details.
[4609] Injil, Revelation 7:17, Isaiah 58:11
[4610] Tawrah, Isaiah 30:8-11, Injil, 2 Timothy 4:3-4.
[4611] Or Qur'an or qur'an. See glossary for more details.
[4612] "Mercy" has a different spelling twice here and in 5 other places. See glossary.
[4613] Injil, Luke 12:16-21
[4614] Injil 2 Corinthians 5:7. The best part of Allah's reward is his presence.
[4615] Arabic /shaytan/. See glossary for more details.
[4616] This may refer to a demonic spirit guide
[4617] Injil, 2 Corinthians 4:3-4
[4618] For "torment" here and in verses 65 and 74, see Tawrah, Isaiah 50:11, Injil, Matthew 18:34, 25:41,46, Luke 16:23-28, Revelation 20:15.
[4619] Injil, Matthew 11:5

# Chapter 43

we will take you<sup>MS</sup> away and take vengeance on them (41) or show you<sup>MS</sup> what we promised them. We will prevail over them. (42) So hold tight to what was inspired to you<sup>MS</sup>. You<sup>MS</sup> are on the straight path.[4620] (43) It is a reminder[4621] for you<sup>MS</sup> and your<sup>MS</sup> people, and you<sup>MP</sup> will be questioned. (44) Ask<sup>MS</sup> the messengers we sent before you<sup>MS</sup>,[4622] "Did we set up other gods[4623] to be worshiped besides the most gracious?" (45) We sent Musa[4624] with our signs to Pharaoh and his nobles. He said, "I am the messenger of the Lord of the universe."[4625] (46) When he brought our signs to them, they laughed at them.[4626] (47) Whenever we showed them signs, they were greater than the previous ones,[4627] and we caught them in torment, so that they may return. (48) They said, "Magician, pray to your<sup>MS</sup> Lord for us according to the covenant he made with you<sup>MS</sup>, and we will be guided."[4628] (49) When we took away the torment from them, they broke their promise.[4629] (50) Then Pharaoh called his people, "My people, am I not king of Egypt[4630] and of these rivers that run underneath me?[4631] Do you<sup>MP</sup> not see? (51) Am I not better than this shameful one who does not make things clear?[4632] (52) Why have gold bracelets not been cast upon him, or angels accompanied him?"[4633] (53) So he made light of his

---

[4620] See glossary for more details, and notes on 3:51, 6:153, 19:36, 36:61, and 43:64 on what the straight path is.

[4621] Arabic /dhikr/. See glossary for more details.

[4622] The only way to ask a messenger who was sent beforehand is to read his book, since he himself is dead.

[4623] Arabic /ilah/ here and in verse 84 (twice). See glossary for more details.

[4624] Moses. See glossary for more details.

[4625] Tawrah, Exodus 3:10

[4626] Tawrah, Exodus 7:13

[4627] This verse talks about the signs being progressively greater. 17:101 mentions nine, and the great sign (79:20) makes a total of ten. This corresponds to the ten signs mentioned in the Tawrah, Exodus 7-12. In the Qur'an 7:107,108, 130, and 133 describe many of these signs. The last sign, probably the same as the "greatest sign" mentioned both in 7:133 and in the Tawrah, Exodus (11:4-5, 12:23,24,29,30) is the blood. The Exodus passages gives the details.

[4628] Tawrah, Exodus 12:32

[4629] Tawrah, Exodus 9:34

[4630] Tawrah, Exodus 6:1

[4631] Tawrah, Exodus 7:20

[4632] Tawrah, Exodus 4:10

[4633] Injil, Matthew 4:11

## Chapter 43

people and they obeyed him. They were unbelieving[4634] people. (54) When they provoked us to anger, we took revenge on them, and drowned them all.[4635] (55) We made them history and a proverb to others.[4636] (56) **25B2** When the son[4637] of Mariam[4638] is cited as an example, your^MS people reject[4639] him.[4640] (57) They said, "Are our gods[4641] better, or he?"[4642] They only want to argue. They are contentious people.[4643] (58)

\*\*\*

He[4644] is only[4645] a servant[4646] we gave blessings. We made him a proverb for the people of Israel.[4647] (59)[4648]

\*\*\*

If we wished, we would have made you^MP into angels ruling on the earth.[4649] (60) He[4650] is[4651] knowledge of the hour,[4652] so do not

---

[4634] Or transgressing or immoral

[4635] Tawrah, Exodus 14:26-31

[4636] Zabur, Psalms 136:15

[4637] Injil, Mark 6:3

[4638] Mary, mother of Jesus. See glossary for more details.

[4639] or hinder

[4640] Injil, Acts 4:10, 2:23,36

[4641] Arabic /ilah/. See glossary for more details.

[4642] i.e. Isa

[4643] Tawrah, Numbers 20:3-13

[4644] i.e. Isa

[4645] Or "truly." Here Isa is called "only" a servant, and elsewhere, Muhammad (ص) is called "only" a warner (79:45, 7:188), but both of them have many other titles in the Qur'an. The phrase translated "only" often has the meaning "truly."

[4646] See glossary. Injil, Philippians 2:6-11, Tawrah, Isaiah 52:13-53:12

[4647] Injil, Luke 2:34

[4648] In this section, there are several ways in which Isa was unique. Isa is the only prophet or messenger who is a proverb (verse 59), is a sign of the last hour, or knows when the last hour will be (61), and commands obedience in the context of the straight path (63). For more information about this subject, see notes at 3:36, 4:158, 5:46,110, 19:19.

[4649] Tawrah, Genesis 1:28. It may be implied that Isa was a regent, though Allah could have made others regents instead of him.

[4650] i.e. Isa

[4651] Or, has. The meaning here could be that Isa's coming back is a sign that the last hour is near, or it could mean that Isa knows when the last hour will be. Injil, Revelation 14:7, Luke 21:28. See note at verse 59.

[4652] Injil, 1 Thessalonians 4:14-17, Matthew 24:30

## Chapter 43

doubt[MP] it,[4653] and follow[MP] me.[4654] This is a straight path.[4655] (61) Do not let Satan block you[MP]. He is a clear enemy to you[MP].[4656] (62) When Isa[4657] brought miracles,[4658] he said, "I have come to you[MP] with wisdom,[4659] and to clarify to you[MP] your[MP] differences,[4660] so fear[MP] Allah and obey[MP] me.[4661] (63) Allah is my Lord and your[MP] Lord,[4662] so worship[MP] him. This is a straight path."[4663] (64) The parties differed among themselves. Woe to the wicked for the torment of a painful day. (65) Do they look for anything except the hour,[4664] which will come upon them suddenly,[4665] without their

---

[4653] i.e. the hour

[4654] i.e. Allah.

[4655] See glossary for more details, and notes on 3:51, 6:153, 19:36, 36:61, and 43:64 on what the straight path is.

[4656] Injil, Revelation 12:9

[4657] Jesus. See glossary for more details.

[4658] The Qur'an lists some of his miracles in 3:49,52, 5:110,112, 19:19,20,24,30-33. Most of the miracles Isa does that are mentioned in the Injil, with the stories behind them, are in the Injil, Matthew 8-11, 14-15,17,21, Mark 1-9,11, Luke 2,4-9,22, John 2,4-6,9,11.

[4659] Injil, Mark 6:2

[4660] Injil, Matthew 19:3-9

[4661] i.e. Isa. Injil, John 5:24. Several prophets tell the people specifically, "obey me." (Nuh 26:108,110, 71:3, Hud 26:126,131, Salih 26:144,150, Lut 26:163, Shuaib 26:179, Harun 20:90, and Isa 3:50, 43:63) Several verses command people to obey "the messenger" (3:32,132, 4:59, 5:92, 8:1,19,46, 24:54,56, 47:33, 58:13, 64:12), most of which probably refer to Muhammad (s). See note at verse 59.

[4662] Injil, John 20:17

[4663] The straight path is mentioned often in the Qur'an (1:7 and 37:118 as "the straight path", 7:16 as "your straight path," 6:126 as "your Lord's straight path," 6:153 as "my straight path," and 2:108,142,213, 3:51,101, 4:68,175, 5:12,16,60,77, 6:39,87,161, 10:25, 11:56, 15:41, 16:76, 121, 19:36,43, 20:135, 22:54, 23:73, 24:46, 28:22, 36:4,61, 38:22, 42:52, 43:43,61,64, 46:30, 48:2,20, 60:1, 67:22 as "a straight path.") However, only 3:51, 6:153, 19:36, 43:61,64, and 36:61 say what the straight path is. This passage is one of the most complete in its explanation, and we can conclude that the straight path includes (from verses 57-64) 1) not rejecting Isa, 2) believing that Isa is a blessed slave, a proverb, and the sign of the hour, 3) not doubting the hour, 4) following Allah, 5) not letting Satan block you, 6) believing that Isa brought miracles and wisdom, 7) believing that Isa came to clarify differences, 8) fearing Allah, 9) obeying Isa, 10) worshiping the one God, who is Isa's Lord and ours, and 11) worshiping Allah. See notes on the other four passages.

[4664] Injil, Revelation 14:7

## Chapter 43

realizing it. (66) Friends will be enemies to each other on that day, except for the reverent. (67) My servants,[4666] you[MP] will not fear or grieve[MP] today (68) since you[MP] believed in our signs and were submitted.[4667] (69) Enter the heavenly garden[4668] gladly, you[MP] and your[MP] wives. (70) They will be served with golden dishes and cups, filled with what their souls desire and what is a delight to the eyes.[4669] You[MP] will be there forever. (71) That is the heavenly garden[4670] which you[MP] have inherited for your[MP] deeds.[4671] (72) You[MP] will have much fruit in it[4672] to eat. (73) Wrongdoers will be in hell's torment forever,[4673] (74) and it will not be lessened. They will be covered with it. (75) We did not wrong them, but they wronged themselves.[4674] (76) They called, "Malik,[4675] let your[MS] Lord kill us."[4676] He said, "You[MP] will remain." (77) We brought you[MP] truth, but most of you[MP] hate the truth.[4677] (78) Did they plan a matter?[4678] We will plan. (79) Do they think that we do not hear their secrets and conspiracies? Yes we do! Our messengers were with them writing it down.[4679] (80) Say[MS], "If the most gracious does have a son, I will be the first worshipper." (81) May the Lord of the heavens and the earth, the Lord of the throne, be glorified above what they describe![4680] (82) Let them go ahead and play until they meet the day they have been promised. (83) He is god in

---

[4665] Injil, 1 Thessalonians 5:3
[4666] See glossary.
[4667] Injil, James 4:7. For "submit," some translators do not translate this. See glossary for more details.
[4668] Arabic /jannah/. See glossary for more details.
[4669] Tawrah, Esther 1:3-8, Proverbs 23:29
[4670] Arabic /jannah/. See glossary for more details. Injil, Revelation 22:2
[4671] Injil, Revelation 22:12
[4672] Injil, Revelation 22:2
[4673] Injil, Revelation 20:10
[4674] 2:57, 3:117,135, 4:64,97, 7:160,177, 9:70, 11:101, 14:45, 16:33,118, 29:40, 30:9, 34:19, 35:32, 65:1, Injil, Revelation 2:23.
[4675] The Qur'an does not explain who Malik is, but it seems he is in charge of hell.
[4676] Injil, Revelation 9:6
[4677] Tawrah, Amos 5:10, Injil, Titus 1:14, John 8:31-47, 17:17, 14:6
[4678] Zabur, Psalms 59:5
[4679] Injil, Revelation 20:12
[4680] The idea of Allah having sexual relations with a woman is disgusting and strongly rejected in all the books.

## Chapter 43

heaven and god on earth, and he is wise[4681] and all-knowing.[4682] (84) Blessed is the owner of the kingdom of the heavens, the earth, and what is between them.[4683] Knowledge of the hour[4684] is with him, and you[MP] will return to him. (85) Those they pray to besides him cannot intercede, except him who bears witness to the truth,[4685] and they know it. (86) If you[MS] ask them, "Who created them?"[4686] They will say, "Allah."[4687] How they lie! (87) And for his saying, "My Lord, these people do not believe. (88) So pardon them,[4688] and say: Peace," they will know. (89)[4689]

---

[4681] Tawrah, Job 9:4, Proverbs 2:6, Jeremiah 9:23-24, Injil, 1 Corinthians 1:21-25, Romans 16:27

[4682] Tawrah, Job 37:16, Isaiah 40:14, Zabur, Psalms 33:13-15, Injil, 1 John 3:20

[4683] Zabur, Psalms 145:11-13

[4684] 43:61, Injil, Revelation 14:7, Matthew 24:36. If the meaning of 43:61 is that Isa is a sign of the hour, then this title of Isa means that Isa is with Allah, which agrees with 3:55 and Injil, Acts 7:55-56

[4685] Injil, John 18:37. This may be a reference to Isa, 4:159. 2:255, 3:49, 5:110, 19:19, 3:45, 20:109, Injil, 1 Timothy 2:5

[4686] Tawrah, Isaiah 40:26

[4687] Tawrah, Isaiah 45:18

[4688] Injil, Colossians 3:13, Luke 17:4, Matthew 18:21-35

[4689] The verses in this chapter that rhyme are put together in paragraphs, separated by ***.

Chapter 44

# Chapter 44 Al-Dukhan[4690]

In the name of Allah, the most gracious and merciful.[4691] HM.[4692] (1) [I swear] by the clear book:[4693] (2) we sent it down[4694] on a blessed night. We were warners. (3) During it, every wise matter is distinguished (4) as a command from us. We were messengers. (5) A mercy[4695] from your^MS Lord. He hears all and knows all, (6) Lord of the heavens, the earth,[4696] and what is between them, if you^MP are certain. (7) He is the only god.[4697] He gives life and causes death,[4698] your^MP Lord and the Lord of your^MP ancestors.[4699] (8) But they are in doubt, playing. (9) Watch^MS for a day when the sky clearly brings forth smoke[4700] (10) that will cover people. This is painful torment. (11) "Our Lord, take away this torment.[4701] We are believers." (12) How should they have the reminder, since a clear messenger has already come to them, (13) and then they turned away from him and said, "A crazy person who was instructed."? (14) We will take away the torment for a little while. You^MP will return. (15) On that day we will attack with the greatest force, and take revenge.[4702] (16) **25B3** Before them, we tested Pharaoh's people when an honored messenger came to them.[4703]

---

[4690] smoke

[4691] Zabur, Psalms 103:8, 145:8. See glossary for more details.

[4692] Here and at the beginning of many chapters there are unvowelled letters of unknown meaning. Numerous theories have been proposed, but there is no agreement on the subject.

[4693] It is unclear what book is being sworn by. In 37:117, the Tawrah is called a similar phrase. If the meaning of /anzala/ in the following verse is figurative and means "reveal", it would refer to one of the former books, since it only makes sense to swear by a different book that the Qur'an was revealed. See following note.

[4694] Or "sent him down." Some believe this refers to Isa. 4:171, Injil, Luke 2:15-20.

[4695] Both the Qur'an (28:86) and Isa (19:21) are called mercy from Allah, so this fits either interpretation.

[4696] Tawrah, Genesis 24:3

[4697] Arabic /ilah/. See glossary for more details.

[4698] Tawrah, 1 Samuel 2:6, Deuteronomy 32:39

[4699] Tawrah, Deuteronomy 6:3

[4700] Injil, Revelation 9:2

[4701] Injil, Revelation 9:5-6

[4702] Injil, Romans 12:19

[4703] i.e. Musa . Injil, Acts 7:35

## Chapter 44

(17) "Restore<sup>MP</sup> Allah's servants to me.[4704] I am a faithful messenger to you<sup>MP</sup>. (18) Do not exalt<sup>MP</sup> yourselves against Allah. I have brought you<sup>MP</sup> clear authority. (19) I take refuge in my Lord[4705] and your<sup>MP</sup> Lord, lest you<sup>MP</sup> stone me. (20) If you<sup>MP</sup> do not believe me, go<sup>MP</sup> away from me." (21) So he prayed to his Lord, "These are wrongdoing people." (22) Take<sup>MS</sup> my servants away at night.[4706] You<sup>MP</sup> will be followed.[4707] (23) Leave<sup>MS</sup> the sea peacefully.[4708] They will be a drowned army.[4709] (24) How many gardens and springs they[4710] left, (25) along with crops, an honored position, (26) and blessings they enjoyed. (27) Thus it happened, and we gave them to other people as an inheritance.[4711] (28) Heaven and earth did not cry over them, and they were not given more time. (29) We rescued the people of Israel from shameful torment,[4712] (30) from Pharaoh. He was exalted and wasteful.[4713] (31) We knowingly chose them above the rest of mankind,[4714] (32) and we gave them signs[4715] with clear trials.[4716] (33) They will say, (34) "This is merely our first death.[4717] We will not be resurrected.[4718] (35) Bring<sup>MP</sup> forth our ancestors, if you<sup>MP</sup> are telling the truth. (36) Are they better, or the people of Tubba and those we destroyed before them? They were wrongdoers. (37) We did not create the heavens, the earth, and what is between them in jest.[4719] (38) We only created them in truth,[4720] but most of them

---

[4704] Tawrah, Exodus 5:1
[4705] Zabur, Psalms 18:2
[4706] Tawrah, Exodus 12:31,42
[4707] Tawrah, Exodus 14:6-8
[4708] Tawrah, Exodus 14:29
[4709] Tawrah, Exodus 14:28
[4710] The reference here is uncertain. One possibility is the people of Canaan, who left gardens, springs, crops, which Allah gave them to the people of Israel. 17:104, Zabur, Psalms 136:21. The other possibility is Pharaoh and his people.
[4711] Zabur, Psalms 136:21
[4712] Tawrah, Isaiah 51:10
[4713] Tawrah, Exodus 5:2, 8:15
[4714] Tawrah, Deuteronomy 7:7-8
[4715] Tawrah, Numbers 14:11
[4716] Tawrah, Exodus 17:7, Deuteronomy 13:3
[4717] Injil, Revelation 20:6
[4718] Injil, Revelation 20:5
[4719] Tawrah, Isaiah 45:18
[4720] Tawrah, Isaiah 45:12

## Chapter 44

do not know. (39) The day of separation is the appointment for all of them.[4721] (40) On that day, no one will help a friend at all.[4722] None will be saved (41) except for the one shown mercy by Allah. He is mighty and merciful.[4723] (42) The zaqqum tree (43) is food for the guilty. (44) It boils like molten brass in the stomach, (45) like boiling water. (46) Take[MP] them and drag[MP] them into the middle of the blazing fire. (47) Then pour[MP] boiling water on their heads as torment. (48) "Taste[MS], since you[MS] are so mighty and generous![4724] (49) This is what you[MP] doubted." (50) The reverent are in a safe place, (51) by heavenly gardens[4725] and springs,[4726] (52) wearing fine silk and brocade and facing each other. (53) Thus it is. We paired them to "hur iin".[4727] (54) They call for all fruits[4728] and are safe. (55) They will not taste death there, except for the first death.[4729] He keeps them safe from the torment[4730] of the blazing fire, (56) grace from your[MS] Lord. That is the great victory.[4731] (57) We made it easier in your[MS] language, so that they may remember. (58) So watch[MS]. They are watching. (59)

---

[4721] Injil, Matthew 25:32

[4722] Tawrah, Isaiah 10:3

[4723] See glossary for more details on "merciful."

[4724] If this is part of the statement to the people in hell, it is said in sarcasm.

[4725] Arabic /jannah/. See glossary for more details.

[4726] Injil, Revelation 22:2

[4727] This phrase is usually translated "and we will marry them to dark-eyed virgins," but the Arabic text does not have the words "dark," "eye," or "virgin". Instead of /'ain/ (eye), the text says /'in/ (wild ox). /hur/ may mean white, but definitely does not mean dark. It is obvious that the meaning is something else. The word /hur/ (translated by some as "virgins") may be related to the Syriac word /hura/ (grape). Some suggest that the meaning "we paired them" may mean "we refreshed them." Thus the meaning might be "we refreshed them with white grapes." Every time this phrase occurs (44:54, 55:20, 56:22), it is in the context of fruit, food and drink. Grapes in the heavenly garden are specifically mentioned in 23:19 and 78:32. See note on 56:22. Furthermore, the idea of virgins for the sexual pleasure of believing men does not fit with the presence of their wives in the heavenly gardens with them (43:70, 36:56), or with equal rewards promised female believers in 40:40, 4:124, 16:97.

[4728] Injil, Revelation 22:2

[4729] Injil, Revelation 2:11, 20:6

[4730] Tawrah, Isaiah 50:11, Injil, Matthew 18:34, 25:41,46, Luke 16:23-28, Revelation 20:15

[4731] Tawrah, Isaiah 25:8, Injil, 1 Corinthians 15:57, 1 John 5:4

# Chapter 44

# Chapter 45 Al-Jathiyah[4732]

In the name of Allah, the most gracious and merciful.[4733] HM.[4734] (1) The revelation of the book is from the Mighty Wise[4735] Allah. (2) The heavens and the earth are signs[4736] for believers.[4737] (3) Your[MP] creation and the living creatures[4738] he spreads around are signs for people who are certain. (4) The difference between night and day,[4739] the provision Allah sends down from the sky that revives the dead ground,[4740] and the change of the winds[4741] are signs for people who comprehend. (5) Those are Allah's signs we recite to you[MS] in truth. After Allah and his signs, what story will they believe in? (6) Woe to every guilty liar (7) who hears Allah's signs[4742] being read to him, then is obstinately proud,[4743] as if he has not heard them. Give his good news – of painful torment.[4744] (8) Whenever he knows anything of our signs, he makes fun of them.[4745] Such people will have shameful torment. (9) Hell will be behind them, and the possessions they have gained will not help them, nor will the helpers they chose besides Allah. They will have great torment. (10) This is guidance, and disbelievers in their Lord's signs will have torment of painful uncleanness. (11) **25B4** Allah has subjected the sea to you[MP], so that ships sail through it by

---

[4732] The kneeler (feminine)

[4733] Zabur, Psalms 103:8, 145:8. See glossary for more details.

[4734] Here and at the beginning of many chapters there are unvowelled letters of unknown meaning. Numerous theories have been proposed, but there is no agreement on the subject.

[4735] Tawrah, Job 9:4, Proverbs 2:6, Jeremiah 9:23-24, Injil, 1 Corinthians 1:21-25, Romans 16:27

[4736] Tawrah, Genesis 1:14

[4737] Zabur, Psalms 111:2

[4738] Tawrah, Genesis 1:24

[4739] Tawrah, Genesis 1:16

[4740] Zabur, Psalms 68:9, Isaiah 55:10-11

[4741] Tawrah, Job 37:9

[4742] Arabic /ayat/ here and in verses 9, 11 and 35. See glossary for more details.

[4743] Tawrah, Proverbs 6:16,17

[4744] For "torment" here and in verses 9-11, see Tawrah, Isaiah 50:11, Injil, Matthew 18:34, 25:41,46, Luke 16:23-28, Revelation 20:15.

[4745] Tawrah, 2 Kings 19:4

## Chapter 45

his command[4746] and you[MP] would seek his grace, so that you[MP] may give thanks.[4747] (12) From himself, he subjected everything in the heavens and the earth to you[MP].[4748] Those are signs to people who consider. (13) Tell believers to forgive[4749] those who do not hope for Allah's days, when he will reward people as they deserve. (14) Whoever does righteous deeds, benefits from it himself, and whoever does bad will have it counted against him.[4750] Then you[MP] will be returned to your[MP] Lord. (15) We gave the people of Israel the book, judgment,[4751] and prophecy,[4752] and we provided them with good things to eat, and we preferred them[4753] above all mankind. (16) We gave them miracles of the command.[4754] They did not differ insolently until after knowledge had come to them. Your[MS] Lord will judge among them on the day of resurrection[4755] about their differences.[4756] (17) Then we set you[MS] on a law of the command, so follow[MS] it and do not follow[MS] the desires of those who do not know. (18) They will not help you[MS] at all against Allah. The wicked help each other, and Allah helps the reverent.[4757] (19) This is evidence to people, and guidance and mercy to people who are certain. (20) Do those who seek bad deeds think that we will treat them like believers who do righteous deeds,[4758] both in life and death? They judge badly. (21) Allah created the heavens and the earth[4759] in truth, so that every soul would be repaid as it deserves. They will not be wronged. (22) Have you[MS] seen someone who knowingly chooses his desire as his god,[4760] while Allah knowingly leads him astray,[4761] blocking his

---

[4746] Zabur, Psalms 107:23
[4747] Injil, 1 Thessalonians 5:18
[4748] Tawrah, Genesis 1:28
[4749] Injil, Colossians 3:13
[4750] Injil, Romans 2:6-10
[4751] See 5:47
[4752] Or prophethood
[4753] Tawrah, Deuteronomy 7:7
[4754] Tawrah, Exodus 31:18
[4755] Tawrah, Daniel 12:2 Injil, Acts 24:15, 1 Corinthians 15:52-54, Revelation 20:11-15
[4756] Injil, Acts 23:7
[4757] Injil, 1 Timothy 2:2
[4758] Here and in verse 30, see Injil, 1 Corinthians 3:8, James 2:14-17, Revelation 19:8.
[4759] Tawrah, Genesis 1:1
[4760] Arabic /ilah/. See glossary for more details. Injil, Philippians 3:19

## Chapter 45

hearing and his heart,[4762] and putting a cover over his sight?[4763] Who will guide him after Allah? Do you[MP] not remember? (23) They said, "This world is all there is. We will die and live. Nothing destroys us except time." They know nothing about that. They merely guess. (24) When our signs and miracles are recited to them, their only excuse is, "Bring[MP] us our fathers if you[MP] are telling the truth." (25) Say[MS], "Allah gives you[MP] life and then death.[4764] Then he will gather[4765] you[MP] on the day of judgment,[4766] of which there is no doubt. But most people do not know. (26) The kingdom of the heavens and the earth is Allah's.[4767] On the day the hour comes, on that day the vain will be lost. (27) You[MS] will see every nation bowing, and every nation[4768] called toward its book, "Today you[MP] are repaid for your[MP] deeds.[4769] (28) This is our book. It speaks the truth against you[MP]. We were recording your[MP] deeds." (29) But their Lord will make the believers who did righteous deeds enter into his mercy. That is the clear victory.[4770] (30) Were my signs not recited to you[MP] disbelievers? But you[MP] were proud, wrongdoing people. (31) When it was said, "Allah's promise is true[4771] and there is no doubt of the hour," you[MP] said, "We do not know what the hour is.[4772] We think it is conjecture and are not certain." (32) The bad deeds they did will appear[4773] and they will be surrounded by what they had made fun of. (33) It will be said, "Today we will forget you[MP] as you[MP] forgot the appointment of this day of yours[MP]. Your[MP] abode will be hellfire,[4774] and you[MP] will

---

[4761] Injil, 2 Thessalonians 2:11, Tawrah, 2 Samuel 22:27, 1 Kings 22:20-23, Ezekiel 14:9
[4762] Tawrah, Exodus 8:15
[4763] Injil, 1 John 2:11
[4764] Tawrah, Deuteronomy 30:19
[4765] Tawrah, Joel 3:11-14, Zephaniah 3:8, Injil, Matthew 25:32, John 15:6, Revelation 16:16
[4766] Injil, Matthew 12:36
[4767] Tawrah, Isaiah 45:12, Zabur, Psalms 24:1, 89:11, Injil, Hebrews 1 10
[4768] Injil, Matthew 25:32
[4769] Injil, Matthew 16:27
[4770] Tawrah, Isaiah 25:8, Injil, 1 Corinthians 15:57, 1 John 5:4
[4771] Tawrah, 2 Samuel 22:31
[4772] Injil, Revelation 14:7
[4773] The verb is masculine and the subject feminine. There may be another meaning.
[4774] Injil, Revelation 14:11

## Chapter 45

have no savior.[4775] (34) That is because you[MP] made fun of Allah's signs and this world[4776] beguiled you[MP]." Today they will not come out of it, and they will not be received favorably. (35) Praise be to Allah, the Lord of the heavens, the Lord of the earth,[4777] the Lord of the universe. (36) The glory[4778] of the heavens and the earth is his,[4779] and he is mighty and wise.[4780] (37)

---

[4775] Tawrah, Isaiah 43:11, Hosea 13:4, Injil, Hebrews 10:26
[4776] Injil, 1 John 2:15-17
[4777] Tawrah, Ezra 5:11
[4778] Or pride
[4779] Zabur, Psalms 148:13
[4780] Tawrah, Job 9:4, Proverbs 2:6, Jeremiah 9:23-24, Injil, 1 Corinthians 1:21-25, Romans 16:27

# Chapter 46 Al-Ahqaf[4781]

**26A1** In the name of Allah, the most gracious and merciful.[4782] HM.[4783] (1) The revelation of the book is from the mighty, wise[4784] Allah. (2) We created the heavens, the earth, and what is between them only in truth and for a specific lifespan.[4785] Disbelievers turn away from the warning they were given. (3) Say[MS], "What do you[MP] think about those you[MP] pray to besides Allah? Show me what they have created on earth.[4786] Do they have other gods in the heavens? Bring me a book before this or some relic of knowledge if you[MP] are telling the truth." (4) Who is further astray than one who prays to gods other than Allah? They will not answer him until the day of resurrection.[4787] They are unaware of their prayers. (5) When people are gathered,[4788] they will be their enemies, and will renounce their worship. (6) When our signs are recited to them as miracles, disbelievers say of the truth that has come to them, "This is clearly magic," (7) or "He invented it." Say[MS], "Even if I invented it, you[MP] cannot do anything to me from Allah. He well knows what you[MP] spew forth. He is an adequate witness between me and you[MP]. He is forgiving[4789] and merciful.[4790] (8) Say[MS], "I am not a new invention among the messengers, and I do not know what will be done to me or to you[MP].[4791] I only follow what I am

---

[4781] Sand dunes
[4782] Zabur, Psalms 103:8, 145:8. See glossary for more details.
[4783] Here and at the beginning of many chapters there are unvowelled letters of unknown meaning. Numerous theories have been proposed, but there is no agreement on the subject.
[4784] Tawrah, Job 9:4, Proverbs 2:6, Jeremiah 9:23-24, Injil, 1 Corinthians 1:21-25, Romans 16:27
[4785] Injil, Matthew 24:35, Revelation 21:1
[4786] Tawrah, Jeremiah 10:11
[4787] Tawrah, Daniel 12:2, Zabur, Psalms 115:4-7, Injil, Acts 24:15, 1 Corinthians 15:52-54, Revelation 20:11-15
[4788] Tawrah, Joel 3:11-14, Zephaniah 3:8, Injil, Matthew 25:32, John 15:6, Revelation 16:16
[4789] Zabur, Psalms 103:3, 130:4, Tawrah, Isaiah 43:25, Exodus 34:7, Injil, Acts 26:18.
[4790] See glossary for more details on "merciful."
[4791] That is, Muhammad (s) did not know whether his eternal destiny would be the heavenly garden or hell.

## Chapter 46

inspired with. I am only[4792] a clear warner."[4793] (9) Say[MS], "What do you[MP] think? If it is from Allah and you[MP] disbelieve in it, yet a witness from the people of Israel testifies to something similar and he believes, while you[MP] are proud?" Allah does not guide wicked people. (10) The disbelievers told the believers, "If it were good, they would have beaten us to it." Since they were not guided by it, they will say "It is an old lie." (11) Before it the book of Musa[4794] [was] a leader[4795] and mercy.[4796] This is a confirming[4797] book in an Arabic language, to warn the wicked and give good news to those who do good deeds. (12) Those who said, "Our Lord is Allah," and are upright shall not fear or grieve. (13) They will go to the heavenly garden[4798] and remain there forever, as a reward for their deeds."[4799] (14) We commanded people to do good to their parents.[4800] Their mothers bore them in pain and gave birth to them in pain.[4801] The pregnancy until weaning lasts thirty months. When he is fully grown and turns forty years old, he said, "My Lord, remind me to give you[MS] thanks for the blessings you[MS] gave me and my parents, and to do righteous deeds that please you[MS]. Give me righteous descendants.[4802] I repent to you[MS], and I have submitted."[4803] (15) For this kind of people, those that go to the heavenly garden,[4804] we accept the best of what they do, and

---

[4792] The word "only" is not to be understood as exclusive. Muhammad (s) has several other titles, including "bearer of good news" (48:8), "testifier" (48:8), Allah's messenger (48:29), prophet (33:45), "witness" (33:45), "caller to Allah by his permission" (33:46), and "shining lamp" (33:46), among others.

[4793] Nuh is also called a clear warner (26:115).

[4794] Moses. See glossary for more details.

[4795] 11:17, Zabur, Psalms 119:29

[4796] 11:17, Zabur, Psalms 119:77

[4797] Here and verse 30 are two of the many times the Qur'an confirms the previous books (2:41,89,91,97,101, 3:3,81, 4:47, 5:48, 6:92, 35:31, 46:12,30).

[4798] Arabic /jannah/. See glossary for more details. Injil, Revelation 22:2

[4799] Injil, Luke 6:35

[4800] Tawrah, Exodus 20:12, Deuteronomy 5:16

[4801] Tawrah, Genesis 3:16

[4802] Tawrah, Proverbs 23:24

[4803] Injil, James 4:7. For "submitted," some translators do not translate this. See glossary for more details.

[4804] Arabic /jannah/. See glossary for more details.

overlook their bad deeds.⁴⁸⁰⁵ That promise they were given is true. (16) As for those who say to their parents, "I am disgusted with youᴰ!⁴⁸⁰⁶ Do youᴰ promise me I can be brought out? Generations before me have passed away." All the while, theyᴰ are praying to Allah. "Woe to youᴹˢ. Believeᴹˢ that Allah's promise is true." They will say, "This is just a bunch of ancient legends." (17) Those are the ones about whom the statement is fulfilled concerning the nations of jinns⁴⁸⁰⁷ and people before them that have passed away and were lost. (18) Everyone has degrees of deeds they did, so we will pay them back for their deeds, and they will not be wronged. (19) On that day, the disbelievers will be shown hellfire. "Youᴹᴾ have wasted yourᴹᴾ good things in yourᴹᴾ earthly life, and youᴹᴾ have enjoyed them. So today, youᴹᴾ will be repaid with contemptible torment⁴⁸⁰⁸ for beingᴹᴾ unjustifiably proud in the land, and for yourᴹᴾ unbelief."⁴⁸⁰⁹ (20) 26A2 Remember Aad's⁴⁸¹⁰ brother, when he warned his people by the sand dunes, since warners had passed away in front of him⁴⁸¹¹ and behind him, "Worship only Allah.⁴⁸¹² I am afraid youᴹᴾ will suffer the torment of a great day." (21) They said, "Have youᴹˢ come to us to lie about our gods?⁴⁸¹³ Bring on what youᴹˢ promise us if youᴹˢ are telling the truth." (22) He said, "Allah only knows. I am conveying the message I was given. I see that youᴹᴾ are ignorant people." (23) When they saw it as a cloud coming toward their valleys, they said, "This is a cloud that will give us rain." Rather it is what youᴹᴾ hastened: a wind with painful torment in it. (24) It will destroy everything by order of its Lord. In the morning, nothing will be left to see but their dwellings. This is how we repay wrongdoing people. (25) We have strengthened them as we have strengthened youᴹᴾ. We gave them hearing, sight, and hearts, but their hearing, sight, and hearts did them no good,⁴⁸¹⁴ since they denied Allah's

---

⁴⁸⁰⁵ Injil, Acts 17:30
⁴⁸⁰⁶ Tawrah, Exodus 21:17
⁴⁸⁰⁷ Or demons. See glossary for more details.
⁴⁸⁰⁸ For "torment" here and in verses 21, 31, and 34, see Tawrah, Isaiah 50:11, Injil, Matthew 18:34, 25:41,46, Luke 16:23-28, Revelation 20:15.
⁴⁸⁰⁹ Or immorality or transgression. Injil, Luke 16:25
⁴⁸¹⁰ Aad is the name of a tribe.
⁴⁸¹¹ Or, "between his hands."
⁴⁸¹² Injil, Matthew 4:10
⁴⁸¹³ Arabic /ilah/. See glossary for more details.
⁴⁸¹⁴ Injil, Romans 11:8

## Chapter 46

signs.⁴⁸¹⁵ So they were surrounded by what they had made fun of. (26) We destroyed the villages around you^MP, and explained the signs, so that they may return. (27) If only the offering and the gods⁴⁸¹⁶ they chose besides Allah had saved them. But they went astray from them. That was the lie they invented. (28) We turned a group of jinns⁴⁸¹⁷ toward you^MS to listen to the Qur'an,⁴⁸¹⁸ and when they came, they said, "Listen." When it was completed, they turned to their people as warners.⁴⁸¹⁹ (29) They said, "Our people, we have heard a book that was revealed after Musa,⁴⁸²⁰ confirming what is in his possession,⁴⁸²¹ guiding to the truth and the straight path.⁴⁸²² (30) Our people, respond to Allah's caller, and believe in him. He will forgive you^MP some of your^MP sins⁴⁸²³ and deliver you^MP from painful torment." (31) Those who do not respond to Allah's caller cannot frustrate [this]⁴⁸²⁴ on earth, and they will have no protector besides him. They have clearly gone astray. (32) ***
Have they not seen that Allah has created the heavens and the earth?⁴⁸²⁵ There was nothing that tired him from their creation.⁴⁸²⁶ He can give life to the dead.⁴⁸²⁷ Indeed, he can do anything.⁴⁸²⁸ (33)
***
On that day, he will show hellfire to the disbelievers. "Is this not real?" They will say, "Yes, [we swear] by our Lord." He will say, "Taste^MP the torment for your^MP disbelief." (34) Endure as the determined messengers endured,⁴⁸²⁹ and do not hasten it for them. On the day they see what they were promised, it will seem to them

---

⁴⁸¹⁵ Arabic /ayat/. See glossary for more details.
⁴⁸¹⁶ Arabic /ilah/. See glossary for more details.
⁴⁸¹⁷ Or demons. See glossary for more details.
⁴⁸¹⁸ Or recitation. See glossary for more details.
⁴⁸¹⁹ Injil, James 2:19
⁴⁸²⁰ Moses. See glossary for more details.
⁴⁸²¹ Or, "between its/his hands" or "in front of it/him."
⁴⁸²² See glossary for more details, and notes on 3:51, 6:153, 19:36, 36:61, and 43:64 on what the straight path is.
⁴⁸²³ Injil, Ephesians 1:7
⁴⁸²⁴ Or, [Allah] or [Allah's plan]
⁴⁸²⁵ Tawrah, Genesis 1:1
⁴⁸²⁶ 2:255
⁴⁸²⁷ Injil, Romans 4:17
⁴⁸²⁸ Tawrah, Job 42:2, Isaiah 14:27, Daniel 4:35, Injil, Matthew 19:26, Mark 10:27, Luke 1:37
⁴⁸²⁹ See "endure" in glossary

Chapter 46

as if they remained only an hour of the day.[4830] [It is] a proclamation. Will he destroy any except unbelieving[4831] people? (35)[4832]

---

[4830] Injil, James 4:14
[4831] Or transgressing or immoral
[4832] The verses in this chapter that rhyme are put together in paragraphs, separated by ***.

# Chapter 47 Muhammad[4833]

In the name of Allah, the most gracious and merciful.[4834] May the works of disbelievers who block [others] from Allah's path go astray.[4835] (1) He has expiated[4836] the bad deeds of believers who do righteous deeds,[4837] who believe in what was revealed to Muhammad,[4838] which is truth from their Lord, and he has made their minds righteous. (2) That is because the disbelievers have followed vain things, while believers follow truth from their Lord. Thus Allah makes proverbs for people. (3) If you[MP] find disbelievers, strike their necks[4839] until, when you[MP] press heavily upon them, you tighten their bonds.[4840] Then afterward either be gracious or [allow] redemption until war lays down its burden. Thus it is. If Allah had willed, he would have been victorious over them, but this was to test[4841] some of you[MP] with each other. The works of those who are killed in Allah's path will not go astray. (4) He will guide them, make their minds righteous, (5) and cause them to enter the heavenly garden[4842] he made known to them. (6) Believers, if you[MP] help Allah, he will help you[MP] and make your[MP] feet firm. (7) May disbelievers be miserable and their works go astray, (8) since they hated what Allah revealed, and he made their deeds in vain. (9) **26A3**

\*\*\*

---

[4833] The name Muhammad, which means "highly praised."

[4834] Zabur, Psalms 103:8, 145:8. See glossary for more details.

[4835] Injil, Matthew 23:13, Luke 11:52.

[4836] Tawrah, Isaiah 27:9, Injil, Romans 3:25, Hebrews 2:17, 1 John 2:2, 4:10

[4837] Here and in verse 12, see Injil, 1 Corinthians 3:8, James 2:14-17, Revelation 19:8.

[4838] Muhammad (s) is mentioned by name here and in three other verses (3:144, 33:40, and 48:29). In addition, he is often referred to, but he is never to be worshiped; he pointed people to Allah. There is no basis in the Qur'an to call Muslims Mohammedans.

[4839]Tawrah, Joshua 10:24. This phrase is often taken out of context. Later in the verse the context of war is mentioned. This cannot be used as a justification for attacking disbelievers in time of peace.

[4840] Tawrah, Joshua 10:30

[4841] Tawrah, Judges 2:22

[4842] Arabic /jannah/ here and in verses 12 and 15. See glossary for more details. Injil, Acts 14:22

## Chapter 47

Have they not walked through the land and seen the end of those before them? Allah destroyed them, and disbelievers will be similar. (10)

\*\*\*

That is because Allah is the believers' protector, while disbelievers have no protector. (11) Allah will cause believers who do righteous deeds to enter heavenly gardens with flowing rivers underneath.[4843] Disbelievers enjoy life and eat just like cattle eat,[4844] and hellfire will be their abode. (12) How many villages stronger than the village you[MS] were expelled from did we destroy, and they had no savior. (13) Are those who trust in a miracle from their Lord like those who think their evil deeds are fair and follow their desires? (14) The heavenly garden the reverent are promised is like rivers of clear water, rivers of unspoiled milk, rivers of delightful wine, and rivers of strained honey. There they will have all kinds of fruit[4845] and forgiveness[4846] from their Lord. Are they like those who are in hellfire forever, given boiling water to drink that tears out their intestines?[4847] (15) Some of them listen to you[MS], and when they go out from you[MS], they say to those who are learned, "What did he say?" Allah has sealed their hearts."[4848] They follow their desires. (16) Those who were guided get more guidance, and he gives them their reverence.[4849] (17) Will they see anything besides the hour coming upon them suddenly?[4850] Its signs have come.[4851] When their reminder comes upon them, what will they do? (18) Know[MS] that Allah is the only god,[4852] and ask[MS] forgiveness[4853] for your[MS] sin[4854] and that of male and female

---

[4843] Injil, Revelation 22:2
[4844] Tawrah, Ecclesiastes 3:18
[4845] Injil, Revelation 22:2
[4846] Injil, Romans 4:7
[4847] Zabur , Psalms 50:22
[4848] Or "What did those whose hearts Allah has sealed say beforehand?"
[4849] Injil, Matthew 13:12
[4850] Injil, 1 Thessalonians 5:3
[4851] The noun here is feminine and the verb masculine. Possibly the meaning is that the signs are people. Injil, Matthew 24:3ff
[4852] Arabic /ilah/. See glossary for more details.
[4853] The belief that all prophets and messengers are sinless is not supported by the Qur'an. For instances of prophets or messengers asking forgiveness or committing sins, see 7:23, 20:121 (Adam), 11:47, 71:28 (Nuh), 26:82, 14:41 (Ibrahim), 28:15-16 (Musa), 7:151, 20:93 (Musa and Harun), 38:24 (Dawud), 38:32,35 (Sulayman), 21:87, 37:142 (Yunus),

believers.[4855] Allah knows your[MP] behavior[4856] and your[MP] dwelling. (19) The believers say, "If only a chapter had been revealed." When a clear chapter was revealed and fighting was mentioned in it,[4857] you[MS] see those with sick hearts[4858] looking at you[MS] as if they were fainting and near death. It is more important for them (20) to be obedient, and to speak kindly. When the matter has been determined, it would have been better for them to have been true to Allah. (21) When you[MP] turned away, could you[MP] have caused destruction on the earth, and cut off[MP] your[MP] relatives? (22) Those are the ones Allah has damned,[4859] made deaf, and blinded. (23)

\*\*\*

Have they not reflected on the Qur'an?[4860] Or are their hearts locked? (24)

\*\*\*

Satan has seduced and given more time[4861] to those who turned back after guidance was made clear. (25) That is because they told those who hated what Allah revealed, "We will obey you[MP] in part of the matter." Allah knows what they conceal. (26) What will happen when the angels cause them to die? They will beat their faces and backs. (27) That is because they followed what enrages Allah and they hate pleasing him, so he has made their deeds to be in vain. (28) Do those with sick hearts[4862] think that Allah will not expose their hatred? (29) If we willed, we would show them to you[MS] and you[MS] would know them by their mark.[4863] You[MS] will know them through the tone of their speech. Allah knows your[MP] deeds. (30) We will test you[MP] to know those who struggle and endure[4864] among you[MP] and we will test your[MP] news. (31) Disbelievers who block [others] from Allah's path and resist the messenger after guidance has been made clear to them will not

---

48:2, 47:19, 40:55, 4:79,106, 9:43, 13:30, 80:1-2, 110:3, 94:2, 23:118, 66:1, 33:37, 8:67, and 9:117 (Muhammad (s).

[4854] Injil, 1 John 1:9
[4855] Injil, 1 John 5:16
[4856] Or "wandering."
[4857] Tawrah, Joshua 1:14
[4858] Tawrah, Jeremiah 8:18, 17:9-10
[4859] Injil, Galatians 3:10
[4860] Or recitation. See glossary for more details.
[4861] See introduction for other ways this verse is translated.
[4862] Tawrah, Jeremiah 8:18, 17:9-10
[4863] Injil, Revelation 13:17, 14:9,11, 16:2, 19:20, 20:4
[4864] See "endure" in glossary

## Chapter 47

harm Allah at all, and he will frustrate their deeds. (32) ٢٦A٤ Believers, obey Allah, obey the messenger, and do not frustrate your[MP] deeds. (33) Allah will not forgive disbelievers who block [others] from Allah's path[4865] and then die while still disbelievers. (34) Do not be[MP] weak or call[MP] for peace,[4866] since you[MP] will be higher,[4867] Allah is with you[MP],[4868] and he will not defraud you[MP] of your[MP] works. (35) This life is play and amusement. If you[MP] believe and are[MP] reverent,[4869] he will give you[MP] your[MP] reward, and will not ask you[MP] about your[MP] money. (36) If he asks you[MP] for it, he will be insistent. You[MP] are miserly and he will expose your[MP] hatred. (37) You[MP] are called to donate in Allah's path.[4870] Some of you[MP] are miserly, and such misers are miserly to the detriment of their own souls.[4871] Allah is self-sufficient[4872] and you[MP] are poor. If you[MP] turn away, he will exchange you[MP] for other people,[4873] who will not be like you[MP]. (38)[4874]

---

[4865] Injil, Matthew 23:13, Luke 11:52.
[4866] Tawrah, Joshua 1:7
[4867] Tawrah, Exodus 14:14
[4868] Injil, Romans 8:31
[4869] Injil, James 2:24
[4870] Injil, 3 John 8
[4871] Injil, 2 Corinthians 9:6
[4872] Or rich.
[4873] Injil, Matthew 21:43
[4874] The verses in this chapter that rhyme are put together in paragraphs, separated by ***.

## Chapter 48: Al-Fath[4875]

In the name of Allah, the most gracious and merciful.[4876] We have given you[MS] an obvious victory, (1) so that Allah may forgive[4877] your[MS] past and future sins; complete his blessings upon you[MS]; guide you[MS] on a straight path;[4878] (2) and rescue you[MS] with a mighty rescue. (3) He it is who sent the presence[4879] into the hearts of the believers, so they would grow in faith. The hosts of heaven and earth belong to Allah. Allah is all-knowing[4880] and wise.[4881] (4) He also did so in order to bring the believing men and women forever into heavenly gardens[4882] with flowing rivers[4883] underneath, and to expiate their bad deeds[4884] from them. This is a great victory[4885] to Allah, (5) that he may torment[4886] hypocritical

---

[4875] The t and the h are separate sounds, not like the th sound in English. Victory or conquest.

[4876] Zabur, Psalms 103:8, 145:8. See glossary for more details.

[4877] The belief that all prophets and messengers are sinless is not supported by the Qur'an. For instances of prophets or messengers asking forgiveness or committing sins, see 7:23, 20:121 (Adam), 11:47, 71:28 (Nuh), 26:82, 14:41 (Ibrahim), 28:15-16 (Musa), 7:151, 20:93 (Musa and Harun), 38:24 (Dawud), 38:32,35 (Sulayman), 21:87, 37:142 (Yunus), 48:2, 47:19, 40:55, 4:79,106, 9:43, 13:30, 80:1-2, 110:3, 94:2, 23:118, 66:1, 33:37, 8:67, and 9:117 (Muhammad (s).

[4878] See glossary for more details, and notes on 3:51, 6:153, 19:36, 36:61, and 43:64 on what the straight path is.

[4879] This word /sakeenah/ (presence) here and in verses 18 and 26 can mean either shekinah (an Arabized word from Hebrew, meaning Allah's presence) or tranquility. Since true tranquility comes from Allah's presence, the two meanings are not contradictory. It is used in 2:248, 9:26,40, 48:4,18,26. In 2:248 it clearly refers to Allah's presence. Tawrah, Numbers 7:89

[4880] Tawrah, Job 37:16, Isaiah 40:14, Zabur, Psalms 33:13-15, Injil, 1 John 3:20

[4881] Tawrah, Job 9:4, Proverbs 2:6, Jeremiah 9:23-24, Injil, 1 Corinthians 1:21-25, Romans 16:27

[4882] Arabic /jannah/. See glossary for more details.

[4883] Injil, Revelation 22:1-2, Tawrah, Ezekiel 47:12

[4884] Tawrah, Isaiah 27:9, Injil, Romans 3:25, Hebrews 2:17, 1 John 2:2, 4:10

[4885] Tawrah, Isaiah 25:8, Injil, 1 Corinthians 15:57, 1 John 5:4

[4886] For "torment" here and in verses 14,16, and 17, see Tawrah, Isaiah 50:11, Injil, Matthew 18:34, 25:41,46, Luke 16:23-28, Revelation 20:15.

men and women and polytheistic men and women, who wrongly think evil thoughts about Allah. They are encircled by evil.[4887] Allah is angry with them, has damned them. He has prepared hell[4888] for them, an evil destiny. (6) The hosts of heaven and earth belong to Allah and Allah is strong and wise.[4889] (7) We have sent you[MS] as a witness, a bearer of good news, and a warner (8) so that you[MP] would believe in Allah and his messenger and aid[4890] him, revere him, and praise him[4891] morning and evening. (9) Those who pledge allegiance[4892] to you[MS] pledge allegiance to Allah, and Allah's hand is upon their hands. Whoever violates[4893] really violates himself. Whoever is faithful to what he promises Allah will receive a great reward from Allah. (10) Those desert nomads[4894] who delay will tell you[MS], "We are busy with our money and our families, so ask forgiveness for us." What they say with their tongues is not what is in their hearts. Say[MS]: "Who can help you[MP] against Allah if he wants to harm you[MP] or benefit you[MP]? Allah is aware of your[MP] deeds. (11) You[MP] thought that Allah's messenger and the believers would never return to their families and this seemed pleasing to you[MP]. You[MP] imagined evil, and you were wicked people." (12) As for those who do not believe in Allah and his messenger, we have prepared a burning fire for disbelievers. (13) The kingdom of the heavens and the earth belongs to Allah.[4895] He has mercy on whoever he wills and he torments whoever he wills.[4896] Allah is forgiving[4897] and merciful.[4898] (14) If you[MP] depart to take spoils, those who delay

---

[4887] Tawrah, Genesis 6:5
[4888] The Arabic word is jahannam, which is related to gehenna.
[4889] Tawrah, Job 9:4, Proverbs 2:6, Jeremiah 9:23-24, Injil, 1 Corinthians 1:21-25, Romans 16:27
[4890] The literal meaning here is reprove or censure, which does not seem to fit, and this word is probably an Arabization of the Hebrew word /'ezr/ (help).
[4891] The "him"s in this verse probably refer to Allah, as this word for praise is not used for people.
[4892] Or proclaim loyalty
[4893] implied object is "his pledge or loyalty"
[4894] Or Bedouins here and in verse 16.
[4895] Tawrah, Isaiah 45:12, Zabur, Psalms 24:1, 89:11, Injil, Hebrews 1:10
[4896] Tawrah, Exodus 33:19, Injil, Romans 9:15,18
[4897] Zabur, Psalms 103:3, 130:4, Tawrah, Isaiah 43:25, Exodus 34:7, Injil, Acts 26:18.
[4898] See glossary for more details on "merciful."

## Chapter 48

will say, "Let<sup>MP</sup> us follow you<sup>MP</sup>." They want to change Allah's word. Say<sup>MS</sup>, "You<sup>MP</sup> will not follow us this way. Allah has said so beforehand." They will say, "So you<sup>MP</sup> are jealous of us." They do not understand much. (15) Say to the desert nomads who delay, "You<sup>MP</sup> will be called to courageous, strong people, either to fight<sup>MP</sup> them or make them surrender. If you<sup>MP</sup> obey, Allah will reward you<sup>MP</sup> well. If you<sup>MP</sup> turn back as you<sup>MP</sup> did before, he will torment you<sup>MP</sup> painfully." (16) Neither the blind nor the lame[4899] nor the sick are obligated. Allah will cause him who obeys him and his messenger to enter heavenly gardens[4900] with flowing rivers[4901] underneath, and will torment him who turns away painfully. (17) **26B1** Allah was pleased with the believers when they pledged allegiance to you<sup>MS</sup> under the tree. He knew what was in their hearts and sent the presence down upon them and rewarded them with a quick victory (18) and much spoils for them to take. Allah is powerful and wise.[4902] (19) Allah promised you<sup>MP</sup> would take much spoils, Then he gave it quickly, and kept people's hands from you<sup>MP</sup> as a sign for the believers and guidance for you<sup>MP</sup> on a straight path.[4903] (20) And others[4904] that you<sup>MP</sup> were unable to get. Allah has surrounded them. Allah can do anything.[4905] (21) If the disbelievers had fought you<sup>MP</sup>, they would have fled, finding neither protector nor savior, (22) as Allah's did in the past. You<sup>MS</sup> will never find a change in Allah's practice. (23) It was Allah who kept their hands from you<sup>MP</sup> and your<sup>MP</sup> hands from them in the heart of Mecca after he gave you<sup>MP</sup> victory over them. Allah sees your<sup>MP</sup> deeds. (24) They are the disbelievers who blocked you<sup>MP</sup> from the sacred place of worship,[4906] so the sacrifice was restrained from its place. If not for the believing men and women you<sup>MP</sup> did not know, you<sup>MP</sup> would have trampled them and been

---

[4899] Tawrah, 2 Samuel 5:6-8

[4900] Arabic /jannah/. See glossary for more details.

[4901] Injil, Revelation 22:1-2, Tawrah, Ezekiel 47:12

[4902] Tawrah, Job 9:4, Proverbs 2:6, Jeremiah 9:23-24, Injil, 1 Corinthians 1:21-25, Romans 16:27

[4903] See glossary for more details, and notes on 3:51, 6:153, 19:36, 36:61, and 43:64 on what the straight path is.

[4904] probably spoils

[4905] Tawrah, Job 42:2, Isaiah 14:27, Daniel 4:35, Injil, Matthew 19:26, Mark 10:27, Luke 1:37

[4906] For "sacred place of worship" here and in verse 27, see Injil, John 4:20-24, Hebrews 8:1-2, 9:24, 10:19-22.

## Chapter 48

shamed unknowingly, in order to bring whoever he wills into his mercy.[4907] If they had been separated, we would have painfully tormented the disbelievers among them. (25) The disbelievers' hearts were furious with the fury of ignorance, so Allah sent his presence on his messenger and the believers, and made them keep the word of reverence, of which they were more worthy and deserving. Allah is all-knowing.[4908] (26) Allah has truly fulfilled the vision to his messenger: you[MP] will certainly enter the sacred place of worship, if Allah wills, safely, with heads shaved[4909] or short-haired, and fearlessly. He knew what you[MP] did not know, and furthermore made it a swift victory. (27) He sent his messenger with guidance and the religion of truth to give it victory over all religion.[4910] Allah is a sufficent witness. (28) "Muhammad,[4911] Allah's messenger,[4912][4913] and those with him are harsh against the disbelievers, and merciful among themselves.[4914] You[MS] see them kneeling and bowing down, seeking grace and pleasure from Allah. The marks of bowing down are on their faces as signs. The Tawrah[4915] compares them to that. The Injil[4916] compares them to a seed that sends forth its stem, and gets strong, thick, and straight on its stalk, thus pleasing the farmers, though the disbelievers are furious at them. Allah has promised the

---

[4907] Tawrah, Exodus 33:19, Injil, Romans 9:15,18
[4908] Tawrah, Job 37:16, Isaiah 40:14, Zabur, Psalms 33:13-15, Injil, 1 John 3:20
[4909] Injil, Acts 18:18, Tawrah, Numbers 6:18
[4910] The probable meaning is "all false religion."
[4911] Muhammad (s) is mentioned by name here and in three other verses (3:144, 33:40, and 47:2). In addition, he is often referred to, but he is never to be worshiped; he pointed people to Allah. There is no basis in the Qur'an to call Muslims Mohammedans.
[4912] Or, Muhammad is Allah's messenger. This verse is the only verse in the Qur'an where the last three words of the Islamic confession occur. Muhammad (s) in this verse and Isa (4:157,171) are the only ones about whom the phrase "[is] Allah's messenger" is used after their names.
[4913] The ones specifically called Allah's messenger in the Qur'an are Muhammad (s) 48:29, 7:158, 33:21,40,53, etc., Musa 61:5, Thamud's messenger 91:13, and Isa 4:157,171, 61:6.
[4914] Or, among them.
[4915] The Law. See glossary for more details.
[4916] Gospel. See glossary for more details.

Chapter 48

believers among them who do righteous deeds[4917] forgiveness and a great reward." (29)

---

[4917] Injil, 1 Corinthians 3:8, James 2:14-17, Revelation 19:8

# Chapter 49 Al-Hujurat[4918]

**26B2** In the name of Allah, the most gracious and merciful.[4919] Believers, do not be forward[4920] in front of[4921] Allah and his messenger. Fear[MP] Allah.[4922] Allah hears all and knows all.[4923] (1) Believers, do not raise your[MP] voices above the prophet's voice, and do not speak[MP] openly[4924] to him as you[MP] do to each other, or your[MP] works will be in vain, though you[MP] do not realize it. (2) Those who lower their voices with Allah's messenger are those whose hearts Allah has tested with reverence. They will have forgiveness and a great reward. (3) Most of those who call to you[MS] from behind the private rooms do not comprehend. (4) If they had waited until you[MS] came out to them, it would have been better for them. Allah is forgiving[4925] and merciful.[4926] (5) Believers, if an unbeliever brings news to you[MP], be clear,[4927] so that you[MP] do not afflict people in ignorance. In that case, you[MP] would regret your[MP] deed. (6) Know that Allah's messenger is among you[MP]. If he were to obey you[MP] in much of the matter, you[MP] would suffer, but Allah made you[MP] love faith, and made it attractive to your[MP] hearts. He made you[MP] hate disbelief, unbelief,[4928] and disobedience. This kind of people are wisely guided. (7) This is Allah's grace and blessings. Allah is all-knowing and wise.[4929] (8) If two parties of

---

[4918] Private rooms
[4919] Zabur, Psalms 103:8, 145:8. See glossary for more details.
[4920] Or "present" The object of what is presented is not stated. According to 58:12, the meaning may be "alms."
[4921] Or, "between the hands of."
[4922] Tawrah, Leviticus 19:14,32
[4923] For "knows all" and "all-knowing" here and in verses 8 and 13, see Tawrah, Job 37:16, Isaiah 40:14, Zabur, Psalms 33:13-15, Injil, 1 John 3:20
[4924] Or, aloud
[4925] Here and in verse 14, see Zabur, Psalms 103:3, 130:4, Tawrah, Isaiah 43:25, Exodus 34:7, Injil, Acts 26:18.
[4926] Here and in verses 12 and 14, see glossary for more details on "merciful."
[4927] Tawrah, Proverbs 1:10
[4928] Or immorality or transgression.
[4929] Tawrah, Job 9:4, Proverbs 2:6, Jeremiah 9:23-24, Injil, 1 Corinthians 1:21-25, Romans 16:27

## Chapter 49

believers fight, reconcile<sup>MP</sup> them.[4930] If one of them is insolent against another, fight<sup>MP</sup> against the insolent party until it returns to Allah's command. If it returns, reconcile<sup>MP</sup> them with justice and equity. Allah loves those who are just. (9) Believers are brothers,[4931] so reconcile<sup>MP</sup> between your<sup>MP</sup> brothers<sup>D</sup> and fear<sup>MP</sup> Allah, so that you<sup>MP</sup> may receive mercy. (10) Believers, do not let<sup>MP</sup> people mock other people who might be better than they. Nor let women mock other women who might be better than them. Do not slander<sup>MP</sup> each other, and do not call<sup>MP</sup> each other bad names. Unbelief[4932] after faith is awful. He who does not repent is wicked. (11) Believers, avoid a lot of speculations.[4933] Some speculations make you guilty. Do not spy or backbite each other. Does anyone want to eat the flesh of his dead brother?[4934] You<sup>MP</sup> would have hated that. Fear Allah.[4935] Allah accepts repentance and is merciful. (12)

\*\*\*

People, we created you<sup>MP</sup> from a male and female[4936] and made you<sup>MP</sup> peoples and tribes,[4937] so that you<sup>MP</sup> could know each other. The godliest among you<sup>MP</sup> toward Allah is the most honorable. Allah is all-knowing and aware. (13)

\*\*\*

**26B3** The desert nomads[4938] said, "We believe." Say<sup>MS</sup>, "You<sup>MP</sup> have not believed. Rather say<sup>MP</sup>: We have submitted.[4939] Faith has not entered your<sup>MP</sup>hearts."[4940] If you<sup>MP</sup> obey Allah and his messenger, your<sup>MP</sup> works will not be diminished at all. Allah is forgiving and merciful. (14) The believers are those who believe in Allah and his messenger, do not doubt, and struggle with their

---

[4930] Injil, Matthew 18:15-17
[4931] Injil, Philippians 4:1, 2 Thessalonians 2:13
[4932] Or immorality or transgression.
[4933] Or, suspicions
[4934] Injil, Galatians 5:15
[4935] Tawrah, Deuteronomy 10:12, Isaiah 29:13, Injil, 1 Peter 2:17, Revelation 14:7
[4936] Tawrah, Genesis 1:27
[4937] Tawrah, Genesis 10:1-32
[4938] Or Bedouins.
[4939] Injil, James 4:7. For "submitted," "submitting," and "submission" here and in verse 17 (twice), some translators do not translate this. See glossary for more details.
[4940] Injil, Acts 15:9

money[4941] and their souls[4942] in Allah's path. They are truthful. (15) Say[MS], "Do you[MP] teach Allah your[MP] religion,[4943] when Allah knows everything in the heavens and the earth? Allah knows everything." (16) They do you[MS] the favor of submitting. Say[MS], "Do not do[MP] me the favor of submission. Rather, Allah did you[MP] the favor of guiding you[MP] to faith, if you[MP] are telling the truth. (17) Allah knows the unseen things of the heavens and the earth.[4944] Allah sees your[MP] deeds." (18)[4945]

---

[4941] Injil, Mark 12:42
[4942] Or selves or lives or persons
[4943] Injil, 1 Corinthians 2:16
[4944] Injil, Matthew 11:25, 2 Corinthians 4:18
[4945] The verses in this chapter that rhyme are put together in paragraphs, separated by ***.

# Chapter 50 Qaf[4946]

In the name of Allah, the most gracious and merciful.[4947] Q.[4948] [I swear] by the glorious Qur'an.[4949] (1)

\*\*\*

They are amazed that a warner from among them has come to them. Disbelievers said, "This is amazing. (2)

\*\*\*

If we die, and are soil, that is a long way off." (3)

\*\*\*

We know what the earth takes away from them, and we have a preserved book. (4)

\*\*\*

They rejected the truth when it came to them. They are in the midst of a confusing matter. (5) Have they not seen how we built and decorated the sky above them without cracks?[4950] (6) We stretched out the earth,[4951] put mountains in it,[4952] and made every kind of delightful plant sprout in it,[4953] (7)

\*\*\*

as a matter of contemplation and a reminder for every repentant servant.[4954] (8)

\*\*\*

We sent down blessed rain[4955] from the sky, and with it sprouted gardens, grain for harvest, (9) tall palm trees with piles of fruit, (10)

\*\*\*

as provision for the servants. We revived a dead town.[4956] That is a resurrection. (11)

---

[4946] The letter q in Arabic

[4947] Zabur, Psalms 103:8, 145:8. See glossary for more details.

[4948] Here and at the beginning of many chapters there are unvowelled letters of unknown meaning. Numerous theories have been proposed, but there is no agreement on the subject.

[4949] Or recitation. See glossary for more details.

[4950] Or, "flaws" or "splits"

[4951] Tawrah, Isaiah 44:24, 51:13

[4952] Zabur, Psalms 65:6

[4953] Tawrah, Genesis 1:11-12

[4954] See glossary for "servant" here and in verses 11 and 29.

[4955] Tawrah, Deuteronomy 28:12, Job 5:10, Joel 2:23, Zabur, Psalms 68:9, Injil, Matthew 5:45

## Chapter 50

\*\*\*

Before them, Nuh's[4957] people[4958] and those of Al-Rass and Thamud[4959] were rejecters, (12)

\*\*\*

as did Aad, Pharaoh,[4960] Lut's[4961] brothers,[4962] (13)

\*\*\*

the people of the wood, and the people of Tubba. Each of them rejected the messengers, and I fulfilled my threat. (14) Did we get tired in the first creation?[4963] They are confused about a new creation.[4964] (15) We created man and know what his soul whispers to him. We are nearer to him than his jugular vein.[4965] (16) When the two receivers[4966] sitting on the right and the left meet, (17) he only says, "He has an observer ready." (18) Then the agony[4967] of death will show the truth. You[MS] wanted to avoid that. (19) Then the trumpet will be blown.[4968] That is the day he threatened. (20) Every soul will come with a driver and a witness. (21) You[MS] were unaware of this, and so we removed your[MS] covering. Your[MS] sight today is sharp. (22) His companion[4969] said, "This is what I have ready." (23) Cast into hell every stubborn disbeliever, (24)

\*\*\*

who hinders good, is a wicked doubter, (25)

\*\*\*

and makes another god[4970] besides Allah.[4971] Cast him into harsh torment.[4972] (26) **26B4** His companion said, "Our Lord, I did not

---

[4956] Town is feminine and dead is masculine. There may be another meaning.
[4957] Noah. See glossary for more details.
[4958] Tawrah, Genesis 6-8
[4959] Thamud and Aad were names of tribes.
[4960] Tawrah, Exodus 4-12
[4961] Lot, nephew of Abraham. See glossary for more details.
[4962] Tawrah, Genesis 19:1-28
[4963] 2:255, 46:33, Zabur, Psalms 121:3,4, Tawrah, Isaiah 40:28
[4964] Injil, 2 Corinthians 5:17
[4965] Tawrah, Jeremiah 23:23-24
[4966] The meaning may be angels.
[4967] Or drunkenness
[4968] Injil, 1 Corinthians 15:52
[4969] This could refer to a spirit guide or a demon that led them astray here and in verse 27.
[4970] Arabic /ilah/. See glossary for more details.

## Chapter 50

make him transgress, but he has gone far astray." (27) He said, "Do not fight in front of me. I sent the threat to you[MP] beforehand. (28) My saying cannot be exchanged, and I do not wrong the servants."[4973] (29) On that day, we will say to hell[FS], "Are you[FS] full?" It[FS] will say, "Are there any more?[4974]" (30) The heavenly garden[4975] will be brought not far from the reverent. (31)
\*\*\*

This is what you[MP] were promised for every contrite keeper,[4976] (32)
\*\*\*

who fears the most gracious in the unseen, and comes with a repentant heart. (33)
\*\*\*

Enter it in peace. That is the day of eternity. (34) They have whatever they want in it, and still more with us.[4977] (35)
\*\*\*

How many generations we destroyed before them, and they were stronger than they! They passed[4978] through the lands. Is there any escape? (36)
\*\*\*

That is a reminder for people who have a heart or listen while he is a witness. (37)
\*\*\*

We created the heavens, the earth, and what is between them in six days,[4979] and we did not become weary.[4980] (38) So endure[4981] what they say, and proclaim your[MS] Lord's praises before sunrise, before sunset, (39)
\*\*\*

---

[4971] Injil, Revelation 21:8
[4972] Tawrah, Isaiah 50:11, Injil, Matthew 18:34, 25:41,46, Luke 16:23-28, Revelation 20:15
[4973] This verse is one of only five verses where the plural form /abid/ is used. All five use the same phrase. This word can also be translated "slaves." The other verses are 8:51, 22:10, 41:46, and 50:29.
[4974] Tawrah, Proverbs 30:16
[4975] Arabic /jannah/. See glossary for more details.
[4976] i.e. keeper of Allah's commandments. Zabur, Psalms 51:17
[4977] Injil, Matthew 19:29, Mark 10:30
[4978] Or, "wandered" or "searched"
[4979] Tawrah, Genesis 1:3-31
[4980] 2:255, 46:33, Zabur, Psalms 121:3,4, Tawrah, Isaiah 40:28
[4981] See "endure" in glossary

## Chapter 50

and at night. Praise him when you are done bowing down. (40)
\*\*\*

Listen on the day the caller calls from nearby. (41)
\*\*\*

The day they hear the cry in truth will be the day of resurrection.[4982] (42)
\*\*\*

We give life and death, and we are [man's] destiny. (43) On that day, the earth will suddenly split away from them.[4983] That is easy for us to gather. (44)
\*\*\*

We know what they say, and you[MS] are not proud[4984] toward them. With the Qur'an,[4985] remind[MS] those who fear my threat. (45)[4986]

---

[4982] Tawrah, Daniel 12:2 Injil, Acts 24:15, 1 Corinthians 15:52-54, Revelation 20:11-15
[4983] Injil, Revelation 16:19
[4984] Or forceful.
[4985] Or recitation. See glossary for more details.
[4986] The verses in this chapter that rhyme are put together in paragraphs, separated by \*\*\*.

Chapter 51

# Chapter 51 Al-Dhariyat[4987]

In the name of Allah, the most gracious and merciful.[4988] [I swear] by the scatterers[FP][4989] that scatter, (1) by the carriers[FP] of heavy burdens, (2) by those[FP] who run easily, (3) and by the dividers[FP] of a matter: (4)

\*\*\*

what you[MP] were promised is true. (5)

\*\*\*

Judgment is coming.[4990] (6)

\*\*\*

[I swear] by the sky with its tracks,[4991] (7)

\*\*\*

you[MP] have a different saying. (8)

\*\*\*

Liars turn away from it. (9)

\*\*\*

May liars[4992] be killed, (10) those who are negligent and confused. (11) They ask when the day of judgment will be.[4993] (12) On that day they will be tested over the fire. (13) "Taste your[MP] testing. This is what you[MP] wanted to hasten." (14) The reverent will be in heavenly gardens[4994] among springs, (15) taking what their Lord gives them. They did good deeds previously.[4995] (16) They slept little at night,[4996] (17) and before dawn they asked forgiveness.[4997] (18) Beggars and the needy had a portion of their money.[4998] (19) For those who are certain, there are signs on the earth (20) and in themselves.[4999] Do you[MP] not see? (21) Your[MP] provision and what

---

[4987] Scatterers[FP]
[4988] Zabur, Psalms 103:8, 145:8. See glossary for more details.
[4989] The reference here could be to the winds that scatter. Zabur, Psalms 1:4
[4990] Tawrah, Joel 2:1
[4991] Or orbits. Zabur, Psalms 19:5
[4992] Or guessers
[4993] Injil, Mark 13:4
[4994] Arabic /jannah/. See glossary for more details.
[4995] Injil, 1 Timothy 6:18
[4996] Zabur, Psalms 119:62
[4997] Zabur, Psalms 5:3
[4998] Tawrah, Isaiah 58:7
[4999] Injil, Romans 1:19-20

## Chapter 51

you[MP] have been promised is in heaven.[5000] (22) So [I swear] by the Lord of heaven and earth, it is true, as you[MP] speak. (23) Have you[MS] heard the story of Ibrahim's[5001] honored guests?[5002] (24) They came to him[5003] and said, "Peace." He said, "Peace to unknown people."[5004] (25) He turned quickly[5005] to his family, brought a fat calf,[5006] (26) and offered it to them.[5007] He said, "Will you[MP] not eat?" (27) He was afraid of them. They said, "Do not be afraid." Then they gave him good news of a knowledgeable boy.[5008] (28) His wife cried out loudly, struck her face, and said, "A barren, old woman."[5009] (29) They said, "This is what your[MS] Lord says.[5010] He is wise[5011] and all-knowing."[5012] (30) 27A1 He said, "Messengers, what do you[MP] have to say?" (31) They said, "We have been sent to wrongdoers,[5013] (32) to send upon them clay rocks,[5014] (33) designated by your[MS] Lord for the wasteful."[5015] (34) So we brought out the believers that were in it,[5016] (35) but found only one family who were submitted.[5017] (36) We left a sign in it[5018] for those who fear painful torment.[5019] (37) Another was Musa,[5020] We sent him to Pharaoh with clear authority, (38) and he

---

[5000] Injil, 1 Peter 1:4
[5001] Abraham. See glossary for more details.
[5002] Tawrah, Genesis 18:1-33
[5003] Tawrah, Genesis 18:2
[5004] Tawrah, Genesis 18:3
[5005] Tawrah, Genesis 18:6
[5006] Tawrah, Genesis 18:7
[5007] Tawrah, Genesis 18:8
[5008] Tawrah, Genesis 18:10
[5009] Tawrah, Genesis 18:12
[5010] Tawrah, Genesis 18:14
[5011] Tawrah, Job 9:4, Proverbs 2:6, Jeremiah 9:23-24, Injil, 1 Corinthians 1:21-25, Romans 16:27
[5012] Tawrah, Job 37:16, Isaiah 40:14, Zabur, Psalms 33:13-15, Injil, 1 John 3:20
[5013] Tawrah, Genesis 18:20
[5014] Tawrah, Genesis 19:24
[5015] Tawrah, Ezekiel 16:49
[5016] Tawrah, Genesis 19:16
[5017] Injil, James 4:7. For "submitted," some translators do not translate this. See glossary for more details.
[5018] Probably the village. Tawrah, Genesis 19:25,28
[5019] Tawrah, Isaiah 50:11, Injil, Matthew 13:34, 25:41,46, Luke 16:23-28, Revelation 20:15
[5020] Moses. See glossary for more details.

turned away to his princes and said, "Either a magician[5021] or crazy." (39) We overtook him and his armies, and left them in the water,[5022] since he was blameworthy. (40) Another was Aad.[5023] We sent a barren wind upon them (41) that left nothing behind. When it came upon them, it made them rot. (42) Another was Thamud. They were told, "Enjoy life for a while." (43) They were insolent towards Allah's command, and lightning[5024] overtook them as they watched. (44) They were not able to stand, and could not defend themselves. (45) Another was Nuh's[5025] people before them. They were unbelievers.[5026] (46) Another is the sky, which we built with hands.[5027] We make things large. (47) We carpeted the earth.[5028] What nice couch spreaders! (48) We created everything in pairs,[5029] so that you[MP] may remember. (49) Flee[MP] to Allah.[5030] I am a clear warner from him to you[MP]. (50) Do not make any other god[5031] besides Allah.[5032] I am a clear warner from him to you[MP]. (51) Thus whenever a messenger came to those before them, they said, "Either a magician or crazy." (52) Did they inherit this from each other? No, they are transgressing people. (53) Turn[MS] away from them. You[MS] are not blameworthy. (54) Remind[MS] them. Reminders are beneficial to believers.[5033] (55) I only created the jinns[5034] and humans so that they would worship me.[5035] (56) I do not want provision from them,[5036] nor do I want them to feed me.[5037] (57) Allah is the strong,[5038] firm provider.[5039]

---

[5021] Tawrah, Exodus 7:11
[5022] Tawrah, Exodus 15:4
[5023] Aad and Thamud were tribes.
[5024] Tawrah, 2 Samuel 22:15
[5025] Noah. See glossary for more details.
[5026] Or transgressing or immoral. Tawrah, Genesis 6:5
[5027] Tawrah, Genesis 1:7-8
[5028] Tawrah, Genesis 1:11-12
[5029] Tawrah, Genesis 7:2, Isaiah 34:15
[5030] Zabur, Psalms 7:1
[5031] Arabic /ilah/. See glossary for more details.
[5032] Tawrah, Exodus 20:4-5
[5033] Tawrah, Deuteronomy 8:2
[5034] Or demons. See glossary for more details.
[5035] Tawrah, Isaiah 43:7
[5036] Tawrah, Isaiah 66:1-2
[5037] Zabur, Psalms 50:12-13
[5038] Tawrah, Job 9:4, Zabur, Psalms 24:8, Injil, Ephesians 6:10, Revelation 18:8

## Chapter 51

(58) Those who are unjust have sins like the sins of their companions.[5040] Let them not hasten me. (59) Woe to the disbelievers for the day they are promised.[5041] (60)[5042]

---

[5039] Zabur, Psalms 136:25
[5040] Injil, Romans 2:1
[5041] Tawrah, Jeremiah 50:27
[5042] The verses in this chapter that rhyme are put together in paragraphs, separated by ***.

Chapter 52

# Chapter 52 Al-Tur[5043]

In the name of Allah, the most gracious and merciful.[5044] [I swear] by the mountain,[5045] (1) by a book, written (2) on a scroll spread out,[5046] (3) by a house built,[5047] (4)
\*\*\*
by a raised ceiling,[5048] (5)
\*\*\*
by a sea filled with water:[5049] (6)
\*\*\*
your[MS] Lord's torment[5050] is inevitable.[5051] (7) There is no defense against it (8)
\*\*\*
on the day the sky is agitated[5052] (9) and the mountains are moved.[5053] (10)
\*\*\*
Woe on that day to the rejecters. (11) They will begin playing (12)
\*\*\*
on the day they will be thrust into the fires of hell.[5054] (13)
\*\*\*
This is the hellfire you[MP] denied. (14) So is this magic? Or do you[MP] not see? (15) Be roasted in it. Whether you[MP] endure[5055] it or not, it is the same for you[MP]. You[MP] are being paid back for your[MP] deeds.[5056] (16) The reverent are in heavenly gardens[5057] of

---

[5043] Mountain
[5044] Zabur, Psalms 103:8, 145:8. See glossary for more details.
[5045] Injil, Hebrews 12:20-22
[5046] This probably refers to the former books, since the Qur'an was not written down until after the death of Muhammad (pbuh). See Tawrah, Exodus 31:18.
[5047] Or "visited"
[5048] Tawrah, Isaiah 42:5, 45:12, 51:13
[5049] Or "waves." Tawrah, Habakkuk 2:14
[5050] For "torment" here and in verses 18 and 47, see Tawrah, Isaiah 50:11, Injil, Matthew 18:34, 25:41,46, Luke 16:23-28, Revelation 20:15.
[5051] Injil, Romans 2:5
[5052] Injil, 2 Peter 3:12
[5053] Injil, Revelation 16:20
[5054] Injil, Matthew 25:46
[5055] See "endure" in glossary
[5056] Injil, Matthew 12:36

## Chapter 52

delight,[5058] (17) rejoicing at their Lord's gifts to them. Their Lord has protected them from the torment of blazing fire. (18) Eat and drink what is wholesome as a reward for your[MP] deeds, (19) reclining on couches lined up. We paired them with "hur iin."[5059] (20) We will unite believers with their seed who followed them in faith.[5060] We will not defraud them[5061] of any of their deeds. Every man is given in pledge for he has earned.[5062] (21) We provided them with fruit and meat as they desire.[5063] (22) There they will dispute over[5064] a cup without vain words or accusations. (23) 27A2 Their fruits,[5065] which are like preserved pearls, will surround them. (24) Some of them go to each other inquiring. (25) They say, "Previously, we were afraid among our people.[5066] (26) But Allah has been gracious to us and protected us from the torment of a hot wind. (27) We prayed to him previously. He is righteous and merciful."[5067] (28) So remind[MS] [people]. By Allah's

---

[5057] Arabic /jannah/. See glossary for more details.

[5058] Injil, John 14:1-3

[5059] This phrase is usually translated "and we will marry them to dark-eyed virgins," but the Arabic text does not have the words "dark," "eye," or "virgin". Instead of /'ain/ (eye), the text says /'in/ (wild ox). /hur/ may mean white, but definitely does not mean dark. It is obvious that the meaning is something else. The word /hur/ (translated by some as "virgins") may be related to the Syriac word /hura/ (grape). Some research suggests that the meaning "we paired them" may mean "we refreshed them." Thus the meaning might be "we refreshed them with white grapes." Every time this phrase occurs (44:54, 55:20, 56:22), it is in the context of fruit, food and drink. Grapes in the heavenly garden are specifically mentioned in 23 19 and 78:32. See note on 56:22. Furthermore, the idea of virgins for the sexual pleasure of believing men does not fit with the presence of their wives in the heavenly gardens with them (43:70, 36:56), or with equal rewards promised female believers in 40:40, 4:124, 16:97.

[5060] Tawrah, 2 Samuel 12:23

[5061] Injil, Romans 3:23, 6:23, 1 Corinthians 3:12-15, Colossians 3:25

[5062] Injil, 1 Corinthians 4:5

[5063] Injil, Luke 22:30

[5064] Or "pass around"

[5065] Most translations have " youths" here but /ghilman/ probably means "the product" in this context, similar to the Arabic phrase "bint al-karma" (literally, daughter of the vine), which means "wine." See 76:19 and 56:18.

[5066] Or "family"

[5067] See glossary for more details on "merciful."

blessings, you^MS are not a fortuneteller or crazy.^5068 (29) Or do they say, "A poet, and we are waiting for time's calamity to fall on him." (30) Say^MS, "Wait. I will wait with you^MP." (31) Or do their dreams command them to do this? Or are they transgressors? (32) Or do they say, "He fabricated it."? No, they do not believe. (33) Let them bring a story like it, if they are telling the truth. (34) Or were they created from nothing? Or are they the creators? (35) Or did they create the heavens and the earth?^5069 No, they are not certain. (36) Or do they have your^MS Lord's storehouses? Or are they sovereign? (37) Or do they have a ladder^5070 on which they listen? Let their listener bring clear authority. (38) Or does he have daughters^5071 and you^MP have sons? (39) Or do you^MS ask them for wages? Have you^MS burdened them with a debt that must be paid?. (40) Or do they have unseen things as they write? (41) Or do they want to plot? Disbelievers will be plotted against. (42) Or do they have a god^5072 besides Allah? May he be glorified^5073 above the gods they worship! (43) If they see a piece of the sky falling, they say, "A heap of clouds." (44) Leave^MS them until they meet their day, when they will faint. (45) On that day, their plots will not help them at all, and they will not be saved. (46) The wicked will have torment besides that, but most of them do not know. (47) Wait^MS for Allah's judgment. Our eyes are upon you^MS. Worship^MS and praise^MS your^MS Lord when you^MS get up (48) and at night. Worship^MS him when the stars go down.^5074 (49)^5075

---

[5068] Or "demonized"
[5069] Tawrah, Jeremiah 10:11
[5070] Tawrah, Genesis 28:12
[5071] Pagan Arabs worshiped goddesses they claimed were Allah's daughters.
[5072] Arabic /ilah/. See glossary for more details.
[5073] Tawrah, Isaiah 2:17
[5074] Zabur, Psalms 119:164
[5075] The verses in this chapter that rhyme are put together in paragraphs, separated by ***.

# Chapter 53 Al-Najm[5076]

In the name of Allah, the most gracious and merciful.[5077] [I swear] by the star when it sets,[5078] (1) your[MP] companion[MS] has not gone astray or been beguiled, (2) nor does he speak out of desire. (3) It is only inspiration, (4) taught by the one mighty in power, (5) who has understanding. So he stood straight[5079] (6) while on the upper horizons. (7) Then he approached and came down, (8) within two bow-shots or closer. (9) Then he inspired his servant. (10) The heart did not lie about what it saw. (11) Do you[MP] dispute with him about what he saw? (12) He saw him on a second descent, (13) at the last lotus tree. (14) That is where the heavenly garden[5080] of refuge is, (15) when the shade covered the lotus tree. (16) His sight did not become dim or wander. (17) He saw some of his Lord's greatest signs. (18) Have you[MP] seen Al-Lat and Al-Uzza, (19) and Manat,[5081] the third, the other one? (20) Do you[MP] have males and he has females? (21) If so, that is an unfair division. (22) They are only names you[MP] and your[MP] ancestors have called them. Allah has not granted them any authority.[5082] They only follow guesses and their souls' desire.[5083] Their Lord has given them guidance. (23) Or do people have what they want? (24) The hereafter and the first world are Allah's. (25) 27A3 How many angels are there in heaven? Their intercession does not help at all, except after Allah gives his permission to the one he wills,[5084] with whom he is pleased.[5085] (26) Those who do not believe in the hereafter give angels female names. (27)

\*\*\*

---

[5076] stars
[5077] Zabur, Psalms 103:8, 145:8. See glossary for more details.
[5078] Or rises
[5079] Or, "sat down"
[5080] Arabic /jannah/. See glossary for more details.
[5081] These three are names of goddesses worshiped by pagan Arabs, who were said to be Allah's daughters.
[5082] Injil, 1 Corinthians 8:4
[5083] Tawrah, Isaiah 40:19-25
[5084] The Qur'an stresses the existence of one intercessor, who has his permission, and with whom he is pleased. See 2:255, Injil, 1 Timothy 2:5.
[5085] 3:49, 5:110, Injil, Matthew 3:17

## Chapter 53

They know nothing about it. They merely follow guessing. Guessing does not prevail against truth at all. (28) So turn away from those who turn away from remembering us, and only want this life. (29)

\*\*\*

That is their goal in knowledge. Your<sup>MS</sup> Lord well knows who has gone astray from his path, and he well knows who is guided. (30) Everything in the heavens and the earth is Allah's,[5086] and he can repay those who do bad deeds for their deeds, and reward those who did good deeds with a good reward.[5087] (31) They avoid major guilt and promiscuity,[5088] but commit some minor ones.[5089] Your<sup>MS</sup> Lord's forgiveness is broad. He knows you well, since he made you from the ground,[5090] for you were fetuses in your mothers' bellies.[5091] So do not justify yourselves.[5092] He knows well who is reverent.[5093] (32) Have you<sup>MP</sup> seen him who turns away, (33) gives little, and is stingy?[5094] (34) Does he know the unseen when he sees? (35) Or has he not been told about what is in the books of Musa[5095] (36) and Ibrahim,[5096] who fully paid his debt: (37) "No one will bear the burden of another,"[5097] (38) "A man gets only what he strives for,"[5098] (39) and "His striving will be seen."?[5099] (40) Then he will be rewarded with a more complete reward.[5100] (41) The end is [going] to your<sup>MP</sup> Lord.[5101] (42) He makes [you] laugh[5102] and cry.[5103] (43) He causes death and gives life.[5104] (44)

---

[5086] Tawrah, Isaiah 45:12, Zabur, Psalms 24:1, 89:11, Injil, Hebrews 1:10
[5087] Injil, Revelation 22:12
[5088] Or lewdness, adultery or abomination
[5089] Zabur, Psalms 19:12,13
[5090] Zabur, Psalms 103:12-14, Genesis 2:7
[5091] Zabur, Psalms 139:13-16
[5092] Injil, Romans 3:28
[5093] Injil, 2 Timothy 2:19
[5094] Tawrah, Proverbs 28:22
[5095] Moses. See glossary for more details.
[5096] Abraham. See glossary for more details.
[5097] Injil, Galatians 6:2,5
[5098] Injil, Luke 14:14
[5099] Injil, 1 Peter 2:12
[5100] Injil, 2 John 8
[5101] Injil, 2 Corinthians 5:10
[5102] Injil, Luke 6:21
[5103] Injil, Luke 6:25
[5104] Tawrah, 1 Samuel 2:6, Deuteronomy 32:39

Chapter 53

He created spouses male and female[5105] (45) from a sperm drop when it is ejaculated.[5106] (46) The latter growth is done by him also.[5107] (47) He gives riches[5108] and gives contentment.[5109] (48) He is Sirius's Lord.[5110] (49) He destroyed Aad[5111] in antiquity, (50) as well as Thamud, whom he did not let remain, (51) and Nuh's[5112] people beforehand.[5113] They were most wicked transgressors.[5114] (52) And he overthrew the lying city,[5115] (53) covering it. (54) Which of your<sup>MS</sup> Lord's benefits do you<sup>MS</sup> doubt? (55) This is a warner, one of the ancient warners.[5116] (56)
\*\*\*

The imminent is drawing near.[5117] (57) Only Allah can keep it away. (58)
\*\*\*

Are you<sup>MP</sup> surprised by this story? (59) Do you<sup>MP</sup> laugh and not cry (60) as you<sup>MP</sup> stand amazed? (61)
\*\*\*

Bow<sup>MP</sup> down and worship<sup>MP</sup> Allah![5118] (62)[5119]

---

[5105] Tawrah, Genesis 1:27
[5106] Tawrah, Genesis 38:9
[5107] Injil, 1 Corinthians 3:7
[5108] Injil, 1 Timothy 6:17
[5109] Injil, 1 Timothy 6:6. This word, in addition to "contentment", has also been translated "little," "poor," "satisfaction," "property," "riches," "gives to hold," "possessions," "causes to possess," "satisfies," "most bountiful," "suffices," "enriches," and "gives possession."
[5110] Tawrah, Job 38:31-32
[5111] Aad and Thamud were tribes.
[5112] Noah. See glossary for more details.
[5113] Injil, Luke 17:27
[5114] Tawrah, Genesis 6:5
[5115] Sodom. Tawrah, Genesis 19:24-25, Deuteronomy 29:23
[5116] Injil, Matthew 16:14
[5117] Injil, Revelation 22:12,20
[5118] Injil, Revelation 22:9
[5119] The verses in this chapter that rhyme are put together in paragraphs, separated by \*\*\*.

# Chapter 54 Al-Qamar[5120]

In the name of Allah, the most gracious and merciful.[5121] The hour is near, and the moon is split. (1) If they see a sign, they turn away and say, "Continued magic." (2) They reject [it] and follow their own desires. Every matter is firmly established. (3) Some tidings with rebukes[5122] came to them. (4) Excellent wisdom. Warnings do not help. (5) Turn[MS] away from them. On the day the caller calls[5123] to something unheard of, (6) 27A4 their sight will be humbled as they come out from the tombs,[5124] as if they were scattered locusts (7) hastening to the caller. The disbelievers will say, "This is a hard day." (8) Before them, Nuh's[5125] people rejected. They rejected our servant and said, "[He is] crazy." He was driven away. (9) He prayed to his Lord, "I am defeated, so defend [me]." (10) We opened the doors of the sky and rain poured forth.[5126] (11) We made the earth gush with fountains,[5127] and the waters met[5128] for a decreed matter. (12) We carried him on a [ship] with boards and caulking.[5129] (13) It sailed with our eyes upon it[5130] as a recompense for him who was disbelieved. (14) And we left it as a sign.[5131] Will anyone remember? (15) What were my torment and my warning like? (16) We have made the Qur'an[5132] easy to remember. Will anyone remember? (17) Aad[5133] rejected. What were my torment and my warning like? (18) We sent a raging wind against them on a continuously unlucky day. (19) It snatched away people as if they were roots of uprooted palm trees. (20) What were my torment and my warning like? (21) We have made

---

[5120] The moon
[5121] Zabur, Psalms 103:8, 145:8. See glossary for more details.
[5122] Or rejection or something forbidden
[5123] Injil, 1 Thessalonians 4:16
[5124] Injil, John 5:28
[5125] Noah. See glossary for more details.
[5126] Tawrah, Genesis 7:11-12
[5127] Tawrah, Genesis 7:11
[5128] Tawrah, Genesis 7:17-19
[5129] Tawrah, Genesis 6:14
[5130] Tawrah, Genesis 8:1
[5131] Tawrah, Genesis 9:12
[5132] Or recitation. See glossary for more details.
[5133] Aad and Thamud were names of tribes.

the Qur'an⁵¹³⁴ easy to remember. Will anyone remember? (22) Thamud rejected the warnings. (23) They said, "Shall we follow a single man from among us? We would be astray and crazy. (24) Has the reminder⁵¹³⁵ been given to him among us all? He is an insolent liar." (25) Tomorrow they will know who the insolent liar is. (26) We will send the camel<sup>F</sup> as a trial to them, so watch them and wait.⁵¹³⁶ (27) Announce to them that the water is apportioned among them, every one present to drink in turn. (28) They called their companion, who took [a sword] and hamstrung [her]. (29) What were my torment and my warning like? (30) We sent a single cry against them, and they were like dry sticks of a cattle-fold builder. (31) We have made the Qur'an⁵¹³⁷ easy to remember. Will anyone remember? (32) Lut's⁵¹³⁸ people rejected the warning. (33) We sent a wind with stones against them – all except for Lut's family, whom we rescued at dawn, (34) as our blessing. This is how we reward those who give thanks. (35) He warned them of our severity, but they doubted the warning.⁵¹³⁹ (36) They asked him [for permission] to sleep with his guest, so we put out their eyes.⁵¹⁴⁰ "Taste my torment and my warning." (37) Continuous torment came to them in the morning.⁵¹⁴¹ (38) "Taste my torment and my warning." (39) We have made the Qur'an⁵¹⁴² easy to remember. Will anyone remember? (40) Warning came to Pharaoh's family. (41) They rejected all our signs,⁵¹⁴³ so we seized them as a mighty, powerful one. (42) Are your<sup>MP</sup> disbelievers any better than those? Or do you<sup>MP</sup> have immunity in the books?⁵¹⁴⁴ (43) Or do they say, "We will all be helped."? (44) The crowd will be defeated and turn back. (45) Their appointment is with the hour, and the hour is very grievous and bitter. (46) Wrongdoers are astray and crazy. (47) On that day, they will be dragged into

---

⁵¹³⁴ Or recitation. See glossary for more details.
⁵¹³⁵ Arabic /dhikr/. See glossary for more details. Here the reminder is given to Thamud.
⁵¹³⁶ Or, "endure."
⁵¹³⁷ Or recitation. See glossary for more details.
⁵¹³⁸ Lot, nephew of Abraham here and in verse 34. See glossary for more details.
⁵¹³⁹ Tawrah, Genesis 19:14
⁵¹⁴⁰ Tawrah, Genesis 19:5,11
⁵¹⁴¹ Tawrah, Genesis 19:23-24
⁵¹⁴² Or recitation. See glossary for more details.
⁵¹⁴³ Arabic /ayat/. See glossary for more details.
⁵¹⁴⁴ Or psalms. Tawrah, Isaiah 28:15

## Chapter 54

hellfire on their faces. "Taste what scorching fire feels like." (48) We have created everything in measure. (49) We have only one command, as the twinkling of an eye.[5145] (50) We have destroyed your[MP] sects. Will anyone remember? (51) Everything they did is in the books.[5146] (52) Everything great and small is written.[5147] (53) The reverent will be in heavenly gardens[5148] by a river,[5149] (54) in an excellent dwelling[5150] with a powerful king. (55)

---

[5145] Injil, 1 Corinthians 15:52
[5146] Or psalms
[5147] Tawrah, Ecclesiastes 12:14
[5148] Arabic /jannah/. See glossary for more details.
[5149] Injil, Revelation 22:2
[5150] Injil, John 14:2-3

Chapter 55

# Chapter 55 Al-Rahman[5151]

**27B1** In the name of Allah, the most gracious and merciful.[5152] The most gracious (1) taught the Qur'an.[5153] (2) He created mankind.[5154] (3) He taught him the proclamation. (4) The sun and moon in a reckoning.[5155] (5) The stars[5156] and the trees[5157] bow down. (6) He raised up the sky[5158] and lowered[5159] the scale.[5160] (7) Do not transgress regarding the balance.[5161] (8) Give a just weight, and do not make the scale lose.[5162] (9) He placed[5163] the earth for creatures.[5164] (10) It has fruits, palm trees with buds, (11) grain with stalks, and food.[5165] (12) Which of your[D] Lord's benefits will you[D] reject? (13) He created mankind from clay[5166] like a potter.[5167] (14) He created jinns[5168] from a flame of fire. (15) Which of your[D] Lord's benefits will you[D] reject? (16) [He is] Lord of both sunrises and both sunsets.[5169] (17) Which of your[D] Lord's benefits will you[D] reject? (18) He loosed both seas to join.[5170] (19) There is a barrier between them neither will pass. (20) Which of your[D] Lord's benefits will you[D] reject? (21) He brings forth pearls and coral from them[D].[5171] (22) Which of your[D] Lord's benefits will you[D] reject? (23) He has vessels high in the seas like mountains.

---

[5151] The most gracious (name of Allah)
[5152] Zabur, Psalms 103:8, 145:8. See glossary for more details.
[5153] Or recitation. See glossary for more details.
[5154] Tawrah, Genesis 1:26-28
[5155] Tawrah, Genesis 1:16-17
[5156] Tawrah, Genesis 1:16
[5157] Tawrah, Genesis 1:12, Psalms 148:9
[5158] Tawrah, Genesis 1:6-8
[5159] Or "placed."
[5160] Tawrah, Isaiah 40:12
[5161] Tawrah, Proverbs 16:11
[5162] i.e. light. Tawrah, Leviticus 19:36
[5163] Or "lowered."
[5164] Tawrah, Genesis 2:8,19
[5165] Tawrah, Genesis 2:16
[5166] Tawrah, Genesis 2:7
[5167] Tawrah, Isaiah 29:16, 45:9, 64:8
[5168] Or demons, here and in verses 33, 39, 56, 74. See glossary for more details.
[5169] Or, "both Easts and both Wests." Zabur, Psalms 75:6, 103:12
[5170] Zabur, Psalms 24:2
[5171] Tawrah, Job 28:18

## Chapter 55

(24) Which of your⁰ Lord's benefits will you⁰ reject? (25) Everyone on it is mortal, (26) but your^MS glorious, honored Lord's face remains.⁵¹⁷² (27) Which of your⁰ Lord's benefits will you⁰ reject? (28) Those in the heavens and the earth ask him.⁵¹⁷³ He has a matter every day.⁵¹⁷⁴ (29) Which of your⁰ Lord's benefits will you⁰ reject? (30) We will settle accounts with⁵¹⁷⁵ you^MP burdensome ones⁰.⁵¹⁷⁶ (31) Which of your⁰ Lord's benefits will you⁰ reject? (32) Jinns and men, if you^MP can pass beyond the borders of the heavens and the earth, then pass. You^MP will not pass except with authority. (33) Which of your⁰ Lord's benefits will you⁰ reject? (34) He will send flames of fire and molten brass against you⁰, and you⁰ will not be helped. (35) Which of your⁰ Lord's benefits will you⁰ reject? (36) When the heavens are split⁵¹⁷⁷ and are rosy like red paint, (37) which of your⁰ Lord's benefits will you⁰ reject? (38) On that day, no human or jinn will be asked about his sin. (39) Which of your⁰ Lord's benefits will you⁰ reject? (40) Wrongdoers will be known by their mark,⁵¹⁷⁸ and will be seized by their hair⁵¹⁷⁹ and feet. (41) Which of your⁰ Lord's benefits will you⁰ reject? (42) This is hell, which wrongdoers denied. (43) They will go back and forth between it and boiling water. (44) Which of your⁰ Lord's benefits will you⁰ reject? (45) For those who fear their Lord's standing,⁵¹⁸⁰ there will be two heavenly gardens.⁵¹⁸¹ (46) Which of your⁰ Lord's benefits will you⁰ reject? (47) Both with branches. (48) Which of your⁰ Lord's benefits will you⁰ reject? (49) There are flowing⁰ springs⁰ there.⁵¹⁸² (50) Which of your⁰ Lord's benefits will you⁰ reject? (51) There are pairs of every kind of fruit⁵¹⁸³ in them⁰. (52) Which of your⁰ Lord's benefits will you⁰ reject? (53) Reclining on couches lined with brocade. The fruit of both heavenly gardens is close by. (54)

---

⁵¹⁷² 1 Timothy 1:17, Revelation 4:11
⁵¹⁷³ Zabur, Psalms 65:2-3
⁵¹⁷⁴ Zabur, Psalms 7:11
⁵¹⁷⁵ Or, "focus on."
⁵¹⁷⁶ Injil, Matthew 18:23
⁵¹⁷⁷ Tawrah, Isaiah 34:4, Injil, Hebrews 1:12
⁵¹⁷⁸ Injil, Revelation 13:17, 14:9,11, 16:2, 19:20, 20:4
⁵¹⁷⁹ specifically forelocks, bangs, or forehead.
⁵¹⁸⁰ Injil, Revelation 15:4, 11:18
⁵¹⁸¹ Arabic /jannah/ here and in verses 54 and 62. See glossary for more details.
⁵¹⁸² Injil, Revelation 7:17
⁵¹⁸³ Injil, Revelation 22:2

## Chapter 55

Which of your[D] Lord's benefits will you[D] reject? (55) In them[FP] are are low-hanging ones[FP] which no men or jinns have previously defiled[5184] previously.[5185] (56) Which of your[D] Lord's benefits will you[D] reject? (57) They[FP] are like rubies and coral. (58) Which of your[D] Lord's benefits will you[D] reject? (59) Will generosity not be rewarded with generosity?[5186] (60) Which of your[D] Lord's benefits will you[D] reject? (61) Below them[D] are two other heavenly gardens. (62) Which of your[D] Lord's benefits will you[D] reject? (63) Lush green[D]. (64) Which of your[D] Lord's benefits will you[D] reject? (65) In them[D] are flowing springs[D]. (66) Which of your[D] Lord's benefits will you[D] reject? (67) In them[D] are fruit, palm trees[5187] and pomegranates. (68) Which of your[D] Lord's benefits will you[D] reject? (69) In them[FP] are beautiful,[FP] wholesome things[FP].[5188] (70) Which of your[D] Lord's benefits will you[D] reject? (71) With white ones,[5189] inside[FP] the tents. (72) Which of your[D] Lord's benefits will

---

[5184] Or "touched."

[5185] Most translations translate this verse "modest spouses previously undeflowered by men and jinns." However, the verse has no word for "spouse." The word usually translated "modest" also means "low" or "short." Thus, the translation "low-hanging ones." (See 6:99, 76:14, where fruits are said to be hanging low) This is more probable given the context of food and drink, and "close by" in verse 54. Grapes in the heavenly garden are specifically mentioned in 23:19 and 78:32. The word /yatmith/ carries the concept of defilement (from a woman's monthly period). Thus the meaning might be "low-hanging [red] grapes." (see also verse 58)

[5186] Injil, Romans 2:7

[5187] i.e. dates

[5188] Or " foods." Some translations add the word "virgins" but this word is not in the text. The word here translated "wholesome things" usually refers to things and not female beings. The same word translated "beautiful" is used of carpets in verse 76.

[5189] Some translations use, "dark-eyed virgins," though the text does not mention dark or eyes or virgins. The word "hur" here may be related to the Syriac word /hura/, which means grapes. Grapes in the heavenly garden are specifically mentioned in 23:19 and 78:32. Thus the meaning here may be "white grapes." See related note at 56:22. Furthermore, the idea of virgins for the sexual pleasure of believing men does not fit with the presence of their wives in the heavenly gardens with them (43:70, 36:56), or with equal rewards promised female believers in 40:40, 4:124, 16:97.

## Chapter 55

you<sup>D</sup> reject? (73) No men nor jinns before them<sup>MP</sup> have defiled[5190] them<sup>FP</sup>. (74) Which of your<sup>D</sup> Lord's benefits will you<sup>D</sup> reject? (75) They<sup>MP</sup> recline on green pillows and beautiful rich carpets. (76) Which of your<sup>D</sup> Lord's benefits will you<sup>D</sup> reject? (77) Blessed be the name of your<sup>MS</sup> glorious, honored Lord.[5191] (78)

---

[5190] The word /yatmith/ carries the concept of defilement (from a woman's monthly period). Crushing red grapes (see note on verse 58) would produce red juice that looks similar.
[5191] Injil, Revelation 4:9

# Chapter 56 Al-Waqiah[5192]

**2782** In the name of Allah, the most gracious and merciful.[5193] When the event happens, (1) no one[FS] can[5194] lie about its happening. (2) It is lowering and raising.[5195] (3)

\*\*\*

When the earth shakes,[5196] (4) and the mountains crumble,[5197] (5) scattered like dust, (6)

\*\*\*

and you[MP] are three pairs. (7) The companions of the right[5198] – what are the companions of the right? (8) The companions of the left[5199] – what are the companions of the left (9)

\*\*\*

and the former ones? The former ones (10) are those brought near[5200] (11) in heavenly gardens[5201] of delight. (12) A crowd of ancient people (13) but few of the latter ones, (14)

\*\*\*

on interwoven couches, (15)

\*\*\*

reclining on them, facing each other. (16) "Wildan mukhalladun"[5202] will surround them (17) in cups and goblets, and

---

[5192] The event
[5193] Zabur, Psalms 103:8, 145:8. See glossary for more details.
[5194] The verb is masculine, but the noun is feminine. There may be another meaning.
[5195] Zabur, Psalms 75:7
[5196] Injil, Revelation 16:18
[5197] Injil, Revelation 16:20
[5198] Injil, Matthew 25:34
[5199] Injil, Matthew 25:41
[5200] This word /muqarrabun/ here, in verse 88, and in 83:21, 28 refers here to the inhabitants of the heavenly garden. Elsewhere in the Qur'an it refers only to the angels (4:172), and Isa (3:45).
[5201] Arabic /jannah/. See glossary for more details.
[5202] Most translations have "Eternal youths" here. However, the word translated "eternal" is not the usual one /khalidun/ which is used 70 times in the Qur'an and means "eternal." Instead, the word /mukhalladun/ is used only here and in 76:19. Some research has suggested that the word may mean "chilled." The word /wildan/ is usually translated "youths" but probably means "the product" in this context, similar to the Arabic phrase "bint al-karma" (literally, daughter of the vine), which means "wine." For

a glass from a clear fountain, (18) from which they will have no hangover, nor pass out, (19) the fruits they choose, (20) the poultry they desire, (21) and "hur iin"[5203] (22) like preserved pearls (23) as a reward for their deeds. (24)

\*\*\*

They will not hear any vain talk or accusations, (25) but only the saying, "Peace, peace." (26)

\*\*\*

The companions of the right – what are the companions of the right? (27)

\*\*\*

By a lotus tree stripped of thorns, (28) a spread-out banana[5204] tree, (29) shade extended, (30)

\*\*\*

water poured out, (31)

\*\*\*

and lots of fruit, (32) which never runs out, nor is forbidden. (33) on raised trellises.[5205] (34)

---

this meaning, see Injil, Matthew 26:28. The traditional translation does not fit the context either here or in 76:19. Here "wildan mukhalladun" are said to be in cups and goblets, and in 76:19, they are compared to scattered pearls, which obviously resemble fruit more than people.

[5203] This phrase is usually translated "dark-eyed virgins," but the Arabic text does not have the words "dark," "eye," or "virgin". Instead of /'ain/ (eye), the text says /'iin/ (wild ox). /hur/ may mean white, but definitely does not mean dark. It is obvious that the meaning is something else. The word /hur/ (translated by some as "virgins") may be related to the Syriac word /hura/ (grape). Thus the meaning might be " white grapes." Every time this phrase occurs (44:54, 55:20, 56:22), it is in the context of fruit, food and drink. Furthermore, the idea of virgins for the sexual pleasure of believing men does not fit with the presence of their wives in the heavenly gardens with them (43:70, 36:56), or with equal rewards promised female believers in 40:40, 4:124, 16:97. The earliest commentaries mention several possible readings of and differing opinions about this phrase, and specifically discuss the problem of how these /hur 'iin/ would be brought to the inhabitants of the heavenly garden by the attendants. The possibility mentioned above is that the reference is not to people but to sparkling white grapes, which look like pearls (verse 23) or eggs (37:49). Grapes in the heavenly garden are specifically mentioned in 23:19 and 78:32. Grapes that are red may be referred to in 55:56-58.

[5204] Or "acacia"

[5205] Or mattresses.

## Chapter 56

\*\*\*

We produced them[FP] (35) and made them[FP] first-fruits,[5206] (36) cool[5207] and juicy,[5208] (37)

\*\*\*

for companions of the right,[5209] (38) a crowd of former ones, (39) and a crowd of the latter ones. (40)

\*\*\*

The companions of the left[5210] – what are the companions of the left? (41)

\*\*\*

In scorching wind and boiling water, (42) in the shade of black smoke, (43) neither cool nor agreeable. (44) Previously they lived luxuriously[5211] (45) and persisted in great wickedness.[5212] (46) They would say, "If we die and are dust[5213] and bones, will we be resurrected? (47) And how about our ancestors?" (48) Say[MS], "The former and the latter (49) will be gathered at a time on a known day.[5214] (50) Then, you[MP] rejecters who went astray (51) will eat from the Zaqqum tree, (52) filling your[MP] bellies with it, (53) followed with a drink of boiling water, (54) that you[MP] will drink like a camel dying of thirst. (55) This is their abode on the day of judgment. (56) We created you[MP].[5215] Will you[MP] not believe? (57) Have you[MP] seen the semen you[MP] ejaculate? (58) Do you[MP] create it, or do we? (59) We decreed death among you[MP], and we are not beaten (60) in replacing the likes of you[MP],[5216] and we will make you[MP] in a manner you[MP] do not know. (61) You[MP] knew about the first creation. Do you[MP] not remember? (62) Have you[MP] seen what you[MP] plow? (63) Do you[MP] sow it or do we? (64) If we had willed,

---

[5206] Many translations have "virgins" but this does not fit the context. The primary meaning of this word is "first fruit."
[5207] Recent research has suggested this meaning, which fits the context well. In verses 42-44, the companions of the left, by contrast, are in hot surroundings.
[5208] See note at 38:52.
[5209] Injil, Matthew 25:34
[5210] Injil, Matthew 25:41
[5211] Injil, Luke 16:19-25
[5212] Injil, Revelation 18:2-3
[5213] Tawrah, Job 10:9
[5214] Tawrah, Joel 3:11-14, Zephaniah 3:8, Injil, Matthew 25:32, John 15:6, Revelation 16:16
[5215] Tawrah, Genesis 1:26-28
[5216] Injil, Matthew 21:43

we would have made it stubble, and you^MP would continue to wonder, (65) "We are in debt, (66) and deprived." (67) Have you^MP seen the water you^MP drink? (68) Did you^MP send it down or did we?^5217 (69) If we had willed, we would have made it bitter.^5218 Will you^MP not give thanks? (70) Have you^MP seen the fire that you^MP kindle? (71) Did you^MP produce the tree for it or did we? (72) We made it a reminder and provision for desert-dwellers. (73) So worship^MS the name of your^MS great Lord.^5219 (74) **27B3** I do not swear^5220 by the stars' falling.^5221 (75) That would be a serious oath, if you^MP only knew. (76) It is a noble recitation^5222 (77) in a hidden book. (78) Only the purified will touch it. (79) A revelation of the Lord of the universe. (80) So will you^MP deceive regarding this saying (81) and make your^MP living by your^MP rejecting? (82) So when it reaches the throat, (83) you^MP will look. (84) We are closer to it than you^MP are,^5223 but you^MP do not see. (85) So if you^MP were not indebted, (87) you^MP would return it if you^MP were telling the truth. (87) But if he were one brought near, (88) rest, food, and a heavenly garden^5224 of delight. (89) As for the companions of the right,^5225 (90) peace to you^MS from the companions of the right.^5226 (91) But if he is a rejecter who went astray, (92) an abode of boiling water, (93) and being roasted in the blazing fire.^5227 (94) This is certain truth, (95) so worship^MS the name of your^MS great Lord.^5228 (96)^5229

---

[5217] Tawrah, Job 5:10
[5218] Tawrah, Exodus 15:23
[5219] Tawrah, 2 Samuel 7:22
[5220] Or, So no, I swear
[5221] Or, the places of the stars. Many interpretations for this phrase have been proposed, including even black holes! Injil, Mark 13:25
[5222] Or qur'an or Qur'an. See glossary for more details.
[5223] Tawrah, Jeremiah 23:23-24
[5224] Arabic /jannah/. See glossary for more details.
[5225] Injil, Matthew 25:34
[5226] Injil, Matthew 25:34
[5227] Injil, Revelation 21:8
[5228] Tawrah, 2 Samuel 7:22
[5229] The verses in this chapter that rhyme are put together in paragraphs, separated by ***.

# Chapter 57 Al-Hadid[5230]

In the name of Allah, the most gracious and merciful.[5231] Let everything in the heavens and the earth praise Allah. He is Mighty and Wise.[5232] (1)

\*\*\*

Everything in the heavens and the earth is his.[5233] He gives and takes life,[5234] and he can do anything.[5235] (2)

\*\*\*

He is the First and the Last,[5236] the Obvious and the Hidden, and he is All-knowing.[5237] (3)

\*\*\*

He created the heavens and the earth

\*\*\*

in six days,[5238] then sat down on the throne.[5239] He knows what enters the earth and what leaves it, what falls from the sky and what ascends to it.[5240] He is with you[MP] wherever you[MP] go. He sees your[MP] deeds. (4) The kingdom of the heavens and the earth is his, and all matters return to Allah. (5) He makes the night enter into the day and the day into the night.[5241] He knows what is in the heart.[5242] (6) Believe[MP] in Allah and his messenger, and donate[MP] a

---

[5230] Iron
[5231] Zabur, Psalms 103:8, 145:8. See glossary for more details.
[5232] Tawrah, Job 9:4, Proverbs 2:6, Jeremiah 9:23-24, Injil, 1 Corinthians 1:21-25, Romans 16:27
[5233] Here and in verse 5, see Tawrah, Isaiah 45:12, Zabur, Psalms 24:1, 89:11, Injil, Hebrews 1:10.
[5234] Tawrah, Deuteronomy 30:19
[5235] Tawrah, Job 42:2, Isaiah 14:27, Daniel 4:35, Injil, Matthew 19:26, Mark 10:27, Luke 1:37
[5236] Tawrah, Isaiah 48:12, Injil, Revelation 22:13
[5237] Tawrah, Job 37:16, Isaiah 40:14, Zabur, Psalms 33:13-15, Injil, 1 John 3:20
[5238] Tawrah, Genesis 1:1-31
[5239] Tawrah, Genesis 2:2-3
[5240] Injil, Acts 1:9-11
[5241] Tawrah, Genesis 8:22
[5242] Tawrah, 1 Samuel 16:7, 1 Chronicles 28:9, Zabur, Psalms 44:21, Injil, Luke 16:15, Romans 8:27, Acts 15:8, 1 John 3:20

## Chapter 57

portion of what he has made you<sup>MP</sup> inherit.[5243] Those who believe and donate will have a great reward. (7)
\*\*\*

What is wrong with you<sup>MP</sup> that you<sup>MP</sup> do not believe in Allah? His messenger calls you<sup>MP</sup> to believe<sup>MP</sup> in your<sup>MP</sup> Lord, and has made a treaty with you<sup>MP</sup>, if you<sup>MP</sup> are believers. (8) He gave miraculous signs to his servant, to bring you<sup>MP</sup> out of darkness into light.[5244] Allah is compassionate and merciful[5245] to you<sup>MP</sup>. (9)
\*\*\*

What is wrong with you<sup>MP</sup> that you<sup>MP</sup> do not spend money in Allah's path, since the inheritance of the heavens and the earth are Allah's?[5246] The one among you<sup>MP</sup> who donates and fights before the victory is not equal to you<sup>MP</sup>. They have a higher rank than those who donate and fight afterwards. Allah promises both of them a reward. Allah is aware of your<sup>MP</sup> deeds. (10)
\*\*\*

Whoever gives Allah a loan will be repaid double, and will have a generous reward.[5247] (11) On that day, you<sup>MS</sup> will see the light from male and female believers shining in front of them and on their right. "Your<sup>MP</sup> good news today is about heavenly gardens[5248] with rivers flowing underneath,[5249] where you<sup>MP</sup> will live forever. This is the great victory."[5250] (12)
\*\*\*

On that day, the male and female hypocrites will say to the believers, "Wait<sup>MP</sup> for us, so we can get some of your<sup>MP</sup> light."[5251] It will be said, "Go back<sup>MP</sup> behind you<sup>MP</sup> and seek<sup>MP</sup> light."[5252] Then a

---

[5243] 2 Corinthians 9:6
[5244] Tawrah, 2 Samuel 22:29, Isaiah 58:10, Zabur, Psalms 18:28, 112:4, Injil, Matthew 4:16, John 8:12, 12:46, Ephesians 5:8, 1 Peter 2:9
[5245] Injil, James 5:11. Here and in verse 28, see glossary for more details on "merciful."
[5246] Injil, 1 Corinthians 6:9-10, Tawrah, 1 Chronicles 29:11-14
[5247] Tawrah, Proverbs 19:17
[5248] Arabic /jannah/ here and in verse 21. See glossary for more details.
[5249] Injil, Revelation 22:1-2, Tawrah, Ezekiel 47:12
[5250] Tawrah, Isaiah 25:8, Injil, 1 Corinthians 15:57, 1 John 5:4
[5251] Injil, Matthew 25:8
[5252] Injil, Matthew 25:9

## Chapter 57

wall will be set up between them, whose door will have mercy on its inside, and torment facing its outside.[5253] (13)

\*\*\*

They will call to them, "Were we not with you[MP]?"[5254] They will say, "Yes, but you[MP] tempted yourselves[MP], waited, and doubted.[5255] Vain desires deceived you[MP] until Allah's command came.[5256] The deceiver deceived you[MP] about Allah.[5257] (14) No ransom will be accepted from you[MP] or the disbelievers today.[5258] Your[MP] abode will be hellfire. It will be your[MP] master[5259] and an awful destiny. (15) 2784

\*\*\*

Has the time not come for believers' hearts to be humble to remember Allah and the truth that was revealed, that they not be like those who were brought the book previously? It seemed like a long time to them, and their hearts grew hard. Many of them were unbelieving.[5260] (16) Know[MP] that Allah revives the dead ground.[5261] We have made the signs clear to you[MP], so that you[MP] would comprehend. (17) Both males and females who give alms to the poor and lend a good loan to Allah will be paid back double, and they will have a generous reward.[5262] (18) Believers in Allah and his messengers are righteous witnesses with their Lord. They will have their reward and their light.[5263] Disbelievers who reject our signs[5264] are going to the blazing fire. (19)

\*\*\*

Know[MP] that this world is a game, an amusement, adornment, boasting among you[MP], and multiplying wealth and children,[5265] like rain whose plants please the disbelievers and then wither, and

---

[5253] Injil, Matthew 25:10-12, Luke 16:19-31. This explains the ancient controversy about predestined /musayyar/ or having free will /mukhayyar/.
[5254] Injil, Matthew 25:11
[5255] Injil, Matthew 25:3,12
[5256] Injil, Matthew 25:3,6
[5257] Injil, Matthew 25:3, 11, 12
[5258] Zabur, Psalms 49:8
[5259] Or "protector" or "companion."
[5260] Or transgressing or immoral
[5261] Tawrah, Isaiah 55:10
[5262] Tawrah, Proverbs 19:17
[5263] Tawrah, Isaiah 50:10
[5264] Arabic /ayat/. See glossary for more details.
[5265] Or possibly, people with no children whose parents have died

## Chapter 57

you[MS] see them turn yellow and crumble. In the hereafter, there will be severe torment,[5266] as well as forgiveness and pleasure from Allah. This world is only enjoyment of vain hopes. (20)

\*\*\*

Strive for forgiveness from your[MP] Lord, and for a heavenly garden as broad as heaven and earth, prepared for believers in Allah and his messengers. That is Allah's grace, that he gives to those he wills. Allah has great grace. (21)

\*\*\*

No affliction on earth or in your souls[MP] will strike unless we created it previously in a book.[5267] That is easy for Allah, (22) so that you[MP] do not grieve over what passed you[MP] by, nor rejoice over what you[MP] have gotten. Allah does not love any proud, boastful people[5268] (23)

\*\*\*

who are miserly and tell people to be miserly.[5269] For those who turn away,
Allah is self-sufficient and praiseworthy. (24)

\*\*\*

We sent our messengers with miracles[5270] and revealed the book and the
scale[5271] with them, so that people would be just. We revealed iron, which is very strong and beneficial to people,[5272] so that Allah would know who would serve him and his messengers in the unseen. Allah is strong[5273] and mighty. (25)

\*\*\*

We sent Nuh[5274] and Ibrahim[5275] and gave their seed[5276] prophecy[5277] and the book. Some of them were guided and many

---

[5266] Tawrah, Isaiah 50:11, Injil, Matthew 18:34, 25:41,46, Luke 16:23-28, Revelation 20:15
[5267] Zabur, Psalms 139:16
[5268] Zabur, Psalms 5:4-5, 11:5, Tawrah, Proverbs 6:16-19
[5269] Tawrah, Proverbs 11:24
[5270] Zabur, Psalms 105:5
[5271] Tawrah, Deuteronomy 32:4
[5272] Tawrah, Genesis 4:22
[5273] Tawrah, Job 9:4, Zabur, Psalms 24:8, Injil, Ephesians 6:10, Revelation 18:8
[5274] Noah. See glossary for more details. Tawrah, Genesis 6:13-22
[5275] Abraham. See glossary for more details. Tawrah, Genesis 12:1-7
[5276] Tawrah, Genesis 12:7, 13:16
[5277] Injil, Matthew 23:29-37

## Chapter 57

of them were unbelieving.[5278] (26) Then we made our messengers follow them. We made Isa[5279] son of Mariam[5280] follow them, and we brought[5281] the Injil[5282] to him, and put compassion[5283] and mercy[5284] into the hearts of those who followed him. They invented monasticism.[5285] We did not ordain it for them, but only seeking Allah's pleasure,[5286] and they were not careful to do that. We gave the believers among them their reward, but most of them were unbelieving.[5287] (27) Believers,[5288] fear Allah[5289] and believe in his messenger. He will give you[MP] a double portion[5290] of his mercy, will give you[MP] light to walk in,[5291] and will forgive you[MP]. Allah is forgiving[5292] and merciful (28) so that the people of the book would know that they have no control over any of Allah's grace. Grace is in Allah's hand and he gives is to those He wills.[5293] Allah has great grace. (29)[5294]

---

[5278] Or transgressing or immoral

[5279] Jesus. See glossary for more details.

[5280] Mary, mother of Jesus. See glossary for more details.

[5281] Most of what all the prophets were given came from Allah orally, and it was later written down. The exception is Musa (Tawrah, Exodus 34:28, Deuteronomy 4:13, 10:4), when Allah himself wrote them on stone tablets.

[5282] Gospel. See glossary for more details

[5283] Injil, Colossians 3:12

[5284] Injil, Matthew 5:7

[5285] Neither the Qur'an nor the former books support monasticism.

[5286] Injil, Matthew 6:33

[5287] Or transgressing or immoral

[5288] Some people think this refers to thte believers referred to in the previous verse, the believers among the Nasara. If this is correct, the messenger referred to would probably be Isa. See 3:53, 4:157,171. Others think the subject changes at this point and the believers are a different group of people, the Muslims, and the messenger referred to is Muhammad.

[5289] Tawrah, Deuteronomy 10:12, Isaiah 29:13, Injil, 1 Peter 2:17, Revelation 14:7

[5290] Tawrah, Isaiah 61:7

[5291] Tawrah, Isaiah 50:10

[5292] Zabur, Psalms 103:3, 130:4, Tawrah, Isaiah 43:25, Exodus 34:7, Injil, Acts 26:18.

[5293] Injil, Romans 9:18

[5294] The verses in this chapter that rhyme are put together in paragraphs, separated by ***.

# Chapter 58 Al-Mujadilah[5295]

**28A1** In the name of Allah, the most gracious and merciful.[5296] Allah has heard the saying of the one[FS] who argues[FS] with you[MS] about her[FS] husband and complains[FS] to Allah. Allah hears your[D] argument. Allah hears all and sees all. (1) As for those of you[MP] who divorce[MP] their[MP] wives,[5297] they[FP] are not their[MP] mothers.[5298] Their[MP] only mothers are those[FP] who gave birth to them[MP]. They[MP] say unlawful sayings, and falsehood. Allah is pardoning and forgiving.[5299] (2) Those[MP] who divorce their[MP] wives and then retract[5300] what they[MP] said must free a slave before they[D] have sex. You[MP] are admonished of that. Allah is aware of your[MP] deeds. (3)
\*\*\*

Those who cannot, must fast[5301] for two consecutive months before they[D] have sex. Those who cannot must feed sixty poor people. That is so that you[MP] will believe in Allah and his messenger. These are Allah's limits. Disbelievers will have painful torment.[5302] (4) Those who oppose Allah and his messenger will be shamed, just like those before them. We have revealed miraculous signs.[5303] Disbelievers will have shameful torment (5)
\*\*\*

on the day Allah resurrects them all, and he tells them what they did. Allah counted it up and they have forgotten it. Allah is witness of everything. (6)
\*\*\*

---

[5295] The arguer[FS]
[5296] Zabur, Psalms 103:8, 145:8. See glossary for more details.
[5297] Tawrah, Deuteronomy 24:1-3
[5298] The word for divorce in these two verses is an abbreviation for the phrase, "Be as my mother's back to me," which was a formula of divorce.
[5299] Here and in verse 12, see Zabur, Psalms 103:3, 130:4, Tawrah, Isaiah 43:25, Exodus 34:7, Injil, Acts 26:18.
[5300] or repeat
[5301] i.e. during daytime hours
[5302] For "torment" here and in verses 5, 15 and 16, see Tawrah, Isaiah 50:11, Injil, Matthew 18:34, 25:41,46, Luke 16:23-28, Revelation 20:15.
[5303] Arabic /ayat/ See glossary.

## Chapter 58

Did you[ms] not think that Allah knows[5304] everything in the heavens and the earth? Whenever three have a private talk, he is the fourth. Whenever five have a private talk, he is the sixth. For any other number less or more than that, he is with them wherever they are.[5305] Then on the day of resurrection,[5306] he will tell them everything they did. Allah knows everything. (7)
\*\*\*

Have you[ms] not seen those who are prohibited from private talks, who then return to what they were prohibited and talk privately of things that bring guilt, hostility, and disobeying the messenger? When they come to you[ms], they greet you[ms] in ways Allah has not greeted you[ms]. They say to themselves, "Why does Allah not torment us for what we say?" Hell, where they will be roasted, is adequate for them. What an awful destiny! (8)
\*\*\*

Believers, when you[mp] hold private talks, do not talk[mp] of things that bring guilt, hostility, and disobeying the messenger. Talk[mp] of righteousness and reverence.[5307] Fear Allah,[5308] to whom you[mp] will be gathered.[5309] (9) Private talks are from Satan, in order to grieve believers. He cannot harm them at all except by Allah's permission.[5310] Let believers trust in Allah.[5311] (10)
\*\*\*

Believers, if you[mp] are told, "Make room in your[mp] assembly," then make[mp] room.[5312] Allah will make room for you[mp].[5313] If you[mp] are told, "Get[mp] up," then get[mp] up. Allah will raise up the believers and the scholars among you[mp] by degrees. Allah is aware of your[mp] deeds. (11)
\*\*\*

---

[5304] For "knows" twice in this verse, see Tawrah, Job 37:16, Isaiah 40:14, Zabur, Psalms 33:13-15, Injil, 1 John 3:20

[5305] Injil, Matthew 18:20

[5306] Tawrah, Daniel 12:2 Injil, Acts 24 15, 1 Corinthians 15:52-54, Revelation 20:11-15

[5307] Injil, Colossians 4:6

[5308] Tawrah, Deuteronomy 10:12, Isaiah 29:13, Injil, 1 Peter 2:17, Revelation 14:7

[5309] Tawrah, Joel 3:11-14, Zephaniah 3:8, Injil, Matthew 25:32, John 15:6, Revelation 16:16

[5310] Tawrah, Job 1:9-12

[5311] Zabur, Psalms 118:5-8

[5312] Injil, James 2:1-9

[5313] Injil, Luke 14:9-10

Chapter 58

Believers, if you<sup>MP</sup> have a private talk with the messenger, bring<sup>MP</sup> alms before[5314] your<sup>MP</sup> private talk. That is better and purer for you<sup>MP</sup>. If you<sup>MP</sup> cannot, Allah is forgiving and merciful.[5315] (12) Are you<sup>MP</sup> afraid to bring alms before your<sup>MP</sup> private talk? If you<sup>MP</sup> do not do it and Allah accepts your<sup>MP</sup> repentance, perform<sup>MP</sup> prayers and pay<sup>MP</sup> the poor-tax. Obey<sup>MP</sup> Allah and his messenger. Allah is aware of your<sup>MP</sup> deeds. (13) 28A2 Have you<sup>MS</sup> seen those who made friends with people that Allah is angry with?[5316] They do not belong to you<sup>MP</sup> or to them.[5317] They knowingly swear to a lie. (14) Allah has prepared severe torment for them. What they do is evil. (15) They used their oaths as a cloak,[5318] and blocked others from Allah's path.[5319] They will have shameful torment. (16) Their money[5320] and their children[5321] will not help them against Allah at all. They are going to hellfire, where they will be forever. (17) On that day, Allah will resurrect them all[5322] and they will swear to him as they swear to you<sup>MP</sup>. They will think they have some basis to stand. Are they not liars? (18) Satan took control of them and made them forget[5323] to mention Allah. They are of Satan's party, and those in Satan's party are lost. (19) Those who oppose Allah and his messenger will be the most abased. (20)

\*\*\*

Allah has written, "My messengers and I will defeat them." Allah is strong[5324] and mighty. (21)

\*\*\*

You<sup>MS</sup> will not find that people who believe in Allah and the last day also love
those who oppose Allah and his messenger, even their fathers, sons, brothers, or relatives.[5325] Allah has written faith on their

---

[5314] For "before" here and in verse 13, it could mean "between the hands of" or "in front of."
[5315] See glossary for more details on "merciful."
[5316] Injil, 1 Corinthians 15:33
[5317] Injil, Luke 9:50, Mark 9:40, Romans 8:31
[5318] Injil, Matthew 23:16-22
[5319] Injil, Matthew 23:13
[5320] Zabur, Psalms 49:7-9
[5321] Or sons
[5322] Injil, John 5:28-29
[5323] Injil, Mark 4:15
[5324] Tawrah, Job 9:4, Zabur, Psalms 24:8, Injil, Ephesians 6:10, Revelation 18:8
[5325] Injil, Luke 14:26, Matthew 10:37

hearts and aided them with a spirit from him.[5326] He will admit them to heavenly gardens[5327] with flowing rivers underneath, where they will live forever. There Allah is pleased with them, and they are pleased with him. They are Allah's party.[5328] Is Allah's party not prosperous? (22)[5329]

---

[5326] Injil, Ephesians 1:13-14
[5327] Arabic /jannah/. See glossary for more details.
[5328] Arabic /hezbollah/
[5329] The verses in this chapter that rhyme are put together in paragraphs, separated by ***.

Chapter 59

# Chapter 59 Al-Hashr[5330]

In the name of Allah, the most gracious and merciful.[5331] Let everything in the heavens and the earth glorify Allah.[5332] He is mighty and wise.[5333] (1)

\*\*\*

He expelled the disbelievers of the people of the book from their homes at the first gathering. You[MP] did not think they would go out, and they thought that their fortresses would defend them from Allah. Allah came upon them where they were not expecting and cast terror into their hearts,[5334] so they and the believers destroyed their houses with their own hands. Consider, you[MP] who can see. (2) If Allah had not prescribed banishment against them, he would have tormented them in this world, and in the hereafter they would have the torment[5335] of hellfire. (3) That is because they contended with Allah and his messenger. Allah will be severe in punishment[5336] to those who contend with Allah. (4)

\*\*\*

The palm trees you[MP] cut down or left[MP] standing on their roots were by Allah's

\*\*\*

permission, in order to shame the unbelieving.[5337] (5)

\*\*\*

Their spoils that Allah gave his messenger from them were not because you[MP] drove horses or camels to him. Rather, Allah gives authority to those of his messengers that he wills. Allah can do anything.[5338] (6)

\*\*\*

---

[5330] The gathering (at the judgment)

[5331] Zabur, Psalms 103:8, 145:8. See glossary for more details.

[5332] Zabur, Psalms 150:6

[5333] Tawrah, Job 9:4, Proverbs 2:6, Jeremiah 9:23-24, Injil, 1 Corinthians 1:21-25, Romans 16:27

[5334] Tawrah, Genesis 35:5

[5335] For "torment" here and in verse 15, see Tawrah, Isaiah 50:11, Injil, Matthew 18:34, 25:41,46, Luke 16:23-28, Revelation 20:15.

[5336] Here and in verse 7, see Injil, Matthew 8:12, 13:42,50, 22:13, 24:51, 25:30, Mark 9:48, Luke 13:28, 19:27.

[5337] Or transgressing or immoral

[5338] Tawrah, Job 42:2, Isaiah 14:27, Daniel 4:35, Injil, Matthew 19:26, Mark 10:27, Luke 1:37

## Chapter 58

The spoils from the inhabitants of the villages that Allah gave his messenger are for Allah, the messenger, relatives, orphans,[5339] the poor, and the travelers,[5340] so that it does not end up among the rich people among you[MP]. Take[MP] whatever the messenger gives you[MP]. Desist[MP] from whatever he forbids you[MP]. Fear[MP] Allah. Allah is severe in punishment. (7)

\*\*\*

[It is] for the poor emigrants who were forced from their homes and their possessions,[5341] who seek Allah's grace and pleasure, helping Allah and his messenger. They are truthful. (8) Those who occupied the house and embraced the faith before them love those who emigrate toward them, and find no need in their hearts for what they have, preferring others above themselves,[5342] even if they are poor.[5343] Those who protect themselves from their souls' covetousness[5344] are successful. (9) Those who came after them say, "Our Lord, forgive us and our brothers who preceded us in faith.[5345] Do not put grudges in our hearts[5346] toward believers. Our Lord, you[MS] are compassionate and merciful.[5347] (10) 28A3 Have you[MS] not seen the hypocrites? They tell their disbelieving brothers among the people of the book, "If you[MP] are expelled, we will go out with you[MP]. We will not obey anyone's orders concerning you[MP]. If you[MP] are attacked, we will help you[MP]." Allah testifies that they are liars. (11) If they are expelled, they will not go out with them, and if they are attacked, they will not help them. If they do help them, they will then turn their backs to them and not be helped. (12) You[MP] are more fearful in their hearts than Allah is. That is because they are people who do not understand. (13) They will not fight against you[MP] all except in fortified cities or behind walls. Their valor among themselves is strong. You[MS] think all of them thus, but their hearts are divided. That is because they are

---

[5339] Tawrah, Job 29:12, Zabur, Psalms 82:3, Injil, James 1:27
[5340] Tawrah, Genesis 14:18-24, 1 Samuel 30:1-31
[5341] Or, money.
[5342] Injil, Philippians 2:3-4
[5343] The verb here is masculine and the noun is feminine. There may be another meaning.
[5344] Injil, Colossians 3:5
[5345] Injil, Hebrews 12:1
[5346] Tawrah, Leviticus 19:18
[5347] Injil, James 5:11. Here and in verse 22, see glossary for more details on "merciful."

people who do not comprehend, (14) like others a short while before them. They tasted the grievousness of their matter, and they will have painful torment, (15) like Satan, when he told the man, "Disbelieve."[5348] When he disbelieved, he said, "I am innocent of you[MS]. I fear Allah,[5349] the Lord of the universe." (16) Their[D] end was in hellfire, where they[D] will be forever. That is how the wicked will be repaid. (17) Believers, fear Allah and let each soul look to what it has prepared for tomorrow.[5350] Fear Allah. Allah is aware of your[MP] deeds. (18) Do not be like those who forgot Allah, and he made them forget their souls. They are unbelieving.[5351] (19) Those that are going to hellfire are not equal to those that are going to the heavenly garden,[5352] who are the winners. (20) If we had revealed this recitation[5353] on a mountain, you[MS] would have seen it humbly split in two out of the fear of Allah. Those are proverbs we give to people, so that they will consider.[5354] (21) He is Allah. He is the only god,[5355] knowing the unseen and the seen. He is the most gracious and merciful.[5356] (22) He is Allah. He is the only god, King,[5357] Holy,[5358] Peace,[5359] Faithful,[5360] Sovereign,[5361] Mighty,[5362] Almighty,[5363] and Proud.[5364] May Allah be glorified above the gods[5365] they worship! (23) He is Allah, the

---

[5348] Tawrah, Genesis 3:1-6
[5349] For "fear Allah" here and twice in verse 18, see Tawrah, Deuteronomy 10:12, Isaiah 29:13, Injil, 1 Peter 2:17, Revelation 14:7.
[5350] Injil, Matthew 6:19-21
[5351] Or transgressing or immoral
[5352] Arabic /jannah/. See glossary for more details.
[5353] Or qur'an or Qur'an. See glossary for more details.
[5354] Tawrah, Proverbs 1:1-7
[5355] Arabic /ilah/ here and in verse 23. See glossary for more details.
[5356] Zabur, Psalms 103:8, 145:8. See glossary for more details.
[5357] Zabur, Psalms 47:7
[5358] Tawrah, Isaiah 6:3
[5359] Tawrah, Isaiah 9:6, 54:10, Zabur, Psalms 29:11, 147:14, Injil, Ephesians 2:14
[5360] Or believer. Jeremiah 42:5, Injil, Revelation 3:14, 19:11
[5361] Injil, Acts 4:24, 1 Timothy 6:15, Revelation 6:10
[5362] Zabur, Psalms 93:4
[5363] Tawrah, Genesis 17:1, 28:3, Zabur, Psalms 91:1, Injil, Revelation 21:22
[5364] Tawrah, Job 22:29, Isaiah 2:12
[5365] Tawrah, Exodus 20:3

## Chapter 58

Creator,[5366] Maker[5367] and Former.[5368] He has the most beautiful names.[5369] Everything in the heavens and the earth glorifies him.[5370] He is Mighty and Wise.[5371] (24)[5372]

---

[5366] Tawrah, Isaiah 43:1,7, 45:18
[5367] Injil, Hebrews 11:10, Job 4:17, Tawrah, Genesis 4:19, Zabur, Psalms 95:6
[5368] Tawrah, Isaiah 43:1,7, 45:18
[5369] Tawrah, Genesis 16:13, 21:33, Deuteronomy 28:58, 1 Chronicles 29:11. The "most beautiful names" are what is commonly known in English as "The 99 names of God," 15 of which are mentioned in verses 22-24. Of the 99 names, 76 are mentioned in the Qur'an. The former books affirm these 76, and mention the rest as well.
[5370] Zabur, Psalms 150:6
[5371] Tawrah, Job 9:4, Proverbs 2:6, Jeremiah 9:23-24, Injil, 1 Corinthians 1:21-25, Romans 16:27
[5372] The verses in this chapter that rhyme are put together in paragraphs, separated by ***.

Chapter 60

# Chapter 60 Al-Mumtahanah[5373]

In the name of Allah, the most gracious and merciful.[5374] Believers, do not choose my enemy and yours<sup>MP</sup> as friends,[5375] giving them friendship though they have disbelieved[5376] in the truth that came to you<sup>MP</sup>, expelling the messenger and you<sup>MP</sup> because you<sup>MP</sup> believe in Allah your<sup>MP</sup> Lord. If you<sup>MP</sup> go out struggling in my path, seeking my pleasure, are you<sup>MP</sup> secretly friends to them[5377] when I know what you<sup>MP</sup> conceal[5378] and what you<sup>MP</sup> announce?[5379] Whoever among you<sup>MP</sup> does this has strayed[5380] from the straight path.[5381] (1)
\*\*\*

If they find you<sup>MP</sup>, they will be enemies to you<sup>MP</sup> and will stretch forth their hands and their tongues against you<sup>MP</sup> for evil. They wish that you<sup>MP</sup> disbelieved. (2)
\*\*\*

Your<sup>MP</sup> relatives and children[5382] will not benefit you<sup>MP</sup> on the day of resurrection.[5383] He will divide you<sup>MP</sup>. Allah sees your<sup>MP</sup> deeds. (3) You<sup>MP</sup> have a good example in Ibrahim[5384] and those that with him, since they told their people, "We are innocent of you<sup>MP</sup> and the gods you<sup>MP</sup> worship besides Allah;. we disbelieve in you<sup>MP</sup>, and between us and you<sup>MP</sup> it seems[5385] that there will be perpetual

---

[5373] The tested one<sup>FS</sup>
[5374] Zabur, Psalms 103:8, 145:8. See glossary for more details.
[5375] Injil, 2 Corinthians 6:14-17
[5376] Injil, 1 Corinthians 15:33
[5377] Injil, 2 Corinthians 6:15
[5378] Injil, Romans 2:16, Zabur, Psalms 44:21
[5379] See also 2:77, 11:5, 14:38, 16:19,23, 27:25,74, 28:69, 36:76, 64:4.
[5380] Injil, 1 Corinthians 15:33
[5381] See glossary for more details, and notes on 3:51, 6:153, 19:36, 36:61, and 43:64 on what the straight path is.
[5382] Or sons
[5383] Tawrah, Ezekiel 14:13-20, Daniel 12:2 Injil, Acts 24:15, 1 Corinthians 15:52-54, Revelation 20:11-15
[5384] Abraham twice in this verse. See glossary for more details. This phrase /uswa hasana/ (good example) is used here and in verse 6 of Ibrahim and those with him, and in 33:21 of Allah's messenger.
[5385] The verb here is masculine and the subject feminine. There may be another meaning or an implied word.

## Chapter 60

enmity and hatred,[5386] until you[MP] believe in Allah alone," except what Ibrahim told his father, "I will ask forgiveness for you[MS], but I cannot help you[MS] with Allah."[5387] Our Lord, we have trusted in you[MS] and turned to you[MS]. You[MS] are the final destiny. (4)

\*\*\*

Our Lord, do not make[MS] us a trial to the disbelievers.[5388] Forgive[MS] us. Our Lord, you[MS] are mighty and wise.[5389] (5)

\*\*\*

You[MP] have a good example in them for those who hope in Allah and the last day.[5390] But for those who turn away, Allah is self-sufficient and praiseworthy. (6) 28A4

\*\*\*

Allah may cause there to be friendship between you[MP] and those of them you[MP] were at enmity with.[5391] Allah is able. Allah is forgiving and merciful.[5392] (7) Allah does not prohibit you[MP] from acting justly and fairly toward those who did not fight you[MP] over religion, and who did not expel you[MP] from your[MP] houses. Allah loves the just. (8) But Allah prohibits you[MP] from being friends with those who fought against you[MP] in religion and expelled you[MP] from your[MP] houses, or assisted in expelling you[MP].[5393] Those who make friends with them are wicked. (9) Believers, if emigrant[FP] believers[FP] come[5394] to you[MP], test them[FP].[5395] Allah knows best about their[FP] faith.[5396] If you[MP] know they[FP] are believers[FS] do not send[MP] them[FP] back[5397] to the disbelievers. They[FP] are not allowed[5398] for them[MP], nor are they[MP] allowed to them[FP].[5399] Give[MP] them[MP][5400]

---

[5386] Injil, 2 Corinthians 6:14-16
[5387] Injil, 1 Timothy 2:5
[5388] Injil, Titus 2:8
[5389] Tawrah, Job 9:4, Proverbs 2:6, Jeremiah 9:23-24, Injil, 1 Corinthians 1:21-25, Romans 16:27
[5390] Injil, Hebrews 13:7
[5391] Tawrah, Proverbs 16:7, Injil, Matthew 5:9, Ephesians 2:14-15
[5392] Here and in verse 12, see glossary for more details on "merciful."
[5393] Tawrah, Proverbs 22:24
[5394] The verb here is masculine and the subject feminine. There may be another meaning or an implied word.
[5395] Injil, 2 Corinthians 2:9
[5396] Injil, 2 Corinthians 13:5, James 1:5, 1 Peter 1:7
[5397] Tawrah, Deuteronomy 23:15
[5398] i.e. in marriage
[5399] Injil, 2 Corinthians 6:14
[5400] i.e. the unbelieving husbands of believing wives

the bride price they<sup>MP</sup> have paid. You<sup>MP</sup> will not be blamed if you<sup>MP</sup> marry them<sup>FP</sup> if you<sup>MP</sup> give them<sup>FP</sup> their<sup>FP</sup> bride price.[5401] Do not retain<sup>MP</sup> guardianship over the disbelievers<sup>FP</sup>. Ask<sup>MP</sup> what you<sup>MP</sup> paid, and let them<sup>MP</sup> ask what they<sup>MP</sup> paid. That is Allah's regulation. He judges among you<sup>MP</sup>. Allah is all-knowing[5402] and wise.[5403] (10) If any of your<sup>MP</sup> wives escape to the disbelievers, and then you<sup>MP</sup> get victory in turn, give<sup>MP</sup> those whose wives have gone away what they<sup>MP</sup> paid. Fear Allah[5404] in whom you<sup>MP</sup> believe. (11) Prophet, if believers<sup>FP</sup> come[5405] to you<sup>MS</sup> and pledge allegiance to you<sup>MS</sup>, provided that they<sup>FP</sup> do not worship<sup>FP</sup> any other gods, do<sup>FP</sup> not steal, do<sup>FP</sup> not commit adultery, do<sup>FP</sup> not kill their children,[5406] do<sup>FP</sup> not invent slanderous things between their hands and legs, and kindly do<sup>FP</sup> not disobey you, then pledge allegiance to them<sup>FP</sup> and ask<sup>MS</sup> Allah's forgiveness for them<sup>FP</sup>. Allah is forgiving and merciful. (12)
***

Believers, do not make<sup>MP</sup> friends[5407] with people Allah is angry with, who despair of the hereafter as do the disbelievers among those in the tombs.[5408] (13)[5409]

---

[5401] "Dowry" is what a bride or her family provides at a wedding. This amount is paid by the bridegroom.
[5402] Tawrah, Job 37:16, Isaiah 40:14, Zabur, Psalms 33:13-15, Injil, 1 John 3:20
[5403] Tawrah, Job 9:4, Proverbs 2:6, Jeremiah 9:23-24, Injil, 1 Corinthians 1:21-25, Romans 16:27
[5404] Tawrah, Deuteronomy 10:12, Isaiah 29:13, Injil, 1 Peter 2:17, Revelation 14:7
[5405] The verb here is masculine and the subject feminine. There may be another meaning or an implied word.
[5406] Or sons
[5407] Injil, 1 Corinthians 15:33
[5408] Injil, 1 Thessalonians 4:13
[5409] The verses in this chapter that rhyme are put together in paragraphs, separated by ***.

# Chapter 61 Al-Saff[5410]

In the name of Allah, the most gracious and merciful.[5411] All that is in the heavens and the earth praises Allah. He is strong and wise.[5412] (1) Believers, why do you[MP] say and do not do[MP]?[5413] (2) Allah hates it greatly when you[MP] say and do not do[MP]. (3)
***
Allah loves those who fight in a row in his path, as if they were a building
joined together. (4)
***
When Musa[5414] told his people, "My people, why do you[MP] harm me when you[MP] know that I am Allah's messenger[5415] to you[MP]?" When they went astray, Allah made their hearts go astray.[5416] Allah does not guide unbelieving[5417] people. (5) When Isa[5418] son of Mariam[5419] said: "People of Israel, I am Allah's messenger to you[MP], confirming that of the Tawrah[5420] which is in my possession,[5421] and giving good news of a messenger coming after me, whose name is most highly praised."[5422] When he came to

---

[5410] Line or row (here, of troops in battle)
[5411] Zabur, Psalms 103:8, 145:8. See glossary for more details.
[5412] Tawrah, Job 9:4, Proverbs 2:6, Jeremiah 9:23-24, Injil, 1 Corinthians 1:21-25, Romans 16:27
[5413] Injil, Matthew 23:3
[5414] Moses. See glossary for more details.
[5415] The ones specifically called Allah's messenger in the Qur'an are Muhammad (s) 48:29, 7:158, 33:21,40,53, etc., Musa 61:5, Thamud's messenger 91:13, and Isa 4:157,171, 61:6.
[5416] see, for example, Tawrah, Exodus 8:32, 9:12
[5417] Or transgressing or immoral
[5418] Jesus. See glossary for more details.
[5419] Mary, mother of Jesus. See glossary for more details.
[5420] The Law. See glossary for more details. Injil, Matthew 5:17-18
[5421] Or, "between my hands" or "in front of me."
[5422] This word can be either a present tense verb, a proper noun, or a comparative adjective. Another translation would be "whose name I praise." A third option is a transliteration, "Ahmad," which common beliefs say is an alternate name for Muhammad (s). Some say that this verse refers to Injil, John 14:16-17, where Isa predicts the coming of another counselor, who would remain with his followers forever, also known as the spirit of truth, whom other people could not accept, because they did not see him or know him, whereas Isa's followers knew him,

them with the miracles, they said, "This is clear[5423] magic." (6) Who is more wicked than him who calls Allah a liar when called to submit?[5424] Allah does not guide wicked people. (7) They want to blow out Allah's light[5425] with their mouths, but Allah will perfect his light, even though the disbelievers hate it. (8) He sent his messenger with guidance and the religion of truth to explain all religion, even though the disbelievers hate it. (9) Believers, shall I show you[MP] a way[5426] that will rescue you[MP] from painful torment?[5427] (10) You[MP] believe in Allah and his messenger and struggle in Allah's path with your[MP] money and your[MP] souls. That is better for you[MP] if you only knew. (11) He will certainly forgive your[MP] sins and cause you[MP] to enter heavenly gardens[5428] with flowing rivers[5429] underneath and fine dwellings in the heavenly gardens of Eden. That is the great victory,[5430] (12) and there another[5431] that you[MP] will love. This is Allah's salvation and a victory that is near.[5432] So give good news to the believers. (13) Believers, be Allah's helpers, as Isa[5433] son of Mariam[5434] asked the disciples,[5435] "Who are my helpers for Allah?" The disciples said, "We are Allah's helpers." Some of the people of Israel

---

because he was with them and would be inside of them. This is obviously not referring to a person, who could be seen and known, but a spirit from Allah, who could be inside them.

[5423] Or clearly

[5424] Injil, James 4:7. For "submit," some translators do not translate this. See glossary for more details.

[5425] See Injil, 1 John 1:5, Matthew 5:14, John 8:12

[5426] or business or trade

[5427] Tawrah, Isaiah 50:11, Injil, Matthew 18:34, 25:41,46, Luke 16:23-28, Revelation 20:15

[5428] Arabic /jannah/ twice in this verse. See glossary for more details.

[5429] Injil, Revelation 22:1-2, Tawrah, Ezekiel 47:12

[5430] Tawrah, Isaiah 25:8, Injil, 1 Corinthians 15:57, 1 John 5:4

[5431] This could mean "benefit." The only word that is mentioned here that would fit otherwise is "garden."

[5432] See Injil, Matthew 19:29

[5433] Jesus. See glossary for more details.

[5434] Mary, mother of Jesus. See glossary for more details.

[5435] Or /hawariyun/ twice in this verse. The reference is to the twelve disciples that Isa sent out as apostles. The Arabic word is of uncertain meaning. Some have suggested that it refers to their arguing, and others to their wearing white robes, or workers in bleaching clothes.

believed and others disbelieved.[5436] We aided the believers against their enemy, and they were victorious.[5437] (14)[5438]

# Chapter 62 Al-Jumuah[5439]

28B1 In the name of Allah, the most gracious and merciful.[5440] Everything in the heavens and on the earth worships Allah, the holy king,[5441] mighty and wise.[5442] (1) He sent a messenger to the Gentiles[5443] from among themselves, reciting his signs to them, purifying them, and teaching them the book and wisdom,[5444] though previously they were clearly astray.[5445] (2) And [sent] others from among them who had not come to them. He is mighty and wise.[5446] (3) That is Allah's grace. He gives it to those he wills. Allah has great grace.[5447] (4) Those who were responsible to carry the Tawrah[5448] and did not carry it are like a donkey carrying scrolls. What an awful proverb for people who rejected Allah's signs.[5449] Allah does not guide wicked people. (5) Say[MS], "Jews,[5450] if you[MP] claim that you[MP], rather than other people, are Allah's helpers, then wish for death if you[MP] are really telling the truth." (6) But they do not wish for it at all because of what their hands have

---

[5436] See Injil, John 6:60-69

[5437] or obvious

[5438] The verses in this chapter that rhyme are put together in paragraphs, separated by ***.

[5439] Friday

[5440] Zabur, Psalms 103:8, 145:8. See glossary for more details.

[5441] Tawrah, Isaiah 43:15

[5442] Tawrah, Job 9:4, Proverbs 2:6, Jeremiah 9:23-24, Injil, 1 Corinthians 1:21-25, Romans 16:27

[5443] Injil, Romans 11:13, 1 Timothy 2:7. Here the meaning of /ummi/ is clearly Gentile, and not illiterate. See 7:157,158

[5444] Injil, Ephesians 3:3-6

[5445] Injil, Ephesians 2:12

[5446] Tawrah, Job 9:4, Proverbs 2:6, Jeremiah 9:23-24, Injil, 1 Corinthians 1:21-25, Romans 16:27

[5447] Injil, Ephesians 1:7, 2:7

[5448] Injil, Romans 3:2

[5449] Tawrah, Numbers 11:20

[5450] Or "those who repented and turned back to the truth." This probably refers to when Jews repented after worshiping the golden calf idol (2:54, 92, 7:138, 148-150, Tawrah, Exodus 32).

## Chapter 62

done.[5451] Allah knows the wicked. (7) Say[MS], "The death you[MP] are fleeing will catch up to you[MP]. Then you[MP] will be returned to him who knows the unseen and the seen,[5452] and he will tell you[MP] your[MP] deeds." (8) Believers, if Friday prayers are called, strive[MP] to remember Allah. Avoid[MP] selling.[5453] That is better for you[MP], if you[MP] only knew. (9) When prayers are finished, spread[MP] forth in the land, seeking Allah's grace. Remember[MP] Allah often, so that you[MP] may prosper.[5454] (10) When they see business or amusement, they go after it and leave you[MS] standing. Say[MS], "What Allah has is better than amusement and than business. Allah is the best provider."[5455] (11)

---

[5451] Injil, Romans 3:9-10
[5452] Injil, Matthew 6:4,6,18
[5453] Tawrah, Nehemiah 13:15-19
[5454] Tawrah, Joshua 1:8,13
[5455] Injil, Matthew 6:25-26

# Chapter 63 Al-Munafiqun[5456]

In the name of Allah, the most gracious and merciful.[5457] When the hypocrites came to you[MS], they said, "We testify that you[MS] are Allah's messenger, and Allah knows that you[MS] are his messenger." Allah testifies that the hypocrites are liars. (1) They have made their oaths a cloak and blocked people from Allah's path.[5458] What they did was bad. (2) That is because they believed, then disbelieved, so their hearts were sealed.[5459] They do not understand. (3) 28B2 When you[MS] see them, you[MS] will be pleased with their bodies, and when they speak, you[MS] will hear their sayings. They are like timber propped up. They think every shout is against them.[5460] They are the enemy, so beware of them. May Allah fight against them.[5461] How they lie! (4) When they are told, "Come, and Allah's messenger will ask forgiveness for you[MP]," they twist their heads and you[MS] see them proudly turning away. (5) Whether you[MS] ask forgiveness for them or not, Allah will not forgive them. Allah does not guide unbelieving[5462] people. (6) They say, "Do not donate to those that are with Allah's messenger until they disperse." The storehouses of the heavens and the earth[5463] are Allah's, but hypocrites do not understand. (7) They say, "If we return to the city, the mightier ones there would expel the humble." Might belongs to Allah, his messenger, and the believers, but the hypocrites do not know. (8) Believers, do not let your[MP] money or your[MP] children[5464] distract you[MP] from remembering Allah.[5465] Those who do that are lost. (9) Donate out of what we have provided you[MP] before death comes to any of you[MF],[5466] and someone says, "If only you[MS] had given me a little more time to give alms and be righteous." (10) Allah will not give

---

[5456] Hypocrites
[5457] Zabur, Psalms 103:8, 145:8. See glossary for more details.
[5458] Injil, Matthew 23:13, Luke 11:52.
[5459] Hebrews 10:26-27
[5460] Tawrah, Proverbs 28:1
[5461] Tawrah, Joshua 23:10
[5462] Or transgressing or immoral
[5463] Tawrah, Job 38:22, Zabur, Psalms 33:7, 135:7, Jeremiah 10:13, 51:16
[5464] or sons
[5465] Tawrah, Exodus 13:3, Injil, Matthew 13:22
[5466] Injil, James 5:1-3

a soul more time once its time comes.[5467] Allah is aware of your[MP] deeds. (11)

---

[5467] Injil, Luke 12:20

## Chapter 64 Al-Taghabun[5468]

In the name of Allah, the most gracious and merciful.[5469] Everything in the heavens and on the earth praises Allah. The kingdom is his,[5470] and praise is his.[5471] He can do anything.[5472] (1) He created you[MP].[5473] Some of you[MP] are disbelievers, and some of you[MP] are believers. Allah sees your[MP] deeds.[5474] (2) He truly created the heavens and the earth,[5475] and he formed you[MP].[5475] He formed you[MP] well,[5477] and he is your destiny.[5478] (3) He knows everything in the heavens and the earth.[5479] He knows what you[MP] conceal and what you[MP] announce.[5480] Allah knows what is in the heart.[5481] (4)

\*\*\*

Have you[MP] not heard the story of the disbelievers beforehand, who tasted the grievousness of their matter? They will have painful torment.[5482] (5)

\*\*\*

That is because messengers used to come to them with miracles and they said, "Should people guide us?" So they disbelieved and

---

[5468] Mutual deception.
[5469] Zabur, Psalms 103:8, 145:8. See glossary for more details.
[5470] Tawrah, 1 Chronicles 29:11
[5471] Zabur, Psalms 147:1
[5472] Tawrah, Job 42:2, Isaiah 14:27, Daniel 4:35, Injil, Matthew 19:26, Mark 10:27, Luke 1:37
[5473] Tawrah, Genesis 1:16-27
[5474] Tawrah, Lamentations 3:50
[5475] Tawrah, Genesis 1:1
[5476] Tawrah, Genesis 2:7
[5477] Tawrah, Genesis 1:31
[5478] Injil, Romans 14:10
[5479] Tawrah, Job 37:16, Isaiah 40:14, Zabur, Psalms 33:13-15, Injil, 1 John 3:20
[5480] See also 2:77, 11:5, 14:38, 16:19,23, 27:25,74, 28:69, 36:76, 60:1.
[5481] Tawrah, 1 Samuel 16:7, 1 Chronicles 28:9, Zabur, Psalms 44:21, Injil, Luke 16:15, Romans 8:27, Acts 15:8, 1 John 3:20
[5482] Tawrah, Isaiah 50:11, Injil, Matthew 18:34, 25:41,46, Luke 16:23-28, Revelation 20:15

Chapter 64

turned away. Allah does not need them.[5483] He is self-sufficient[5484] and praiseworthy.[5485] (6)

\*\*\*

Disbelievers claim that they will not be resurrected. Say[MS]: Oh yes, [you will. I swear] by my Lord. You[MP] will be resurrected[5486] and then you[MP] will be told your[MP] deeds. That is easy for Allah. (7) Believe in Allah, his messenger, and the light we revealed.[5487] Allah is aware of your[MP] deeds.[5488] (8)

\*\*\*

On that day, he will gather you[MP] for the day of gathering.[5489] That is the day of mutual deception. Allah will expiate[5490] the bad deeds of those who believe in him and do righteous deeds.[5491] He will cause them to enter heavenly gardens[5492] with flowing rivers underneath,[5493] where they will live forever. That is the great triumph. (9)

\*\*\*

Disbelievers who reject our signs[5494] will be in hellfire, where they will be forever.[5495] It is an awful destiny. (10)

\*\*\*

He does not make calamities happen except by Allah's permission. Allah guides the heart of believers in him.[5496] Allah knows everything. (11) Obey[MP] Allah and obey[MP] the messenger. If you[MP] turn away, our messenger's only responsibility is to proclaim clearly.[5497] (12) Allah is the only god.[5498] Let the believers trust in

---

[5483] Tawrah, Job 35:7
[5484] Injil, Acts 7:49
[5485] Zabur, Psalms 147:1
[5486] Injil, John 5:29
[5487] Injil, John 1:8-9
[5488] Injil, Luke 12:2
[5489] Tawrah, Joel 3:11-14, Zephaniah 3:8, Injil, Matthew 25:32, John 15:6, Revelation 16:16
[5490] Tawrah, Isaiah 27:9, Injil, Romans 3:25, Hebrews 2:17, 1 John 2:2, 4:10
[5491] Injil, 1 Corinthians 3:8, James 2:14-17, Revelation 19:8
[5492] Arabic /jannah/. See glossary for more details.
[5493] Injil, Revelation 22:2
[5494] Arabic /ayat/. See glossary for more details.
[5495] Injil, Revelation 14:10, 22:10
[5496] Zabur, Psalms 32:8
[5497] Injil, Luke 7:27
[5498] Arabic /ilah/. See glossary for more details.

Allah. (13) Believers, there will be enemies to you[MP] among your[MP] own wives and children.[5499] Beware[MP] of them.[5500] If you[MP] will pardon them, overlook them,[MP] and forgive[MP] them, then Allah will be forgiving[5501] and merciful.[5502] (14) Your[MP] money and your[MP] children are a trial.[5503] There is a great reward with Allah.[5504] (15) So fear Allah[5505] as much as you[MP] can, listen[MP], obey[MP], and donate[MP]. It is better for your[MP] souls.[5506] Those who are kept safe from their soul's covetousness[5507] will be prosperous. (16) If you[MP] give Allah a good loan, he will pay you[MP] back double,[5508] and will forgive you[MP]. Allah is grateful and gentle.[5509] (17) He knows the unseen and the seen,[5510] and is mighty[5511] and wise.[5512] (18)[5513]

---

[5499] Or sons here and in verse 15. Injil, Matthew 24:10, 10:21,35,36 Deuteronomy 13:6

[5500] Tawrah, Deuteronomy 13:8

[5501] Zabur, Psalms 103:3, 130:4, Tawrah, Isaiah 43:25, Exodus 34:7, Injil, Acts 26:18.

[5502] See glossary for more details on "merciful."

[5503] Injil, 1 Timothy 6:10, Luke 14:26, Matthew 10:37

[5504] Injil, Matthew 5:12

[5505] Tawrah, Deuteronomy 10:12, Isaiah 29:13, Injil, 1 Peter 2:17, Revelation 14:7

[5506] Or, and donate what is good for your souls (or selves, or each other).

[5507] Injil, Ephesians 5:5

[5508] Tawrah, Proverbs 19:17

[5509] Zabur, Psalms 45:4, 145:17, Injil, Matthew 11:29, Galatians 5:22

[5510] Injil, Acts 15:8

[5511] Zabur, Psalms 93:4

[5512] Tawrah, Job 9:4, Proverbs 2:6, Jeremiah 9:23-24, Injil, 1 Corinthians 1:21-25, Romans 16:27

[5513] The verses in this chapter that rhyme are put together in paragraphs, separated by ***.

# Chapter 65
# Chapter 65 Al-Talaq[5514]

**28B3** In the name of Allah, the most gracious and merciful.[5515] Prophet, when you[MP] divorce wives, divorce[MP] them[FP] according to their[FP] term. Calculate their term and fear[MP] Allah, your[MP] Lord. Do not expel[MP] them[FP] from their[FP] houses. They[FP] should not go out unless they[FP] have clearly committed promiscuity.[5516] Those are Allah's limits, and those who exceed Allah's limits[5517] have wronged themselves.[5518] You[MS] do not know whether Allah will bring about a matter after that. (1) When they[FP] have completed their term, either keep them[FP] kindly or part[MP] from them[FP] kindly. Have just people[MD] among you[MP] testify, and call witnesses to give evidence before Allah.[5519] Believers in Allah and the last day are admonished to do that. Allah will make a way of escape[5520] for those who fear Allah.[5521] (2) He will provide for them in ways they were not counting on.[5522] Allah is enough for those who trust in him. Allah will bring his matter to a conclusion. Allah has assigned a measure to everything. (3) If you[MP] doubt regarding those[FP] of your[MP] wives who despair[FP] of having more periods, and those[FP] who have not yet had periods, then their[FP] term is three months. The term for those who are pregnant is until they give

---

[5514] divorce
[5515] Zabur, Psalms 103:8, 145:8. See glossary for more details.
[5516] Or lewdness, adultery or abomination. See Injil, Matthew 5:32, 19:9.
[5517] Injil, Matthew 5:32, 19:9, Mark 10:11-12, Luke 16:18
[5518] The injustice/wickedness, disbelief/ungratefulness, evil, unrighteousness/sin, or lostness of mankind is mentioned in a number of verses in the Qur'an as well as in the previous books. Injustice or wickedness: 2:57, 3:117,135, 4:64,97, 7:160,177, 9:70, 10:44, 11:101, 14:34,45, 16:33,61,118, 29:40, 30:9, 33:72, 34:19, 35:32, 43:76, 65:1, Tawrah, Genesis 6:5, Job 25:4, Injil, Acts 3:26, disbelief or ungratefulness: 14:34, 17:67, 22:66, 42:48, 43:15, 80:17, Injil, Hebrews 3:19, Evil: 12:53, Tawrah, Jeremiah 17:9, Injil, Matthew 15:19, Mark 7:21, unrighteousness or sin: 91:8, Tawrah, 1 Kings 8:46, Ecclesiastes 7:20, Injil, Romans 3:9-19, 5:12, lostness: 103:2, Tawrah, Jeremiah 50:6, Injil, Luke 19:10, Romans 3:23, 6:23
[5519] Tawrah, Deuteronomy 24:1
[5520] Injil, 1 Corinthians 10:13
[5521] For "fear Allah" here and in verses 5 and 10, see Tawrah, Deuteronomy 10:12, Isaiah 29:13, Injil, 1 Peter 2:17, Revelation 14:7.
[5522] Tawrah, Genesis 22:8,14

birth. Allah will make his command easy for those who fear him.[5523] (4) This is Allah's command which he has revealed to you[MP]. Allah will expiate the bad deeds[5524] of those who fear Allah, and greatly increase their rewards. (5)

House[MP] them[FP] where you[MP] used to live according to your[MP] means. Do not harm[MP] them[FP] to trouble them[FP]. If they[FP] are pregnant, provide[MP][5525] for them[FP] until they[FP] give birth. Pay them[FP] their[FP] wages[5526] if they[FP] nurse the baby for you[MP], and counsel[MP] among yourselves[MP] kindly. If it is difficult for you[MP], another[FS] will nurse[FS] him. (6)

Those who are wealthy should pay from their wealth, and those whose finances are tight should pay from what Allah has given them.[5527] Allah does not make a soul responsible for more than it has been given.[5528] After a time of want, Allah will give plenty.[5529] (7) How many villages were insolent towards the command of their Lord and his messengers? We gave them a severe reckoning, and gave them horrible torment, (8) so they tasted the grievousness of their matter. Their matter ended in loss. (9) Allah has prepared them harsh torment,[5530] so you[MP] thinkers, fear Allah. Allah has revealed a reminder[5531] for believers, (10) a messenger reciting Allah's signs as miracles to you[MP], to bring out believers who do righteous deeds[5532] from darkness into the light.[5533] He will admit believers in Allah who do righteous deeds into heavenly gardens[5534] with flowing rivers underneath,[5535] where they will live

---

[5523] Injil, 1 John 5:3
[5524] Tawrah, Isaiah 27:9, Injil, Romans 3:25, Hebrews 2:17, 1 John 2:2, 4:10
[5525] Or donate
[5526] Tawrah, Exodus 2:9
[5527] Injil, 2 Corinthians 8:12
[5528] Injil, 2 Corinthians 8:12-13, 1 Corinthians 10:13
[5529] Philippians 4:11-12
[5530] Tawrah, Isaiah 50:11, Injil, Matthew 18:34, 25:41,46, Luke 16:23-28, Revelation 20:15
[5531] Arabic /dhikr/. See glossary for more details.
[5532] Injil, 1 Corinthians 3:8, James 2:14-17, Revelation 19:8
[5533] Tawrah, Isaiah 9:2
[5534] Arabic /jannah/. See glossary for more details.
[5535] Injil, Revelation 22:2

forever and ever.[5536] Allah will provide well for them. (11) Allah created seven heavens[FP], and earths similar in number to them[FP].[5537] The command is revealed among them[FP], so that you[MP] may know that Allah can do anything,[5538] and Allah knows everything. (12)[5539]

---

[5536] Injil, Matthew 25:34,46

[5537] The word "them" referring to heavens, is the word used for thinking beings. This may be because the heavens are considered to actively obey Allah.

[5538] Tawrah, Job 42:2, Isaiah 14:27, Daniel 4:35, Injil, Matthew 19:26, Mark 10:27, Luke 1:37

[5539] The verses in this chapter that rhyme are put together in paragraphs, separated by ***.

# Chapter 66: Al-Tahrim[5540]

**28B4** In the name of Allah, the most gracious and merciful.[5541] Prophet, why do you[MS] forbid what Allah has allowed for you[MS]? You[MS] are trying to please your[MS] wives.[5542] Allah is forgiving[5543] and merciful.[5544] (1) Allah has decreed that you[MP] break your[MP] oaths. Allah is your[MP] master. He is all-knowing[5545] and wise.[5546] (2)
\*\*\*

When the prophet told some of his wives a saying in secret, and then she told it, and then Allah informed him of it, he made some of it known and disclaimed some of it. When he told her about it, she said, "Who told you[MS] that?" He said, "The all-knowing, aware one told me." (3) If you[D] repent to Allah, your[D] hearts[P] have listened. If they[5547] defend[MD] each other against him, Allah is his master, along with Jibril[5548] and the righteous believers, and after that, the angels are a support. (4)
\*\*\*

If he divorces you[FP],[5549] his Lord may exchange for him better wives[FP], who submit[FP] and believe[FP], are submissive[FP], repentant[FP], worshipful[FP], who travel[FP], widows[FP] and virgins[FP]. (5)
\*\*\*

Believers, guard yourselves[MP] and your[MP] families from hellfire, whose fuel is people and rocks. There are severe, strong angels over it who do not disobey[MP] what Allah commands them, but do[MP]

---

[5540] Forbidding

[5541] Zabur, Psalms 103:8, 145:8. See glossary for more details.

[5542] Injil, 1 Corinthians 7:33

[5543] Zabur, Psalms 103:3, 130:4, Tawrah, Isaiah 43:25, Exodus 34:7, Injil, Acts 26:18.

[5544] See glossary for more details on "merciful."

[5545] For all-knowing here and in verse 3, see Tawrah, Job 37:16, Isaiah 40:14, Zabur, Psalms 33:13-15, Injil, 1 John 3:20

[5546] Tawrah, Job 9:4, Proverbs 2:6, Injil, Jeremiah 9:23-24, Injil, 1 Corinthians 1:21-25, Romans 16:27

[5547] The verb here is either in the third person masculine dual perfect tense, or in the imperfect tense with two missing letters. The context is second person feminine dual. The reason is unknown.

[5548] the archangel Gabriel

[5549] This verse is in the feminine plural, whereas the previous verse addresses two women.

## Chapter 69

as they are told. (6) Disbelievers, do not make excuses today. You[MP] are being repaid for your[MP] deeds.[5550] (7)

\*\*\*

Believers, repent[MP] sincerely toward Allah, that your[MP] Lord may expiate your[MP] bad deeds[5551] and admit you[MP] to heavenly gardens[5552] with flowing rivers[5553] underneath. On that day, Allah will not shame the prophet nor those who believed with him. Their[MP] light proceeds between their[MP] hands, and with oaths[5554] they[MP] say: "Lord, perfect our light and forgive us. You[MS] can do anything."[5555] (8) Prophet, struggle against the disbelievers and the hypocrites and be tough with them. They will dwell in hell, an awful destiny." (9)

\*\*\*

Allah gave a parable to the disbelievers: Nuh's[5556] wife and Lut's[5557] wife.[5558] They were married[5559] to two of our righteous servants,[5560] but they betrayed them. Their husbands could not help them at all with Allah. It was told them both, "Enter hellfire along with others who enter." (10) Allah gave a parable to the believers: Pharaoh's wife, who said, "Lord, build me a house in heaven[5561] with you[MS], and rescue me from Pharaoh and his work, and rescue me from wicked people," (11) and Mariam,[5562] daughter of Imran,[5563] who guarded her chastity,[5564] so we

---

[5550] or used to do

[5551] Tawrah, Isaiah 27:9, Injil, Romans 3:25, Hebrews 2:17, 1 John 2:2, 4:10

[5552] Arabic /jannah/. See glossary for more details.

[5553] Injil, Revelation 22:1-2, Tawrah, Ezekiel 47:12

[5554] or, and in their right hands

[5555] Tawrah, Job 42:2, Isaiah 14:27, Daniel 4:35, Injil, Matthew 19:26, Mark 10:27, Luke 1:37

[5556] Noah. See glossary for more details.

[5557] Lot, nephew of Abraham. See glossary for more details.

[5558] Tawrah, Genesis 19:26, Injil, Luke 17:32

[5559] or, were under

[5560] See glossary.

[5561] or the garden

[5562] Mary, mother of Jesus. See glossary for more details.

[5563] The Injil does not give the name of Mary's father. She was a relative of Elizabeth, a descendant of Harun, whose father was Amram, so this phrase could either refer to her father, or her ancestor.

[5564] Or genitals or vulva. The meaning is she was a virgin. Injil, Luke 1:34

breathed of our spirit⁵⁵⁶⁵ into her womb. She believed in⁵⁵⁶⁶ the words of her Lord and of his books,⁵⁵⁶⁷ and she was devout."⁵⁵⁶⁸ (12)⁵⁵⁶⁹

# Chapter 67 Al-Mulk⁵⁵⁷⁰

**29A1** In the name of Allah, the most gracious and merciful.⁵⁵⁷¹ Blessed be the One with the kingdom⁵⁵⁷² in his hand. He can do anything.⁵⁵⁷³ (1) He created death and life⁵⁵⁷⁴ to test you^MP, to see which of you^MP have the best deeds. He is mighty⁵⁵⁷⁵ and forgiving.⁵⁵⁷⁶ (2) He created seven heavens on top of each other. You^MS do not see anything uneven in the most gracious's creation. Look again. Do you^MS see a flaw?⁵⁵⁷⁷ (3) Then look^MS twice again, and your^MS sight will be turned about, driven away, and fatigued. (4) We have decorated the lower heaven with lamps⁵⁵⁷⁸ and made them things to throw at the devils,⁵⁵⁷⁹ for whom we have prepared the torment⁵⁵⁸⁰ of burning fire. (5) The torment of hell awaits disbelievers in their Lord. It is an awful destiny.⁵⁵⁸¹ (6) When they

---

⁵⁵⁶⁵ Injil, Luke 1:35. Isa and Adam are the only ones who came about through Allah's spirit. See 32:9, 38:72, and 15:29 for Adam and here and 21:91 for Isa.

⁵⁵⁶⁶ Or, "confirmed."

⁵⁵⁶⁷ Injil, Luke 1:45

⁵⁵⁶⁸ Injil, Luke 1:38

⁵⁵⁶⁹ The verses in this chapter that rhyme are put together in paragraphs, separated by ***.

⁵⁵⁷⁰ Kingdom

⁵⁵⁷¹ Zabur, Psalms 103:8, 145:8. See glossary for more details.

⁵⁵⁷² Tawrah, 1 Chronicles 29:11

⁵⁵⁷³ Tawrah, Job 42:2, Isaiah 14:27, Daniel 4:35, Injil, Matthew 19:26, Mark 10:27, Luke 1:37

⁵⁵⁷⁴ Tawrah, 1 Samuel 2:6

⁵⁵⁷⁵ Zabur, Psalms 93:4

⁵⁵⁷⁶ Zabur, Psalms 103:3, 130:4, Tawrah, Isaiah 43:25, Exodus 34:7, Injil, Acts 26:18.

⁵⁵⁷⁷ Tawrah, Genesis 1:31

⁵⁵⁷⁸ Tawrah, Genesis 1:16

⁵⁵⁷⁹ Arabic /shayatin/. See glossary for more details. Injil, Revelation 12:4

⁵⁵⁸⁰ For "torment" here and in verses 6 and 28, see Tawrah, Isaiah 50:11, Injil, Matthew 18:34, 25:41,46, Luke 16:23-28, Revelation 20:15.

⁵⁵⁸¹ Injil, Revelation 20:10

## Chapter 69

are thrown into it, they will hear it sigh as it boils. (7) It almost sounds furious. Whenever a group is thrown into it, its guards will ask, "Did a warner not come to you^MP?" (8) They will say, "Yes. A warner came to us, but we rejected him and said, "Allah has not revealed anything." "You^MP have greatly strayed." (9) They said, "If only we had heard or understood, we would not have gone to the burning fire." (10) They confessed their sins.[5582] Away with those who are going to the burning fire! (11) Those who are afraid of their Lord in the unseen[5583] will have forgiveness and a great reward. (12) Whether you^MP keep your^MP saying secret or make^MP it public, he knows what is in the heart.[5584] (13) Does the creator,[5585] who is kind[5586] and aware, not know?[5587] (14) He made the earth for you^MP to plow,[5588] so walk in its fields and eat of his provision. Everyone will be gathered[5589] to him. (15) Are you^MP safe from the one in heaven opening up the earth to swallow you^MP[5590] as it shakes? (16) Or are you^MP safe from the one in heaven sending a sandstorm of pebbles against you^MP? You^MP will know what my warner is like. (17) Those who were before them rejected. What a denial they got from me! (18) Have they not seen the birds above them lined up and flapping?[5591] Only the most gracious holds them up.[5592] He sees everything. (19) What army of yours^MP can save you^MP apart from the most gracious? Disbelievers are deluded. (20) Who is your^MP provider if he withholds his provision?[5593]

\*\*\*

They obstinately persist in insolence and flee. (21)

\*\*\*

---

[5582] Injil, James 5:16
[5583] Injil, 1 Peter 1:8
[5584] Tawrah, 1 Samuel 16:7, 1 Chronicles 28:9, Zabur, Psalms 44:21, Injil, Luke 16:15, Romans 8:27, Acts 15:8, 1 John 3:20
[5585] Tawrah, Isaiah 43:7
[5586] Zabur, Psalms 145:17
[5587] Tawrah, Job 37:16, Isaiah 40:14, Zabur, Psalms 33:13-15, Injil, 1 John 3:20
[5588] Tawrah, Genesis 2:15
[5589] Here and in verse 24, see Tawrah, Joel 3:11-14, Zephaniah 3:8, Injil, Matthew 25:32, John 15:6, Revelation 16:16
[5590] Tawrah, Numbers 16:30-32
[5591] Or gliding, or pulling in (their wings)
[5592] Injil, Matthew 6:26, 10:29
[5593] Injil, Matthew 6:25-26

## Chapter 69

Does he who walks grovelling on his face have better guidance than him who walks rightly on the straight path?[5594] (22) Say[MS], "He created you[MP] and gave you[MP] hearing, sight, and hearts. How little you[MP] give thanks! (23) Say[MS], "He created you[MP] on the earth[5595] and you[MP] will be gathered to him." (24) They will say, "When will this promise be, if you[MP] are telling the truth?" (25) Say[MS], "Only Allah knows.[5596] I am only a clear warner." (26) When they see it come near, disbelievers will scowl, and they will be told, "This is what you[MP] claimed." (27) Say[MS], "What do you[MP] think? Whether Allah destroys me and those that are with me or whether he has mercy on me, who will save disbelievers from painful torment?" (28) Say[MS], "He is the most gracious. We believe in him and trust in him. You[MP] will know who is clearly astray." (29) Say[MS], "What do you[MP] think? If your[MP] water seeps into the ground, who will bring you[MP] clear spring water?" (30) [5597]

---

[5594] See glossary for more details, and notes on 3:51, 6:153, 19:36, 36:61, and 43:64 on what the straight path is.
[5595] Tawrah, Genesis 2:15
[5596] Injil, Matthew 24:36, Mark 13:32
[5597] The verses in this chapter that rhyme are put together in paragraphs, separated by ***.

Chapter 69

# Chapter 68 Al-Qalam[5598] or Nun[5599]

**29A2** In the name of Allah, the most gracious and merciful.[5600] N.[5601] [I swear] by the pen and they write, (1) you[MS] are not possessed,[5602] by the blessings of your[MS] Lord. (2) You[MS] will not have a diminished reward. (3) You[MS] have a great natural disposition.[5603] (4) You[MS] will see and they will see (5) which of you[MP] is demented. (6) Your[MS] Lord well knows[5604] those who have strayed from his path, and he well knows those who are guided. (7) Do not obey[MS] the rejecters. (8) They wish you[MS] would deceive, so they could deceive, too. (9) Do not obey any shameful swearers, (10) slanderers, liars, and gossips, (11) hinderers of good, aggressors, the guilty, (12) violent, and above all that, ignoble.[5605] (13) Someone with money and children[5606] (14) will say, "Ancient legends" when our signs are recited to him. (15) We will brand him on the nose. (16) We tested them as we tested the owners of the garden, when they swore they would gather fruit in the morning (17) and they did not make an exception.[5607] (18) As they were sleeping, a walker from your[MS] Lord walked around them, (19) and in the morning it seemed all gathered. (20) They called to each other in the morning, (21) "Go to your[MP] fields in the morning if you[MP] want to gather." (22) So they went off talking softly, (23) "Do not let any needy person enter it today against your[MP] will." (24) So they went off purposefully and determined. (25) When they saw it, they said, "We have gone astray. (26) We have been prevented." (27) The most moderate of them said, "Did I not tell you[MP], are you[MP] not going to glorify Allah?" (28) They said, "May our Lord be glorified! We were evildoers." (29) They

---

[5598] The pen (for writing)
[5599] The letter N
[5600] Zabur, Psalms 103:8, 145:8. See glossary for more details.
[5601] Here and at the beginning of many chapters there are unvowelled letters of unknown meaning. Numerous theories have been proposed, but there is no agreement on the subject.
[5602] By demons. Or, crazy.
[5603] Or, morality.
[5604] Tawrah, Job 37:16, Isaiah 40:14, Zabur, Psalms 33:13-15, Injil, 1 John 3:20
[5605] Injil, Romans 1:29-31
[5606] Or sons
[5607] Probably "if Allah wills" Injil, James 4:13-16

came toward each other, blaming each other. (30) They said, "Woe to us. We were transgressors. (31) Maybe our Lord will exchange it for good to us. We will earnestly pray to our Lord." (32) That is what torment is like. The torment[5608] of the hereafter will be greater, if they only knew it. (33) The reverent will have heavenly gardens[5609] of delight with their Lord.[5610] (34) Shall we make submitted[5611] ones equal to wrongdoers? (35) What's wrong with you[MP]? How do you[MP] judge? (36) Do you[MP] have a book you[MP] study? (37) You[MP] should have whatever you[MP] choose in it. (38) Or do you[MP] have oaths that are valid against us until the day of resurrection?[5612] You[MP] would have whatever you[MP] judge. (39) Ask[MS] them which of them guarantees that. (40) Or do they have partners?[5613] Let them bring their partners if they are telling the truth. (41) On that day, legs will be bared, and they will be called to bow down, but they will not be able to. (42) Their gaze will be humbled, and they will be abased. They were called to bow down when they were healthy. (43) Let me alone with the rejecters of this story. We will gradually punish them in ways they do not know. (44) I will give them time, because[5614] my trap is firm. (45) Did you[MS] ask them for payment so they are burdened by debt? (46) Or is the unseen theirs, and they are writing it down? (47) Endure[5615] your[MS] Lord's judgment, and do not be like the one in the whale,[5616] who called out in his oppression.[5617] (48) If blessings from his Lord had not come to him,[5618] he would have been left disgraced in a deserted place.[5619] (49) But his Lord chose him[5620]

---

[5608] Tawrah, Isaiah 50:11, Injil, Matthew 18:34, 25:41,46, Luke 16:23-28, Revelation 20:15

[5609] Arabic /jannah/. See glossary for more details.

[5610] Zabur, Psalms 16:11

[5611] Injil, James 4:7. For "submitted," some translators do not translate this. See glossary for more details.

[5612] Tawrah, Daniel 12:2 Injil, Acts 24:15, 1 Corinthians 15:52-54, Revelation 20:11-15

[5613] The meaning may be "other gods"

[5614] Or, I will dictate to them that

[5615] Or, "wait for."

[5616] The reference is to Yunus. See glossary for more details. Tawrah, Jonah 1:17-2:10

[5617] Tawrah, Jonah 2:1-9

[5618] Tawrah, Jonah 2:10

[5619] Tawrah, Jonah 2:2-7

[5620] Tawrah, Jonah 3:2

and made him righteous.[5621] (50) Disbelievers almost made you[MS] slip by their glances when they heard the reminder.[5622] They said, "He is possessed."[5623] (51) It is only a reminder[5624] for all creatures. (52)

# Chapter 69 Al-Haqqah[5625]

**29A3** In the name of Allah, the most gracious and merciful.[5626] The inevitable. (1) What is the inevitable? (2) How can you[MS] know the inevitable? (3) Thamud and Aad[5627] rejected the knocker. (4) Thamud were destroyed by the thunderstorm, (5) and Aad were destroyed by a gale, a furious, violent wind. (6) He made it last a grueling seven nights and eight days, and you[MS] see its people lying prostrate as if they are wasted palm tree roots. (7) Do you[MS] see anything left of them? (8) Pharaoh[5628] and overthrown cities[5629] before him were at fault. (9) They disobeyed their Lord's messenger, and were seized by great punishment.[5630] (10) When the water rose up, we carried you[MP] in the ark[5631] (11) to make it a reminder for you[MP], and to make attentive ears aware. (12) When the trumpet is blown with a single blast,[5632] (13) the earth and the mountains will be picked up together and thrown down once and pounded to dust,[5633] (14) on that day the event will happen. (15) The sky will be split and torn on that day.[5634] (16) Angels will be at its sides, and on that day, eight will carry your[MS] Lord's throne above them. (17) On that day you[MP] will be exposed and nothing of yours[MP] will be hidden.[5635] (18) Those who are given their books in

---

[5621] Tawrah, Jonah 4:10-11
[5622] Arabic /dhikr/. See glossary for more details.
[5623] By demons. Or, crazy.
[5624] Arabic /dhikr/. See glossary for more details.
[5625] The inevitable (probably referring to the day of judgment)
[5626] Zabur, Psalms 103:8, 145:8. See glossary for more details.
[5627] Thamud and Aad are tribes, here and in the following two verses.
[5628] Tawrah, Exodus 7-14
[5629] Probably Sodom and Gomorrah. See 9:70 and Tawrah, Genesis 19
[5630] Tawrah, Exodus 14, Genesis 19
[5631] Tawrah, Genesis 7-8
[5632] Injil, 1 Corinthians 15:52
[5633] Injil, Revelation 21:1, Hebrews 1:11-12
[5634] Injil, Hebrews 1:10-12
[5635] Injil, Luke 12:3, Hebrews 4:13

## Chapter 69

their right[5636] hands will say, "Take and read my book. (19) I imagined I was going to meet my reckoning." (20) He will have a pleasing life (21) in a high heavenly garden,[5637] (22) where the bunches of fruit are hanging down nearby. (23) "Eat[MP] and drink[MP] in health for your[MP] deeds beforehand in past days." (24) Those who are given their books in their left hands[5638] will say, "I wish I had not been given my book (25) and did not know my reckoning. (26) I wish it had killed me. (27) My money did not help me. (28) My authority has been destroyed." (29)
\*\*\*

Take him and chain him, (30) roast him in the blazing fire, (31) then march him with a seventy-cubit-long chain. (32)
\*\*\*

He did not believe in the great[5639] Allah, (33) nor did he urge anyone regarding feeding the poor.[5640] (34) So he has no friend here today, (35) nor any food besides pus, (36) which only the guilty eat. (37) No! I swear[5641] by what you[MP] see (38) and what you[MP] do not see. (39) It is the saying of an honored messenger. (40) It is not the saying of a poet. How little you[MP] believe! (41) Nor is it the saying of a soothsayer. How little you[MP] remember! (42) A revelation of the Lord of the universe. (43)
\*\*\*

If he had fabricated some sayings against us, (44)
\*\*\*

we would have taken him by his right hand (45) and cut his aorta. (46) None of you[MP] could have stopped it. (47) It is a reminder for the reverent. (48) We know that some of you[MP] are rejecters.[5642] (49) It is a cause of sighing for disbelievers. (50) It is certain truth. (51) Glorify the name of your[MS] great[5643] Lord. (52)[5644]

---

[5636] Injil, Matthew 25:34
[5637] Arabic /jannah/. See glossary for more details.
[5638] Injil, Matthew 25:41-46
[5639] Zabur, Psalms 145:3
[5640] Injil, Luke 14:13, 19:8
[5641] Or, I do not swear
[5642] Injil, John 6:64
[5643] Zabur, Psalms 145:3
[5644] The verses in this chapter that rhyme are put together in paragraphs, separated by \*\*\*. In addition, several words have been altered to fit the rhyme (verses 19, 20, 25, 26, 28, 29)

# Chapter 70 Al-Marij[5645]

In the name of Allah, the most gracious and merciful.[5646] A questioner asked about torment[5647] that will happen (1) to the disbelievers. There is no defending against it,[5648] (2)

\*\*\*

from Allah, who has ladders.[5649] (3)

\*\*\*

The angels and the spirit ascend[5650] to him on a day that is fifty thousand years long. (4)

\*\*\*

So endure[5651] patiently. (5) They think it is far in the future, (6) and we think it will be soon.[5652] (7)

\*\*\*

On that day, heaven will be like brass[5653] (8) and the mountains will wither.[5654] (9)

\*\*\*

No one will ask his friend. (10)

\*\*\*

They will make them see. The wrongdoer will wish he could be redeemed from that day's torment by his children[5655] (11) his girlfriend,[5656] his brother, (12) his family that cared for him, (13) or anyone on earth, that they would rescue him. (14)

\*\*\*

No! It is the flame (15) that plucks out for grilling, (16) calling[5657] those who turn back, turn away, (17) gather, and are miserly. (18)

29A4

---

[5645] Ladders, or stairways
[5646] Zabur, Psalms 103:8, 145:8. See glossary for more details.
[5647] For "torment" here and in verse 11, see Tawrah, Isaiah 50:11, Injil, Matthew 18:34, 25:41,46, Luke 16:23-28, Revelation 20:15.
[5648] Injil, 1 Thessalonians 5:3
[5649] Tawrah, Genesis 28:12
[5650] Injil, John 1:51
[5651] See "endure" in glossary
[5652] Injil, Revelation 22:20
[5653] Tawrah, Deuteronomy 28:23, Leviticus 26:19
[5654] Or, be like wool.
[5655] Or sons
[5656] i.e. sexual partner.
[5657] Or, you call

# Chapter 70

\*\*\*

Mankind were created very impatient: (19) impatient when touched by evil, (20) and stingy when touched by good. (21)

\*\*\*

The exceptions are those who perform prayers; (22) who are regular in performing their prayers; (23) whose money has a known right (24) for the beggar and the needy; (25) who believe in the day of judgment;[5658] (26) who are afraid of their Lord's torment, (27) since their Lord's torment is not secure; (28) who guard their chastity[5659] (29) from all but their wives and the slave girls they own, thus avoiding blame, (30) since those who seek more than that are transgressors;[5660] (31) who are careful in their pledges and their promises; (32) who testify uprightly;[5661] (33) and who protect the performance of their prayers. (34) They will be honored[5662] in heavenly gardens.[5663] (35) What is wrong with the disbelievers? They hasten to you[ms] (36) in crowds on the right and on the left. (37) Do they all aspire to be admitted to the heavenly garden of delight? (38) No! We created them from what they know. (39) No. I swear[5664] by the Lord of the sunrises and the sunsets,[5665] we are able (40) to exchange them for [others] better than they are.[5666] We are not preceded.[5667] (41) So let them discuss and play until they meet the day they are promised. (42) On that day,[5668] they will be brought out of the tombs quickly,[5669] like they were hastening to a goal.[5670] (43) Their gazes will be humbled and abasement will afflict them.[5671] That is the day they were promised. (44)[5672]

---

[5658] Zabur, Psalms 1:5, Injil, 1 John 4:17
[5659] or genitals
[5660] Injil, 1 Thessalonians 4:3-6
[5661] Or, who give testimony. Tawrah, Exodus 20:16
[5662] Injil, Matthew 25:21
[5663] Arabic /jannah/ here and in verse 38. See glossary for more details.
[5664] Or I do not swear.
[5665] Or Easts and Wests. Injil, Luke 13:29
[5666] Injil, Matthew 21:43
[5667] Or beaten (as in a race).
[5668] Injil, Romans 2:16
[5669] Injil, John 5:28,29
[5670] Or a marker
[5671] Injil, 1 John 2:28
[5672] The verses in this chapter that rhyme are put together in paragraphs, separated by \*\*\*.

Chapter 71

# Chapter 71 Nuh[5673]

In the name of Allah, the most gracious and merciful.[5674] We sent Nuh[5675] to his people: "Warn your[MS] people[5676] before painful torment[5677] seizes them." (1) He said, "My people, I am a clear warner to you[MP]: (2) worship[MP] Allah, fear[MP] him, and obey[MP] me.[5678] (3) He will forgive you[MP] your[MP] sins[5679] and give you[MP] more time for a specific span. When the time Allah's has set comes, it cannot be postponed, even if you[MP] knew." (4)

\*\*\*

He said, "My Lord, I called my people night and day. (5) My calling only made them run away more. (6) Whenever I call them to your[MS] forgiveness, they put their fingers in their ears, cover themselves with their garments, insist, and are proud. (7) Then I called them publicly. (8) I announced it to them and told them in secret. (9) I said: Ask your[MP] Lord for forgiveness. He is quite forgiving.[5680] (10) He sends abundant rain[5681] from the sky on you[MP]. (11) He provides you[MP] with money and children,[5682] and makes gardens and rivers for you[MP]. (12) What is wrong with you[MP] that you[MP] do not hope for Allah's honor?[5683] (13) He created you[MP] in stages.[5684] (14) Have you[MP] not seen how Allah created seven

---

[5673] Noah
[5674] Zabur, Psalms 103:8, 145:8. See glossary for more details.
[5675] Noah. See glossary for more details.
[5676] Tawrah, Genesis 6:13
[5677] Tawrah, Isaiah 50:11, Injil, Matthew 18:34, 25:41,46, Luke 16:23-28, Revelation 20:15
[5678] Several prophets tell the people specifically, "obey me." (Nuh 26:108,110, 71:3, Hud 26:126,131, Salih 26:144,150, Lut 26:163, Shuaib 26:179, Harun 20:90, and Isa 3:50, 43:63) Isa is the only one who commands obedience in the context of the straight path. Several verses command people to obey "the messenger" (3:32,132, 4:59, 5:92, 8:1,19,46, 24:54,56, 47:33, 58:13, 64:12) , most of which probably refer to Muhammad (s).
[5679] Injil, Luke 11:4
[5680] Zabur, Psalms 103:3, 130:4, Tawrah, Isaiah 43:25, Exodus 34:7, Injil, Acts 26:18.
[5681] Tawrah, Deuteronomy 28:12, Job 5:10, Joel 2:23, Zabur, Psalms 68:9, Injil, Matthew 5:45
[5682] Here and in verse 21, or "sons."
[5683] Injil, Romans 2:4
[5684] 80:18-19

## Chapter 71

heavens on top of each other? (15) He made the moon to be light in them, and made the sun a lamp.[5685] (16) Allah makes you sprout like plants from the ground. (17) Then he returns you[MP] to it, and brings you[MP] forth from it.[5686] (18) Allah made the earth a carpet for you[MP], (19) so that you[MP] would walk on paths and roads[5687] in it. (20) Nuh[5688] said, "My Lord, they disobeyed me and followed one who did not give them more money or children, but only loss. (21) They plotted greatly (22) and said: Do not forsake[MP] your[MP] gods,[5689] and do not forsake[MP] Wadd, Suwaa, Yaghuth, Yaouq, or Nasr.[5690] (23) They led many astray. The wicked only stray further. (24) They were drowned and made to enter hellfire for their guilt. They found no helpers besides Allah. (25) Nuh[5691] said, "My Lord, do not leave homes for the disbelievers on the earth. (26) If you[MS] leave them alone, they will lead your[MS] servants astray, and their children will all be unrighteous and disbelieving. (27) My Lord, forgive[MS] me,[5692] my parents, believers who enter my house, and the rest of the believers, both male and female. Give the wicked nothing but destruction."[5693] (28)[5694]

---

[5685] Tawrah, Genesis 1:16-18
[5686] Tawrah, Genesis 3:19.
[5687] Or mountain passes.
[5688] Noah. See glossary for more details.
[5689] Arabic /ilah/. See glossary for more details.
[5690] These names mean Destroyer, Night Group, Helper, Deterrer, and Eagle.
[5691] Noah. See glossary for more details.
[5692] The belief that all prophets and messengers are sinless is not supported by the Qur'an. For instances of prophets or messengers asking forgiveness or committing sins, see 7:23, 20:121 (Adam), 11:47, 71:28 (Nuh), 26:82, 14:41 (Ibrahim), 28:15-16 (Musa), 7:151, 20:93 (Musa and Harun), 38:24 (Dawud), 38:32,35 (Sulayman), 21:87, 37:142 (Yunus), 48:2, 47:19, 40:55, 4:79,106, 9:43, 13:30, 80:1-2, 110:3, 94:2, 23:118, 66:1, 33:37, 8:67, and 9:117 (Muhammad (s).
[5693] Tawrah, Genesis 6:13
[5694] The verses in this chapter that rhyme are put together in paragraphs, separated by ***.

Chapter 72

# Chapter 72 Al-Jinn[5695]

29B1 In the name of Allah, the most gracious and merciful.[5696] It was inspired to me that a group of jinns[5697] listened. They said, "We have heard an amazing[5698] recitation[5699] (1) that calls to right guidance, and we have believed in it. We will not worship any gods besides our Lord. (2) May our Lord's majesty be exalted. He has not chosen a girlfriend[5700] or a boy.[5701] (3) Our foolish one[5702] said extravagant lies against Allah.[5703] (4) We did not think that people and jinns would tell lies about Allah. (5) Some men[5704] took refuge in[5705] male jinns, who made them more evil.[5706] (6) They thought, as you[MP] thought, that Allah would not resurrect anyone.[5707] (7) We touched the sky and found that it was full of strong guards[5708] and shooting stars. (8) We sat on chairs near it to hear. Those who listen now will find shooting stars waiting in ambush for them. (9) We do not know whether evil is desired for those on earth or if their Lord wants right guidance for them. (10) Some of us are righteous, and some of us are not. We followed different ways.[5709] (11) We did not think that we'd be able to thwart Allah on earth, nor to thwart him by fleeing. (12) When we heard guidance, we believed in it.[5710] Whoever believes in his Lord will not fear deficiency or oppression. (13) Some of us are

---

[5695] Demons
[5696] Zabur, Psalms 103:8, 145:8. See glossary for more details.
[5697] Or demons, here and in verses 5 and 6. See glossary for more details.
[5698] Or "strange"
[5699] Or qur'an or Qur'an. See glossary for more details.
[5700] i.e. sexual partner. All the books reject the idea of Allah having a sexual partner.
[5701] All the books reject the idea of Allah producing a boy, or choosing a boy.
[5702] Possibly a reference to Satan
[5703] Injil, John 8:44
[5704] Or "human men"
[5705] Injil, 1 Corinthians 10:20
[5706] Or "more foolish" or "oppressed them more"
[5707] Injil, 2 Peter 3:4
[5708] Tawrah, Genesis 3:24
[5709] Injil, Revelation 12:4
[5710] Tawrah, Isaiah 50:5, 30:20-21

## Chapter 72

submitted[5711] and some of us are unjust.[5712] Whoever submits seeks right guidance.[5713] (14) The unjust are fuel for hell."[5714] (15) \*\*\*

If they had been upright on the way, we would have given them abundant water (16) to test them with it. Whoever turns away from remembering his Lord will be made to walk in severe torment.[5715] (17) Places of worship are for Allah, so do not pray[MP] to other gods besides Allah.[5716] (18) When Allah's servant stood up to pray[5717] to him, they were nearly a crowd against him. (19) \*\*\*

Say[MS], "I pray to my Lord and I do not worship any other gods besides him." (20) Say[MS], "I cannot harm you[MP] or give you[MP] right guidance." (21) Say[MS], "No one will deliver me from Allah.[5718] I will not find any refuge besides him.[5719] (22) [I only have] for a proclamation from Allah and his messages. Whoever disobeys Allah and his messenger will go to the fires of hell and will remain there forever and ever.[5720] (23) When they see what they were threatened with, they will know who is weakest as a savior and least in number." (24) Say[MS], "If I only knew whether what you[MP] are promised will come soon or whether my Lord will give it some more time! (25) He knows the unseen. He does not show anyone his unseen things, (26) except for the messenger he is pleased with.[5721] He walks in front of him[5722] and behind him observing, (27) so that he would know that they have delivered their Lord's

---

[5711] Injil, James 4:7. For "submitted" and 'submits" in this verse, some translators do not translate this. See glossary for more details.

[5712] Or "just"

[5713] Tawrah, Proverbs 3:5-6

[5714] Injil, Revelation 20:14-15

[5715] Tawrah, Isaiah 50:11, Injil, Matthew 18 34, 25:41,46, Luke 16:23-28, Revelation 20:15

[5716] Tawrah, Exodus 20:1-2

[5717] Injil, Matthew 6:5. Some take the word /qaam/ to mean "was resurrected" and propose the translation When Allah's servant was resurrected and prayed to him, they almost worshipped him.

[5718] Tawrah, 1 Samuel 4:8

[5719] Tawrah, 2 Samuel 22:3

[5720] Injil, Matthew 25:46

[5721] This seems to be a reference to Isa, because no other messenger knows what is unseen. He is called both "the messenger" and he proclaimed to people what was unseen. See 3:49, 4:171, 3:53, Injil, Luke 6:8

[5722] Or, "between his hands."

## Chapter 72

messages. He comprehends what they have, and counts everything by number."[5723] (28)[5724]

---

[5723] Injil, Matthew 10:30

[5724] The verses in this chapter that rhyme are put together in paragraphs, separated by ***.

Chapter 73

# Chapter 73 Al-Muzzammil[5725]

In the name of Allah, the most gracious and merciful.[5726] Wrapped up one, (1)
\*\*\*

get up[MS] at night,[5727] for most of it, (2) half of it, give (3) or take a little, and chant[MS] the Qur'an.[5728] (4) We will give you[MS] heavy sayings. (5) The beginning of the night is more commonly trodden, and straighter in speech. (6) In the day, you[MS] have a long time occupied with worldly affairs.[5729] (7) Remember your[MS] Lord's name and devote[MS] yourself[MS] totally to him.[5730] (8) [He is] Lord of the East and the West;[5731] he is the only god.[5732] Choose[MS] him as a protector. (9) Endure[MS][5733] what they say, and separate[MS] from them graciously. (10) Leave[MS] the rejecters who received blessings to me, and give them a little more time. (11)
\*\*\*

We have fetters, a blazing fire, (12) food that sticks in the throat, and painful torment[5734] (13)
\*\*\*

on a day the earth and the mountains shake,[5735] and the mountains will be poured out as sand.[5736] (14) We sent you[MP] a messenger who witnessed against you[MP], as we sent a messenger to Pharaoh.[5737] (15) Pharaoh disobeyed the messenger[5738] and we overtook him with chastisement. (16)
\*\*\*

---

[5725] Wrapped up
[5726] Zabur, Psalms 103:8, 145:8. See glossary for more details.
[5727] Injil, 1 Thessalonians 5:6
[5728] Or recitation. See glossary for more details.
[5729] Injil, Philippians 3:19
[5730] Zabur, Psalms 37:5
[5731] Or, "sunrise and sunset." Injil, Matthew 24:27
[5732] Arabic /ilah/. See glossary for more details.
[5733] See "endure" in glossary
[5734] Tawrah, Isaiah 50:11, Injil, Matthew 18:34, 25:41,46, Luke 16:23-28, Revelation 20:15
[5735] Injil, Revelation 16:18
[5736] Injil, Revelation 16:20
[5737] Acts 7:35
[5738] Tawrah, Exodus 8:15

Chapter 73

How will you<sup>MP</sup> be protected when you<sup>MP</sup> disbelieve in a day that makes children[5739] gray-haired? (17)

\*\*\*

Then the heavens will be split. Its promise will be fulfilled. (18) This is a reminder. All who will it choose a path to their Lord. (19)

**29B2**

\*\*\*

Your<sup>MS</sup> Lord knows that you<sup>MS</sup> and a group that are with you<sup>MS</sup> get up less than two-thirds of the night, half of it, or a third of it. Allah determines the night and the day.[5740] He knows that you<sup>MP</sup> will not count it, and he accepts your<sup>MP</sup> repentance, so read[5741] what you<sup>MP</sup> can of the Qur'an.[5742] He knows that some of you<sup>MP</sup> are sick, and others are traveling in the land, seeking Allah's grace. Yet others are fighting in Allah's path. So read<sup>MP</sup> what you can of it, perform<sup>MP</sup> prayers, and pay<sup>MP</sup> the poor-tax. Give<sup>MP</sup> Allah a good loan.[5743] You<sup>MP</sup> will find the good[5744] that you<sup>MP</sup> send ahead for your<sup>MP</sup> souls to be with Allah. It is better and greater in reward,[5745] so ask<sup>MP</sup> forgiveness from Allah. Allah is forgiving[5746] and merciful.[5747] (20) [5748]

---

[5739] or sons

[5740] Tawrah, Genesis 1:4-5

[5741] The word for read here only means read, not recite. Since this verse commands Muhammad (ص) and those with him to read, he must have known how to read. See note at 7:157.

[5742] Or recitation. See glossary for more details.

[5743] Tawrah, Proverbs 19:17

[5744] Tawrah, Proverbs 16:20

[5745] Injil, 2 Timothy 1:12

[5746] Zabur, Psalms 103:3, 130:4, Tawrah, Isaiah 43:25, Exodus 34:7, Injil, Acts 26:18.

[5747] See glossary for more details on "merciful."

[5748] The verses in this chapter that rhyme are put together in paragraphs, separated by \*\*\*.

Chapter 74

# Chapter 74 Al-Muddathir[5749]

In the name of Allah, the most gracious and merciful.[5750] Shrouded one, (1) stand up, warn, (2) and magnify your[MS] Lord.[5751] (3) Purify your[MS] garments,[5752] (4) and get rid of all impurity.[5753] (5) Do not be[MS] generous in order to get[MS] more.[5754] (6) Endure[MS][5755] for your[MS] Lord's sake.[5756] (7) When the trumpet sounds,[5757] (8) that day will be a hard day (9) for disbelievers. [It will] not be easy. (10)
\*\*\*

Let[MS] me alone with the only one, whom I created. (11) I have given him much money (12) and children[5758] as witnesses. (13) I have prepared well for him.[5759] (14)
\*\*\*

Then he is greedy for me to increase them. (15)
\*\*\*

No. He was stubborn regarding our signs. (16) I will make him tired going uphill.[5760] (17)
\*\*\*

He thought and planned. (18) May he be killed![5761] How he planned! (19) May he be killed! How he planned! (20) Then he looked, (21) frowned, and scowled. (22) Then he turned around, was proud, (23) and said, "This is only magic that is related. (24) This is only human speech." (25) I will roast him in scorching fire. (26) How can you[MS] know what scorching fire is? (27) It will not keep alive, nor will it leave alone. (28) It darkens[5762] people. (29) It has nineteen over it; (30) we only made angels responsible for hellfire, and we only made their term a temptation for disbelievers,

---

[5749] Shrouded
[5750] Zabur, Psalms 103:8, 145:8. See glossary for more details.
[5751] Zabur, Psalms 40:16
[5752] Injil, Revelation 3:18, Tawrah, Isaiah 64:6, 61:10
[5753] Injil, Colossians 3:5, Tawrah, Isaiah 1:18, Proverbs 20:9
[5754] Injil, 1 Timothy 6:5
[5755] See "endure" in glossary
[5756] Injil, 1 Corinthians 15:58
[5757] Injil, Revelation 8:7-11:15
[5758] Or, "sons."
[5759] Tawrah, Job 21:7-13
[5760] Or, more and more.
[5761] Zabur, Psalms 104:28,29
[5762] Or possibly, clarifies to.

## Chapter 74

so that those who were given the book would be certain, so that believers would increase in faith, so that those who were given the book and the believers would not doubt, and so that those with sick hearts[5763] and disbelievers would say, "What does Allah mean by this proverb?"[5764] Thus Allah leads astray those he wills,[5765] and guides those he wills.[5766] Only he knows the armies of your[MS] Lord.[5767] They are only a reminder to people. (31) No. [I swear] by the moon, (32) by the night when it retreats, (33) and by the morning when it shines, (34) it is one of the biggest matters, (35) a warning to people, (36) to one among you[MP] who wills to go forward or stay behind. (37)

\*\*\*

Every person is indebted for his deeds.[5768] (38)

\*\*\*

But not companions of the right hand[5769] (39) as they ask in heavenly gardens[5770] (40) about the wrongdoers, (41)

\*\*\*

"What made you[MP] go to scorching fire?" (42)

\*\*\*

They said, "We did not perform prayers, (43) we did not feed the needy,[5771] (44) we engaged in vain discussion with others, (45) we rejected the day of judgment,[5772] (46) until certainty came upon us." (47) The intercession of the intercessors will not benefit them.[5773] (48) What is wrong with them that they turn away from the reminder, (49)

\*\*\*

as if they were donkeys running away, (50) escaping from a lion? (51) No. Every man of them wants to be given unfolded pages.[5774] (52) No. They do not fear the hereafter. (53) No. It is a reminder.

---

[5763] Tawrah, Jeremiah 8:18, 17:9-10
[5764] Injil, Matthew 13:10-17
[5765] Injil, 2 Thessalonians 2:11, Tawrah, 2 Samuel 22:27, 1 Kings 22:20-23, Ezekiel 14:9
[5766] Injil, Romans 9:18
[5767] Zabur, Psalms 24:10, Injil, Matthew 26:53
[5768] Injil, Romans 3:23, Tawrah, Ecclesiastes 7:20.
[5769] Injil, Matthew 25:34
[5770] Arabic /jannah/. See glossary for more details.
[5771] Injil, Matthew 25:42
[5772] Injil, Luke 21:34
[5773] Tawrah, 1 Samuel 2:25, Jeremiah 7:16
[5774] Or "books."

Chapter 74

(54) Whoever wills will remember it. (55) They will not remember it unless Allah wills that. He is worthy of reverence and worthy of forgiveness. (56)[5775]

---

[5775] The verses in this chapter that rhyme are put together in paragraphs, separated by ***.

## Chapter 75 Al-Qiyamah[5776]

**29B3** In the name of Allah, the most gracious and merciful.[5777] I do not swear[5778] by the day of resurrection,[5779] (1) nor do I swear[5780] by the blameworthy[5781] soul.[5782] (2) Do people think we will not gather their bones?[5783] (3) Yes [we will.]. We can [even] form his fingertips.[5784] (4) But people want to act unrighteously in front of him, (5) asking, "When is the day of resurrection?"[5785] (6)
\*\*\*

When sight is dazzled, (7) the moon is eclipsed,[5786] (8)and the sun and moon are gathered,[5787] (9) on that day, people will say, "Where is the escape[5788] route?" (10) No. There is no refuge.[5789] (11) On that day, the abode[5790] will be to go to your[MS] Lord. (12) People will be told on that day what they did before and after.[5791] (13)
\*\*\*

People will be evidence against themselves (14) even if they make excuses. (15) Do not move your[MS] tongue to hasten it.[5792] (16) We have to gather it and recite it. (17) When we recite it, follow its reading.[5793] (18) Then we have to clarify it. (19) No. But you[MP]

---

[5776] resurrection
[5777] Zabur, Psalms 103:8, 145:8. See glossary for more details.
[5778] Or, "No. I swear"
[5779] Here and in verse 6, for "day of resurrection," see Tawrah, Daniel 12:2 Injil, Acts 24:15, 1 Corinthians 15:52-54, Revelation 20:11-15
[5780] Or, "And no, I swear"
[5781] Or blaming.
[5782] Tawrah, Ezekiel 18:20
[5783] Tawrah, Ezekiel 37:1-10
[5784] Injil, 1 Corinthians 15:35-48
[5785] Injil, 2 Peter 3:4
[5786] Injil, Revelation 6:12
[5787] Tawrah, Isaiah 13:10, Injil, Revelation 6:12
[5788] Hebrews 2:3
[5789] Injil, Revelation 6:16
[5790] Or stability
[5791] Injil, Romans 14:12
[5792] Injil, 2 Peter 3:12
[5793] Or qur'an or recitation. See glossary for more details. Injil, James 1:21-25, John 5:24

## Chapter 75

love what is transitory, (20) and forsake the hereafter.[5794] (21) On that day, faces will be shining,[5795] (22) looking at their Lord.[5796] (23) Other faces will be dismal, (24) thinking that calamity will happen[5797] to them. (25)

\*\*\*

No. When it reaches the breastbone (26)

\*\*\*

and "Who is the enchanter?" is said, (27) he thinks that it is the end,[5798] (28) and legs are turned to each other. (29) On that day, they will be driven to your[MS] Lord. (30)

\*\*\*

He did not believe[5799] or pray, (31) but he rejected and turned away. (32) Then he went to his family haughtily,[5800] (33) woe to you and woe to you[MS], (34) then woe to you and woe to you[MS]. (35) Do people think that they will be left alone? (36) Were they not a sperm in an ejaculated drop of semen? (37) Then they were a clot of blood he created and formed,[5801] (38) and he made from it the spouses[D], male and female.[5802] (39) Is such a one not able to revive the dead?[5803] (40) [5804]

---

[5794] Injil, 2 Corinthians 4:18
[5795] Injil, 2 Corinthians 3:13
[5796] Injil, 2 Corinthians 3:18, Zabur, Psalms 34:5
[5797] The noun here is feminine and the verb is masculine. There may be an alternate meaning.
[5798] Or separation or parting.
[5799] Yusuf Ali translates this "So he gave nothing in Charity."
[5800] Or quickly
[5801] Zabur, Psalms 139:13-16
[5802] Tawrah, Genesis 1:27
[5803] Injil, 2 Corinthians 4:14
[5804] The verses in this chapter that rhyme are put together in paragraphs, separated by \*\*\*.

# Chapter 76 Al-Insan[5805] or Al-Dahr[5806]

In the name of Allah, the most gracious and merciful.[5807] Has there ever been a time when mankind was not remembered? (1) We created mankind from a drop of sperm, a mixture. We will test him. We gave him hearing and seeing. (2) We guided him on the path to see whether he would give thanks or be ungrateful. (3) We have prepared shackles, chains, and a burning fire for the disbelievers. (4) The righteous will drink from a cup mixed with camphor.[5808] (5) They will drink from a spring that Allah's servants cause to flow. (6) They fulfill their vows, and fear a day of widespread evil. (7) They feed the poor, the orphan, and the prisoner out of love.[5809] (8) "We feed you[MP] for Allah's sake. We do not want any reward or thanks from you[MP]. (9) We fear a dismal, calamitous day from our Lord." (10) Allah protected them from that day's evil[5810] and granted them brightness and happiness. (11) For their endurance,[5811] Allah rewarded them with a heavenly garden[5812] and silk. (12) They will recline there on couches and will not see the sun or cold. (13) Its shade will draw near them, and the clusters will be hanging low.[5813] (14) They will be surrounded by silver vessels and crystal goblets, (15) the goblets of silver measured carefully. (16) There they will be given drink from a cup mixed with ginger, (17) [from] a spring called Salsabil. (18) **29B4** Wildan mukhalladun[5814] will surround them. If you[MS]

---

[5805] mankind
[5806] The era.
[5807] Zabur, Psalms 103:8, 145:8. See glossary for more details.
[5808] Arabic /kafur/, from which this English word comes. The meaning here is probably the healthful properties the resin of this tree produces.
[5809] Injil, Matthew 25:31-36, James 1:27
[5810] Injil, Matthew 6:34
[5811] See "endure" in glossary, here and in verse 24.
[5812] Arabic /jannah/. See glossary for more details.
[5813] See 6:99, and notes at 37:48, 38:52, 55:56
[5814] Most translations have "Eternal youths" here. However, the word translated "eternal" is not the usual one /khalidun/ which is used 70 times in the Qur'an and means "eternal." Instead, the word /mukhalladun/ is used only here and in 56:17. Some research has suggested that the word may mean "chilled." The word /wildan/ is usually translated "youths" but probably means "the product" in this context, similar to the Arabic phrase "bint al-karma" (literally, daughter of the vine), which means "wine." For

## Chapter 75

were to see them, you<sup>MS</sup> would think they were scattered pearls. (19) When you<sup>MS</sup> look, you<sup>MS</sup> see pleasure and a great kingdom.[5815] (20) They will have green silk robes and brocade, and wear silver bracelets. Their Lord gives them pure drink. (21) "This is your<sup>MP</sup> reward. Your<sup>MP</sup> efforts are gratefully accepted." (22) We revealed the Qur'an[5816] to you<sup>MS</sup>, (23) so endure until your<sup>MS</sup> Lord's decision. Do not obey the guilty or disbelievers among them. (24) Remember your<sup>MS</sup> Lord's name morning and evening, (25) and bow down to him at night, worshiping him all night long.[5817] (26) They love what is transitory and leave behind them a weighty day. (27) We created them and strengthened their joints. If we will, we will exchange them.[5818] (28) This is a reminder. Whoever wills to chooses a path to his Lord. (29)

\*\*\*

You<sup>MP</sup> will not will it unless Allah wills it. Allah is all-knowing[5819] and wise.[5820] (30) He makes those he wills enter his mercy, but he has prepared painful torment[5821] for the wicked. (31)[5822]

---

this meaning, see Injil, Matthew 26:28. The traditional translation does not fit the context here, which compares the /wildan/ to scattered pearls, nor 56:18, which says they are in cups and goblets.
[5815] Injil, Matthew 25:34
[5816] Or recitation. See glossary for more details.
[5817] Zabur, Psalms 119:62,160
[5818] Injil, 1 Corinthians 15:42-54
[5819] Tawrah, Job 37:16, Isaiah 40:14, Zabur, Psalms 33:13-15, Injil, 1 John 3:20
[5820] Tawrah, Job 9:4, Proverbs 2:6, Jeremiah 9:23-24, Injil, 1 Corinthians 1:21-25, Romans 16:27
[5821] Tawrah, Isaiah 50:11, Injil, Matthew 18:34, 25:41,46, Luke 16:23-28, Revelation 20:15
[5822] The verses in this chapter that rhyme are put together in paragraphs, separated by \*\*\*.

# Chapter 77 Al-Mursalat[5823]

In the name of Allah, the most gracious and merciful.[5824] [I swear] by the messengers[FP][5825] sent to benefit,[5826] (1) the storms[FP] with gusts, (2) the scatterers[FP] that spread abroad, (3) the separaters[FP] that distinguish,[5827] (4) and those who[FP] speak reminders, (5) excuses, or warnings: (6) ***
What you[MP] have been promised will happen. (7) ***

So when the stars are obliterated, (8) the heavens split,[5828] (9) the mountains uprooted,[5829] (10) when the time of the messengers[MP] is set,[5830] (11) until what day are they postponed? (12) ***

Until the day of separation! (13) How can you[MS] know the day of separation?[5831] (14) ***

Woe to the rejecters on that day.[5832] (15) Did we not destroy the men of old? (16) Then we made the latter ones follow them. (17) Thus we do with wrongdoers. (18) Woe to the rejecters on that day. (19) Did we not create you[MP] from shameful water?[5833] (20) We made it in a secure place[5834] (21) for a known decree.[5835] (22)

---

[5823] the messengers[FP]. The meaning could be angels or winds. Verse 2 suggests the latter and verse 4 the former. See Injil, Hebrews 1:7, where they are connected.
[5824] Zabur, Psalms 103:8, 145:8. See glossary for more details.
[5825] Injil, Hebrews 1:7, Zabur, Psalms 104:4
[5826] Some translations render this word "successively."
[5827] Injil, Matthew 13:41
[5828] Injil, Hebrews 1:10-12
[5829] Tawrah, Isaiah 54:10
[5830] The verb used here is for unthinking beings, so possibly the winds are meant.
[5831] Injil, Matthew 25:32
[5832] The text does not say what they rejected here and in verses 19, 28, 34, 37, 40, 45, 47, and 49. Most likely the meaning is either "the day of separation" (verse 13), hell (verse 29), or "Allah's signs," which are very frequently mentioned in the Qur'an as being rejected by disbelievers. See "sign" in glossary.
[5833] i.e. semen
[5834] i.e. the womb. Zabur, Psalms 139:13-16
[5835] Or period of time (the nine months of pregnancy). Tawrah, Job 39:2

## Chapter 77

We determined it. What good determiners! (23) Woe on that day to the rejecters. (24)

\*\*\*

Did we not make the earth a place for gathering together (25) both the living and the dead? (26) We made lofty mountains in it, and gave you[MP] fresh water. (27)

\*\*\*

Woe on that day to the rejecters. (28) Go to what you[MP] rejected. (29)

\*\*\*

Go to the shadow with three parts, (30) which gives no shade or benefit from the flame. (31)

\*\*\*

It sparks like a palace,[5836] (32) like yellow camels. (33) Woe to the rejecters on that day. (34) This is a day they will not speak. (35) They will not be allowed to give excuses. (36) Woe to the rejecters on that day. (37) This is the day of separation. We have gathered[5837] you[MP] along with the men of old.[5838] (38) If you[MP] have a plot, plot against me. (39) Woe to the rejecters on that day. (40) The reverent will be in shade, by springs, (41) with whatever fruit they desire. (42) "Eat and drink in health for your[MP] deeds.[5839] (43) This is how we reward those who do good." (44) Woe to the rejecters on that day. (45) Eat and enjoy life for a while.[5840] You[MP] are wrongdoers. (46) Woe to the rejecters on that day. (47) If they are told, "Kneel," they do not kneel. (48) Woe to the rejecters on that day. (49) What story will they believe in after that?[5841] (50)[5842]

---

[5836] Other translations render this word, "tree trunks," "logs," "forts," or "dry faggots."

[5837] Tawrah, Joel 3:11-14, Zephaniah 3:8, Injil, Matthew 25:32, John 15:6, Revelation 16:16

[5838] Injil, Matthew 25:32

[5839] Injil, Matthew 25:34-36

[5840] Injil, Luke 12:19

[5841] Injil, Luke 16:29-31

[5842] The verses in this chapter that rhyme are put together in paragraphs, separated by \*\*\*.

Chapter 78

# Chapter 78 Al-Naba'[5843]

**30A1** In the name of Allah, the most gracious and merciful.[5844] What are they asking each other about? (1) About the great news (2) that they differ about. (3) No, they will know. (4) Again, no, they will know. (5)

\*\*\*

Have we not made the earth wide, (6) and the mountains pointed? (7) We created you[MP] in pairs,[5845] (8) and gave you[MP] rest in sleep.[5846] (9) We made the night a covering, (10) and the day for livelihood.[5847] (11) We built seven strengths[5848] over you[MP], (12) and set a burning lamp.[5849] (13) We sent down abundant water from the presses[5850] (14) to make seeds and plants sprout, (15) as well as thickly-planted gardens. (16) The day of separation[5851] is a fixed time, (17) a day when the trumpet will be blown,[5852] and you[MP] will come in waves.[5853] (18) Heaven will be opened and will be like doors, (19) and the mountains will be moved[5854] and will be like mirages. (20) Hell will be an ambush, (21) an abode for transgressors, (22) where they will remain for ages.[5855] (23) They will taste neither coolness nor a drink there,[5856] (24) rather boiling water and pus, (25) a suitable repayment. (26) They were not hoping for a reckoning, (27) and they rejected our signs.[5857] (28) We have counted everything in a book,[5858] (29) so taste it, and

---

[5843] the news item
[5844] Zabur, Psalms 103:8, 145:8. See glossary for more details.
[5845] Tawrah, Genesis 7:2, Isaiah 34:15-16
[5846] Zabur, Psalms 127:2
[5847] Zabur, Psalms 104:23
[5848] possibly the skies or heavens
[5849] i.e. the sun
[5850] the reference is to clouds
[5851] Injil, Matthew 25:32
[5852] Injil, Revelation 11:15
[5853] Injil, Matthew 25:32
[5854] Injil, Revelation 16:20
[5855] Injil, Matthew 25:46
[5856] Injil, Luke 16:24
[5857] Arabic /ayat/. See glossary for more details.
[5858] Injil, Revelation 20:12

## Chapter 78

you<sup>MP</sup> will not get more of anything except torment.[5859] (30) The reverent have a refuge, (31) gardens and grapes, (32) juicy and ripe,[5860] (33) and cups that are full.[5861] (34) They will not hear vanity or lies (35) as a reward, a gift, and a reckoning from your<sup>MS</sup> Lord, (36) the Lord of the heavens, the earth, and what is between them, the most merciful. They can say nothing to him (37) on the day the spirit and the angels[5862] are lined up. None will speak except he who has the most merciful's permission,[5863] and he will say the truth.[5864] (38) That is the true day, so whoever wants to will choose an abode by his Lord. (39) We have warned you<sup>MP</sup> of imminent torment, on a day when a man will see what he has done. The disbeliever will say, "I wish I were soil."[5865] (40)[5866]

---

[5859] For "torment" here and in verse 40, see Tawrah, Isaiah 50:11, Injil, Matthew 18:34, 25:41,46, Luke 16:23-28, Revelation 20:15.

[5860] Most translations have "full-breasted girls of similar age." This is unlikely since there are no words in the verse corresponding to "breasted," "girls," or "age" and in light of the context, with fruit in the previous verse and drink in the following verse. The word "full" with reference to fruit conveys "juicy," and /atrab/ can be understood to mean "ripe."

[5861] Zabur, Psalms 23:5

[5862] Injil, Revelation 5:11

[5863] This may be a reference to Isa, whom the Qur'an emphasizes six times that he had Allah's permission (3:49 and 5:110).

[5864] Isa is called the "saying of truth" 19 34 so this may be a reference to him.

[5865] Tawrah, Hosea 10:8

[5866] The verses in this chapter that rhyme are put together in paragraphs, separated by ***.

551

# Chapter 79 Al-Naziat[5867]

In the name of Allah, the most gracious and merciful.[5868] [I swear] by those who snatch suddenly,[5869] (1) those[FP] who draw out smoothly, (2) those[FP] who swim,[5870] (3) those[FP] who precede, (4) and those[FP] who direct matters: (5) on the day the trembler[FS5871] trembles,[5872] (6) followed by the follower,[FS5873] (7) on that day, hearts will palpitate, (8) and their[5874] sight will be humbled.[5875] (9) They will say, "Have we been returned in our former condition, (10) even though our bones had rotted?"[5876] (11) They said, "Then that is a losing return. (12) It is a single cry." (13) They are wakeful.[5877] (14)

\*\*\*

Have you[MS] heard the story of Musa?[5878] (15) His Lord called him in Tuwa, the
holy valley, (16) "Go[MS] to Pharaoh.[5879] He is a tyrant. (17) And say[MS]: "Can you[MS] be purified? (18) I will guide you[MS] to your[MS] Lord and you[MS] will fear." (19) So he showed him the great sign,[5880] (20) but he rejected and disobeyed.[5881] (21) Then he turned away quickly, (22) gathered [people], and called out. (23)

---

[5867] the (female) snatchers, possibly angels
[5868] Zabur, Psalms 103:8, 145:8. See glossary for more details.
[5869] possibly angels, here and in the next four verses, though the words are feminine plural.
[5870] Injil, Revelation 14:6
[5871] possibly the trumpet blast that signals the day of resurrection
[5872] Tawrah, Joel 2:1
[5873] possibly another trumpet blast on the day of resurrection. Injil, 1 Corinthians 15:52
[5874] This could refer to the eyes of the hearts or the eyes of the tremblers.
[5875] Tawrah, Isaiah 2:17
[5876] Injil, 2 Corinthians 4:14, Tawrah, Ezekiel 37:3
[5877] possibly "at the judgment"
[5878] Moses. See glossary for more details.
[5879] Tawrah, Exodus 3:10
[5880] This verse talks about the greatest sign. 17:101 mentions nine, so there are a total of ten. This corresponds to the ten signs mentioned in the Tawrah, Exodus 7-12. In the Qur'an 7:107,108, 130, and 133 describe many of these signs. The last sign, probably the same as the "greatest sign" mentioned both in 7:133 and in the Tawrah, Exodus (11:4-5, 12:23,24,29,30) is the blood. The Exodus passages gives the details.
[5881] Tawrah, Exodus 14:5

## Chapter 79

He said, "I am your^MP most high lord." (24) So Allah seized him as an example of punishment[5882] in the hereafter as well as in this world. (25) That is a moral for those who fear. (26)

\*\*\*

Is your^MP nature stronger, or the sky's, which he built?[5883] (27) He raised its ceiling and leveled it, (28) darkened its night and brought forth its dawn.[5884] (29) Then he spread out[5885] the earth. (30) He brought forth its water and pastures from it,[5886] (31) and founded the mountains[5887] (32)

\*\*\*

as pleasure for you^MP and your^MP cattle. (33)

\*\*\*

When the great disaster comes, (34) on that day people will remember what they were striving for, (35) and the blazing fire will be evident for those who see. (36) For those who transgress (37) and prefer this world, (38) the blazing fire will be their abode. (39) But for those who fear their Lord's status and forbid people from their passion, (40) heaven will be their abode. (41)

\*\*\*

They ask you^MS about the hour, "When it will be fixed?" (42) What are you^MS that you^MS should remember it? (43) Its end is your^MS Lord's. (44) You^MS are only a warner for those who fear it. (45) When they see it, it will seem to them that they only remained [on earth] for an evening or its dawn. (46)[5888]

---

[5882] Tawrah, Exodus 14:26-29
[5883] Tawrah, Genesis 1:7-8
[5884] Tawrah, Genesis 1:4-5
[5885] Tawrah, Isaiah 37:16. Or possibly, "made like an egg."
[5886] Tawrah, Isaiah 30:23
[5887] Zabur, Psalms 65:6
[5888] The verses in this chapter that rhyme are put together in paragraphs, separated by \*\*\*.

Chapter 80

# Chapter 80 Abasa[5889]

**30A2** In the name of Allah, the most gracious and merciful.[5890] He[5891] frowned and turned away[5892] (1) when the blind man came to him. (2) How could you[MS] know whether he would be purified, (3) or remember, and the reminder benefit him? (4) But as for self-sufficient one (5) you[MS] receive him with honor. (6) It is not your[MS] fault that he does not purify himself. (7) But as for him who comes seeking (8) and fearing, (9) you[MS] ignore him. (10)
\*\*\*

No! It is a reminder. (11) He who wants to will mention[5893] it (12) in honored books (13) that are lifted up and purified (14) by the hands of scribes (15) who are noble and righteous. (16) May mankind be killed! How disbelieving he is![5894] (17) From what did he create him? (18) From a drop of semen he created him and decreed him. (19) Then he made his path easy, (20) made him die, and buried him, (21) then when he wills, he will resurrect him. (22) No! He has not fulfilled what he commanded him. (23) Let man look at his food. (24)
\*\*\*

---

[5889] he frowned

[5890] Zabur, Psalms 103:8, 145:8. See glossary for more details.

[5891] traditionally understand as referring to Muhammad (s).

[5892] The belief that all prophets and messengers are sinless is not supported by the Qur'an. For instances of prophets or messengers asking forgiveness or committing sins, see 7:23, 20:121 (Adam), 11:47, 71:28 (Nuh), 26:82, 14:41 (Ibrahim), 28:15-16 (Musa), 7:151, 20:93 (Musa and Harun), 38:24 (Dawud), 38:32,35 (Sulayman), 21:87, 37:142 (Yunus), 48:2, 47:19, 40:55, 4:79,106, 9:43, 13:30, 80:1-2, 110:3, 94:2, 23:118, 66:1, 33:37, 8:67, and 9:117 (Muhammad) (s).

[5893] Or remember

[5894] The injustice/wickedness, disbelief/ungratefulness, evil, unrighteousness/sin, or lostness of mankind is mentioned in a number of verses in the Qur'an as well as in the previous books. Injustice or wickedness: 2:57, 3:117,135, 4:64,97, 7:160,177, 9:70, 10:44, 11:101, 14:34,45, 16:33,61,118, 29:40, 30:9, 33:72, 34:19, 35:32, 43:76, 65:1, Tawrah, Genesis 6:5, Job 25:4, Injil, Acts 3:26, disbelief or ungratefulness: 14:34, 17:67, 22:66, 42:48, 43:15, 80:17, Injil, Hebrews 3:19, Evil: 12:53, Tawrah, Jeremiah 17:9, Injil, Matthew 15:19, Mark 7:21, unrighteousness or sin: 91:8, Tawrah, 1 Kings 8:46, Ecclesiastes 7:20, Injil, Romans 3:9-19, 5:12, lostness: 103:2, Tawrah, Jeremiah 50:6, Injil, Luke 19:10, Romans 3:23, 6:23

## Chapter 80

We poured out water, (25) split the earth, (26) and caused seeds to sprout in it, (27) as well as grapes, clover, (28) olives, palms, (29) thick gardens, (30) fruit, and plants, (31)

\*\*\*

as enjoyment for you<sup>MP</sup> and your<sup>MP</sup> cattle. (32)

\*\*\*

So when the deafening sound comes, (33) on a day when a man flees from his brother, (34) mother, father, (35) partner,[5895] and children,[5896] (36)

every man among them will have enough to keep him busy. (37)

\*\*\*

Some faces will shine on that day, (38) laughing and rejoicing at the good
news. (39) Other faces will have dust upon them (40) and be covered with blackness. (41) Those are the disbelievers and the unrighteous. (42)[5897]

---

[5895] i.e. sexual partner
[5896] or sons
[5897] The verses in this chapter that rhyme are put together in paragraphs, separated by \*\*\*.

# Chapter 81 Al-Takwir[5898]

In the name of Allah, the most gracious and merciful.[5899] When the sun is folded up,[5900] (1) when the stars fall,[5901] (2) when the mountains pass away,[5902] (3) when pregnant camels are neglected, (4) when the beasts are gathered, (5) when the seas swell,[5903] (6) when souls are united,[5904] (7) and when the daughter buried alive is asked, (8) "What sin were you[MS] killed for?" (9) When the books are opened,[5905] (10) when the sky is removed,[5906] (11) when the blazing fire burns fiercely,[5907] (12) and when heavenly garden is brought near,[5908] (13) then the soul will know what it has brought.[5909] (14)

\*\*\*

No. I[5910] swear by the stars[5911] (15) which move and are hidden, (16) the night when it comes on suddenly,[5912] (17) and the morning when it breathes: (18)

\*\*\*

it is the saying of an honorable messenger, (19) who has power at the firm throne. (20) [He is] obeyed and faithful. (21) Your[MP] companion is not crazy.[5913] (22) He has seen him at the clear

---

[5898] being folded up
[5899] Zabur, Psalms 103:8, 145:8. See glossary for more details.
[5900] or "darkened" Hebrews 1:12
[5901] Injil, Matthew 24:29
[5902] Injil, Revelation 16:20
[5903] Injil, Luke 21:25
[5904] or married. The idea is probably "re-united with their bodies" Injil, Revelation 20:4
[5905] Injil, Revelation 20:12
[5906] Hebrews 1:12, Pslam 102:26-27
[5907] Injil, Revelation 21:8
[5908] Injil, Revelation 21:2
[5909] Injil, Luke 14:14
[5910] Or "I do not"
[5911] or planets or hiders. See *Injil*, Jude 13. Some say this refers to black holes, which move and are invisible (see verse 16). Since the word "hidden" in verse 16 is related to the word "to sweep", these people see the characteristic of black holes to sweep everything into them alluded to here.
[5912] or attacks
[5913] or demon-possessed

## Chapter 81

horizon. (23) He is not greedy[5914] for the unseen. (24) It is not a damned devil's saying. (25) Where are you[MP] going? (26) It[5915] is only a reminder[5916] to mankind, (27) to each of you[MP] who wills to be upright. (28) You[MP] only will [it] if Allah, the Lord of the universe, wills [it]. (29)[5917]

---

[5914] some old manuscripts have "suspicious"
[5915] or "he"
[5916] Arabic /dhikr/. See glossary for more details.
[5917] The verses in this chapter that rhyme are put together in paragraphs, separated by ***.

# Chapter 82 Al-Infitaar[5918]

**30A3**In the name of Allah, the most gracious and merciful.[5919] When the sky is torn in two,[5920] (1) when the planets are scattered, (2) when the seas flow,[5921] (3) when the graves are scattered,[5922] (4) a soul will know its former and latter works.[5923] (5)

\*\*\*

Man, what seduced you[ms] away from your generous Lord, (6)

\*\*\*

who created you[ms],[5924] formed you[ms],[5925] and dealt justly with you[ms]?[5926] (7) He put you together in the shape he willed.[5927] (8)

\*\*\*

No. You reject the judgment. (9) There are keepers over you, (10) honorable scribes, (11) who know your[mp] deeds. (12) The righteous are in delight,[5928] (13) and the unrighteous are in the blazing fire, (14) being roasted in it on the day of judgment. (15) They will not be absent from it.[5929] (16) How can you[ms] know the day of judgment?[5930] (17) Yes, how can you[ms] know the day of judgment? (18)

\*\*\*

On that day, no soul will be able to do anything for another. The command on that day is Allah's. (19)[5931]

---

[5918] being torn
[5919] Zabur, Psalms 103:8, 145:8. See glossary for more details.
[5920] Injil, Hebrews 1:12, Zabur, Psalms 102:26-27
[5921] or, "flow together" or "explode"
[5922] Injil, Matthew 27:52
[5923] see 48:2 for a similar phrase
[5924] Tawrah, Genesis 1:27
[5925] Tawrah, Genesis 2:7
[5926] Zabur, Psalms 145:17
[5927] Zabur, Psalms 139:13
[5928] also used for heaven
[5929] Injil, Matthew 25:41
[5930] Injil, 2 Peter 3:7, 1 John 4:17
[5931] The verses in this chapter that rhyme are put together in paragraphs, separated by \*\*\*.

# Chapter 83 Al-Mutaffifun[5932]

In the name of Allah, the most gracious and merciful.[5933] Woe to the wrongdoers. (1) When they receive a measure from people, they take it in full, (2) but when they give them a measure or weigh it out for them, they make them lose. (3) Do they think that they will not be resurrected[5934] (4) for a great day, (5) the day when people will stand before the Lord of the universe? (6) No! The book of the unrighteous is imprisoned.[5935] (7) How can you[MS] know what imprisoned is? (8) It is a numbered book. (9) Woe to the rejecters on that day . (10) They reject the day of judgment. (11) The only rejecters are all those who are guilty and hostile. (12) If our signs are recited to them, they say, "Ancient legends." (13) No, but rather what they gained has covered[5936] their hearts. (14) No. They will be shut out from their Lord on that day, (15) and then be roasted in the blazing fire. (16) Then it will be said, "This is what you[MP] denied." (17) No, the book of the righteous is in the heights. (18) How can you[MS] know the heights? (19) It is a numbered book. (20) Those who are brought near[5937] will see it. (21) The righteous are in delight,[5938] (22) looking from couches. (23) You[MS] see in their faces the brightness of delight. (24) They are given a drink of sealed rahiq.[5939] (25) It is sealed with musk. Let the competers[5940] compete for that. (26) It is mixed with a beverage[5941] (27) from a spring where those brought near drink. (28) Wrongdoers laugh at believers. (29) If they pass them, they wink. (30) When they turn back to their families, they do so jesting. (31) When they see them, they say, "These have gone astray." (32) They were not sent to them as guardians. (33) Today,

---

[5932] Cheaters or those who give short measure
[5933] Zabur, Psalms 103:8, 145:8. See glossary for more details.
[5934] Or sent
[5935] Or in Sijjin here and in verse 8. Injil, Jude 6
[5936] Other translations say "rusted in" Injil, James 5:3, Matthew 6:19-21, Luke 18:22,23, 1 Timothy 6:10
[5937] Besides the righteous here, verse 28, and in 56:11,88, angels (4:172) and Isa (3:45) are the only ones also called "brought near."
[5938] i.e. the garden
[5939] This may be wine.
[5940] Or strivers or aspirers. Tawrah, Isaiah 5:22
[5941] Or tasnim

Chapter 83

believers will laugh at disbelievers, (34) looking from couches. (35) Have disbelievers been repaid for their deeds? (36)

# Chapter 84

# Chapter 84 Al-Inshiqaq[5942]

30A4 In the name of Allah, the most gracious and merciful.[5943] When the sky is split (1) and listens to its Lord, and it must; (2) when the earth is spread out, (3) casts out what is in it, and makes itself empty, (4) listens to its Lord, and it must; (5)
***
Man, you[MS] are laboring for your[MS] Lord,[5944] and you will meet him. (6) He who is given his book in his right hand (7)
***
will be given a light reckoning,[5945] (8) and happily return to his family. (9)
***
As for him who is given his book behind his back, (10)
***
he will call for destruction (11) and be roasted in a burning fire. (12) He was happy among his family. (13)
***
They thought they would not return, (14)
***
but [they were wrong]; their Lord sees them. (15)
***
No. I[5946] swear by the sunset, (16) the night and what it gathers, (17) and the moon when it is full: (18) You[MP] will ride one level above another.[5947] (19)
***
What is wrong with them that they do not believe? (20) When the Qur'an[5948] is read, they do not bow down. (21) Disbelievers are rejecters, (22) and Allah knows what they hoard.[5949] (23) Give them good news: of painful torment,[5950] (24) except for believers

---

[5942] Being split
[5943] Zabur, Psalms 103:8, 145:8. See glossary for more details.
[5944] Injil, 1 Corinthians 15:58
[5945] Injil, Luke 12:48
[5946] or "I do not"
[5947] or "stage after stage"
[5948] Or recitation. See glossary for more details.
[5949] or "hide" as in thoughts
[5950] Tawrah, Isaiah 50:11, Injil, Matthew 18:34, 25:41,46, Luke 16:23-28, Revelation 20:15

Chapter 84

who do righteous deeds.[5951] They will have an undiminished reward. (25)[5952]

---

[5951] Injil, 1 Corinthians 3:8, James 2:14-17, Revelation 19:8
[5952] The verses in this chapter that rhyme are put together in paragraphs, separated by ***.

# Chapter 85 Al-Buruj[5953]

In the name of Allah, the most gracious and merciful.[5954] [I swear] by the sky with the constellations. (1)
***
the promised day, (2) the witnesser and the witnessed: (3) May those of the trench be killed, (4) [those of] the fire that was fueled, (5) as they sat by it (6) and witnessed what they did to the believers. (7) They took revenge on them just because they believed in mighty,[5955] praiseworthy[5956] Allah. (8) Everything in the heavens and the earth is his.[5957] Allah is a witness[5958] of everything. (9)
***
Those who tested the male and female believers and then did not repent[5959] will have hell's torment,[5960] and the fire's torment. (10)
***
Believers who do righteous deeds[5961] will have heavenly gardens[5962] with flowing rivers underneath.[5963] That is the great victory.[5964] (11)
***
Your[ms] Lord's vengeance is severe. (12) He creates and restores. (13) He is forgiving[5965] and loving, (14) and has the glorious throne.[5966] (15) He accomplishes what he wants.[5967] (16) Have

---

[5953] constellations
[5954] Zabur, Psalms 103:8, 145:8. See glossary for more details.
[5955] Tawrah, Genesis 49:24
[5956] Zabur, Psalms 113:3
[5957] Tawrah, Isaiah 45:12, Zabur, Psalms 24:1, 89:11, Injil, Hebrews 1:10
[5958] Tawrah, Jeremiah 29:23
[5959] Zabur, Psalms 7:12-13
[5960] For "torment" twice in this verse, see Tawrah, Isaiah 50:11, Injil, Matthew 18:34, 25:41,46, Luke 16:23-28, Revelation 20:15.
[5961] Injil, 1 Corinthians 3:8, James 2:14-17, Revelation 19:8
[5962] Arabic /jannah/. See glossary for more details.
[5963] Injil, Revelation 22:1-2, Tawrah, Ezekiel 47:12
[5964] Tawrah, Isaiah 25:8, Injil, 1 Corinthians 15:57, 1 John 5:4
[5965] Zabur, Psalms 103:3, 130:4, Tawrah, Isaiah 43:25, Exodus 34:7, Injil, Acts 26:18.
[5966] Tawrah, Isaiah 6:1, Injil, Revelation 4:2
[5967] Zabur, Psalms 135:6

## Chapter 85

you[MS] heard the story about the army, (17) about Pharaoh[5968] and Thamud?[5969] (18)

\*\*\*

Disbelievers reject continually, (19)

\*\*\*

and Allah surrounds them

\*\*\*

from behind.[5970] (20)

\*\*\*

It is a glorious recitation[5971] (21)

\*\*\*

on a preserved tablet.[5972] (22)[5973]

---

[5968] Tawrah, Exodus 6-14
[5969] Thamud is the name of a tribe.
[5970] Zabur, Psalms 89:31-32
[5971] Or Qur'an or qur'an. See glossary for more details.
[5972] Tawrah, Exodus 31:18
[5973] The verses in this chapter that rhyme are put together in paragraphs, separated by \*\*\*.

# Chapter 86 Al-Tariq[5974]

In the name of Allah, the most gracious and merciful.[5975] [I swear] by the sky and the morning star. (1) How can you[ms] know about the morning star?[5976] (2) ***
It is a piercingly bright star. (3)
***
Every soul has a guardian.[5977] (4)
***
Let every person look to what he was created from.[5978] (5) He was created from flowing water (6)
***
that comes from between the loins[5979] and the sternum.[5980] (7)
***
He is able to return him (8) on the day secrets are tested. (9) He will have no power or savior.[5981] (10) By the sky to which it[5982] returns,[5983] (11) and the earth which is split, (12)
***
it is a saying that distinguishes. (13)
***
It is not a joke. (14)

They plot, (15) and I plot, (16) so give the disbelievers extra time. Give them a little time.[5984] (17)[5985]

---

[5974] The morning star, or a night visitor or knocker. Some believe this refers to a pulsar. Its pulsating (verses 1-2) can be compared to knocking, and its radiation is piercing (verse 3).
[5975] Zabur, Psalms 103:8, 145:8. See glossary for more details.
[5976] Injil, 2 Peter 1:19, Revelation 2:28, 22:16
[5977] Tawrah, Ezekiel 28:14-16, 1 Peter 2:25
[5978] Tawrah, Genesis 6:7
[5979] Tawrah, Leviticus 15:16
[5980] Zabur, Psalms 139:13,15
[5981] Zabur, Psalms 49:8-9
[5982] or they. The reference could be to rain.
[5983] Tawrah, Isaiah 55:10-11
[5984] Injil, Romans 3:25
[5985] The verses in this chapter that rhyme are put together in paragraphs, separated by ***.

# Chapter 87 Al-Aala[5986]

**30B1** In the name of Allah, the most gracious and merciful.[5987] Praise the name of your[MS] highest Lord, (1) who created and shaped, (2) who determined He and guided, (3) who brought forth the pasture (4) and made it dark stubble. (5) We will dictate to you[MS], so do not forget (6) anything but what Allah wills. He knows what is plain and what is hidden.[5988] (7) We will make it easy for you[MS] to be at ease. (8) Remind [them] if the reminder is beneficial. (9) He who fears will remember. (10) The most wretched will avoid it- (11) he who is roasted in the biggest fire of hell. (12) Then he will neither die nor live in it. (13) Success[5989] is for him who is purified, (14) who remembers Allah's name and performs prayers. (15) But you[MP] prefer the present life, (16) whereas the hereafter is better and more lasting.[5990] (17) This is truly in the first books, (18) the books of Ibrahim[5991] and Musa.[5992] (19)

---

[5986] The Highest
[5987] Zabur, Psalms 103:8, 145:8. See glossary for more details.
[5988] Injil, Revelation 2:23
[5989] Tawrah, Joshua 1:8
[5990] Injil, 1 John 2:15-17
[5991] Abraham. See glossary for more details. Tawrah, Genesis 12:1-7
[5992] Moses. See glossary for more details.

# Chapter 88 Al-Ghashiyah[5993]

In the name of Allah, the most gracious and merciful.[5994] Have you[MS] heard the story of the covering? (1) On that day, faces will be humbled, (2) working, and weary, (3) roasting in a hot fire,[5995] (4) given drink from a boiling spring.[5996] (5)

\*\*\*

They have no food except daria,[5997] (6) which neither nourishes nor satisfies the hunger. (7)

\*\*\*

On that day, faces will be blessed,[5998] (8) pleased with their efforts,[5999] (9) in a high heavenly garden,[6000] (10) where they do not hear vanity. (11) In it are running springs, (12) raised trellises,[6001] (13) cups in place, (14) cushions lined up, (15) and rich carpets spread out.[6002] (16)

\*\*\*

Do they not see how the camels were created,[6003] (17) how the sky was raised,[6004] (18) how the mountains were erected,[6005] (19) and how the earth was spread out?[6006] (20)

\*\*\*

Remind[6007] them. You[MS] are one who reminds. (21) You[MS] are not in control over them, (22) except for those who turn away and disbelieve (23) Allah will torment them greatly.[6008] (24)

---

[5993] the covering, sometimes used of the day of judgment
[5994] Zabur, Psalms 103:8, 145:8. See glossary for more details.
[5995] Injil, Luke 3:17
[5996] or vessel
[5997] The reference is uncertain, and it may not be an earthly food. It may refer to the durian fruit family, which has thorns on the outside and a strong stench. It is banned in Southeast Asia from hotels and public transportation.
[5998] Or smooth, soft, or joyful
[5999] Injil, Ephesians 6:8
[6000] Arabic /jannah/. See glossary for more details.
[6001] Or beds
[6002] Injil, John 14:2-3
[6003] Tawrah, Genesis 1:24-25
[6004] Tawrah, Isaiah 40:22,26
[6005] Zabur, Psalms 65:6
[6006] Zabur, Psalms 136:6
[6007] Cheaters or those who give short measure

## Chapter 88

\*\*\*They will return to us, (25) and we will be responsible for reckoning with them.[6009] (26) [6010]

---

[6008] Tawrah, Isaiah 50:11, Injil, Matthew 18:34, 25:41,46, Luke 16:23-28, Revelation 20:15

[6009] Injil, Hebrews 9:27

[6010] The verses in this chapter that rhyme are put together in paragraphs, separated by \*\*\*.

# Chapter 89 Al-Fajr[6011]

In the name of Allah, the most gracious and merciful.[6012] [I swear] by the dawn, (1) ten nights, (2) the even and the odd,[6013] (3) and the night when it passes. (4) Is there an oath in that for one who understands? (5)
\*\*\*

Did you[MS] not see what your[MS] Lord did to Aad,[6014] (6) Iram at the column? (7) Nothing similar was created in the land. (8) And [what he did to] Thamud, who hollowed out rocks in the valley? (9) And Pharaoh of the pyramids?[6015] (10) All of them were tyrants in the land. (11) They caused great destruction in it, (12) so your[MS] Lord poured a scourge of torment on them. (13) Your[MS] Lord is observing. (14)
\*\*\*

When a man is tried by his Lord, and he honors him and provides blessings for him, he says, "My Lord honored me."[6016] (15) But when he tries him and is sparing with his provision, he says, "My Lord dishonored me." (16)
\*\*\*

No! You[MP] do not honor the orphan.[6017] (17) Nor do you[MP] encourage feeding the poor. (18)
\*\*\*

You[MP] consume their inheritance like collected food. (19) You[MP] love money greatly.[6018] (20) No! If the earth is utterly pulverized (21) and your[MS] Lord and the angels come in rows,[6019] (22) and hell is brought out on that day, mankind will remember. How will he have a reminder? (23)
\*\*\*

---

[6011] dawn

[6012] Zabur, Psalms 103:8, 145:8. See glossary for more details.

[6013] or double and single

[6014] Aad and Thamud are names of tribes.

[6015] or tent-pegs. The meaning of this word is something pointed. It is used elsewhere in the Qur'an of mountains (78:7), and since the only "mountains" Pharaoh was around would have been the pyramids, this is probable. "Tent-pegs" makes no sense as an epithet of Pharaoh.

[6016] Tawrah, Deuteronomy 26:19

[6017] Injil, James 1:27

[6018] Injil, Luke 16:10-14, 12:15, 1 Timothy 6:10, Matthew 6:24

[6019] Injil, Mark 13:27

Chapter 89

He will say, "I wish I had prepared my life." (24)
\*\*\*

On that day, no one will torment with his torment. (25) None will bind his bonds.[6020] (26)
\*\*\*

Peaceful soul[FS], (27) return[FS] to your[FS] Lord,[6021] content[FS] and pleasing[FS], (28)
\*\*\*

and enter[FS] along with my servants.[6022] (29) Enter[FS] my heavenly garden.[6023] (30)[6024]

---

[6020] Injil, Matthew 18:18
[6021] Zabur, Psalms 116:7
[6022] See glossary.
[6023] Arabic /jannah/. See glossary for more details.
[6024] The verses in this chapter that rhyme are put together in paragraphs, separated by \*\*\*.

Chapter 90

# Chapter 90 Al-Balad[6025]

**30B2** In the name of Allah, the most gracious and merciful.[6026] No, I swear[6027] by this land (1) as you[MS] are an inhabitant on this land, (2) and by a father and what he has fathered: (3) We have created man in misery. (4) Does he think no one can overpower him? (5)
\*\*\*

He says, "I have destroyed much wealth." (6)
\*\*\*

Does he think no one has seen him? (7)
\*\*\*

Did we not give him two eyes, (8) a tongue and two lips? (9) We have guided him on the two paths, (10)
\*\*\*

and he did not charge the ascent.[6028] (11) How can you[MS] know the ascent? (12) Freeing a servant (13) or feeding someone on a day of famine, (14) an orphan relative (15) or a poor man in the land. (16) Then he was a believer who commanded endurance[6029] and mercy. (17) Those are going to heaven.[6030] (18) Disbelievers in our signs[6031] are the damned,[6032] (19) who will be covered with hellfire. (20) [6033]

---

[6025] The city, land, or country
[6026] Zabur, Psalms 103:8, 145:8. See glossary for more details.
[6027] Or, I do not swear
[6028] Injil, Matthew 7:13-14
[6029] See "endure" in glossary
[6030] or, owners of the right hand. Injil, Matthew 25:34-40
[6031] Arabic /ayat/. See glossary for more details.
[6032] Or, owners of the left hand. Injil, Matthew 25:41-46
[6033] The verses in this chapter that rhyme are put together in paragraphs, separated by \*\*\*.

# Chapter 91 Al-Shams[6034]

In the name of Allah, the most gracious and merciful.[6035] [I swear] by the sun and its dawn, (1) by the moon which follows it, (2) by the day which reveals it, (3) by the night which covers it, (4) by the sky and what built[6036] it, (5) by the earth and what spread it out, (6) and by a soul and what shaped it. (7) So he showed its unrighteousness[6037] and reverence to it. (8) Blessed is he who purifies it.[6038] (9) He who corrupts it will be disappointed. (10) Thamud[6039] rejected it in its transgression (11) since the most wretched of them were sent forth. (12) Allah's messenger[6040] said, "Allah's female camel and its watering." (13) They rejected him and they hamstrung her, so their Lord obliterated them for their sin, and leveled them. (14) He does not fear its results. (15)

---

[6034] The sun

[6035] Zabur, Psalms 103:8, 145:8. See glossary for more details.

[6036] The reference could be to materials, as the word is "what," not "who."

[6037] The injustice/wickedness, disbelief/ungratefulness, evil, unrighteousness/sin, or lostness of mankind is mentioned in a number of verses in the Qur'an as well as in the previous books. Injustice or wickedness: 2:57, 3:117,135, 4:64,97, 7:160,177, 9:70, 10:44, 11:101, 14:34,45, 16:33,61,118, 29:40, 30:9, 33:72, 34:19, 35:32, 43:76, 65:1, Tawrah, Genesis 6:5, Job 25:4, Injil, Acts 3:26, disbelief or ungratefulness: 14:34, 17:67, 22:66, 42:48, 43:15, 80:17, Injil, Hebrews 3:19, Evil: 12:53, Tawrah, Jeremiah 17:9, Injil, Matthew 15:19, Mark 7:21, unrighteousness or sin: 91:8, Tawrah, 1 Kings 8:46, Ecclesiastes 7:20, Injil, Romans 3:9-19, 5:12, lostness: 103:2, Tawrah, Jeremiah 50:6, Injil, Luke 19:10, Romans 3:23, 6:23

[6038] Tawrah, Proverbs 20:9.

[6039] The name of a tribe

[6040] The ones specifically called Allah's messenger in the Qur'an are Muhammad (s) 48:29, 7:158, 33:21,40,53, etc., Musa 61:5, Thamud's messenger 91:13, and Isa 4:157,171, 61:6.

# Chapter 92 Al-Layl[6041]

In the name of Allah, the most gracious and merciful.[6042] [I swear] by the night when it covers, (1) by the day when it appears, (2) and by what[6043] created male and female. (3) Your[MP] striving is divided. (4) But to him who gives and is reverent (5) and gives alms kindly[6044] (6) we will ease his way toward ease. (7) But to him who is stingy, desires riches,[6045] (8) and rejects kindness, (9) we will ease his way to difficulty.[6046] (10) His money will not help him when he dies.[6047] (11) Guidance is our responsibility. (12) The hereafter and the present are ours. (13) I warned you[MP] about a flaming fire, (14) which roasts only the most wretched one, (15) he who rejected and turned away.[6048] (16) The godliest people will avoid it. (17) They give their money as poor-tax, (18) and give no blessings to anyone for a reward, (19) but only seek their highest Lord's face. (20) They will be pleased. (21)

---

[6041] The night
[6042] Zabur, Psalms 103:8, 145:8. See glossary for more details.
[6043] The reference here is unclear, since it uses the word "what" instead of "who."
[6044] See introduction for other ways this verse is translated.
[6045] Injil, 1 Timothy 6:10
[6046] Injil, Luke 16:19-31
[6047] Zabur, Psalms 49:6-8
[6048] Injil, Revelation 21:8

## Chapter 93 Al-Duha[6049]

In the name of Allah, the most gracious and merciful.[6050] [I swear] by the early morning, (1) and by the night when it is dark: (2) your[MS] Lord did not leave you[MS] or hate [you]. (3) The hereafter is better for you[MS] than the first world. (4) Your[MS] Lord will give to you[MS], so you'll[MS] be satisfied. (5) Did he not find you[MS] an orphan and shelter [you]?[6051] (6) He found you[MS] lost, and guided [you].[6052] (7) He found you[MS] poor, and enriched [you].[6053] (8)

\*\*\*

Do not overpower[MS] the orphan. (9) Do not reproach[MS] the beggar.[6054] (10)

\*\*\*

So speak about your[MS] Lord's blessings.[6055] (11)[6056]

---

[6049] Early morning
[6050] Zabur, Psalms 103:8, 145:8. See glossary for more details.
[6051] Injil, Romans 8:14-15
[6052] Injil, Luke 15:4
[6053] Injil, 1 Corinthians 9:8-11
[6054] Injil, Matthew 5:42
[6055] Injil, 1 Corinthians 2:12
[6056] The verses in this chapter that rhyme are put together in paragraphs, separated by \*\*\*.

# Chapter 94 Al-Inshirah[6057] or Al-Sharh[6058]

**30B3** In the name of Allah, the most gracious and merciful.[6059] Have we not opened up your[MS] heart[6060] (1) and taken away from you[MS] your[MS] burden[6061] (2) which had strained your[MS] back?[6062] (3) We increased your[MS] fame.[6063] (4)

\*\*\*

There is ease along with difficulty. (5) There is ease along with difficulty. (6)

\*\*\*

So when you[MS] finish, stand up (7) and desire your[MS] Lord.[6064] (8)[6065]

---

[6057] being opened up
[6058] opening up
[6059] Zabur, Psalms 103:8, 145:8. See glossary for more details.
[6060] or chest or breast
[6061] Injil, Matthew 11:28-30 The belief that all prophets and messengers are sinless is not supported by the Qur'an. For instances of prophets or messengers asking forgiveness or committing sins, see 7:23, 20:121 (Adam), 11:47, 71:28 (Nuh), 26:82, 14:41 (Ibrahim), 28:15-16 (Musa), 7:151, 20:93 (Musa and Harun), 38:24 (Dawud), 38:32,35 (Sulayman), 21:87, 37:142 (Yunus), 48:2, 47:19, 40:55, 4:79,106, 9:43, 13:30, 80:1-2, 110:3, 94:2, 23:118, 66:1, 33:37, 8:67, and 9:117 (Muhammad (s).
[6062] Tawrah, Isaiah 10:27
[6063] Or reminder. Injil, John 3:25-30
[6064] Zabur, Psalms 63:1-2
[6065] The verses in this chapter that rhyme are put together in paragraphs, separated by \*\*\*.

Chapter 95

# Chapter 95 Al-Tin[6066]

In the name of Allah, the most gracious and merciful.[6067] [I swear] by the fig, the olive,[6068] (1) Mount Sinai,[6069] (2) and this secure land:[6070] (3) we have created people in the best form[6071] (4) and then returned them to the lowest of the low.[6072] (5) But as for the believers who do righteous deeds,[6073] they will have an unfailing reward.[6074] (6) So what is still making you[MS] deny judgment[6075]? (7) Is Allah not the wisest[6076] ruler?" (8)

---

[6066] the fig
[6067] Zabur, Psalms 103:8, 145:8. See glossary for more details.
[6068] Tawrah, Deuteronomy 8:8
[6069] Sinai in this verse is actually Sineen for the sake of the rhyme.
[6070] The reference could be to a country or a city
[6071] Tawrah, Genesis 1:26-28
[6072] Tawrah, Isaiah 2:9
[6073] Injil, 1 Corinthians 3:8, James 2:14-17, Revelation 19:8
[6074] Injil, Hebrews 9:15
[6075] or religion
[6076] Tawrah, Job 9:4, Proverbs 2:6, Jeremiah 9:23-24, Injil, 1 Corinthians 1:21-25, Romans 16:27

# Chapter 96 Al-Alaq[6077]

In the name of Allah, the most gracious and merciful.[6078] Read[MS] in the name of your[MS] Lord who created, (1) created people from a clot. (2)
\*\*\*

Read[MS], and your[MS] Lord is the most generous. (3)
With a pen,[6079] he taught- (4) taught people what they did not know.[6080] (5)
\*\*\*

No! People are transgressors. (6) They think they have no needs. (7) You[MS] will return to your[MS] Lord. (8) Have you[MS] seen him who forbids (9) a servant[6081] from praying? (10) Do you[MS] think he is guided (11) or commands reverence? (12) When he rejects and turns away, do you[MS] think (13) that he does not know that Allah sees? (14)
\*\*\*

No! If he does not stop, we will drag him by his hair,[6082] (15) by his lying, guilty hair. (16) Let him call those he calls. (17) We will call the reverent ones.[6083] (18)
\*\*\*

No! Do not obey him, but bow down and come near. (19)[6084]

---

[6077] clot
[6078] Zabur, Psalms 103:8, 145:8. See glossary for more details.
[6079] The reference may be to the books he revealed.
[6080] Zabur, Psalms 94:10
[6081] See glossary.
[6082] specifically forelocks, bangs, or forehead.
[6083] Some translators put "guardians of hell", "braves of the army", "angels of hell" or "guardians"
[6084] The verses in this chapter that rhyme are put together in paragraphs, separated by \*\*\*.

# Chapter 97 Al-Qadr[6085]

In the name of Allah, the most gracious and merciful.[6086] We have revealed him[6087] on the night of destiny.[6088] (1) How can you[MS] know the night of destiny? (2) The night of destiny is better than a thousand months. (3) The angels and the spirit descended[6089] during it with their Lord's permission for every matter. (4) It is peace[6090] until the coming of the dawn.[6091] (5)

---

[6085] decree or destiny

[6086] Zabur, Psalms 103:8, 145:8. See glossary for more details.

[6087] or it. Some translators believe this refers to the night when Isa was born. Most believe it refers to the revelation of the Qur'an.

[6088] This word, /qadr/ is a synonym for the word predestined /maqdiy/ in the Qur'an. /Maqdiy/ is only used twice, 1) to refer to hellfire (19:71) and 2) to refer to Isa's being a mercy from Allah and a sign to the universe (19:21). This lends support to the translators who believe that this verse refers to Isa's birth.

[6089] Another indication that the reference in this chapter is to Isa is the record of the angels descending at night and announcing the birth of Isa (Injil, Luke 2:8-14)

[6090] This is a further indication that the reference of this chapter might be Isa. He is the only one called the prince of peace (Tawrah, Isaiah 9:6), and the only giver of peace in the Injil (Injil, John 14:27) and the Qur'an (19:33).

[6091] Injil, 2 Peter 1:19

# Chapter 98 Al-Bayyinah[6092]

In the name of Allah, the most gracious and merciful.[6093] The disbelievers among the people of the book and the idolaters were not separated until the miracle came to them. (1) A messenger from Allah reads purified pages (2) in which are valuable books. (3) Those who were given the book did not separate until the miracle came to them. (4) They were only commanded to worship Allah sincerely in religion[6094] as monotheists, to perform prayers,[6095] and to pay the poor-tax.[6096] That is valuable religion.[6097] (5) The disbelievers among the people of the book[6098] and the idolaters will be in the fires of hell forever.[6099] They are the most evil of all creatures. (6) Believers who do righteous deeds[6100] are the best of all creatures. (7) Their reward will be with their Lord:[6101] heavenly gardens[6102] of Eden with flowing rivers[6103] underneath where they will live forever.[6104] Allah is pleased with them and they also with Allah. That is [the reward] of him who fears his Lord. (8)

---

[6092] miracle
[6093] Zabur, Psalms 103:8, 145:8. See glossary for more details.
[6094] Injil, Matthew 4:10
[6095] Injil, Matthew 6:5-8
[6096] Injil, Luke 11:42
[6097] Injil, James 1:27
[6098] Those people who have a book from Allah are not saved if they do not believe in it.
[6099] Injil, Matthew 25:41
[6100] 2:62, 5:69, Injil, 1 Corinthians 3:8, James 2:14-17, Revelation 19:8
[6101] Injil, Colossians 3:23-24
[6102] Arabic /jannah/. See glossary for more details.
[6103] Injil, Revelation 22:1-2, Tawrah, Ezekiel 47:12
[6104] Injil, 1 Corinthians 2:9

# Chapter 99 Al-Zalzalah[6105]

In the name of Allah, the most gracious and merciful.[6106] When there is a serious earthquake,[6107] (1) when the earth brings forth its weights, (2) and when people say, "What is wrong with it?", (3) on that day, it will speak of its news (4)

\*\*\*

that your[MS] Lord inspired. (5)

\*\*\*

On that day, all people will scatter forth to see their works.[6108] (6)

\*\*\*

Those who do a speck of good will see it,[6109] (7) and those who do a speck of evil will see it.[6110] (8)[6111]

---

[6105] earthquake

[6106] Zabur, Psalms 103:8, 145:8. See glossary for more details.

[6107] Injil, Matthew 27:51-54, 28:1-2

[6108] Injil, Matthew 25:31-46

[6109] Injil, Hebrews 6:10

[6110] Injil, John 5:29

[6111] The verses in this chapter that rhyme are put together in paragraphs, separated by \*\*\*.

# Chapter 100 Al-Adiyat[6112]

In the name of Allah, the most gracious and merciful.[6113] [I swear] by the chargers[6114] who pant, (1) who kindle fires as they strike, (2) who attack in the morning, (3) who raise dust (4) as they go into the midst of a crowd. (5)
\*\*\*

Truly mankind is ungrateful to his Lord. (6) He is witness of that. (7) He[6115] strongly loves wealth. (8) 30B4
\*\*\*

Do they not know that when those in the tombs are scattered (9) and the secrets of the heart are made manifest,[6116] (10) that on that day, their Lord will be aware of them? (11)[6117]

---

[6112] chargers, enemies, attackers, misdeeds. The context implies horses.
[6113] Zabur, Psalms 103:8, 145:8. See glossary for more details.
[6114] Tawrah, Job 39:19-25
[6115] i.e. man. This verse could also mean "He (Allah) strongly loves goodness."
[6116] Injil, 1 Corinthians 14:25
[6117] The verses in this chapter that rhyme are put together in paragraphs, separated by \*\*\*.

# Chapter 101 Al-Qariah[6118]

In the name of Allah, the most gracious and merciful.[6119] Doomsday! (1) What is doomsday? (2) How can you[MS] know what doomsday is? (3)

\*\*\*

[It is] a day when people will be like scattered moths (4)

\*\*\*

and the mountains like carded wool. (5)

\*\*\*

He whose balances are heavy[6120] (6) will have a pleasing life, (7) but he whose balances are light[6121] (8) will have the abyss as his mother. (9) How can you[MS] know what that is? (10) [It is] scorching fire[6122]! (11)[6123]

# Chapter 102 Al-Takathur[6124]

In the name of Allah, the most gracious and merciful.[6125] Gathering up [possesions] distracts[6126] you[MP] (1) until you[MP] go to[6127] the graveyards. (2)

\*\*\*

No! You[MP] will know. (3) No again! You[MP] will know. (4) No! If you[MP] knew with certainty, (5) you[MP] would see the blazing fire. (6) Then your[MP] eyes would certainly see it. (7) Then you[MP] will be asked on that day about delight. (8)[6128]

---

[6118] doomsday, the last judgment, or disaster
[6119] Zabur, Psalms 103:8, 145:8. See glossary for more details.
[6120] i.e. with many good deeds
[6121] i.e. with few good deeds. Zabur, Psalms 62:9, Tawrah, Daniel 5:27
[6122] Injil, Mark 9:43
[6123] The verses in this chapter that rhyme are put together in paragraphs, separated by \*\*\*.
[6124] proliferation or gathering up (of possessions)
[6125] Zabur, Psalms 103:8, 145:8. See glossary for more details.
[6126] Injil, Luke 12:16-21
[6127] literally visit
[6128] The verses in this chapter that rhyme are put together in paragraphs, separated by \*\*\*.

# Chapter 103 Al-Asr[6129]

In the name of Allah, the most gracious and merciful.[6130] [I swear] by the afternoon. (1) People are really lost,[6131] (2) except for the believers who do righteous deeds[6132] and continue[6133] in truth[6134] and endurance.[6135] (3)

# Chapter 104 Al-Humazah[6136]

In the name of Allah, the most gracious and merciful.[6137] Woe to every backbiting slanderer[6138] (1) who gathers money and stores it up.[6139] (2) He thinks that his money will make him immortal.[6140] (3) Never! He will be thrown into the crushing fire. (4) How can you[MS] know the crushing fire? (5) [It is] Allah's fire that is kindled.

---

[6129] Mid-afternoon; the word also means era. Since other chapters in the Qur'an have specific references to time of day (chapter 92 means "night," 89 means "dawn," 93 means "early morning," and 113 means "daybreak,") it is probably that this one also means "afternoon" rather than "era."

[6130] Zabur, Psalms 103:8, 145:8. See glossary for more details.

[6131] The injustice/wickedness, disbelief/ungratefulness, evil, unrighteousness/sin, or lostness of mankind is mentioned in a number of verses in the Qur'an as well as in the previous books. Injustice or wickedness: 2:57, 3:117,135, 4:64,97, 7:150,177, 9:70, 10:44, 11:101, 14:34,45, 16:33,61,118, 29:40, 30:9, 33:72, 34:19, 35:32, 43:76, 65:1, Tawrah, Genesis 6:5, Job 25:4, Injil, Acts 3:26, disbelief or ungratefulness: 14:34, 17:67, 22:66, 42:48, 43:15, 80:17, Injil, Hebrews 3:19, Evil: 12:53, Tawrah, Jeremiah 17:9, Injil, Matthew 15:19, Mark 7:21, unrighteousness or sin: 91:8, Tawrah, 1 Kings 8:46, Ecclesiastes 7:20, Injil, Romans 3:9-19, 5:12, lostness: 103:2, Tawrah, Jeremiah 50:6, Injil, Luke 19:10, Romans 3:23, 6:23

[6132] Injil, 1 Corinthians 3:8, James 2:14-17, Revelation 19:8

[6133] Tawrah, Ezekiel 18:14-17

[6134] Injil, John 8:32-36

[6135] See "endure" in glossary

[6136] The slanderer

[6137] Zabur, Psalms 103:8, 145:8. See glossary for more details.

[6138] Tawrah, Proverbs 10:18

[6139] Injil, James 5:3

[6140] Injil, Luke 12:16-21

(6) It penetrates the hearts, (7) and engulfs them (8) in broad columns. (9)

# Chapter 105 Al-Fil[6141]

In the name of Allah, the most gracious and merciful.[6142] Did you[MS] see what your[MS] Lord did to those with[6143] the elephant? (1) Did he not make their plot go astray?[6144] (2) He sent flocks of birds upon them, (3) who threw rocks of baked clay upon them, (4) and made them like stalks of grain that were eaten up.[6145] (5)

# Chapter 106 Al-Quraysh[6146]

In the name of Allah, the most gracious and merciful.[6147] For a pact with the Quraysh, (1)
\*\*\*

their pact for winter and summer trips. (2)
\*\*\*

Let them worship the Lord of this sanctuary, (3)
\*\*\*

who fed them to ward off hunger[6148] and kept them safe to ward off fear.[6149] (4)[6150]

---

[6141] The elephant
[6142] Zabur, Psalms 103:8, 145:8. See glossary for more details.
[6143] or the owners of
[6144] or astray
[6145] Tawrah, Genesis 41:7, Joel 1:10,17, Hosea 8:7
[6146] the name of the tribe to which Muhammad (s) belonged
[6147] Zabur, Psalms 103:8, 145:8. See glossary for more details.
[6148] Zabur, Psalms 145:16
[6149] Zabur, Psalms 46:1-2
[6150] The verses in this chapter that rhyme are put together in paragraphs, separated by \*\*\*.

Chapters 107-108
# Chapter 107 Al-Maoun[6151]

In the name of Allah, the most gracious and merciful.[6152] Have you[MS] seen him who rejects religion?[6153] (1) He rebuffs the orphan (2) and does not urge others to feed the needy.[6154] (3) Woe to those who perform prayers, (4) who are absent-minded when they perform prayers,[6155] (5) who are hypocritical,[6156] (6) and who forbid devotion. (7)

# Chapter 108 Al-Kawthar[6157]

In the name of Allah, the most gracious and merciful.[6158] We have given you[MS] an abundance,[6159] (1) so perform your[MS] prayers to your[MS] Lord and slaughter [an animal]. (2) He who hates you[MS] will be mutilated.[6160] (3)

---

[6151] Devotion, alms, aid, or utensils.
[6152] Zabur, Psalms 103:8, 145:8. See glossary for more details.
[6153] Or [the day of] judgment
[6154] Injil, James 1:26,27
[6155] Injil, Matthew 6:4-7
[6156] Injil, Matthew 23:13-32
[6157] Abundance. Some say this is the name of a river in paradise.
[6158] Zabur, Psalms 103:8, 145:8. See glossary for more details.
[6159] Injil, 2 Corinthians 9:10-11
[6160] Either physically (of a limb, for example), or by being childless.

# Chapter 109 Al-Kafiruun[6161]

In the name of Allah, the most gracious and merciful.[6162] Say[MS]: "Disbelievers, (1) I do not worship what you[MP] worship, (2)
\*\*\*

nor do you[MP] worship what I worship. (3)
\*\*\*

I do not worship what you[MP] worshiped, (4)
\*\*\*

nor do you[MP] worship what I worship.[6163] (5)
\*\*\*

You[MP] have your[MP] religion and I have my[6164] religion." (6)[6165]

# Chapter 110 Al-Nasr[6166]

In the name of Allah, the most gracious and merciful.[6167] When Allah's salvation[6168] and victory[6169] come, (1)
\*\*\*

and you[MS] see people entering[6170] into Allah's religion by droves, (2) then extol your[MS] Lord's praises and ask his forgiveness.[6171] He accepts repentance.[6172] (3)[6173]

---

[6161] Disbelievers
[6162] Zabur, Psalms 103:8, 145:8. See glossary for more details.
[6163] Tawrah, Isaiah 40:18-29
[6164] or "a"
[6165] The verses in this chapter that rhyme are put together in paragraphs, separated by \*\*\*.
[6166] Victory or salvation
[6167] Zabur, Psalms 103:8, 145:8. See glossary for more details.
[6168] Zabur, Psalms 18:2
[6169] Tawrah, Isaiah 25:8, Injil, 1 Corinthians 15:57, 1 John 5:4
[6170] Injil, Matthew 7:13-14
[6171] Injil, 1 John 1:8-10 The belief that all prophets and messengers are sinless is not supported by the Qur'an. For instances of prophets or messengers asking forgiveness or committing sins, see 7:23, 20:121 (Adam), 11:47, 71:28 (Nuh), 26:82, 14:41 (Ibrahim), 28:15-16 (Musa), 7:151, 20:93 (Musa and Harun), 38:24 (Dawud), 38:32,35 (Sulayman), 21:87, 37:142 (Yunus), 48:2, 47:19, 40:55, 4:79,106, 9:43, 13:30, 80:1-2, 110:3, 94:2, 23:118, 66:1, 33:37, 8:67, and 9:117 (Muhammad (s).
[6172] See glossary on "repentance." Tawrah, Jonah 3:10

Chapters 111-112

# Chapter 111 Al-Lahab[6174], Abu Lahab[6175], or Al-Masad[6176]

In the name of Allah, the most gracious and merciful.[6177] May Abu Lahab's hands be destroyed and may he be destroyed.[6178] (1) May his money and his income not suffice him.[6179] (2) He will be roasted in a flaming fire,[6180] (3) along with his wife the wood-carrier (4)
\*\*\*
with a palm-fiber rope around her neck. (5)[6181]

# Chapter 112 Al-Ikhlas[6182] or Al-Tawhid[6183]

In the name of Allah, the most gracious and merciful.[6184] Say[MS], he only is Allah,[6185] (1) Allah is the everlasting refuge.[6186] (2) He did not beget,[6187] nor was he born. (3) He is incomparable.[6188] (4)

---

[6173] The verses in this chapter that rhyme are put together in paragraphs, separated by \*\*\*.
[6174] The flame
[6175] Father of Lahab, who was Muhammad's (s) uncle. A man in the Arab world is still called, "Father of [oldest son]."
[6176] Palm fiber
[6177] Zabur, Psalms 103:8, 145:8. See glossary for more details.
[6178] Tawrah, Proverbs 14:11
[6179] Zabur, Psalms 109:10
[6180] There is a word play here, as the name Lahab means flame
[6181] The verses in this chapter that rhyme are put together in paragraphs, separated by \*\*\*.
[6182] Sincerity
[6183] unity (belief in the oneness of Allah)
[6184] Zabur, Psalms 103:8, 145:8. See glossary for more details.
[6185] Or, "He is Allah, One," or "He is the one Allah." Tawrah, Deuteronomy 6:4, Injil, Mark 12:29, 1 Timothy 2:5. See "god" in glossary.
[6186] Zabur, Psalms 46:1
[6187] This term refers to physical/sexual procreation. All the books reject the idea of Allah begetting children sexually.
[6188] Or none is equal to him. Tawrah, Isaiah 40:18-29

# Chapter 113 Al-Falaq[6189]

In the name of Allah, the most gracious and merciful.[6190] Say[MS], "I take refuge in the Lord of the daybreak,[6191] (1) from the evil of his creation,[6192] (2)

\*\*\*

from the evil of dusk[6193] when it settles, (3)

\*\*\*

from the evil of women spitting on knots, (4) and from the evil of an envier when he envies.[6194] (5)[6195]

# Chapter 114 Al-Nas[6196]

In the name of Allah, the most gracious and merciful.[6197] Say[MS], "I seek the protection[6198] of the Lord of mankind,[6199] (1) the king of mankind,[6200] (2) the god[6201] of mankind,[6202] (3) from the evil whispers of the sneaking whisperer,[6203] (4) who whispers into the hearts[6204] of mankind, (5) by jinns[6205] and people."[6206] (6)

---

[6189] Daybreak
[6190] Zabur, Psalms 103:8, 145:8. See glossary for more details.
[6191] Tawrah, Job 38:12
[6192] Tawrah, Isaiah 45:7
[6193] Tawrah, Proverbs 7:6-23
[6194] Injil, Matthew 20:1-16, Romans 1:29, James 3:14-16
[6195] The verses in this chapter that rhyme are put together in paragraphs, separated by \*\*\*.
[6196] Mankind
[6197] Zabur, Psalms 103:8, 145:8. See glossary for more details.
[6198] Zabur, Psalms 59:16
[6199] Romans 10:12
[6200] Zabur, Psalms 47:7
[6201] Arabic /ilah/. See glossary for more details.
[6202] Tawrah, Jeremiah 32:27
[6203] i.e. the devil
[6204] Or chests or breasts
[6205] Or demons. See glossary for more details.
[6206] Injil, 2 Timothy 4:18

# Appendix 1: Examples of differences in various translations of the Qur'an

Mariam (19): 10b
/qaala aayatuka alla tukallima nnaasa thalaatha layaalin sawiyyan/

"Said He, Thy sign is that thou shalt not speak to men, though **being without fault**, three nights." (Arberry)

"He said, Thy sign is that thou shalt not speak to men for three nights, **(though) sound**." (Palmer)

"Your sign is that for three days and nights, He replied, you shall be bereft of speech, **though otherwise sound in body**." (Dawood)

"He said, thy token is that thou, **with no bodily defect**, shalt not speak unto mankind three nights." (Pickthall)

"He said, Your sign shall be not to speak to people for three **full** nights." (Khalidi)

"He said, your sign is that you will not speak to the people for three nights **consecutively**." (Monotheist)

"Thy sign, was the answer, shall be that thou shalt speak to no man for three nights, **although thou art not dumb**." (Yusuf Ali)

"He said, Your sign is that you shall speak to no man for three nights, **although you are not dumb**." (Ozek)

"He said, Your sign will be that you will not speak to any people for three nights **in a row**." (Irving)

"He said, Your sign is that you will not [be able to] speak to anyone for three **full [days and]** nights." (Abdul Haleem)

"Your sign, He said, is that you will not be able to speak to people for three nights." **[not translated]** (Unal)

"He said, Your sign is that you will not be able to speak to the people three nights **while in sound health**." (Shakir)

"Your sign shall be that you not speak to people for three nights **in a row**." (Cleary)

# Appendix 1

"Said [the angel]: Thy sign shall be that for **full** three nights **[and days]** thou wilt not speak unto men." (Asad)

"He said, Your sign is that you will not speak to the people for three nights **consecutively**." (Yueksel)

"He said, 'Your sign will be that you will not speak to anyone for three **consecutive** days and nights, **although sound in body**.'" (Khan)

"The answer was, "Your Sign shall be that you shall not speak to mankind for three nights, **even though you are not dumb**.'" (Ahamed)

"Your sign is that you will not talk to anybody for three nights, **although you are sound of body**." (Fakhry)

"He said, Your sign is that you will not speak to the people for three nights, **[being] sound**." (Saheeh Intl.)

## Appendix 1

Muhammad (47):25(b)
/ash-shaitaanu **sawwala** lahum **wa'amla** lahum/

"Satan it was that **tempted** them and **Allah respited** them." (Arberry),

"Satan **induces** them, but **[Allah] lets** them **go on for a time**." (Palmer),

"**seduced** by Satan and **inspired** by him." (Dawood),

"Satan has **seduced** them, and **He giveth them the rein**." (Pickthall)

"Satan it was who **tempted** them and **gave** them **false hope**." (Khalidi),

"**Iblis** has **enticed** them and **led them on**." (Monotheist),

"**The Evil One** has **instigated** them and **buoyed** them **up with false hopes**." (Yusuf Ali),

"Satan has **made their way easy and prolonged from them false hopes**." (Ozek),

"Satan has **seduced** ... and he is **dictating** to them." (Irving),

"...are **duped** and **tempted** by Satan." (Abdel Haleem),

"Satan has **seduced** them; he has **implanted in them long-term worldly ambitions**." (Unal),

"**The Shaitan** has **made it a light matter** to them; and He **gives them respite**." (Shakir),

"Satan has **made suggestions** to them and has **encouraged** them."(Cleary)

"Satan has **embellished their fancies** and **filled them with false hopes**." (Asad)

"**The devil** has **enticed** them and **led them on**." (Yueksel)

"Satan has **embellished their fancies** and God **gives them respite**." (Khan)

"**The Satan** has **misguided** them and **built them up with false hopes**." (Ahamed)

"It was Satan who **insinuated** them and **deluded** them." (Fakhry)

"Satan **enticed** them and **prolonged hope** for them." (Saheeh Intl.)

# Appendix 1

Al-Layl (92):6
/wasaddaqa bilhusna/

"and confirms the reward most fair," (Arberry)

"And believes in the best" (Palmer)

"and believes in goodness," (Dawood)

"And believeth in goodness;" (Pickthall)

"And believes in God's reward," (Khalidi)

"And trusts in goodness." (Monotheist)

"And (in all sincerity) testifies to the Best,-" (Yusuf Ali)

"And believes in the best," (Ozek)

"and acts charitably in the highest manner" (Irving)

"who testifies to goodness-" (Abdel Haleem)

"And affirms the best (in creed, action, and the reward to be given)," (Unal)

"And accepts the best," (Shakir)

"trusting in the happy end,"(Cleary)

"And believes in the truth of the ultimate good" (Asad)

"Trusts in goodness." (Yueksel)

"And believes in the truth of what is right," (Khan)

"And (in all sincerity) accepts and follows the best-" (Ahamed)

"And believes in the fairest reward." (Fakhry)

"And believes in the best [reward]." (Saheeh Intl.)

Appendix 2
# Appendix 2: Glossary:

Aaron: see Harun

Abraham: see Ibrahim

acceptor of repentence: see repent

Adam: (The first man Allah created) It seems that the Arabic form could have been transliterated from either the Hebrew /Adam/ or the Greek /Adam/. This name in the original language meant "red" or "earthy." This name is used in the Qur'an 25 times. The passages that refer to him are 2:30-41, 3:33-34,59, 5:27, 7:19-27, 17:11,61, 18:50, 20:115-123. His story is mentioned in the Tawrah, Genesis 1:26 - 5:5, and he is mentioned elsewhere in the Tawrah 3 times, and in the Injil in Luke 3:38, Romans 5:14, 1 Corinthians 15:22,45, 1 Timothy 2:13-14, and Jude 14.

Alexander (the Great): see Dhul-Qarnayn

Allah: (God) is the transliteration in English of the word in Arabic for the Almighty, All-knowing Creator of the universe, the only God, He who is worthy of all praise, worship and honor, Allah most gracious and merciful.

/Allah/ is the equivalent of "God" as understood properly in the previous books. It is used 2697 times alone in the Qur'an. All Arabic-speaking Muslims, Arabic-speaking Christians, and Arabic-speaking Jews use the word /Allah/ for God, and it is used in Arabic versions of all the books, Qur'an, Law, Psalms, and Gospel. It is the linguistic equivalent to /elohim/ in Hebrew, which is the word used in the Law for God 7007 times. Jesus used /elo(h)i/ to talk to Allah in the Injil (Mark 15:34).

Many consider Allah not just a title denoting God, but the *name* of God in Arabic, similar to /yahweh/ in the Law. This has grammatical validity, since neither of those names have a feminine or plural, nor can they be used with a pronoun (e.g. *my* Allah). However, there is no widespread agreement on this subject.

The Qur'an strongly affirms that Allah is the same God worshiped by true Christians, Jews, and Muslims. See 10:90, 29:46, 73:9 among many other verses listed under "god" in this glossary.

Al-Taghut: see false gods

## Appendix 2

Alyasa: (Elisha, servant of Elijah and later a prophet himself) It seems that the Arabic form was transliterated from the Hebrew /Alyasha'/ instead of the Greek /Elisaie/. This name in the original language meant "God is my salvation." This name is used in the Qur'an 2 times. His story is in the Tawrah, 1 Kings 19:16 through 2 Kings 13:21, and he is mentioned once in the Injil, Luke 4:27.

Ayyub: (Job, the prophet known for patience) It seems that the Arabic form was transliterated from the Hebrew /Ayub/ instead of the Greek /Iob/. This name in the original language meant "returning." This name is used in the Qur'an 4 times. His story is in the Tawrah, Job 1-42, and he is elsewhere mentioned twice in the Tawrah, Ezekiel 14:14,20, and once in the Injil, James 5:11.

Bible: This word is not used in the any of the books, but it is used by many people to refer to the Tawrah, Zabur, and Injil all together. (q.v.)

blazing fire: /al-jahim/ This word for hell is used 26 times in the Qur'an.

bottomless pit: /hawiya/ This word for hell occurs once, in 101:9 and is related to air or emptiness.

burning fire: /al-sa'ir/ This word for hell is used 16 times in the Qur'an.

Christ: see Messiah

Christian: /al-nasara/ This word refers to those of the Christian religion, but its origins are not clear. Some have suggested that the word is derived from Nazareth, the town where Isa was brought up, as is implied in the Injil, Matthew 2:23, Acts 24:5. Others believe that it is because of the Arabic word /ansar/ (helpers/servants) used in 61:14, 3:52. In the Injil, the followers of Christ are usually called believers, disciples or followers, so this is quite possible.

Criterion: /al-furqan/ This word comes from the root word meaning difference, and seems to mean what differentiates good and evil. In 2:185, it refers to the Qur'an, and in 2:53, 21:48, it refers to the Tawrah.

crushing fire: /al-hutama/ This word for hell occurs only in 104:4,5. It is from the word for crushing.

David: see Dawud

## Appendix 2

Dawud: (David, king of the people of Israel and father of Solomon) It seems that the Arabic form was transliterated from the Hebrew /Dawod/ instead of the Greek /Dauid/. This name in the original language meant "beloved." This name is used in the Qur'an 16 times. The passages that refer to Dawud are: 2:251, 4:163, 5:78, 6:84, 17:55, 21:78-80,105-106, 27:15-16, 34:10-13, 38:17-26,30. His story in the Tawrah is in 1 Samuel 16:13 through 1 Kings 2:10 and 1 Chronicles 9:22 - 29:30. In addition, he is mentioned elsewhere 204 times in the Tawrah, 87 times in the Zabur, and 59 times in the Injil.

day of resurrection: /yawm al-qiyamah/. The Qur'an refers to the day of resurrection /yawm al-qiyamah/ 10:60 et al., the day of judgment /yawm al-din/ 15:35 et al, the last day /al-yawm al-akhir/ 2:8 et al., that day /yawma'idhin/ 11:66 et al., a great day /yawm azim/ 10:15, et al., a painful day /yawm alim/ 11:26, 43:65, a great day /yawm kabir/ 11:4, a grievous day /yawm 'asib/ 11:77, a day that surrounds /yawm muhit/ 11:84, a day that will be witnessed /yawm mashhud/ 11:103, and many more ways of describing it. These all refer to the day of resurrection, but focus on different aspects of it.

demon: see jinn

destruction/destroy: /fasaad, yafsid/. This word has the meaning of destruction or corruption. When used of a location, it is generally translated "destroy" or "destruction," but when it is used of people, it is generally translated "corrupt" or "corruption."

devils/a devil: /shaytan/shayatin/ This is the same word as the one translated "Satan" but without the definite article. It seems that the Arabic form was probably transliterated from the Hebrew /shatan/ and not the Greek /satanas/. This name in the original language meant "adversary." This name is used in the Qur'an 6 times in the singular (devil) and 18 times in the plural (devils). See also jinn and Satan. The name Iblis we have left in Arabic.

Dhul-Kifl: (Ezekiel, a prophet) The origin of the Arabic form is unknown. It does not seem to have any relation to the Hebrew /yahazqael/ or the Greek /iezekiel/. This name in the original language meant "dedicated." This name is used in the Qur'an 2 times in 21:85 and 38:48, and twice in the Tawrah as well, in Ezekiel 1:3, 24:24. Some commentators think this is a name of Obadiah.

## Appendix 2

Dhul-Qarnayn: (Some people think this refers to Alexander the Great, the greatest king of the Greeks. Another view is that it refers to Cyrus, king of Persia) The Arabic term means "he of the two horns." Horns are symbols of power. He is mentioned three times in the Qur'an, in 18:83,86,94, and is prophesied of in *Tawrah*, Daniel 11:3 (Alexander), and Isaiah 45:1 (Cyrus).

disbelief/disbelieve(r): /kufr/. This word has the meaning of "knowing and rejecting," though the root meaning is also connected with ungratefulness and covering of the truth.

donate: /anfaqa/ This word literally meaning spend, but is used for spending money to benefit the poor or spending it to accomplish Allah's will.

Elijah: see Ilyas

Elisha: see Alyasa

endure: /yasbur/ This word can also mean to be patient. Since the Qur'an usually uses this in the context of enduring trials and difficulties, and since "patience" today usually implies waiting but not necessarily suffering, we have translated this word "endure." See Zabur, Psalm 55:12, Injil, Matthew 5:4,11-12, 10:22, 24:13, 1 Corinthians 9:12, 10:13, 2 Corinthians 1:6, Colossians 3:13, 2 Timothy 2:24, Hebrews 11:37, James 1:12, 5:7,11, 1 Peter 2:20, Revelation 2:2.

Enoch: see Idris

false gods: /al-taghut/ This word is used in the Qur'an 8 times, and can be either singular or plural. It means anything that is falsely worshiped, and thus can refer to Satan as well.

the flame: /laza/ This word for hell occurs only in 70:15, with a related term used in 92:14.

God: see Allah and god

god: /ilah/ This word is used 147 times in the Qur'an. It is from the same root as /allah/ but can be singular, dual, or plural, masculine or feminine. It refers to anything that people worship, whether false (20:88, 37:36) or true (10:90, 29:46).

The Qur'an, Tawrah, Zabur, and Injil agree that there is only one God. (*Qur'an*: 2:133,163,163,255, 3:2,6,18,18,62, 4:87,171, 5:73, 6:19,102,106, 7:59,65,73, 85,158, 9:31,129, 10:90, 11:14,50,61,84, 13:30, 14:52, 16:2,22,51, 18:110, 20:8,14,98,

Appendix 2

21:25,87,108, 22:34, 23:23,32,116, 27:26, 28:70,88, 29:46, 35:3, 37:4,35, 38:65, 39:6, 40:3,62,65, 41:6, 44:8, 47:19, 59:22,23, 64:13, 73:9, *Tawrah*: Exodus 8:10, 9:14, Deuteronomy 4:35,39, 6:4, 33:26, 1 Samuel 2:2,2,2, 2 Samuel 22:7, 1 Kings 8:60, 2 Kings 19:19, 1 Chronicles 17:20, 2 Chronicles 14:11, Isaiah 37:16,20, 43:10,11, 44:6,8, 45:5,6,14,18,21,21, 46:9,9, Daniel 3:29, Hosea 13:4, Joel 2:17, Micah 7:18, *Zabur*: Psalms 86:8,10, *Injil*: Matthew 19:17, Mark 10:19, 12:29,32, Luke 18:19, John 5:44, 10:30, 17:3,4,22, Romans 3:30, 16:27, 1 Corinthians 8:4,6, Galatians 3:20, Ephesians 4:6, 1 Timothy 1:17, 2:5, 6:15, James 2:19, Jude 25, Revelation 15:4)

Gog and Magog: see Yajuj and Majuj

Goliath: see Jalut

Gospel: see Injil

hajj: (pilgrimage) This is the word used for the complete pilgrimage that is done at the appointed time. See minor pilgrimage. Tawrah, Exodus 23:17, 34:23-24, Leviticus 23:4-37, Deuteronomy 12:11, 16:16, Isaiah 4:5, Joel 2:16, Zabur, Psalms 84:7, Injil, John 12:20, Acts 8:27

Harun: (Aaron, brother of Moses) It seems that the Arabic form was transliterated from the Greek /Aaron/ instead of the Hebrew /Ahron/. This name in the original language meant "enlightened," "exalted," or "high mountain." This name is used in the Qur'an 20 times. His story is in the Tawrah, Exodus 4:14 through Numbers 33:39, and he is mentioned 40 other times in the Tawrah, 8 in the Zabur, and 4 in the Injil.

heavenly garden(s): see jannah

hell: /jahannam/ This is the usual word for hell, and is related to the Hebrew word /gehennom/ "valley of Hinnom (or possibly wailing)" for hell. It is used 77 times in the Qur'an.

hellfire: /al-naar/ This word literally means "the fire" and is used 104 times in the Qur'an to mean the fire of hell. When this is not the meaning, it is translated "fire" (41 times). The Qur'an often states that hellfire is eternal, and those who are in it will not escape (2:167,217,257,275, 3:24,116, 4:14, 5:37, 6:128, 7:36, 9:17, 10:27, 13:5, 18:53, 58:17, 59:17, 64,:20, and many others.)

## Appendix 2

Iblis: (the devil) This name or title is derived from the Greek /diabolos/, which means "he who throws [trouble] between [people]." It is used 11 times in the Qur'an.

Ibrahim: / (Abraham) There are two forms of orthography of this word in the Qur'an, /ibrahim/ and /ibraheem/ possibly parallel to the names Abram and Abraham (see Tawrah, Genesis 17:5). It seems that the Arabic forms were transliterated from the Hebrew /Abraham/ instead of the Greek /Abraam/. This name in the original language meant "father of a multitude." This name is used in the Qur'an 69 times. Passages that refer to Ibrahim are: 2:124-140,255-260, 3:33,65-68,84,95-97, 4:54,125,163, 6:74-84,161, 9:70,114, 11:69-76, 12:6,38, 14:35-41, 15:51-60, 16:120-123, 19:41-50,58, 21:51-73, 22:26,43,78, 26:69, 29:16-27,31-32, 33:7, 37:83-113, 38:45, 42:13, 43:26-28, 51:24-34, 53:37, 57:26, 60:4, 87:19, and Tawrah, Genesis 11:26-25:8. He is also referred to in the Tawrah 65 times, in the Zabur 4 times, and in the Injil 68 times.

Idris: (Enoch, father of Methuselah and great-grandfather of Noah) The origin of the Arabic form is unknown. It does not seem to have any relation to the Hebrew /hanukh/ or the Greek /enokh/. This name in the original language meant "dedicated." This name is used in the Qur'an 2 times. Some commentators think this is a name of Ezra. His story is in the Tawrah, Genesis 5:18-24, and he is mentioned one other time in the Tawrah and 3 times in the Injil.

Ilah: see god

Ilyas: (Elijah, a prophet) It seems that the Arabic form was transliterated from the Greek /ilias/ instead of the Hebrew /elihu/. This name in the original language meant "God is he." This name is used in the Qur'an 2 times. In addition, another form of the word might refer to Elijah in 37:130. His story is in the Tawrah, 1 Kings 17:1 through 2 Kings 2:11, and he is elsewhere referred to 13 times in the Tawrah and 29 times in the Injil.

Injil: (gospel) The Arabic word Injil is from the Greek word /evangelion/ which means "gospel" or "good news." It refers to what is known today as the New Testament, though many people assume it means just the life of Christ as contained in Matthew, Mark, Luke and John. The Qur'an states that Allah gave Jesus the good news. (5:46). Jesus promised that God's spirit would later reveal further parts of the good news to his various followers. (Injil, John 14:26, 16:12-13)

## Appendix 2

Isa (or Esa or Issa): (Jesus) It seems that the Arabic form was transliterated from the Greek /isous/ instead of the Hebrew /yehoshua/. This name in the original language meant "God saves." This name is used in the Qur'an 25 times and in the Injil 911 times.

Isaac: see Ishaq

Ishaq: /is-haq/ (Isaac, second son of Abraham) It seems that the Arabic form (pronounced is-hak, not ish-ak) was transliterated from the Hebrew /yits-haq/ instead of the Greek /isak/. This name in the original language meant "he laughs." This name is used in the Qur'an 17 times. His story is in the Tawrah, Genesis 17:19-21, 21:3-35:29, and he is elsewhere mentioned 36 times in the Tawrah, once in the Zabur, and 20 times in the Injil.

Ishmael: see Ismail

Islam: see submitted

Ismail: (Ishmael, oldest son of Abraham) It seems that the Arabic form was transliterated from the Hebrew /yishmael/ as well as the Greek /ismail/. This name in the original language meant "Allah hears." This name is used in the Qur'an 12 times: 2:125,127,133,136,140, 3:84, 4:163, 6:86, 14:39, 19:54, 21:85, 38:48. His story is in the Tawrah, Genesis 16, 17 and 25, and is referred to five other times in the Tawrah.

Jacob: see Yaqub

Jalut: /jalut/ (a giant whom Dawud killed). This name is mentioned three times in the Qur'an (2:249,250,251), and is related to the Hebrew/golyath/ and may mean "conspicuous." In the Tawrah his story is mentioned in 1 Samuel 17:1-58.

Jannah: /al-jannah/ This word has the meanings of heaven (the eternal abode of the righteous) and garden. When the reference is to a place on earth, we have translated it "garden" but when the reference is to the hereafter, we have translated it "heavenly garden."

Jesus: see Isa

Jethro: see Shuaib

jihad: see struggle

jinn: (demon). This word is the source of the English word genie, which however has a different connotation. Though not exactly equivalent, it is dynamically closest to the English word demon.

Some object to this translation, saying that jinn in the Qur'an, while mostly evil, are sometimes good (see 27:17,39, 34:12, 72:11), while demons in the Law and Gospel are always evil. However, a careful study of the Law and the Gospel shows that there were demons or evil spirits that accomplished Allah's will (Tawrah, 1 Samuel 16:14, 19:9, 1 Kings 22:23, 2 Chronicles 18:22, Injil, 2 Corinthians 12:7-9).

The word translated "demonized," is from the same root (literally jinn-ed) and also means "crazy." See also Iblis and Satan.

Job: see Ayyub

John (the Baptist): see Yahya

Jonah: see Yunus

Joseph: see Yusuf.

Law: see Tawrah

Lot: see Lut

love: In the Qur'an, Allah is twice called "loving" /Al-Wadud/, one of the 99 names of Allah. In addition, it says Allah loves certain people: those who do good 2:195, 3:134,148, the repentant 2:222, the purifiers 2:222, 9:108, those who keep their oaths 3:76, the reverent 3:76, 9:4,7, those who endure 3:146, those who trust him 3:159, the generous 5:13,93, the just 5:42, 49:9, 60:8, those who fight in his path 61:4, and those who love him 5:54. For those Allah loves in the other books, see Tawrah, Deuteronomy 23:5, 33:3, 2 Chronicles 2:11, Proverbs 3:12, 15:9, Hosea 13:1, Injil, 2 Corinthians 9:7, Hebrews 12:6, John 3:35, 5:20, 10:17, 14:21,23, 16:27.

The Qur'an also says Allah does not love certain other people: aggressors 2:190, the wicked 3:57,140, 42:40, disbelievers 2:176, 3:32, 22:39, 30:45, traitors 4:107, 8:58, 22:39, the proud, 4:36, 16:23, 57:23, the boastful 4:36, 57:23, the guilty 2:176, 4:107, destroyers 5:64, transgressors 5:87, 7:55, and wasters 6:141, 7:31. For those Allah does not love in the other books, see Zabur, Psalms 5:4-5, 11:5, Tawrah, Proverbs 6:16-19.

## Appendix 2

Lut: /Lut/ (Lot, nephew of Abraham) It seems that the Arabic form was transliterated from the Hebrew /Lot/, which has a parallel letter to the Arabic /ta'/ instead of the Greek /Lot/, which does not. This name in the original language meant "covered." This name is used in the Qur'an 27 times. His story is in the Tawrah, Genesis 11:27 - 13:14, 14:12-16, 19:1-36. He is elsewhere mentioned twice in the Tawrah, once in the Zabur, and three times in the Injil.

Mariam: (Mary, mother of Jesus) The vowelling in Arabic suggests that the Arabic form was transliterated from the Greek /Mariam/ instead of the Hebrew /Miriam/. This name in the original language meant "myrrh" or "bitter." This name is used in the Qur'an 34 times. Mariam is the only woman whose name is given in the Qur'an. Isa is thus the only person in the Qur'an who is called by his mother's name (since he had no physical/sexual father). Her story is mentioned in the Injil, Matthew 1:16-2:23, Luke 1:27-2:51, and she is mentioned four other times in the Injil. Her becoming the mother of Jesus is prophesied in the Tawrah, Isaiah 7:14. She is called the daughter of Imran in 66:12 and 3:35-36. There is a similarly-named person in the Tawrah (Exodus 6:20, Numbers 26:59) called Amram, who is the father of Harun, Musa, and Miriam (same spelling in Arabic as Mariam.) If the same person is intended, this may refer to Mariam's descent from the priestly line of Harun, as her relative Elizabeth was descended from Harun, son of Amram (Injil, Luke 1:5,36). Mariam's father is not mentioned in the Injil, though Joseph (Injil, Matthew 1:16) and Heli (Injil, Luke 3:23) have been suggested.

Mary: see Mariam

mercy /rahmah/ Allah's mercy is a predominant theme in all the books, mentioned in the Qur'an over 200 times and over 200 times in the Tawrah, Zabur, and Injil. See, for example, Tawrah, Exodus 34:6, Numbers 14:18, Deuteronomy 4:31, 2 Samuel 24:14, Nehemiah 9:17, Isaiah 54:7, Lamentations 3:22, Daniel 9:9, Joel 2:13, Jonah 4:2, Zabur, Psalms 25:6, 86:15, 103:8, 145:8, Injil, Luke 1:50, 2 Corinthians 1:3, Ephesians 2:4, and James 5:11. Mercy in Arabic is a broader term than in English, and includes the concepts of grace, kindness, and forgiveness as well as mercy.

The word "mercy" has feminine gender except in 7 instances, 2:218, 7:56, 11:73, 19:2, 30:50, 43:32 (twice), where it is spelled /rahmat/, and it is given masculine gender. The reason is not known.

## Appendix 2

messenger: /rasul/ There are many messengers mentioned in the Qur'an but only three are called "the messenger": Muhammad (s) in 7:157, etc., Musa in 73:16 and Isa in 3:53. Only two are called "Allah's messenger" in the Qur'an: Muhammad in 48:29 and Isa in 4:157,171. The word means one who is sent. Isa is called Allah's messenger messenger in Injil, Hebrews 3:1, and Musa in Exodus 3:13-15.

Messiah: /Al-Masih/ The Arabic word Masih comes from the Hebrew word /Mashiakh/. The English equivalent, Christ, comes from the Greek word /khristos/. It is a title, not a name. This title means, "he who was anointed (Arabic /masaha/) with oil as God's appointment as prophet, priest, and king." Oil is several times connected with God's spirit (Tawrah, 1 Samuel 16:13, Isaiah 61:1, Zechariah 4:11-14; see Qur'an 2:87,253,5:110.) In the Tawrah, prophets, priests, and kings were anointed with oil to show God's appointment to their jobs, but only the Messiah had all three roles in one person. As a prophet, he delivered Allah's message (19:30, 3:49, Injil, Matthew 13:57, 21:11,46). As a priest, he interceded (which requires a close relationship to Allah, sinlessness, and Allah's permission 2:255, 3:49, 5:110, 19:19, 3:45, Injil, Hebrews 6:20). Also as a priest, he offered sacrifice (3:55, 5:117, 37:107, Injil, Hebrews 9:26, 10:5,12). As a king he was to be obeyed (see 3:50-51, 43:61-64, Injil, Revelation 17:14). This title is used 11 times in the Qur'an and 521 times in the Injil. Isa is the only one in the Qur'an who is called Messiah.

Methuselah: see Salih

millah: see spiritual path

minor pilgrimage: /al-umra/ This is a partial pilgrimage that is done at a different time of year than the appointed one. It is used twice in the Qur'an.

miracle: /bayyinah/. This word comes from the root "clear" and we have translated it miracle. It probably implies that the miracle makes Allah's character clear.

Moses: see Musa

most gracious and merciful: /al-rahman al-rahim/ These two words are from the same root (mercy). Some explain them as "full of mercy" and "mercy-giving", or alternatively, "he who has mercy" and "he who shows mercy". Since these expressions are awkward in an English translation, we have used the familiar expression

## Appendix 2

"gracious and merciful." "Gracious" implies Allah giving men the good reward they do not deserve and "merciful" implies Allah not giving men the evil repayment they do deserve. "Gracious" and "merciful" together cover the lexical meaning of the two Arabic terms together.

Muhammad: (also transliterated Mohamed and many other ways) This is an Arabic name, and it means "highly praised." This name is used in the Qur'an 4 times, in 3:144, 33:40, 47:2, 48:29, but he is referred to hundreds of times by titles.

Musa: (Moses) It seems that the Arabic form was transliterated from the Hebrew/Mosheh/ instead of the Greek /Mosis/. This name in the original language meant "drawn out [of the water]." This name is used in the Qur'an 136 times. The passages that mention Musa are: 2:51-71, 87,92,108,136,246,248, 3:84, 4:153,164, 5:20-26, 6:84,91,154, 7:103-160, 10:75-89, 11:17,97,110, 14:5-8, 17:2,101-104, 18:60-82, 19:51-53, 20:9-98, 21:48, 22:44, 23:45-49, 25:35-36, 26:10-68, 27:7-14, 28:3,48,76, 29:39, 32:23, 33:7,69, 37:114-122, 40:23-37,53, 41:45, 42:13, 43:46-55, 46:12,30, 51:38-40, 53:36, 61:5, 79:15-26, 87:19. His story is in the Tawrah, Exodus 2:10 - Deuteronomy 34:5, and he is also referred to 117 times elsewhere in the Tawrah, 8 times in the Zabur, and 80 times in the Injil.

Muslim: see submitted

names of God, 99 The Qur'an mentions the "beautiful names" in 7:180, 17:110, 20:8 and 59:24, but does not give a list. There are several lists with minor variations. Of the names on the most commonly-accepted list, the Qur'an has 76 of them. All 99 are found in each of the Tawrah, the Zabur, and the Injil.

Nasara: see Christian

New Testament: see Injil

Noah: see Nuh

Nuh: (Noah) It seems that the Arabic form was transliterated from the Hebrew /nuh/ and from the Greek /noe/. This name in the original language meant "rest." This name is used in the Qur'an 43 times. Passages that refer to Noah are: 3:33, 4:163, 7:59-64,69, 9:70, 10:71-73, 11:25-49,89, 14:9, 17:3,17, 19:58, 21:76-77, 22:42, 23:23-30, 25:37, 26:105-122, 29:14-15, 33:7, 37:75-83, 38:12-14, 40:5,31, 42:13, 50:12, 51:46, 53:52, 54:9-15, 57:26, 66:10, 71:1,21-28. His story is in the Tawrah, Genesis 5:29

## Appendix 2

through 9:29. He is also mentioned 10 other times in the Tawrah and 8 times in the Injil.

Old Testament: see Tawrah

patience see endure

perform prayers: /yusalli/ This word is used for ritual prayers. /yad'u/ is used for private petitions and is translated "pray". See Tawrah, 2 Kings 17:36, 1 Chronicles 16:29, Daniel 6:11-14, Zabur, Psalms 29:2, 96:9, 99:5,9, 132:7, Injil, Matthew 6:5-15, 1 Thessalonians 5:17, Jude 20.

pilgrimage: see hajj

poor-tax: /al-zakah/ This word refers to the required portion (traditionally 2.5% yearly) of the assets that are given to the poor. The verb from which this noun is derived means "to purify," and an alternative translation could be "capital purification," meaning that once the sacred portion has been removed, the rest is pure. See Tawrah, Deuteronomy 14:28-29, 26:12, Injil, Matthew 19:21, Mark 12:42-43, Luke 19:8, Acts 11:29, Romans 15:26, 2 Corinthians 8:14-15, 9:12. . There is a separate word, /yatasaddaq/ or /sadaqat/, that is used for voluntary alms to the poor, for instance in 9:58.

prayer: see perform prayers

presence: /sakeenah/ This word can be either the Arabized form of the Hebrew word /shekinah/ (meaning Allah's presence – see 2:248), or tranquility. Since true tranquility comes from Allah's presence, the two meanings are not contradictory.

promiscuous: /fahish/ This word has connotations of lewdness or adultery.

Psalms: see Zabur

Qur'an /al-qur'an/ (recitation, reading, or lectionary). An alternative spelling is Koran. Some translations of the Qur'an do not transliterate this word, but actually translate it, which helps clarify the meaning. The Qur'an several places uses the word qur'an indefinitely, as "a qur'an/recitation" (10:61, 13:31, 17:88), referring to other qur'ans, and "this qur'an/recitation" (6:19, 10:37, 12:3, 17:9,41,89, 18:54, 25:30, 27:76, 30:56, 34:31, 39:27, 41:27, 43:31, and 59:21), to distinguish it from other qur'ans/recitations (10:15). This implies that "qur'an" is used to mean "recitation," "reading," or even "lectionary." Lectionary

## Appendix 2

(something read in parts) is very probable, since the Qur'an is divided into 30 sections. In these cases the word /qur'an/ has been translated as recitation. Elsewhere, when the Arabic says the Qur'an, it has been transliterated as Qur'an.

The Qur'an describes itself as qur'an of the dawn (17:78), an Arabic qur'an (12:2, 10:113, 39:28, 41:3, 42:7, and 43:3) as opposed to a foreign qur'an (41:44), a clear qur'an (15:1, 36:69) as contrasted with other qur'ans/readings that are not clear, a noble qur'an (56:77), the great qur'an (15:87), a wonderful or strange qur'an (72:1), and a wise qur'an (36:2). In 75:18, the word "qur'an" is clearly used to mean "reading," and not "qur'an."

The Qur'an directed Muhammad (s) that when he read the Qur'an, he should seek God's protection from Satan (16:98), and if this was a good principle for him to follow, the rest of us should do the same.

realize: /yash'ur/ It is used 25 times in the Qur'an and has the idea of sensing.

recitation: /qur'an/ see Qur'an

reflect on: /yatadabbar/ It is used 4 times in the Qur'an, always with an object.

remember/remind: /dhakara/ and other verbal forms: This word can also have the meaning of "mention." Five times in chapter 19, Allah commands, "Remember in the Book about...", referring to Mariam, Ibrahim, Musa, Ismail, and Idris. It seems that the original receipients of the Qur'an were more familiar with the stories in the previous books than people today, and they got the message just by telling them, "remember."

reminder: /dhikr/ This word, which means "reminder" or "mention" or "remembrance," is assumed by many who have not studied the Qur'an closely to refer to the Qur'an exclusively. In many verses, it clearly refers to the Qur'an (3:58, 16:44, 21:24,50, 36:69, 43:5,44, 68:51,52). In others, the context is unclear but may refer to the Qur'an (12:104, 20:99, 23:71, 38:87, 65:10, 81:27). Parts of the Qur'an are considered "reminders" in 21:2 and 26:5, and the Qur'an contains "reminders" in 21:10 and 38:1.

However, sometimes this word clearly refers to other books. In 7:63 the "reminder" is given to Nuh. In 7:69, it is given to Hud. In 21:48, it is given to Musa and Harun. In 54:25, it is given to Thamud. In 15:6, it is given to former nations. In 37:168,

Appendix 2

it is given to the men of old. In 21:105, it is prior to the Zabur (about 1600 years before the Hijra). Former people forgot the "reminder" in 25:18 and possibly 38:8. The story of Zakariyya is considered a "reminder" in 19:2. Ismail, Alyasa, and Dhu-Al-Kifl are connected with the "reminder" in 38:48, and all the wicked seem to have been led astray in 25:29. Other verses (36:11, 37:3, and 41:41) are unclear in reference.

In 16:43 and 21:7, those who received the Qur'an are told to ask the people of the reminder if they do not know something. Obviously they were not supposed to ask themselves. This other group, the people of the reminder, had received that previously.

In 15:9, in the context of the reminder given to former nations (15:6), the Qur'an says that Allah revealed the reminder, and he will protect it.

repent: /yatubu/ This word is related to the Hebrew word /shub/. Both the Qur'an and the previous books use this term for people and for Allah. When used of people, the word means being sorry for doing something wrong, changing one's mind about it, and resolving not to repeat it. When used of Allah, it conveys the idea of Allah being sorry and compassionate toward a repenter, and accepting his repentance, just as does the word /neham/ in the Law. In neither case does it imply that Allah made a mistake. Therefore, we have translated it "to accept repentance" when used of Allah, and the name /al-tawwab/ as "acceptor of repentance."

reveal: /anzala/ or /nazzala/ This word contains the picture of sending down or lowering, and sometimes is translated that way when the meaning is literal (e.g. 5:112). When used of revelation of the books, it is translated "reveal." Generally, /nazzala/ refers more to verbal, literal, or word-for-word inspiration, and /anzala/ refers most to inspiration of the meaning but not the specific words. /nazzala/ is used for the inspiration of the Tawrah (3:93), the Book (in general) in 2:176, and the Qur'an (17:106, 47:2, 76:23). /anzala/ is used of the Tawrah in 3:3, 5:44, the Injil in 3:3, the previous book (in general) in 57:25, and the Qur'an in 2:41, 5:48, 10:94, 12:2, 14:1, 16:64, 20:113, etc. The two uses are contrasted in 4:136, where /nazzala/ is used of the Qur'an and /anzala/ is used of the previous book.

Reverent: /taqiy/, and the associated nouns and verbs. The Arabic word describes a person who both fears or reveres Allah and does what is right, is pious and has a noble character. When it has the

## Appendix 2

direct object "Allah" we have translated it "to fear Allah." When the object is a person or a thing, we have translated it "to guard against."

Salih: (Methuselah, grandfather of Noah) It seems that the Arabic form was transliterated and shortened from both the Hebrew /methushalah/ and the Greek /mathusala/. This name in the original language meant "his death will bring." This name is used in the Qur'an 9 times. Other identifications are possible. His story in the Tawrah is in Genesis 5:21-27, and he is elsewhere mentioned in Tawrah, 1 Chronicles 1:3 and Injil, Luke 3:37.

Satan: /al-Shaytan/ It seems that the Arabic form was probably transliterated from the Hebrew and not the Greek. This name in the original language meant "adversary." This name is used in the Qur'an 64 times. /Al-Taghut/ is also translated Satan 3 times (4:51,60,76) See also jinni and Devil.

Saul: see Talut

save, savior: /yansur/nasir/naseer/. This word also has the meaning of giving victory, protecting and helping.

say /qul/ This word is almost always translated as the masculine singular command of "to say," but it may also be a transliteration from the Hebrew word /qol/ which can mean "Listen." (See Isaiah 52:8, NET, RSV, and NASB)

scorching fire: /saqar/ This word for hell is used 4 times in the Qur'an.

self-sufficient: /al-ghani/ This is one of the "99 names of God." When used of people, the meaning is "rich." It is used of Allah in 2:263, 267, 3:97, 4:131, 6:133, 10:68, 14:8, 22:64, 27:40, 29:6, 31:12, 26, 25:13, 39:7, 47:38, 57:24, 60:6, and 64:6.

servant: /abd/ This word sometimes means "slave," (generally referring to people who were slaves of other people), sometimes "servant," and other times, "worshiper." This word has two separate plurals with two different meanings. When the plural is /abid/ is used, the meaning is generally "servant" or "slave." This plural is used only five times in the Qur'an, in 3:182, 8:51, 22:10, 41:46, and 50:29, though the singular also has this meaning sometimes. When the plural is, /ibad/ the meaning is generally "worshiper." In this translation, we have generally used "servant", since "slave" implies servitude against one's will. Allah does not force anyone to worship or serve him. This Arabic word /abd/ and

## Appendix 2

the corresponding words in the Law /abd/ and the Gospel /doulos/ have similar ranges of meaning.

shayatin see devil

shaytan see devil and Satan

Shuaib: (Jethro, Musa's father-in-law), also called /Hobab/ (Tawrah, Judges 4:11) and /Reuel/ (Tawrah, Exodus 2:18). The origin of the Arabic form is unknown. It does not seem to have any relation to the Hebrew /Yathru/ or the Greek /Iothor/. Jethro means "dedicated." This name is used in the Qur'an 11 times. His story is in the Tawrah, Exodus 18:1-12.

sign: /ayah/. This word can mean miracle or verse as well. For consistency, we have translated it as sign, or when the context requires it, verse. See miracle. The Qur'an has harsh words to say about those who deny, reject, or disbelieve in Allah's signs. They will have severe torment (3:4, 6:49,93), will be roasted in blazing fire (4:56, 5:10,86, 57:19), will be deaf and dumb in the darkness (6:39), will have awful torment (6:157), will lose their souls (7:9), will go to hellfire forever (7:35, 41:28, 64:10, 90:20), will have heaven's doors closed against them (7:40), will be forgotten by Allah (7:51, 20:126-127), will be lost (10:95), will live in hell (17:97,98, 18:106, 78:21-28) will be in continual burning fire (17:97,98), will have shameful torment (22:57), will despair of Allah's mercy (29:23), will have painful torment (29:23, 31:7, 45:8), will have an evil end (30:10), will be brought into torment (30:16), will be losers (39:63 ), will have torment of painful uncleanness (45:11), and will be damned (90:19).

In this world, those who have rejected Allah's signs have experienced harsh punishment (3:11), a swift reckoning (3:19), collapse of their dwellings (3:112), drowning (7:64,136, 10:72, 21:77), being cut off (7:72), being seized for their sins (8:52, 54:42), being destroyed for their sins (8:54, 25:36), curse (11:59-60), and tasting shameful torment (41:16). They are promised that they will be gradually punished (7:182), they will not be guided (12:104), and their works will be in vain (18:105). With all these warnings, it is wise for us to know and believe Allah's signs.

Most of the signs the Qur'an mentions have to do with creation and life that all men can observe the creation of the heavens and the earth, the difference of night and day, ships sailing the sea, the rain Allah sends down, sending every kind of animal into the earth, sending off the winds, and the clouds between the sky and the earth (2:164, 10:5), splitting the seed and the date pit, bringing forth the living from among the dead, bringing forth the dead from among the living, splitting the morning, making the night quiet, making the sun and moon a reckoning, guidance of the stars, creation of mankind from one soul, rain down bringing forth all kinds of plants, herbs, seeds, and fruits (6:95-99).

However, Allah gave many more specific signs to his messengers (peace be upon them all), and no messenger ever brought a sign except with Allah's permission 13:38, 40:78. These are the signs Allah gave the various messengers, in rough chronological order: *Adam*: clothing of reverence 7:26. *Salih*: a female camel 7:73, 11:64, destruction of the wicked 27:45-52, 26:158. *Nuh*: the ark 7:64, 29:15, 54:15, drowning of the wicked 25:37, 26:119-121. *Lut*: stones raining down 15:61-76, 26:167-174, 29:31-35, 51:32-37. *Musa*: the flood, the locusts, the lice, the frogs, and the blood, detailed signs 7:133, drowning of the wicked 26:67, some of Allah's greater signs 20:23, the great sign 79:20, nine signs 17:101, his staff becoming a serpent 7:106-107, 20:17-21, his hand becoming white but unharmed 20:22. *Shuaib*: torment of the wicked 26:188-190. *The prophet of the people of Israel* (Samuel) the ark of the covenant, 2:248. *Zakariya*: not speaking for three days 3:41, 19:10. *Isa*: creating a bird, healing the man born blind and the leper, giving life to the dead, telling people what they ate and stored, confirming the Tawrah, permitting forbidden things, 3:49-50, sending down a table from heaven 5:113. Interestingly, Isa is the only prophet or messenger who *is himself* a sign. He and his mother Mariam are both signs 19:21, 23:50. *Hud*: 26:139 destruction of the wicked. Note: *Muhammad* did not have a sign 6:37,109, 7:203, 10:20, 13:27, 20:133, 21:5, and therefore was rejected often 6:124. The reason the Qur'an gives for not giving signs is that the disbelievers would still have rejected him 30:58, 37:14, 54:2. However, 3:58, 12:1-2, 26:192-197, 41:3 seem to refer to the Qur'an as a sign.

slave: see servant

Solomon: see Sulayman

spiritual path: /millah/ This word is used in the Qur'an 15 times, most often about Ibrahim. Several times it refers to Ibrahim's being a monotheist as a description of his spiritual path (2:135,

## Appendix 2

3:95, 4:125, 6:161, 16:123). 22:78 describes those who follow Ibrahim's path as submitted ones /muslimun/. When not describing Ibrahim's path it can be positive (12:38), neutral (2:120), or negative (7:88-89, 12:37, 38:7).

straight path: /al-sirat al-mustaqim, sawa' al-sabil/ There are two words used in the Qur'an for "path" /sirat and sabil/ and two words used for "straight" (sawa' and mustaqim) in this expression.

The straight path is mentioned often in the Qur'an (1:7 and 37:118 as "the straight path", 7:16 as "your straight path," 6:126 as "your Lord's straight path," 6:153 as "my straight path," and 2:108,142,213, 3:51,101, 4:68,175, 5:12,16,60,77, 6:39,87,161, 10:25, 11:56, 15:41, 16:76, 121, 19:36,43, 20:135, 22:54, 23:73, 24:46, 28:22, 36:4,61, 38:22, 42:52, 43:43,61,64, 46:30, 48:2,20, 60:1, 67:22 as "a straight path") However, only 3:51, 6:153, 19:36, 43:61,64, and 36:61 tell what the straight path is. See notes on these five passages.

struggle: The Arabic word /jihad/ means struggle, not holy war, and is used in the Qur'an four times only (9:24, 22:78, 25:52, and 60:1). The verbal form is more common. There are several aspects of struggle mentioned in the Qur'an: struggle in Allah's path by seeking his pleasure (2:218, 4:95, 5:54, 8:72,74,75, 9:19,20,24,41, 49:15, 60:1, 66:11), struggle by emigrating (2:218, 8:72,74,75, 9:20,81, 16:110), struggle by believing (2:218, 8:72,74,75, 9:19,20,44,88, 49:15, 60:1, 61:11) struggle by spending money and sacrificing one's own life (4:95, 8:72, 9:20,41,44,81, 49:15, 61:11), struggle by being patient (3:142, 16:110, 47:31), struggle by sheltering refugees (8:72, 74), struggling by not sitting idle (4:95, 9:81,86), struggle by giving (29:69), struggle in Allah by prayer, giving, and trusting in Allah (22:78, 29:69), struggle to encourage (29:8), and struggle by being righteous (9:44), struggle against unbelievers, whom Allah (not people) will punish (9:73, 25:52, 66:9), None of these verses about struggle have anything to do with killing people. The Qur'an is very clear that the true enemy of the believers is Shaitan (2:168,208, 5:91, 6:142, 7:22, 12:5, 17:53, 28:15, 35:6, 36:60, 43:62).

submission: /islam/. See submitted

submitted: /muslim/ and /islam/ In some cases, it can be more active, as in "surrendered." Most translators translate this word either "submitted" or "surrendered," or put this meaning in a footnote. Some translators choose not to translate this word at all, but just transliterate it /muslim/. Translators do similar things with the word /islam/.

However, this gives the wrong impression, that those the Qur'an refers to are the same as those who call themselves Muslims today. Many Muslims today are merely cultural Muslims, and have never submitted their lives to Allah. Some even live totally opposed to the Qur'an's teaching.

Islam as it has developed over the last 14 centuries has added many traditions to the words of the Qur'an, and so Islam today implies something very different from the original meaning of Islam (submitted) in the Qur'an.

In addition, the original Qur'anic use of the Arabic word /muslim/ is very different from the common understanding of the word today (at best, followers of Muhammad (s) in 21st century Islam; at worst, terrorists).

A study of the Qur'anic use of this word shows that the meaning "followers of Muhammad" is not intended, since many other people and groups are described by the Arabic word /muslim/ in the Qur'an: Noah (10:72), Abraham (3:67, 4:124, 37:103), Abraham's son (37:103), Joseph (12:101), Pharaoh (10:90), the people of Israel (10:83), the queen of Sheba and Solomon (27:44), the prophets (5:44), the disciples of Jesus (3:52, 5:111), and all in heaven and earth (3:83). These all lived hundreds or thousands of years before the birth of Muhammad (s), so none of them were followers of Muhammad (s), since he had not yet been born. In addition, 28:53 refers to those who were submitted before the Qur'an.

Therefore, the most precise meaning in the Qur'an of the Arabic word /muslim/ is "submitted," and we have chosen to translate that original meaning.

Sulayman: (Solomon, son of David) It seems that the Arabic form was transliterated from the Greek /salomon/ instead of the Hebrew /shalmah/. This name in the original language meant "peace." This name is used in the Qur'an 17 times. His story in the Tawrah is mentioned in 1 Kings 1:1 - 11:43 and 1 Chronicles 22:1 through 2 Chronicles 9:31, and he is referenced in the Injil 11 times.

Talut: (Saul, the first king of the people of Israel). This name is used only in 2:247,249 and is not derived from either the Hebrew /shaul/ or the Greek /saoul/. His story is mentioned in the Tawrah,

Samuel 9:1 through 2 Samuel 1:27, and he is mentioned in the Injil only in Acts 13:21. Other instances of Saul in the Injil refer to the man later known as Paul.

Tawrah: (The Law) This word is taken from the Hebrew /torah/ although the usage is slightly different. In the Qur'an, the Arabic word Tawrah is always presented as the book Allah revealed to the people of Israel in general, and not just what was revealed to Musa. There are no specific verses in the Qur'an that mention both the word Tawrah and Musa, though many people assume that Tawrah refers only to what are known as the five books of Musa. Thus it refers to what is known today as the Old Testament, or the Tanakh, and contains all revelation before Isa. Its usage parallels the usage of /ho nomos/ in the Gospel, where it sometimes refers to the books of Musa (Injil, Luke 2:23) and sometimes to all that Allah revealed to the people of Israel (Injil, John 15:25 refers to the Psalms, and Injil, 1 Corinthians 14:21 to the book of Isaiah).

thinkers: /ulu al-albab/ Literally, possessors of minds (or hearts). This phrase is used in the Qur'an 16 times.

torment: /adhab/ This word also means "torture," but "torture" is usually physical, while the torment unbelievers will suffer can also be psychological, emotional, or shameful.

unbelief: /fisq/ This word also can mean transgression or immorality.

understand: /yafqah/ Used 20 times in the Qur'an. A related word today is used for a religious scholar. /ulu al-nuha/ (20:54,128) and /dhu mirrah/ (53:6) are also translated this way.

we "We" is used throughout the Qur'an when Allah speaks, both with verbal forms and the pronouns "we", "our," and "us." This is most probably the "royal we" as used by a king (or queen) when referring to himself. It does not imply that Allah is not one. See under "god" above.

worship: /ya'bud/ See servant.

Yahya: (John the Baptist, son of Zechariah). He is sometimes called the Baptizer or the Baptist because he immersed people in water when they repented. Injil, Matthew 3:1-6. The origin of the Arabic form is uncertain, but probably is related to the Hebrew /yuhanan/ instead of the Greek /yuannis/. In older Arabic Bibles, this name is spelled /yuhanna/, which has the same undotted form

Appendix 2

as /yahya/ .This name in the original language meant "God's grace." This name is used in the Qur'an 5 times. Passages that refer to Yahya are: 3:39, 6:85, 19:5-15, 21:90. His story in the Injil is told in Matthew 3:1-4:12, 9:14-17, 11:2-18, 14:2-10, 16:13-14, 17:10-13, 21:25-32, Mark 1:1-14, 6:14-29, 8:27-28, 11:30-32, Luke 1:13-80, 3:2-20, 5:33, 7:18-35, 9:7-9,18-20, 11:1, 16:16-17, 20:4-8, John 1:6-40, 3:23-4:1, 5:33-36, 10:40-41, Acts 11:16, 13:24-25, 19:4. His coming is prophesied in the Tawrah, Isaiah 40:3-5, Malachi 3:1, 4:5-6.

Yajuj and Majuj: (Gog and Magog). The origin of the Arabic spelling could have come from the Greek /Gog kai Magog/ or the Hebrew /Gog wa Magog/. These are mentioned only in 18:94 and 21:96, and seem to refer to nations or leaders of nations. Gog is mentioned in the Tawrah, 1 Chronicles 5:4, Ezekiel 38:2,3,14,16,18,21, 39:1(twice), 11 (twice), and Injil, Revleation 20:8. Magog is mentioned in Tawrah, Genesis 10:2, 1 Chronicles 1:5, Ezekiel 38:2, 39:6, and Injil, Revelation 20:8.

Yaqub: (Jacob, son of Isaac and grandson of Abraham) It seems that the Arabic form was transliterated from the Hebrew /ya'qub/ instead of the Greek /yakob/. This name in the original language meant "he supplants" or "he grasps the heel." This name is used in the Qur'an 16 times. His story is in the Tawrah, Genesis 25:26-49:33, and he is also mentioned in the Tawrah 132 times, the Zabur 34 times, and the Injil 26 times.

Yunus: (Jonah, the prophet swallowed by a whale or large fish) It seems that the Arabic form was transliterated from the Greek /iunas/ instead of the Hebrew /yunah/. This name in the original language meant "a dove." This name is used in the Qur'an 4 times. The passages that refer to Yunus are 4:163, 6:86-87, 10:97-98, 37:139-148. He is also called /Dhu-Al-Nun/ (he of the fish) in 21:87-88, and /sahib al-hut/ (he of the whale) in 68:48-50. His story is in the Tawrah, Jonah 1-4 and 2 Kings 14:25, and he is mentioned in the Injil in Matthew 12:39-41, 16:4, Luke 11:29-32.

Yusuf: /Yusuf/ (son of Jacob, grandson of Isaac, and great grandson of Abraham) It seems that this name was probably transliterated from the Hebrew /yusif/ more than the Greek /yosif/. In the original language, this name meant, "he adds." It is used in the Qur'an 27 times. His story is in the Tawrah, Genesis 37-50.

Zabur: /al-zabur/ (Psalms) This refers to the book of the Psalms, especially the Psalms of David. The word /ketubim/ to Jews is

## Appendix 2

broader than this, and includes other writings by Solomon and others. It is possible that the word /al-hikmah/ "wisdom" refers to the Psalms in 3:48.

zakah: see poor-tax.

Zakariyya: (Zechariah, father of John the Baptist) It seems that the Arabic form was transliterated fromthe Hebrew /zakariyah/ instead of the Greek /zakhariyas/. This name in the original language meant "Allah remembered." This name is used in the Qur'an 7 times. His story is mentioned in the Injil in Luke 1:5-80.

Zechariah (father of John the Baptist): see Zakariyya

Made in the USA
Coppell, TX
24 February 2026

72270312R00351